Language: Structure and Use

PROGRAM AUTHORS

Language: Structure and Use

Grades 7–12

Thomas L. Clark
University of Nevada
Las Vegas, Nevada

Ronald L. Cramer
Oakland University
Rochester, Michigan

Chris Welles Feder
New York, New York

Shirley C. Fencl
Special School District of St. Louis County
Florissant, Missouri

Roseann Dueñas Gonzalez
University of Arizona
Tucson, Arizona

Dorothy M. Griffin
Evanston Township High School
Evanston, Illinois

Ruby P. Herlong
Saluda High School
Saluda, South Carolina

Mary Hynes-Berry
Ancona Montessori School
Chicago, Illinois

Dale R. Jordan
Jordan-Adams Learning Center
Oklahoma City, Oklahoma

Karen J. Kuehner
Glenbrook South High School
Glenview, Illinois

Lida Lim
Burlingame Public Schools
Burlingame, California

Tara McCarthy
Woodstock, New York

Norman C. Najimy
Pittsfield Public Schools
Pittsfield, Massachusetts

Neil E. Nakadate
Iowa State University
Ames, Iowa

Paul E. Pesce
Wilbraham Junior High School
Wilbraham, Massachusetts

John Prejza, Jr.
Burlingame Public Schools
Burlingame, California

John T. Reque
Evanston Township High School
Evanston, Illinois

James R. Shay
University of Texas
Austin, Texas

E. Brooks Smith
Wayne State University
Detroit, Michigan

DeWayne Triplett
Northern Illinois University
De Kalb, Illinois

Gladys V. Veidemanis
Oshkosh North High School
Oshkosh, Wisconsin

Language: Structure and Use

Karen J. Kuehner
John T. Reque

Scott, Foresman and Company
Editorial Offices: Glenview, Illinois

Regional Sales Offices: Palo Alto, California •
Tucker, Georgia • Glenview, Illinois •
Oakland, New Jersey • Dallas, Texas

ISBN: 0-673-10273-4

Printed in the United States of America.

12345678910 VHS 89888786858483828180

Contents

The first four units of this book consist entirely of review exercises.

UNIT ONE GRAMMAR REVIEW

UNIT SIX COMPOSITION

ABCDE
FGHIK

Unit One Grammar Review

LMNO
PQRST
VXYZ

CHAPTER 1 Parts of Speech

The terms in **boldface** in the directions for the following exercises refer to entries in the Language Handbook.

PART 1 Nouns

• **EXERCISE 1. Common and proper** Divide a sheet of paper into two columns across, labeling the first column **Common noun** and the second column **Proper noun**. Then list the nouns in the following sentences under their appropriate category. The figure in parentheses indicates the number of nouns in each sentence.

Example: According to Grandfather, the play was completed before the referee blew the final whistle. (4)

Answer:

Common noun	**Proper noun**
play, referee, whistle	Grandfather

1. Theodore Roosevelt was nationally famous long before he led his regiment on a cavalry charge up San Juan Hill. (4)

2. The capitol was built of marble from a quarry in the southern part of the state. (5)

3. A yowling cat can keep a family awake for hours. (3)

4. The tape on the package was coming loose, and the contents had begun to protrude through the open lid. (4)

5. A Zen question from Japan asks, "What is the sound of one hand clapping?" (4)

6. The audience gave the young singer a standing ovation for his performance. (4)

7. Ed, give me that bottle of Buzz-off before you sit down. (3)

8. The narrow-gauge train that runs between Durango and Silverton has often appeared in movies about the early days of the West. (6)

• **EXERCISE 2. Concrete and abstract** Divide a sheet of paper into two columns across, labeling the first column **Concrete words** and the second column **Abstract words**. Then list the nouns in the following sentences under their appropriate category. The figure in parentheses indicates the number of nouns in each sentence.

Example: The principle of *détente* appeals to people who are concerned about relations between countries with different philosophies. (6)

Answer:

Concrete words	**Abstract words**
people, countries	principle, *détente*, relations, philosophies

1. The strength and freshness of the portrait appealed to the imagination of the art critic. (5)

2. With unexpected ingenuity, Victoria solved every problem that occurred during her first overnight camping trip. (4)

3. Socrates, the philosopher, often argued with his followers about the nature of truth and beauty. (6)

4. Without some form of legal system, civilization would soon disintegrate into anarchy and chaos. (5)

5. The dilapidated stable was soon to be torn down since the new owner intended to build a tennis court. (3)

6. With her ability and drive, Martina should become a top executive in the company. (5)

7. At the height of the storm, the force of the wind threatened to topple a massive tree in the front yard. (6)

8. A process that would liquefy coal might provide one solution to the energy crisis. (4)

PART 2

Pronouns

• **EXERCISE 3. Personal and possessive** Divide a sheet of paper into two columns across, labeling the first column **Personal pronouns** and the second column **Possessive pronouns**. Then list the pronouns in the following sentences under their appropriate category. The figure in parentheses indicates the number of pronouns in each sentence.

Example: I was amazed the monkey accepted Yolanda's treat, while it ignored yours and mine. (4)

Answer:

Personal pronouns	**Possessive pronouns**
I, it	yours, mine

1. As we walked closer to the edge of the Grand Coulee Dam, even Greta's cynical brother was impressed. (1)

2. I feel certain that you're wearing Penny's raincoat and she's wearing mine. (4)

3. They ran across the busy street, heedless of the traffic. (1)

4. Before Anne agreed to baby-sit for the Glanvilles, she asked me if I had met them. (4)

5. "Excuse me, sir, but the first two seats are ours and the two just behind the pillar are yours." (3)

6. The restaurant manager conceded that the fault for the mix-up in the reservations was his and promised that we could call him any time for a free dinner. (3)

7. According to Mrs. Nazarian, the black car had originally been hers, but a friend borrowed it when he took a job in Iowa. (3)

8. Let's ask Burt if he will let us ride to the picnic with him; once we eat, you can ask Alex to give you a ride home. (7)

• **EXERCISE 4. Relative, reflexive, and indefinite** Identify only the relative, reflexive, and indefinite pronouns in the following sentences. List each pronoun, along with its classification. Use the abbreviations "Rel" for **Relative pronouns**, "Ref" for **Reflexive pronouns**, and "Ind" for **Indefinite pronouns**. The figure in parentheses indicates the number of specified pronouns in each sentence.

Example: After talking with someone who had seen the movie, Leo decided to see it for himself. (3)

Answer: someone, Ind; who, Rel; himself, Ref

1. The frantic fly shook itself loose from the spider's web. (1)

2. All of the packages that had been mailed from Chicago arrived within a week. (2)

3. Miyo asked herself the meaning of the verse from Matthew: "Many are called but few are chosen." (3)

4. Anyone who can already ride a horse should not enroll in the beginners' class. (2)

5. Scientists discussed among themselves the problem that had led to the breakdown of the reactor. (2)

6. Some of the substitutes whom the school had hired were retired teachers. (2)

7. The coach said, "Everyone on this team must stop and ask herself whether the championship is worth fighting for." (2)

8. Several of the prizewinning quilts were purchased by people who appreciated fine needlework. (2)

• **EXERCISE 5. Interrogative and demonstrative** Identify the interrogative and demonstrative pronouns in the following sentences. List each pronoun, along with its classification. Use the abbreviations "Int" for **Interrogative pronouns** and "Dem" for **Demonstrative pro-**

LANGUAGE NOTES

Dear Human Being...

If you have ever puzzled over which salutation to use in a letter to a recipient whose gender is unknown to you, you may agree with Sam Levenson.

The English language does not possess a word which can linguistically and humanistically bridge the gap between male and female without detracting from either. What is lacking is not a third gender word but a unifying one, a word rich enough in meaning to describe a totally mature human being, who can with joy rather than conflict express the essence of being at one and the same time masculine, feminine, paternal, maternal, whose strength is shown through tenderness, who can see any member of the human race as "bone of my bones, and flesh of my flesh," who espouses the cause of Human Lib.

nouns. The figure in parentheses indicates the number of interrogative or demonstrative pronouns in each sentence. Hint: Do not confuse demonstrative pronouns with demonstrative adjectives.

Example: Who opened that window? (1)
Answer: Who, Int

1. What was the name of the song you were singing? (1)
2. These are the kinds of complaints that occur most often. (1)
3. Who said that is the station offering free record albums to the first five callers? (2)
4. Whom will you select as a delegate to the convention? (1)
5. Pointing to one stack of cassette tapes, Manny said, "I listened to those last night." (1)
6. Whoever wrote this essay about soybeans? (1)
7. Whatever will we do with these six antique mustache cups that Helen found? (1)
8. This is the kind of weather I like–warm, breezy, clear. (1)

PART 3
Verbs

• EXERCISE 6. Action and linking List and identify the verbs in the following sentences, writing "A" for an **Action verb** and "L" for a **Linking verb**. The figure in parentheses indicates the number of verbs in the sentence.

Example: Nicole polished the silver for the party. (1)
Answer: polished, A
Example: The new telephone is in the corner of the kitchen. (1)
Answer: is, L

1. Mr. Kutsa, an official of an independent truckers' organization, opposed further interstate commerce regulations. (1)
2. In the lobby of the National Gallery of Art, the group of Swiss tourists patiently awaited a guide. (1)
3. In 1948, that car cost $1,875; today, the same car in mint condition is a valuable $17,000 classic. (2)
4. The patrolman copied the license number of the gray van in his small black notebook. (1)
5. The cabinetmaker seemed absorbed in her work, but she still heard everything in the shop. (2)
6. Two natural fibers are wool and cotton; silk, a third natural fiber, is the most expensive of the three. (2)
7. Addy located an early city plan of New Orleans in a file folder that contained other, similar documents. (2)
8. During the winter months Monarch Pass was isolated because of heavy snow. (1)

• **EXERCISE 7. Auxiliary** List each **Auxiliary verb** in the following sentences.

Example: She could not get her kite off the ground.
Answer: could
Example: The President will be attending a press conference later this afternoon.
Answer: will be

1. We are going to climb Long's Peak this weekend unless there is too much to do here at the ranch.
2. The problem of international terrorism should concern everyone.
3. Has the mail come yet this morning?
4. The two ushers were carefully dismantling the theater marquee.
5. I can help with the bake sale before and after school if you need me.
6. Shall I carry out the garbage now or later?
7. Tom will probably be elected to the student council this year unless he decides not to run.
8. If you haven't changed your mind about the trip, we will be leaving shortly after 6:00 A.M. tomorrow.

PART 4
Adjectives

• **EXERCISE 8.** List every **Adjective** in the following sentences. (There are four adjectives in each sentence.) Disregard such words as *a, an,* or *the.*

Example: Hal couldn't decide between a blue cotton shirt or a hand-knitted fisherman's cardigan.
Answer: blue, cotton, hand-knitted, fisherman's

1. The Sunday brunch at the new restaurant was lavish but relatively inexpensive.
2. The wooden crate seemed large, but we found it was too small for a dozen bowls.
3. The saxophone player in the back row of the band played the difficult solo and then waved to the appreciative fans.
4. The blue storage silos represent an extensive investment, but at present they are practically empty.
5. The hitchhiker looked tired and forlorn as he stood on one shoeless foot.
6. The only sounds in the large lecture room were the voice of the lecturer and the steady scratching of pens.
7. When the old beagle became weak and ill-tempered, Grandpa tried to make him into a reliable watchdog.

8. The history book contains excellent illustrations; they are clear and, occasionally, quite humorous.

PART 5

Adverbs

• **EXERCISE 9.** List each **Adverb** in the following sentences. The figure in parentheses indicates the number of adverbs in the sentence.

Example: We stopped briefly in Tucson to visit Ned's elderly uncle. (1)
Answer: briefly

1. We were utterly dumfounded when our idea for the float was unanimously accepted. (2)
2. She looked up slowly and fearfully. (3)
3. Claire was rather quiet throughout the meeting, but afterwards, when we discussed the issue of salary increases, she spoke eloquently in favor of them. (3)
4. The guide pointed south and said, "If you'll follow that path carefully, it will take you almost to the falls." (3)
5. Although I've seen *The Wizard of Oz* often, the only character that consistently delights me is the Cowardly Lion. (2)
6. The theater critic thought highly of the scenery, but he was not too impressed with either the leading man or lady. (3)
7. Mark had never considered bricklaying when he was choosing a career; then he discovered how well it paid. (4)
8. The union's counterproposal was not radically different from its initial demands, but the negotiators gladly accepted it. (3)

PART 6

Prepositions

• **EXERCISE 10.** List each **Preposition** in the following sentences. The figure in parentheses indicates the number of prepositions in the sentence.

Example: The profession of dentistry involves long hours and demands a keen interest in people. (2)
Answer: of, in

1. During the course of the year Lori helped her puppy grow into a well-trained pet. (3)
2. The cake with the fancy decorations came from a bakery located near the drugstore. (3)
3. Merchants in the local shopping center reported that orders for jeans had increased markedly since Memorial Day. (3)

4. The disturbance at the Civic Center began before eleven, rose to its noisiest height around noon, and was over shortly after one. (5)

5. The young lieutenant planned to resign from the Navy in August since at that time her second tour of duty would be over. (4)

6. Rushing through the line, the quarterback on the opposing team raced toward the goal. (3)

7. After he steamed off the wallpaper above the fireplace, Rich discovered, beneath the final layer, an original mural that might have been painted by Diego Rivera, the famous Mexican painter. (3)

8. In 1946, at the invitation of President Truman, Winston Churchill came to Fulton, Missouri, and delivered his famous "Iron Curtain" speech. (4)

PART 7

Conjunctions

• **EXERCISE 11.** List and identify the **Conjunctions** in the following sentences, writing "CC" to identify the four **Coordinating conjunctions**, "COCO" to identify the four pairs of **Correlative conjunctions**, "CA" to identify the four **Conjunctive adverbs**, and "SC" to identify the four **Subordinating conjunctions**.

Example: Dust and grime covered the windowsill.
Answer: and, CC
Example: Mr. Andrews was both secretary and treasurer of the local chapter of Elks.
Answer: both-and, COCO
Example: John graduated from West Point in June; then he was assigned to Fort Leonard Wood in Missouri.
Answer: then, CA
Example: Because she liked outdoor work, Liza applied for a position as a forester in the Wasatch Mountains.
Answer: Because, SC

1. Steve held two jobs in addition to going to night school; consequently, he was nearly always tired.

2. In the cold mountain air Kirk not only wore long underwear, but he also put on two pairs of insulated gloves.

3. The governor requested a special election when the lieutenant-governor resigned to become a federal judge.

4. Enrico wasn't willing to cheat on the test, nor would he help Ted to cheat.

5. The bandleader told the players to be ready to play either "Hail to the Chief" or the national anthem of Mexico.

6. If you decide to go to the rodeo, remember to be home by ten.

7. The writing of the paper took four hours; the typing, however, took nearly six.

8. Sally liked Jane's living room, but she especially admired her kitchen.

9. The owners of the rug company wanted a phone number that people could easily remember; therefore, they were delighted with 227-7387, a number that spells CARPETS.

10. The horse shied either at a rabbit or at a snake.

11. In August, Dr. Williamson will finish her research at the Johnson Library in Austin, and her husband will participate in a project sponsored by the National Disease Center in Atlanta.

12. Although we counted the gate receipts three times, we couldn't agree on the total.

13. Our guide's nationality was neither Bohemian nor Croatian.

14. You might miss the turn to the fairgrounds unless you keep track of the mileage.

15. During the frigid winter months, ice forms over small ponds; indeed, in subzero weather the ice is often six or eight inches thick.

PART 8

Interjections

• **EXERCISE 12.** List each **Interjection** in the following sentences. One sentence contains no interjection.

Example: Oh, is that the way that computer works?
Answer: Oh

1. When Professor Higgins in *My Fair Lady* hears Eliza speak in her cockney accent, he says, "Heavens, what a noise."

2. Gosh, you didn't really see that rock star in person, did you?

3. "What," he asked icily, "did you intend to do with that canoe?"

4. Oh, that iodine really stings.

5. Good grief, can't you even stay awake five minutes?

6. Wow, come over here and look through the microscope.

7. My, I can't get over your resemblance to your mother.

8. Hey! Where do you think you're going?

CHAPTER

2 The Structure of the Sentence

The terms in **boldface** in the directions for the following exercises refer to entries in the Language Handbook.

PART 1

Simple and Compound Subjects

• EXERCISE 1. List and identify the **Subject**, simple or compound, in the following sentences. Write "S" for simple and "C" for compound.

Example: The antique wooden chair had been painted bright red.
Answer: chair, S
Example: After dinner, Dad and Uncle Pete played a game of chess.
Answer: Dad, Uncle Pete, C

1. Marta strummed two or three bars of an ancient Gaelic song.
2. At the end of the cooking demonstration, the chef offered samples of Peking duck to everyone in the room.
3. Would the room look less cluttered without that pair of wing chairs?
4. Only after a direct order from military headquarters was the reserve unit dispatched to the second front.
5. One of the keys on Mr. Daniel's key ring fits every door in this building.
6. Over the heads of the spectators floated hundreds of brightly colored balloons.
7. Coughing and wheezing, the exhausted firefighter staggered from the lobby into the fresh air.
8. In Florida, there are miles of beaches and acres of orange groves.

9. Both the *Washington Post* and the *Christian Science Monitor* are consistently named in lists of outstanding newspapers.

10. Jane's best pair of earrings dropped behind the dresser and were lost for more than two weeks.

11. At the height of the fad, thirteen girls and nine boys crowded into the phone booth.

12. After less than two hours in the sun, the leaves and stem of the Hawaiian ti plant burned and shriveled.

PART 2

Simple and Compound Predicates

• **EXERCISE 2.** List and identify the **Predicate**, simple or compound, in the following sentences. Write "S" for simple and "C" for compound.

Example: The flowered blue sheet has been badly ripped.
Answer: has been ripped, S
Example: The man next door died and left his library to the local high school.
Answer: died, left, C

1. Janet is amazingly naïve for a high-school senior.

2. After this next commercial I will drive downtown and get the cleaning.

3. The haughty lady in the large black hat demanded her money.

4. That flickering light has bothered me for at least a week.

5. Sarah was working for her father as a cashier.

6. The new baby laughs constantly and coos occasionally.

7. Have you considered the cost of the dinner to each individual?

8. One of the most breathtaking sights in the entire exhibit was the gold mask.

9. At Annapolis on graduation day, the cadets toss their hats into the air and then spend hours retrieving them.

10. By Sunday morning, your uncle and I will have been on our fishing trip for at least two days.

11. In ceramics class the students rolled clay into long noodlelike shapes and then formed graceful pots.

12. The prices of paperback books will undoubtedly be higher next year.

PART 3

Subject/Verb/Direct Object

• **EXERCISE 3.** Divide a sheet of paper into three columns across. In the first column write the **Subject** of each sentence. In the second,

LANGUAGE NOTES

Honest Ads

OK, so it's only two ads, but they've appeared within a day of each other and if the momentum holds, we could have a trend on our hands.

I'm talking about an ad to sell a house and another seeking employment that have dared use a refreshing and unique approach to advertising: honesty.

The first ad was out of London and was placed by a man trying to sell his house. His ad read: "Two-and-a-half bedroom box located in suburbia, miles from any pretty country, yet lacking the cultural facilities of any decent sized town. Pocket handkerchief garden that floods in winter, acid soil suited only to rhododendrons and thistles."

"It's convenient, expensive, and dirty. The whole in terrible decay."

The second ad was placed by a woman newspaper executive who had had a hard day and decided to place an ad in the Job Wanted Female classification in Florida. She wrote:

"WANTED: EASY JOB: Educated, experienced woman wants what most people want—a high-paying job in an advisory role, three days a week with long lunch breaks, good benefits, including one-month vacations and a secretary. Does not do windows."

I told my husband what I'd really like to see is an ad under Used Cars that reads:

"We don't want to be your friend. We just want to sell you a car. We have the second-best deal in town with no intention of matching another offer. For this week and for as many weeks as it takes to unload it, we have a 4-door, undependable gas hog that needs brakes, tires, and a mechanic for an owner. Has a lot of toys under the hood (also in the back seat and trunk) and has been owned by everyone in town. We're pushing this turkey because it makes our lot look shabby."

My husband winced. "Who would buy a car with a pitch like that?"

"We did."

–Erma Bombeck

write the **Verb**. In the third, write the **Direct object**. All but three of the sentences contain a direct object.

Examples: Carmen packed her suitcase for the trip to Atlantic City.
The ad promised a free pizza to all honor students.

Answers:	**Subject**	**Verb**	**Direct Object**
	Carmen	packed	suitcase
	ad	promised	pizza

1. The lifeguard hurled the life preserver into the deep end of the pool.
2. Have you seen my pearl necklace anywhere in the room?
3. Lynn always complies readily with her friends' requests for help.
4. The street vendor was selling hot dogs and hot chestnuts to an eager crowd.
5. Martha gave one of the most impressive election speeches of the entire campaign.
6. The mirror in the fun house dramatically distorted Fran's shape.
7. A silver medal he just might win.
8. The garden hose had been coiled neatly underneath the faucet.
9. Have the principal and the dean given their approval for this absence?
10. Napoleon's forces were decisively beaten at Waterloo.

PART 4
Subject/Verb/Object/Complement

• **EXERCISE 4.** Divide a sheet of paper into four columns. In the first column write the **Subject** of each sentence. In the second, write the **Verb**. In the third, write the **Direct object**. In the fourth, write the **Subject complement**. Three of the sentences contain neither a direct object nor a subject complement.

Examples: Yuri stopped the argument between the two students.
His apology was heartfelt and sincere.

Answers:	**Subject**	**Verb**	**Direct object**	**Subject complement**
	Yuri	stopped	argument	
	apology	was		heartfelt, sincere

1. The two investigators interrogated Al about the accident at the intersection.
2. The First National Bank had been designated the executor of Mrs. Corl's estate.
3. Throughout the entire parade my youngest sister marched in a downpour of rain.
4. Larry recited the Gettysburg Address to the entire student body.
5. The naval officer is the husband of Mr. Laski's sister-in-law.

6. The ex-coach's speech on sportsmanship was understated but quite inspiring.

7. The new ice-skating rink will probably not be open until February.

8. In early December many popular gift items become quite scarce.

9. That city is one of the country's largest manufacturers of junior apparel.

10. By evening many of the dead branches on the oak tree had been removed.

11. At the sound of another cat's meow, the belligerent Siamese flicked its tail angrily.

12. The telephone next door has been ringing for at least an hour.

13. Marco hit his forehead in exasperation.

14. The records in the cabinet and the books on the shelves were evidence of his interest in music and literature.

15. Venison often tastes odd to people.

PART 5

Direct and Indirect Objects

• **EXERCISE 5.** List the italicized words. Then identify the word by writing "DO" for **Direct object** or "IO" for **Indirect object**. In one sentence the italicized word is neither.

Example: Mr. Diaz gave the parking lot *attendant* a dollar.
Answer: attendant, IO
Example: Anita should embroider another *pillow* for her mother.
Answer: pillow, DO

1. The butcher had saved *Mrs. Mulligan* three pounds of stew meat.

2. Please copy your chemistry *notes* for the review session.

3. Uncle Ferdinand handed *me* a slice of Lady Baltimore cake.

4. The director of our zoo studied zoology for many *years.*

5. Don't tell *him* any confidential information.

6. Roger paid *Carrie* an extravagant compliment for her work on the sophomore float.

7. Juan contributed twenty *hours* of his time to the recycling center.

8. At the historical society, you can see *letters* and *memorabilia* from the early days of the republic.

9. The malfunctioning lawn mower gave *Mrs. Frederick* fits.

10. The teachers' association awarded the *valedictorian* a full-year scholarship to the state university.

PART 6

Object Complements

• **EXERCISE 6.** List the **Object complement** in the sentence. For the one sentence that does not contain an object complement, write "None."

Example: We seniors considered Homecoming Week a success.
Answer: success

1. The high winds and waves made the ocean crossing a disaster.
2. The Costas named their younger boy Mark.
3. Charles Dickens found writing quite lucrative.
4. One of the great mansions of Newport, Rhode Island, was named after my great-uncle.
5. Alida Pruitt just painted her kitchen red, pink, and orange.
6. As a joke, all the members of the team dyed one lock of their hair green.
7. Because of his many childhood illnesses, some people thought Theodore Roosevelt a sissy.
8. The critic labeled the multi-million dollar film boring.

CHAPTER 3 Phrases, Clauses, and Kinds of Sentences

The terms in **boldface** in the directions for the following exercises refer to entries in the Language Handbook.

PART 1 Phrases

• **EXERCISE 1. Prepositional phrases** List each **Prepositional phrase** in the following sentences. There are thirty prepositional phrases in all.

Example: Mimi looked like a ballet dancer as she went through her exercises before the long hall mirror.
Answer: like a ballet dancer; through her exercises; before the long hall mirror.

1. Since September, the importer had been marketing elaborately molded candles from Bavaria; indeed, they were among his most popular items.
2. To the golfer's disgust his ball rolled past the green and into a small pond.
3. Shortly after midnight a slim figure crept beneath the lighted window; within the house a second shape moved up the stairs and along the dark corridor toward the bedroom.
4. We played a vigorous game of racquetball on Wednesday at noon and, against all odds, trounced our opponents.
5. Under difficult conditions and without much hope for survival, the mountaineers built a fire between two rocks and warmed themselves during the long night.

With sixty staring me in the face, I have developed inflammation of the sentence structure and a definite hardening of the paragraphs.

James Thurber (in 1955)

6. Behind the deserted house was an ancient wooden barn that might have been built around 1850, for it had a faded hex sign on it that had been painted by hand.

7. Who besides you would be willing to drive cross-country with only fifty dollars in her purse?

8. Over the three-month period, half-a-million dollars of the taxpayers' money had been spent to restore the historical courthouse.

• **EXERCISE 2. Participles** List each **Participle** in the following sentences. In parentheses, write the noun or pronoun each participle modifies.

Example: The frightened child cowered before the snarling dog.
Answer: frightened (child); snarling (dog)

1. His condescending attitude infuriated me.

2. The kite, wheeling and dipping, finally rose on a gust of wind.

3. Despite his expertise, the locksmith could not get his key into the frozen lock.

4. Juanita's use of the Heimlich maneuver instantly aided the choking man.

5. The insurance company reimbursed Patrick for his stolen camera.

6. The radio operator tried to tell the captain about the sinking ship not far from them.

7. The test-weary students considered the pounding noise an unnecessary distraction.

8. With his daughter's help, Max fixed the broken water pipe.

• **EXERCISE 3. Participles and participial phrases** List each **Participle** or **Participial phrase** in the following sentences. In parentheses, write the noun or pronoun it modifies. Some sentences may contain more than one participle or participial phrase.

Example: The polished crystal glinted in the lighted cabinet.
Answer: polished (crystal); lighted (cabinet)
Example: Running steadily, Jack won the race.
Answer: Running steadily (Jack)

1. Smiling, he walked slowly toward the podium.

2. Digging carefully, the archaeologist uncovered a valuable pre-Columbian cup.

3. The tiny river meandering through the foothills bubbled its way toward the plain.

4. Dan admired the excellence of the roads running through Kansas.

5. With hot compresses I lessened the pain shooting through my arm.

6. The young musician accepted the award sponsored by the Friends of Music League.

LANGUAGE NOTES

Sesquipedalian

Each of the following numbered items is a familiar adage rewritten in deliberately difficult language. See if you can match the difficult versions with the original sayings.

1. Judicious and accurate appraisal of the meritoriousness, or otherwise, of the internal content of a specific tome would be totally devoid of feasibility, were it to be predicated exclusively upon an assessment of purely external evidence.

2. A rotatorily locomotive dornick is consummately incapable of bryophytic accumulation.

3. Continuing physical possession, *sans* detriment, of a gâteau, is unquestionably incompatible with ingestion thereof.

4. Remoteness from immediate presence generates increscent cardiac amatoriousness.

5. Unoccupied physical manual equipment is inevitably presented with opportunities for employment, by Mephistophelean intervention.

6. An omnifariousness of alternatives and diversifications endows mortal existence with piquancy.

7. It would be an insuperably problematical proposition to justify any divergence between inspissated liquid preparations designed to accompany calorically treated anserine creatures respectively of feminine and masculine gender.

8. Calligraphic instruments predominate over mere weaponry.

–Roy Ward Dickson

A. Sauce for the goose is sauce for the gander.
B. Absence makes the heart grow fonder.
C. Variety is the spice of life.
D. You cannot judge a book by its cover.
E. A rolling stone gathers no moss.
F. You cannot have your cake and eat it too.
G. Idle hands are the devil's workshop.
H. The pen is mightier than the sword.

7. The student getting the fewest wrong answers will be excused from the next major quiz.

8. Tossing and turning, I rumpled the sheets right off the bed.

9. The counselor hired as a specialist in career education proved to be quite helpful to many of the graduating seniors.

10. The movie star entered a restaurant known for its celebrities and fine food.

11. We estimated more than ten thousand ducks migrating south for the winter.

12. Neither Frank nor John could decipher the hastily written note.

• EXERCISE 4. Gerunds List each **Gerund** and indicate its function in the sentence. Use the following abbreviations: "S" for subject; "DO" for direct object; "SC" for subject complement; "OP" for object of a preposition; "A" for appositive; "IO" for indirect object.

Example: I enjoy driving but not on icy roads.
Answer: driving, DO
Example: Steve indicated his agreement by nodding and smiling.
Answer: nodding, smiling, OP
Example: Careful listening is a skill to be cultivated.
Answer: listening, S

1. Laughing is sometimes a good way to ease tension.

2. It may seem obvious, but the principal job of a salesperson is selling.

3. Frank believes he can cheer himself up by whistling.

4. After an analysis of the nature of the soil, the mining engineer strongly recommended strip-mining.

5. His careful questioning was evidence of long hours of preparation.

6. After Peter ran for five minutes on a treadmill, the physician examined him and gave jogging his approval.

7. Seeing is believing, or so various camera manufacturers would like us to believe.

8. Have you tried dieting?

9. I devote a great deal of time and money to my hobby, baking.

10. We were amazed at the tremendous bill we received for our winter heating.

11. The professor's main duty, lecturing, was so time-consuming that he had only a few hours for consultations with students.

12. Chemical spraying is frowned on by many home gardeners.

• EXERCISE 5. Gerunds and gerund phrases List each **Gerund phrase** in the following sentences and indicate its function. In one case there is a simple one-word **Gerund**. Use the following abbreviations: "S" for subject; "DO" for direct object; "SC" for subject complement; "OP" for object of a preposition; "A" for appositive; "IO" for indirect object. Two sentences contain neither a gerund nor a gerund phrase.

Example: We began cleaning the filthy oven.
Answer: cleaning the filthy oven, DO
Example: We liked the idea of owning our own busines.
Answer: owning our own business, OP
Example: Lounging around is just asking for trouble.
Answer: Lounging around, S; asking for trouble, SC
Example: Has your father given retiring any thought?
Answer: retiring, IO

1. Climbing Mount Everest is possible but extremely hazaı

2. We enjoyed seeing the slides of her trip to Kenya.

3. Pablo took seriously his weekly chores of stoking the furn cleaning out the ashes.

4. During the scavenger hunt, leaving clues for others was forbidden.

5. Aunt Evelyn noted that her favorite pastime, tap-dancir once again becoming popular.

6. My idea of a pleasant summer evening is barbecuing s chicken and eating it outdoors.

7. Hal got his present position by watching carefully all notices the company employment opportunity board.

8. Doug was planning an addition to his extensive trainin program.

9. Creating an elaborate costume is no problem for an avid masquerade party-goer.

10. Eating well is no different from traveling well; it merely takes money, discrimination, and luck.

11. The images in the kaleidoscope are changing with every movement of the cylinder.

12. Monica felt well rewarded after receiving an A in biology.

13. The Democratic leadership opposed the ratifying of the treaty.

14. Sam's most annoying habit was changing his mind continually.

15. Exposing your face to too much sun will rob your skin of valuable moisture.

• **EXERCISE 6. Gerunds and participles** Identify each **Gerund** and **Participle** in the following sentences, listing the word and its appropriate label. Write "G" beside gerunds and "P" beside participles. Hint: One sentence contains a two-word participle.

Example: Traveling from coast to coast, Marcella was accustomed to meeting new people.
Answer: Traveling, P; meeting, G

1. "Dancing keeps me trim," said the agile octogenarian.

2. You seem to have an unusual capacity for eating rich foods.

3. Removing his jacket, Lars dove into the lagoon to rescue the drowning youngster.

4. Elsa found the task of rebuilding the old television set challenging.

5. Without hesitating a moment, the small child picked herself up and resumed roller-skating.

6. Thinking the concert was over, he began applauding the soloist, causing an embarrassing moment in the audience.

7. Looking for the stolen ring was as difficult as finding a needle in a haystack.

8. Awakened from his nightmare, Kurt found himself walking in his sleep.

9. I find walking at a brisk pace tremendously exhilarating.

10. She appeared to enjoy playing the trombone; but later she said that this activity was not a rewarding one for her.

11. His batting average is low, but his fielding can't be beaten.

12. Having campaigned for nearly a year, the aspiring politician finally decided to withdraw from the race.

• **EXERCISE 7. Infinitives** List the **Infinitive** in each sentence and then indicate its function in the sentence. Use the following abbreviations: "S" for subject; "DO" for direct object; "SC" for subject complement; "M" for modifier.

Example: To err is human.
Answer: To err, S
Example: I decided to go, but the bus had already left.
Answer: to go, DO

1. To communicate requires great effort on the part of the deaf.
2. Haven't you found a book to read yet?
3. All the apples at the bottom of the barrel started to rot.
4. One method of toning the muscles is to exercise.
5. Only one of the staff officers wanted to retreat.
6. To breathe is a basic bodily necessity.
7. The cat to buy is the little calico in the corner of the cage.
8. The thermometer outside the back door seems to be frozen.

• **EXERCISE 8. Infinitives and infinitive phrases** List the **Infinitive** or **Infinitive phrase** in each sentence and indicate its function in the sentence. Use the following abbreviations: "S" for subject; "DO" for direct object; "SC" for subject complement; "M" for modifier. One of the sentences contains neither an infinitive nor an infinitive phrase.

Example: When she couldn't find enough lemons to make a pie, Mrs. Jarman decided to serve ice cream instead.
Answer: to make a pie, M; to serve ice cream instead, DO
Example: *To Catch a Thief* is the name of both a book and a film.
Answer: *To Catch a Thief,* S

1. After the last performance, the students were asked to return all costumes borrowed from the costume room.

2. My father's latest edict is to limit my telephone conversations to six minutes.

3. To die honorably was the wish of every Roman soldier.

4. We finally received visas to visit East Germany and Poland.

5. To write a hit song has been Ray's ambition since high school.

6. Have you tried to scrape off those barnacles?

7. In addition to maintaining the machinery, Fred's secondary responsibility is to schedule the overtime.

8. On a trampoline a gymnast needs spotters to prevent accidents.

9. To have been the recipient of a Congressional Medal of Honor had thrilled my father.

10. The damage left by the spring floods was appalling to see.

11. The purpose of the speech was to interest young people in government service.

12. With the playing of the national anthem, the audience rose to attention.

• **EXERCISE 9. Appositives** List the **Appositives** that appear in the sentences and in parentheses indicate the word each modifies.

Example: Mrs. Roberts, our next-door neighbor, is nearly sixty.
Answer: neighbor (Mrs. Roberts)
Example: The novel, an exciting mystery, sold more than 350,000 copies in its first month.
Answer: mystery (novel)

1. The stars of the movie, Paul Newman and Robert Redford, made a guest appearance to promote attendance.

2. Frank Lloyd Wright, the world-famous architectural innovator, designed more buildings than he saw completed.

3. My history teacher cannot decide who was the greater orator, Winston Churchill or Daniel Webster.

4. The owner of the hardware store, a slight little man, lifts incredibly heavy sacks of cement every day.

5. He plays the viola, a stringed instrument larger than a violin.

6. The license plate read "New Mexico, Land of Enchantment."

7. Sloth, one of the seven deadly sins, simply means laziness.

8. Patronage jobs, those given to party faithfuls, are slowly being replaced by civil service positions.

PART 2

Clauses

• **EXERCISE 10. Adverb clauses** List each **Adverb clause** in the following sentences.

Example: When the cake fell, my brother's face fell too.
Answer: When the cake fell

Example: I can go only if we double date.
Answer: if we double date.

1. I will assent to your going if your father agrees.
2. As long as his food is well prepared, my cousin George eats heartily.
3. The plane arrived later than we had expected.
4. The tycoon had made his money by selling whenever the market was particularly active.
5. Because their baby-sitter called, the Kowalczuks left early.
6. Will you mind waiting while we pay the electric bill?
7. Although the troops settled into a fairly straight line, the drill sergeant wasn't too impressed with their posture.
8. The inexperienced diver grimaced in pain as he belly-flopped.
9. The regulations forbid talking after the fire drill begins.
10. Nelida, a shortstop, is always nervous before the first pitch of the game is thrown.
11. The fanciful gardener told us to prune the bush until it cried.
12. Arriving after the crowd had dispersed, Mark wondered about their purpose in gathering.

• **EXERCISE 11. Adjective clauses** List the **Adjective clause** in each sentence and indicate in parentheses the word each clause modifies. Hint: Some clauses are not introduced by a relative pronoun or relative adverb. When you list such a clause, insert the word that has been omitted and underline it.

Example: The fisherman described the fish that got away.
Answer: that got away (fish)
Example: Can you identify the woman who left this message?
Answer: who left this message (woman)
Example: The congratulatory telegram we sent to Jill cost more than six dollars.
Answer: that we sent to Jill (telegram)

1. The acoustical engineer who planned the sound system was delighted with its success.
2. Kiyo handed me the magazine that contained my article about preserving fresh fruits and vegetables.
3. The Stradivarius violin was a gift the wealthy industrialist had given to the museum.
4. Parkinson's Law, which states that work will expand to fill the time allotted, is usually referred to in jest.
5. The reporter wrote a scathing article about the people he had interviewed during the course of his research.
6. Hunting with a bow and arrow is a skill that I do not have.
7. Do you remember the time when you bowled a perfect game?
8. Charlie Jaeger is one salesman for whom I have great respect.

9. A point in the Rocky Mountains where water flows either to the east or to the west is called the Continental Divide.

10. The wrestler Larry beat earlier in the season had greatly improved.

11. Curling is a sport that came to America from Scotland.

12. The Gold Rush attracted people whose dream was instant wealth.

• **EXERCISE 12. Noun clauses** List the **Noun clause** in each sentence and indicate its function. Use the following abbreviations: "S" for subject; "SC" for subject complement; "O" for object; and "A" for appositive. Explain the precise function of those clauses that function as objects.

Example: What the painting meant was explained in the guidebook.
Answer: What the painting meant, S
Example: Hawaii, where I spent my vacation, is truly beautiful.
Answer: where I spent my vacation, A
Example: Judd's friends were interested in how he caught the fish.
Answer: how he caught the fish, O (object of the preposition *in*)
Example: Dusting whatever she could reach, Jenny finished quickly.
Answer: whatever she could reach, O (object of the participle *Dusting*)
Example: A doctor is what her parents hoped she would be.
Answer: what her parents hoped she would be, SC

1. Carolina mentioned that she had earned a black belt in karate.

2. Have you done any further thinking about what I suggested?

3. Where my date had learned about fixing a car engine was a mystery to me.

4. Camping, which I've done since childhood, is my favorite form of relaxation.

5. Because she wished to economize, the woman was accustomed to selecting whichever items were on sale.

6. When Stonehenge was built remains a matter of controversy.

7. Because Jim couldn't decide which offer to accept, he kept both teams in suspense.

8. The old trapper enjoyed telling why he had settled in the area.

9. Give that old sofa to whoever asks for it.

10. Where the valuable book had been hidden was a question for the head librarian to answer.

11. The insurance policy states precisely what the company will and will not pay.

12. One of the main topics at the conference was whether the police should have the right to stop and search suspected lawbreakers.

13. The excuse given by most students was that they had the flu.

14. Whatever you can give will be deeply appreciated.

15. One act was enough for the critic to know if the play would be a hit.

PART 3

Kinds of Sentences

• **EXERCISE 13. Classified by purpose** Classify the following sentences according to their *purpose*: **Declarative**, **Imperative**, **Interrogative**, or **Exclamatory**.

Example: Stop that mischief.
Answer: imperative

1. Hank spends hours studying for his weekly calculus test.
2. Were you able to jot down the license number before the car pulled away?
3. What a handsome man!
4. The young nuclear biologist explained the bases for his various theories.
5. Wait until your number is called, please.
6. Has the new fire detector been installed yet?
7. Please unload the dishwasher before you leave for work.
8. The ream of paper appeared to be quite discolored.

• **EXERCISE 14. Simple and compound sentences** Identify the following sentences according to their *structure:* **Simple sentence** or **Compound sentence**. Hint: Don't be misled by a compound subject or a compound verb.

Example: He admired the Fonz, a popular television character created by Henry Winkler.
Answer: simple
Example: A person without feelings may be indifferent to much of life, but a person with too many feelings may be overwhelmed by life.
Answer: compound

1. The circus elephant lumbered down Broad Street and then stopped to drink from the fountain in the middle of the square.
2. Typing her novel for six hours at a time made Clarissa an efficient typist, but it did little for her posture.
3. The young newlyweds established a savings account at the bank, for they wanted to buy some property on a nearby lake.
4. Has either you or your sister ever paddled a canoe?
5. The historic cemetery, overgrown with weeds and largely neglected, lay to the north of the town.
6. A statue commemorating the battle and designed by a famous sculptor served as the focal point for the rally.
7. In the early years of the Republic, the major goal was economic independence; later, men like Noah Webster brought the country together by encouraging cultural achievements.

8. The pirates of the sixteenth and seventeenth centuries robbed and pillaged the ships and people of many nations.

9. To make certain of the plan's secrecy, Ralph pretended to go to bed and Enrique stayed in plain sight of his parents.

10. According to the Bible, the lilies of the field toil not, and neither do they spin.

11. The books to read are listed at the end of the chapter.

12. Every year the salmon of the Columbia River travel all the way to the ocean and back again.

• **EXERCISE 15. Complex sentences** Identify each **Complex sentence** by writing its **Subordinate clause**. Some of the clauses are not introduced by a relative pronoun or relative adverb. When you list such a clause, insert the word that has been omitted and underline it. Hint: Two sentences have more than one subordinate clause. Three of the sentences are not complex.

Example: The stained-glass window, which had shattered during the storm, was priceless.
Answer: which had shattered during the storm
Example: Fran asked if the luggage store could stamp her initials on the attaché case.
Answer: if the luggage store could stamp her initials on the attaché case
Example: After we completed the float, we celebrated our accomplishment with a good night's sleep.
Answer: After we completed the float

1. Tom assumed that we all had an excellent sense of direction.

2. After he explained how the rigging worked, the window washer invited us to join him as he washed windows on the sixtieth floor.

3. Ms. Padilla must be very small if she uses only one yard of material for a pair of slacks.

4. The explanation that he provided proved to be satisfactory.

5. The usher I asked about curtain time gave me a hurried reply.

6. It must be exhilarating to win a gold medal in the Olympics.

7. If you can hold the frame straight, I can measure the distance from the frame to the ceiling.

8. Jogging along the beach, Bailey found a seashell that contained a live crab.

9. The detective discovered what the rest of the investigators had overlooked.

10. The will, when it was finally read, established the identity of the mysterious benefactor.

11. Mr. Choi, a member of the town council for over thirty years, ran the business in partnership with his wife.

12. Delighted with the friendliness of the people she had met, Meg was eager to return to Europe.

13. The grizzly bears who prowl around Yellowstone Park in the mornings are probably the ones we were warned about by the guide.

14. Picking up her knitting, Donna tried to remember the pattern but finally had to get up and find the pattern book.

15. Lynn's attitude toward school changed when she made the debate team.

• **EXERCISE 16. Compound-complex sentences** Identify each **Compound-complex sentence** in the following examples. Then list the **Main clause** and the **Subordinate clause** from these sentences under their appropriate headings. There are four compound-complex sentences.

Example: The mistletoe that grew wild in the swamp was lovely, but we could not stop to admire it.

Answers:

Main clause	Subordinate clause
The mistletoe . . . was lovely; we could not stop to admire it.	that grew wild in the swamp

1. We waited until the tugboat passed the levee; then we returned to the house.

2. He was charged with theft, but further investigation revealed his innocence.

3. The mechanic who worked on the assembly line was so dependable that he was made a supervisor; two years later he became a vice-president.

4. The superintendent spoke eloquently to the graduating seniors.

5. The dress rehearsal we attended was four hours long, but the final performance lasted only three hours and ten minutes.

6. When the trooper stopped Sally for speeding, his tone of voice was stern but his eyes were twinkling.

7. An extremely high-minded individual, Eduardo takes seriously both his family and his civic responsibilities.

8. By the end of the day, Alden wanted nothing more than to go to bed; he had cleaned the basement and the garage, planted more than fifty tulip bulbs, pruned the bushes by the front door, and carried three bags of debris to the curb.

• **EXERCISE 17. Four sentence structures** Classify the following sentences according to their structure: **Simple**, **Compound**, **Complex**, **Compound-complex**.

Example: Although the play was a great success, the cast party failed because everyone was exhausted.

Answer: complex

Example: *Pride and Prejudice,* to my mind Jane Austen's most enjoyable novel, is about the manners and morals of a small segment of English society in the early nineteenth century.

Answer: simple

1. While ironing the new curtains, Mildred discovered a flaw running through the fabric both crosswise and lengthwise.

2. The golden canary chirped and sang under the baleful glare of the tortoise-shell cat, but the little bird knew that its days were numbered.

3. Cracking and popping his gum, Raymond distracted the other students and forced the instructor to request that he get rid of it.

4. The fabulous ruby lay winking on the velvet cushion, tempting the unscrupulous and the honest alike.

5. The scissors I purchased last week already need sharpening.

6. To ensure the secrecy of the code, one unit knew the ciphers for the first half of the alphabet, and the other unit knew those for the second half.

7. Lucy said it was the worst baby-sitting job of her life, for the baby cried for a solid hour before finally falling asleep.

8. It is the royal monogram on the bottom of this teacup that makes it so valuable, not the gold-trimmed rim and handle.

9. Is the boy running in the marathon your neighbor, or is he the new minister's son?

10. A bay colt with a white blaze down its face came dancing out of the barn beside its mother, the big gray mare.

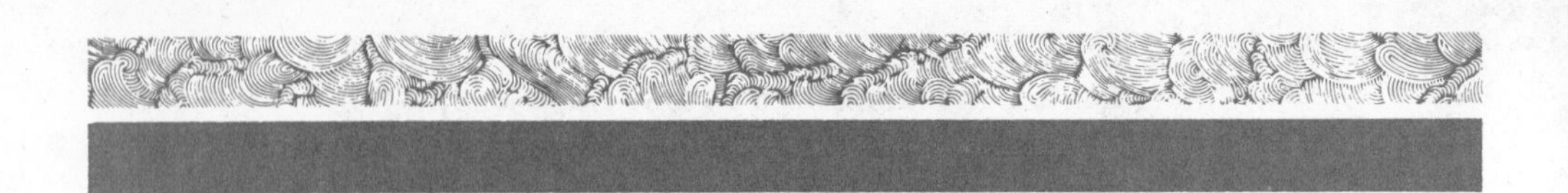

CHAPTER 4 Sentence Effectiveness

The terms in **boldface** in the directions for the following exercises refer to entries in the Language Handbook.

PART 1 Sentence Errors

• **EXERCISE 1. Sentence fragments** Each of the following items contains a complete sentence and an italicized **Sentence fragment**. Eliminate the fragment by rewriting the item as a single sentence, adding a comma where necessary, and omitting any unnecessary words.

Example: As the runners headed for the finish line, Wayne redoubled his effort. *And, to everyone's delight, won the race.*
Answer: As the runners headed for the finish line, Wayne redoubled his effort and, to everyone's delight, won the race.
Example: Mrs. Quan stood in a long line at the main post office. *Waiting to buy a sheet of newly issued stamps.*
Answer: Mrs. Quan stood in a long line at the main post office, waiting to buy a sheet of newly issued stamps.

1. On her vacation last summer, Paula stopped in Hannibal, Missouri. *The town where Mark Twain's boyhood home is located.*

2. A careful buyer of a used car generally checks the mileage, the state of the interior, the tightness of the steering wheel. *And, especially, the condition of the tires.*

3. It was easy to choose between the two pairs of sunglasses. *Since one was two dollars cheaper than the other.*

4. Richard skillfully transferred the trout from the frying pan to a hot platter. *And then deftly deboned it in one quick movement.*

5. Janelle felt foolish. *Wearing the Bride of Dracula costume.*

6. In his letter of application, David said he would come for an interview. *Whenever it was convenient.*

7. Around the corner wobbled the last of the bicycle-race contestants. *His hair plastered to his head and his face wet with exertion.*

8. By mid-October, Mr. Laskey had cut back his prize rosebush to a height of eleven inches. *And packed it in a three-inch covering of straw.*

9. The clown offered my brother a ride on a pinto pony. *The one with red tassels on its harness.*

10. *The racing car that had been developed by a group of unknowns and tested by two experienced drivers.* It may win the Monte Carlo Grand Prix.

• **EXERCISE 2. Comma splices and run-ons** Decide which of the following sentences are correctly punctuated and which contain a **Comma splice** or a **Run-on sentence**. Correct the comma splice by writing the word before the comma (in run-on sentences you will have to supply the comma), the comma itself, and an appropriate coordinating conjunction (*and, or, for,* or *but*). If the sentence is correct, write "Correct."

Example: Buy a hot dog from that street vendor, you will find out what a really good hot dog tastes like.
Answer: vendor, and
Example: After we had visited the top of the Washington Monument, we decided next to visit the National Gallery, then the Smithsonian Institution.
Answer: Correct

1. The auditor carefully went over his figures he could not find his error.

2. When the firefighters finally returned from their call, their pot roast was cold, the beans were soggy, and the salad, wilted.

3. Mr. Propper is almost pleased that his car has been stolen, now he can buy one that will be more economical to run.

4. The drought has nearly burned up the grass on the fairways, the maintenance crew has kept the greens watered.

5. Standing before the hidden camera, the shopper said, "This one on the right is the margarine this one on the left is the butter."

6. Center the large oil painting above the fireplace group the small prints together on the side wall near the window.

7. The Ace Heating Company installed a new water heater in Mrs. Malugen's basement, at no cost they hauled the old heater away.

8. Please separate your white shirts from your red towels you may end up with lurid pink shirts.

9. When he finished setting up the lights, the photographer shot more than twenty pictures of the boy and his sister.

10. Put sufficient postage on that letter, the post office will return it to you.

• **EXERCISE 3.** Decide where in the following sentences a **Semicolon** is needed to eliminate a **Comma splice** or a **Run-on sentence**. In some cases you will need to supply a **Comma** to set off **Conjunctive adverbs**. Write the word preceding the mark to be added, along with the appropriate punctuation mark and the word following the mark. If a sentence is correct, write "Correct." Hint: You may wish to review the following section on the punctuation of **Conjunctive adverbs** in the Language Handbook: **Comma**, section **2**.

Example: The farmer carefully measured the dimensions of the stall, then he began to estimate the amount of straw he would need.
Answer: stall; then
Example: Mount Kilimanjaro, the highest mountain in Africa, is located in northeast Tanzania, it is more than nineteen thousand feet high.
Answer: Tanzania; it
Example: Fran's typewriter was a large, heavy machine, as a result she rarely bothered to carry it to the store for a cleaning.
Answer: machine; as a result, she

1. When the hurricane suddenly headed north, the radio stations began broadcasting the news consequently everyone was prepared for the storm and no one was injured.

2. The winter had been severe, nevertheless the newly planted trees survived.

3. If you decide to go into medicine, however, this nursing home job will have been excellent preparation.

4. Impressed with the efficiency of the movers, Vivian agreed to recommend them to several of her friends.

5. Mr. Santini had put more than thirty coats of shellac on the bowl still he thought it should have two or three more coats.

6. The rugs from China are usually made of silk, the rugs from Morocco however are more likely to be wool.

7. Ernie was disconcerted by the questions from the class, for he thought he had covered the problems that were being raised.

8. Although Mr. Szabo tried to discourage his wife from buying the old roll-top desk, she thought it was worth the money the wood alone was worth the price the dealer was asking.

9. After the noise-abatement committee met with the airport manager, he instructed all planes to cut their noise by 50 percent the committee however was still not satisfied.

10. The farmer agreed that contour plowing was unquestionably better for the soil, nevertheless he missed the long, straight rows.

11. Thad carefully guided the mower near the fence, making certain that he did not get too close to chip the paint, then he turned off the mower, got down on his hands and knees, and hand-clipped the remaining grass.

12. After signing more than four hundred diplomas, the principal threw down the pen, sighed, and sat back in his chair.

LANGUAGE NOTES

Little Red Revisited

Once upon a point in time, a small person named Little Red Riding Hood initiated plans for the preparation, delivery, and transportation of foodstuffs to her grandmother, a senior citizen residing at a place of residence in a forest of indeterminate dimension.

In the process of implementing this program, her incursion into the forest was in mid-transportation process when it attained interface with an alleged perpetrator. This individual, a wolf, made inquiry as to the whereabouts of Little Red Riding Hood's goal as well as inferring that he was desirous of ascertaining the contents of Little Red Riding Hood's foodstuffs basket, and all that.

"It would be inappropriate to lie to me," the wolf said, displaying his huge jaw capability. Sensing that he was a mass of repressed hostility intertwined with acute alienation, she indicated.

"I see you indicating," the wolf said, "but what I don't see is whatever it is you're indicating at, you dig?"

Little Red Riding Hood indicated more fully, making one thing perfectly clear—to wit, that it was to her grandmother's residence and with a consignment of foodstuffs that her mission consisted of taking her to and with.

At this point in time the wolf moderated his rhetoric and proceeded to grandmother's residence. The elderly person was then subjected to the disadvantages of total consumption and transferred to residence in the perpetrator's stomach.

"That will raise the old woman's consciousness," the wolf said to himself. He was not a bad wolf, but only a victim of an oppressive society, a society that not only denied wolves' rights, but actually boasted of its capacity for keeping the wolf from the door. An interior malaise made itself manifest inside the wolf.

. . . .

Little Red Riding Hood achieved his presence.

"Grandmother," she said, "your ocular implements are of an extraordinary order of magnitude."

"The purpose of this enlarged viewing capability," said the wolf, . . .

—Russell Baker

From "Little Red Riding Hood Revisited" by Russell Baker, NEW YORK TIMES MAGAZINE, January 13, 1980.

• **EXERCISE 4. Misplaced and squinting modifiers** The following sentences contain **Misplaced modifiers** or **Squinting modifiers**. Rewrite each sentence so that the modifying word or phrase is correctly placed.

Example: Gertrude spied the rare bird with the new binoculars that she had bought on sale.
Answer: With the new binoculars that she had bought on sale, Gertrude spied the rare bird.
Example: George spotted a clump of mushrooms raking the leaves.
Answer: Raking the leaves, George spotted a clump of mushrooms.

1. Elias failed to see the woman who was standing outside the hotel because of the rain.
2. The lion was captured by an experienced hunter in a net.
3. Marilyn entertained the relatives who lived near her last week.
4. The manager of the hamburger stand said at noon the boys could leave.
5. We recommended a new detergent for the clothes with special additives.
6. The fire chief said near dawn the fire had ignited and burned for an hour before the alarm went off.
7. The clown in the red costume circled the arena on a white horse standing on his hands.
8. I can instruct you on how to pack for your trip abroad in five minutes.
9. She told us stories about how she walked to school in two-foot snow drifts nearly every day.
10. Eva and Arne spied four fat robins on their way to the park.

• **EXERCISE 5. Dangling modifiers** The following sentences contain **Dangling modifiers**. Rewrite each sentence to eliminate the dangling modifier. You may need to rephrase the modifier or the main sentence.

Example: Looking west toward the foothills, the sun nearly blinded Paco.
Answer: Looking west toward the foothills, Paco was nearly blinded by the sun.
Example: By installing deadbolts on all doors, the danger of burglary can be significantly reduced.
Answer: By installing deadbolts on all doors, a homeowner (or: you) can significantly reduce the danger of burglary.

1. While driving to Hartford, the storm that had been threatening finally broke.
2. After planting the seeds only last week, the appearance this morning of some small green shoots amazed Frank.
3. To avoid further lawsuits, all models made after June fifteenth of this year were recalled and their carburetors replaced.

> *Words have weight, sound, and appearance; it is only by considering these that you can write a sentence that is good to look at and good to listen to.*
> W. Somerset Maugham

4. Seeing the long line at the box office, the question was not whether we could get four tickets but whether we could get any at all.

5. When introduced, *Motor Trend* magazine said the Fantasy combined fuel economy with the latest in engineering.

6. Because of a heavy weekend work schedule, my social life had come to a virtual standstill.

7. Although carefully tended by a professional gardener, I thought the formal gardens were sterile and uninteresting.

8. To enjoy a picnic to its fullest, lots of food and insect repellent are necessary.

9. Currently a packer in a paper products factory, Jim's ambition is to manage a men's store.

10. Washed frequently, you will find that your car may be worth about two hundred dollars above the list price when you trade it in.

11. Having won the debate tournament, the girls, we thought, would be glad to be seen with two such intelligent competitors.

12. While talking with his friends, the topic of sports inevitably came up.

PART 2

Sentence Style

• **EXERCISE 6. Parallel constructions** Each of the following sentences contains grammatical constructions that are not parallel. Rewrite the sentences, using **Parallel constructions**.

Example: Mac's principal is kind and knowledgeable and has a lot of compassion.

Answer: Mac's principal is kind, knowledgeable, and compassionate.

Example: She asked that the room be straightened, that he carry out the garbage, and the wood be chopped.

Answer: She asked that the room be straightened, the garbage carried out, and the wood chopped.

1. One speaker has some annoying mannerisms: whistling through his teeth, he says "uh" or "ah" between sentences, and gesturing wildly.

2. Next semester I will either sing in the choir, join the conservation club, or I will play lead clarinet in the marching band.

3. The television director was delighted with the star; she was cooperative, talented, and she was always on time.

4. The personnel director not only promised the applicant the job, but the opportunity to buy some shares in the company.

5. Although she is nearly eighty years old, the spry old woman likes water-skiing, planting her own vegetable garden, and to ride in local parades.

6. This article tells all about arthritis–how it affects a person, the rapid rate of its onset, and treating it.

7. Calculus homework has always been easier for me than my cousin Yoshiko.

8. Elaine had to decide whether to stay home and finish her health paper or should she accept the invitation to baby-sit.

9. After her summer job as a book shelver, Marnie concluded it was better to work steadily than at a furious pace.

10. Book reviewers across the country have praised the novel for the vividness of its characters, the battle scenes are quite accurate, and it is appealing to a wide audience.

• **EXERCISE 7. Deadwood** Rewrite the following sentences to eliminate the **Deadwood**.

Example: The salesclerk in the camera department looked with a horrified expression on his face as the young boy knocked a display table over on its side.

Answer: The camera salesclerk looked horrified (or: in horror) as the young boy knocked over a display table.

1. At the final conclusion of the disco contest of dancing, the two twins were each awarded with a trophy.

2. In the warranty that came along with the toaster, it guaranteed that any defective parts that needed replacing would be provided at no cost.

3. The young teen-ager asked whether if he waited for and took the 22 bus which stopped at the corner, would it take him on out to the airport.

4. Due to the fact that the auto mechanic wanted to make additional sums of money, the shop manager scheduled him for overtime of at least ten hours every week.

5. If Rod's condition of health undergoes a change, then I make the recommendation that you should pick up the phone and call me.

6. The famous French writer of novels was to all intents and purposes without speech at the myriad number of huge skyscrapers in New York.

7. Jimmy didn't like to work alone by himself, so he hoped that his father would be able to help him with the final assembling of the model of the airplane.

8. When the experienced mountain climber heard a faraway rumbling in the distance, he paused and tried to come to a decision as to whether he should continue on or stop and camp.

• **EXERCISE 8. Creating smooth sentences** Some of the following items contain a series of short, choppy sentences; some are composed of long, stringy sentences. Each should be revised. Tighten the structure by combining elements; by using **Verbals** (a **Participle**, **Gerund**, or **Infinitive**) where appropriate; by creating more complex sentences; or by dividing ideas into more than one sentence.

Example: It is a summer day and Tom has been told to go outside and whitewash the fence and that is a task he doesn't like, but he goes out and then some of his friends come along and they begin to taunt him, so Tom in a very clever way makes them envy him and in a little while the friends are painting Tom's fence for him.

Answer: One summer day Tom is told to whitewash the fence, a task he doesn't like. When some friends taunt him, Tom cleverly turns their taunts into envy and soon the friends are painting his fence.

1. Becky was driving west in her station wagon. Her station wagon began to choke. Then it began to sputter. Then some steam emerged from under the hood. Becky stopped on the shoulder of the road. She let the motor get cooler.

2. Mrs. Isaacs often stumbled over the garden hose. She suggested to her husband that they purchase a hose reel. They called the store and asked the store to deliver the reel to their house. Mr. Isaacs discovered he would have to assemble the hose reel.

3. The *Mona Lisa* is probably the most famous painting in the world. It was painted by Leonardo da Vinci. He painted during the period called the Italian Renaissance.

4. Wendell is my eight-year-old neighbor boy, and he plays on a summer baseball team, and that particular team practices in a park, and the park is three miles from Wendell's house.

5. The Social Security Administration wrote Sylvia a letter. In it they answered the questions she had asked them in a letter. They said she was eligible for benefits. But she first had to work forty quarters. They said that a part of her monthly contribution would support the Medicare program. They said that her children would be protected if she became disabled.

6. The composer wrote a violin concerto, and it was premiered recently, and at the end of the concert the composer thanked the conductor and he also thanked the soloist.

7. We used to live in Naples, Florida, and our house was not far from our grandmother's house, and my younger sister, Julie, she used to talk on the phone to Grandmother nearly every day, but now we live in Minnesota, but Julie still tries to call Grandmother.

8. Inez went to a stereo store, and she asked a salesperson to demonstrate various speakers, and then she asked for the advantages and disadvantages of each speaker, and eventually she decided to wait a few more months, and then she would buy.

PART 3

Passive and Active Voice

• **EXERCISE 9.** Each of the italicized verbs in the sentences below is in the **Passive voice**. Change the verb to **Active voice** and rewrite the sentence.

Example: When the quarterback overthrew his tight end, the ball *was intercepted* by an alert safety who ran nearly ten yards before he was brought down.

Answer: When the quarterback overthrew his tight end, an alert safety intercepted the ball and ran nearly ten yards before he was brought down.

1. Every spring the flowering cherry trees *are seen* by millions of visitors to Washington, D.C.

2. The final coat of car wax *was applied* by Wendy and Dave.

3. On one rainy Saturday, all of Beethoven's symphonies *were heard* by Claudine.

4. The cycle *was* skillfully *eased* into an opening in the lane to his right by Otis.

5. The instructions to the graders indicated that spelling errors on essay tests *were to be marked* by the grader.

6. While the anesthesiologist checked the patient's pulse rate, the surgeon *was helped* into her gloves by one of the nurses.

7. As soon as it *was learned* by the hero that the heroine was in danger, he alerted the sheriff and then set out for the ranch.

8. The dresses that *had been chosen* by the bride for her bridesmaids are going to be made of red velvet.

Chapter 1 The Parts of Speech

Write the part of speech of each underlined word in the sentences that follow. The underlined word will be a noun, pronoun, verb, adjective, adverb, preposition, conjunction, or interjection.

Example: This is not my idea of an ideal summer day.
Answers: pronoun, adverb, adjective

1. Soon after the auditions, the judges named Janet the winner.
2. Gosh, the last time that my team won the cup was ten years ago; however, the coach has already predicted another cup this year.
3. The strength of the hot Florida sun gave Chris a terrible sunburn, for he had not used any lotion.
4. After he had seen all of the shows for the new season, the critic wrote regretfully, "This is another disastrous year for our television viewers."
5. Who is the one who said, "There's a sucker born every minute"?

Chapter 2 The Structure of the Sentence

Write the name of each underlined item in the sentences that follow. The underlined item will be a verb, subject, direct object, indirect object, subject complement, object complement, prepositional phrase, or appositive phrase.

1. In her haste to answer the phone, Linda tripped over the extension cord.
2. This small group of engineers are considered experts in their field.
3. Katy called her pet iguana Lester Christopher, her great-grandfather's name.
4. The team voted Henry most valuable player and presented him with the game ball.
5. On St. Patrick's Day, the city's favorite holiday, the river was dyed green.
6. The unsuspecting victim of fraud could be you, Cindy.
7. In frustration, Ed gave the knob a turn and it fell off.
8. Luis hoisted the saddle onto the skittish Appaloosa.
9. Bella sent her mother a gorgeous pin, a topaz surrounded by four tiny diamonds.
10. Ranching is still important in many parts of this state.

Chapter 3 Phrases, Clauses, and Kinds of Sentences

A. Identify the underlined verbal phrases as gerund, participial, or infinitive phrases.

1. To perform at Carnegie Hall was the ambition of every singer at the audition.
2. Marathon running has become a national pastime.
3. Obsessed by his mission, the romantic young man wanted above all else to meet the person with the magical voice.
4. Reading great works of literature is a lifetime endeavor.

5. The cake, heaped high with strawberries and whipped cream, is for Lucy's birthday.

6. Skipping along the aisles of the supermarket, the small girl upset a pyramid of soup cans.

B. Indicate whether the underlined subordinate clauses are adverb, adjective, or noun clauses.

1. When Mike Della was in the first grade, he ate his erasers.

2. Emily said that the movie was too contrived to be believable.

3. This is the article that explains how to fold napkins in the shape of flowers.

4. Ferdinand's Farrago, which sells everything from macramé to mung beans, will move to another location in September.

5. This is the corner of the garden where he has planted tomatoes and radishes.

6. If the rain lets up by noon, we can still go to the concert in the park.

C. Identify each of the following sentences as either simple, compound, complex, or compound-complex.

1. When the doctor returns my call, be sure to get the message.

2. After sleeping all night on the bus, Rita found the idea of a breakfast stop appealing.

3. The chaperons tried to find an inexpensive restaurant where everyone could eat, but it was so early that no place was open.

4. I could swear that this pothole in the street wasn't here yesterday; nor do I recall seeing that bent street sign.

5. Jordan and he planned to awake early and leave for Louisville on the early train.

6. Whatever will I do with the four baby robins that I found just beyond the hedge in the front yard?

7. I can be at your house by noon, or we can meet at the pool.

8. Jane agrees with you but still refuses to take sides.

Chapter 4 Sentence Effectiveness

Each of these sentences contains one of the following: comma splice, deadwood, dangling modifier, unparallel construction, run-on. Identify the error in each sentence.

1. The fact of the matter is that Jack is lazy but bright.

2. Stuffed with a foot of salami, we gawked at the sandwich.

3. If you study diligently, work efficiently, and are doing a wide amount of reading, you should have little trouble passing this course in science.

4. I'll warn you about one thing, go over each question carefully before filling out the answer card.

5. My mother says, "The proof of the pudding lies in the eating" I agree with her philosophy.

Perfect Score: 70

Unit Two Usage Review

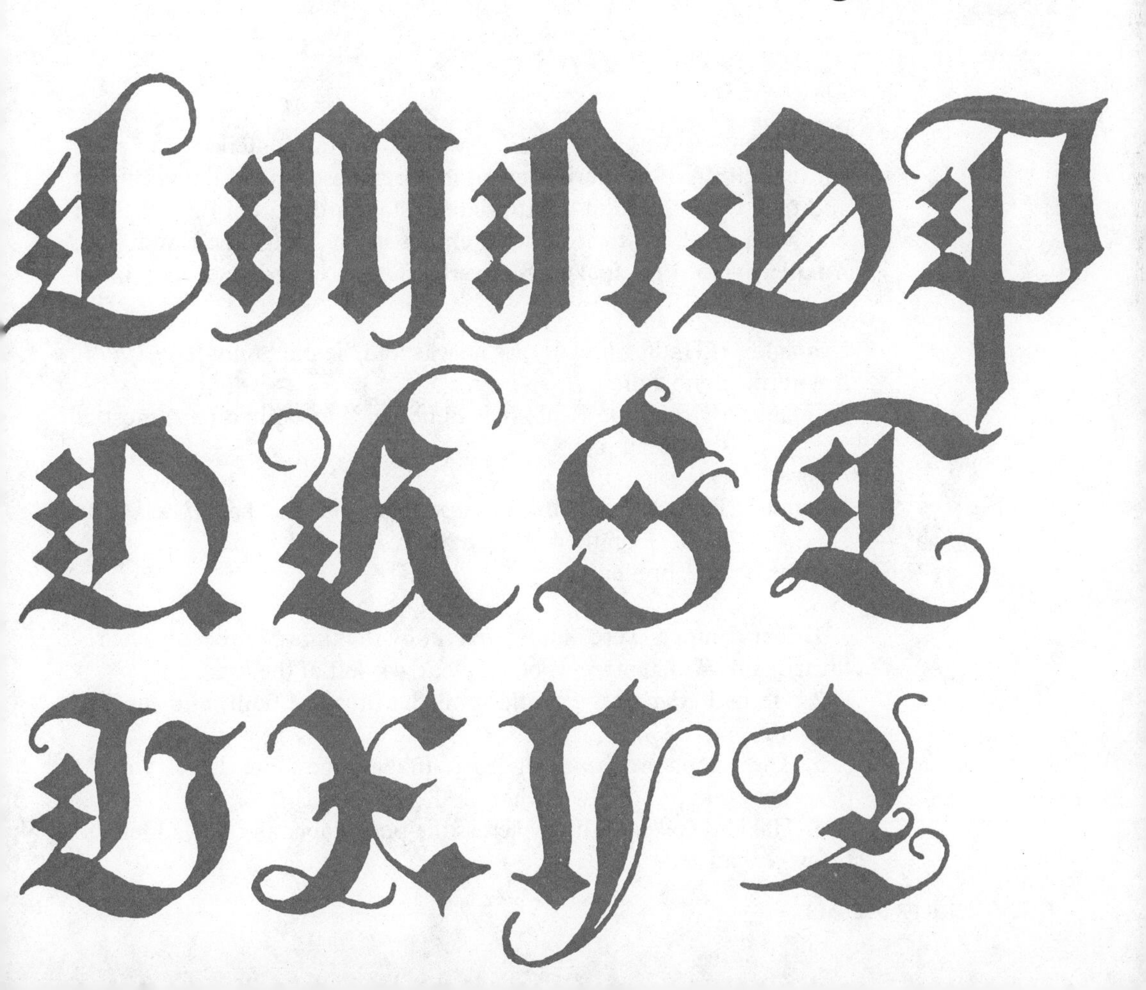

CHAPTER

5 Verb Problems

The terms in **boldface** in the following exercises refer to entries in the Language Handbook.

PART 1

Principal Parts of Verbs

• **EXERCISE 1. Irregular verbs** In the following sentences, the present tense form of the verb is given in parentheses. Read the sentences and then write the form appropriate in standard written English. You may wish to review the following entries in the Language Handbook: **Auxiliary verb**; **Principal parts of verbs**; **Tenses of verbs**, sections **1** and **2**.

Example: If Hadley had (*do*) as he was told, he might not have (*fall*).
Answer: done, fallen
Example: By the time Paula (*come*) home, Warren had (*eat*) most of the pecan pie.
Answer: came, eaten
Example: The next day Brigid (*see*) that someone had (*break*) the padlock on the basement door.
Answer: saw, broken

1. The campers were almost (*freeze*) by the time Manuel and Al returned and (*throw*) more wood on what was left of the fire.

2. He had (*shake*) the bottle until the pressure built, and the cap (*fly*) off.

3. The telephone (*ring*) at least fifteen times, but Ethel was so (*wear*) out that it didn't wake her.

4. Hal had (*swim*) halfway across the pool when, all of a sudden, he (*grow*) exhausted.

5. If he could have (*steal*) into the room without anyone seeing him, he probably would have (*tear*) up the photograph.

6. Ray had (*draw*) a picture of a hummingbird that was one of the best Elena had ever (*see*).

7. Jim arrived last night and (*come*) over, but he hasn't (*speak*) to your father about a job yet.

8. After the rodeo queen had (*ride*) past the reviewing stand, the visiting judge said, "You know, I could have (*swore*) she winked at me!"

9. The woman (*become*) very angry when she (*see*) that the sweaters had (*shrink*).

10. Ivan (*begin*) to think that he should have (*take*) the exam after all.

11. He (*do*) his best, but he couldn't have (*run*) any faster.

12. The soprano said that after she had (*sing*) the solo, she had (*go*) offstage.

13. Later I learned that if I had (*choose*) the silver bracelet, the salesclerk would have (*give*) it to me for half price.

14. When you think of all the sandwiches he had (*eat*) and all the lemonade he had (*drink*), he should have (*sink*) the minute he (*dive*).

15. If we had (*drive*) any nearer the edge of the cliff, the car might have (*go*) over.

• **EXERCISE 2. *Lay* and *lie*** Write the correct, standard form of **lay** (*lay, laid, laid, laying*) or **lie** (*lie, lay, lain, lying*) for each blank in the following sentences.

Example: She ______ the key on the edge of the counter whenever she comes in the back door.

Answer: lays

Example: Sam was certain he had seen the cat ______ in the space between the windowsill and the screen.

Answer: lying

1. Yesterday, the dog ______ under the porch for most of the day.

2. When he heard what was being said about me, Cliff soon ______ the rumors to rest.

3. When I saw the twins, they ______ peacefully in their father's arms.

4. She had to ______ on the floor since her mattress had not come.

5. Nina assured me that she had ______ the binoculars on the dashboard.

6. The golden retriever fetched the ball and ______ it at the small boy's feet.

7. Tell me where you have ______ the morning paper, please.

8. Last week Dad and I ______ the new linoleum that Mother had chosen.

9. Although the boxcar had fallen into the ravine and is now ______ on its side, the wrecking crew anticipates no problem in retrieving it.

10. She had just ______ down when the telephone rang.
11. The tiger is still ______ near the back of its cage.
12. You shouldn't have ______ so long in that broiling sun.
13. Until it was weaned, the young puppy usually ______ as close to its mother as possible.
14. ______ still; the doctor will be in shortly to examine your leg.
15. When the bird sees fresh food in its dish, it ______ its head to one side and sings happily.

• **EXERCISE 3. Troublesome verb pairs** Write the correct verb for each of the following sentences. You may wish to review the following entries in the Language Handbook: **bring**, **take**; **learn**, **teach**; **leave**, **let**; **rise**, **raise**; **sit**, **set**.

Example: Once the bread had (*rose, risen*), it was ready for the oven.
Answer: risen
Example: Mrs. Franklin asked her son to (*sit, set*) in another room since she wanted to move the living-room furniture.
Answer: sit

1. When you come in, please (*bring, take*) the clothes basket and (*sit, set*) it on the kitchen table.
2. Mrs. DeVito said she would (*learn, teach*) me how to make a cake with self-(*rising, raising*) flour.
3. Alyson (*learned, taught*) me how to trim poodles last week; this week I intend to (*sit, set*) down with the veterinarian and discuss my career plans.
4. Claude, (*leave, let*) me wash the outside of the windows while you (*bring, take*) the ratchet screwdriver back to Mr. Mendel.
5. We (*sat, set*) by the kitchen window, talked about the matters of the day, and watched the moon slowly (*rise, raise*) above the placid lake.
6. My parents won't (*leave, let*) me have the fireworks, so I must (*bring, take*) them back to Mr. Cizsek.
7. The horticulture teacher (*learned, taught*) his students how to (*sit, set*) out plants to take full advantage of the sun.
8. The lecturer (*sat, set*) his notes on the lectern and waited for one of the students to (*rise, raise*) a question.
9. (*Leave, Let*) me help you with the multiplication tables; in return, you can (*learn, teach*) me the state capitals.
10. When I asked if he would (*bring, take*) his book on home construction to the meeting, Eric (*raised, rose*) from the sofa and sauntered to the bookcase.

PART 2
Verb Tenses

• **EXERCISE 4. Uses and sequences** For each of the following sentences, write the appropriate form of the verb given in parentheses. In the two cases where both options are correct, write the word "Correct." You may wish to review the following entry in the Language Handbook: **Tenses of verbs**, sections **2** and **3**.

Example: Yesterday, at precisely 6:32, the sun (*rose, rises*).
Answer: rose
Example: By the end of next week, Franny and Sean (*will have driven, have driven*) through more than forty states.
Answer: will have driven
Example: Kristin wanted to visit Sweden since both sets of her grandparents (*emigrated, had emigrated*) from there.
Answer: had emigrated

1. The influenza epidemic of 1918 began in March; by November, when it disappeared, more than 21 million people (*died, had died*).
2. (*Will you have written, Will you write*) your English paper before your history research is due?
3. Homer's *Iliad,* a long poem dealing with the Trojan War, (*was, is*) one of the landmarks of Western literature.
4. By the time Sumi returned with an extension ladder, the baby robin (*hopped, had hopped*) back along the limb to the nest.
5. Raoul (*wonders, wondered*) if he'd left instructions for the carpenter.
6. Over the last forty centuries the "General Sherman," a massive redwood tree in California's Sequoia National Park, (*grew, has grown*) to a height of over 272 feet.
7. What Lincoln (*had said, said*) in a few short minutes at Gettysburg is considered one of his most eloquent speeches.
8. Before the French paid him to help with General Washington's Continental Army, Baron von Steuben (*had served, served*) with the Prussian army.
9. "Ladies and Gentlemen, I have a little invention that, if purchased, (*revolutionizes, will revolutionize*) your lives!"
10. The President (*stated, has stated*) on several occasions that he intends to cut federal spending.
11. The cat's contented purring suggested that it (*had recently been fed, was recently fed*).
12. The world traveler reported that many times she (*saw, had seen*) the Taj Mahal by moonlight.
13. When the concert next Saturday is over, I (*shall have played, have played*) my violin for the last time.
14. A dedicated opera lover, Marina (*has attended, attends*) performances at La Scala, Covent Garden, and the Metropolitan.
15. Before Kennedy promised that Americans would land on the moon, space scientists (*had known, knew*) that it could be done.

• **EXERCISE 5. Verbals** Write the standard form of the verb in parentheses in each of the following sentences. You may wish to review the following entry in the Language Handbook: **Tenses of verbs**, section **4**.

Example: She had hoped (*to buy, to have bought*) a genuine Australian opal.
Answer: to buy
Example: (*Riding, Having ridden*) in college, Vera already owned a fine pair of leather boots.
Answer: Having ridden

1. (*Having sat, Sitting*) in the doorway, Glenda could see how cloudy the sky was becoming.
2. (*Being given, Having been given*) two quarts of strawberries, Henry leafed through his cookbook in search of a recipe for chocolate fondue.
3. (*Writing, Having written*) the conclusion of his research paper, Tom went back to check the accuracy of several footnotes.
4. The two librarians had planned (*to have visited, to visit*) the famous Reading Room of the British Museum.
5. An experienced caddy, Marshall was embarrassed (*to have been hit, to be hit*) in the arm by a stray golf ball yesterday.
6. (*Having admired, Admiring*) a similar antique teapot in the Frick Museum, Mrs. Hernandez was delighted with the one we gave her.
7. Michelangelo's sixteenth-century painting of the *Creation of Man* is known (*to have taken, to take*) many years of arduous work.
8. (*Ripping, Having ripped*) the hem of her dress, Laurie sidled to the back of the room and stood against the wall.
9. When she heard about the scholarship for the children of World War II veterans, Tina asked (*to have been considered, to be considered*).
10. Would the curator have liked (*to photograph, to have photographed*) the painting before it was sent to the restorer?

PART 3
The Subjunctive

• **EXERCISE 6.** In each of the following sentences, list the verb in parentheses that is most appropriate in formal English. You may wish to consult the following entry in the Language Handbook: **Subjunctive**.

Example: If the Cardinals (*was, were*) at home this weekend, we might have gone to a ball game.
Answer: were
Example: The young couple requested that the entire marriage ceremony (*is, be*) no longer than an hour.
Answer: be

1. Dr. Chung is insisting that my father (*get, gets*) a second opinion.
2. If she (*would have, had*) sold the painting, the room would now seem terribly empty.

3. Aunt Florence said that if she (*was*, *were*) thirty again, she would doubtless live her life in exactly the same way.

4. If that chair (*wasn't*, *weren't*) so near the fireplace, you wouldn't be so hot.

5. Andrea cooks as though butter (*was*, *were*) still twelve cents a pound.

6. If John Adams (*was*, *were*) alive today, would he recognize the country he helped bring into being?

7. The judge requested that the jury (*is*, *be*) selected before the end of the court session.

8. The plane would have been on time if the weather (*would not have*, *had not*) been so turbulent.

9. The Senate Foreign Affairs Committee demanded that the top secret document (*be*, *is*) produced for the hearings.

10. If the rain (*would have*, *had*) come earlier, the grass might not be quite so brown.

Our doubts are traitors,
And make us lose the good we oft might win
By fearing to attempt.

William Shakespeare

CHAPTER 6 Subject-Verb Agreement

The terms in **boldface** in the following exercises refer to entries in the Language Handbook.

PART 1

General Problems with Agreement

• EXERCISE 1. Read the following sentences to determine subject-verb agreement. Write the verb in parentheses that best completes each sentence according to formal English. You may wish to review the Language Handbook for entries under **Agreement**, sections **1a**, **1b**, **1c**, and **1i**; **there is, there are**; **together with**.

Example: This dress with the designer label (*cost, costs*) far too much money.
Answer: costs
Example: Neither Ann nor Tony (*has, have*) any idea of the time.
Answer: has
Example: After supper, Andy and, I think, Jane (*is, are*) going to the movies.
Answer: are

1. The fiction shelves in the public library (*was, were*) filled with novels written by authors from dozens of countries.

2. Before the invasion of Normandy in 1944, meteorologists who were experts in their field (*was, were*) asked about probable landing conditions.

3. Table lamps using a three-way bulb (*has, have*) been on sale at a 10 percent discount.

4. Neither Ted nor his teammates (*was, were*) planning to attend the banquet.

5. Charlie (*doesn't, don't*) often go fishing alone.

6. There (*is, are*) probably four or five items on the agenda.

7. (*Has, Have*) Mr. Estes, president of Scavengers, Inc., determined where the sunken man-of-war might be located?

8. The old-fashioned inkstand and the quill pen (*suggest, suggests*) that the owner of the house loves antiques.

9. A high wind riffling the water in the lagoon and scattering sand in everyone's face often (*signal, signals*) a weather change.

10. Near the corner drugstore, Mr. Jimenez and his wife, an expert and efficient cook, (*operate, operates*) a hot-dog stand.

11. (*Was, Were*) the speakers scheduled to arrive by car or by bus?

12. There (*is, are*) usually solutions to virtually all problems.

13. At the end of the week either the manager or one of his assistants (*distribute, distributes*) the work schedule for the next week.

14. If the towels and the washcloth (*doesn't, don't*) get dry, we will hang them outside and let the wind dry them.

15. Here (*is, are*) the lawn furniture that I liked.

16. A mask from the South Seas, along with two feather capes made in Peru in the eighteenth century, (*was, were*) featured in the article on the museum's primitive art collection.

17. At the top of the attic stairs (*sit, sits*) a trunk filled with family pictures and a suitcase containing Great-grandma's pioneer diary.

18. The fighter, together with his trainer, (*is, are*) holding a press conference at 5:30 P.M. today.

19. Neither of these cake recipes (*require, requires*) any shortening.

20. Under one of those two beds (*is, are*) the box of winter blankets that need to be cleaned.

• **EXERCISE 2.** Write the verb in parentheses that best completes each sentence so that there is subject-verb agreement. You may wish to review the following entries in the Language Handbook: **Agreement**, sections **1e**, **1f**, **1h**, and **1j**; **one of those who**.

Example: Seven dollars (*was, were*) more than Ray wanted to pay for ten pounds of birdseed.
Answer: was
Example: *Heroic Deeds* (*tell, tells*) the story of a young Italian who makes and loses a fortune in the shipping business.
Answer: tells
Example: Physics (*has, have*) been called the aristocrat of the sciences.
Answer: has

1. Six months (*seem, seems*) a long time to wait for a response.

2. Annette is the only one of Pat's sisters who (*know, knows*) how to change a tire.

3. *The Adventures of Tom Sawyer* (*tell, tells*) about one of the most delightful characters in American fiction.

4. Val is the only one of those girls who (*demand, demands*) constant attention.

5. "Pomp and Circumstance" by Sir Edward Elgar (*was*, *were*) the recessional at the graduation ceremony.

6. Ten kilowatts (*is*, *are*) all the power the generator could produce.

7. After the weather report on our local radio and television stations (*come*, *comes*) the international news.

8. Two thirds of a yard, or twenty-four inches, (*is*, *are*) more than adequate to make four napkins.

9. "Terry and the Pirates," the most exciting of all the radio adventure stories broadcast during the '30s and '40s, (*captivate*, *captivates*) youngsters today just as it originally did.

10. Is it true that measles in children (*isn't*, *aren't*) nearly so dangerous as measles in adults?

PART 2

Collective Nouns

• **EXERCISE 3.** The subjects in the following sentences are **Collective nouns**. Write the correct verb in each item. You may wish to review the following Language Handbook entry: **Agreement**, section **1d**.

Example: The committee (*has*, *have*) voted to do away with expensive decorations for the dance.
Answer: has
Example: The Central High Band (*was*, *were*) debating about which routine to perform in the Thanksgiving Day parade.
Answer: were

1. The angry swarm of bees (*is*, *are*) headed in this direction.

2. In the stuffy room the jury (*was*, *were*) arguing about the integrity of the last witness for the prosecution.

3. Taking advantage of the time-out, the team (*was*, *were*) talking over the new play.

4. Ignoring a hundred years of tradition, the club (*has*, *have*) invited a woman to become a member.

5. In one smooth wave, the audience (*was*, *were*) standing and cheering the opera diva.

6. Grazing peacefully on the hillside, the flock of sheep (*was*, *were*) unaware of the wolf's presence.

7. The family (*is*, *are*) agreed among themselves not to contest the will.

8. An unruly mob (*is*, *are*) a difficult problem for police to handle.

9. Since hearing the news about the spectacular sale, a crowd from all parts of the city (*has*, *have*) assembled outside the store.

10. The troop of Scouts (*was*, *were*) discussing whether to camp at the river's edge or on the hillside above it.

11. Martha's herd of Charolais cattle (*has*, *have*) been sold for a record market price.

12. A family, as defined by numerous sociologists, (*consist*, *consists*) of a minimum of two people.

LANGUAGE NOTES

NEWS

Legend has it that *New York Tribune* editor Horace Greeley insisted that *news* was plural, and once wired a reporter: "Are there any news?" The prompt, if apocryphal, reply: "Not a new."

–William Safire

CHAPTER 7 Pronoun Problems

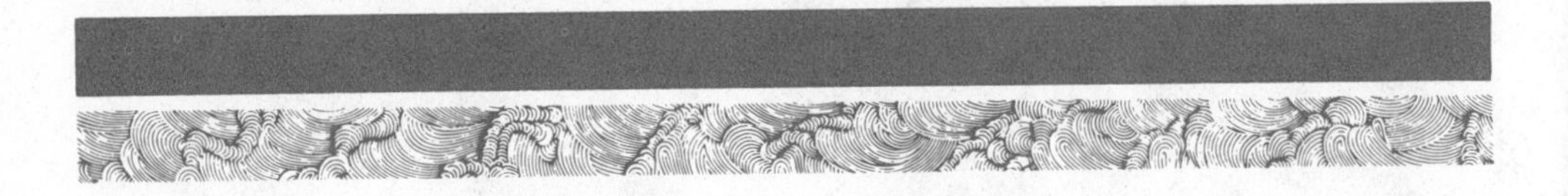

The terms in **boldface** in the following exercises refer to entries in the Language Handbook.

PART 1

Indefinite Pronouns

• EXERCISE 1. Read the following sentences to determine subject-verb agreement. Write the verb in parentheses that best completes each sentence according to formal English. You may wish to review the following entry in the Language Handbook: **Agreement**, sections **1g** and **2b**.

Example: Several pages of the book (*was*, *were*) missing.
Answer: were
Example: (*Has*, *Have*) any of this dinner been made with butter?
Answer: Has

1. Not one of the lifeguards at the beach this summer (*has*, *have*) had to rescue a swimmer from drowning.

2. Some of the cotton material imported from Italy (*was*, *were*) used for her wedding dress.

3. Each of the lions (*was*, *were*) basking in the morning sun.

4. I wondered if all of the cookies that Mark had baked last night (*was*, *were*) gone.

5. To help solve the oil shortage, many of the governors from the western states (*is*, *are*) recommending a ban on all dune buggies.

6. Few of the mechanics (*know*, *knows*) how to repair my great-grandmother's Packard touring car.

7. Everybody at the ceremonies (*was*, *were*) admiring the precision of the twenty-one-gun salute.

8. Not one of the oranges that I ate (*was, were*) as juicy as the ones we grow at home.

9. Anyone who helps clean up the parks (*is, are*) eligible for our community Good Citizen Award.

10. No one that I talked to (*has, have*) visited the Republic of San Marino, the oldest republic in the world.

11. Most of the scratches on the wooden desk (*has, have*) been the result of natural wear and tear.

12. Somebody in the tenor section of the chorus (*sing, sings*) slightly off-key.

PART 2

Personal Pronouns

• **EXERCISE 2.** Complete each of the following sentences with the singular or plural **Personal pronoun(s)** appropriate in formal English. You may wish to review the following entry in the Language Handbook: **Case**.

Example: For treasurer and program director our local League of Women Voters nominated Shelly Baum and (*I, me*).

Answer: me

Example: Although Yang Cha had had the idea in the first place, it was (*we, us*) who actually stripped and painted the antique chairs.

Answer: we

1. Rico and (*she, her*) customized the 1955 DeSoto that they had found in an old garage on her grandfather's property.

2. When Ralph moved to Pittsburgh, he took the butcher block table that (*he, him*) and his dad had made.

3. Mrs. Latta complimented Marge and (*I, me*) on the completeness of our job applications.

4. Although Louie smiled and waved, in the darkness Mrs. Stapleton couldn't see that it was (*he, him*).

5. Grandma divided her second-best set of dishes between my sister and (*I, me*).

6. Since I had never met my brother's father-in-law, I didn't know whether the man in the tweed sport coat was (*he, him*) or not.

7. At the drag strip where they had once raced, the manager greeted Pam and (*he, him*) with open arms.

8. Lying at the bottom of the pileup were the tight end and (*I, me*).

9. After Maria's laughing comment to us, we suspected it was (*she, her*) who had decorated the car.

10. At Wake Island, nearly 2,000 miles west of Hawaii, the pilot emerged from the cockpit, walked down the aisle, and asked if (*we, us*) boys were enjoying the flight.

11. Asked whether she was going to marry the man whom she'd been seeing, the widow replied, "That's strictly between (*he, him*) and (*I, me*)."

12. To Ramon and (*she, her*) fell the task of collecting the tickets.

13. While the boys did the cooking for the annual picnic, to (*us, we*) girls fell the task of chopping wood for the fire.

14. Had it been (*they, them*) who sent us this book, we would certainly have found a gift card.

15. Did the additional weight in your trunk cause either you or (*he, him*) to have trouble steering the car?

PART 3

Who and Its Forms

• **EXERCISE 3.** The blank space in each of the sentences below requires one of the forms of the relative pronoun **who**: *who, whom, whose, whoever, whomever.* Write the word that is appropriate in formal English.

Example: The lawyer did not know ______ was filing the case.
Answer: who
Example: The specialist ______ the company hired to oversee the installation of the computer was eminently qualified.
Answer: whom

1. Wendy knew a woman ______ vocation was mending broken dolls.

2. The dazzling ballerina was the daughter of a woman ______ own career had also been in dance.

3. I read about the man ______, according to the *Guinness Book of Records*, holds the record for the highest dive ever made into shallow water—a 40-foot dive into 12½ inches of water.

4. Now that we have an official contract for drilling, you may hire ______ applies for a job.

5. Have you ever met anyone ______ had been invited to the White House as an official adviser?

6. Major Henry Wayne was the man ______ the army sent to North Africa to buy camels for use in the western United States.

7. The carpenter ______ you hired to build the shelves in your basement has mitered the corners perfectly.

8. You may distribute these posters for the rummage sale to ______ you wish.

9. In late August the football coach had more than ten candidates for quarterback; by the beginning of the season he was down to three ______ were eligible.

10. The pianist ______ Tom had studied with when he was in high school had recommended that he continue his studies after he graduated.

11. The woman ______ I believe will be chosen to christen the new aircraft carrier is the daughter of the Chief of Naval Operations.

12. The ambassador, ______ government had only recently been formed, sent invitations to nearly everyone of importance.

13. The committee had commissioned a painting from an artist ______ they thought would do an outstanding job.

14. "In the final quarter, get the ball to ______ has the best chance of making a basket," the coach advised.

15. At the political rally we heard a speaker ______ many people think will be our next mayor.

PART 4

Antecedents

• **EXERCISE 4.** For each of the following sentences choose the pronoun that is most appropriate in formal English. You may wish to review the following entries in the Language Handbook: **Agreement**, section **2**; **Antecedent**.

Example: Mr. Holloway asked the attendant at one of the local service stations if (*they, he*) expected another delivery before the end of the month.

Answer: he

Example: If a team member wins, (*they, he or she*) should donate the trophy to our school.

Answer: he or she

1. As the teacher requested, every girl in the class had (*their, her*) gym clothes freshly washed and pressed for Field Day.

2. Neither of the companies showed a profit during (*its, their*) first year of expansion.

3. I spoke with the person who had telephoned the office this morning, but (*they, she*) had failed to leave (*her, their*) number.

4. If one is a hemophiliac (*you, he*) should be prudent about participating in certain activities.

5. After they constructed the canoe according to the directions in the kit, Jules and Laura asked if we wanted to test the result of (*their, his*) efforts.

6. Department store managers must be calm at all times; in addition (*you, they*) must be able to anticipate customers' needs.

7. The radio station manager said that neither of the groups performing at the concert had recorded (*their, its*) songs but that a recording session had been planned for the near future.

8. The insurance executive asked, "Can you make certain that every woman in the office signs (*her, their*) entitlement card before leaving work on Friday?"

9. Yesterday at his favorite restaurant, Larry ate three pieces of pie; (*you, he*) shouldn't do that while trying to lose weight.

10. The rapidity with which the students can dismantle and reassemble a motor is a good test of (*your*, *their*) mechanical skill.

11. Unless cooks have actually served a ten-course dinner, (*they*, *you*) have no idea of the effort and organization it takes.

12. Neither of the men brought (*their*, *his*) lunch to work today.

PART 5

Reference of Pronouns

• **EXERCISE 5. Vague and indefinite pronouns** Each of the following sentences contains a problem concerning the **Reference of pronouns**. If the pronoun reference is vague, replace the pronoun with a more specific noun. If the pronoun reference is indefinite, eliminate the pronoun entirely. Rewrite each sentence.

Example: The swimming team has been quite successful, but it is a sport which attracts few spectators.

Answer: The swimming team has been quite successful, but swimming is a sport which attracts few spectators.

Example: John D. Rockefeller is credited with having enormous foresight and a thorough grasp of the oil business, which made him both envied and admired.

Answer: John D. Rockefeller is credited with having enormous foresight and a thorough grasp of the oil business, two qualities that made him both envied and admired.

Example: In the program notes, it tells that the symphony was composed in less than three days.

Answer: The program notes tell that the symphony was composed in less than three days.

1. Because Anna had admired Mrs. Osborn's teaching, Anna decided that she would become one.

2. Since football is a contact sport, they are constantly improving the padding and helmets worn by the players.

3. In the movie *The Sting*, it shows two men who pull off a complicated hoax.

4. Jody loved to sew, but she rarely wore them once they were done.

5. Before turning in my term paper, I asked my father to help me with the proofreading and it pleased him enormously.

6. Delivering the mail is a tiring task, but in my neighborhood they do an excellent job.

7. The advertisement stipulated a high-school diploma, but that was not my situation.

8. During the 1950s, many Westerners went uranium prospecting, but it was difficult to find.

9. Debra looked for three hours but she couldn't find her glasses; unfortunately, as she pointed out, she needed them to find them.

10. Although he admitted he had never been on one, Dino thought that hunting was cruel and inhuman.

11. Duane was anxious to learn some hang-gliding techniques, since it was very popular in his part of the country.

12. Franz's father, who had studied violinmaking at a famous school in Germany, said that they often spend more than six months working on a single instrument.

• **EXERCISE 6. Ambiguous pronouns** Each of the following sentences contains a problem with the **Reference of pronouns**. Rewrite each sentence so that its meaning is clear. Although each sentence can be written in more than one way to avoid ambiguity (two interpretations are possible), you need write only one sentence for each number. You may wish to review the following entry in the Language Handbook: **Ambiguity**, section **1**.

Example: Mary did not want to be partners with Tanya in the tennis tournament, since she was a much better singles player.

Answer: Mary did not want to be partners with Tanya in the tennis tournament, since Mary was a much better singles player. [Or: Mary did not want to be partners with Tanya in the tennis tournament, since Tanya was a much better singles player.]

1. The party was the same day as the class picnic, so we had to miss it.

2. Dale wanted to contact Sati as soon as he arrived in town.

3. After her meal she ordered dessert, although it was tasteless.

4. Carla decided to take the small part in the play, although it was poorly written.

5. Sheila laughed heartily at Ms. Netterling because she had a good sense of humor.

6. Minutes after the tractor crashed through the fence, it shuddered and collapsed into the field of soybeans.

7. Mother pressed an extra twenty dollars into Gertrude's hand even though she disliked special treatment for anybody.

8. Kay refused to share a locker with Virginia although she always said hello to her in the halls.

CHAPTER 8 Problems with Modifiers

The terms in **boldface** in the following exercises refer to entries in the Language Handbook.

PART 1

Linking Verbs

• **EXERCISE 1.** List the **Adverb** or **Adjective** that completes the sentence according to formal English. You may wish to review the following entries in the Language Handbook: **bad**, **badly**; **good**, **well**; **Linking verb**.

Example: Pat realized she had not been responsible for the loss, but she still felt (*bad*, *badly*) about the ring's disappearance.
Answer: bad
Example: Mother stuffed the turkey with a sausage dressing, but all of us thought the dressing tasted (*odd*, *oddly*).
Answer: odd
Example: Despite her long stay in the hospital, Sarah insisted that she felt (*good*, *well*) enough to travel.
Answer: well

1. Although she was not particularly frightened of it, Brenda said the boa constrictor felt (*strange*, *strangely*).

2. Everyone at the wedding commented on how (*beautiful*, *beautifully*) the soloist had sung.

3. While it was brewing, the coffee smelled (*wonderful*, *wonderfully*).

4. My mother jokingly commented that a typical mother always feels as (*bad*, *badly*) as any one of her children feels.

5. With its flaky golden crust and juicy filling, the apple pie looked (*appetizing, appetizingly*).

6. We were surprised that the fireplace worked so (*good, well*) after the chimney cleaner had finished cleaning the flue.

7. Mort often acts as (*peculiar, peculiarly*) as his brother.

8. He felt (*bad, badly*) because he couldn't invite everyone to dinner.

9. The great cathedral at Chartres rose (*majestic, majestically*) above the surrounding fields.

10. Brett commented that this year's raspberry crop tasted as (*sweet, sweetly*) as any he had ever eaten.

11. Asked what it felt like to be a newly naturalized citizen, Mr. Varela said smilingly, "It feels (*good, well*) to be a part of this wondrous nation!"

12. After examining some of her dress designs, the manufacturer told Gail that her dresses could be produced (*cheap, cheaply*).

13. Don had been feeling (*bad, badly*) about coming in fourth until the coach told him that the third-place winner had been the preceding year's winner.

14. The lizard appeared (*sluggish, sluggishly*) as it lay in the warm, morning sun.

15. When their teacher left the room, the boisterous kindergartners behaved so (*bad, badly*) that the principal had to come in and quiet them.

PART 2

Comparison of Adjectives and Adverbs

• **EXERCISE 2.** In the following sentences choose the adjective or adverb form in parentheses that is appropriate in standard written English. You may wish to review the following entry in the Language Handbook: **Comparison of adjectives and adverbs**.

Example: Please don't feel you have to buy the (*cheapest, cheaper*) of the two coats.
Answer: cheaper
Example: The two boxes on the left are, I think, (*equaller, more equal*) in size than the two on the right.
Answer: more equal

1. Which of the last five calculus problems did you think was the (*least, less*) difficult?

2. The agile dancer in the second row kicked (*vigorouser, more vigorously*) than any other dancer.

3. Of the two cages we were considering, the (*smallest, smaller*) was the (*better, best*) bargain.

4. These pears seem (*riper, more riper*) than the ones we bought last week.

5. Of the three brothers who occupy the room, Neal keeps it (*neatest, more neat*).

6. The new jet engines that have recently been developed run (*more noiselessly, more noiseless*) than the older models.

7. The pillow at the back of the rocker is (*more fatter, fatter*) than the one in the seat.

8. I never thought I'd see anyone who danced (*more clumsily, more clumsier*) than I.

9. Sally readily agreed that she felt (*most secure, more secure*) in the water than in the gondola of a hot-air balloon.

10. This is the (*worse, worst*) winter we've had since 1967.

11. Which manufacturer invested (*most heavily, more heavier*)–Acme, Best, or Consolidated?

12. In the darkness it was difficult to tell which one of the three children was sleeping (*more soundly, most soundly*).

PART 3

Modifiers Used with Gerunds

• **EXERCISE 3.** Complete each sentence by choosing the word that is appropriate in formal English. You may wish to review the following entry in the Language Handbook: **Gerund**, section **3**.

Example: I must admit that the sight of (*you, your*) manipulating a unicycle made us laugh.

Answer: your

1. I was delighted at (*him, his*) knowing about the obscure artist.

2. (*Brian, Brian's*) refusing the award made sense to those who knew his feelings about public acclaim.

3. (*Mia, Mia's*) fidgeting detracted from her fine speech.

4. We were counting on the (*mayor, mayor's*) approving our budget.

5. Charles was the only debater who noticed (*your, you*) avoiding the question.

6. Ms. Alvarez criticized (*me, my*) being late.

7. The agent insisted on the importance of the (*singer, singer's*) getting sufficient rest before a performance.

8. I consider (*you, your*) scowling at dinner an unfavorable judgment on my cooking.

CHAPTER 9 Word Choice

The exercises in this chapter are designed to help you distinguish among words that are commonly confused. In the first part, you will be dealing with homophones, words that sound alike but are spelled differently. In the second part, you will be dealing with words that are commonly confused.

Each of the words or groups of words in **boldface** is listed in the Language Handbook.

PART 1

Homophones

• **EXERCISE 1.** Write the one word from the pair in parentheses that best completes each sentence: **born**, **borne**; **capital**, **capitol**; **complement**, **compliment**; **council**, **counsel**; **lead**, **led**; **principal**, **principle**.

Example: The atomic age, according to contemporary scientists, was (*born*, *borne*) in a laboratory located at the University of Chicago.
Answer: born
Example: The (*capital*, *capitol*) of Finland is the city of Helsinki.
Answer: capital
Example: Aaron thanked the man for his sincere (*compliment*, *complement*).
Answer: compliment
Example: The (*council*, *counsel*) debated for three weeks before deciding on a downtown parking policy.
Answer: council
Example: The assault on San Juan Hill was (*lead*, *led*) by Theodore Roosevelt.
Answer: led

Example: The (*principle*, *principal*) of the high school required all students to attend the assembly.
Answer: principal

1. Many foreigners are surprised that the (*capital*, *capitol*) of the United States is not New York City.

2. After the understudy acknowledged her eighth curtain call, the director said to the producer, "Tonight, a star was (*borne*, *born*)."

3. At the end of the play, Hamlet was (*borne*, *born*) on the shoulders of four captains to his last resting place.

4. With their domes and classical columns, the (*capital*, *capitol*) buildings of many states suggest the ancient rather than the modern world.

5. Had the country listened to the (*council*, *counsel*) of its leading ecologists, many of its larger cities might now be free from pollution.

6. The (*council*, *counsel*) listened to the proposal by the Commissioner of Parks for increased staff and maintenance.

7. Jorge's grandmother laughed and said, "The greatest (*complement*, *compliment*) a cook can receive is an empty plate."

8. You will find that gold jewelry will (*complement*, *compliment*) a beige outfit better than silver jewelry will.

9. The physics teacher spent half of the class period explaining the (*principal*, *principle*) of electromagnetism.

10. During the long drive across Texas, the trail boss's (*principal*, *principle*) worry was lack of water.

11. The documents for the time capsule were first placed in a (*lead*, *led*) box before being buried beneath the cornerstone.

12. The pass receiver (*lead*, *led*) his nearest pursuer by more than ten yards.

• **EXERCISE 2.** Write the word from the pair or group in parentheses that best completes each sentence: **stationary**, **stationery**; **their**, **there**, **they're**; **to**, **too**, **two**; **your**, **you're**.

Example: If (*your*, *you're*) planning (*to*, *too*, *two*) attend the testimonial dinner, please bring (*your*, *you're*) spouse and at least (*to*, *too*, *two*) other people.
Answer: you're, to, your, two
Example: Eleanor said that the (*stationary*, *stationery*) store did not carry the line of get-well cards that she preferred.
Answer: stationery

1. The captain was (*to*, *too*, *two*) busy watching the treacherous reefs (*to*, *too*, *two*) notice the storm approaching from the west.

2. After the wind died down, the flag at the top of the pole hung virtually (*stationary*, *stationery*).

3. Mrs. Trejo shook her head and said, "I think (*your*, *you're*) wrong about the Victors. (*Their*, *There*, *They're*) moving to Houston, not Dallas."

LANGUAGE NOTES

Folk etymology is the term for the creation of new words by mistake or misunderstanding or mispronunciation. *Tawdry,* for example, came from Saint Audrey's, a place where cheap merchandise was sold. In today's language, *harebrained* is often giddily and irresponsibly misspelled *hairbrained,* perhaps on the notion that the hair is near the brain.

The slurred *and* is one of the prolific changers of phrases. When *hard and fast* is spoken quickly, it becomes *hard 'n fast,* which sometimes gets transformed to *harden-fast rules.* In the same way, the old *whole kit 'n caboodle* is occasionally written as *kitten caboodle,* a good name for a satchel in which to carry a cat.

–William Safire

4. If the space between the (*to, too, two*) thermal panes widens and one of the panes cracks, (*your, you're*) insurance policy will cover replacement.

5. The building over (*their, there, they're*) on (*their, there, they're*) right is the DeYoung Museum.

6. Four members of the League of Women Voters discussed the results of (*their, there, they're*) investigation of the personal property tax laws.

7. Glaring at her angry son, Mrs. Svoboda said, "(*Your, You're*) not going (*to, too, two*) spend the summer on a dude ranch and that's that!"

8. "Please let me go to the fair! I want to go (*to, too, two*)!" cried the child wildly.

9. One of the legends about this haunted mansion states that during the day the statues remain (*stationary, stationery*), while at night they step from (*their, there, they're*) pedestals and move among the rooms.

10. It was (*their, there, they're*), on that very spot, that my great-grandfather built his first house after arriving in the United States.

11. Do you prefer monogrammed or plain (*stationary, stationery*)?

12. Do you agree with the quotation that states, "You can't be (*to, too, two*) rich or (*to, too, two*) thin"?

PART 2

Words Commonly Confused

• **EXERCISE 3.** Write the word from either pair that best completes each sentence: **accept**, **except**; **adapt**, **adopt**. In some sentences you will have to change the form of the word you choose.

Example: Tim and Sonja _____ Phum Thi Kim, who had come to the United States as a refugee in 1977.

Answer: adopted

Example: When the television station received more than ten thousand complaints, the station manager realized that the public would not _____ the new weather reporter.

Answer: accept

1. After the first snows had fallen, all the hiking trails _____ those on the lowest slopes were closed to the public.

2. Many cooks find it difficult to _____ their recipes to the metric system of measurement.

3. Has the box office announced when it will be _____ orders for next Saturday's concert?

4. Athletes from every western country _____ Bulgaria were participating in the Olympic trials.

5. When it appeared at their door for the fourth morning in a row, the family realized that the dog had _____ them.

For last year's words belong to last year's language
And next year's words await another voice.

T. S. Eliot

6. Orchestra conductors for a ballet or opera company know that they must ______ the tempo of the music to the performers.

7. As a foreign exchange student, Moira knew that she would have to ______ many invitations to speak to civic groups.

8. The student council discussed the three resolutions which had been submitted and officially ______ the one written by Francine.

• **EXERCISE 4.** Write the one word from the following pair that best completes each sentence: **affect**, **effect**. In some cases you will have to change the form of the word you choose.

Example: The music had a decided ______ on the mood of the audience.
Answer: effect
Example: The heavy rain seemed to ______ the moods of everyone who scurried along the street.
Answer: affect

1. The biologist's somber statements were designed to ______ the attitude and behavior of everyone in the room.

2. The thunder and lightning had had a definite ______ on the dog; it cowered under the bed until long after the last raindrop fell.

3. According to Mrs. Levy, the purpose of the boycott on flour was to ______ a change in the store's pricing policy.

4. Knowing that certain colors ______ people's attitudes toward their surroundings, the interior designer chose cheerful yellows and tranquil blues for the hospital's corridors.

5. ______ an accent, Jaime tried to convince the antique dealer that he knew a great deal about European paperweights.

6. The research project was designed to discover whether people's complexions were ______ by the eating of certain foods.

7. We inquired what ______ the low water table would have on the supply of water.

8. It is not easy to ______ a change in the rules of professional football.

9. The eerie sound of the oboe was ______ the young children in the audience; they either sat on the edges of their chairs or moved closer to their parents.

10. The devaluation of the dollar could have a disastrous ______ on the U.S. economy.

11. One of life's little domestic mysteries is why the adding of a bright blue substance to wash water should have the ______ of whitening the wash.

12. Most authors are delighted to appear on talk shows since public appearances ______ the sales of their books substantially.

• **EXERCISE 5.** Write the following word or phrase that best completes each sentence: *all-around, all right, already, all ready, all to-*

gether, altogether. You will find these words in the Language Handbook listed under **all and its compounds**.

Example: The head designer had ______ approved the drawing, but it still had to be submitted to the engineering department.
Answer: already
Example: Instead of individual pictures, Grandmother wanted the family to stand ______.
Answer: all together

1. Since he had ______ seen the new sculpture gallery, Steve said he would meet us later in the lobby near the museum store.
2. Tammy was stunned when she was named ______ senior athlete at yesterday's assembly.
3. After examining the fabric label, the fire chief said the material met the safety requirements and would be ______ for us to order.
4. The platoon sergeant asked his men if they would be ______ for the fifteen-mile march within the hour.
5. Before the start of the game, both the defensive and offensive teams stood ______ for an official photograph.
6. The paramedic hovered anxiously by the nurse's station, waiting to inquire if his patient would be ______ after yesterday's relapse.
7. Although Mickey had ______ eaten three hot dogs, he claimed that he was still hungry.
8. The teacher asked whether everyone in the class was ______ to begin the examination.
9. Although she had trained for months, Maureen thought it ______ improbable that she would win the competition.
10. The color of the new carpeting is ______, but there are several curious holes.
11. Dad was ______ to put the hamburgers on the grill when he saw our neighbor's dog running away with two patties in its mouth.
12. The young couple were so preoccupied that the waiter thought it ______ possible that they were unaware the restaurant was closing.

• **EXERCISE 6.** Write the one word from either pair that best completes each sentence: **allude, refer**; **allusion, illusion**. In some cases you will have to change the form of the word you choose.

Example: The speaker ______ directly to the Alamo in his speech celebrating Texas independence.
Answer: referred
Example: The ______ of a rich vein spurred the eager young miner to spend all his time digging for silver.
Answer: illusion

1. Exhausted and thirsty from the drive through the desert, the trucker believed he had seen a service station, but it turned out to be only an ______.

2. The philanthropist, who wished to remain anonymous, was embarrassed when the speaker ______ to him by name.

3. Bonnie gave the ______ of calmness, although she later confessed that she had been nervous.

4. The warden promised the new inmate that no guard would even ______ to the nature of his crime.

5. In the title of his book *Of Mice and Men*, Steinbeck used an ______ to a line from one of Robert Burns's poems.

6. The reporter probably meant John Dean when he ______ to the "man who had pointed out the cancer growing on the Presidency."

7. Scaled-down furnishings give this room the ______ of being much larger than it actually is.

8. When the master of ceremonies spoke of the greatest male comedian of our time, each of the comedians at the head table assumed the ______ was to himself.

9. Although she did not ______ to me by name, most of my friends knew from the clues given that I was the Mystery Student.

10. As a young woman, Blanche ______ to opera as a ridiculous form of the arts; as she grew older, however, she developed a serious interest in it.

• **EXERCISE 7.** Write the word from either pair that best completes each sentence: **among**, **between**; **amount**, **number**.

Example: In typing his term paper, Robin had left out a ______ of footnotes.
Answer: number
Example: You will find the whole cloves on the second shelf ______ the cinnamon and the dill.
Answer: between

1. Once the results of the primary were clear, the voters were left with a choice ______ one candidate who had never held public office and another who had once been accused of fraud.

2. "Calm down, miss," said the woman in the Lost and Found Department. "I'm certain you'll find your keys ______ the things in this box."

3. Mrs. Keough was astonished at the ______ of dust that had accumulated in the filter.

4. To the meeting of the OPEC nations, Sheik Yamani had brought a ______ of critical questions.

5. ______ the debris in the attic, we found a handsome and ornate picture frame.

6. The Hruskas divide their time ______ their apartment in Florida and their summer home in the Poconos.

7. The homeowner complained about the excessive ______ of noise coming from the house two doors away.

8. Bring a sufficient ______ of books or you may be bored.

• **EXERCISE 8.** Write the word from the pair in parentheses that best completes each sentence: **advice**, **advise**; **device**, **devise**; **disinterested**, **uninterested**.

Example: A conflict of that intensity can probably be resolved only by (*disinterested, uninterested*) parties.
Answer: disinterested
Example: Sam and David may be too stubborn to accept any (*advice, advise*).
Answer: advice

1. The bird was clever enough to (*device, devise*) a way of getting out of its cage.

2. Allan's younger sister tried to tell him about the new friend she had met, but Allan was too (*disinterested, uninterested*) to pay any attention.

3. As the most (*disinterested, uninterested*) bystander, Mr. Feldman was asked to give his impression of the cause of the accident.

4. The swimming coach had hoped to (*device, devise*) a series of exercises that would get the swimmers back into shape for the season.

5. If John is smart, he will ask for some (*advice, advise*) from the local Legal Aid Society.

6. Mr. Moss developed a small (*device, devise*) that would lengthen the life of a washing machine significantly.

7. The law assumes that as a member of a school faculty, a teacher is not sufficiently (*disinterested, uninterested*) to be eligible to run for the Board of Education.

8. The diplomat felt he must (*advice, advise*) his country that a trade agreement could improve relations immeasurably.

9. Alistair, a bow and arrow enthusiast, worked all summer to (*device, devise*) an arrow that would work like a boomerang.

10. Although she had asked her mother's opinion on the proper clothing for a weekend in New York, Sophia disregarded the (*advice, advise*) she received.

11. Harley fell asleep during the movie not because he was (*disinterested, uninterested*), but because he had had little sleep the night before.

12. One of the functions of the guidance department is to (*advice, advise*) students about future career choices.

• **EXERCISE 9.** Write the word from either pair that best completes each sentence: **emigrate**, **immigrate**; **ensure**, **insure**. In some cases you will have to change the form of the word you choose.

Example: The DiFiores ______ from Italy to California in the 1880s.
Answer: emigrated
Example: To ______ fair treatment of each customer, the baker asked each person to take a number as he or she entered.
Answer: ensure

1. The huge diamond had originally cost a million dollars, but it was now ______ for more than twice that amount.

2. The government representative indicated that thousands of refugees wished to ______ to Canada or to the United States.

3. One theory of the origin of Native Americans argues that they ______ from northern Asia across the Aleutian Islands.

4. If you wish to ______ the arrival of that letter, send it by registered mail.

5. During the potato famines of the nineteenth century, many people ______ from Ireland to other English-speaking countries.

6. In the early nineteenth century many English prisoners were asked to choose between hanging and ______ to Australia.

7. Lloyd's of London has traditionally been the company which would ______ anything–a dancer's legs, a pianist's hands, or a shipment of valuable minerals.

8. After World War II, many Jewish people wished to ______ from Europe to the newly formed country of Israel.

9. Most states have laws which make it mandatory for drivers to be adequately ______.

10. To ______ the success of their first space probe, the NASA scientists worked many years.

• **EXERCISE 10.** Write the word from either pair that best completes the sentence: **notorious**, **famous**; **lose**, **loose**. In some cases you will have to change the form of the word you choose.

Example: Few things create more noise and chaos than a fox ______ in a henhouse.

Answer: loose

Example: The FBI produced evidence that the man had been a ______ criminal.

Answer: notorious

1. In her younger days, Grace had been a world-______ singer, but now she was a character actress in a popular soap opera.

2. Annette sighed, "If I keep on ______ things this year, the insurance company will probably cancel my policy."

3. During World War II, when the government feared careless talk might lead to sabotage, one poster read, "______ lips sink ships."

4. When it became known that the man was a ______ card shark, no casino in Las Vegas would allow him to play.

5. Once the German shepherd was ______, he ran in determined pursuit of the squirrel that had been tormenting him.

6. Gita read everything she could find about the legendary exploits and dissolute life of the ______ Don Juan.

7. The most ______ marine biologist of our time is Jacques Cousteau.

8. Nervous about appearing before the group, Mal was especially concerned that he would ______ his place in the book from which he was to read.

• **EXERCISE 11.** Write the word from the pair that best completes each sentence: **imply**, **infer**. In some cases you will have to change the form of the word you choose.

Example: From the expression on her father's face, Elena ______ that he had been amused by her comment.
Answer: inferred
Example: Mr. Marini strongly ______ that I would be fired if I came to work late.
Answer: implied

1. "Young man," the irate motorist said, "are you ______ that I deliberately backed into your car?"

2. Hank ______ from its appearance and behavior that the puppy had been well treated.

3. From the description the caller gave, Mrs. Vargas ______ that his poor television reception was probably caused by an inadequate or malfunctioning antenna.

4. Seeing the trail of sand leading from the back door to the shower stall, Mr. Butterfield could ______ that his daughter had spent the day at the beach.

5. The prosecutor ______ from the witness's hesitation that the witness might be withholding valuable information.

6. The fan yelling from just above the dugout strongly ______ that the umpire had poor vision.

7. From diaries and journals of the period, the historian was able to ______ that drought, not disease, had led to the decline of the settlement.

8. Every time that actor makes a gesture or lowers his voice, he ______ an entire range of complex emotions.

• **EXERCISE 12.** Write the word from either pair that best completes the sentence: **nauseated**, **nauseous**; **moral**, **morale**.

Example: Residents of the area complained bitterly about the ______ odor rising from the city dump.
Answer: nauseous
Example: The lawyer argued that the case had both legal and ______ implications.
Answer: moral

1. Since roller coasters invariably made Sue ______, she decided to have an ice-cream cone while the others waited in line.

2. The writer believed that no novel deserved to be called great unless it dealt with universal ______ issues.

3. After their fifth straight win, the ______ of the team was high.

4. The six-car accident on the freeway was the most ______ sight the reporter had ever witnessed.

5. The supervisor was told that the ______ of her crew might be improved if she were more liberal in her praise.

6. After his one attempt to eat them, Oscar said the oysters had ______ him.

7. Emily has such an intense fear of flying that she finds even an airport itself ______.

8. Far too many people believe that it is impossible for a person to be ______ if he or she is involved in politics.

• **EXERCISE 13.** Write the word from either pair that best completes the sentence: **precede**, **proceed**; **prophecy**, **prophesy**; **than**, **then**. In some sentences you will have to change the form of the word you choose.

Example: Donna Andersen's name ______ Donna Anderson's in the alphabetical listing of students.
Answer: preceded [Or: precedes]
Example: Margie's older sister lives in Bogotá, more ______ three thousand miles away from the rest of the family.
Answer: than
Example: The ______ of the oracle at Delphi were generally stated in quite ambiguous words.
Answer: prophecies

1. The plumber could not ______ with the repair until the part he had ordered arrived from the manufacturer.

2. At basketball practice Mr. Myers spent most of the first hour working on free throws; ______ he drilled the team on rebounds.

3. Since you are shorter, Bob, why don't you ______ Kent in the line?

4. At the beginning of each decade, reporters ask eminent people to ______ what will occur in the ensuing years.

5. Terry and Chiyo ______ to the first house, hoping that the occupant would have the first item on their scavenger-hunt list.

6. When Jocasta heard the ______, she gave her son Oedipus to a shepherd with instructions that the baby be destroyed.

7. This sundae contains more ______ six hundred calories.

8. Occasionally the first-grader had difficulty remembering that *i* ______ *j* in the English alphabet.

9. Depending on the week she picks the grapes, Aunt Tillie's homemade grape juice is sweeter some years ______ others.

10. In Shakespeare's *Julius Caesar*, the soothsayer ______ that harm will come to Caesar, but Caesar chooses to ignore him.

11. After carefully cleaning the press, the master engraver ______ placed the copper plate into position.

12. At the end of the editorial, the announcer said that the ______ statement had represented the views of the management.

13. The salesperson thought that the jacket was a size larger ______ Fred needed.

14. The demonstrators had been ______ toward the municipal building when a police officer asked them to halt their march.

15. The clairvoyant was certain her ______ would come true.

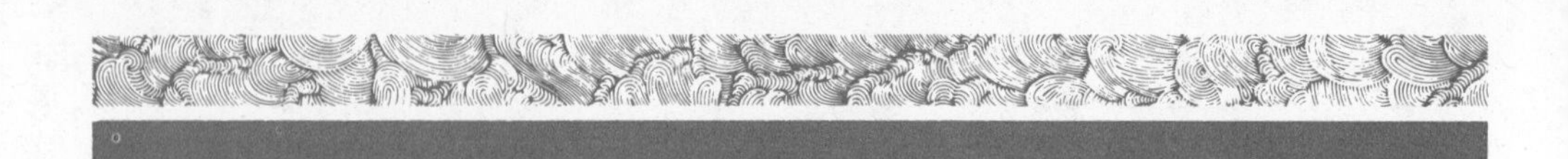

CHAPTER 10 Conventions of Usage

The exercises in the first part of this chapter are designed to help you recognize the difference between formal and informal English. The second part focuses on appropriate prepositions. Part three deals with nonstandard English.

Each of the words or phrases in **boldface** is listed in the Language Handbook. You may wish to review the entry before completing the exercise.

PART 1

Troublesome Words and Expressions

• EXERCISE 1. Write the one phrase from either pair that would be used in formal English: **center around**, **center on** or **center in**; **each other**, **one another**. In some cases you will have to change the form of the word.

Example: Courteously, the various speakers applauded ______.
Answer: one another
Example: As the title of the book suggests, the action of Conrad's *Lord Jim* is ______ the title character.
Answer: centered in [Or: centered on]

1. The two boxers shook ______ hands clumsily.

2. The decorator had planned the room so that attention would be ______ the large portrait hanging above the mantel.

3. The ultimate responsibility for the decision was ______ the chairman of the board.

4. Although none of the four tennis players had ever met before, they knew ______ by reputation.

5. Until the curtain rose for the first act, Steve's interest had been ______ his date.

6. The bus driver and the passenger glared at ______ contemptuously; finally the passenger produced a token and sat down.

7. The three printers who had helped produce the prizewinning brochure congratulated ______ on their achievement.

8. The authority to continue or call off the game was ______ one person.

• **EXERCISE 2.** Write the one word from either pair that completes the sentence in formal English: **farther**, **further**; **healthful**, **healthy**.

Example: If the next gasoline pump is ______ than six miles, we will never get there.
Answer: farther
Example: Winnie was certain that her homemade bread contained more ______ ingredients than any commercially made loaf.
Answer: healthful

1. Have you had the opportunity to think ______ about the terms of the offer?

2. To the small boy, distances were incomprehensible; he thought New York City was no ______ from Salt Lake City than San Francisco was.

3. Congratulations, Mr. Herman. Your ______ appearance should convince people to exercise more regularly.

4. The nutritionist attempted to explain to the audience the necessity for a ______ diet.

5. "Marry you!" the cashier exclaimed. "Nothing could be ______ from my thoughts."

6. Mr. Elliott irritated the guest of honor ______ by mispronouncing her name.

7. Mrs. Steiger was agreeably surprised to discover that Milwaukee is no ______ than seventy-five or eighty miles from Chicago.

8. With his twinkling eyes and firm skin, the septuagenarian looked as ______ as any fifty-year-old.

9. When the government banned cyclamate, claiming that it had no ______ properties, the general public was suspicious of the evidence.

10. According to many pediatricians, a chubby child is not always a ______ child.

• **EXERCISE 3.** Write the one word from either pair that completes the sentence in formal English: **if**, **whether**; **last**, **latest**.

Example: The ______ figures from the Department of Labor indicate that unemployment fell slightly during the summer.
Answer: latest
Example: The headwaiter asked ______ we wanted to sit near the windows or the salad bar.
Answer: whether

1. As we walked toward the stables, Juan asked ______ I had ever ridden on an English saddle.

2. According to the coach's instructions, the ______ person in was responsible for securing the oars and locking the boathouse.

3. The ______ increase in the prime lending rate has made the purchase of a home all but impossible for many people.

4. ______ you have the proper wrenches, I'll be happy to tighten the bolts on that air conditioner.

5. When he was ready to resume dictating, Mr. Hansen asked his secretary to reread his ______ several sentences.

6. Inga doesn't know ______ she has the stamina to become a photographer's model.

7. To understand the ______ developments in music, the choral director discovered she needed to know more about the use of electronic devices.

8. ______ she sells her quota of magazines or not, Priscilla will still have earned a number of valuable prizes.

• **EXERCISE 4.** Write the one word from either pair that completes the sentence in formal English: **less**, **fewer**; **like**, **as**, **as if**, **as though**.

Example: The Department of Agriculture reports that there are ______ family-owned farms now than ever before.

Answer: fewer

Example: Will arrived fifteen minutes late for the service, just ______ Ida had said he would.

Answer: as

1. If you're going to make lemonade again this afternoon, please put ______ sugar in it.

2. Angela was not pleased when her brother told her that she looked ______ a scarecrow; she thought her weight loss made her look quite attractive.

3. Although Marco backed the car into the garage ______ he had always done, he heard the sound of something being dragged under the bumper.

4. There were ______ accidents at that year's Indianapolis 500 than ever before.

5. From the early returns of several key districts, it appears ______ the incumbent is going to be returned to office.

6. The travel agent noted that ______ people were booking tickets for Europe; instead, the fashionable place to visit seemed to be the South Seas.

7. We had become so accustomed to Millie's long hair that when she had it cut last year, she looked ______ she had been scalped.

8. The jeweler assured Mr. Corso that he would have ______ trouble with his watch if he had it cleaned every year.

• **EXERCISE 5.** Write the one word from either pair that completes the sentence in formal English: **mutual**, **common**; **try and**, **try to**.

Judge Strikes Blow for Literacy

While eating lunch, Champaign County Circuit Court Judge Robert Steigmann found the grammar of a bread label in contempt for reading "25 percent less calories." He notified the offending bakery of its misdemeanor, and a few months later received a new loaf of bread with "25 percent fewer calories" on the wrapper. It came inside an engraved bread box reading "To Teach Is to Learn Twice, Thank You." The president of Interstate Brands also had written Steigmann that "hopefully, your comments will encourage us and our package designers to upgrade the state of the art." Now, if only the judge could outlaw such clichéd jargon . . .

Champaign-Urbana (Ill.) NEWS-GAZETTE, October 13, 1979.

Example: Once the two antagonists finally met, they discovered even more grounds for their ______ antagonism.
Answer: mutual
Example: While Marian secures the spinnaker, you ______ keep the boom from shifting.
Answer: try to

1. As they approached the shooting gallery, Kevin turned to his father and asked, "Would you ______ win that large stuffed panda for me?"
2. In most states there is ______ cooperation between local and state police agencies.
3. Although the two countries had often differed in their methods of government, they had a ______ enemy that held them together.
4. The two principals agreed that one of their ______ problems was a lack of funds for the support of girls' athletics.
5. When Ms. Mavrelis tore her new tweed overcoat on a nail, she asked if the local cleaners would ______ reweave the tear.
6. The judges of the final debate had some difficulty declaring a winner; both teams had been so skilled that there was virtually a ______ destruction of arguments.
7. Margo, who had not touched a piano in nearly four years, said she would ______ learn the concerto in time for the concert.
8. When the two men realized they had a ______ interest in farming, they began to exchange information.

PART 2
Idiomatic Prepositions

• **EXERCISE 6.** List the prepositions that most appropriately complete each of the following sentences. Before you begin, you may wish to review the entry on **Preposition** in the Language Handbook. (The idiomatic uses of prepositions that are not covered in the entry should be available in either a good dictionary or a dictionary of synonyms.)

Example: The kangaroo is an animal peculiar (*to*, *in*, *by*) Australia.
Answer: to
Example: Myra's supervisor observed that she was extremely perceptive (*for*, *in*, *on*) financial matters.
Answer: in
Example: We learned that Shakespeare's plays have been translated (*into*, *in*, *on*) virtually every language, including pidgin English.
Answer: into

1. Wally was so engrossed (*with*, *for*, *in*) the television program that he failed to hear the doorbell.
2. Though Mr. Kim said Tom's question was not relevant (*for*, *in*, *to*) the discussion, Tom continued to press for an answer.

3. If you walk through our backyard, please be wary (*about, toward, of*) the dog; she distrusts strangers.

4. Our stingy neighbor was averse (*against, from, to*) spending either time or money on the improvement of his property.

5. Logically, it is silly to be envious (*toward, of, about*) the good fortune of others; psychologically, however, such an attitude is understandable.

6. The field officers on the right flank reported that their forward troops were particularly vulnerable (*to, for, in*) bombardment.

7. The arrogant architect thought that the drawing by his young assistant was devoid (*in, with, of*) all grace or style.

8. People who are neglectful (*about, with, of*) their responsibilities may find they are given fewer and fewer.

9. Can you tell me if the pineapple is native (*of, to, in*) Hawaii?

10. As his ballooning figure indicated, Bill had too great a fondness (*of, for, to*) banana cream pie.

11. During the twentieth century the horse has been superseded (*with, by, because of*) the automobile.

12. The exuberant four-year-old, excited by his birthday celebration, was forgetful (*with, of, about*) his manners.

13. Accustomed to being obeyed, the retired general was highly intolerant (*toward, with, of*) his wife's opposition to his decision.

14. The actor refused the part in the film, saying that he was repelled (*at, by, with*) the idea of working with a snake.

15. When he realized what his practical joke had caused, Stan repented (*of, about, for*) his actions.

PART 3

Nonstandard English

• **EXERCISE 7.** The following sentences contain examples of nonstandard English. Correct the part of the sentence that contains nonstandard expressions by writing the words before and after the problem and correcting the problem itself. You may wish to review the following entries in the Language Handbook: **a, an**; **Double negative**; **kind, sort**; **nohow**; **nowheres**; **them**; **this here, that there**.

Example: We looked in every room in the house, in the basement, and in the yard, but the poodle was nowheres around.
Answer: was nowhere around
Example: He handed me a apple that he had just picked.
Answer: me an apple
Example: That there road is terribly bumpy.
Answer: That road
Example: He couldn't barely reach the elevator buttons.
Answer: He could barely [Or: He couldn't reach]
Example: I can't use those kind of wrench on my car.
Answer: use this kind [Or: use that kind]

No one who cannot limit himself has ever been able to write.
Nicolas Boileau

1. Until we visited the zoo, none of us had ever seen a anteater.

2. Jamie couldn't solve hardly any of this week's math problems.

3. Don't you think them kind of candlesticks would look nice on the living-room mantel?

4. The cherry table, which the store assured us had been delivered, was nowheres to be found.

5. Those kind of remarks are quite out of place in a formal assembly such as this one.

6. Now, this here rosebush is a hardy perennial and should bloom five or six months of the year.

7. Until he gets his new trifocal lenses, Uncle Bliss can't read the small print in the newspaper nohow.

8. Despite the money he had made as a peach picker, Dennis didn't have nothing good to say about the work.

9. Cicadas, at least these here kind, can keep you awake.

10. The shepherd estimated that if the chinook wind blew any harder, more than half of them sheep would panic and fall into the snow-filled arroyo.

11. The automobile slowly picked its way through an number of deep and treacherous potholes.

12. If you don't watch carefully, you can catch that there rope on the pommel and pull yourself off the horse.

13. These sort of sprinklers will last for at least ten years.

14. Shaking off the catcher's signal, the pitcher told himself that he didn't never pitch a low curve to a southpaw.

15. Mr. Van was upset when the plumber called and said that because of a personal problem, he couldn't come nohow.

Chapter 5 Verb Problems

A. In the following sentences, the present tense form of the verb is given in parentheses. Read the sentence and then write the form appropriate in standard written English.

1. Although Ralph had (*take*) gloves, he had not (*wear*) them.

2. The lifeguard (*lead*) the paramedics to the place where the swimmer had last been (*see*).

3. Lill had (*rise*) shortly before sunrise and (*go*) to the beach.

4. Have you (*speak*) to Curt as you have (*do*) in the past?

5. The insurance agent has (*write*) a description of the plants that had been (*steal*) from the florist.

6. The winds had (*blow*) so fiercely that a branch on the oak tree had (*fall*) into the driveway, narrowly missing our new car.

7. Mr. Carlisle could have (*swear*) the alarm had not (*ring*).

8. If he had (*know*) that it was octopus, would he have (*eat*) it?

B. Write the verb or verb form that is appropriate in formal English for each of the following sentences.

1. Please pick up the clothes (*laying, lying*) on the floor and (*bring, take*) them down to the basement.

2. After they (*rose, raised*) the price of candy, Grandmother (*learned, taught*) us to make our own.

3. The Spanish teacher (*announced, has announced*) on several occasions that she intends to give pop quizzes.

4. Annette had planned (*to enter, to have entered*) a school of nursing, but she finally decided to become a doctor.

5. If the reporter (*was, were*) more dedicated, he would have (*knowed, known*) more about the topic he was investigating.

6. When the golfers complete this last hole, they (*will have played, have played*) more than six consecutive hours.

7. The firm's insurance company insisted that the coverage for industrial accidents (*be, is*) increased at least 50 percent.

8. (*Losing, Having lost*) the field glasses he had borrowed, Ray went to more than a dozen stores looking for a similar pair.

Chapter 6 Subject-Verb Agreement

Write the correct verb form for each of the following sentences.

1. The speakers of Ann's stereo system (*sound, sounds*) good in the new apartment.

2. There (*is, are*) more than enough pie for everyone.

3. In the new wing of the museum, the store and the sculpture gallery (*share, shares*) the space equally.

4. (*Hasn't, Haven't*) the election judges finished counting yet?

5. Neither the weight nor the design of the fabric (*please, pleases*) the tailor.

6. Two-thirds of a cup of oil (*is, are*) all the recipe calls for.

7. The cast of the spring musical (*agree, agrees*) the set could be struck within eight hours of the final curtain.

8. *Positive Forces* (*was, were*) recently reprinted as a paperback.

Chapter 7 Pronoun Problems

Write the appropriate pronoun form for each of the following sentences according to formal English.

1. See if that's (*he, him*) at the back door.

2. The woman (*who, whom*) had sold us the cat inquired about it.

3. Liberty Savings and Loan raised (*their, its*) interest rates.

4. If one is allergic to penicillin, (*you, he or she*) should alert a doctor.

5. Most of the people (*who, whom*) we met in Africa earn less than $1,000 per year.

6. The job of choosing the band was assigned to Ned and (*I, me*).

7. If students haven't learned to study in high school, (*they, you*) may find college difficult.

8. If you were (*I, me*), would you accept the offer?

Chapter 8 Problems with Modifiers

List the adverb or adjective form that completes the sentence according to formal English.

1. Which of the two cars is the (*more, most*) economical?

2. Tia Dolores thought the chili tasted (*sharp, sharply*) enough.

3. My employer disliked (*me, my*) arriving late every day.

4. The rock band played (*good, well*) during each of its six sets.

5. You shouldn't feel (*bad, badly*); it was an accident.

6. Why does he always dress so (*conspicuous, conspicuously*)?

Chapter 9* Word Choice

Write the one word from the pair in parentheses that completes the sentence according to formal English.

1. Is (*there, their*) no way to (*ensure, insure*) that the package will arrive by Monday morning?

2. If (*fewer, less*) than three qualified people from within the company apply for the new positions, we will (*except, accept*) applications from people outside the company.

3. From the tone of Nan's report, Alice (*implied, inferred*) that Nan was angered by the decision of the town (*council, counsel*).

4. Mother was (*all ready, already*) to leave when Marshall asked (*if, whether*) she had either money or credit cards.

5. Mr. Dura (*alluded, referred*) to Lascaux Cave as one of the more (*famous, notorious*) examples of primitive art.

6. The (*last, latest*) issue of the magazine included an article on the (*affect, effect*) of plastic on home decoration.

7. If you'd taken (*your, you're*) own (*advice, advise*), you never would have tried (*to, too*) ski under such dreadful conditions.

8. If you rearrange the agenda so that item 4 directly (*precedes, proceeds*) item 9, then item 4 would (*complement, compliment*) item 9.

Perfect Score: 66

---

*There is no test on Chapter 10.

Unit Three Mechanics Review

CHAPTER 11 Three Areas of Mechanics

The terms in **boldface** in the directions for the following exercises refer to entries in the Language Handbook.

PART 1

Capitalization

• **EXERCISE 1.** Some of the words in the following sentences need to be capitalized. Write these words, supplying **Capital letters** where needed.

Example: grocery shopping at one local store can be a culinary adventure; one aisle is filled with such delicacies as chinese condiments, italian cooking oil, moroccan orange slices, and english fruitcakes.
Answer: Grocery, Chinese, Italian, Moroccan, English
Example: after the author of the article "new talents in music" hailed her carnegie hall debut, jacqueline called her mother, who lived in a small town in the south, and read the review.
Answer: After, New, Talents, Music, Carnegie Hall, Jacqueline, South
Example: "my topic this tuesday," the speaker announced, "is the effect of the reformation on the arts; in addition, i will begin a discussion of the tenets of protestantism."
Answer: My, Tuesday, Reformation, I, Protestantism

1. unlike thanksgiving, which is always celebrated on the fourth thursday in november, easter can occur in either march or april.

2. until sears tower was completed, the twin towers of the world trade center were the highest buildings in either the eastern or western hemisphere.

3. when she was traveling through northern italy, sister mary margaret made a special trip to assisi, the birthplace of saint francis.

4. most of the new york delegation to the 1932 democratic convention arrived at union station on the famous twentieth century limited.

5. in the midst of the civil war, lincoln signed the emancipation proclamation, but the war went on for several years until lee finally surrendered and the confederacy fell.

6. the president's airplane is now called by the dignified name of *air force one,* but the first presidential plane–it belonged to franklin roosevelt–was called *sacred cow.*

7. after completing a history course, my uncle enrolled in three english courses: shakespeare seminar 306, the literature of south america 399, and an advanced course in composition.

8. from many miles above the earth, the astronauts of the apollo mission reported seeing a variety of blue colors ranging from cobalt to aegean to aquamarine.

9. to his archaeology professor, randy said, "excuse me, sir, but i'd like you to meet rabbi and mrs. levine. the rabbi is quite interested in your excavations at masada and would like to know if you have unearthed any examples of roman weapons."

10. this last autumn robert and his cousin michael picked more than forty bushels of jonathan apples, and between halloween and armed forces day their mothers canned more than a hundred quarts of applesauce.

11. during our visit to london, we saw the changing of the guard at buckingham palace, attended a play at the shaftesbury theatre, shopped on bond street, ate at a restaurant in the savoy hotel, and took a boat trip up the thames.

12. my great-grandfather had booked passage from europe on the *titanic,* but fortunately great-grandmother insisted on sailing on the *mauretania.*

13. the byrnes placed their canoe on the top of their ford station wagon, wedged the aaa maps of the northeast under a visor, and tossed the collected plays of bernard shaw onto the back seat. (they were driving to niagara and planned to see two plays at the shaw festival near there.)

14. on the northwest corner of arsenal street and tower grove avenue stands the second congregational church where henry ward beecher, a nineteenth-century abolitionist, is reputed to have preached; the church itself has been preserved as a landmark.

15. madge's english teacher said, "and now, i'd like to read you part of a poem that's so bad, it's good. listen to the poem; then try to explain my paradoxical statement: 'and did young stephen sicken,/ and did young stephen die?/ and did the sad hearts thicken,/ and did the mourners cry?' " –Samuel L. Clemens, THE ADVENTURES OF HUCKLEBERRY FINN, 1885.

PART 2

Plurals of Nouns

• **EXERCISE 2. Plurals ending in *s* or *es*** Write the plurals of the following nouns, using your dictionary when you are uncertain. The words followed by an asterisk have two acceptable plurals; give both of them. You may wish to review the following entry in the Language Handbook before beginning this exercise: **Plurals of nouns**, sections **1**, **2**, **3**, **4**, and **5**.

Examples:	veto	lunch	mutiny	bread	life
Answers:	vetoes	lunches	mutinies	breads	lives

1. tornado*	**6.** crash	**11.** lobby	**16.** desperado*
2. proof	**7.** Emily	**12.** knife	**17.** ditch
3. gypsy	**8.** thief	**13.** curio	**18.** armory
4. wallet	**9.** stucco*	**14.** waltz	**19.** grief
5. raisin	**10.** tax	**15.** oyster	**20.** shovel

• **EXERCISE 3. Other plural formations** Write the plurals of the following nouns, using your dictionary when you are uncertain. The words followed by an asterisk have two acceptable plurals; give both of them. You may wish to review the following sections in the Language Handbook before beginning this exercise: **Plurals of nouns**, sections **6**, **7**, **8**, and **10**. For further assistance use a dictionary.

Examples:	basis	ox	armband	moose
Answers:	bases	oxen	armbands	moose

1. Chinese	**6.** louse	**11.** maid of honor	**16.** criterion*
2. appendix*	**7.** get-together	**12.** antenna*	**17.** plateau*
3. tooth	**8.** trout	**13.** father-in-law	**18.** heir apparent
4. woman	**9.** virtuoso*	**14.** court-martial	**19.** drive-in
5. larva	**10.** foot	**15.** sheep	**20.** stadium*

PART 3

Possessives

• **EXERCISE 4.** The italicized item in each of the following groups tells what is owned. The second item names the owner or owners. Write the possessive form of the owner followed by the name of the thing owned. You may wish to review the following entry in the Language Handbook: **Possessive case**.

Example: *book* Charles
Answer: Charles's book [Or: Charles' book]
Example: *feeling* everyone
Answer: everyone's feeling

There is no subject so old that something new cannot be said about it. Dostoevsky

Example: *vacation* a month
Answer: a month's vacation
Example: *novels* Hawthorne and Melville
Answer: Hawthorne's and Melville's novels
Example: *car* the Blisses
Answer: the Blisses' car

1. *bottles* the babies
2. *responsibilities* the men
3. *lawsuit* Barbara
4. *plan* my brother-in-law
5. *music* Elton John and the Beatles
6. *taxes* the year
7. *ring* someone
8. *catalog* Horner
9. *strategy* a commander
10. *rest* a minute
11. *gifts* the alumni
12. *report* a gun
13. *house* the Cyruses
14. *honking* the geese
15. *campaign* the Attorney General
16. *product* Harris and Sneed
17. *time* an hour
18. *guess* anyone
19. *lease* the owner
20. *importance* the phenomena
21. *trainer* the porpoises
22. *screams* Agnes and Inez
23. *labor* a day
24. *decks* a man-of-war
25. *fault* no one

• **EXERCISE 5.** Some of the words in the following sentences require an **Apostrophe**. Write these words, adding apostrophes where needed. Hint: In some cases with **Plurals of nouns**, the apostrophe is optional; in such instances be consistent in your use or omission of the apostrophe.

Example: Ill show you Lennys poetry from the 1970s, but remember that its not his best work.
Answer: I'll, Lenny's, 1970s (or: 1970's), it's
Example: Whod guess thered be three YMCAs within walking distance of Lincolns downtown area.
Answer: Who'd, there'd, YMCAs (or: YMCA's), Lincoln's

1. Although the art historians specialty is painting, hes also interested in Persian miniatures and Japanese netsukes.

2. During the late 1960s and early 1970s Americas involvement in the Vietnam war increased significantly.

3. Every time she saw asterisks (*s) in her textbook, Leahs eyes automatically dropped to the bottom of the page.

4. During its grand opening sale the supermarket gave three months groceries to one shopper each week.

5. Jane, in your essay on Buddhism, you have more than five misspelled *Buddha*s; nobody elses paper had quite so many.

6. If youre going to repaint the house numbers on the Lutzes mailbox, remember to leave more space this time between the two 3s.

7. Isaac Isherwoods father spent over one hundred dollars on an engraved watch for his son, but the jeweler mistakenly engraved it with 2 *i*s instead of 2 *I*s.

8. There were only 2 As awarded to the entire class of M.A.s.

LANGUAGE NOTES

CONTRACTIONS
CONTRACTIONS
C'NTR"CT'NS
C'NTR'CT'NS

Contractions have been used in English as long as there have been words to contract. Many contractions which were used centuries ago are no longer seen or heard today. Two from old English which are nearly obsolete are *doff* (do off) and *don* (do on). *Doff,* according to the Oxford English Dictionary, means "to put off or take off from the body. . . ." and *don* means just the opposite of *doff.* Shakespeare's writings are full of contractions. Some we no longer use, as *scape* for escape in "Safe scape the King." Others are common today: "What's the matter?" "Who's within!" "Here's a skull now." " 'Tis for the head."

CHAPTER 12 Punctuation

The terms in **boldface** in the directions for the following exercises refer to entries in the Language Handbook.

PART 1

End of Sentence Punctuation

• **EXERCISE 1.** Decide which mark should be used at the end of each of the following sentences. Some numbered items contain more than one sentence. Write the word preceding the punctuation to be added and the appropriate mark–**Period**, **Exclamation mark**, **Question mark**, **Dash**, or **Ellipsis**. If you think a sentence could end with more than one mark, write both and be prepared to defend your answer.

Example: Did you order this book on the U.S. National Parks
Answer: Parks?
Example: Look out for that truck It nearly hit that car
Answer: truck! car! [Or: car.]
Example: Lois ordered a red telephone for her kitchen
Answer: kitchen.
Example: "If you'll wait just a minute," she said, "I'm certain Mr. Flynn is "
Answer: is——" [Or: is. . . ."]
Example: Son, your mother and I wish you'd stay home for the summer Keep in mind that a rolling stone
Answer: summer. stone. . . . [Or: stone——]

1. The electrical circuit that controls the outdoor lights seems to have a defect

2. That man walking into the laundromat is Mr. Elizabeth, are you listening to me

3. Ow Every time I try to hit this tack, I hit my finger instead

4. You did say Dad's boss was coming to dinner tonight, didn't you

5. If you hadn't been greedy, you might have shot both those ducks Remember, a bird in the hand

6. And now, my fellow countrymen, you are probably asking yourselves what I intend to do about inflation

7. Ron, you look marvelous How many pounds have you lost

8. If I take this left path, can I reach the glacier before noon

9. Is there anyone here who remembers which countries were involved in the Battle of Trafalgar Oh, good

10. Now, dump the cut grass into the rest of the mulch Yes, did you have a question

11. Twice a year you must remove the grate that covers the motor and

12. Nonsense I distinctly remember telling you that last week

13. What will she do with her plants when she flies to Japan

14. Did you say that Winston Churchill was the author of that quotation Everyone knows it was Abraham Lincoln who said, "A house divided "

15. Young man, you have the car back by midnight or

PART 2

Commas

• **EXERCISE 2. In a compound sentence** Decide in which of the following items commas are needed to separate the main clauses in a **Compound sentence**. Then write the word that should be followed by a **Comma**, the comma itself, and the **Coordinating conjunction**. If the sentence is not compound and no comma is needed, write "None." You may wish to review **Comma**, section **1**, in the Language Handbook.

Example: The front-door key wasn't on the key ring nor was it in any of the usual hiding places.

Answer: ring, nor

Example: Dean offered to accompany his Aunt Donna and his Uncle Jim said he would be a fine escort.

Answer: Donna, and

1. The airplane hadn't even taken off yet the woman in seat 16-D was complaining of being airsick.

2. In the crawl space underneath the house the exterminator looked for signs of a skunk's nest and for any evidence of cracks in the foundation.

3. We refuse to give up hope for a miracle is always possible.

4. By noon, Norma had shopped for the groceries and picked up the cleaning and made a list of things to do but she still had not heard from Ralph.

5. The student couldn't remember Professor Kaplan's name nor could he recall the name of his new book.

6. The floor refinishers offered to sand off the old varnish and to refinish the hardwood floors.

7. All of the garden flowers were in bloom but the roses were particularly glorious.

8. On their way to the recycling center they met Bill and Steve and Susan gave him their bundles of paper and their sack of cans.

9. Jess had signed a contract with the Jets or the Rams would have certainly tried to draft him.

10. Mr. Barnhart turned off the ignition switch but for nearly half a minute the car continued to run.

11. The downpour occurred in the middle of our vacation so the carpets got soaked.

12. Tim had waited for the train was rarely on time.

• **EXERCISE 3. In a series** Read the following sentences and decide where commas or semicolons are needed to separate items in a series. Write any word that should be followed by a punctuation mark, along with the appropriate mark. You may wish to review **Comma**, section 3, in the Language Handbook. Hint: Use the "close" style of adding a comma before the last item in a series.

Example: Before distinguishing himself in World War I, Harry Truman, who was later to become President, had been a timekeeper for a railroad construction gang a mailroom clerk and a bookkeeper.

Answer: gang, clerk,

Example: Composer Frederick Loewe and lyricist Alan Jay Lerner were responsible for the creation of *Brigadoon,* a musical about a mythical Scottish village that appears once every one hundred years *Paint Your Wagon,* a musical about the California Gold Rush era and *My Fair Lady,* a musical about the transformation of a cockney flower girl into a proper English lady.

Answer: years; era;

1. Mr. Nemo told the realtor that he was interested in buying a house that was modern roomy and economical.

2. At a recent family reunion, Jake talked with Uncle Jasper, who was a test pilot for the Navy Aunt Winnie, who ran a travel agency in Buffalo and his cousin Erv, who had organized a successful management consultant firm.

3. According to the title page in this book, the publishers have offices in Glenview, Illinois Dallas, Texas Oakland, New Jersey Tucker, Georgia and Palo Alto, California.

4. The mystery guest on the television quiz show said he had choreographed shows on Broadway in nightclubs and in large amphitheaters such as the Municipal Opera in St. Louis.

5. Novels poems essays short stories and plays are all examples of the main divisions of literature.

6. Jane arose about two in the morning and decided to close the windows in the kitchen to get a drink of water and to check on the new puppies.

7. The freshmen elected an excellent slate of officers: Don Steinhorn, president Gerry Skubic, vice-president Jerome Rugan, secretary and Arliss Parenti, treasurer.

8. Because the setting is delightful the instructors are excellent and the opportunities are unparalleled, the music camp attracts applicants from throughout the country.

9. Designing the set building it and painting it are the major responsibilities of the technical director of a play.

10. During the past several years we have had such foreign students in our school as Pepe, a Mexican Inga, an Austrian and Ian, a Scot.

11. The body stores iron primarily in the liver spleen blood and bone marrow.

12. The survey team divided its respondents into three discrete groups: women who were married and working women who were unmarried and working and women who were married and not working.

• **EXERCISE 4. To set off introductory clauses and phrases** Read the following sentences and decide where commas are needed to set off introductory clauses and verbal phrases. Then write the last word of the clause or phrase and the comma that should follow it. If a sentence does not require a comma, write "None." You may wish to review **Comma**, sections **4** and **8**, in the Language Handbook.

Example: After he finished the gutters no longer leaked.
Answer: finished,
Example: Sliding into home Ron scored the winning run.
Answer: home,

1. While waiting for the pictures to develop Ed did his exercises.

2. To check the cleanliness of the barracks the sergeant ran a white-gloved hand over the tops of the lockers.

3. Before he went to bed Brian read the last act of *King Lear*, one of Shakespeare's greatest tragedies.

4. Changing a tire was something of a challenge to Kay.

5. If you can understand this explanation calculus should cause you no problems.

6. After advertising for a used stove Mrs. Dietzler was amazed that she had had only three responses.

7. To find an honest man is not as difficult as Diogenes thought.

8. After engraving the trophy Mr. Ruiz polished it once again and wrapped it carefully in a soft cloth.

9. When Mary called the bear looked up from the garbage can and slowly turned its head in her direction.

10. When coordinating the colors in a room you need to decide first on one dominant hue.

11. To bring up the heavy chest the diver needed two winches and a strong rope.

12. If you like the type for the wedding announcements can be smaller or larger.

• **EXERCISE 5. To set off interrupting elements** Read the following sentences and decide where commas are needed to set off interrupting elements, appositives, and contrasting expressions. Then write any word that should be followed by a comma, and the comma itself. You may wish to review the following sections in the Language Handbook: **Comma**, sections **2**, **6**, and **7**.

Example: Mrs. LaFleur the owner of the craft store gives lessons in weaving and needlepoint.
Answer: LaFleur, store,
Example: Well if you do plant strawberries, put them near the barn.
Answer: Well,
Example: Carlotta you're going to put this money in the bank aren't you?
Answer: Carlotta, bank,
Example: For dessert the kids preferred ice cream not fresh fruit.
Answer: cream,

1. "All right anyone who has worked on the rings is automatically in the intermediate gymnastics class."

2. Fred a railroad buff organized a short trip on the stretch of line between town and the old mining camp.

3. It was nearly four in the morning I guess before we had finished unloading the fish and securing the lines.

4. The winners of decathlons have to be versatile don't they?

5. One of the simplest but most useful of all inventions however is the pencil with attached eraser.

6. This particular bread is quite healthful since it calls for honey not granulated sugar.

7. The last six items on the menu are not available sir.

8. The mayor has called this meeting friends to discuss the problem of pollution.

9. You don't really think this house is haunted do you?

10. The bakery will be out of doughnuts by now I suppose.

11. The deadline for the paper was only a suggestion not an order wasn't it?

12. Although they both had to catch an early flight, it was Larry not Wendell who seemed concerned about rising at dawn.

13. Could you help Mr. Adamic Karl with his easel and paintbox?

14. The *Wall Street Journal* a newspaper specializing in business and economics reporting has won several Pulitzer Prizes.

15. Naomi you're too young to enter the barrel race, but you could qualify I think for the tug-of-war.

• **EXERCISE 6. To set off nonrestrictive phrases** Decide which of the modifying phrases in the following sentences are nonrestrictive and should be set off by commas. Then write any word that should be followed by a comma, and the comma itself. Write "None" if a sentence does not require a comma. You may wish to review **Comma**, section **5**, in the Language Handbook.

Example: The poetry read in class yesterday was written by Poe.
Answer: None
Example: The other automatic garage door equipped with a UHF digital control and a time-delayed light was the one we decided to have installed.
Answer: door, light,

1. The sea gulls wheeling and turning floated on the invisible wind.

2. Muriel has a date with the boy running for the goal line.

3. This edition of *Gulliver's Travels* despite its yellowed pages and small print was being offered for more than $5,000.

4. The bundle of new bills dropped by the thief had been taken to the police station as evidence.

5. The men exhausted but exhilarated by the applause agreed to return to the studio for further demonstrations of their phenomenal barbershop harmony.

6. The man with his hand in the air has been trying to capture the auctioneer's attention for some time.

7. The name Horatio given to him by his maternal grandmother had been replaced by the nickname "Hulk."

8. The train rumbled closer its whistle cutting the air.

9. Tomatoes grown in your own garden always seem tastier than those bought in a store.

10. The leopard crouching beneath a low bush watched the antelope as it picked its dainty way toward the waterhole.

11. The club manager believed that Janet making her first appearance as a professional singer was destined to be a star.

12. Catalog sales first popularized by a large national store now account for a significant share of the commercial market.

• **EXERCISE 7. To set off nonrestrictive clauses** Locate each **Adverb clause** or **Adjective clause** in the following sentences; then decide which of the clauses are nonrestrictive and should be set off by commas. Write any word that should be followed by a comma, and the comma itself. Write "None" if a sentence does not require a comma. You may wish to review **Comma**, section **5**, in the Language Handbook.

Example: On the third week in June which was long before their usual arrival the Robinsons drove into the small fishing resort.
Answer: June, arrival,
Example: The Grandview Stables which had been the site of a terrible fire was back in operation within a month.
Answer: Stables, fire,
Example: Is Red Skelton the comedian who is such a superb pantomimist?
Answer: None
Example: One of the squirrels whom we called Charlie ate all the birdseed.
Answer: squirrels, Charlie,

1. The uniforms since they had been purchased with municipal funds were stored in the basement of the city hall.

2. The two-story yellow house which was built at the turn of the century by a lumber magnate has been turned into a local historical museum.

3. Dr. McKeon's rule was that anyone who made an appointment was billed whether the appointment was kept or not.

4. The photographer who had been engaged to take pictures at the wedding had once worked for a large newspaper.

5. The biscuits that Katie served for breakfast were light and crisp probably because she had used her grandmother's recipe.

6. You cannot fix a dripping faucet unless you have proper tools.

7. The mine workers would not reenter the shaft no matter how safe the engineer said it was.

8. The coelacanth one of a variety of fish that scientists believed had been extinct for more than seventy million years was brought to the surface of the Indian Ocean in December, 1938.

9. Rico's Pizza Parlor became an immediate success though Rico himself had never made a pizza before he opened the restaurant.

10. The Rosetta stone which Napoleon brought back from his Egyptian campaign provided the world with the first translation of ancient Egyptian writing.

11. Mozart who was a child prodigy began performing and composing at an extremely young age.

12. By six o'clock when the evening rush hour was at its height there was a four-mile backup at the Olive Street intersection.

13. A senator who chairs a senate committee has more power than any member of that committee.

14. At the Outward Bound camp Tom's fellow campers would not let him fail at anything no matter how inadequate or inept he felt.

15. The marchers who had come from every state in the Union held a midnight vigil at the Washington Monument.

• **EXERCISE 8. Routine uses** Decide where commas are needed in the following sentences. Write the word or figure that should be followed by a comma, and the comma itself. You may wish to review **Comma**, section **9**, in the Language Handbook.

Example: The Board of Education designated June 15 1985 as the date for the closing of the venerable old school.
Answer: June 15, 1985,
Example: To get a copy of the bill Burton wrote to the Senate Documents Room United States Capitol Washington D.C. 20510.
Answer: bill, Room, Capitol, Washington, .

1. Lamar wrote to Dean Howard Findley 3810 Cullen Street Houston Texas 77004 to thank him for his interest and to accept the scholarship offer.

2. Mark Twain was born November 30 1835 and died April 21 1910; coincidentally, the years of his birth and death were years when Halley's comet flashed across the sky.

3. The author of the first book I read was Mary McCarthy, the second Henry F. Baxter Ph.D.

4. The first measurements of the Arctic Ocean suggested that it extended for nearly 3600000 square miles and that roughly two-thirds of it was covered with ice.

5. Dear Mother
Could you please send me your recipe for brownies?

6. Dr. Martin Luther King Jr. was the victim of an assassination in 1968.

7. One of my friends prefers modern furniture, another Victorian.

8. Mr. Tillapaugh instructed his secretary to close his business letters with these words: "Very truly yours R. J. Tillapaugh."

9. In October 1938 the young Orson Welles starred in a radio broadcast that purported to be a newscast about the invasion of earth by Martians.

10. Both Evanston Illinois and Evanston Wyoming were founded by John Evans, a man who also founded two universities and two seminaries and even had a famous Colorado peak named for him.

• **EXERCISE 9. For clarity** Read the following sentences and decide where commas are needed to separate words that might be mistakenly run together when read for the first time. Then write the word that should be followed by a **Comma**, and the comma itself.

There are two good things in life, freedom of thought and freedom of action.
W. Somerset Maugham

Example: Next to the man who had rescued the girl the mayor gave the city's highest award.
Answer: Next, girl,
Example: If you and your brother are playing play to win.
Answer: playing,

1. When focusing Dan discovered that his new glasses got in the way of the viewer.

2. When you are choosing choose a pattern that will blend with the tweed in your new topcoat.

3. If you like the doorman will park your car for you.

4. After we locate this address book me on the first flight going to Patagonia.

5. Not more than three weeks after Bud was asked to be the best man at their wedding.

6. Mary thought she would detest the camping trip to Yellowstone, but ever since she has been eager to go camping again.

7. During the Christmas holiday shopping is Wynn's major source of entertainment.

8. With those lamps can turn on and off automatically.

9. To the allergic kittens are often as much a danger as are full-grown cats.

10. Below the foothills slowly gave way to the vast plains beyond.

PART 3

Semicolons

• **EXERCISE 10. In compound sentences** Read the following sentences and decide where a **Semicolon** is needed to separate main clauses. Write each word that should be followed by a semicolon and the punctuation mark itself. You may wish to review **Semicolon**, section **1**, in the Language Handbook.

Example: The auditorium is too small to hold the entire student body therefore, the assembly this afternoon will be limited to seniors and juniors.
Answer: body;

1. The doctor believed deeply in reverence for life accordingly, he refrained from stepping on an ant or swatting a mosquito.

2. Originally, the Hollywood movie studios were run by powerful individuals now they seem to be little more than the holdings of large conglomerates.

3. The young congresswoman objected strongly to the pay raise that Congress voted itself in fact, she tried to introduce a bill that would make the raise illegal.

4. Take down the washing before you lead those horses through the yard otherwise, the clothes will get dirty again.

LANGUAGE NOTES

Lewis Thomas writes about semicolons, but watch his use of the last punctuation mark in the excerpt. Does it leave you dangling, expecting more?

I have grown fond of semicolons in recent years. The semicolon tells you that there is still some question about the preceding full sentence; something needs to be added; . . . It is almost always a greater pleasure to come across a semicolon than a period. The period tells you that that is that; if you didn't get all the meaning you wanted or expected, anyway you got all the writer intended to parcel out and now you have to move along. But with a semicolon there you get a pleasant little feeling of expectancy; there is more to come; read on; it will get clearer.

. . . .

Sometimes you get a glimpse of a semicolon coming, a few lines farther on, and it is like climbing a steep path through woods and seeing a wooden bench just at a bend in the road ahead, a place where you can expect to sit for a moment, catching your breath. Commas can't do this sort of thing; they can only tell you how the different parts of a complicated thought are to be fitted together, but you can't sit, not even take a breath, just because of a comma,

5. Dr. Barnitz had been considered for posts in the foreign service, in the Justice Department, and in the judiciary in the end, however, he was passed over entirely.

6. Jessie spent nearly two days scraping the loose paint finally, she was ready to prime the surface.

7. Mrs. Lawrence is reputed to spend a great deal of money on her wardrobe consequently, we were not surprised when she was voted one of the best dressed women in town.

8. Mr. Petrie complained loudly about the tax levy he was, nonetheless, one of the first to pay his bill.

• **EXERCISE 11. In series and between clauses** Decide where a **Semicolon** should replace a comma in the following sentences. Then write each word preceding the semicolon, along with the semicolon itself. You may wish to review **Semicolon**, sections **2** and **3**, in the Language Handbook.

Example: I ate three pieces of cake, Jack, two, and Cheryl, only one.
Answer: cake; two;
Example: Sheila, my lab partner in chemistry, worked on the last experiment for three days, but the results were inconclusive, she confided to me later.
Answer: days;

1. She had written three novels by the time she was twenty-five: *Samantha, the Surprise Egg*, *Beloit, My Birthplace*, and *Jodhpur Dickens, Teen-age Jockey*.

2. The Ritz, an old theater on Chestnut Street, just held a film festival of old horror movies, including *Frankenstein*, *The Curse of Frankenstein*, and *Dracula*, and the crowds, as we expected, were tremendous.

3. When Katy was a child, her family made many weekend trips to visit relatives in Janesville, Wisconsin, Rockford, Illinois, and Springfield, Illinois.

4. Among the illustrious graduates of Hill Park High School, Class of 1976, who attended the reunion were Arlo Ganz, a graduate student in business, Mollie Urlinger, a representative for IBM, and yours truly, an aspiring actor.

5. Ronald Tonelli, first baseman for the Lodgers, signed a contract, but he wouldn't reveal his salary, despite many questions from the press.

6. My cousin, who drives a bus on Clark Street, knows many of his passengers by name, and several of his passengers pooled their money to buy him a Christmas present.

7. I recognized only three names on the slate: Pam Perkins, a candidate for president, Toni Varsegi, a candidate for treasurer, and Rex Stacey, a candidate for secretary.

8. My sister, who oversleeps at least twice a week, was advised by Mrs. Leacock, her boss, to buy a reliable alarm clock, and we agreed it would be a wise investment.

PART 4
Dashes

• **EXERCISE 12.** Decide where a **Dash** should be inserted in the following sentences. Then write the word preceding the punctuation mark to be added, the dash itself, and the word following the dash.

Example: Now, ladies and gentlemen, I give you the man who made this championship a reality Coach Allen.
Answer: reality–Coach

1. The Holy Roman Empire was a loosely organized empire John, please don't tap that pen on your desk which existed from the ninth or tenth century until 1806.
2. When the contralto finished the final song of her recital, the audience clamored for the one encore they had come to hear "Che Faro Senza, Eurydice."
3. Ten years after their moonwalk, the three astronauts well, actually, they're now ex-astronauts appeared on television to reminisce about their experience.
4. To be a successful husband and father, a man should cultivate gentleness, empathy, and compassion; for these qualities and I particularly want to emphasize this are not characteristics that should be the exclusive province of women.
5. In her French cooking class Mother finally achieved the highest accolade of all a compliment on her sauces.
6. Good heavens, I don't think that man sees the car in back of
7. The French expression *touché* it means "a touch" in case you're wondering, Hans originally came from fencing and indicated that one's opponent had penetrated one's defense.
8. Frank emptied the contents of his jeans pockets on the table, and we were awed at the variety coins, paper money, a driver's license, keys, old ticket stubs, and a rabbit's foot.

PART 5
Parentheses

• **EXERCISE 13.** Decide where **Parentheses** should be inserted in the following sentences. Then write the parentheses and the words or items that they enclose.

Example: The statistics indicating a halt in growth of the company see Chart I have been disputed by the business manager.
Answer: (see Chart I)

1. Tolstoy is reputed to have had three criteria for judging the worth of a work of art: 1 What was the artist's intent? 2 Did the artist accomplish that intent? 3 Was it worth the doing?

2. As long as you wear that chartreuse cap and I'll bet you wear it until June people will laugh.

3. Wentworth Pfister "Slats" to his friends is here.

4. Oxy and the Morons the little-known country-and-western band I told you about will play here tonight.

5. My favorite books mysteries, detective stories, and fantasies are exclusively fiction.

6. My best friend we called her "Pinky" in grade school has lovely red hair.

7. A compound sentence see page 60 is made up of two or more independent clauses.

8. They say, "Diamonds are a girl's best friend," but I've never had any diamonds, not friends, that is.

9. If you aren't sure how to spell *hors d'oeuvres* and no one ever is consult a dictionary.

10. They say that two can live as cheaply as one I never know who *they* are, but I don't believe it.

PART 6

Colons

• **EXERCISE 14.** Decide where a **Colon** is needed in the following sentences. Then write any word that should be followed by a colon, and the colon itself.

Example: Mr. Torres's advanced English class read four literary masterpieces last semester *Crime and Punishment,* a brilliant psychological study; Gustave Flaubert's *Madame Bovary,* a classic of the French school of realism; Jane Austen's gentle satire of the English middle class, *Pride and Prejudice;* and Herman Melville's brooding novel of good and evil, *Moby Dick.*

Answer: semester:

Example: To conclude her paper opposing capital punishment, Mary Jo cited the following biblical verse "Shall mortal man be more just than God? Shall a man be more pure than his maker?"

Answer: verse:

1. Nearly every schoolchild is familiar with Caesar's terse summary of his Pontic campaign "I came; I saw; I conquered."

2. Dear Sir

Under separate cover we have mailed copies of our article on the installation of a septic field, which appeared in *The Homeowner's Magazine*, 25 40–42.

3. The printed program categorized the annual supporters of the symphony according to the size of their donation Guarantors, people who contributed more than $5,000; Patrons, those who gave between

LANGUAGE NOTES

Lewis Thomas comments on the use of parentheses. (H. W. Fowler was the author of a classic language reference work.)

There are no precise rules about punctuation (Fowler lays out some general advice (as best he can under the complex circumstances of English prose (he points out, for example, that we possess only four stops (the comma, the semicolon, the colon and the period (the question mark and exclamation point are not, strictly speaking, stops; they are indicators of tone (oddly enough, the Greeks employed the semicolon for their question mark (it produces a strange sensation to read a Greek sentence which is a straightforward question: Why weepest thou; (instead of Why weepest thou? (and, of course, there are parentheses (which are surely a kind of punctuation making this whole matter much more complicated by having to count up the left-handed parentheses in order to be sure of closing with the right number (but if the parentheses were left out, with nothing to work with but the stops, we would have considerably more flexibility in the deploying of layers of meaning than if we tried to separate all the clauses by physical barriers (and in the latter case, while we might have more precision and exactitude for our meaning, we would lose the essential flavor of language, which is its wonderful ambiguity))))))))))))).

$1,000 and $4,999; Donors, those pledging between $500 and $999; and Members, the largest group, supporters who subscribed between $250 and $499.

4. Civilians talk of eating dinner at 630, but the military would say 1830.

5. Spoonerisms are sometimes defined as inside-out expressions; they are named after the Reverend William Spooner, an English professor, who once chided a student with this reproach "You have deliberately tasted two worms and you can leave Oxford by the town drain."

6. Before opening the swimming pool, the lifeguard had several duties to perform he was to sweep and scrub the dressing rooms, check the chlorine level of the water, and straighten the lounge chairs around the deck.

7. On the cornerstone of the new School of Law are written these words by the famous jurist Sir William Blackstone "It is better that ten guilty persons escape than one innocent suffer."

8. The note made quite clear what the children were to do Mary was to put her toys away; Andy, to wash and dry the dishes; and Ben, to wrap the garbage and take it to the front curb.

PART 7

Underlining

• **EXERCISE 15.** Copy and underline any titles, words, letters, and figures from the following sentences that should be italicized. You may wish to review the following entries in the Language Handbook: **Titles of books, articles, etc.**; **Underlining**.

Example: One of the most perceptive books about the United States ever written, Democracy in America, contains the observations of Alexis de Tocqueville, a Frenchman who traveled to this continent in the mid-nineteenth century.

Answer: Democracy in America

Example: When you add the suffix -able to the word notice, do you drop or retain the e?

Answer: -able, notice, e

1. One of the forerunners of such magazines as Woman's Day or Vogue was Godey's Lady's Book, which had a circulation of 150,000 by 1860.

2. I liked Anne Tyler's short story "With All Flags Flying" better than her novel Searching for Caleb.

3. Originally dedicated to Napoleon, this work by Beethoven is normally referred to as the Emperor Concerto.

4. The famous tale about Rip van Winkle was the concluding piece in a collection of writing entitled The Sketch Book.

5. Olga, I think you'd better proofread your papers more carefully. You have consistently misspelled the words receive and deceive because you've reversed the e and the i.

6. There was an article in Art News about Hogarth's series of drawings, The Rake's Progress.

7. Detectives in television dramas sometimes refer to the MO of a criminal. The letters come from the Latin term modus operandi, which means "method of working."

8. Leon didn't know which album to buy: the new recording of Mozart's opera Don Giovanni or an album of John Philip Sousa's marches.

9. The movie Head over Heels was based on Ann Beattie's novel Chilly Scenes of Winter.

10. The bank discovered that the check originally written for only thirty dollars had been altered; someone had changed the 3 to an 8 and had then tampered with the written figure.

11. When a managing editor of the Los Angeles Times objected to a statement in one of the daily comic strips, he directed that the strip be omitted from all editions of the paper.

12. I think he meant the word dander instead of dandruff when he said, "You really got my dandruff up."

PART 8

Hyphen

• **EXERCISE 16.** Decide where a **Hyphen** should be inserted in the following sentences. Then write the word or words that require a hyphen. You should have a total of eighteen hyphens.

Example: The students recorded their answers to the test on self correcting answer sheets.
Answer: self-correcting

1. Told to number off, the thirty four eager campers instantly be gan to shout out alternate numbers.

2. The local power company estimated a one fifth increase in power usage for the humid summer months.

3. Mrs. Goldman's sister in law invited Mrs. Goldman to spend her hard earned money on a vacation at a balloon ranch in central Colorado.

4. When the washing machine overflowed and water got under the newly laid linoleum, we had to relay it with a stronger adhesive.

5. Janet stood in front of the full length mirror in the living room hall, but she still couldn't quite see if her hem was even.

6. You'll have to reform that clay into a larger bowl.

7. This is my hot fudge sundae.

8. When the ex ball player walked onto the brightly lighted in field, the fans gave him a twelve minute standing ovation.

9. Since the end of World War II, American foreign policy has been strongly anti isolationist, a significant departure from its pre war position.

10. The losing candidate had won a majority of votes only in the forty eighth and forty ninth wards.

PART 9

Quotation Marks

• **EXERCISE 17.** Copy the sentences, adding **Quotation marks** and any other punctuation that is needed. You may wish to review the following entries in the Language Handbook, paying particular attention to the capitalization of words in quotations: **Quotation marks**; **Capital letters**, sections **1a** and **1b**.

Example: If the victim is bleeding from an artery the instructor said you may have to apply a tourniquet.

Answer: "If the victim is bleeding from an artery," the instructor said, "you may have to apply a tourniquet."

Example: It was Wordsworth in his poem The Tables Turned who said Books! 'Tis a dull and endless strife.

Answer: It was Wordsworth in his poem "The Tables Turned" who said, "Books! 'Tis a dull and endless strife."

1. Tighten the lug with that lug wrench the mechanic said as he held the tire firmly in place.

2. Is this the week of the Chaplin Festival at the Museum of Modern Art I've never seen any of his movies Mark said but they're reputed to be among the finest of all silent films.

3. The announcer stated we interrupt this program to bring you an important announcement.

4. What's making Erica so uncomfortable is it the noise or something she ate the neighbor inquired.

5. Written thirty years ago these words by E. B. White are just as applicable today everybody likes to hear about a man laying down his life for his country but nobody wants to hear about a country giving her shirt for her planet.

6. That stings exclaimed Juan are you certain you don't have a disinfectant that won't hurt quite so much.

7. Mandy shouted hey Lyle I overheard Mrs. Cervantes say Lyle is probably going to win the award for most outstanding athlete Lyle I think that's great!

8. To be or not to be said the actor is probably the most famous line in all of Shakespeare.

9. In a speech to the U.S. Senate on March 14, 1834, Henry Clay proclaimed the arts of power and its minions are the same in all countries and in all ages.

10. And now said the attorney continuing his interrogation of the witness tell us what you saw after you heard the scream.

PART 10

Unnecessary Punctuation

• **EXERCISE 18.** Each of the following sentences contains one or more unnecessary punctuation marks. Rewrite each sentence, omitting any punctuation that is not needed, adding any that is needed, and correcting any that is wrong. You may wish to review in the Language Handbook each area of punctuation covered in this chapter.

Example: A successful and provocative playwright. George Bernard Shaw came to the theater "late in life"; he was in fact over forty before he wrote his first drama.

Answer: A successful and provocative playwright, George Bernard Shaw came to the theater late in life; he was, in fact, over forty before he wrote his first drama.

Example: After the young man said that "he had worked on an oil-tanker," Mr Runkle regarded his daughter's friend with more interest.

Answer: After the young man said that he had worked on an oil tanker, Mr. Runkle regarded his daughter's friend with more interest.

1. The magazine that first brought the subject to the world's attention, was so important to the case, that the lawyer entered a copy as evidence in the trial.

2. The dress, that Mrs. Lincoln had worn to her husbands first presidential inauguration, was displayed in a second-floor case.

3. Grandmother agreed that Dickens's novel David Copperfield, had been her favorite; but she still loved weeping over "Oliver Twist." A novel that has been made into a successful musical play!!!

4. When the ushers cleaned the balcony they found not only gum stuck to the seats, but, also, at least a bushel basket's worth of gum wrappers lying, on the floor.

5. The two expressions, that most irritated the speech teacher, were, "You know," and *I mean*.

6. The older paramedic called the hospital, while the younger one was taking the victim's blood pressure, and calming the victim's wife.

7. With an expression of delight, on his face, Dirk said "that his blind date had been a real "winner"."

8. The letter from the housing office advised Martha to bring her own sheets towels desk lamp and pillow, when she came to register.

9. The 1889, flood in Johnstown Pennsylvania caused the loss of twenty-two hundred lives, and, the property damage was estimated at more than ten million an enormous sum in those days.

10. Who wrote the book when it was published and where it was published,–all these are the kinds of data a simple bibliography should contain!

11. At the end of the unit, on satiric poetry, Mr. DeLesseps read: *The Unknown Citizen* a short poem by W. H. Auden.

12. The President turned his attention to domestic problems, when his pact with the nonaligned nations' seemed certain of Congressional approval.

Chapter 11 Three Areas of Mechanics

A. In each of the following items, decide whether or not the underlined letters should be capitalized. Write only the words that should be capitalized, being sure to capitalize them.

1. "My family has led a romantic life," exclaimed tatiana. "My great-grandmother eloped with a french count when she was sixteen.

2. By the time she was twenty, they had lived in london, paris, and the american south.

3. They named their plantation belle chance and raised guernsey cattle and thoroughbred racehorses.

4. Aunt Beatrice, their oldest daughter, was a suffragette and ran a fancy millinery shop on fifth avenue in new york until she married a captain in the navy. Then she wrote the *jolly jeremiah* series of books for children.

5. My uncle alex became a senator in washington, d.c., and spoke out in favor of the eighteenth amendment to the constitution, supported the founding of the league of nations, and taught a course in russian literature at william and mary college every spring."

6. "You should teach a course in genealogy yourself," interrupted Burt, "but why don't you just write a best seller entitled *family roots: tough old coots to tender young shoots?*"

B. The italicized item in each of the following groups tells what is owned. The second item names the owner or owners. Write the possessive form of the owner followed by the name of the thing owned.

Example: *den* the foxes
Answer: the foxes' den

1. *cars* my brother-in-law
2. *hat* a witch
3. *seed catalog* Wilson and Roth
4. *pause* an instant
5. *lenses* the glasses
6. *squeaks* the mice
7. *irresponsibility* someone
8. *harness bells* a horse

C. For each item, write the correct form of the word or phrase in parentheses.

1. As we cycled around the pond, the (*geeses, geese's*) honking faded away.

2. The two (*Amies, Amys*) both received (*As, A's*) on the last test.

3. We were awakened at dawn by the (*mooses', moose's*) calls.

4. Both (*navies, navys*) concealed the number of (*men-of-war, man-of-wars*) they were building.

5. Although (*Arliss's, Arlisses*) father collects (*knifes, knives*), she herself can't tell a bowie from a grapefruit blade.

6. The application form asks that we list our (*hobbys, hobbies*).

7. (*Grandmothers, Grandmother's*) are some of the most comforting people in the world.

8. A (*gypsie's, gypsy's*) caravan nowadays is more likely to be silver-gray metal than brightly painted wood.

Chapter 12 Punctuation

A. Each of the following numbers refers to a place where punctuation may or may not be needed. Write the number followed by the name of the appropriate punctuation: colon, comma, end punctuation, quotation marks, semicolon, or no punctuation.

a. Adele claimed ___(1) that she overheard Miss Carson say ___(2) ___(3) I quit ___(4) ___(5)

b. The signal agreed upon was ___(6) ___(7) One if by land ___(8) two if by sea ___(9) ___(10)

c. On our marathon drive from Boston to San Francisco ___(11) we stayed with friends in Richmond ___(12) Indiana ___(13) Hays ___(14) Kansas ___(15) and Price ___(16) Utah ___(17)

d. The pig ___(18) with the straight tail ___(19) is a family pet ___(20) named Hilda ___(21)

e. Arthur Conan Doyle ___(22) tiring of his creation ___(23) Sherlock Holmes ___(24) killed him off ___(25) however ___(26) popular demand forced ___(27) Doyle to resurrect Holmes in a later story ___(28)

B. Follow the directions given for **A**, using the following punctuation: apostrophe, colon, dash, hyphen, quotation marks, and no punctuation.

a. Somerset Maugham ___(1) s famous short story ___(2) Rain ___(3) was made into a full ___(4) length movie.

b. ___(5) Oh, Laddie! Marigold! Why did you ever run away from home? ___(6) sobbed the child, clutching the collies ___(7) ruffs.

c. Before the Battle of Hastings ___(8) Mark, are you getting this? ___(9) William vowed to build an abbey if his forces ___(10) were victorious.

d. ___(11) Would you say that Poe ___(12) s ___(13) The Raven ___(14) is one of the most often ___(15) quoted poems? ___(16) asked Laura.

Perfect Score: 117

ABCDE
FGHIJK

Unit Four Language and Thinking

LMNOP
QRSTU
VWXYZ

CHAPTER 13 Word Origins

When terms appear in **boldface** in the directions for the following exercises, they refer to entries in the Language Handbook. Use a good dictionary whenever you feel it is necessary.

PART 1

Latin and Greek Roots

• EXERCISE 1. The items below consist of common Latin or Greek roots plus their italicized definitions. Use a good dictionary to list at least five common English words derived from these root words. Then add a colon and define each of your words.

Example: ject–*throw*
Answers: conjecture: "a guess"
dejected: "in low spirits"
eject: "to drive out or expel"
interject: "to insert abruptly"
project: "an undertaking" (noun) or
"to devise or to throw forward" (verb)
Some additional possibilities:
reject: "to throw away as useless"
inject: "to fill by forcing in liquid"
abject: "wretched"

1. dict–*say, speak*
2. spec, spic, or spect–*look at*
3. mar–*sea*
4. port–*carry*
5. civi–*citizen*
6. derm–*skin*

7. chron–*time*
8. pod or ped–*foot*
9. micro–*small*
10. meter–*measure*

PART 2

Words from Old and Middle English

• **EXERCISE 2.** Match the number of each word in column 1 with the letter of its description in column 2. Then add a colon and define each word in column 1. Use a good dictionary whenever you feel it is necessary. Number 1 has been done for you.

Example: 1. knave
Answer: 1. c: "rascal"

1. knave
2. hone
3. glower
4. trivet
5. hussy
6. scythe
7. swath
8. thatch
9. gewgaw
10. gore

a. from OE, based on a Latin word meaning "to cut"
b. from a ME word meaning "housewife"
c. from OE *cnafu* meaning "boy"
d. Part of this OE word means "three."
e. This ME word refers to a way of looking at someone.
f. As a noun this word comes from an OE word meaning "dirt." As a verb this word comes from a ME word meaning "spear."
g. This word from OE could refer to a roof or to hair.
h. from an OE word meaning "track" or "trace"
i. The first syllable of this word from ME rhymes with *you.*
j. from an OE word meaning "stone"

PART 3

Borrowed Words

• **EXERCISE 3. From French** The following **Borrowed words** and phrases are from French. Write the word, a colon, and a current English definition. Use a good dictionary whenever you feel it is necessary.

Example: faux pas
Answer: faux pas: "slip in speech"; "breach of etiquette"
Example: risqué
Answer: risqué: "somewhat improper or suggestive"

Example: sabotage
Answer: sabotage: "damage done" (noun) or "to damage or destroy" (verb)

1. adroit
2. passé
3. coup
4. apropos
5. *déjà vu*
6. laissez faire
7. savoir-faire
8. amateur
9. rendezvous
10. cul-de-sac
11. gourmet
12. cliché
13. boutonniere
14. ragout
15. avant-garde
16. en masse
17. gaffe
18. *raison d'être*
19. gauche
20. carte blanche

• **EXERCISE 4. From other languages** The following **Borrowed words** come from a number of languages. Write each word, the language or languages from which it comes, and its present definition. Use a good dictionary in answering.

Example: adobe
Answer: adobe: Spanish from Arabic, "brick made of sun-dried clay" or "structure made of such bricks"

Example: dilettante
Answer: dilettante: Italian from Latin, "a dabbler in art or science"

Example: ersatz
Answer: ersatz: German, "a substitute or imitation that is usually inferior"

1. mugwump
2. thug
3. assassin
4. kowtow
5. alligator
6. cockroach
7. boomerang
8. slalom
9. checkmate
10. bantam (fowl)
11. juke (box)
12. babushka
13. taboo
14. safari
15. kibitzer
16. junta
17. jodhpur
18. spiel
19. waffle
20. banjo

Spanish is the language for lovers, Italian for singers, French for diplomats, German for horses, and English for geese.
Spanish proverb

CHAPTER 14 Using Words

The terms in **boldface** in the directions for the following exercises refer to entries in the Language Handbook. Use a good dictionary whenever you feel it is necessary.

PART 1
Denotation

• EXERCISE 1. Each of the words listed below has more than one **Denotation**. Use a good dictionary to help you write three sentences illustrating various definitions of the word. You may change the tense or the number of the word. Underline the word in each sentence.

Example: line
Answers: Tad lined the ball over the right-field fence.
Line this box with velvet.
They bowled a line before the other team arrived.
Some additional possibilities:
Tell us the meaning of line 16 in this poem.
The toy shop carries six lines of ship models.
Elizabeth I was the last of the Tudor line since she had no children.
Stretch that line from the corner of the house to the oak tree.
Can you see that line of trees in the distance?

1. iron
2. measure
3. draft
4. gorge
5. branch
6. hatch
7. fall
8. jam

PART 2

Connotation

• **EXERCISE 2.** Decide the **Connotation**–favorable, unfavorable, or neutral–of each italicized word. Then answer the question that follows each pair of sentences.

Example: "Do you think the flowers in the centerpiece are *colorful*?" "Yes, I think the arrangement is very *gaudy*." (Which word is more favorable?)
Answer: colorful
Example: "That company needs *aggressive* salespeople." "Oh, their salespeople are *pushy* enough." (Which term is more neutral?)
Answer: aggressive

1. "The Arabs whom he led admired T. E. Lawrence (Lawrence of Arabia) for his *reckless* actions." "I thought they appreciated his *adventurous* deeds." (Which word is more favorable?)
2. "In the Wells family, the grandmother is the most *dominant* person." "Yes, she's quite an *overbearing* woman." (Which word is more favorable?)
3. "Dr. Reston is being quite *pig-headed* about his retirement." "Yes, he has always been a *determined* man." (Which word is more neutral?)
4. "Wendell's *casual* handling of the situation helped defuse a tense moment." "Yes, Wendell does have a marvelously *haphazard* approach to emotional stress." (Which word is more favorable?)
5. "The Senate disapproved of the appointment of Tom Smith, one of the President's former *cronies*." "Yes, many senators voted against this former business *associate* of the President." (Which word is more neutral?)
6. "Angela is quite *particular* about her appearance." "Yes, I've always thought she was a *fussy* person." (Which word is more neutral?)
7. "When that world leader was assassinated, his *disciples* tried to carry on his policies." "Do you think other *henchmen* were faithful to his philosophy?" (Which word is more favorable?)
8. "Be careful when you handle that figurine; it's quite *fragile*." "Yes, I can see how *flimsy* it is." (Which word is more favorable?)
9. "Jack spends his weekends *gallivanting* from one activity to another." "Yes, he does seem to be *moving* from one distraction to another." (Which word is more neutral?)
10. "The sales manager endorsed Phil's *plans* to increase sales." "Yes, he said they were clever *schemes*." (Which word is more neutral?)
11. "Andrew is a *shrewd* investor in the market." "Yes, he has a reputation for being quite *crafty*." (Which word is more favorable?)

12. "Mr. Taylor is a well-paid *bureaucrat*." "Yes, I'd heard he was a well-paid *administrator*." (Which word is more neutral?)

13. "Jan is absolutely *fanatic* on the subject of the Jets." "Yes, I'd heard she was *dedicated* to that team." (Which word is more favorable?)

14. "Were you able to *persuade* him?" "Yes, we *brainwashed* him easily." (Which term is more neutral?)

15. "If you've never heard him *rant*, you are in for a treat." "Yes, I had heard that he could *speak* eloquently." (Which word is more favorable?)

PART 3

Euphemisms

• EXERCISE 3. Each of the italicized words or expressions in the following sentences is a **Euphemism**. Write the word or phrase that is euphemistic, a colon, and a more straightforward word or expression.

Example: As a result of his *violent physical altercation,* Doug could hardly *ingest.*

Answer: violent physical altercation: fight; ingest: eat.

1. If the storm windows are not installed by November, you should complain to the *custodial engineer.*

2. For the small, hot back bedroom on the second floor, Mr. Hale purchased a *preowned* air conditioner.

3. Since the evidence had been obtained by *electronic surveillance,* the judge dismissed the charges.

4. In an attempt to keep the city clean, the Department of Streets and Sanitation placed three *ecological receptacles* on every city block.

5. To prevent another *extensive civil disturbance*, five hundred more police officers were assigned to patrol the parade route.

6. His story was so bizarre that we were quite sure he was *tampering with the truth.*

7. Frightened by the *severe economic downswing*, Mr. Taylor wondered whether he should sell or keep his second car.

8. Dillard's Emporium has a new department: clothes for the *full-figured* woman.

9. Once the lieutenant discovered the extent of the enemy's forces, he ordered a hasty *strategic withdrawal.*

10. When Mr. Murty *went to his reward*, the neighborhood helped his widow with the *interment* expenses at the local *memorial park*.

PART 4

Big Words and Trite Expressions

• EXERCISE 4. The following sentences contain italicized examples of **Big words** and **Trite expressions**. Revise each sentence, substituting for the italicized words less formal or less hackneyed words that convey the same meaning.

Example: From the *apogee* of the hill, Lord Raglan could see that the Russians had *extirpated* his valiant Light Brigade *as quick as a wink.*

Answer: From the top of the hill, Lord Raglan could see that the Russians had wiped out (or: destroyed, annihilated) his valiant Light Brigade quickly.

1. Glenn, one of the ranch hands, *avouched* that riding the pinto would be *as easy as falling off a log.*

2. *Scared out of his wits*, Lloyd looked down the length of the ski jump; he knew, however, that if he refused to jump, he would be forever accused of *pusillanimity.*

3. The FBI tried to decipher the *recondite* sentence although one agent *had a sneaking suspicion* that he would never understand the last four words.

4. Returning from a week at the summer resort, Susan *penned* an *encomium* to the manager: "I had *the time of my life.* Thank you for making my vacation so pleasant."

5. The vice-president in charge of programing knew she had at least one *ace in the hole* for the fall television season: a comedy series featuring a young man and Rover, his *faithful canine friend.*

6. Although Mrs. Nellis *elucidated* her plans to Diane, her favorite niece, she asked Diane to keep those plans secret until *the time was ripe.*

7. Martin was *nervous as a cat* before the ceremony; as a result, he *let go in one ear and out the other* everything his best man said.

8. For several weeks, negotiations for the contract moved *at a snail's pace* with neither side willing to talk seriously; after a four-day *hiatus*, however, the two sides finally agreed on terms.

9. The baseball scout *descried* the hopeful young pitcher and sadly informed him that against professional batters, the young man would be *a fish out of water.*

10. Rosa objected to the way the speaker *rode roughshod over* the audience during the *interrogation and riposte* period.

11. Life on a sailing ship at the end of the nineteenth century was not *a bed of roses;* sailors knew the truth of the old *apothegm:* "The captain of a ship is all-powerful."

12. By *putting his shoulder to the wheel*, Terry *meliorated* his class rank considerably.

PART 5

Misused Words

• **EXERCISE 5.** In fourteen of the following sentences a word has been misused. Write the word and a colon; then substitute a more ap-

LANGUAGE NOTES

Can you replace each misused word with one that makes sense?

The Chiverless Knight

David, who had grown up in a pedantry, was always reading about the days of Chiverless Knighthood, and dreaming up stories in which he himself played a heroic role. In one he was strolling through a woodland, strumming his peccadillo, when he came to a shady arbitrary in which a beautiful maiden was gathering colorful chameleons and weaving them into garlands.

Suddenly a huge orthodox charged out of the woods straight toward the maiden. There was no time for the knight to be

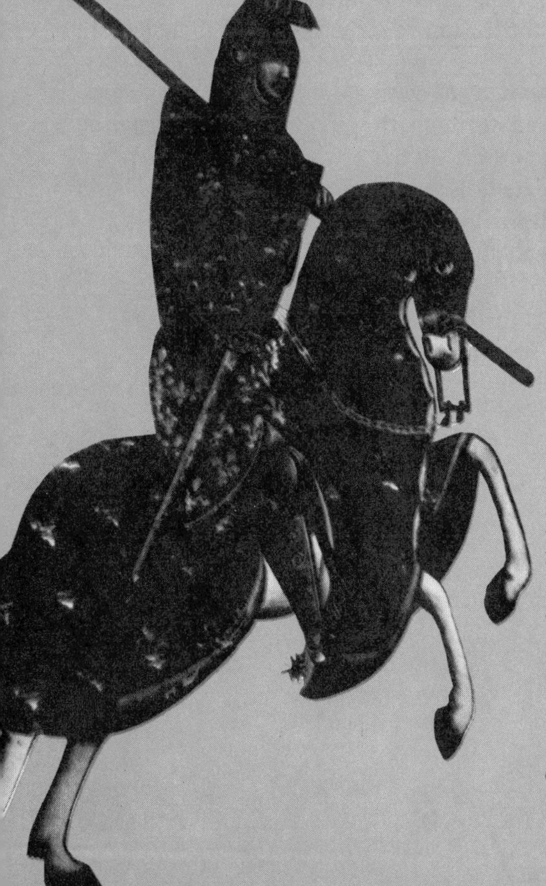

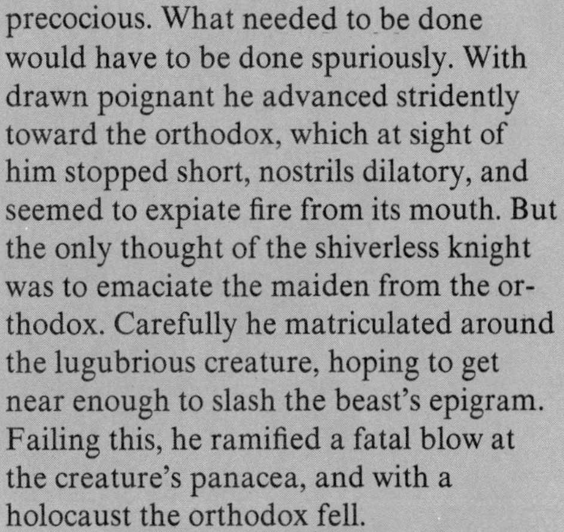

precocious. What needed to be done would have to be done spuriously. With drawn poignant he advanced stridently toward the orthodox, which at sight of him stopped short, nostrils dilatory, and seemed to expiate fire from its mouth. But the only thought of the shiverless knight was to emaciate the maiden from the orthodox. Carefully he matriculated around the lugubrious creature, hoping to get near enough to slash the beast's epigram. Failing this, he ramified a fatal blow at the creature's panacea, and with a holocaust the orthodox fell.

The maiden, who at sight of the terrible incarceration had been monetarily overcome with nostalgia, recovered quickly, and wished to show her gratuity to the knight. At her bequest he accompanied her to the paragon where she lived. Her father, the pariah of the realm, gave a huge fiasco in honor of the hero. Her fiancé, indigent over the favor accorded the knight, plotted to have the newcomer expedited, and even planned a cursory murder. But the plot was flustrated, and in his disparity the thwarted suitor plunged a dagger into his epitome and shortly afterward exhumed.

The pariah, already in his adage, had long been looking for a man of sufficient inertia and ambiguity to take his place, and with the anonymous consent of his whole diatribe he gave his realm and his daughter to the Chiverless Knight.

–Amsel Greene

propriate word. For the sentence that has no misused word, write "Correct."

Example: Mary always took for granite that she would graduate from high school.
Answer: granite: granted

1. The frail young woman had a medical problem–a congenial heart defect–that prevented her from participating in sports.

2. We checked the voracity of his statements by calling the hotel he claimed to have stayed in.

3. After the fright she had received, it was amazing that Ella regained her composition so quickly.

4. The steward had promised we would land momentously, but we circled the field more than thirty minutes before touching down.

5. Marshall said that the trek into the desert would be ardent, but none of us expected it to be as exhausting as it was.

6. As one method of conserving energy, the federal government has been encouraging homeowners to increase the amount of isolation.

7. The hallmarks of a typical murder mystery are a baffling crime, numerous false clues, and an ingenuous solution.

8. Every spring the sight of young lambs gambling on the green meadow delighted the farmer and his children.

9. Beginning with *Oklahoma!* the corroboration of Rogers and Hammerstein produced many memorable musicals.

10. Because it had been bottled improperly, the apple juice failed to foment at the correct rate.

11. Josie was incredulous when she received the news of her award.

12. The Lopatos wandered through the great bizarre of Istanbul, stopping at one stall after another and bartering with the owner.

13. After two weeks of heated discussion, the legislators passed a bill outlawing corpulent punishment in the schools.

14. Your dinner was delicious, but I wish I hadn't gouged myself on three desserts.

15. Has everyone been appraised of the change in plans?

CHAPTER 15 Figurative Language

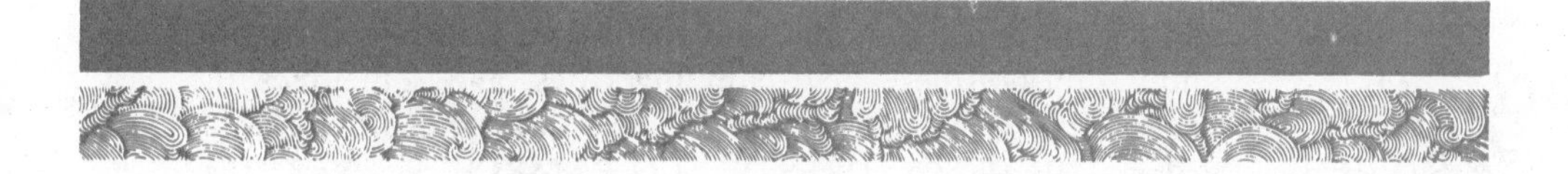

The terms in **boldface** in the directions for the following exercises refer to entries in the Language Handbook.

PART 1 Imagery

• **EXERCISE 1.** The following descriptive passages are rich in **Imagery**. Read each passage and determine the sense(s) to which it mainly appeals: sight, sound, touch, taste, smell, kinesthetic. Name the sense and write the words or phrases from the passage that especially appeal to this sense.

Example: I hung my jacket on a nail and began thoughtfully to unbutton my shirt. It was when I was pulling it over my head that I noticed Mr. Alderson's nose wrinkling. The farm men, too, began to sniff and look at each other wonderingly. Mrs. Hall's bath salts, imprisoned under my clothing, had burst from their bondage in a sickly wave, filling the enclosed space with their strident message. Hurriedly I began to wash my arms in the hope that the alien odour might pass away but it seemed to get worse, welling from my warm skin, competing incongruously with the honest smells of cow, hay, and straw. –James Herriot. ALL CREATURES GREAT AND SMALL. New York: St. Martin's Press, Inc., 1972.

Answer: smell: nose wrinkling; sniff; bath salts; sickly wave; strident; alien odour; competing with the honest smells of cow, hay, and straw.

> Any euphemism ceases to be euphemistic after a time and the true meaning begins to show through. It's a losing game, but we keep on trying.
> Joseph Wood Krutch

1. The grind of gears came, meaning he was halfway up the hill, and the new engine scream pulling down to a low, pained roar, another shift, to low, to low-low, the pounding throb—far away, though—and then the purr at the peak of the hill and the purr rising, pulling back against the thrust, strangling itself on the downgrade. –John Gardner. NICKEL MOUNTAIN. New York: Alfred A. Knopf, Inc., 1973.

2. He found a half-pint bottle of whipping cream in the refrigerator and took it, guiltily, with a loaf of stale white bread, into the back. Pouring some cream into a saucer, he soaked it up with bread, greedily wolfing the cream-laden bread. –Bernard Malamud. THE ASSISTANT. New York: Farrar, Straus & Giroux, Inc., 1957.

3. The heat of June grew until the shady yards gave up the smell of the damp soil, of underground, and the city—Pluto kingdom of sewers and drains, and the mortar and roaring tar pots of roofers, the geraniums, lilies-of-the-valley, climbing roses, and sometimes the fiery devastation of the stockyards stink when the wind was strong. –Saul Bellow. THE ADVENTURES OF AUGIE MARCH. New York: The Viking Press, 1953.

4. His lungs ached. The blood stopped in his veins, his eyes burned, his brain plunged faster than his stomach. –Tim O'Brien. GOING AFTER CACCIATO. New York: Delacorte Press/Seymour Lawrence Books, 1978.

5. The clouds over the land now rose like mountains and the coast was only a long green line with the gray blue hills behind it. The water was a dark blue now, so dark that it was almost purple. As he looked down into it he saw the red sifting of the plankton in the dark water and the strange light the sun made now. –Ernest Hemingway. THE OLD MAN AND THE SEA. New York: Charles Scribner's Sons, 1952.

6. All the rest of the knuckles were covered with scars and cuts, old and new. I remember the palm was smooth and hard as bone from hefting the wooden handles of axes and hoes, not the hand you'd think could deal cards. The palm was callused, and the calluses were cracked, and dirt was worked in the cracks. –Ken Kesey. ONE FLEW OVER THE CUCKOO'S NEST. New York: The Viking Press, 1962.

7. The driver and the passenger were standing in the street looking at the car; it had big wheels with pneumatic tires and wooden spokes painted in black enamel. It had brass headlamps in front of the radiator and brass sidelamps over the fenders. It had tufted upholstery and double side entrances. –E. L. Doctorow. RAGTIME. New York: Random House, Inc., 1975.

8. The dry wind roughened her lips and parched her nostrils. –Wallace Stegner. ANGLE OF REPOSE. New York: Doubleday & Co., Inc., 1971.

9. But once I went to investigate an obvious accident—the darkness suddenly streaked with headlights pointing straight up and exploding; the silence pierced with a metal screaming and the shriek of ground glass. –John Irving. THE WORLD ACCORDING TO GARP. New York: E. P. Dutton, 1978.

10. But the only music from the deep that night was the murmur of the tide on the shingle; and somewhere much farther out, the dimly raucous cries of the gulls roosting on the calm water. –John Fowles. THE FRENCH LIEUTENANT'S WOMAN. Boston: Little, Brown & Company, 1969.

11. The bread was brown and shining, with a woven plait on top of it, its crust a perfect brittle glaze, yellow-brown like a harvest offering. –Margaret Drabble. THE REALMS OF GOLD. New York: Alfred A. Knopf, Inc., 1975.

12. [Apple pie has a] thick flaky pastry and hunks of sweet apple bathed in a syrup; rich but sturdy dough filled with finely sliced tart apples seasoned with cinnamon; an upper and lower crust in a traditional pie pan; an upper crust only, in a deep dish; a bottom crust with crosses of dough over the filling. . . . –M. F. K. Fisher. "Apple Pie," ESQUIRE, December, 1975.

PART 2

Simile and Metaphor

• **EXERCISE 2.** The following sentences contain examples of **Simile** and **Metaphor**. Identify the figure of speech in each sentence and indicate what is being compared. One of the items contains a simple comparison; for this item write "None."

Example: The highway is a ready cake mix of snow, ice, sand, salt and trouble. –E. B. White. "The Railroad," THE POINTS OF MY COMPASS. New York: Harper & Row, Publishers, Inc., 1962.

Answer: Metaphor: Highways in winter are being compared to cake mixes since both are "frosted" with various ingredients.

Example: Over the fields, when we came out of the woods, the thin trails of blue smoke were as motionless as cobwebs. –Ellen Glasgow. "Jordan's End," THE SHADOWY THIRD AND OTHER STORIES. New York: Doubleday & Co., Inc., 1923.

Answer: Simile: Trails of blue smoke are compared to cobwebs since both are delicate, fragile, and motionless.

Example: He arrived in Segovia early one Sunday morning. It was filled with sunlight, the clouds were silk-white in the mountain air. Their shadows wandered over the slopes of the bare sierra like creatures that crept and warmed themselves on the soil and rock. –Saul Bellow. "The Gonzaga Manuscripts," SEIZE THE DAY. New York: The Viking Press, 1954.

Answers: Metaphor: The whiteness of the clouds is compared to the whiteness of silk. There is also the suggestion that both items are delicate and glistening.
Simile: The shadows of the clouds are compared to small mountain creatures.

1. She went up on her knees, bowed over, and began to scrub again, with new energy. She was really a network of thin taut ligaments and long muscles elastic as woven steel. –Katherine Anne Porter. "Holiday," THE ATLANTIC MONTHLY, December 1960.

2. The dry season had already begun; the river was shoal in places, with sand bars lengthening at the bends, and sunken trees emerging like great black feeding reptiles of another age. –Peter Matthiessen. AT PLAY IN THE FIELDS OF THE LORD. New York: Random House, Inc., 1965.

3. Piling into the locker room after the three-hour practice, the players smelled like men who had not had a bath in weeks.

4. Mrs. May's bedroom window was low and faced on the east and the bull . . . stood under it, his head raised as if he listened–like some patient god come down to woo her–for a stir inside the room. –Flannery O'Connor. "Greenleaf," EVERYTHING THAT RISES MUST CONVERGE. New York: Farrar, Straus & Giroux, Inc., 1965.

5. Then the rain comes like a burst of tears; and the wind blows the wicker baskets over, and the tin cans from inside them roll about the porch floor. The tin cans and the wicker stands and the swinging baskets make a clatter like a jazz band. –Peter Taylor. "Sky Line," A LONG FOURTH AND OTHER STORIES. New York: Harcourt Brace Jovanovich, Inc., 1941.

6. The little children came too, like a bouncing stream overflowing the fields, and set upon the men, the women, the dogs, the rushing birds, and the wave-like rows of earth, their little voices almost too high to be heard. –Eudora Welty. "Livvie," THE WIDE NET AND OTHER STORIES. New York: Harcourt Brace Jovanovich, Inc., 1943.

7. Then they watched the Texan descend, carrying a looped-up blacksnake whip, and go around to the rear of the herd and drive it through the gate, the whip snaking . . . in methodical and pistol-like reports. –William Faulkner. "Spotted Horse," THE HAMLET. New York: Random House, Inc., 1940.

8. The future was a vast hollow sphere, strangely soundless, uninhabited without incident or detail. . . . –Katherine Anne Porter. SHIP OF FOOLS. Boston: Little, Brown & Company, 1962.

9. We keep stores of discarded words around, out beyond the suburbs of our minds, stacked like scrap metal. –Lewis Thomas. THE MEDUSA AND THE SNAIL. New York: The Viking Press, 1979.

10. A stuffed moose of a warm woman with a tabbycat face charged in on swollen feet. –J. F. Powers. "Prince of Darkness," PRINCE OF DARKNESS AND OTHER STORIES. New York: Doubleday & Co., Inc., 1946.

PART 3

Personification, Hyperbole, and Understatement

• **EXERCISE 3.** Each of the following sentences contains one of the following **Figures of speech**: **Personification**, **Hyperbole** (overstatement), or **Understatement (Litotes)**. Identify each figure of speech. If the figure is personification, indicate what is being personified and how.

Example: The leaves clung, whispering and talking when the wind blew. . . . –Sherwood Anderson. "Brother Death," DEATH IN THE WOODS. New York: Liveright Publishing Corporation, 1933.

Answer: Personification: The leaves, like people, whisper and talk as they cling.

Example: For his daughter's wedding Mr. Gresham threw a small reception for six hundred of his closest associates.

Answer: Understatement

1. "Nobody was su'prised when Dolly blew into the dinin' room with it–a rock that Ike'd bought off'n Diamond Joe the first trip to New York. Only o' course it'd been set into a lady's-size ring instead o' the automobile tire he'd been wearin'." –Ring Lardner. "Alibi Ike," ROUND UP. New York: Charles Scribner's Sons, 1929.

2. Today's language is the result of an interminable series of small blunders, one after another, leading us back through a near infinity of time. The words are simply let loose by all of us, allowed to fly around out there in the dark, bumping into each other, mating in crazy ways, producing wild, random hybrids, beyond the control of reason. –Lewis Thomas. THE MEDUSA AND THE SNAIL. New York: The Viking Press, 1979.

3. Presenting the watch to the retiring employee, the president of the company said, "Ladies and Gentlemen. This man has accomplished a small feat. He has never missed a day of work in forty-three years."

4. The trail moved up the dry shale hillside, avoiding rocks, dropping under clefts, climbing in and out of old water scars. –John Steinbeck. "Flight," THE PORTABLE STEINBECK. New York: The Viking Press, 1946.

5. Pauline had been rather busy that day. She had canned eighty-four jars of tomatoes, driven the fifty-two miles to town, and captured a burglar.

6. Day after day and night after night there was nothing round the ship but the howl of the wind, the tumult of the sea, the noise of water pouring over her deck. There was no rest for her and no rest for us. She tossed, she pitched, she stood on her head, she sat on her tail, she rolled, she groaned, and we had to hold on while on deck and cling to our bunks when below. . . . –Joseph Conrad. "Youth," YOUTH: A NARRATIVE, AND TWO OTHER STORIES. Edinburgh 1902, New York, 1903.

7. The last case of dynamite is packed, the percussion caps are wired, and the men all move back out of danger. Ol' Paul looks around and hollers: "Let her go!"

Well sir, the shock throws every man in camp flat on his back, knocks the cupolas off three barns in Iowa, and the smoke and dust go up in a column thirty-four miles high. –Glen Rounds. "Why There Are No Trees on the Desert," OL' PAUL, THE MIGHTY LOGGER. New York: Holiday House, Inc., 1976.

8. Two colossal historical incidents took place yesterday, incidents which must go echoing down the corridors of time for ages, incidents which can never be forgotten while histories shall continue to be written. Yesterday, for the first time, business was opened to commerce by the Marconi Company and wireless messages sent entirely across the Atlantic, straight from shore to shore; and on that same day the President of the United States for the fourteenth time came within three miles of flushing a bear. –Mark Twain. "The Hunting of the Cow," MARK TWAIN IN ERUPTION. New York: Harper & Row, Publishers, 1922. Reprinted by permission.

9. Winner of the prestigious title of all-conference back, president of the senior class, and valedictorian of his graduating class, Elliott was considered a fairly good prospect for admission to the state university.

10. The bamboos take an easier way, they bend to the earth and lie there, creaking, groaning, crying for mercy. The contemptuous wind passes, not caring for these abject things. –Jean Rhys. WIDE SARGASSO SEA. New York: W. W. Norton & Company, Inc., 1966.

11. He said he had been captain of ships that had turned bottom upward and sailed along to their destinations on their masts. He said that he had leaned his back against a hurricane. –Constance Rourke. "Davy Crockett: Sunrise in His Pocket," DAVY CROCKETT. New York: Harcourt Brace Jovanovich, Inc., 1934.

12. Before retiring for the night, Grevelle ate several sandwiches, drank a bottle of fresh milk, and polished off the better part of a cherry pie. "What I like," Grevelle observed, "is a snack to settle the stomach."

PART 4

Mixed Figures of Speech

• **EXERCISE 4.** Each of the following sentences contains a **Mixed figure of speech**. In each item identify the two elements whose combination results in the mixed figure of speech.

LANGUAGE NOTES

At the Mad Hatter's tea-party,
Alice, of Wonderland fame,
learned about the importance of word order.

The Hatter opened his eyes very wide on hearing this; but all he *said* was, "Why is a raven like a writing-desk?"

"Come, we shall have some fun now!" thought Alice. "I'm glad they've begun asking riddles–I believe I can guess that," she added aloud.

"Do you mean that you think you can find out the answer to it?" said the March Hare.

"Exactly so," said Alice.

"Then you should say what you mean," the March Hare went on.

"I do," Alice hastily replied; "at least–at least I mean what I say–that's the same thing, you know."

"Not the same thing a bit!" said the Hatter. "Why, you might just as well say that 'I see what I eat' is the same thing as 'I eat what I see'!"

"You might just as well say," added the March Hare, "that 'I like what I get' is the same thing as 'I get what I like'!"

"You might just as well say," added the Dormouse, who seemed to be talking in his sleep, "that 'I breathe when I sleep' is the same thing as 'I sleep when I breathe'!"

"It *is* the same thing with you," said the Hatter, and here the conversation dropped, . . . –Lewis Carroll

Lewis Carroll. From "A Mad Tea-Party," ALICE'S ADVENTURES IN WONDERLAND, 1865.

Example: The Department of Energy had devised a game plan for the allocation of resources, but when the world price of oil rose, the scenario had to be revised.

Answer: The writer has mixed a sports metaphor (game plan) with one of filmmaking (scenario).

1. When it looked as though he was finally down for the count, Sam played his trump card.

2. When Fletcher, who was normally a quiet man, took the bull by the horns and began explaining, we could see he was going too far out on a limb.

3. Nicky thought he had the contract all sewed up, but when the board of directors looked over the terms, the agreement came unglued.

4. Jeannie had the answer on the tip of her tongue, but when Mrs. Oliveras called on her, it stuck in her throat.

5. The defendant spun a web of lies that was finally unhinged when an eyewitness came forward to testify.

6. When Alec decided to begin his own business, his wife thought he was opening a can of worms; but Alec, who had great faith in his ability to succeed, said that troubles were nothing to be afraid of and that he'd cross that bridge when he came to it.

7. My sister gave me such a stony gaze, I thought I'd melt right there on the spot.

8. I think it was her nerves of steel that helped her sail through the exam.

9. Asked about her many years as a hostess in an exclusive restaurant, Miss Collins smiled and said, "When I remember all the faces I've seated. . . ."

10. "I will leave no stone unturned in finding the fly in the ointment," he said.

PART 5

Allusions

• **EXERCISE 5.** Each of the italicized words in the following sentences is an **Allusion** that is figurative. Identify the source of the allusion: mythology, literature, the Bible, history. Then indicate its appropriateness to the content of the sentence. Use a good dictionary or reference book to look up any allusion that is not familiar to you. Hint: Two of the allusions might be considered both historical and literary since they deal with actual people who influenced the world of literature.

Example: During the last few months of Nixon's presidency, General Haig–according to one contemporary chronicler–played *Richelieu* to Nixon's *Louis XIII*.

Answer: History: Richelieu was a French cardinal and statesman who virtually controlled France for eighteen years during the reign of Louis XIII. Since Nixon conceded that during his last months in office he spent an inordinate amount of time dealing with the accusations leveled against him, Haig is reputed to have made many significant national decisions during that time.

Example: When his ship got off-course, struck a reef, and ripped its keel, the captain began to suspect that he had a *Jonah* on board.

Answer: The Bible: Jonah was a biblical character whose disobedience toward God brought disaster to a ship. Today the word connotes any person believed to bring bad luck to an enterprise.

Example: When I had spent all my savings on an outfit for homecoming, Mother said, "Don't worry, *Micawber,* something will turn up."

Answer: Literature: Wilkins Micawber, a character from Dickens's *David Copperfield*, divided his time between a shabbily genteel existence and debtors' prison. He seemed unaware of his dire circumstances, cheerfully waiting for "something to turn up."

1. As the fighter's business manager and *Boswell*, Greg accompanied the heavyweight on all tours, making notes in small notebooks during the day and transcribing them at night.

2. When he attended the U.S. Army War College, Bill had to design plans for both an attack and a retreat. His offensive plan was praised, but the class thought that his retreat might result in another *Dunkirk*.

3. The substitute letter carrier limped into the post office and sighed, "Why didn't anyone tell me about that *Cerberus* at the corner of Chestnut and Lilac Lane?"

4. Although Mrs. McGarrett had the patience of *Job,* even she grew exasperated at the lawyer's request for another continuance.

5. To many movie fans, the actor appears to be the image of a *Byronic* hero, but when he laughs in that high, infectious giggle, he shatters the image.

6. Shaking his head in bewilderment, the judge thought to himself, "Not even *Solomon* could come to a wise decision in this case."

7. After being expelled from the Soviet Union, Alexander Solzhenitsyn found his own *Elba* on an estate in New England.

8. The team's manager said, "Boys, you deserve to celebrate, but if this party turns into a *Donnybrook*, you'll have to pay for the damages."

9. To become a doctor takes years of study and training during which the student must avoid the *Scylla* of despair and the *Charybdis* of overconfidence.

10. Some of the nuclear scientists responsible for the creation of the atomic and hydrogen bombs were afraid that the result of their work would be nothing short of *Armageddon*.

CHAPTER 16 Thinking Logically

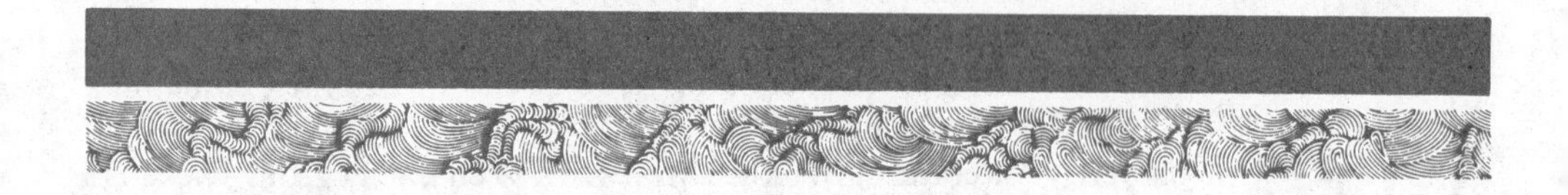

The terms in **boldface** in the directions for the following exercises refer to entries in the Language Handbook.

PART 1

Fact and Opinion

• EXERCISE 1. Each of the following items contains either a **Statement-of-fact** or a **Statement of opinion**. Write the number of each item. Then write "S-F" for statements-of-fact, "S-O" for statements of opinion, and "Both" for statements that contain both fact and opinion. Remember: A statement-of-fact need not be true. It must, however, be a statement whose truth or falsity can be established.

Example: The flowering begonia, a fast-growing perennial, will thrive in either sun or shade.
Answer: S-F
Example: Children who deliberately set fires will probably grow into adult pyromaniacs, arsonists, or both.
Answer: S-O

1. The U.S. Army volunteer system has been so inefficient and ineffectual that the country should immediately reinstate the mandatory draft.

2. The company that first produces an electric automobile with a range greater than five hundred miles will certainly make a huge profit.

3. Although the interstate route to Cheyenne is six miles shorter than the foothills route, the latter has much more interesting scenery.

4. Poison ivy is recognizable by its six-pointed leaf with small red spots near each tip.

5. The best American musical is *My Fair Lady*, with *Candide* and *The Music Man* running close seconds.

6. In the mid-fifties, Edmund Hillary, a New Zealand mountaineer, became the first man to climb Mt. Everest.

7. For a housewife who wants a profitable career but does not want to work from nine to five, the best choice is selling real estate.

8. Of the four precious gems–diamonds, emeralds, sapphires, and rubies–the emerald is the most expensive.

9. Last year's Superbowl game was the dullest one yet with its lackluster playing and a 0–7 score.

10. You will find a description of the House of Usher on page 217 of your literature anthology.

PART 2

Inductive and Deductive Reasoning

• **EXERCISE 2.** The following are examples of **Inductive reasoning**. Read each item carefully. Then decide whether sufficient information has been given to reach a valid generalization.

Example: On the first day of class at a large metropolitan high school, Ida sees a sophomore student rudely bump into a classmate in the corridor. A week later Ida sees two other sophomores elbow their way to the front of the cafeteria line–and immediately she generalizes: "Sophomores! They don't have any manners."

Answer: Invalid generalization. Three sophomores, however rude, represent only a small part of the class. Such a sweeping generalization about all sophomores is not backed by sufficient evidence.

1. Randy eats tacos, burritos, enchiladas, and refried beans every chance he gets. He eats at his favorite restaurant, Taco Loco, twice a week. That guy really likes Mexican food.

2. We are told that five years ago the literary magazine had to be discontinued for lack of student support. But times have changed. A poll taken at the last meeting of the Writers' Club disclosed that 96 of its 123 members want, and promise to subscribe to, a monthly literary magazine. So the faculty can rest assured on this point: 75 percent of the student body, at the very least, will back the project by buying subscriptions.

3. Three students from my high school spent their vacation in the Bahamas, five went to Florida, and six or seven flew to New York to see plays and to visit the museums. Two stayed home only because they couldn't find anybody to take care of their private stables. It would appear that they come from fairly affluent backgrounds.

4. The detective observed that the thief must have entered through the kitchen window and exited through a bedroom window, for a pane was out of the kitchen window and the dust on the windowsill beneath the open bedroom window had clearly been disturbed. Further, there were footprints from the kitchen to the bedroom.

5. Artie won the canoe race during the final days of camp. Then he took second place in the archery contest. And he finished his sweep by putting his tent up in record time and catching and cooking the largest northern pike of the summer. You can see why he was selected as camper of the year.

6. It isn't the teen-agers–it's the elderly drivers who are the real menace on our streets and highways. Why, last week alone the *Evening News* reported four accidents that involved drivers from sixty-six to seventy years of age. We need a new state law: no man or woman over sixty-five should be given a driver's license.

7. There are never any knickknacks on Mrs. Greenberg's shelves; the work surface in the kitchen is devoid of any cannisters or plates; and there is nothing lying around in any of the rooms; in fact, nothing is ever out of place. You can tell that Mrs. Greenberg is a woman who dislikes clutter.

8. To collect data for an article on ecology, a student reporter spends an afternoon walking along the west fork of a river near his school. During the course of his walk, he notices a bright-blue liquid pouring from the local textile firm into the river. When he asks to see the plant manager for an explanation of what he has observed, he is told that the manager is "much too busy" to see him. Disturbed by the blue liquid and by the rebuff, the reporter writes, as the introductory sentences for his article: "Industry in Midville is behaving in a grossly irresponsible manner toward our environment–in particular, toward the Axehead River. And, what's worse, local industry is 'much too busy' to talk about it."

• **EXERCISE 3.** The following are examples of **Deductive reasoning**. Analyze the arguments to determine which are valid and which are invalid–and why. In analyzing each item, (1) translate the argument into a full syllogism; (2) check the truth of the premises; (3) check the correctness of the reasoning. You may wish to review **Syllogism** in the Language Handbook.

Example: [From a sports page] All members of this sports-page staff agree that this year's team is a sure-fire cinch to win the state trophy, because these athletes have what all champions have–a fighting spirit and great teamwork.

Answer: The argument can be translated into the following syllogism:

All teams that win championships are teams that have a fighting spirit and great teamwork.

Our team is a team that has a fighting spirit and great teamwork.

Therefore our team is a team that will win the championship.

Facts do not cease to exist because they are ignored.
Aldous Huxley

Here we can accept both premises as true. But when we check the reasoning, we find that it is fallacious—that the conclusion does not *necessarily* follow from the premises. The major premise tells us only that all championship-winning teams have a fighting spirit and great teamwork; it does not say that all teams with a fighting spirit and great teamwork win championships. It is quite possible, then, that our team—in spite of its spirit and teamwork—will *not* be a championship team.

1. [Overheard on a bus] "I say that Martinez is *not* a great writer and I can prove it. Not one of the many books she has written has become a best seller. You don't have to take my word for it; I can show you the best-seller lists from *Publishers Weekly* for the last five years."

2. The new white slacks Nan is wearing are so wrinkle-free that they can't be made of pure cotton.

3. [Said at a board meeting] "Ladies and gentlemen, I can explain what's wrong. A study of these reports shows clearly that all TV shows which emphasize the sensational get high ratings—impressively high. As long as this executive board persists in its policy of producing only programs of intellectual appeal—programs that do not emphasize the sensational—our shows will *never* achieve high ratings."

4. [Overheard in a personnel office] "How did I know that applicant lied about his having worked at the Parkerwurst Company in Boston these past three years? It's elementary, my dear Ms. Watson. In the course of our interview I found out that he didn't know what all proper Bostonians know—that *tonic* is their word for *soda pop.*"

5. [Overheard in an elevator] "What's wrong with believing in astrology? Lots of famous people have believed in astrology. J. P. Morgan believed in astrology—in fact, he made a fortune on the stock market by following his astrologer's advice. And if it was good enough for J. P. Morgan, it's sure good enough for me!"

6. [From a conversation at a football game] "The Bears win the championship? You've got to be kidding! Those bums haven't had a decent shot at it for the past ten years."

7. [From a conversation at a P.T.A. meeting] "My poor Ramona has been really burning the midnight oil for her trigonometry course. Frankly, I don't understand why she wanted to take that course in the first place. After she graduates, she's going to help her father and me run our business. And who needs trigonometry in an ice-cream parlor?"

8. [Overheard on a commuter train] "Senator Blank was found guilty on that income-tax evasion charge? Well, I'm not surprised. He's a politician, isn't he?"

9. [From a book review] In his preface to *The Liberal Takes the Stand* the author states explicitly that he is a liberal. But his book makes it quite clear that, by his own definition, he is not a true liberal. "All liberals," he says, "are open-minded to ideas which challenge tradition." Yet in three spots that I can point out, he shows himself to be extremely narrow-minded in his sarcastic condemnation and savage rejection of certain suggested reforms.

10. Melissa, the youngest daughter, did not set the table, for she always puts all the utensils to the left of the plate.

PART 3

Fallacies in Reasoning

• **EXERCISE 4. Hasty generalization and either-or argument** The following items illustrate two fallacies in reasoning: the **Hasty generalization** and the **Either-or argument**. Identify the fallacy by writing "hasty" or "either-or." Explain the flaw in logic represented by each statement.

Example: Unless the city council approves the change in the curfew, the instances of vandalism will continue to rise.

Answer: Either-or: The statement presents two alternatives: Change the ordinance affecting curfew or accept increasing vandalism. It ignores such other alternatives as augmenting the police force, installing more lights in neighborhoods where vandalism is high, beginning a program to educate the public on how to avoid vandalism, or initiating stiffer fines for vandalism.

Example: Ida said she was never going to southern California again; it rained on all six days of her vacation there.

Answer: Hasty: On the basis of a short visit, Ida concluded that rain falls constantly in southern California. Her experience has been too brief to warrant such a generalization.

1. Gene, an avid reader of murder mysteries, prides himself on solving the case by the end of the first sixty pages. But I don't think he's such a great sleuth; he was wrong about the last two books he has read.

2. Mother said that anyone who would own a second-hand car is a fool or a saint.

3. No one answered when we rang the doorbell, so we decided that the Lums must have closed the cottage and returned home.

4. Mollie had bought a new rubber plant to replace the one that had died. She watered it every other day, and when it, too, died, she decided that she must have overwatered it.

5. Lindsey always brings dried fruits, nuts, and soybeans in her lunch. I'm glad I'm not a vegetarian like she is.

6. Mr. Kahn couldn't decide whether Van, who sat on the bench instead of joining in the game, was sick or whether he simply disliked Mr. Kahn's coaching.

7. When, at her birthday party, Kathy ignored the present that her uncle had given her, he was quite distressed. He had thought she would enjoy having her own pocket calculator.

8. There are only two ways to make a fortune: you can inherit money, which many people do; or you can enter a lucrative business and be sharper than any of your competitors.

9. There are two schools of thought on writing. One contends that the best way to learn to write well is to write on a regular basis—preferably every day. Another school suggests that writing once a week or less is equally effective, but only if you combine your writing with a rigorous program of revision.

10. When Mark found that two of the apples at the top of the barrel were wormy, he told the produce manager to get rid of the entire barrel.

• **EXERCISE 5. Other fallacies** The following items illustrate these fallacies in reasoning: **Begging the question**, the **Post hoc fallacy**, **Ignoring the question**, and the **Argumentum ad hominem**. Write the number of the item; then identify the fallacy. Be ready to explain your choice for each item. You may wish to review these fallacies in the Language Handbook.

Example: When Dr. Ferris congratulated Louise on her excellent dental checkup, she was delighted though not surprised. Shortly after a previous visit, she had purchased both an electric toothbrush and a water spray, and she knew these had done the trick.

Answer: *Post hoc*: The assumption is that the purchase of the electric toothbrush and the water spray has had a direct effect on the health of her teeth. Though both articles may have had some effect, there are other possible explanations. Tooth decay rarely progresses constantly, particularly with regular checkups. It is often allied with the general health and age of the person and the kind of food he or she eats. The two articles may have had a contributory effect, but it would be fallacious to assume that they were the sole cause of an excellent checkup.

1. Ladies and Gentlemen of the City Council. The Neighborhood Federation asks you to vote against the building of this twenty-two-mile strip of concrete known as the Prairie Highway. In the long history of this fair city, we have had an equally long history of pride in our neighborhoods and of concern for our public parks. Many of your council members come from these neighborhoods; you've played on the fields in our wonderful parks. You've watched little acorns, both literally and figuratively, grow into mighty oaks. Concrete, ladies and gentlemen, does not grow. It merely sits there, or it quietly crumbles. I urge you, then, to vote against stagnation and erosion. Vote for growth. Defeat this proposal. We do not need this long gray line!

2. Clarice wouldn't dream of seeing that new movie at the Bijou. She said the leading man has been married three times and, supposedly, he's lost more than a fortune at the gaming tables in Las Vegas.

3. For Eli's friend Mark, a budding young painter, marriage has certainly been a professional as well as a personal boon. Since marrying Elma Fleig, Mark has had his work displayed in a large New York gallery; several international critics have praised his work; and he now commands more than a thousand dollars for even a small canvas.

4. The school board did not wish to hire the inexperienced young man as administrator because he lacked the background for running the large district. After all, someone who has not already headed a large district could not make judgments and decisions or face the problems that inevitably arise in such a job.

5. Bret complained that he had never had any trouble with his back until he bought that new, low-slung sports car. "Driving in style," he said, "just isn't worth the backache it causes."

6. Dear Madam:

I am responding on behalf of the entire library board to your letter objecting to a book in the library's collection. May we suggest that, in this instance, your request for the removal of the book is ill-advised. The book in question was written by a member of this community, an outstanding citizen of the most impeccable moral character. He has selflessly contributed both time and money to the support of the library and to the expansion of its collection. Secondly, the author himself presented the library with copies; they cost the taxpayers not one red cent. Finally, the book itself has been extremely popular. At no time since we acquired it, have there been fewer than six people on the waiting list. For these reasons, the board has instructed me to inform you that the book will not be removed.

7. I think that English homework takes too much time because it consumes most of the evening.

8. I refuse to read Belinda Muckridge's new book *Why Countries Allow War*. She has never served in the army and has been on the battlefield only in the capacity of a reporter. Let writers who want to make informed comments about war be those soldiers who have actually fought in the war. Muckridge and those other "experts" who pretend to understand war should observe the rule: "Fight before you write."

Chapter 14* Using Words

A. Each of the following numbered sets contains one word that has a *favorable* connotation, one that is more *neutral,* and one that is *unfavorable.* Next to the word, write "F," "N," or "U" to indicate its connotation.

1. impetuous foolhardy brave
2. cold reserved dignified

B. Write a straightforward word or phrase for the italicized euphemisms and big words in the following sentences.

1. When John was *de-hired,* he decided he'd better *investigate other employment opportunities.*

2. Mark, a modern Robin Hood, specialized in *the unauthorized expropriation of money.*

C. Choose the most appropriate word for the misused italicized word in each of the following sentences.

1. After listening to his spooky tale of an encounter with Bigfoot, we began our midnight walk home with great *tribulation.*
(a) trenchancy **(b)** trepidation **(c)** travesty

2. Algebra I is a *perquisite* for Algebra II.
(a) persecute **(b)** prerogative **(c)** prerequisite

Chapter 15 Figurative Language

A. Identify the one sense (sight, sound, touch, taste, or smell) to which the imagery in the following passage does *not* make an appeal.

As he gazed into the cobalt-blue Tibetan sky, Nicholas sensed that his quest for the snow leopard was nearing an end. With his numbed fingers he clutched at the rock surface and pulled himself behind the boulder. From nearby he heard a soft, padded rustling, like dust gently stirred by a feather. Then suddenly the breeze wafted to him a pungent odor that warned him the leopard was near.

B. Identify the figure of speech–simile or metaphor–in the following sentence and indicate what is being compared.

Peter Jenkins, the chief of British Intelligence, was an owl in the espionage aviary, for he was nocturnal in his habits, acute in his perceptions, and both silent and seemingly wise in hunting prey.

C. Identify the type of figure of speech–personification, hyperbole, or understatement–in the following sentences. Identify as "literal" the one sentence that does not make use of figurative language.

1. Lily, landlubber though she is, bought a boat that rivals the *Titanic* in size, accessories, and accommodations.

2. She set out on a cruise with a crew of volunteers made up of her friends.

---

*There is no test on Chapter 13.

3. The cruel sea battered Lily's boat mercilessly.

4. The storm caused a little damage to Lily's boat: a leaking hull, an engine that wouldn't work, and a broken rudder.

D. In the following sentence two metaphors are used to describe one country, resulting in a mixed figure of speech. Identify the two metaphors.

Sergei Oblonsky warned from exile that the Russian bear was on the prowl and that unless the western nations acted together it would soon wrap its coils around yet another country.

Chapter 16 Thinking Logically

A. Write "S-F" for a statement-of-fact and "S-O" for a statement of opinion.

1. Francis Marion, an American general in the Revolutionary War, was called "the Swamp Fox."

2. Fujiyama, an extinct volcano near Tokyo, is the most beautiful mountain in the world.

B. The following items illustrate these logical fallacies: Hasty generalization, Either-or argument, Begging the question, the *Post hoc* fallacy, Ignoring the question, and *Argumentum ad hominem.* Identify the specific fallacy in each item.

1. Matthew must not be fond of desserts–he passed up a second helping of Kate's delicious cheesecake.

2. In attempting to draw Professor Natenshon out on the subject of evolution, the questioner stated that the professor must choose to be on the side of either the apes or the angels.

3. Every American student should be required to learn a foreign language because in our modern world it is absolutely essential to know more than one language.

4. Our city made a big mistake in electing Diane Burns mayor. Six weeks after she was sworn in three major industries moved out, the school system was bankrupt, and property taxes went up.

5. *Eat Your Heart Out* should win the Pulitzer Prize for fiction: it's been on the best-seller list for three months, it's going to be made into a movie, and its author has overcome a great deal of adversity in her life.

6. Professor Eckhart's criticisms of the advertising industry are completely unwarranted. But what else could one expect from a member of the intelligentsia who is opposed to free enterprise?

Perfect Score: 28

Unit Five Test-taking

CHAPTER 17 Tips for Taking Tests

No matter what direction you follow after high school, you will encounter tests of one kind or another that require you to use your language skills. If you apply for a job, your prospective employer may ask you to take a proficiency test to determine whether you have the necessary job skills. If you go on to college, you will take a number of placement tests in your first few weeks; these tests may determine what level and type of courses you can take during your first year or two of study. If you go into the armed forces, you will be faced with various types of competency tests during your first weeks of training. In many trades and professions, promotion is won only through the passing of some type of test. Ours is a test-oriented society, and, like it or not, success in today's world is partially determined by how well you "test."

You may have been warned before taking a test that "There is no way to prepare for this test." In one sense this is true, but there are, in fact, many things you can do before and during a test that can improve your performance.

Things to do before the test

1. Even if you have had experience with multiple-choice tests (such as the Scholastic Aptitude Test), it may be helpful to review, during the weeks before you take the test, some test formats you are likely to encounter. A number of helpful books available in stores and libraries contain advice and examples of full-length tests. Practice and some careful working through of the examples, with particular attention to the type of mental gymnastics you are asked to perform, can be of real benefit. Knowing what to expect on a particular type of test will make you more confident, which, in turn, should help you do better. Furthermore, research has shown that practice in test-taking, by itself, can significantly improve test scores.

2. Don't try to cram during the last few days or nights before the test. Reading through a 3,000 word vocabulary list the night before a language-aptitude test probably will do more harm than good. The best thing you can do immediately before an important test is to relax, get a good night's sleep, and eat a good breakfast before setting out.

Things to do when you take the test

1. Come into the testing place on time with as relaxed and positive an attitude as you can manage. Dress comfortably and sensibly and be prepared to sit for a long period. Pick a place where you will be as comfortable as possible and where you can best concentrate.

2. Think positively about the test and your own abilities. There's probably a good deal you already know that can be of help on any test. If you are at first stumped by a question, use your common sense and apply your own experience. Often this approach will help you solve a problem that at first seems impossible.

3. Read *all* the directions and be sure you understand them. Do *all* the sample questions before starting the test, even if you are sure you know how to do them. More tests are failed because the directions are not followed than from almost any other cause. Also note carefully the time limits for the test, or for each of its sections. Note the number of items you have to complete within these limits, so that you can pace yourself. (Remember, some tests are designed so that it is virtually impossible to complete all the items within the time limit. If this is the case, the directions will give you some warning. But it is still important to pace yourself, since your score will be based on the number of items you have completed correctly.)

4. Once you start the test, keep going. Do not linger too long on any one question. If you cannot answer a question after a reasonable amount of time, skip it and try to come back to it later. In order to locate quickly and efficiently those items you have skipped, place a small check mark beside the number of each skipped item on your answer sheet.

5. Mark the answers clearly. Do not make more than one mark on any one item (you can't fool the computer). Pay particular attention to the correspondence between the number of the test item and the number on the answer sheet. Check this correspondence at intervals, say every ten items or so. If you answer the question correctly, but put your mark in the wrong line or wrong row, the computer will mark your answer wrong. One small error in your marking of answers can cause you to do poorly on a test.

6. If you finish the test with a few minutes to spare, use that time to check and recheck your work. Look for answers you may have skipped, those that are unclearly marked, or those you have some hesitations about. Often a few extra moments spent checking out a test can pay dividends in higher scores.

Things not to do when you take the test

1. Whatever happens, don't panic. If something seems wrong with your test (sometimes a page or a section is missing, and occasionally people have been given the wrong test), or if your chair is impossibly wobbly, or all three of your pencils' points snap in the first thirty seconds, get the attention of the person in charge of the test and explain your problem.

2. Don't watch the clock. Check your progress from time to time, or at the halfway point, and speed up if necessary.

3. Don't let yourself be distracted. If you are seated next to an uncomfortably hot radiator or near someone who sneezes every thirty seconds, or if you find yourself in any other circumstance that tends to break your concentration, ask to be moved.

4. Don't be a perfectionist. Choose the best or most likely answer from among the choices given, even if it is not phrased exactly the way you would like. Don't take time to write comments on your test or answer sheet.

5. Don't shuffle things around while you take the test. This breaks your concentration and wastes time. Position yourself so that you are comfortable, with your test booklet and answer sheet laid out on a flat surface so that you can look from one to the other without having to move either.

CHAPTER 18 Reading Comprehension Tests

Most tests of verbal skill contain a major section on reading comprehension. Because reading difficulty may vary with the type of material to be read, these tests usually include selections from a variety of subjects, such as science, history, literature, and philosophy.

The questions based on the selections also vary in difficulty. Some questions merely require an understanding of the factual material in the selection. Others, more difficult, may ask you to interpret and analyze what you have read. Still others may evaluate your ability to apply and test principles discussed by the author. And some questions may even require that you judge the author's treatment of the material or evaluate the author's ability to use evidence to support general statements.

Here is a typical exercise dealing with reading comprehension. Following this test are the answers, along with an explanation of what skill each question is designed to test.

Example: *Directions:* Read the following passage and then answer the questions that follow it by choosing the best among the four suggested answers for each question. Write the letter of your choice after the appropriate question number on your paper. Answer questions only on the basis of what is stated or implied in the passage.

> We do not have heroes any longer, or perhaps it is more accurate to say, we do not make heroes anymore. There are some who do not mind this, and even think we may be safer without heroes. But even they acknowledge that the absence of heroes is a mark of our age, telling us something about the kind of people we are. It is more than a century since Carlyle wrote *On Heroes, Hero-worship, and the Heroic in History,* in which he lamented, "I am well aware that in these days, Hero-worship, the thing I call Hero-worship, professes to have gone out, and finally ceased." He called Napoleon "our last Great Man," because the (5)

modern age "as it were denies the existence of great men: denies the desirableness of great men." In all of this he was putting his finger, as he often did, on a characteristic of the age that was just beginning, one that our own century has only confirmed. Carlyle is himself something of a heroic writer, with whom, for that reason, we cannot come to grips. 10

A society that has no heroes will soon grow enfeebled. Its purposes will be less elevated; its aspirations less challenging; its endeavors less strenuous. Its individual members will also be enfeebled. They will "hang loose" and "lay back" and, so mellowed out, the last thing of which they wish to hear is heroism. They do not want to be told of men and women whose example might disturb them, calling them to effort and duty and sacrifice or even the chance of glory. "We have a great many flutes and flageolets [small wind instruments]," said Emerson, "but not the sound of any fife" to summon us. More than a century later, we hardly have even flutes and flageolets, but we do have a great many guitars. Heroes need other music than strumming. 15 20 25

"Not only is a hero needed, but a world fit for him; a world not of *Valets*," said Carlyle again. As we read the word, his finger seems pointed at us, at our own world. If we no longer have any heroes, it may not be because no one is fit to be a hero, but because we are not fit to recognize one. It may even be that the powers-that-be in our societies do not want us to have heroes. Heroes are against things-as-they-are. They break through the pattern of valetdom, the ruck that most of us accept out of indifference or weariness. They say that things aren't necessarily so, that they can be altered if we strain to change them. All heroes are rebels–which does not mean that all rebels are heroes–and as rebels they are spirited. Our times are dispirited. 30 35

We need to begin with a model.

1. According to the writer of this passage, the modern age has existed for

A. over a century
B. the past five decades
C. at least 300 years
D. twelve generations

2. The author considers the sound of a fife

A. a reminder of Napoleon
B. a symbol of the modern age
C. a rousing call to action
D. soothing music for our modern age

3. What is meant in line 25 by "Heroes need other music than strumming"?

A. Heroes lack the time to listen to music.
B. Heroic actions will not be brought about by a gentle summons.
C. The modern hero is represented by the rock star.
D. Heroes are willing to make great sacrifices.

---

4. The author states all of the following *except*:
A. We may not be able to recognize a hero.
B. Modern heroes may not actually exist.
C. Heroes always provide a stabilizing influence on society.
D. Powerful people may not want heroes.

5. In this passage, the word *Valets* (line 27) probably refers to
A. weak people
B. talented leaders
C. stubborn peers
D. eager sympathizers

6. One can conclude that the writer of this passage is
A. furious
B. lighthearted
C. indifferent
D. critical

7. The main idea of this passage may be best expressed as:
A. Heroes are no longer necessary.
B. No one is fit to be a hero today.
C. Napoleon was our last great hero.
D. Our present age does not encourage heroism.

Answers: In answering the questions about the preceding passage, notice that initially several of the choices offered seem correct. Upon closer examination, however, you can distinguish the one correct answer from those that merely repeat conspicuous phrases, contain irrelevant statements, or twist the original thought. Some answers may be relatively easy to determine; others may require careful deduction or inference making. Different questions are designed to pinpoint particular reading-comprehension skills.

Question 1 tests your ability to find specific details. The first paragraph of the passage states that Carlyle wrote about the modern age over a century ago, so that choice *B* can be immediately eliminated. Later in the paragraph, we learn that the modern age was just beginning during Carlyle's time, thus eliminating choices *C* and *D*. From the information provided, you can determine that choice *A* is correct.

Question 2 requires that the reader make some inferences. There is no connection made in the passage between the fife and Napoleon or the modern age; thus choices *A* and *B* are incorrect. The end of paragraph 2 implies that the guitar, not the fife, provides soothing music for the modern age, thus eliminating choice *D*. Choice *C* is the correct answer. Notice Emerson has observed that a fife no longer summons us.

Question 3 is slightly more difficult, since it requires you to interpret figurative language. Choices *A* and *C* can be eliminated because no evidence in the passage is provided to support them. Although there is some basis provided in the passage for the statement in choice *D*, this statement has no bearing on the phrase in question 3. In order to confirm that choice *B* is correct, a reader should recognize that, in the context of the second paragraph, the gentle sound of strumming would soothe people rather than provide a call to action.

Question 4, with its signal word *except*, requires you to locate the one incorrect answer. All the statements, with the exception of choice *C*, can be found in the passage. Not only does choice *C* not appear in the passage; it is the very opposite of what the author has stated. Heroes are against things-as-they-are; they break through patterns; they question things and work for change–qualities that are anything but stabilizing. One other thing to note in choice *C* is the word *always*. Be wary of answers that include superlatives such as *best* or *worst*, or of all-inclusive words such as *every*, *always*, and all-exclusive words such as *never* or *none*. Whenever such words appear, reread the paragraph to ascertain whether or not these words are correctly used.

Question 5 tests your ability to determine the meaning of unfamiliar words, as used in the passage. By examining the context in which the word appears, you can get a general idea of the author's meaning. Because Carlyle says that Valets would not appear in a world fit for heroes, you can assume that this term does not refer to talented leaders or eager sympathizers. And because the author remarks that the pattern of valetdom is accepted out of indifference or weariness, you can eliminate stubborn peers, leaving *A* as the correct answer.

Question 6 tests your ability to ascertain the author's tone or attitude toward the subject. While the tone is too strong to be called *lighthearted* or *indifferent*, it is too mild to be considered *furious*. Choice *D* best expresses the author's tone.

Question 7 tests your ability to state the main idea of a passage. In the opening sentence, the author observes that we do not have, nor do we make, heroes. Choice *D* seems most compatible with the main idea, as stated in this topic sentence. Nowhere in the passage do we read that heroes are no longer necessary, eliminating choice *A*. If you examine choice *B* in its original context, you will notice that the statement is qualified by the phrase "it may not be because." Thus, choice *B* is incorrect as it stands. Although choice *C* appears in the passage, it clearly does not embody the main idea, since it concerns only one particular hero.

• **EXERCISE 1.** *Directions*: Read the following passage and then answer the questions that follow it by choosing the best among the four suggested answers. Write the letter of your choice after the appropriate number on your paper. Answer questions only on the basis of what is stated or implied in the passage.

> Bumblebees have suffered in this century by comparison with the honeybee, whose spectacular powers of information-handling and social management have constituted some of the major discoveries in ethology. Bumblebees, by contrast, live nowhere near as corporate an existence. Their hierarchies are much less rigid; the queens and work- 5 ers do not look very different from each other, and even among what differences do exist there is a wide range of individual variation. In honeybees the castes are more distinct and there are no intermediate

I wish he would explain his explanation. Lord Byron

forms. Bumblebees do not pool information about new food sources, or recruit helpers as honeybees do. Adults rarely regurgitate food for 10 other adults or try to groom them, and social relations are generally more volatile. Bumblebee queens hold their rank by physically harassing competitors, those bees with developing ovaries. When bumblebee colonies grow larger than a few hundred members the queen loses control of the hive and the workers begin to eat her eggs and to lay eggs of 15 their own, which she in turn tries to eat. Honeybee queens control nests of up to 40,000 members with powerful, behavior-modifying drugs that keep the workers tranquilized and docile.

Most biologists betray the unconscious assumption that a complicated social organization is an achievement, and that bumblebees, in 20 comparatively simple colonies, have somehow *failed*. . . . [But at least one biologist] maintains that an elaborate social order makes for a garrison state in perpetual energy crisis. Large societies in a fixed location tend to deplete the neighborhood of whatever resources the society needs, so that the environment is at least intermittently impoverished. 25 One way of dealing with the prospect of depleted energy is to stockpile resources when they become available, building huge reserves. The reserves in turn attract predators, which make an expensive defense establishment necessary, which increases the drain of local resources, and 30 so on.

From this perspective, the bumblebees are a great success. They have achieved a modest social order without committing themselves to the costly business of supporting a large standing army. They have managed this by learning how to forage successfully in weather that keeps most other species of bees in the hive. Bumblebees evolved in 35 the Arctic, and there they acquired the two traits that have freed them from a rigid social discipline: the knack of foraging among widely scattered and minute food sources, and a profound control over the generation and loss of body heat. They work hard, foraging for longer hours during the day than honeybees and visiting two to three times as many 40 flowers in a given period. Thus they have a steady income, and are not obliged to accumulate surpluses as protection against future shortage, which would attract skunks and foxes. Honeybees did not evolve this flexibility because they arose in tropical Asia. They adapted to capitalizing quickly on the discovery of major finds, such as large flowering 45 trees, and are thus committed to a corporate, garrison existence.

1. In comparison to honeybees, bumblebees have all of the following *except*:

A. a less corporate existence
B. more effective methods of information-sharing
C. less rigid hierarchies
D. less distinct castes

---

2. The queen bumblebee
   A. controls workers by tranquilizing them
   B. thrives in nests of over a thousand workers
   C. survives by physically harassing rivals
   D. is an expert in social management

3. Honeybees have a "perpetual energy crisis" because
   A. they stockpile resources that attract predators
   B. they do not support a large standing army
   C. they exhaust themselves in gathering food
   D. they work fewer hours during the day than do bumblebees

4. Which of the following is *not* mentioned in the passage as contributing to make bumblebees successful foragers?
   A. They have a profound control over the generation and loss of body heat.
   B. They can gather food from scattered and minute sources.
   C. They require less food for sustenance than do honeybees.
   D. They work longer hours and visit more flowers than do honeybees.

5. Which of the following describes the "garrison state" mentioned in lines 22–23?
   A. "huge reserves" (line 27)
   B. "a modest social order" (line 32)
   C. "a large standing army" (line 33)
   D. "a steady income" (line 41)

6. Which of the following contributes to the "steady income" mentioned in line 41?
   A. future shortages
   B. the knack of foraging among scattered food sources
   C. accumulated surpluses
   D. capitalizing quickly on the discovery of major finds

CHAPTER 19 Error Recognition

PART 1

Correction Choice

The purpose of error-recognition items is to determine whether you can spot mistakes in areas such as mechanics, grammar, or usage. These tests operate under the assumption that if you can find mistakes, you can correct them. For example, you might be tested on spelling by being asked to locate the one misspelled word in each group of five:

Examples:

1. A. truly B. until C. layed D. every E. delay
2. A. either B. wierd C. seize D. receive E. niece
3. A. occurred B. weather C. nickel D. accommodate E. supercede
4. A. villain B. tragedy C. forty D. awkward E. priviledge
5. A. precede B. definite C. seperate D. metaphor E. necessary

Answers: 1. C; 2. B; 3. E; 4. E; 5. C

In another type of error-recognition test, you are given sentences with parts that are underlined and lettered. In some of these sentences one, and only one, of the underlined parts is incorrect and needs changing. In other sentences, none of the parts needs changing. You are asked to indicate which one, if any, of the underlined parts you think should be changed.

Examples:

1. He would of [A] given us boys [B] first prize had it not been [C] for our falling [D] in the first part of the competition. No error. [E]

2. You may not believe her and I, but my grandmother already called the attendance office to say that we should be excused regardless of the mixup. No error.

(A: may not; B: her and I; C: already; D: regardless; E: No error.)

3. If we cannot raise that window, the only route that will ensure our escape is to jump off of the loading platform. No error.

(A: raise; B: ensure; C: our escape; D: off of; E: No error.)

Answers:

In sentence 1, the verb phrase should be *would have*, not *would of*, which is nonstandard usage; the answer is *A*. In sentence 2, *her and I* should be *her and me*, with both pronouns in the objective case following the verb; the answer is *B*. In sentence 3, *off of* is nonstandard usage; the preposition *off* is correct; the answer is *D*.

• **EXERCISE 1.** Each of the following sentences contains four underlined items, one of which *may* be incorrect. If an underlined item contains an error, mark the letter on your paper. If there is no error in any underlined item, mark *E* on your paper.

1. If I were she, I would postpone graduating high school until next year so that I could play a few more roles in theater productions. No error.

(A: If I were she; B: graduating; C: so that; D: could play; E: No error.)

2. As he was lying under the car, the principal walked by, recognized his fancy boots, and proceeded to compliment him on his auto mechanics trophy. No error.

(A: lying; B: principal; C: proceeded; D: compliment; E: No error.)

3. Just between you and me, I think the judges gave Anne fewer points then she expected. No error.

(A: between; B: you and me; C: fewer; D: then; E: No error.)

4. They gave only one reason why whoever accepts the award should give it to the school instead of keeping it for theirself. No error.

(A: only; B: whoever; C: accepts; D: theirself; E: No error.)

5. Since you have been given more responsibility on the job, you had ought to ask for a raise. No error.

(A: Since; B: have been given; C: had ought; D: raise; E: No error.)

In another exercise item, you are required to choose from among a number of possibilities the one best correction or improvement of an underlined word or phrase. Since some of the underlined items are correct as they stand, one of the possibilities offered is NO CHANGE.

Examples:

1. The moped is theres, not Bob's.

A. theirs
B. their's
C. there's
D. they'res
E. NO CHANGE

2. When you layed that book on the counter, did you know it was overdue?

A. lay
B. laid
C. had lain
D. were lying
E. NO CHANGE

Answers:

In sentence 1, you must first distinguish between homonyms and then choose the correct possessive form of the pronoun; the answer is *A*. In sentence 2, you must first distinguish between two verb forms and then select the proper spelling and tense of the verb; the answer is *B*.

• **EXERCISE 2.** Write the letter of the best correction for the underlined section in each of the following sentences. If the underlined section is correct, write the letter that indicates NO CHANGE.

1. It finally snowed, however, not enough fell for good skiing.

A. snowed; however,
B. snowed; however;
C. snowed however,
D. snowed; however
E. NO CHANGE

2. By the time I awake, the sun arises.

A. will rise
B. will have risen
C. will be raised
D. will have arose
E. NO CHANGE

3. Elena's senior activities include playing clarinet in the orchestra, editor of the yearbook, and running hurdles on the track team.

A. yearbook editor
B. yearbook editing
C. to edit the yearbook
D. editing the yearbook
E. NO CHANGE

4. Although semester exams are required of all freshmen, sophomores, and juniors, they are not required of seniors second semester.

A. a senior doesn't have to take exams second semester
B. second semester exams don't apply to you if you're a senior
C. seniors don't second semester
D. us seniors don't have to take them second semester
E. NO CHANGE

5. On the three-week exchange trip to Spain, we will attend school like we do here in the United States.

A. as we do
B. as if we do
C. just like we do
D. as though we do
E. NO CHANGE

PART 2

Selecting Acceptable Sentences

Another type of exam tests your ability to judge an entire sentence in terms of grammar, usage, and style. You will have to determine any incorrect items yourself, since items that might contain errors are not underlined. On one such exam you are required to select from among several possibilities the best sentence according to formal written English.

Examples:

1. A. Pulling the steering wheel too far to the right, the car jumped the curb.
B. Neither the principal nor the dean have given permission for the dance.
C. Going ice skating sounded easier than it turned out to be.

2. A. Miss Willard gave the seating chart to Joanne and I to take to the office.
B. If he were going to school in the 1950s, he would have to observe a dress code.
C. Ian prefers traveling in the summer rather than to work at home with his brother.

Answers: In the first example, item *C* is correct. Sentence *A* contains a dangling modifier, and in sentence *B* the *neither/nor* construction requires a singular verb. In the second example, item *B*, in which the subjunctive form is used correctly, is right. In sentence *A*, the use of the nominative case *I* as the object of the preposition *to* is incorrect. In sentence *C*, the gerund *traveling* and the infinitive *to work* are not parallel constructions.

• **EXERCISE 3.** For each group of sentences, write the letter of the item that is correct according to standard written English.

1. A. The next step in developing pictures is where you remove the film from the fixer.
B. The reason they canceled the volleyball game was because of last night's storm.
C. My going to camp tomorrow has caused problems with the work schedule at the restaurant.
2. A. The Crosses, our next-door neighbors, paid Paula and me to mow their lawn while they were on vacation.
B. So far in her auto maintenance class, Laura has learned how to clean spark plugs and changing an oil filter.
C. No sooner had we started the race when a rabbit dashed across our path.
3. A. Not one of the club members have entered the contest.
B. Having never been to Washington, the Lincoln Memorial impressed me most.
C. Hernando's experiences in the Marine Corps were different from what his father had told him to expect.

PART 3
Sentence Completion

In another related type of test item, you are provided with a sentence beginning and offered a choice of three or four endings, one of which is correct. This form may test items such as coordination and subordination of sentence parts, pronoun reference or agreement, and parallel structure.

Examples:

1. Mike got up early to open the restaurant,
A. but his first customer was already waiting at the door.
B. while his first customer was already waiting at the door.
C. so that his first customer was already waiting at the door.

2. Dickinson's poetry is filled with riddles, personifications, and subtle rhymes;
A. this makes her work difficult to read.
B. these elements make reading her work difficult.
C. it makes her work difficult to read.

3. The yearbook staff decided to raise the extra money by holding a car wash,
A. selling candy, and increased advertising.
B. candy sales, and an advertising increase.
C. selling candy, and increasing advertising.

Answers: In sentence 1, *A* completes the sentence correctly because *but* shows the right connection between the clauses. In sentence 2, *B* is the right answer because it avoids the vague pronoun references of *this* or *it*. In sentence 3, *C* completes the sentence correctly because *selling candy* and *increasing advertising* are participial phrases that are parallel to *holding a car wash.*

• **EXERCISE 4.** Select the ending that completes each sentence according to standard written English.

1. Braking too quickly on the slick pavement,
A. the car swerved into a tree.
B. he swerved the car into a tree.
C. and swerving, the car hit a tree.

2. My New Year's resolutions were the following:
A. to keep my room neat; watching my weight; and the debate team.
B. keeping my room neat; watching my weight; and to make the debate team.
C. to keep my room neat; to watch my weight; and to make the debate team.

3. I spend too much money on records and movies,
A. which my family disapproves of.
B. a practice that my family disapproves of.
C. and my family disapproves of it.

4. It makes more sense for me to rewire this lamp than
A. to throw it away.
B. throwing it away.
C. to be throwing it away.

5. Rafting down the Wolf River,
A. dangerous rocks began to appear.
B. there were dangerous rocks.
C. we saw dangerous rocks.

CHAPTER 20 Organizing Sentences

PART 1
Scrambled Sentences

Another type of exam, consisting of paragraphs in which the sentences have been scrambled, tests your ability to organize ideas into a logical sequence. In order to arrange these sentences in the proper sequence, you must note the relationships between certain ideas, the connecting words in sentences, and other clues such as logical order. To successfully complete this kind of test, you must understand the principles involved in constructing a coherent paragraph.

For this test format, a rather complicated answer form is provided to ensure that you get full credit for every relationship that you indicate correctly, even though your answer as a whole may not be perfect.

Example: *Directions*: The sentences that follow are not in their proper order. Read them and decide how they should be arranged to make a well-organized paragraph. Do not leave out any sentence. Jot down on scratch paper the correct order of the sentences, and then answer the questions that follow.

In answering the questions, use *X* to mean that no sentence follows. If you have arranged the sentences in a group to read in the order *B*, *C*, *A*, *D*, you will answer the question "Which sentence did you put after *D*?" by writing *X*.

A. Fearful that the earth would be enveloped by deadly gases in its flowing tail, people bought comet pills to ward off its effects, and held end-of-the-world gatherings.

B. In fact, NASA is planning a scientific welcoming party in space. . . .
C. In 1985, when the comet returns—as it does every three-quarters of a century—it should get a friendlier reception.
D. When Halley's Comet last streaked across the skies in 1910, it was for many an unwelcome visitor.

1. Which sentence did you put first?
2. Which sentence did you put after *A*?
3. Which sentence did you put after *B*?
4. Which sentence did you put after *C*?
5. Which sentence did you put after *D*?

The logical order for these sentences is *D*, *A*, *C*, *B*.

Answers: If you completed this example correctly, the answers on your test sheet would read *D*, *C*, *X*, *B*, *A*. Note that the order of your answers is not the same as the order of the sentences in the unscrambled paragraph.

This sample paragraph uses chronological order as the basis for its structure. The first step in handling this type of exercise item is to read through all the sentences and to find the one that logically comes first. From this, the pattern of the other sentences can be worked out by recognizing the various connecting words and other sentence links. In putting scrambled sentences in their proper order, you will find it necessary to work backward as well as forward to arrive at a logical paragraph.

• **EXERCISE 1.** Follow the directions on page 153 for rearranging in coherent order the following scrambled sentences:

A. They counted a total of just under 4 million people, although President Washington suspected that this was an undercount.
B. Despite this reduction, however, in 1940 a question about income was added to the census.
C. Today's citizens, who may balk at answering questions about income, could face a fine of $100 if they refuse to complete the form or supply false information.
D. Although this original census asked only 6 questions, by 1890 there were over 400 questions for some heads of households.
E. Fortunately, that same year the electric tabulating machine was introduced, making it easier to count this unwieldy number of questions.
F. In August 1790, the first U.S. census takers began counting the American people—a project that took 18 months.
G. By the next census, however, the large number of questions had been reduced drastically.

---

1. Which sentence did you put first?
2. Which sentence did you put after *A*?
3. Which sentence did you put after *B*?
4. Which sentence did you put after *C*?
5. Which sentence did you put after *D*?
6. Which sentence did you put after *E*?
7. Which sentence did you put after *F*?
8. Which sentence did you put after *G*?

PART 2

Sentence Outlines

Another test calls for rearrangement of scrambled sentences into a sentence outline. From a list of sentences, you are asked to organize the material into a related pattern, much as you would do when writing a sentence outline for a research paper.

Example: *Directions*: Read the following statements carefully, paying attention to their relationship to one another. Then, next to the number of each statement, mark the appropriate letter.
A, if the statement contains the central idea around which most of the other statements can be grouped
B, if the statement contains a main supporting idea of the central idea
C, if the statement contains an illustrative fact or a detailed piece of evidence
D, if the statement is irrelevant to the other material

1. It is a wise idea to investigate the policies of different insurance companies since some companies place a student with a B average into a lower risk category.
2. It is usually better to buy from a reputable used car dealer who offers a warranty than from a private owner.
3. In shopping for a used car, economy-minded teen-agers must consider not only the price of the car but also the best deal on car insurance.
4. Since the price of a new car is prohibitive for most teen-agers, they should look for a good deal on a used car.
5. The cost of car insurance may be greater than the cost of a used car.
6. Many high schools now discourage students from driving to school by limiting parking permits to those with part-time jobs.
7. Even with a good academic record, however, boys will usually pay at least $300 more a year for car insurance than girls.

Answers: 1. *B*; 2. *B*; 3. *A*; 4. *B*; 5. *C*; 6. *D*; 7. *C*
In arranging the sentences into an outline, you will have only one sentence labeled *A* because there can be only one central idea. In this

Man is a rational animal who always loses his temper when he is called upon to act in accordance with the dictates of reason. Oscar Wilde

case, sentence 3 expresses the main idea: shopping for the best deal on a car and car insurance for a teen-ager. Three sentences function as subtopics of the main idea: sentence 1 on investigating insurance companies; sentence 2 on buying from a reputable used car dealer; and sentence 4 on buying a used car. These three sentences would be marked *B*. Two sentences, adding specific detail, would be marked *C*: sentence 5 on the high cost of insurance and sentence 7 on high insurance costs for boys. Sentence 6 is irrelevant and would be marked *D*.

• **EXERCISE 2.** Using the directions on page 155, mark the following sentences *A*, *B*, *C*, or *D* to indicate how they would fit into a coherent sentence outline.

1. A campus visit should be made when classes are in session.
2. Talking with guidance counselors, college admissions representatives, and other experts will provide useful information about what colleges want.
3. Students who don't go to college often earn just as much as those who get college degrees.
4. Brochures sometimes try to "sell" a college, however.
5. Visiting colleges can provide information that can help in narrowing the college application decision.
6. Early graduation from high school appeals to a few seniors every year.
7. College brochures and catalogs provide a solid beginning to the application process.
8. Applying to college is a complicated process that requires careful investigation.

CHAPTER

21 Style and Appropriateness

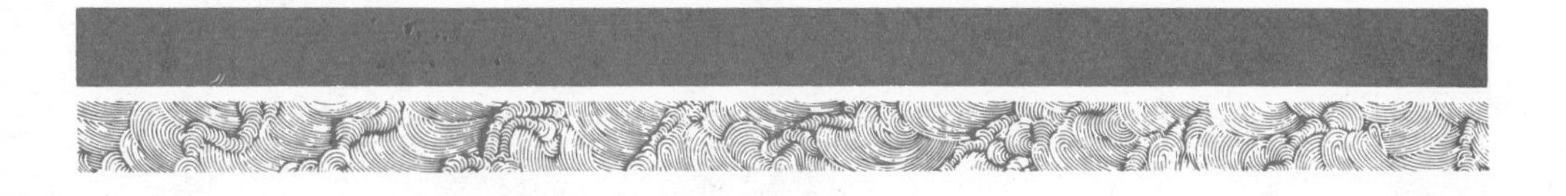

Your ability to recognize in prose or poetry elements of style, such as tone, figurative language, diction, and rhythm, may be tested in several ways.

PART 1

Prose Passages

One type of examination includes several passages of prose with words or phrases removed at intervals. On these exams, you are asked to complete the passage with items you consider most appropriate in style and meaning.

Example:

I lingered round them, under that benign sky: watched the moths fluttering among the heath and hare-bells, listened to the soft wind ______1______ through the grass, and wondered how any one could ever imagine unquiet slumbers for the ______2______.

–Emily Brontë, *Wuthering Heights*

1. A. roaring
B. as it tippytoed
C. breathing
D. as it hesitated

2. A. dead folks
B. sleepers in that quiet earth
C. decaying bodies in their graves
D. criminals hanged for murder

Answers:

For the first item, *C* is the correct answer. Answer *A* contradicts the peaceful image of the passage, *B* is incorrect in form and diction, and *D* is not in keeping with the meaning or the rhythm of the passage. In the second item, the answer is *B*. *A* is incorrect in diction, *C* departs from the tone of the passage, and *D* contradicts the meaning of the passage.

• **EXERCISE 1.** Write the letter of the answer that best completes each item.

I went to the woods because I wished to live deliberately, to front only the essential facts of life, and see if I could not learn what it had ____1____, and not, when I came to die, discover that I had not lived. I did not wish to live what was not life, living is so dear; nor did I wish to practice resignation, unless it was ____2____. I wanted to live deep and suck out all the marrow of life, to live so sturdily and so Spartanlike as to put to rout all that was not life, to cut a broad swath and shave close, ____3____, and reduce it to its lowest terms, and if it proved to be mean, why then to get the whole and genuine ____4____ of it, and publish its meanness to the world; or if it were sublime, to know it by experience, and be able to give a true account of it in my ____5____.

–Henry David Thoreau, *Walden*

1. A. to profit me from
B. to teach
C. to help me get by
D. hidden under its carpet

2. A. quite necessary
B. a viable alternative
C. the right kind
D. the best deal I could get

3. A. to manipulate life into a defensive situation
B. knocking some sense into life
C. to beat the life out of life
D. to drive life into a corner

4. A. cheapness
B. horror
C. meanness
D. obscurity

5. A. next excursion
B. life following this current one
C. memoirs
D. journey to the Happy Hunting Ground

PART 2

Poetry Selections

Another test of your sensitivity to style and appropriateness uses selections from poems with single lines omitted. You are asked to select the correct missing line from several choices. The incorrect lines may be inappropriate in tone, diction, meaning, or rhythm.

Example:

The Riddle we can guess
We speedily despise–
Not anything is stale so long
______________________.

A. As Yesterday's surprise–
B. As Children with large eyes–
C. If it eventually tries–
D. That nifty thoughts surmise–

Answer:
In this example, the correct line is *A*. Line *B* makes no sense in meaning, line *C* is inconsistent with the other three lines in rhythm, and line *D* is inappropriate in diction.

• **EXERCISE 2.** Write the letter of the line of poetry that best completes each passage.

1. With rue my heart is laden
  For golden friends I had,
For many a rose-lipt maiden
  And many a lightfoot lad.

By brooks too broad for leaping
  The lightfoot boys are laid;
The rose-lipt girls are sleeping
______________________.

A. Where moonbeams never played.
B. On yonder hill in the shade.
C. In fields where roses fade.
D. In dresses that are frayed.

---

2. He clasps the crag with crooked hands;
Close to the sun in lonely lands,
Ring'd with the azure world, he stands.

The wrinkled sea beneath him crawls;
He watches from his mountain walls,
____________________________.

–Alfred, Lord Tennyson,
"The Eagle"

A. And like a thunderbolt he falls.
B. His mate flies by; to her he calls.
C. The pretty plain, the happy halls.
D. The planets are gleaming like golden balls.

3. I strove with none, for none was worth my strife:
Nature I loved, and next to Nature, Art:
I warmed both hands before the fire of Life;
____________________________.

–Walter Savage Landor,
"On His Seventy-fifth Birthday"

A. And that philosophy is smart.
B. They say I've put the horse before the cart.
C. You can follow me too; take heart.
D. It sinks; and I am ready to depart.

4. Fear no more the heat 'o the sun,
Nor the furious winter's rages;
Thou thy worldly task hast done,
Home art gone, and ta'en thy wages;
Golden lads and girls all must,
____________________________.

–William Shakespeare, *Cymbeline*

A. Face the music, as is just.
B. Fading and tarnish, turn to trust.
C. As chimney-sweepers, come to dust.
D. Meet their maker–if they're just.

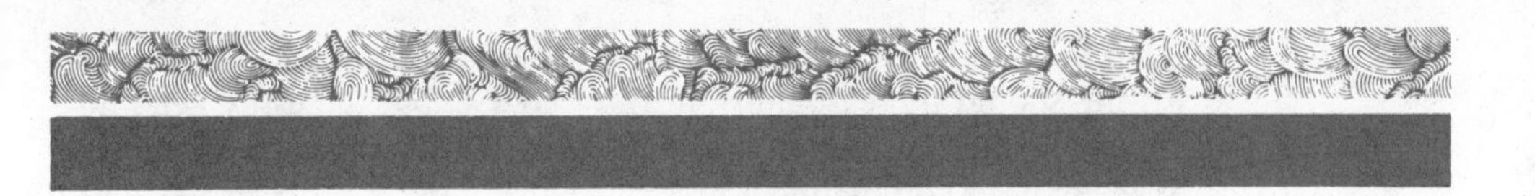

CHAPTER 22 Essay Exams

PART 1
Writing Samples

In language-effectiveness tests, you will be asked to write a brief essay on a general topic–one that does not require specialized knowledge or information. Time does not permit a long essay on this kind of test, which is usually limited to 30 minutes. You may be asked to write only one paragraph; in any case, you probably won't have time for more than three.

Your essay should demonstrate your ability to write a coherent, intelligent piece of prose about a given topic in a limited amount of time. Correct mechanics, spelling, grammar, and usage are essential. In writing an essay of this kind, keep in mind these guidelines:

- Study the question or statement carefully. Be sure you understand exactly what you are asked to do. Failure to follow directions could lead you off the track or disqualify your answer.
- Do not waste time repeating the question or statement verbatim or writing a long introduction. Get to the point immediately. Develop your thesis–the main point that you are making–within the first two or three sentences of your essay.
- Sketch out a rough outline mentally or on paper to help you organize your material. The deductive approach is usually effective and direct: make a general point and support it with specific evidence. Or you may wish to rephrase the question or statement in the form of a topic sentence.
- Write as concretely as possible. The question will normally be broad enough to allow you to draw upon material from various sources.

Who you gonna believe, me or your own eyes?
Chico Marx

• Do not assume you will be able to rewrite your essay. Your handwriting should be reasonably clear, of course, but the essay need not appear in the polished manuscript form that is expected when you have not been writing under pressure.

Here is an example of a statement designed to produce a writing sample. Read the statement carefully; then study the three essays following it. Apply the writing sample guidelines to these essays as you read them.

Example: *Directions*: In a one-paragraph essay, discuss your personal position in regard to the following quotations from two Presidents. Explain not only what you think about the change in our economic situation but also what you are doing about it. Support your general comments with concrete examples. Develop a topic sentence at the beginning of your essay that covers the entire paragraph.

Keep in mind that approximately twenty-five years have intervened between the time that these statements were made. During these years the generous spending of a consumer society has begun to give way to thrift because of an energy crisis and high prices.

"Buy anything."

—President Eisenhower, 1950s

"Eliminate waste."

—President Carter, 1980s

Answers:

Essay 1

Overall I'm a thrifty guy. I believe in saving as much money as possible, whenever possible. In this day and age with the economy suffering from inflation, I must be sure not to "buy anything," as President Eisenhower said, but instead "eliminate waste," according to President Carter's current words. Knowing nothing of today's energy crisis, Eisenhower's words made sense to people during the 1950s. Possibly this is what led today's society to desperately search for a way to replenish our countries dwindling energy resources. If only they had been wiser in their spending, they could have prevented today's consumer problems. With this in mind, I play my part in obeying President Carter's request. Our house temperature is lowered, making our heating bill less. I make sure that I don't leave any unneccesary appliances or lights on which would waste badly needed electricity. Our car is seldom used, hopefully stopping our dependence on foreign oil. As for luxuries such as food, I save coupons and when we go shopping, we use them. We also look for the best buys and bargains. We don't buy junk food anymore. This might only save a few pennies here and there, but it all adds up. By saving as much money as possible and making a few sacrafices, we can still live an ordinary and definitely satisfactory life. —Ben Segedin

Essay 2

My position between these two quotes leans more toward the "Buy anything" by President Eisenhower. I think the change in the last twenty-five years is not surprising. Because if millions of people are going to buy everything their is bound to be a shortage somewhere along the line. When it comes time for me to change I don't think I will. Due to my shortage of money one might think I should, but since I don't have to support anybody and my dad lends me a couple bucks here and there, whats the point in changeing. But if you do support a family and you don't have spare bucks coming in then there should be a definite change. Because less you waste the more we have. –Ron Cassata

Essay 3

The price rise and the energy crisis that America now faces have caused people to reevaluate their financial situations; but although they have begun cutting back in certain areas, Americans are still spending too much money. The most obvious example of cutting back is the automobile. Several years ago, no one thought about gas prices, car pools, or walking short distances. Today people buy gas-saving cars, ride the bus, bike, and walk in an attempt to lessen our dependence on foreign oil. Nevertheless, people are remiss in other areas. Americans are a "credit-happy" people, paying a great deal of interest on items they seldom need and can ill afford. In addition, they eat out frequently, generally paying higher food prices than they would if they ate at home. Although I seldom eat out and refuse to pay four dollars for a movie, I am less thrifty in other areas. I tend to buy expensive clothes, but I tell myself that since I've stopped growing, clothes are a long-range investment. My mother, who clips coupons and buys many food items in case lots for discount prices, reminds me to be more frugal. Next year, when I'm off at college balancing my own budget, I will undoubtedly be forced to be more thrifty. Right now I'm afraid that the cost of living is going to rise so much that by the time I'm ready to raise a family, I'll be quite unable to support one. Meanwhile, I make small sacrifices and view my occasional indulgences, like those of all Americans, as a way to help me get through hard economic times. –Heather Nobels

Essay 1 is a fairly successful response to the question, but the beginning is weak and there are errors in mechanics (note, for example, the dangling modifier in sentence 4) and spelling. There is a thesis or topic sentence–the third sentence of the paragraph–but the writer wastes the next two sentences with a vague comment on current problems. Only about halfway through the paragraph does the writer begin to get specific in a personal response to the topic, as requested in the directions. The details used by the writer effectively illustrate methods to economize. But the conclusion seems to accept the economic situation, although the writer has earlier complained about it. The style of the paragraph is generally clear, marred by a few clichés such as "In this day and age" and "save a few pennies." The essay would earn a medium score.

Essay 2 begins with a clear topic sentence or thesis. But its third sentence is illogical, assuming that high consumption automatically means shortages. More seriously, the essay offers no personal examples of how the writer is dealing with the problem presented in the question. The writer's shift from first person to second person in the last sentence is confusing. The paragraph contains two sentence fragments, several spelling errors, and generally faulty mechanics. It would receive a low score on an evaluation.

Essay 3 begins with a clear but general topic sentence, establishing the contrasting ideas of "cutting back" and "spending too much money." Both the Eisenhower and the Carter philosophies are illustrated with examples throughout the essay. Rather than discussing these contrasting philosophies separately, however, the writer has chosen to weave them together. Transitional words such as *Nevertheless, In addition,* and *Meanwhile* signal whether there will be a continuation or a change of thought. The writer seems in control of the material, expressing ideas in a competent style characterized by good word choice and a variety of sentence structures. Mechanics and spelling are good. The essay would receive a high score.

PART 2

The Essay Question

Questions that appear on mid-term or semester exams often require an essay of several paragraphs which may take an hour or 90 minutes to write. In this type of essay question you are required to apply reading material to a fresh situation. You may be asked, for example, to explain how this material illustrates a general concept or idea, or you may be required to compare and contrast ideas within the material. An effective essay answer, then, involves more than a simple rehashing of the material you have read, for it requires that you shape and select material in order to substantiate your ideas.

The following is an essay written by Tracy, a high-school senior, on a 60-minute semester exam for an English class. Students were to choose examples from any two literary works (out of a list of twenty titles) to illustrate a quotation. Tracy chose as her examples Henrik Ibsen's play *A Doll's House* and Henry James's novel *Daisy Miller*.

Example: *Directions*: Write an essay in which you use two characters from different works that you have read for first-semester English to document the following quotation. Your examples may come from reading for class assignments or from your outside reading. You may compare and contrast the two characters you choose or may simply present them as two separate examples of the quotation. In developing your essay, pay particular attention to the last sentence of the quotation and remember that in literature a "life" is created by an author.

> All lives are interesting; no one life is more interesting than another. Its fascination depends on how much is revealed and in what manner. –Mavis Gallant. From "Paul Leautaud, 1872–1956," THE NEW YORK TIMES BOOK REVIEW, September 9, 1973.

Answer:

As makers of literary beings, authors enjoy a certain power; they are free to create people as they please and they alone have control over precisely what the world will ever know of these people. Perhaps it was with this thought in mind that someone stated, "All lives are interesting," adding that the fascination of those lives "depends on how much is revealed and in what manner." The accuracy of this observation becomes clear when one focuses on some of the lives created by authors and on the authors themselves. Daisy of Henry James's *Daisy Miller* and Nora of Henrik Ibsen's *A Doll's House* are both interesting women, but Daisy is highly enigmatic while Nora is more open. Bringing these women to life within a year of each other (1878 and 1879), James and Ibsen use sharply different approaches in revealing characters who still fascinate us over a century later.

Handled skillfully, both enigma and openness can be fascinating. Both Winterbourne and the reader find themselves drawn to Daisy Miller, partly because she is such a closed character. Though talkative–indeed, "she chatters"–she does not discuss her true thoughts and feelings. We learn of Daisy as James arranges for us to hear choice comments by Mrs. Walker, who finds her immoral, and by Winterbourne's aunt, Mrs. Costello, who thinks her "hopelessly vulgar" for being "intimate" with her family's Italian courier. We are tantalized by their comments, but James refuses to reveal Daisy fully, confining us instead to the point of view of a tortured Winterbourne, who, like ourselves, strives to learn who Daisy really is. James contrasts her apparent brazenness to the coy, almost schemingly maidenlike blushes of the Geneva ladies, yet leaves us wondering whether Daisy is simply a bit crude or absolutely unaware of the rigid European social structure into which she has plunged. Only at her death does James allow us the satisfaction of a slightly closer look at Daisy; she calls out in her delirium that they must tell Winterbourne she was *not* engaged to Giovanelli, and at her graveside Giovanelli tells Winterbourne she was one of the most innocent women he'd known. Thus James leads us on with clues to Daisy's character, finally revealing her naive purity while at the same time preserving his carefully drawn enigma. For Winterbourne, the truth about Daisy comes too little–and too late.

Ibsen, on the other hand, allows us a much clearer look into Nora's personality at the opening of *A Doll's House*, yet we find this forthright view of a dynamic woman as intriguing as any element of mystery might have been. While Daisy's fascination lies in James's reserve in displaying her character indirectly, Nora's appeal lies in Ibsen's direct presentation of the changes she undergoes. As Nora progresses from the macaroon-sneaking "little skylark" of her husband Torvald to the realization that even though she committed forgery and risked blackmail to save his life, he blames her for disobeying him, we watch her horror at this discovery and her resolve to take action. We are fascinated as she abandons Torvald and their children to become Nora, not Nora-mother or Nora-wife. Ibsen's development of Nora kindles our interest because we watch her learn the truth step by step and we sympathize with this woman's desire to become a person in her own right. Having shared her self-analysis and self-discovery so directly, we are ready to help her close that door.

Authors face an infinite combination of possibilities as they create lives; their success depends on how they match the impression they strive for with their means of achieving it. In *Daisy Miller* James tantalizes us with an enigmatic style because he wants us to feel that the tragedy of Daisy is Winterbourne's failure to understand her. In *A Doll's House* Ibsen outlines Nora in detail because he wants us to share the victory she wins through self-understanding. James and Ibsen have created wisely; in each case, character matches manner. –Tracy Ronvik

Tracy's essay should be judged on the basis of how well it deals with the topic. The introductory paragraph announces the specific examples to be discussed: Daisy and Nora. It includes a thesis statement in the fourth sentence: "Daisy of Henry James's *Daisy Miller* and Nora of Henrik Ibsen's *A Doll's House* are both interesting women, but Daisy is highly enigmatic while Nora is more open." The initial paragraph, then, announces both the focus and the structure of the essay.

Following the instructions, Tracy discusses in the body of her essay (1) how much of a life the author reveals and (2) the manner of doing so. She has chosen two characters that lend themselves to contrast. In the first body paragraph she establishes how Henry James develops Daisy's character indirectly in order to intrigue the reader, and in the second body paragraph she shows how Henrik Ibsen uses an opposite approach in developing the character of Nora.

Tracy also pays attention to the final hint in the instructions, "in literature a 'life' is created by an author," since she focuses on James and Ibsen throughout her essay. Her concluding paragraph continues that focus as it summarizes what she has said and synthesizes the significance of the quotation as it applies to James's Daisy and Ibsen's Nora.

Tracy's essay, with its perceptive insights, effective use of detail, and mature writing style, deserves a high grade.

Unit Six Composition

CHAPTER 23 The Techniques of Writing

PART 1

The Topic Sentence and Transitions

Most prose writing builds around the paragraph, a collection of sentences developing a main point. The sentence that expresses the central idea of a paragraph is called its *topic sentence.* (See **Topic sentence** in the Language Handbook.) In this paragraph from *The Last Cowboy* by Jane Kramer, locate the topic sentence and determine how the other sentences relate to it. Look for *transitions,* words and phrases that establish connections between sentences. (See **Transitions** in the Language Handbook.)

(1) Last year, Americans ate twenty-seven billion pounds of beef—a hundred and twenty-nine pounds per capita—and the "new ranching," as it is practiced today in the Texas Panhandle and across a good part of the Western plains, supports and speculates on their enormous appetite. **(2)** It will probably go on supporting that appetite until no one can afford the cost, in dollars and in lost protein, of the seven or eight pounds of grain that a steer consumes to put on one pound of weight in a feedyard pen. **(3)** The economics of feeding cattle is simple. **(4)** A weaned calf grows steadily and naturally on grass, but a seven-hundred-pound yearling grazing through a dry-grass season with the help of a little daily protein supplement does well simply to maintain the weight it has. **(5)** It would take two more years of grazing under the best conditions to bring that yearling's weight up to the thousand and fifty or eleven hundred pounds that packers claim is the right weight, in terms of efficient family cuts, for slaughtering. **(6)** And during those

years that steer would be taking up valuable range space from a younger, faster-growing animal–and yielding in the end the dry, sinewy beef that cowboys like but almost no one else wants to eat. **(7)** Farmers have always fed grain to their cattle–at least in winter. **(8)** Ranchers have been feeding grain to steers for rapid gain and rich, tender beef ever since the range was fenced and they could no longer drive their herds north summers, following the grass season across a thousand miles. **(9)** Twenty years ago–when Panhandle ranching was entirely cow-calf ranching, and no one had even thought of using his ranch as a way station for Okie calves en route to a feedyard–ranchers were shipping their steers to be fed in yards in Colorado and Arizona or California, or consigning them to stock farmers in Kansas, Illinois, Iowa, and Nebraska, to be fed with the farmer's own corn and silage. **(10)** But twenty years ago people ate far less beef than they do now. **(11)** Feed grains were plentiful and cheap then, and so was oil for the tractor fuel and the fertilizers a farmer needed to produce that grain.
–Jane Kramer. THE LAST COWBOY. New York: Harper & Row, Publishers, Inc., 1977.

The opening sentence of this eleven-sentence paragraph functions as the topic sentence because it establishes the subject: the "new ranching" method of raising beef cattle. The other sentences support the topic sentence in two ways. Sentences two through six develop information about the process of feeding beef cattle; sentences seven through eleven report background on feeding practices prior to the "new ranching." Transitions between sentences in the paragraph include several devices:

- word repetition: *appetite* (sentences 1 and 2); *yearling* (sentences 4 and 5)
- pronouns and demonstrative adjectives: *It* (sentence 2); *those years* (sentence 6); *that grain* (sentence 11)
- synonyms: *steer, cattle, beef cattle* (used throughout)
- links through time: *two more years* (sentence 5); *Twenty years ago* (sentences 9 and 10)
- change of viewpoint: *but* (sentences 4 and 10)

• **EXERCISE 1.** Choose one topic sentence from the following list and develop it into a paragraph of about 200 words. Underline the transitional devices you have used to connect sentences and ideas.

- The lyrics of much contemporary music provide glib answers to difficult questions.
- One sure key to social success is the ability to make small talk.
- Fame does strange things to some people.
- Beware of the person who has many friends.
- A good book demands much of its reader.
- Money may not buy happiness, but it can provide some worthwhile substitutes.
- A car can be a bane and a blessing to a teen-ager.
- Taking risks is an essential part of life.

PART 2
Detail and Imagery

When you write, your choice of detail controls the message you give to your reader. The more specific your choice of words, the more precisely your reader will understand what you are saying. Language that appeals to the senses is called *imagery.* (See **Imagery** in the Language Handbook.) Note the use of imagery in the following selection by Hal Borland. To which senses does he appeal?

November

November is berry-bright and firelight-gay, a glittering night, a crisp blue day, a whispering wind and a handful of determined fence-row asters. It is a lithe hemlock in a green lace party dress, and a clean-limbed gray birch laughing in the wind. It is apple cider with champagne beads of authority. It is a gray squirrel in the limber top of a hickory tree, graceful as the wind; it is a doe and her fawns munching windfall winesaps in the moonlit orchard. November is a handful of snowflakes flung over a Berkshire hilltop, and a woodchuck sniffing the wind and retreating to his den to sleep till April.

Our northern land begins to tuck itself in for the winter. Frost, wind and rain bring down the leaves and the season's coverlet starts to take shape in the woodland. It is still restless, the gusting wind rustling and shifting the leaves even in the hillside thickets, strewing them over the meadows, heaping them in the fence corners. Sometimes it seems that the leaves themselves are restless, reluctant to be earth-bound. After all, they are winged and they had an airy lifetime, and now they are free to ride each passing breeze. But the restlessness will pass. In a few more weeks they will settle down to blanket the earth, to dull the fang of frost for the wild seed and root and bulb.

November is the evening of the year, the bedtime of the green and flowering world. Now comes the time for sleep, for rest. The coverlet is being spread. Next should come the lullaby; but the lullaby singers have all gone south. The pines and the hemlocks will whisper good night instead. –Hal Borland. "November," THE GOLDEN CIRCLE: A Book of Months. New York: Thomas Y. Crowell, Publishers.

1. Find three images, each one appealing to a different sense, in Borland's essay.

2. Explain how each italicized word in the following phrases contributes to a particular image:
determined fence-row asters
the *limber* top of a hickory tree
the *fang* of frost

3. A writer may arrange words so that their sounds and rhythms appeal to a reader's senses. What effect do the rhythms and sounds of words in the first sentence have on you?

• **EXERCISE 2.** Now try developing your own imagery through use of specific words and details. Write a paragraph or two in which you use imagery to create a specific impression about a general topic like Borland's November. Use another month if you wish, or perhaps a day of the week, a season, or a holiday. You might choose images that appeal to a single sense, like sight, or to a variety of senses as Borland has done.

PART 3

Mood

The atmosphere or climate of feeling in a literary work is called *mood.* The writer's choice of setting, objects, details, images, and words all contribute in creating a particular mood. The following two paragraphs are from *The Hound of the Baskervilles,* a Sherlock Holmes mystery by Arthur Conan Doyle. As you read them, try to determine the mood the author has created.

> The avenue opened into a broad expanse of turf, and the house lay before us. In the fading light I could see that the centre was a heavy block of building from which a porch projected. The whole front was draped in ivy, with a patch clipped bare here and there where a window or a coat of arms broke through the dark veil. From this central block rose the twin towers, ancient, crenellated, and pierced with many loopholes. To right and left of the turrets were more modern wings of black granite. A dull light shone through heavy mullioned windows, and from the high chimneys which rose from the steep, high-angled roof there sprang a single black column of smoke.

The dining room, which opened out of the hall, is described as:

> . . . a place of shadow and gloom. It was a long chamber with a step separating the dais where the family sat from the lower portion reserved for their dependents. At one end a minstrel's gallery overlooked it. Black beams shot across above our heads, with a smoke-darkened ceiling beyond them. With rows of flaring torches to light it up, and the colour and rude hilarity of an old-time banquet, it might have softened; but now, when two black-clothed gentlemen sat in the little circle of light thrown by a shaded lamp, one's voice became hushed and one's spirit subdued. A dim line of ancestors, in every variety of dress, from the Elizabethan knight to the buck of the Regency, stared down upon us and daunted us by their silent company. We talked little, and I for one was glad when the meal was over and we were able to retire into the modern billiard-room and smoke a cigarette. –Sir Arthur Conan Doyle. THE HOUND OF THE BASKERVILLES. John Murray Publishers, Ltd.

1. How would you describe the mood of this selection? What words and details contribute to this mood?

2. In what way do descriptions of the time of day and the decor of the house contribute to this mood?

• **EXERCISE 3.** Using Doyle's paragraphs as an example, write two or three descriptive paragraphs (200–300 words) in which you try to create a specific mood, such as melancholy or gloom. You may never have visited a mysterious old mansion, but you probably have experienced a dark, rainy night in a place that seemed to come alive with strange noises, or perhaps you once had dinner at a friend's house where the atmosphere was strained or sad. No matter what mood you decide to create, choose words, a setting, objects, and details that will re-create your feelings for the reader.

PART 4

Tone

An author's attitude toward a subject and an audience is called *tone.* Such an attitude can be described by words such as *serious, cynical, humorous, bitter, joyful,* and *fanciful.* The following excerpts are taken from "The Wonderful Old Gentleman," a short story by Dorothy Parker. In the story, a married couple, the Bains, and Mrs. Bain's sister, Mrs. Whittaker, sit together in the Bains' shabby living room awaiting the imminent death of the women's father. The Bains have cared for the old man in their house for the past five years.

As you read, try to determine the tone of the passages. What is the author's attitude toward Mrs. Whittaker?

> As soon as she had heard that the Old Gentleman was dying Mrs. Whittaker had come right over, stopping only to change her dress and have her dinner. . . .
>
> She graciously patronized the very chair she now sat in, smiled kindly on the glass of cider she held in her hand. The Bains were poor, and Mrs. Whittaker had, as it is ingenuously called, married well, and none of them ever lost sight of these facts.

1. What does the first sentence tell us about Mrs. Whittaker?

2. The author says Mrs. Whittaker "graciously patronized the very chair" she sat in. What does that phrase tell us about her attitude toward her poorer relations? about the author's attitude toward Mrs. Whittaker?

> Mrs. Whittaker's dress was always studiously suited to its occasion; thus, her bearing had always that calm that only the correctly attired may enjoy. She was an authority on where to place monograms on linen, how to instruct working folk, and what to say in letters of condolence. The word *lady* figured largely in her conversation. . . . Mrs. Bain looked at her sister's elaborately curled, painstakingly brown coiffure, and nervously patted her own straggling hair, . . .
>
> [Mrs. Whittaker] took a small bite of cooky.
>
> "*Awfully* good," she said. She broke into a little bubbly laugh, the laugh she used at teas and wedding receptions and fairly formal din-

ners. "You know," she went on, as one sharing a good story, "he's gone and left all that old money to me." -Dorothy Parker. LAMENTS FOR THE LIVING. New York: Viking Penguin Inc. Copyright 1930 by Dorothy Parker. Copyright renewed © 1958 by Dorothy Parker. Reprinted by permission of Viking Penguin Inc.

1. What is revealed about Mrs. Whittaker through her appearance? her words? her behavior?

2. Choose one of the following words, or one of your own, to describe Parker's tone in these passages: *angry, concerned, fanciful, amused, satirical, critical.* Explain your choice.

• **EXERCISE 4.** Using the preceding passages as examples, write several paragraphs (200–300 words) about a subject (person, place, or thing) toward which you have a definite attitude. Your attitude may be admiring, critical, or amused, for example. Make this attitude clear by choosing a situation, details, words, and a particular focus that suit your tone. Try to make your tone consistent throughout the essay.

PART 5
Style

Every competent writer has a purpose for writing and chooses a tone, words, details, images, and sentence patterns to serve that purpose. The manner in which writers use words, images, and rhythms to serve their purposes is called *style.* As you read the following paragraphs by Edward Hoagland, be aware of his style:

> I used to love to get into the thick of crowds. I loved the subway rush hour, the crush at ticket windows, the squeeze of New Year's Eve on Forty-second Street, or the night street market in Boston. I felt enlarged, recharged by these mob scenes, much as I did when climbing on a mountainside. The tussling beefiness of everybody poured into me like broth; I felt exuberant, enhanced by the soul-mix. I liked losing control of where my feet took me, I liked swimming against the tide and with the tide. I liked feeling united with many, many other men, becoming all together as big as Gulliver, sprawled bulkily and uncoordinatedly along the street. And though I'd seen mobs behave savagely, some of my experience was of the moments when, on the contrary, a benign expressiveness, even a kind of *sweetness,* is loosed–when life seems to be an unmixed good, the more the merrier, and each man rises to a sense of glee and mitigation, alleviation or freedom which perhaps he wouldn't quite dare feel alone. The smiling lightness, infectious blitheness, the loose exultant sense of unity in which sometimes a mass of people as a whole seem to improve upon the better nature of the parts–this intrigued me. Figuratively it manifests itself for instance in the extraordinary quality that singing by a congregation acquires. The humdrum and unlovely voices gradually merge into a sweet, uniquely pristine note, a note angelic-sounding, hardly believable. Looking about, one can't see who in particular might have such a

voice; everybody in the pew wears an expression as if he were about to sneeze, and squawks at least a little. It is a note created only when hundreds sing. It needs them all; no single person is responsible, any more than any individual in a roaring mob lends that its bestiality.

Just as with other natural wonders of the world to which one relinquishes oneself, instead of feeling smaller, I often felt bigger when I was packed into a multitude, and taking for granted the potential for mayhem of crowds, of which so much has been written, I was fascinated instead by the clear pealing gaiety, the swelling savory relief and regenerative power that sometimes over-rides the anxieties we suffer from when we're alone and lets us stand there beaming on the pavement with twenty thousand other people. It's like riding in surf, it's like a Dantean ascent one circle up. Suddenly we *like* all of these strangers–even the stranger in ourselves–and seem to see a shape to life, as if all the exertions of the week really were justified and were a source of joy. –Edward Hoagland. THE COURAGE OF TURTLES. New York: Random House, Inc. Copyright © 1971 by Edward Hoagland. Reprinted by permission of Random House, Inc., and the Lescher Agency.

1. Imagine that the beginning of the selection by Hoagland had been written another way. Compare the original five sentences to the following version in terms of use of detail, word choice, and sentence patterns:

> I used to like being in the middle of a large number of people. It reminds me of once when I climbed on a mountainside. Just wandering around makes me feel good, when there are other people around. I think when folks are together, they are happier and can accomplish more than when they are alone.

2. All of the following are items in the Language Handbook that deal with matters of style. Choose five of these items and read their entries in the Language Handbook. Then discuss these items as they apply to Hoagland's paragraphs.

Allusion	Figures of speech	Repetition
Connotation	Hyperbole	Transitions
Denotation	Imagery	Usage
Diction	Imitative words	

3. Why do you think Hoagland chose this particular style to convey his ideas? Given his subject, do you think this style serves his purpose? Explain.

• **EXERCISE 5.** Rewrite one of the assignments that you have done for one of the preceding exercises in this chapter. Adopt a style–graceful, simple, comic, formal, lively–that you think will best convey your ideas. Choose words, sentence patterns, sounds, rhythms, imagery, and a tone that suit your purpose. When you have finished, share your writing with the class, asking them to describe your writing style.

LANGUAGE NOTES

English 104
June 1, 1607

Composition by Will Shakespeare

Ref
Too much subjunctive

If it were done when 'tis done, then 'twere well
It were done quickly; if the assassination
Could trammel up the consequence, and catch
With his surcease success; that but this blow
Might be the be-all and the end-all here,
But here, upon this bank and shoal of time,
We 'ld jump the life to come. But in these cases
We still have judgment here; that we but teach
Bloody instructions, which, being taught, return
To plague the inventor; this even-handed justice
Commends the ingredients of our poisoned chalice
To our own lips.

Dead

Big W

avoid repetition.

Clarify

Don't begin sentence with conjunction

Too strong. Use annoy or bother.

C-

Macbeth, act 1, scene 7

Will,
Do not use contractions in formal writing. Avoid figurative language until you can use it more skillfully and precisely. After all, how can justice commend ingredients? Next time, find a more pleasant topic.

PART 6
Revision

The following is a description of her grandfather written by Betsy and returned with critical remarks by her teacher. In order to understand the abbreviated remarks on the theme, you may wish to refer to **Correction marks** in the Language Handbook. In addition, you may wish to review the following entries in the Language Handbook:

Ambiguity	Deadwood
Comma splice	Parallel constructions
Dangling modifiers	Reference of pronouns

Frag
Dang
Ref
Dead
Big W
R O
Pn
Apos
CS, Sp
Apos
Par
avoid repetition and short, choppy sentences

Whittling a block of maple, Gramps sits on the front steps of our porch by a dilapidated red Ford pickup. Click, click, click; his rhythm is perfect. Steady slow scrapes on a curious chunk of wood, hard and fine-grained. Gleaming in the sunlight, he makes his knife give life to the chunk of wood. Sometimes he just sits still, while it lies forgotten in his hand. Owing to the fact that he was injured in the Second World War, the index finger on his left hand stops before the top joint. At times I envy his Utopian tranquillity and universal creativity. But he whittles with dexterity he never seems to lose his rhythm. Gramps has whittled many items for me; a tiny basket made from a hazelnut, a nesting hen made from a log, and a 10-inch B for my name made from a two-by-four. Sometimes Gramps eyes glaze over, he stops and fingers his knife with a carressing gesture. Its times like this when he seems to be meditating on the past—as a private in the service where pals called him Whittles, serving as president of the school board, and when he had a story published in a national magazine.

My gramps has lived with wood so long that in his old age he's beginning to resemble it. He has grainy skin. He has dark-stained hands and appears to be varnished. I'll bet if you could take a cross section of Gramps, like they do with old trees, you could see many concentric circles of growth rings. –Betsy Laski

1. Comment on Betsy's general use of detail and imagery. Do you think it is vivid? effective?

2. Has Betsy succeeded in giving you some clear impressions of her grandfather? Why or why not?

3. Do you consider this a good piece of writing? Explain.

• **EXERCISE 6.** Revise Betsy's essay according to the correction marks given in the margin.

CHAPTER 24 Functional Writing

When you write formal letters, explain a process, give directions, or write applications for a job or for college, you are required to communicate specific information in a limited amount of space. In such writing, your purpose and your audience are prescribed. While functional writing may not always allow you to be creative, it puts special demands on your ability to write clearly and concisely.

PART 1
Letters

A formal letter requires a style that gets to the point quickly, states your purpose clearly, and establishes a tone that fits the circumstances of the communication. In a *business letter,* you should address your reader in a formal but not stuffy manner, explaining your purpose in crisp, simple prose. (See **Business letters** in the Language Handbook.) Jim, a high-school senior, wrote the following letter to schedule a visit to a college:

Box 342
Middletown, Montana 59801
October 10, 1980

Dr. Marina Hilstron, Dean of Admissions
Lincoln College
Metropolis, Montana 59715

Dear Dean Hilstron:

Thank you for the catalogs about Lincoln and the financial aid information. I have discussed with my parents your invitation to visit the campus, and they have suggested Friday, October 26, when we do not have school because of our district teachers' convention.

I plan to drive to Metropolis that morning with Lewis Clark, who is also interested in applying to Lincoln. We should arrive by noon, and we would appreciate the opportunity to visit some afternoon classes, especially in biology, Lewis's major interest, and forestry, my tentative course of study.

Your offer of overnight housing in a campus dorm is accepted and appreciated. We look forward to seeing you on October 26.

Sincerely yours,

James J. Hillman

1. Why is it important to acknowledge something you have received in the mail, as Jim has done?

2. Do you think Jim effectively states his purpose in this letter? Why or why not?

Informal or friendly letters vary widely in style, according to purpose and audience. You may not thank your grandmother for a birthday gift in quite the same style as you write to your younger sister at summer camp. Adjusting language and tone to the occasion is the secret of an informal letter. Here is a letter Maria wrote to a French student who will be staying with her on a three-week exchange program:

Dear Veronique,

Your list of what to bring to the U.S. is fine except for film. My cousin works at a photo supply store, and he can get film for you at the wholesale price, so don't bother to bring any. Yes, the raincoat should be warm enough; April isn't usually very cold in Indiana, but if the weather gets bad we'll lend you something.

The plans for going to Washington for Easter vacation have worked out, and I'm really excited you'll be able to see such a French-looking city while you're here. We couldn't get train reservations—our rail system isn't as efficient as yours—but I think you'll like the all-night bus ride. That way we can afford to fly back.

My mother told her sixth-grade class that you'd speak to them about France some day while you're here. I think they want to hear about Joan of Arc and Napoleon and people like that. Hope you won't mind.

We'll meet your plane in Chicago on Saturday, March 29, at 1:45 P.M. Look for me when you get to customs. I'll be in the balcony above you.

Love,

Maria

Somebody's boring me...I think it's me.

Dylan Thomas

• **EXERCISE 1.** Write a business letter of at least three paragraphs, following the Language Handbook form carefully. Develop your own topic or choose from one of these:

• Explain to a college admissions office why you have decided not to attend that college, even though you've been admitted.
• Complain to the sales manager of an automobile agency about problems with the car that you have recently purchased.
• React to an article in your school or community newspaper by writing a letter to the editor.

• **EXERCISE 2.** Assume that as an apprentice advice columnist you must write a reply to the following letter. Addressing yourself to the three points made by "Been There," write a letter of response that either supports or rejects this method of coping with a younger brother.

Dear Ann Landers:

It was quite obvious from your answer to "Hanging by a Thread and Suffering in Alexandria" that you never have had a brat for a little brother.

The young lady stated she was punished each time the brat started hollering because the little liar said she hit him.

The solution is obvious. The next time the brat starts to holler, she should hit him in the mouth. He will still holler, but at least he won't be lying when he says she hit him. When he gets tired of being hit, he will leave her alone.

This solution will accomplish a number of worthwhile objectives. First and foremost, it will improve her life immeasurably.

Second, it will teach the brat how life works (i.e., if you bother people and bear false witness you tend to get hit in the mouth a lot).

Third, the older sister will have a golden opportunity to show her mother that the girl has a mind of her own and will no longer tolerate prejudicial treatment.

Been There

PART 2

Explaining a Process

Writing that explains a process requires a simple, clear style to show a reader how to do something. The steps must be presented in the proper sequence so that the reader can visualize the process, or actually perform these steps. The following is an explanation of the Heimlich Maneuver, a method for rescuing food-choking victims devised by Dr. Henry J. Heimlich, a Cincinnati surgeon:

> To perform the so-called Heimlich Maneuver with the victim standing or sitting, the rescuer (who will be male for grammatical simplicity) stands behind the victim (or the victim's chair) and wraps his arms around the victim's waist. Then with the thumb side of his fist placed slightly above the victim's navel and slightly below the rib cage, the rescuer grabs his own fist with his other hand and presses into the victim's abdomen with a quick upward thrust, repeating the process several times if necessary. With the victim lying on his back, the rescuer faces the victim and kneels astride his hips. Then with one hand on top of the other, the rescuer places the heel of his bottom hand slightly above the navel, slightly below the rib cage, and again, delivers one or more quick upward thrusts to the victim's abdomen. If alone, a victim may perform the Heimlich Maneuver on himself. –"Four Minutes to Live . . . This Maneuver Can Save You," SCIENCE DIGEST, July 1977. Reprinted by permission from SCIENCE DIGEST. Copyright © 1977 The Hearst Corporation. All Rights Reserved.

If you feel that you could perform this process after reading the explanation carefully, the paragraph has done its job. Note that the word *Then* is used to signal the proper order of steps. In more complicated directions, other signal words, such as *now, first, next,* and *finally,* can serve to order the steps. Although explaining the proper sequence of steps in the Heimlich Maneuver can be a life-and-death matter, the explanations of other processes are intended merely to inform or entertain. The following describes how over seventy years ago Carl Akeley, a naturalist and taxidermist, mounted skin on a papier-mâché manikin of an elephant for display in a museum:

> It is a problem successfully to bring out of Africa the skin of an elephant in condition fit to mount. These huge hides are from an inch to two inches in thickness when removed from the carcass. They are cut in five or six pieces and immediately work must be started in the dense wet bamboo forests to pare the skin down by hand to a thickness of about one half inch. These are then heavily salted and loosely rolled together, bound securely in native cloth, and made ready for transportation many miles to the nearest point where oxen could be secured. Each section would weigh several hundred pounds and be carried by eight or ten native porters for the magnificent sum of thirty cents per month–and grub.

To mount "green" skins is not practical, so Akeley developed a special method of tanning never before used. As a result the elephant skins were turned into a high grade leather hide presenting the same exterior as worn by [the elephant] "Tembo" in his native haunts—sparse, stiff hairs, wrinkles, warts, tick-holes and all. The big sections of skin were first laid in their proper position on the finished manikin and by means of huge syringes somewhat like the present day auto grease gun, a mixture of hydrated plaster of Paris and glue was shot in under the skin through small slits easily closed, and then the skin modeled into shape with numerous wrinkles as in actual life, the plaster of Paris and glue hardening and holding the skin in exact position. Akeley did practically all of this modeling with his own hands. The edges of each section were then sewed together with hidden stitches and filled with colored beeswax so that when finished even the most critical eye could not detect the seams. As a rural visitor once said, "That old bull looks just like he growed into his hide." –C. L. Dewey. "My Friend Ake," NATURE MAGAZINE, December 1927. Copyright 1927 by American Museum of Natural History. Reprinted with permission.

• **EXERCISE 3.** Write an essay in which you explain to the members of your English class a process. Decide before you begin whether class members should be able to repeat the process once they have read your description or whether your audience should simply find the essay informative and interesting. In any event, make sure that the sequence of steps is clear. Choose a topic you are well acquainted with.

PART 3

Job Application

A job application essay is usually a part of a personnel form that asks for specific background information such as education and work experience. Because your response is limited to the space on the form, it must be tightly written. Those who read your essay will try to determine from it something about your personality and your writing ability. Although those who screen your application may not demand a sophisticated writing style, they will expect accuracy in matters such as spelling, grammar, mechanics, and usage. But the major purpose of the essay is to determine your suitability for the particular job. Therefore, in this kind of essay you need to indicate that you have a solid understanding of the nature of the job and a confidence about your ability to perform it. Read the following job application essays:

> I feel that my nine years of employment at various stables qualifies me for the position of head instructor at Heathcliff Riding Academy. I have taught equitation and hunt seat for four years, and the majority of my pupils have placed well in their categories in various horse shows.

First I teach them the fundamentals of horse care, from the cleaning of the tack to the feeding patterns of each horse. My pupils are not permitted to mistreat or punish their horses.

Another of my chief concerns is the safety of the riders. It is important to evaluate the ability of riders in controlling different horses and to give them mounts that they can safely handle. The pupils will then progress to more difficult horses as their performances improve. I think I work well with horses as well as people. I own a palomino quarter horse and have successfully trained him from a colt to a good, dependable hunter. Through training my own horse, I have acquired patience—a quality essential in teaching pupils to ride. I would like to run my own riding academy some day, and the position as head instructor at Heathcliff would be excellent training for that long-range goal. –Jocelyn Zilliac

I would like to become an aid at Children's Hospital because I like children (although I can't say I've always liked hospitals). My past jobs have been as a checkout clerk at a supermarket, a waitress, and a baby-sitter. I enjoy working with people of all ages and ethnic backgrounds. I have also worked as a volunteer for the Latino Advocate Office in my community, where I helped Latinos with their problems—from interpreting a utility bill to providing emergency housing. My family speaks Spanish at home, and I also speak fair French and a few phrases in Polish. You might not have many French people coming into the hospital, but I'm sure there are many patients who speak Spanish because I read a recent survey to that effect. If I were hired, I'd be working with small children, although I'm not sure just what I'd be doing. But as I said, I do like children and where there's a will, there's a way. My grandmother says I have a great deal of patience, although I tend to get out of sorts with my younger sister. My eventual career goal is to become a pediatrician, so I feel that this position would introduce me to hospital activities in an effective manner while I am still in high school.

–Maureen Combs

Evaluate each of the preceding essays according to the following:

1. Spelling, grammar, mechanics, usage
2. A tight writing style

3. Applicant's understanding of the nature of the job
4. Applicant's confidence about performing the job

• **EXERCISE 4.** Write a paragraph in which you explain your reasons for wanting a particular job, either one that you might like to hold now or in the future. Use one of the following suggestions, or one of your own:

- Explain your reasons for wanting to join the state highway patrol.
- Discuss your qualifications for the position of recreational director in the summer youth program.
- Besides the financial considerations, why are you seeking a career in real estate?
- How do you expect the postal service position for which you are applying to benefit you in terms of your long-range career goals?

PART 4

College Application

In a college application essay, you are asked to respond to a topic that is general enough to permit individual reaction but specific enough to reveal how well you structure your writing. Your audience for this essay is a small group of college admissions personnel who will be evaluating your essay along with those of many high-school seniors. A college application essay should have a clear focus and include well-chosen examples that strengthen your observations. Its tone should convey to your audience a sense of how you see yourself. In this essay you need to demonstrate your readiness for college in both an educational and a social sense.

As you read Rob's college application essay, note the correction marks beside the first two paragraphs. Keep in mind that the entire essay needs editing and rewriting. The topic: "We would like to know what you have been thinking about recently. Please comment on, or discuss, some matter that adds to what you have already told us on the rest of the application."

	After nine years of cooking with my family
Dang	in the kitchen at home, on the backyard brick
	barbecue my brother and I designed and built,
	and over an open fireplace in my family's cabin
Sp	in northern Maine, there is a corellation between
lc	cooking and preparing for college and Life.
Awk	To successfully make a meal, one must not
	just take recipe in hand and set off in the general
	direction of a finished product. But one must
Frag	think and plan. In order that mistakes might be
Wordy	prevented. So, too, succeeding in life demands
	that one prepare in advance to anticipate those

obstacles which one may experience and must overcome. Then when they are experienced, they can be overcome.

Before starting to cook, utensils and ingredients must be chosen with care. Just as a well-designed food processor and a wide selection of fresh food aids one in preparing tastier foods faster, a good school and a wide variety of courses give one the basic ingredients to succeed in Life. At my school I learned a love for learning for its own sake and the self-dissipline needed for studying. The study of mathematics and science courses are the background upon which I will build at college for a career in medicine, just as a well-selected tray provides the base for an elegant entree.

Organization and following directions carefully are two more things I have learned from my years of cooking. At the same time, however, I have learned that experimentation is important to the creative side of cooking, no new recipes are ever developed by following only the old ones. So it is with Life. We'd still be living in caves if Man had not tried to change things for the better.

As food is necessary to life and health, so a formal education is for taking one's place in society and the affairs of the community and the world. The menu must be balanced with thought given to assuring one has enough vitamins, minerals, and proteins. So one's education should be balanced with proper attention given to fields of study outside one's immediate interests. One should include liberal and fine arts courses even when persuing a career in science. And finally, to close this, one must remember that just as a few spices and sweets enliven a meal, fun and a sense of humor should be stirred in for a fulfilling college experience and after it.

Rob has drawn an analogy between his cooking and his thoughts about education and life in general. (See **Analogy** in the Language Handbook.) The admissions board members who read his essay might well think his approach to the essay topic fresh and original. The essay fulfills the requirements of the topic by relating both what Rob has been thinking about and what his avocation is.

His essay, however, is seriously flawed. There are problems not only with mechanics, usage, and spelling, but also with style. As you read the first two paragraphs again, note the specific errors the marginal correction marks refer to. (See **Correction marks** in the Language

Handbook.) Compare the first two flawed paragraphs with the edited and rewritten paragraphs following:

> For nine years I have cooked in such diverse places as my family's kitchen, on the backyard brick barbecue my brother and I designed and built, and over an open fireplace in our cabin in northern Maine. I now realize that there is a correlation between cooking and preparing for college and life.
>
> When I prepare a meal, having a recipe at hand and a finished product in mind are not enough. I must also plan carefully in order to prevent foolish mistakes. Forethought and preparation are necessary for one's nonculinary future too. These plans may not assure success, but they will help one anticipate and overcome the obstacles that are inevitable in every life.

In the rewritten paragraphs, Rob has made the corrections indicated by the marginal correction marks:

- He has replaced the sentence containing the dangling modifier with two shorter sentences.
- He has corrected the spelling of *correlation.*
- He has used a lower-case *l* when writing *life.*
- He has replaced the sentence fragment with a complete sentence.
- He has generally eliminated deadwood and revised awkward writing.

• **EXERCISE 5.** Using the following guidelines, edit and rewrite the final three paragraphs of Rob's essay:

1. Evaluate Rob's essay in terms of mechanics, usage, and spelling, making corrections where they are necessary. Watch for comma splices, unnecessary capital letters, lack of subject-verb agreement, and dangling modifiers. Check the spelling of any words you are not sure of.

2. The focus of Rob's essay is his analogy between cooking and education and life. Do you think he has included enough specific examples to support the focus? Are the examples Rob does include good ones? For example, is there a clear and sensible analogy between college courses as the basis for a career and a tray as the base for an entree?

3. The tone of Rob's essay is generally serious and thoughtful, with touches of humor. He displays originality in developing an analogy between cooking and life. In your rewriting of Rob's essay, try to retain his tone, but eliminate anything you judge to detract from that tone. Keep in mind that he wants to present himself as a good prospect for college.

CHAPTER 25 Writing About Yourself

PART 1

A Childhood Experience

At first thought, writing about yourself seems easy. After all, on what subject do you have more information? But because you know so much about yourself, you must limit the focus of your topic, presenting only information that contributes to your point. After determining the focus, you must choose details and a setting that reinforce the impression you wish to convey. And you should choose a tone that suitably expresses your ideas. Or maybe it is more exact to say that a tone will choose you, since your tone often evolves quite naturally once you have begun to write. Consider how one writer deals with these three elements–setting, detail, and tone–in the following selection:

> There was a heavy fig tree on the lawn where the house turned the corner into the side street, and to the front and sides of the fig tree were three live oaks that hid the fig from my aunts' boardinghouse. I suppose I was eight or nine before I discovered the pleasures of the fig tree, and although I have lived in many houses since then, including a few that I made for myself, I still think of it as my first and most beloved home.
>
> I learned early, in our strange life of living half in New York and half in New Orleans, that I made my New Orleans teachers uncomfortable because I was too far ahead of my schoolmates, and my New York teachers irritable because I was too far behind. But in New Orleans I found a solution: I skipped school at least once a week and often twice, knowing that nobody cared or would report my absence. On those days I would set out for school done up in polished strapped shoes and a prim hat against what was known as "the climate," carrying my books and a little basket filled with delicious stuff my Aunt Jenny and Carrie, the cook, had made for my school lunch. I would round the corner of the side street, move on toward St. Charles Avenue, and sit on a bench

as if I were waiting for a streetcar until the boarders and the neighbors had gone to work or settled down for the post-breakfast rest that all Southern ladies thought necessary. Then I would run back to the fig tree, dodging in and out of bushes to make sure the house had no dangers for me. The fig tree was heavy, solid, comfortable, and I had, through time, convinced myself that it wanted me, missed me when I was absent, and approved all the rigging I had done for the happy days I spent in its arms: I had made a sling to hold the school books, a pulley rope for my lunch basket, a hole for the bottle of afternoon cream-soda pop, a fishing pole and a smelly little bag of elderly bait, and a pillow embroidered with a picture of Henry Clay on a horse that I had stolen from Mrs. Stillman, one of my aunts' boarders; and I drove a proper nail to hold my dress and shoes to keep them neat for the return to the house.

It was in that tree that I learned to read, filled with the passions that can only come to the bookish, grasping, very young, bewildered by almost all of what I read, sweating in the attempt to understand a world of adults I fled from in real life but desperately wanted to join in books. -Lillian Hellman. AN UNFINISHED WOMAN. Boston: Little, Brown & Company, 1969.

1. What is the writer's setting in this reminiscence? Keep in mind that setting comprises details of both place and time.

2. We hear about the fig tree in the first paragraph of the selection. At what point do we learn its full significance to the writer?

3. What are some details the writer lists about her setting-out-for-school appearance? about the contrivances in the fig tree?

4. How would you characterize the writer's attitude toward this time in her life? Does she seem to look back on this period regretfully or pleasantly? Does she regard the fig tree as a happy, enriching childhood experience or as an unhappy retreat from the realities of her childhood? Explain. List some words or phrases that reveal to you the tone of the paragraphs.

• **EXERCISE 1.** Write an essay describing a situation from your childhood about which one of the following comments could be made–or another of your own choosing. Select a setting, details, and a tone that seem suitable to the comment that you choose.

• "She's (He's) my best friend, but I don't really like her (him)."
• "I have never been able to establish a meaningful relationship with Brussels sprouts (cats, maps, high heels, recorded messages, a typewriter)."
• "So you want to make a twelve-year-old genius into a full-time college student."
• "Ballet dancing (snow, oatmeal, summer camp, a paper route) is highly overrated."
• "After this experience, I must admit that looks can be deceptive."
• "That's absolutely the weirdest outfit I've ever seen."
• "Honest, I'll never, never do it again."

PART 2

A Revealing Incident

Have you ever had an experience in which you came to a new and perhaps a not so welcome understanding about yourself? Writers often describe such moments of truth, seeking to make readers understand and perhaps recognize in themselves the characteristic described. As you read the following selection, try to determine its tone. What was the writer's prevailing feeling when the incident occurred? What is his feeling now that it is past?

Friday, I Was Mugged

There were two of them. . . . They were both about eighteen or nineteen. One of them was wearing a loose shirt or jacket with large gray and white checks. Subject One was a little shorter and heftier, I think, than Subject Two. And that is all on earth I could tell the police about being mugged and robbed. . . .

As muggings go, my little mugging was not much. Unlike a dear friend in Richmond, who two years ago was beaten to a bloody pulp, I was not hurt. Unlike an off-duty police officer in Washington that same day, I was not shot dead. . . . Mine was a routine instance of what the police call "robbery, fear."

But it was not routine to me. On this particular Friday morning, I parked my car on Virginia Avenue a block away from the *Washington Star.* The street runs under an elevated freeway at this point. It is always shadowy. . . .

I finished my work at the *Star* and exactly at noon I left the building and walked through a fine drizzle toward my car. The street was empty. I unlocked the door on the driver's side, tossed a briefcase onto the passenger seat, got behind the wheel and started to close the door. There was a large body blocking it in an open position. This was Subject One.

"The money," he said. . . . "Your money, man." His right hand was in his pocket, holding a short, solid object. . . . I thought it was a pistol. . . . He jabbed me on the arm. He might have been talking to an exceptionally stupid child. Separating each word with rising urgency: "Give me the money! Give me the money."

"Take it easy," I mumbled. I reached into my breast pocket, took out my billfold, and pulled out three or four $10 bills. He snatched them from my hand. "The whole thing," he said. Now he was speaking faster. "Gimmee the thing." He grabbed the billfold.

He noticed a watch on my left wrist. "The watch! Take it off!" He jabbed again with his concealed right hand. . . .

At last the strap came free. He seized the watch and spun around. So far as I can recall, his companion had said not one word. The two of them ran off, loping more than running, across a playground. . . . I ran back to the *Star*, crying "police!" at the top of my lungs.

Funny thing. I was able to call my secretary and to tell her calmly to get at the business of reporting the stolen credit cards and driver's license. Then shock set in. Shock, humiliation, shame, rage, tears, aching legs, tightness in the chest, slurred speech. I could not get my breath. It is an awful thing, a terrifying thing, to be dominated, to be helpless, to know stark, sobbing fear. . . .

I am in my fortieth year as a newspaperman. We newsmen are supposed to have exceptional powers of observation. I could not tell the police whether the two men had mustaches; I could not describe the pants they were wearing. I never saw their faces clearly. . . .

Twenty-four hours later, as I write, I am still shaky. I fantasize: I had hidden a pistol on the floor of the car, and instead of supinely handing over my billfold I had made a lightning grab for my gun, shot the two punks in their bellies, and laughed as they fell to the pavement. . . .

–James J. Kilpatrick. "On Being Mugged," January 17, 1980. © 1980 Universal Press Syndicate. Reprinted by permission of the author.

1. In the preceding essay, what does the setting contribute to the incident the writer describes?

2. Why doesn't the writer more closely describe his two assailants? What details about the mugging does he describe in detail?

3. Characterize the contrasting tones of the last two paragraphs of the selection.

• **EXERCISE 2.** Write an essay describing an incident in which you learned something about yourself–either good or bad. Describe the setting in which this incident occurred and provide details to make the event vivid for your readers. Adopt a tone that is compatible with the impression you wish to convey.

PART 3

A Humorous Anecdote

Not all essays about yourself need be serious. A personal essay that entertains through humor uses the same elements as a serious essay–setting, detail, and tone–to achieve its effect. Consider this example from Dan, a high-school senior:

Feet: Grin and Bare Them

The following information appears on page 25 of the school handbook: Shoes must be worn at all times in school. Any student without shoes is subject to disciplinary action. The steps to be taken are (1) personal counseling; (2) notification of parents; (3) etc. . . .

For quite a while I was fascinated with the thought of step one, the personal counseling session for a student caught shoeless. A counseling session? Look in the handbook if you don't believe me. What is there to be discussed? Then, one day last week, my curiosity was satisfied.

"We caught another one," said a security monitor as she dragged me in to the counseling office.

"Good," said my counselor, Mr. Archie Supports. "Now, Dan, I am your friend. I want to help you. But first, you must tell me what is causing you to sublimate your feelings toward wearing shoes."

Having imagination, it takes you an hour to write a paragraph that, if you were unimaginative, would take you only a minute. OR you might not write the paragraph at all. Franklin P. Adams

"Because it's hot out!"

"Sounds like a serious one," said the monitor. "Shall I send for the principal?"

"No, get the school psychologist, Dr. Sock," said Mr. Supports. "I see from your referral that Mr. Foote kicked you out of class."

"Yeah," I said. "And I'm not gonna wear any shoes!"

"All right, young man, you leave me no other choice."

"You mean—"

"Yes. I want you to look at your feet. I want you to probe your sole. Look how big they are. Your big toe is like Paul Bunion. (I was later told this procedure is the latest thing: joke therapy.) Or am I just being corny? You're just a loafer—"

"Stop!" I screamed.

"Want a penny, loafer? Don't tread on me, young man, or I'll have that flatfoot in here. Barefootedness is your archenemy."

"Ohhhh, . . ." I groaned, barely conscious. "I feel like such a heel."

"It's worked!" cried the monitor.

"Let's see," said my counselor. "How do you feel about shoes now, young man?"

"They're my sole concern," I muttered.

"He's cured," said the counselor. -Dan Greenberger

1. For what kind of audience does Dan's essay seem intended? How do you know?

2. Did you laugh? Why or why not?

3. In what way does the title establish the kind of humor Dan uses throughout? Do you think he is an effective punster?

4. Do you think that the experience really occurred, that the entire incident is made up, or that the essay combines reality with exaggeration? Explain.

• **EXERCISE 3.** Now write a humorous essay with you as the protagonist. Develop your own topic or use one of the following comments as a base:

• "I don't care if you are offering one million; I'm not interested."
• "I've learned never to trust anyone with red hair (galoshes, a parrot, a pet rock)."
• "I guess it's true–you are what you eat."
• "I warned you that mystery novels (crossword puzzles, pretzels, telephones, dog biscuits, double features) are addictive."
• "Look, I know this sounds a bit bizarre, but I really do have a talking plant (stubborn pair of ears, phobia about small dogs, recurrent dream about eating my hat)."

CHAPTER 26 Writing About Other People

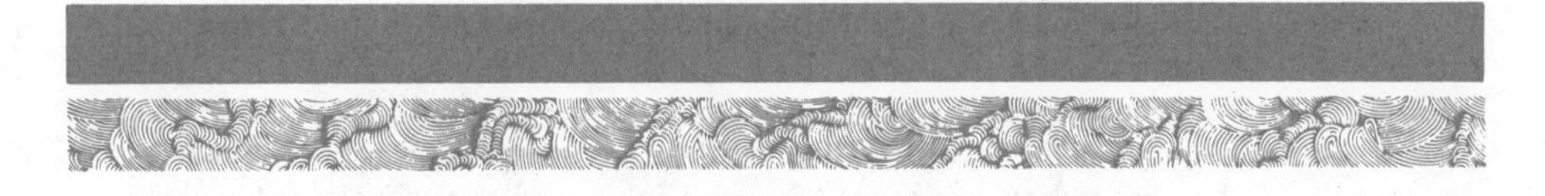

You may have already had occasion to write about people. Once out of school, you will probably have even more occasion to describe others in writing. Medical personnel write about their patients, social workers write about their cases, teachers and neighbors write recommendations and references for students. When you are writing in a special or professional capacity about another person, both the subject and focus are prescribed and your writing will be generally factual. On other occasions, however, you may be asked to write imaginatively about someone, choosing your own subject, focus, and details. In such cases, you may wish to portray someone through one of three approaches: a sketch, an interview, or a profile. Let's examine them one by one.

PART 1
A Sketch

A *sketch* is a brief description of another person that emphasizes a particular element of behavior or character. Like a cartoonist or caricaturist, a writer of a sketch may highlight certain qualities of the subject through emphasis or exaggeration. Because of its brevity and its limited focus, a sketch provides an incomplete portrait. Yet these very limitations allow writers a great deal of freedom in selecting and presenting information. Like most essays, a sketch, however brief, develops a main point, or *thesis.* Through selection of detail, word connotation, and sentence pattern, the writer's tone contributes to the thesis. Consider these opening paragraphs of three sketches:

> Mr. Eduardo Cerello, my former violin professor, was an arrogant, unfeeling human being. His temper was forever erupting, and he had

no patience with students, especially ones like me who never used to practice. When he became excited, his words would be stressed by tapping his bow on my head. These are only a few reasons why my three years of studying with him were so miserable. He had many other faults that caused my strong feeling of dislike for him and my eventual departure from his studio. –Stephanie Miller

Kitty Kramer has been a member of the club that we belong to up in Michigan for as long as I can remember. Every time I saw her around the club I was always curious about what she was like until I finally was able to meet her three summers ago. The first year I met her, Kitty was seventy years old, but her looks made her appear older. Her face was so wrinkled that she looked like an old man; it showed that she had led a strong, hard life in the out-of-doors. She was the mother of five, four girls and a boy, and the grandmother of nineteen. –Linda Heiberger

He struts in, mirror glasses flashing. "Hi there," he says, leaning across the counter with an attempt at a devilish grin. But the maroon bagger's vest ruins the effect and John gives up the charade. Laughing, he pulls off the glasses, leaving his hair wilder than it had been a few minutes before. "So, how's life?" he asks cheerfully. John's mood is always happy; he is the ideal person to deal with all the old ladies who forget to weigh their fruit, lose their carts, and ask for shopping bags after the order has already been packed. –Maureen Mayday

Let's examine each of these opening paragraphs to see how effectively it introduces the sketch.

In the opening sentence of her sketch, Stephanie expresses a strong, direct attitude toward her violin teacher. In addition, we learn that Cerello's hot temper may be justified, since Stephanie didn't practice. The reader should recognize that sketches like Stephanie's may be colored by the writer's feelings and viewpoint, which in turn provide a distinctive tone. This paragraph could be sharpened by adding more detail. One strong image, "his words would be stressed by tapping his bow on my head," is weakened by use of the passive voice.

Linda does not develop a strong attitude about Kitty Kramer in this paragraph; we are told only that she is curious about her subject. The paragraph would be more vivid with the addition of more descriptive details about Kitty's appearance. The end of Linda's paragraph is weak, since the focus changes from Kitty to her family–a shift that does not advance her character.

Maureen's paragraph about John, her co-worker in a supermarket, is effective because it successfully integrates many details. In just a few lines she uses most of the techniques available to a writer who sketches another person:

1. She shows John in action: "struts," "pulls off the glasses."

2. She quotes him: "Hi there," "So, how's life?"

3. She uses gestures and body language: "devilish grin," "leaning across."

4. She describes physical appearance: "hair wilder than . . . before."

5. She mentions clothing: "mirror glasses," "maroon bagger's vest."

6. She supplies direct comment: "ideal person."

7. She relates John to his environment: "deal with all the old ladies. . . ."

Maureen has sketched quickly and strongly here. Her use of detail enriches the picture, and her verbs, all in the present tense, intensify the action of her scene.

• **EXERCISE 1.** Write a one-paragraph sketch about a person, highlighting a particular quality, mannerism, or feature. Choose words, details, and a tone that contribute to this sketch. Use some of the devices Maureen has employed in describing John, her co-worker.

PART 2

An Interview

Often, the best way to acquire information or to learn the opinions of others is to talk with them directly. Such conversations, intended for a specific purpose, are called *interviews.* Once you have chosen the person you wish to interview, you should do some preliminary research on both the person and the topic to be discussed. Because interviews may entertain as well as inform an audience, you will want to determine beforehand the purpose of the interview. Thoughtful interview questions, written out in advance, should be open-ended to produce interesting, informative answers rather than yes-or-no responses. Don't stick too rigidly to your written questions once the interview begins, since other questions may occur to you as the interview proceeds. Take notes carefully, and do not hesitate to ask the interviewee to clarify or repeat a comment. Be careful to write down responses verbatim and in quotation marks if you think you might quote them directly in your written report. Exact quotations will be essential when you write out the interview, so accuracy is imperative. You may wish to ask permission to tape the interview, especially if the topic is complex. Once you have completed the interview session, write up a report as soon as you can so that the information doesn't go stale.

The following is based on an interview of civil rights leader Jesse Jackson by a high-school senior.

Jackson Speaks Out

Deep in the heart of Operation PUSH headquarters on Chicago's South Side, sitting behind a cluttered, L-shaped desk in an office glazed with service awards and golden athletic trophies, the Reverend Jesse Jackson is almost always busy. Today is no different.

Our conversation was regularly interrupted by urgent telephone calls and other items Jackson faithfully attended to. Nevertheless, the man some call "the black Moses" found time to discuss his favorite topic, the state of education in America today.

"Teachers must be perceived as caring and concerned about the whole student and not just about the subject they are teaching," insisted Jackson. "We must broaden our thrill zone. We must have chemistry teachers who can motivate us to know that there is a thrill in working out a chemical composition," he observed.

"For it is just as exciting to score high on a national exam as it is to shoot well in a championship ball game," said Jackson, who, in fact, accomplished both feats himself as a high-school student.

"Administrators are the real key, though," asserted the Baptist minister. "The principal sets the pace in any given school. He must be a moral authority who teaches discipline."

Parent and community participation in the educational process are also crucial, noted Jackson, himself the father of five. "Parents," he said, filling the room with a bellowing voice, "must monitor their children's study hours and come visit the school as often as possible."

Jackson pointed out that community participation is a problem. "Administrations have isolated the school from the community," he said. "Much of the disruption in schools is the result of community alienation from the school."

The school's attitude toward disruptive students ought to be redemptive, not punitive, according to Jackson, who used an analogy to illustrate his point. "If the coach says, 'Run five miles,' no one gets angry, for you perceive that running five miles is for therapeutic purposes and not because the coach is being punitive. Therefore, the coach can be absent and the captains will run the team five miles, because self-discipline is learned, and the by-product of learning is development, something you will need for the rest of your life."

Students must become more dedicated toward receiving an education, Jackson continued, noting that he advocates "at least two hours of study each night with the radio and TV off."

But Jackson's most pressing educational goal is desegregation. "We must convince everybody that there is a mutual advantage in cultural diversity," he stressed. "People really need to appreciate other people during their formative years."

Jackson closed the interview with a firm handshake. As I left his office, he was on the phone again, preparing for a press conference to be held during his lunch hour. That sounds about right for Jesse Jackson, a man who has little time to spare. –Norman Atkins

1. What does this sketch reveal about Jesse Jackson's appearance? his actions? his thoughts?

2. What do the following details indicate to you about the interviewee: "bellowing voice"; "firm handshake"; "a man who has little time to spare"?

3. Why do you think this interview relies so heavily on direct quotes?

4. What research about Jackson and the topic of discussion does the writer appear to have done before the interview took place?

5. Pose three questions that the interviewer might have asked to obtain Jackson's responses.

6. Does the interview seem to have a focus? If so, what is it?

• **EXERCISE 2.** Choose a person you wish to interview. Then do some preliminary research on both the person and the topic to be discussed. Decide what audience will ultimately read this interview. Devise appropriate, open-ended interview questions. When you conduct the actual interview, take notes carefully, writing down any comments in quotation marks that you might eventually quote verbatim. Examine your notes while the interview is still fresh in your mind, making a follow-up call to clarify any areas that seem vague as you read your notes. Then complete the interview by writing it up.

PART 3

A Profile

A *profile,* which is a brief biography or characterization of a person, combines the techniques used in writing a sketch and an interview. A profile records a person's behavior, background, words, attitudes, or opinions. Because it does not confine the reader to a brief and limited impression, as a sketch does, a profile adds a dimension to the subject. Although longer than a sketch, a profile must still retain a consistent tone and a sense of direction. Consider Jim's profile of Bob Otto, a man with whom he worked at a gas station:

"It's Hard, It's Hard"

Bob Otto was born in the backwoods of Mississippi, and even after many years in the North, he still maintains his drawl. When first meeting him, most people see an illiterate old hillbilly, but he surprises them with an intelligence and wit that few people could match. My contact with Bob was crammed into a two-month period, nine hours a day, when we worked together last summer at a gas station.

The first few days I worked with Bob I stayed a distance away from him. Bob is a straightforward person, unafraid to tell anyone what he thinks, and this includes bosses, customers, and fellow workers. Many times I saw Bob tell off a customer. Every other morning a surly man would come in to buy gas. I suppose Bob had planned to say something this particular morning because as the man rolled down his window Bob said, "Boy, am I glad to see you."

"Why?" asked the man.

"Because now I don't have to take any of your bunk for another two days." With that the man drove off so flustered he forgot to buy any gas.

During the time we worked together, Bob quit the job twice to make a point to the boss, but he never told me the point. Maybe the point was that Bob doesn't adjust to people—people adjust to Bob. After I got used to how Bob liked to handle the business, he stopped being critical of me and started talking about other subjects besides the weather and baseball. He seemed to be reaching out to me in friendship, and from then on he was like a big brother. He told jokes nonstop, except when he was giving advice. I could ask or tell him anything. Because he was such a direct person, he expected others to be frank with him too.

Bob's pride in his job was his strong point. From the way he bounced from car to car, I could tell he took pride in the service he gave. His generosity also had pride in it; it showed when he gave me food or information or even a laugh. But his pride also seemed to give him a foolish courage. As he told me, "I'll take 'em on, no matter what size."

Bob's past ties in with his personality on the job. I placed his age at about fifty-five, and for fourteen of those years he drove a diesel truck cross-country. That was where he picked up most of his jokes, he told me, exchanging them with other truck drivers. But it was also while driving a truck that he became unable to adjust to other people's habits. "Too much time alone," he said. "Couldn't compromise my life or work style."

Finally Bob became an alcoholic. He went to live in a house where the other residents were alcoholics too. The purpose of the house was to help these people overcome their problem, Bob told me, and the rule was that everyone in the house had to be very direct with the other residents. I believe that living in the house is what made Bob so straightforward.

Bob's pride seems to stem from the fact that he has pulled himself out of the gutter and is on his way back. A job in a gas station isn't much when you're Bob's age, but you wouldn't know that to watch him shine a windshield or drain a crankcase. "It's hard, it's hard," he said about getting himself back together. Thanks, Bob. –Jim Votanek

1. What do you learn from this profile about Bob Otto's behavior? his background? his opinions?

2. Do you think that the quotations Jim has used in the profile are well chosen? Why or why not?

3. After reading this profile, one student commented: "I feel I know Bob, but I can't visualize him." Do you think this is a valid observation? Explain.

4. Choose a word to describe Jim's tone in this profile and explain your choice.

• **EXERCISE 3.** Write a profile of someone you know in which you combine your observations about that person's character with descriptions of behavior, direct quotations, biographical information, and whatever other evidence might be useful to support your observations. Do not try to write a chronological biography; instead, build your profile around an element of character, background, talent, or any other quality that you find especially interesting about that person.

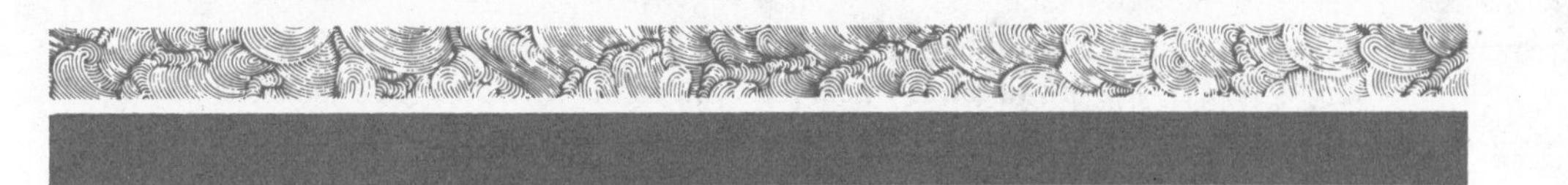

CHAPTER

27 Writing About Places, Words, Activities, and Things

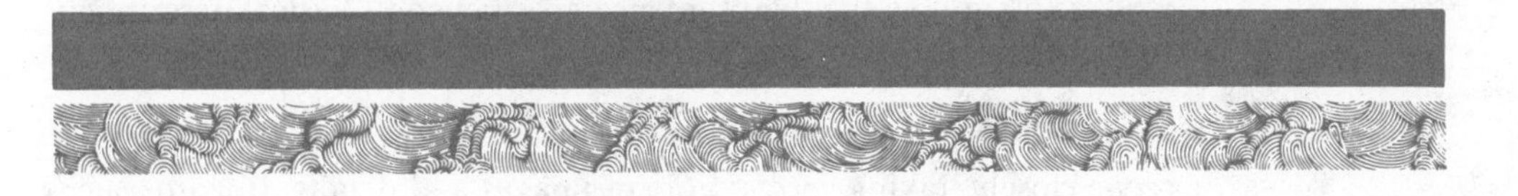

PART 1

Writing About Places

One effective way to write about a place is to use the techniques of a movie camera. Like the camera, you can linger over a scene, zoom in on a detail, draw back from a subject, or shift your focus abruptly. And like a camera, you cannot rely on words like *beautiful* or *mysterious* to evoke emotional responses, but must portray these qualities through specific detail. Remember that your work must have a direction, just as a movie does. Your writing should go somewhere, taking a reader along. Note how the use of camera techniques enriches this description of a New York City scene:

> From the south side of a block in the West Eighties, one can see the backs of several empty tenements whose rear windows once looked at the backs of other tenements, now torn down. If anyone were to look out these windows now, he would see a vacant lot: litter; bits of brick; weeds and wild flowers; bottles and cans. As we walked along the block one afternoon—an eerie place—we heard high, wailing sounds coming from one of the hollow buildings. The sounds—a mixture of howling, baying, and yipping—were oddly musical, and seemed to have some pattern. We stopped and looked for the source of the cries. All we saw was a long stick waving this way and that between the black chimneys on the rooftop. Then we caught a glimpse of a man's head for an instant. A flight of pigeons—forty or fifty of them—swirled over the building, then banked away in seeming response to the waving

stick and the odd, compelling cries. The pigeons swept overhead, crossing the street, then curved back to the rooftop again; the stick waved; the cries sent them off in another direction. They soared up into the flawless blue sky, then swung around, headed for the roof once more. From where we stood watching and listening, next to the vacant lot, it seemed as if the man on the roof—with only a stick and a musical score of his own composition—was conducting the entire sky. —"Notes and Comment" from "The Talk of the Town," THE NEW YORKER, October 22, 1979. Reprinted by permission; © 1979 The New Yorker Magazine, Inc.

1. Cite some strong visual and auditory images from the preceding essay.

2. How is the idea of movement conveyed? Note in particular the use of verbs in describing the pigeons.

3. Assume you were filming this scene at a distance, using long, sweeping shots. Where would you stop the camera to emphasize a detail? Where would you zoom in for a close-up shot?

4. Explain how the final sentence goes beyond physical description to make an interpretative statement.

• **EXERCISE 1.** Pick a scene you would like to describe. View this scene closely, taking special note of images and details. If words such as *pretty* or *depressing* occur to you, determine what concrete details will create the same impression for your reader. Decide how to move your description along, choosing items such as action verbs, sentence length, and shifts in focus to convey motion. End your description with a general comment on the significance of the scene.

The following was written by Frier, a high-school senior:

123 S. Carolina St., Louisiana, Missouri

You are in Illinois. You pass the last cornfield and a village named Pike Station, which smells of pigs. You ascend the only hill in the entire state and approach the shining hot steel bridge. You can smell the green, murky life of the river, only yards away. You cross the bridge and the steel hums beneath your tires. You are in Missouri. The green, billowing bluffs are a relief from the torrid cornfield flatness of the state. Louisiana, Missouri, population 5,000. This is my town. You turn left immediately and turn right on Georgia Street. You continue down Georgia to the Dairy Queen. You buy a 30¢ chocolate chip cone and pat Butch, the Dairy Queen's stray dog. You find Eighth Street, which runs into Georgia, and walk down Eighth to S. Carolina. On the corner there is a house. That's my house.

The house is painted white, and it has always been in my family. We've had it for about one hundred years. We've had the property for longer than that. It is a farmhouse without a farm. White wooden shingles cover the exterior. Long ago my great-great-grandfather, who lost two fingers in the Civil War, converted the second floor into an apartment. It is no longer an apartment, but the second floor is still used. It serves as attic and cobwebbed playground. A large, southern porch skirts the front of the house. A copy of the *Press-Journal* lies rolled near the door. It is Sunday afternoon and you hear the soft swish of cars on Georgia Street. The air smells of cut grass and a hint of rain. The address numbers say "123," a magic combination. The doorbell chimes. The house, the lot, both loom in bittersweet memory—weddings, funerals. I have seen them here. The house is saturated with the remnants of tears shed during the situations that have become the stanchions of my experience.

You take off your jacket, and the Missouri sun beats on. You enter the house. Central air conditioning—the space is cool and southern. The dining room also serves as a hall. The ceiling is high. The air smells of holiday and quiet worry. Dark-stained table, dark-stained cabinet with collection of antique fruit plates, great-great-grandma's crocheted tablecloth, filmy curtains. The bathroom door rests shut, directly to your left. Go to the kitchen. Modest white refrigerator, white stove, the noble instruments of grandmotherhood. Green Coke bottles on the windowsill filter light onto oilcloth where fresh fruit lives in a bowl. Liquor locked and out of reach in white cabinet. Have a Coke, 8 ounce size—magic. Go to the den. TV, great old chairs, the old, old desk. Above the TV there are pictures and framed documents that amount to a pictorial history of the family. Three-fingered Jack McCollister, his son Frank who ran off with a dancing girl, old Taylor Frier whose surname I now bear as my first, they all live above the television. The desk. My great-grandfather handed me a pearl-handled pen-knife when I was eight years old. He stood at this desk and told me that it was a large responsibility and that I better not lose it. I lost it. He never found out. Into the parlor. Antique chairs, end tables, two hide-a-bed sofas, tall curtained windows. There is a fireplace that no longer operates. It is marble and has a gas jet and artificial logs. Above it hangs an original Currier & Ives print of a steamboat race. I love it.

And so night falls and you must leave. You can hear the distant frustrated roar of broken teen-age mufflers in the bowling alley parking lot. You cross the bridge, past the River-View Motel, across the river into Illinois. You leave Elysium to sort itself out; skyscrapers call. –Frier McCollister

1. What images in Frier's work evoke the sharpest emotional response from you? Why?

2. In what various ways does Frier achieve a sense of movement in this selection?

3. Note the following in Frier's writing: length of sentences; "sentences" that lack a verb; matter-of-fact reporting; use of concrete detail. Given these elements, how would you describe Frier's style?

4. In what way does Frier's style suit his subject? Would the poetic style of Hal Borland (see page 170) have served Frier's purposes in this selection? Why or why not?

5. Use your own word or one of the following to describe the tone of this essay: *indignant; humorous; scornful; fanciful; nostalgic.* What words and details help to establish this tone?

• **EXERCISE 2.** Write an essay in which you describe a place that you know or remember well. Decide before you begin whether the purpose of your essay is to inform, to entertain, or to persuade. Devise a topic sentence that announces the place you will describe and states your attitude toward the place. Use specific words, sentence structure, and imagery to produce an overall tone and to make the place vivid to your reader.

PART 2

Writing About Words

Words, like people, can be vital and interesting; and, like people, words may acquire a personality or a reputation of their own. On occasion, you may want to write about specific words, defending them, disclaiming them, or explaining them. The writer of the following essay seeks acceptance for a word that has inspired controversy among language purists.

Abandon Hope

Evidently, the word *hopefully* has become the litmus test to determine whether one is a language snob or a language slob.

Angrily, traditionalists hold that the word is an adverb, usually intended to modify a verb. In the sentence "He will look at me hopefully," the verb *to look* is modified by *hopefully*, to mean that the look will contain hope. Purists reject "Hopefully, he will look at me" because it is confusing. Does it mean "with hope in his eyes" or "I hope he will look at me"? They argue that when you mean to say "it is hoped" or "I hope," you should come out and say those words, and not cloak your hopes in a fuzzy *hopefully* that can be misinterpreted.

Additionally, the anti-dangling-adverb crowd insists that *-ly* has a use in helping understanding and should not be corrupted. For example, if you say "Close the door tight," the adjective *tight* modifies the noun *door,* thus describing accurately the desired condition of the door; but if you say, "Close the door tightly," the adverb *tightly* modifies the verb *close*, and does not describe the door.

Coolly, and against all that good sense, the language slob replies, "What most people use becomes 'correct,' and most people use *hopefully* to mean 'one hopes.' To wrinkle your nose at common usage is to be a language snob."

Fortunately, we do not have to choose up sides on the basis of slob versus snob, descriptive versus prescriptive linguistics, to deal with *hopefully*.

Basically, I use *hopefully* to mean "it is to be hoped" not because I accept loose new standards, but because I embrace time-tested and readily understood usage. The English language has been using adverbs to qualify a whole following clause or sentence for centuries; with one deft daub, an adverb can quickly and vividly color a sentence that follows, infusing the words that come after it with a meaning that otherwise would have to be evoked with a long and often awkward qualifier. The anti-*hopefully* brigade wishes a word like *hopably* existed, to do for *hopefully* what *regrettably* does for *regretfully*, but (one regrets) *hopably* is not a word—so it makes no sense to keep fighting the extended use of *hopefully*.

Importantly, the editor of *Webster's New World Dictionary*, David Guralnik, agrees: "Happily, there are many precedents for such a usage," he writes. "Presumably, purists howled when each one first appeared. Probably time will take care of *hopefully* as well."

Doubtlessly, my deliberate decision to adopt *hopefully* in its sentence-coloring sense, and to defend it vigorously as structurally correct rather than to accept it listlessly as common sloppy usage will be attacked by people who get their kicks out of hanging out on old ramparts. But while they're knocking *hopefully*, they'll have to deal with the deliberately dangling adverbs that begin every paragraph in this entry. –William Safire. "Abandon Hope," from On Language, NEW YORK TIMES MAGAZINE, May 20, 1979. © 1979 by The New York Times Company. Reprinted by permission.

1. Would you say that the tone of the previous essay is *witty*? *serious*? *outraged*? *lighthearted*? Referring to the essay itself, explain how one of these words (or a word of your own) characterizes the tone.

2. Do you think that the technique revealed in the last sentence helps the writer in making a case for *hopefully*? Why or why not?

One need not always write about words in a serious manner. Here is a paragraph on the supposed origin of the phrase "devil may care":

> During the Middle Ages in Porkpie, a duchy of Treelip noted for its exportation of turnip greens, baldness was considered a mark of good breeding. The first thing a mother asked (after "Where's my breakfast") when a newborn was placed in her arms was, "Is my wee Eggbert (or Hercules, or Mahinda) bald," knowing the baby's future depended on the answer. And, often as not, the answer was, "Not by a hair." Women had their heads shaved, making potholders and stuffed animals out of their tresses. In short, hair was considered a punishment, a curse of the devil. Hairied people told hair-raising stories of police hairassment. Head-shaving replaced hot-fudging as a national pastime, and shave-offs, razor-ins, and pluck-outs provided public entertainment much as tax evasion does today. But one spring morning a hirsute young swain declared baldly: "It bothers me not that the devil make hair," and refused to have his head shaved. Whereupon everyone in the kingdom began chanting, "Devil make hair, devil make hair," and staged a grow-in. And that's how we got the expression. Of course, the spelling has changed a bit, but then only part of the alphabet had been invented by the Middle Ages. –Hazel Dare

• **EXERCISE 3.** Write an essay in which you imaginatively trace the origin of a well-known word or phrase such as one of the following: *jump on the bandwagon, the cat's pajamas, apple pie order, bring home the bacon, bats in one's belfry, spill the beans, pass the buck, go Dutch treat, face the music, go out on a limb, a fine kettle of fish, take the cake.* Adopt a humorous tone and be as fanciful as you wish.

> It took me fifteen years to discover I had no talent for writing, but I couldn't give it up because by that time I was too famous.
>
> Robert Benchley

Words often have personal meanings for people, which go beyond their dictionary definitions. You may wish to describe a word in terms of your own private associations. Here is one writer's definition of the word *jogger*:

Enigma in Motion: What Really Makes Joggers Go Running?

(1) Every neighborhood has at least one. He materializes out of the shadows–puffing, wheezing. His feet slap against the pavement like a metronome. His unshaven face has the martyred look of an El Greco painting, with eyes staring ahead as if a banana peel (to which he is reasonably well resigned) awaits him over the next rise.

(2) The Jogger belongs to the morning-twilight people: The perky little lady who wraps her husband's London Fog coat over her night-gown and walks her Pekingese "Drat"; the newsboy on a blue wreck of a bike who throws his paper into the shrubbery and flees, whistling.

(3) Why does the Jogger run? Certainly not for pleasure in any of the usual senses of the word. He has his official explanation, for the world and for himself as well. He is "giving himself a workout." He is "keeping himself in shape." He is just "shedding a few pounds." All the common-sense arguments of hygiene get enlisted.

(4) But more is going on here. In an hour or so the Jogger will be standing on a train station platform in a dark suit with a rolled news-paper beside a lot of other men in dark suits with rolled newspapers. The sun will be in the sky, and in the full light he will pass inspection as a member of a particular community–never mind which–on the way to a particular job–never mind doing what. He will be into his role as citizen, as jobholder, just as when he comes home he will be into his role as husband-and-father.

(5) But for the moment, here in the morning twilight, as he commits the primary act of putting one foot in front of the other–fast–the Jog-ger is being nothing but himself. A member of the species in sneakers and gym suit: He-who-runs.

(6) The Capes, the Colonials, the English Tudors he jogs past might as well be straw huts along the Congo or Arab tents in the desert. For the Jogger is a man out of his context.

(7) What is the Jogger running from? The real question is: What is he running toward? Is this man in a schoolboy's outfit running back toward his childhood? Left, right. Left, right. Toward a world of play, where objectives were simple–like, get up the hill?

(8) Or perhaps the Jogger is running back further than that. Perhaps he is a time machine, jogging back to a kind of primal self: The first pursuer, or maybe the first escaper.

(9) Heavy! Mystical! No wonder the Jogger keeps things simple. A workout is a workout is a workout. Right? Can't a man take in a little fresh air without founding a philosophy?

(10) Still, to the nonjogger, who (unlike the Jogger) can't just run away from the question, the Jogger remains an enigma. Look at him as he wobbles over the hill and dale–one of life's pilgrims on double time. But what's the quest? Where's the grail? What beat is this man picking up as his sneakers slap-slap, turning Ravel's *Bolero* into a soft-shoe routine?

(11) The Jogger is a mime whose gestures seem to signal meanings, even if neither he nor we know the code. Doomed to journeys rather than destinations, he plods on. Other runners race against competitors, or at least the clock. Other runners have a finish line. Not the Jogger.

(12) He no longer belongs to that kind of time, that kind of space. Condemned to endless repetition, forever on the shake, he runs as if by perpetual motion he will sooner or later discover his direction. He runs as if he cannot help himself.

(13) He is a messenger from the Plains of Marathon who has forgotten his message and to whom it must be delivered. But he keeps on running anyway.

(14) The world is nothing but the ground he runs upon. He becomes nothing but his feet.

May he trip over no tricycles.

May he be bitten by no dogs.

May he run in peace.

May he find peace in running. –Melvin Maddocks. "Portrait of a Jogger." Reprinted by permission from THE CHRISTIAN SCIENCE MONITOR.

1. What does each of the following labels tell us about the jogger?
"a man out of his context" (paragraph 6)
"a time machine" (paragraph 8)
"one of life's pilgrims on double time" (paragraph 10)

2. For what reasons might the jogger be running, according to this essay?

3. In paragraph 1, the jogger is described with the words *puffing* and *wheezing*. In the same paragraph, the actual rhythms of jogging are suggested with the description of feet that "slap against the pavement like a metronome." Find other words or phrases in the essay that convey an image or the rhythms of a jogger.

• **EXERCISE 4.** Write an essay in which you define a word according to the personal associations it has for you. You may wish to convey its special meaning through labels and titles, such as the previous essay does, or through word choice or a style that reinforces its meaning. For example, you might describe your special connotations for a telephone by choosing sounds and rhythms that suggest a phone ringing; or you might describe the soothing sounds of the sea in rhythms that suggest the lapping of water. Whatever word you choose, use details to explain why it has personal significance for you. You may wish to write about one of the following words or to choose one of your own: *snake, typewriter, soap, a particular fruit or vegetable, tree, calories, leather, nightmares, childhood, first bicycle, exams, summer, rain, television.*

PART 3

Writing About Activities or Things

An essay about something concrete, inanimate, or impersonal–for example, an object, an item, or an activity–requires more than a dictionary definition or a list of characteristics. You can make such a subject come alive through your style, tone, word choice, and use of detail. Here is an essay on a familiar subject, handwriting:

Nowadays, Writing Is Off the Wall

Nearly everyone has had the frustration of receiving a phone message, restaurant bill, mechanic's receipt or note from the boss that turns out to be about as easy to decipher as Egyptian hieroglyphics. Weaned as they are on telephones, typewriters, computer printouts and other communications gadgetry, Americans have simply forgotten how to write clearly—when they write at all. So bad is the situation that the Writing Instrument Manufacturers Association, which annually celebrates John Hancock's birthday, Jan. 23, as National Handwriting Day, has decided that it is "hopeless" to go on using the occasion to promote legibility in signatures. But the retreat is only partial. Says Frank L. King, W.I.M.A.'s executive vice-president: "We may have weakened on signatures, but not on anything else. We will continue to vigorously provoke people's awareness of bad handwriting."

By W.I.M.A.'s reckoning, business loses as much as $200 million yearly as a result of illegible records and messages. Sloppily filled-out returns hamper tax collection, while indecipherable addresses account for much of the 38 million pieces of mail that wind up in dead-letter offices at a cost of nearly $4 million a year for extra handling.

Rotten writing is scarcely a new problem. Napoleon's script was so miserable that one of his generals once mistook a letter of his for battle orders. Charles Hamilton, a Manhattan dealer in autographs and manuscripts, contends that writer Gertrude Stein's oblique prose style may be explained by the fact that compositors often misread her cryptic script. Poet William Butler Yeats often could not read his own work. Horace Greeley, the editor of the old New York *Tribune*, had a notoriously illegible scrawl. He once scribbled a note to a reporter telling him he was fired for incompetence; so indecipherable was the missive that for years afterward the man was able to pass it off as a letter of recommendation.

What dismays pen- and pencil-makers today is that woeful writing seems to be spreading. Particularly upsetting is the poor example being set by the White House. Among recent Presidents, Richard Nixon's script was barely legible, while John Kennedy's was so erratic that he seldom signed his own name the same way twice. Though Jimmy Carter's hand is clear, it seems almost juvenile when compared with the elegant, flowing scripts of early Chief Executives like George Washington and Thomas Jefferson.

Among professionals, doctors continue to live up to their reputation as the worst scribblers. A study published in the American Medical Association's *Journal* reports that at one hospital 33% of all the physicians' notes were essentially illegible (general surgeons and urologists were the worst offenders; gynecologists and cardiac surgeons did somewhat better). *Pharmacy Times* magazine regularly reproduces particularly hopeless prescriptions.

Beyond the fact that much less communication is handwritten now than it was in the days of the quill pen, experts point to several causes of scriptural sloppiness. Some blame a spreading weakness of will.

Says Sam Toombs, a Houston psychologist: "Bad handwriting is a way of saying something and taking it back at the same time. People scrawl signatures on material for which they don't want to be held responsible." Others cite the hurried nature of modern society, in which speed is given a higher priority than clarity. Pen-makers decry poor instruction: while courses in calligraphy are gaining in popularity among adults, schools have de-emphasized instruction in penmanship. Promoters of good script point out that at schools in Oregon, where italic handwriting is taught as a way to instill clarity, students not only develop superior penmanship but get higher-than-average grades all round.

No purist on penmanship, W.I.M.A.'s King admits to a feeling that script that is just a little sloppy may indicate "a more complex and exciting person." Nonetheless, W.I.M.A. recommends 17 steps toward more legible handwriting, including: "Slow down. Sit properly. Watch out for tricky letters . . . *a, e, t* and *r* cause the most difficulty." And at the end of the list: "Think of the person receiving what you write, and be merciful." –"Nowadays, Writing Is off the Wall," TIME, January 28, 1980. Reprinted by permission from TIME, The Weekly Newsmagazine; Copyright Time Inc. 1980.

1. In what way does the writer of this essay use the following to enliven the subject of handwriting: people in history; humor; contemporary details and current facts?

2. Do you think the purpose of this essay is to entertain, to instruct, or to do both? Explain.

• **EXERCISE 5.** Choose one of the following items and write an essay about it in which you present factual information to your reader in an interesting manner. You may expand the topic by discussing how it relates to present society, to history, or to the arts. Use library research, as well as your own observations, to enliven the topic. Your essay should be approximately 500 words.

Here are several places to begin research on this essay: unabridged dictionaries, the *Oxford English Dictionary*, Bartlett's *Familiar Quotations*, *Shakespeare Concordance*, *Bible Concordance*, *Readers' Guide to Periodical Literature*, other magazine indexes, general and specialized encyclopedias, *Dictionary of Symbols*, art books, photography books, advertising, works of art and literature that you already know. Check the card catalog for other books more specialized than these reference sources.

Your essay need not contain formal footnotes. Instead, attribute information within the text itself, by quoting source, author, and page numbers in a running citation.

balloon	chain	fence	knife	ring
bicycle	cloak	fountain	lace	scales
boat	clock	gate	lamp	screen
boomerang	crown	goblet	mask	sword
bowl	crutch	gun	mirror	table
bridge	cup	hat	necklace	umbrella

CHAPTER **28 Writing About Ideas**

Of the many types of writing that deal mainly with ideas, three will be treated in this chapter: persuasive writing, critical writing, and analytical writing in the form of explication. You will frequently encounter persuasive and critical writing in forms such as ads and reviews. Since these types of writing can influence you, you should be able to evaluate the ideas they express. On the other hand, while you may seldom encounter an explication in your nonacademic life, you will undoubtedly be called upon to write an explication if you go on to college. Additionally, the analytic process of explication provides a valuable step-by-step approach for attacking any difficult subject.

PART 1

Writing to Persuade

Persuasive writing, designed to convince a reader to agree with a particular view, takes many forms—from advertising copy to newspaper editorials to political brochures. Although the writers of commercials, campaign speeches, and legal arguments may seek to persuade by loading words and slanting facts, persuasive writing can be based on sound logic and honest arguments. Whatever its style, persuasive writing will generally include four basic characteristics: (1) It directs its appeal to a particular audience; (2) It establishes a consistent tone in order to provoke the desired response; (3) It states its position early in the essay; (4) It supplies specific evidence to support its position. Using these guidelines, evaluate the following essay by Mark, a high-school senior:

> Although our student body has various channels for expressing its concerns, it has overlooked a powerful supplement to the student council and principal's advisory committees—electing an eighteen-year-old to the Board of Education. Ours would not be the first school in the area with a recent graduate on the board; Ranes

Township and Seabard are currently reaping the advantages of a younger board member's insights. Each district elected an eighteen-year-old board member a year ago.

An eighteen-year-old board member, fresh from the halls of MHS, would perceive school problems from the perspective of the student; his or her knowledge and attitudes would be a by-product of four years' close contact with the school. Such a board member would supply an awareness of student reaction and participation that could separate a successful policy change from an unsuccessful one. Furthermore, students could comfortably approach a young board member with their problems and concerns, creating a valuable two-way exchange. This direct feedback would prove extremely useful to other board members who don't have the time or image to develop rapport with students in order to assess their viewpoints.

A young board member could also soften student antagonism toward the school administration by giving students an indirect though integral role in decisions affecting their future. By helping to relieve students of the feeling that people who run the school don't care about them, a young board member might pave the way toward more mutual cooperation between students and adults at MHS.

If the student body intends to support a candidate for the school board, it must hurry because there is only one month left until election day. The requirements for board candidacy are simple: The candidate must (1) be at least eighteen years old; (2) have been a school district resident for at least one year; (3) be a registered voter. The candidate must also intend to live in the Middletown area for the length of the term—four years. In addition, all candidates must file for candidacy by March 23 with petitions containing fifty signatures.

In neglecting to find and nominate a student candidate for the election, MHS students will forfeit a major opportunity for a direct voice to express their concerns about the state of the school. If we are sincere about wanting to help run MHS, what better way to do so than electing one of ourselves to the Board of Education. –Mark Epstein

1. Do you think that Mark has presented his case in a convincing manner? Evaluate his essay, using the four basic characteristics of persuasive writing, listed at the beginning of the chapter, as guidelines.

2. What word would you use to describe the tone of this essay? To whom do you think Mark is directing his observations?

• **EXERCISE 1.** Now write your own essay, designed to persuade. Assume that you have been asked to write a guest editorial for the school or community newspaper. Choose an appropriate topic and apply the guidelines at the beginning of this chapter for writing the persuasive essay. Your essay should be from 300 to 500 words.

PART 2

Critical Writing

Writing that criticizes evaluates a subject, presenting both its negative and positive qualities. A reader often relies on critical writing in making certain decisions. Is the product worth buying? Is the book worth reading? Is the concert worth hearing? Much critical writing deals with the arts—film, painting, music, theater, literature—but it may also evaluate such diverse subjects as athletics, restaurants, and consumer products. An effective critical essay should accomplish the following:

1. It gives the reader a general idea of the subject being discussed. (It need not explain an entire plot, for example, but it should present a basic summary of events, leaving any surprise elements, such as an unexpected ending, for readers to discover themselves. In addition, the critic may supply any relevant background that helps put the work in context: for example, some commentary on an era during which a historical novel is set.)

2. It describes some of the techniques used. (How has the conductor, the coach, the designer, or the chef produced particular effects?)

3. It provides comment on items that are especially significant, or it highlights noteworthy elements that readers might miss on their own. (A critic might point out a rather subtle motif that runs throughout a play or a dance scene in a revue that is done with extraordinary precision and grace.)

4. It uses details from the topic or work to substantiate observations or opinions. (What qualities make this pocket calculator the best you can buy for the money? Why is this rock group's latest album inferior to its previous ones?)

5. It develops an attitude toward the subject. (Most critical writing takes the form of a mixed review, noting both positive and negative qualities of the subject. Yet after having read a critical review, a reader should know whether or not the critic was favorably disposed toward the subject. Often movie or restaurant critics use a star rating system—usually from zero to four stars—to evaluate subjects.)

The following is a review of a 1968 film version of *Romeo and Juliet*, directed by Franco Zeffirelli:

Zeffirelli's *Romeo and Juliet* will surely do much to reawaken a youthful identification with the aristocratic "star-crossed lovers" who have been so long in the limbo of Required Reading. . . . With a charged, witty camera, Zeffirelli has managed to make the play alive and wholly contemporary without having had to transfer the action to a modern setting. Romeo and Juliet appear afresh as two incredibly articulate but believably agonized teen-agers whose turf happens to be Quattrocento Verona. Too young to buck the Establishment–the Italian city-state with its machinery of epic feuds and rituals–they are finally undone by their passions. Death enlarges them when they abolish their parents' hate. They become, as Juliet's father puts it in the play's epilogue, "the poor sacrifices of our enmity."

Instead of simply duplicating the first-folio on film, Zeffirelli and his two co-writers, Franco Brusati and Masolino d'Amico, have blithely excised and elided speeches, transposed lines, eliminated characters. It is a dangerous game, rewriting Shakespeare, but *Romeo and Juliet* proves that it can be played and won. An even greater risk was to give the leading roles to a pair of youthful unknowns with virtually no acting experience: Juliet is a tremulous 16-year-old, Olivia Hussey; Romeo is Leonard Whiting, 17. Both look their parts and read their lines with a sensitivity far beyond the limitations of their age.

Equally impressive is John McEnery, 25, who plays Mercutio not as a witty, lascivious buffoon but as a possessed genius who has lounged too long with his inferiors. His delivery of the Queen Mab speech is a masterpiece of abstracted art. Teetering on madness, he spouts the words as if emerging from a lifelong nightmare. Zeffirelli, however, seems to have had better luck in casting youth than age. Pat Heywood's Nurse is a cockney caricature. And Milo O'Shea's Friar Laurence is a characterization lost somewhere in the middle distance, not deeply enough involved with the lovers nor sufficiently removed to act as a chorus of comment.

As in his *The Taming of the Shrew*, starring the Burtons, Zeffirelli dazzles the eye with a virtuoso use of color. His camera is a Renaissance palette. Courtiers stride by in the muted gold and crimsons of Piero della Francesca; cobblestones and horsemen diminish into the serene infinities of Uccello. Visually, Shakespeare has never been better realized–and seldom has he had so sensitive a collaborator.

1. Evaluate this review using as guidelines the five points listed for critical writing.

2. Do you think the critic has given away too much information in revealing the deaths of the young couple? Why or why not?

3. How would you characterize the general attitude of the critic toward this movie?

• **EXERCISE 2.** Assume you have been asked to write a critical review for your school newspaper. Choose as a topic a movie, play, book, concert, art exhibit, record album, or a consumer product (such as a used car, a stereo, or a moped) that seems appropriate.

PART 3

Explication

In order to understand some works of literature, especially poems, you may have to do a close analysis, perhaps even a line by line or a word by word study. Such analysis is called *explication*. Although such detailed study would seldom be possible or necessary for a longer work such as a novel, it is often a valuable way of approaching a dense or difficult poem. Read the following poem and the explication of it:

IX

He woke in terror to a sky more bright
Than middle day; he heard the sick earth groan,
And ran to see the lazy-smoking cone
Of the fire-mountain, friendly to his sight
As his wife's hand, gone strange and full of fright; 5
Over his fleeing shoulder it was shown
Rolling its pitchy lake of scalding stone
Upon his house that had no feet for flight.
Where did he weep? Where did he sit him down
And sorrow, with his head between his knees? 10
Where said the Race of Man, "Here let me drown"?
"Here let me die of hunger"?—"let me freeze"?
By nightfall he has built another town:
This boiling pot, this clearing in the trees.

This poem describes the effects of a volcano, although this phenomenon is never actually mentioned by name. Instead, phrases are used that suggest strong visual images: the "lazy-smoking cone" and the "fire-mountain." These metaphors present more memorable pictures than the mere word *volcano* would have done. Many other figures of speech appear in the poem. The earth is personified as sick and groaning. The personified mountain, once friendly, has "gone strange and full of fright." The imagery in line 7 appeals to the sense of sight, as well as that of touch (*scalding*) and smell (*pitchy*); in addition, the word *Rolling* conveys the idea of movement.

The poet relies quite heavily on the sounds of words. Lines 4, 5, 6, and 8 are alliterative (*fire, friendly, full, fright, fleeing, feet, for,* and *flight*). The long, slow sounds in the phrase "lazy-smoking cone" suitably express the lingering scene of a pre-volcanic mountain. Phrases are repeated in lines 9–12 ("Where did he"; "let me") to make the man's plight more dramatic.

The poem is well suited to the sonnet structure. The first 8 lines describe the volcano, the next 4 portray the man's dilemma in the wake of disaster, and the final 2 present the man's resolution. Once the disaster has been described, the focus shifts to the man who has been

---

forced to flee from his home. A series of questions are posed to suggest possible reactions to this disaster: Did he weep and sorrow? Did he succumb to the forces that commonly destroy human beings–drowning, starvation, freezing? Has he given in to adversity, as suggested in the repeated phrase "let me"? But the resolution in the last two lines reveals him to be a survivor. Time is telescoped ("By nightfall") in a description of his efforts to rebuild what he has lost. Two aspects of civilization are suggested by metaphors: cooking ("This boiling pot") and building ("this clearing in the trees"). This man will recover and rebuild.

In determining the full significance of this poem, one must call to mind the title of the series from which it comes: *Epitaph for the Race of Man.* An epitaph is a brief statement in memory of a dead person, usually placed on a tombstone. This poem, then, especially its last two lines, serves as commentary on all human beings. The human race, with its ability to survive disaster and rebuild life, will endure.

Evaluate this explication in the light of the following guidelines:

1. Has the explication made this poem clear?

2. Has the explication dealt with technical devices (poetic forms, figurative language, word choice, use of sound), in the light of their contribution to the poem?

3. Is the explication arranged in some order? (For example, some explicators approach a poem line by line; others organize paragraphs according to specific poetic devices in the poem.)

4. Has the explication offered commentary on the significance of the poem, providing some clues as to why the poem was written?

• **EXERCISE 3.** Using the previous explication as a guide, write an explication of the following poem. Note that this poem directly follows the previous sonnet by Millay in *Epitaph for the Race of Man.* Note also that the form and theme of the two sonnets are similar, and feel free to use any information in your own explication from the one that has been done for you.

X

The broken dike, the levee washed away,
The good fields flooded and the cattle drowned,
Estranged and treacherous all the faithful ground,
And nothing left but floating disarray
Of tree and home uprooted,—was this the day 5
Man dropped upon his shadow without a sound
And died, having laboured well and having found
His burden heavier than a quilt of clay?
No, no. I saw him when the sun had set
In water, leaning on his single oar 10
Above his garden faintly glimmering yet . . .
There bulked the plough, here washed the updrifted weeds . . .
And scull across his roof and make for shore,
With twisted face and pocket full of seeds.

CHAPTER 29 The Research Paper

You have to write a research paper. It's part of the course, and probably the longest, most complicated piece of writing you'll be asked to do all year.

Research takes time. For that reason you will need a few weeks to do this project. Research also involves a variety of tasks. You have to find information, organize it, and present it in a clearly written form that interests your reader. Because so much time and effort go into a research paper, it is important that you begin the project with an understanding of the steps that are required to complete such an assignment.

Why write a research paper? Like any other assignment, the purpose is partly to help you develop skills that you can continue to use after high school. You will apply the techniques of research in almost any career you enter and in some hobbies and leisure-time activities as well. Some fields, such as law, journalism, and laboratory science, may require almost constant research. Others, such as business, advertising, and medicine, may require frequent research. More immediately, a research project improves your study skills because it requires you to initiate and carry through a complex assignment within a specific time limit.

The research paper needs to be thought of as a step-by-step process so that its size does not overwhelm you before you get started. The process can be divided into six parts:

1. Developing a topic: you decide on a subject that is narrow enough to develop in a paper of the required length.

2. Locating information: you search for evidence to support the point that you want to make in the paper.

3. Reading and taking notes: you perform the actual research work by collecting the evidence that you will need.

4. Organizing the paper: you outline the basic structure for reporting your research.

5. Writing the first draft: you make the preliminary written report of your research.

6. Writing the final draft: you polish the preliminary report and submit it in correct form complete with the necessary citations for your research.

As you work through these steps toward your own completed research paper, you can benefit from the experiences of three students—Sara, Margaret, and Phil—who have followed the six steps in writing their papers.

PART 1

Step One: Developing a Topic

When you begin to develop a topic for your research paper, try to choose a subject that grows from your own interests and knowledge. The assignment will be more successful if you are working on something that genuinely interests you. A subject that you already know something about will help you to get started on the research process. You should also do some preliminary research to make sure that adequate material is available on the topic. Finally, the topic ought to be one about which you can develop a point of view, for a definite attitude toward your material will give shape to your paper.

Ideas for research-paper topics that fulfill these requirements can come from a variety of sources. Your own reading—assigned or independent—may give you suggestions. So will TV shows, movies, and other entertainment or cultural experiences. Your hobbies, your part-time job, your extracurricular activities, and your career goals can all provide possibilities for research-paper topics.

Sara is fascinated by unsolved mysteries, although she prefers those of nature to those of the occult or supernatural. Her favorite high-school subject is biology, and she works part-time in a tropical fish store. She has seen a TV show on Bigfoot and read about the Abominable Snowman, but, after reading an article in *National Geographic*, she decides that the Loch Ness monster might be the best possibility for research. In addition, her interest in oceanography makes the Loch Ness monster a particularly good choice.

Margaret's teacher requires a literary topic for the research-paper assignment and suggests that the students develop their papers from a list of twentieth-century fiction that he hands out. Margaret has read several of the books, but she decides that Sherwood Anderson's collection of short stories, *Winesburg, Ohio*, would make a good basis for her research paper because she has recently studied one of the stories in class and is curious about its symbolism.

Phil plans a career in architecture, so he wants to do his paper on that topic. He has read several books about Frank Lloyd Wright, but he thinks that anything he might use to develop a paper about Wright seems already to have been written. Then he recalls that a house in his neighborhood was designed by a pupil of Wright's, and he wonders if it might not be possible to write his paper about that house. His teacher thinks the topic will be too narrow, so Phil decides to expand it by investigating all examples of the Prairie style of architecture, designed by Wright and other architects, in his community.

The efforts of Sara, Margaret, and Phil suggest that developing a research-paper topic is a process of reduction. Each began with a general idea and narrowed it to a specific focus. Sara narrowed her idea from mysteries of nature to the Loch Ness monster; Margaret, from literature to symbolism in *Winesburg, Ohio*; Phil, from architecture to Prairie style houses in one community. At this point they do not yet have complete topics, but they can now do some preliminary research to determine whether enough material exists on what they want to write about.

Some browsing in the card catalog in the school library, in the *Readers' Guide to Periodical Literature*, or in the stacks should suggest how much material is available. (See **Card catalog** and **Readers' Guide** in the Language Handbook.) If too much material is available, Sara, Margaret, and Phil may have to narrow their topics further. If very little material appears, their topics may need to be broadened, or even abandoned.

• **EXERCISE 1.** Write down three to five general topics. Develop them into research-paper topics by narrowing them in two or three stages to specific topics. For example: abstract art–abstract art in the United States–the works of Jackson Pollock. Work from the following list or generate your own topics. Choose your topics carefully because one of them will be the topic of your research paper.

Abstract Art	First Aid	Plastics
Advertising	Folklore	Poetry
Agriculture	Foreign Trade	Political Parties
Anthropology	Futurism	Prisons
Archaeology	Government Secrecy	Psychology
Armed Services	Higher Education	Race
Aviation	History	Recreation
Ballet	Homemaking	Religion
Careers	International Law	Science Fiction
Ceramics	Labor Unions	Shakespeare
Children	Language	Skiing
Cinema	Macramé	Social Work
Cities	Mass Media	Sports
Civil Service	Medicine	Sports Cars
Conservation	Music	Superstitions
Crime	Mythology	Taxes
Ecology	Nuclear Power	Teaching the Handicapped
Economics	Olympics	Television
Energy	Outer Space	Thanatology
Famous Outlaws	Photography	Women's Rights

Developing the Controlling Purpose Although Sara, Margaret, and Phil now seem to have topics that they can work on, each of them still needs to restrict the subject and develop an attitude toward it in order to give the research paper a focus, called a *controlling purpose.* In order to produce a paper of from 1,500 to 3,000 words–five to ten typewritten pages–it will be necessary to define the limits of the topic, partly through further narrowing, partly through aiming the research efforts toward a specific end. What about the Loch Ness monster? What about the symbols in *Winesburg, Ohio*? What about Prairie style architecture in one community? Sara, Margaret, and Phil will need to formulate controlling purposes before they know just what kind of research to do.

Setting up a controlling purpose has a twofold value. First, it assures from the outset that you have an idea you want to communicate about your topic. Second, as you research the paper, the controlling purpose acts as a guide helping you recognize the kind of information the reader needs to understand your idea, while eliminating material that doesn't relate clearly to your topic. As you continue to learn more about your subject, the controlling purpose may have to change. Perhaps the material that you need to support your topic cannot be found. Perhaps you come across other material that you prefer to use, but it doesn't fit your original plan. Don't hestitate to make changes when such things happen. A researcher must be flexible.

Having decided on their respective topics, Sara, Margaret, and Phil now need to determine an attitude about their topics to produce a controlling purpose. Sara is sure the Loch Ness monster exists, but she cannot prove it with the evidence she has found thus far. Rather than try to prove the monster does or does not exist, Sara decides to show her readers that increased efforts by scientists point toward its existence. Thus she has given her research efforts a focus.

Margaret knows that Anderson's use of symbols in *Winesburg, Ohio* interests her because she sees a pattern in them. She isn't sure she understands the symbols, however, so she thinks that a comparison of her own ideas about them with the ideas of literary critics may show her whether she is right. Because she feels the symbols develop Anderson's characters in the book, she decides to try to examine their effect on characterization in Anderson's writing.

Phil becomes more and more enthusiastic about Prairie style houses as he locates several of them in his community. He wonders why more houses of this style weren't built in the neighborhood. He decides to combine a description of the growth of Prairie architecture in the community with an analysis of why that growth came to an end.

At this point, then, the controlling purposes of Sara, Margaret, and Phil read like this:

- Sara: How are modern methods of discovery helping to prove the existence of the Loch Ness monster?
- Margaret: What are the contributions of the symbols in Sherwood Anderson's *Winesburg, Ohio* to his development of characters?

I love being a writer. What I can't stand is the paperwork.
Peter De Vries

• Phil: Which houses are examples of the Prairie style in this community and why weren't more of them built?

At this point in your research-paper project, the controlling purpose should be thought of as a rough guideline. Phrasing it as a question will help you focus your research toward the answer; nevertheless, you will very likely do more investigation than will be needed for your paper.

• **EXERCISE 2.** Spend some time thinking about and doing preliminary research on two of the topics you developed in Exercise 1. Write a statement to express a controlling purpose for each of them. Phrase each controlling purpose as a one-sentence question. Be prepared to explain to your class how the controlling purpose narrows the topic and how it illustrates an attitude toward that topic. For example, if the topic is the works of Jackson Pollock, the controlling purpose might be: How do Pollock's later works forecast a new direction in the development of abstract art in the United States?

Decide on the topic and controlling purpose that you wish to research for your paper. Keep in mind that it is a preliminary controlling purpose and may change as your research develops new directions for investigation.

PART 2

Step Two: Locating Information

Once you have established the preliminary controlling purpose of your research paper, you are ready to begin in earnest locating information to support it. This process is the foundation of research. Finding information is something that you have been doing all your life, of course, but for a research paper you must restrict your search to a specific topic. It may help you to remember that there are only three ways of gaining information: personal observation and experimentation, listening to other people, and reading. While all three methods may be required for your research paper, reading will usually dominate your investigation.

Sara, Margaret, and Phil had already begun to locate information when they developed a preliminary controlling purpose. Each of them used what he or she already knew to formulate a topic. Sara has read a magazine article that she might be able to use in her paper. Margaret has already read *Winesburg, Ohio*. She will need to reread it with her controlling purpose in mind. Phil has read three books on Frank Lloyd Wright and one on architects who adapted his designs. He is familiar with one example of Prairie style architecture, and in a brief conversation with the owner of the house he has learned the addresses of several other houses to look at.

All three students now turn to the school library in their search for other possible sources of information. Each will make a *working bibliography*: a list of books, articles, pamphlets, and other sources that are likely to deal with their topics. The students won't be absolutely sure just how useful each source is until it has been located and examined. The working bibliography is thus a list of potential sources, some of which will actually contribute to the research paper and some of which will not. Those that are used in the paper will be cited in a list of sources at the end of the paper; this final list is called a *bibliography*. (See **Bibliography** in the Appendix.)

Your working bibliography will come from these sources in the library:

The card catalog. Use the card catalog to locate books on your topic. Check under all the headings you can think of that relate to your subject. Sara looks under "Loch Ness," "Monsters," "Scotland," and "Prehistoric Animals." When she decides that a book sounds useful, she adds it to her list, writing down author, title, publication information, and the library call number. (See **Card catalog** in the Language Handbook.)

The Readers' Guide to Periodical Literature. The *Guide* lists articles from over 150 magazines. Sara finds a number of recent articles by checking the *Guide*, but Margaret has no luck at all, for her topic, symbolism in *Winesburg, Ohio*, doesn't seem to fit the *Guide*'s sources. Phil locates two articles under the heading of "Prairie Style Architecture" in the *Guide*: one in *House and Garden* and the other in *American Heritage*. Whatever your topic, add to your list articles that you think will be useful, writing down the author (if given), title (in quotes), name of magazine (underlined), volume number, date, and page numbers.

Other magazine indexes. Specialized magazines are sometimes indexed in a form similar to the *Readers' Guide*. For example, Margaret finds articles about Anderson in the *Humanities Index*, which lists articles from journals and periodicals in such subject areas as literature, language, philosophy, religion, the performing arts, archaeology, history, and folklore. Sara locates material that may help her in the *General Science Index*, which lists articles from 89 periodicals in the sciences. Phil is able to find possible sources in the *Social Science Index*, which covers articles from over 200 publications in the social sciences, including anthropology, medicine, psychology, political science, economics, environmental science, geography, law, and sociology.

Other major magazine indexes include the *Education Index*, which lists articles in education magazines, and *Consumer Index*, a guide to articles on consumer information in 107 magazines. Ask your librarian for other magazine index possibilities. Although *National Geographic* has published two volumes that index its own articles, one from 1888 to 1946, the other from 1947 to 1976, most magazines do not publish their own indexes. But many magazines annually include an index in the last edition of a volume that lists the articles published during that year.

The New York Times Index. This index lists alphabetically summaries of articles appearing in the *New York Times*. If the summary sounds appropriate, check to see if your library has the complete article on microfilm. Volume, date, page, and column where the article appears in an edition are listed after the summary. If the article appears in a Sunday edition, a Roman numeral is used to identify the section of the paper in which it can be found. Sara finds this entry in the *Index* for 1976:

> **LOCH Ness Expedition, Academy of Applied Science/New York Times. See also** Loch Ness Monster
> **LOCH Ness Monster**
> ....
> **Academy of Applied Science (Boston, Mass) and NY Times to undertake most thorough and technologically sophisticated investigation to date in order to identify elusive and unexplained phenomenon usually referred to as Loch Ness Monster; . . .** (L), My 28,1:5; . . .

The symbols My 28, 1:5 tell Sara that she will find the complete article in the May 28 edition of the newspaper on page one, column 5. The symbols (S), (M), and (L) are used to indicate the length of the article: short, medium, or long.

Most other newspapers are not formally indexed. If you are investigating a topic in which newspaper research is likely to be significant, check with the librarian about other newspaper indexes. Even though such indexes may not be available, some librarians recommend the *New York Times Index* as a useful guide for locating articles in other newspapers on the same day or slightly later, especially when the news article has had national or international scope.

The Vertical File Index. Published monthly, this index lists pamphlets that have been published on a broad variety of topics. Many of these pamphlets will be on file in your library's vertical or pamphlet file, usually in large filing cabinet drawers. If you want a pamphlet that is not in the file, the *Index* will tell you where to send for it and will indicate if there is a charge.

The Monthly Catalog of United States Government Publications. This source lists additional pamphlet titles published by the United States Government Printing Office. You can locate these pamphlets the same way you do those in the *Vertical File Index*.

Encyclopedias. A general encyclopedia, usually published in several volumes, contains articles on a broad variety of topics, usually written by experts in the various fields of knowledge that are included. Some well-known general encyclopedias include *Encyclopedia Americana, Collier's Encyclopedia, Compton's Encyclopedia, Encyclopaedia Britannica, Encyclopedia International, Merit Students Encyclopedia,* and *World Book Encyclopedia*. Each is published in a number of volumes. One-volume encyclopedias of general information include the *New Columbia Encyclopedia* and *Random House Encyclopedia.*

Encyclopedia articles are sometimes too general to supply the specific information that you may need for a research paper. But they can be useful in supplying background information on a topic that may give you ideas about further developing it. And the articles often contain a list of other reading on the subject. An encyclopedia article on

Frank Lloyd Wright, for example, leads Phil to several books that will possibly contribute to his investigation of Prairie style architecture.

A specialized encyclopedia, which may be published in several volumes or as a single book, contains articles on a specific field of knowledge. Like a general encyclopedia, it may be most helpful in providing background information on a topic and leading the researcher to further material. The range of specialized encyclopedias is remarkable. Here are a few examples: *Encyclopedia of Bioethics, Encyclopedia of Environmental Sciences, Encyclopedia of Human Behavior, Encyclopaedia Judaica, Encyclopedia of Philosophy, Encyclopedia of Transportation, Encyclopedia of Witchcraft and Demonology.*

Dictionaries. Dictionaries define words and phrases. While you may use a standard dictionary to establish a working definition of an important word or phrase in your research, other dictionaries of a more specialized nature may also be useful. Margaret uses the *Dictionary of Symbols* to gather background information about the general symbolic meaning of three of Anderson's symbols in *Winesburg, Ohio:* hands, walls, and rain.

Book Review Digest. This index lists the reviews that were published about a book upon its first appearance. Annual volumes have been published since 1905. Margaret looks under Anderson in the 1919 volume and finds a synopsis of six reviews published about *Winesburg, Ohio*, shortly after its publication that year. Three of them will be hard to locate, since they appeared in local newspapers or obscure periodicals, but Margaret finds that the other three appeared in well-known magazines that she can locate.

Other written sources may also provide information for your research paper. Because Margaret's topic is a literary one, her teacher tells her to look for a *critical edition* or a *casebook*. A critical edition contains the complete text of a work of literature–usually a novel but perhaps an epic poem, a collection of lyric poetry, or a work of nonfiction–and a collection of essays and articles about the work. This material has been assembled by an editor to provide the reader with commentary on the literary work along with the text itself. A *casebook* is similar to a critical edition. It does not contain the literary work itself, however, but only essays and articles that have been written about it. A casebook may focus on a specific work of literature or upon one author's collected works.

Margaret is able to locate a critical edition of *Winesburg, Ohio* that contains the text itself plus twenty essays about it by literary critics. She realizes that she has a gold mine of possible information in one location. Indeed, two of the early reviews of *Winesburg, Ohio* that she had discovered in *Book Review Digest* have been reprinted in this critical edition, saving her the trouble of looking for them in the periodicals that originally published them in 1919.

Local newspaper files can sometimes supply information on a topic if you have the patience to look through information that has not been indexed. Phil learns from a book on the history of his community that the weekly newspaper printed detailed reports of Prairie style houses as they were built during the 1920s. The school librarian suggests that he try the public library for its files of that newspaper, or even the local newspaper office itself. Some newspaper offices will permit you to use their libraries–called morgues in newspaper jargon–for independent research projects.

• **EXERCISE 3.** Using the resources discussed in the preceding section, begin to compile a working bibliography for one of the topics and its controlling purpose that you developed in Exercise 2. Divide your source materials into books, periodical articles, encyclopedia and dictionary entries, pamphlets, and a miscellaneous category that might include such items as interviews, personal observations, letters, or even the back covers of record albums. Contribute to a class list of specialized sources that class members have found helpful. Add to this list information about local libraries and other possible sources that you have found useful.

PART 3

Step Three: Reading and Taking Notes

Even before you complete a working bibliography, you probably have begun to read and take notes on the sources you have located. Because you have much to read, you should develop an ability to skim material quickly in order to judge its value to your research paper. As she begins to read for her paper on the Loch Ness monster, Sara uses a number of techniques that enable her to skim the material quickly to determine its relevance to her paper.

The first potential source that Sara discovers in her search for material is a book that she locates under the subject heading "Monsters" in the card catalog of her school library. Its title, *In Search of Lake Monsters,* and another heading, "Loch Ness Monster," that the card catalog lists for the same book, suggest to Sara that the book may be useful. She locates the book on the library shelf and sits down to skim through it for a few minutes. First she checks the publication date; it is 1974, which suggests that the book contains reasonably recent material on her topic. Next she looks at the table of contents. The book is divided into eighteen chapters, three of which seem to pertain directly to Sara's topic as suggested by the chapter titles: "Loch Ness Enigma: a Real Monster?", "Loch Ness Enigma: in Eclipse," and "Loch Ness Enigma: Under Survey."

Before she turns to these chapters, however, Sara checks the back of the book to see whether it has an index. A five-page index includes the entry "Loch Ness Monster" and refers her to pages in the chapters on that topic plus one or two other places in the book. Sara also looks to see if the book includes a bibliography, which she finds just before the index. She finds a number of entries in the twelve-page bibliography that seem to refer to the Loch Ness monster. But several of the titles are in foreign languages, many others seem to come from old English and Scottish newspapers, and most of the books about the Loch Ness monster carry the names of English publishers. Sara does write down the name of one book published in the United States and the title of one article that appeared in *Harper's Magazine* in 1956. But she decides not to write down the other possible sources for her working bibliography yet because they may be unobtainable and she can always return to *In Search of Lake Monsters* if she decides to utilize its bibliography later on.

After looking at the chapter headings, index, and bibliography, Sara begins to read the introduction and the pertinent chapters of the book as quickly as possible. At this stage of her reading, she does not take notes; rather, she looks for basic ideas in the material that will give her a sense of what the book is about and what the author's viewpoint toward the topic seems to be. In skimming the book in this manner, Sara focuses on a number of clues to the content:

• She pays close attention to the topic sentences of paragraphs (often the first sentence of each paragraph), because the topic sentences give her an idea of what the paragraphs are about.

• She looks carefully at the final sentence of a paragraph as another place where the author may make a particularly significant point.

• She watches for subheads within chapters as guidelines to the subtopics into which the author may divide his material.

• She notes that the author is writing in the first person and watches for references to "I" since they express his opinion about the material.

• She keeps an eye on names of persons and places, looking for repetition as a clue to importance.

• She looks carefully at illustrations or charts because they suggest material that the author considers of major importance.

• She watches for words and phrases that imply significance: for example, "Here we have important testimony about the animal's limbs and way of moving."—Peter Costello, *In Search of Lake Monsters* (New York: Coward, McCann & Geoghegan, 1974), p. 36.

• She tries to form an impression of the author's method of organizing his material; in this case he seems to be using a general chronological approach, beginning with early reports of the Loch Ness monster and proceeding to report developments in information about the monster in the time sequence in which they occurred.

Because Sara is still relatively unfamiliar with her topic, this first job of skimming a source is a somewhat slow process for her. But as she becomes more and more familiar with the basic material on the topic, she will be able to skim more quickly because she will not have to pause to recognize basic information that will repeat itself on occasion. For example, the first time Sara encounters the word *plesiosaur*, she has to slow down to determine just what it is. But after that, the word does not cause her to hesitate.

Art is limitation; the essence of every picture is the frame.
G. K. Chesterton

After skimming the three chapters of *In Search of Lake Monsters* that deal with her topic, Sara pauses to recall what the author is saying. It seems to her that he is trying to summarize information about the monster from the earliest reports about it until the early 1970s, when his book was published. She realizes that the first chapter on the monster recounts some of the early reports of its existence but dates the first serious modern interest in it from 1933, when a number of sightings provoked an interest by British newspapers and magazines. Early photographs encouraged that interest, Sara notes. The second chapter seems to Sara to develop the theories of a number of zoologists and other naturalists about the monster. The third chapter continues to emphasize scientific efforts to find the monster by reporting the first real expeditions for that purpose. On page 97 Sara notices a quote made in 1962 that seems significant: "The Loch Ness monster is no longer the silly [tourist] season joke it once was, but a serious problem receiving careful investigation." By the end of this chapter, she remembers, the author has begun to summarize his report on the monster, and she makes a mental note to review that last part of his material carefully when she rereads the chapters.

Having taken an hour to complete the process of skimming about one hundred pages of *In Search of Lake Monsters*, Sara decides the source is worth taking notes on for a number of reasons:

- She understands the author's material fairly well. Because she doesn't have to struggle to figure out what he is saying, she feels she can cope with this topic.
- She believes that the author has given a good deal of information in a relatively brief space. He has referred to much of the earlier literature on the monster, saving her the difficulty of finding it for herself.
- She thinks the author has stressed the scientific efforts at discovering the monster rather than individual speculations about its identity. Sara feels that she would like to emphasize similar material in her own paper.

Note Taking Returning to the book the next day, Sara is now prepared to take notes on the chapters she has skimmed. Note taking puzzles some students who don't see why they simply cannot pile the books and magazines in front of them and write a paper directly from the sources at hand. There are three main reasons this approach won't work: (1) Some sources cannot be taken out of the library. Some material may be photocopied, of course, but that can be expensive. (2) Spreading out the contents of many sources may be confusing. Writing the paper will require that you zigzag from source to source, and the sheer bulk of material from perhaps fifteen different places would get in your way. (3) Merely stacking up the sources prevents any assimilation of their content, an essential process that must precede the writing of your paper.

The third reason really explains the major value of taking notes. In writing a research paper, you draw upon a number of sources, using them to support your controlling purpose. Although you did not generate the source material, you have provided the idea for the paper, and such an idea requires a unique framework upon which to develop the points you are going to make. Therefore you will need to reprocess the sources in order to make them support your ideas; the original sources cannot simply be left as they were first written because in that form they supported someone else's ideas. So the note-taking process begins the effort at building something new—your research paper—from material that exists in a number of scattered places.

As you take notes, you will need to fill out two kinds of cards: *bibliography cards* and *note cards*. Your cards should measure 3″ x 5″ or 4″ x 6″; a heavy brown packet or envelope will keep them neat. You might use colored bibliography cards and white note cards for easy distinction. Use ink because pencil will smudge as the cards are handled.

Each source that might go into your paper must be listed on a bibliography card, which should be filled out before you begin to take notes on that source. Here are samples from Sara's cards to show the correct form for books and magazines:

Bibliography card for a book:

Source number	②
Author	Meredith, Dennis L.
Title	Search at Loch Ness
Publisher	Quadrangle Books/The New York Times Book Company
Place and date	New York, 1977
Call number, location	001.944 CHS Library

Bibliography card for a magazine article:

	③
Author	Ellis, William S.
Title	"Loch Ness: The lake and the legend"
Magazine	National Geographic
Volume and Pages	Vol. 151, No. 6 pp. 759-779
Date	June 1977
Location	Personal copy

For encyclopedia articles, dictionary entries, and pamphlets, follow the form shown in these samples from Phil's and Margaret's cards:

Bibliography card for an encyclopedia article:

Author	(no author)	①
Title	"Wright, Frank Lloyd"	
Encyclopedia	Encyclopaedia Britannica (Macropaedia)	
Volume and Pages	Volume 19, p. 1029	
Place and Date	Chicago, 1979	
Location	MHS library	

Bibliography card for a dictionary entry:

Author	Cirlot, J. E.	①
Title	"Hand"	
Dictionary	A Dictionary of Symbols	
Volume and Pages	(no volume) pp. 130-131	
Publisher	Philosophical Library	
Place and Date	New York, 1962	
Location	CHS library	

Bibliography card for a pamphlet:

Author	(no author)	②
Title	"Evanston Architecture: a Sampler of Self-Guided Tours"	
Publisher	City of Evanston Planning Dept.	
Place and Date	Evanston, Ill., 1974	
Location	Evanston Public Library	

Note that when information is not available from a particular source, as in the encyclopedia and pamphlet cards (no author) and the dictionary card (no volume number), Phil and Margaret indicate the absence of this information. In that way they won't think they've forgotten to list the information when they come to it later.

Because several of his sources will be personal interviews, Phil needs to develop a bibliography card for an interview:

	③
Interview subject	Keith, Catherine V.
Interview topic	Personal interview about her Prairie style home, 2227 Simpson Street, Evanston, Illinois
Date	Feb. 4, 1980
Location	Evanston, Illinois (taped)

Phil indicates on the card that he taped the interview.

For essays from a casebook or critical edition, use the form illustrated by this card from Margaret's packet:

	②
Author	Rideout, Walter B.
Title	"The Simplicity of Winesburg, Ohio"
Book, Editor, Pages	Sherwood Anderson's Winesburg, Ohio: Text and Criticism, ed. John H. Ferres, pp 287-300.
Publisher	The Viking Press
Place and Date	New York, 1966
Call number	813/AN
Location	CHS library

Notice that each bibliography card has been given a circled identification number in the upper right corner. This *source number* is different for each bibliography card. It is a kind of code that facilitates your reference work. Thus, if you fill out twenty-three bibliography cards, number them from 1 to 23. The call number and location abbreviation at the bottom of each card will tell you where to find the source should you need to return to it for additional notes.

As you begin to read and take notes, be sure to put the source number from the bibliography card on all the note cards taken from that source. If the source of bibliography card number 14 produces twenty note cards, each note card should have the number 14 in the upper right corner. When you begin to shuffle the cards in the process of organizing your paper, that number will tell you the source of each note, making it easier for you to give proper footnote and bibliography credit.

Once you have skimmed a source to determine its value for your paper, you are ready to begin taking notes on it. Be selective. Take notes only when you think you might be able to use the material. Granted, that's difficult to predict at this early stage of research, and you'll find yourself with more notes than you need at times. But as you polish your research skills, you will become a keener judge of just what to take notes on.

Besides the source number, each note card you fill out needs a heading of some kind, called a guideline (sometimes called a slug or slugline), and the page number from which you have taken notes. The guideline should suggest a subtopic of your paper. For example, (using LNM as an abbreviation for Loch Ness monster), Sara uses guidelines such as *Origins of LNM, LNM Sightings, Photographing LNM,* and *LNM Biological Theories*. Here is an example of a note card that she fills out from *In Search of Lake Monsters:*

Source number

Guideline
Note

Echo-soundings of LNM ①

ship Rival III obtained e-s of large object 480 feet below surface December '54; technicians examined graph: said it seemed to be one large object, not a shoal of fish.... E-s do not show object shape— only presence, size, density

Page number
Comment by Sara

p. 82
[he doesn't fully define an e-s]

On this note card Sara includes the source number of the bibliography card to tell her from which source the note comes. She abbreviates the information she wants as much as she can: for example, *e-s* for *echo-sounding*. She is careful to specify the page number on which the material is found so that she can footnote it properly if she uses it in her research paper. And she adds a reminder to herself in brackets at the bottom of the card to indicate that she isn't quite sure just what an echo-sounding is.

Except for material that you think you might quote directly, the note cards should be filled out in your own words, not those of the source. Direct quotes will not appear frequently in your paper, so copy them sparingly on note cards. Quote directly only when you feel that the author's style is as valuable as the meaning. Sometimes a direct quote conveys more authority from a source than a rephrasing would. But be careful to quote exactly every word and punctuation mark, and enclose the words in quotation marks so that you remember they are quoted directly. Sara wants to keep the flavor of this description from *In Search of Lake Monsters* of a land sighting of the Loch Ness monster:

Source number

Guideline

Direct Quote

LNM Sightings ①
Arthur Grant, medical student, Jan. 5, 1934:
"I had a splendid view of the object. In fact, I almost struck it with my motorcycle. It had a long neck and large oval-shaped eyes on the top of a small head. The tail would be from five to six feet long and very powerful; the curious thing about it was that the end was rounded off; it did not come to a point. .... Knowing something of natural history, I can say that I have never seen anything in my life like the animal I saw. It looked like a hybrid—a cross between a plesiosaur and a member of the seal family."
P. 46

Note that the ellipsis within the quote reminds Sara–and alerts the reader–that something has been omitted from the quotation. (See **Ellipsis** in the Language Handbook.)

Most of your notes will not be verbatim quotes from a source. Rather, they will be rephrased versions of that source in your own words. You will wish to take advantage of the paraphrase and the précis as forms of restating material when you take notes. (See **Paraphrase** and **Précis** in the Language Handbook.) A paraphrase involves a restatement of the author's ideas in your own words and simplified form. Read the source two or three times; then develop a version that says essentially the same thing in your own language. The result forces you to understand what you have read because you have rewritten it in words more natural to you. Here is an example from Sara's research:

> *Original version:* "There is no need to invent a new animal to explain the beast. As many have said, the beast in the loch has a remarkable resemblance to a plesiosaur, a long-necked, flippered reptile that hunted fish in ancient seas. One particular type of plesiosaur, the elasmosaur, is the best candidate of the lot. The elasmosaur, with its extremely long neck, containing 76 vertebrae, and its broad, flat, inflexible trunk has been described as looking like a snake pulled through the body of a turtle. It flourished during the Cretaceous Period from 135 million to 65 million years ago, apparently dying out in the mysterious cataclysm that abruptly ended the golden age for dinosaurs.
>
> At 40 feet, the elasmosaur was the right length to be the beast in the loch. And, as with the beast in the loch, it propelled itself with pow-

erful strokes of its large flippers, its round body and stubby tail being of little use in swimming. Although many plesiosaurs had long lizard-like heads, the elasmosaur possessed a smaller, rounder head as the beast is said to have. The elasmosaur fed on fish, whipping its long neck through the water to snare its prey. The beast in the loch has been seen to behave similarly. Many have reported sighting the hump of the beast, floating motionless in the water, suddenly dashing off and submerging, as if the animal were making a quick lunge to snare a fish."—Dennis Meredith, *Search at Loch Ness* (New York: Quadrangle, 1977), pp. 120–121.

Sara's note card paraphrase:

Biological theory—elasmosaur ②

Many believe LNM a plesiosaur, flippered reptile with long neck. Elasmosaur, a type of plesiosaur, seems most like LNM. It has long neck (76 vertebrae) and broad, flat trunk. Lived during Cretaceous period, from 135 to 65 million years ago. 40 ft. long—same size as LNM moved with flippers as LNM appears to do. Had small round head, as LNM seems to. Fed on fish, using neck to reach for them—LNM seems to do this. May explain sudden movement of humps: LNM lunging to snare fish.

pp. 120-121

While a paraphrase restates the author's ideas in your own words, a précis summarizes those ideas. It produces a condensed version of the original material by concentrating on the main idea of the author and omitting most examples and illustrations. Supporting details do not go into a précis; the main points may simply be listed on your note cards or phrased in sentence form. Here is another paragraph from Sara's research in Meredith's book:

Original version: "Despite the remarkable similarities between the beast in the loch and the elasmosaur, there are "minor" difficulties. For one thing, an elasmosaur–beast would have had to survive without detection during centuries of human exploration of the oceans, no mean feat for an air-breathing creature. Also, paleontologists have pointed out that skeletal remains of plesiosaurs indicate that they could not raise their flippers above the level of their shoulders. This means that they were probably poor divers, spending most of their time paddling about on the surface of ancient seas—very unlike the beast in the loch, which is seldom seen on the surface. And, finally, plesiosaurs were warm–water creatures, presumably unable to regulate their internal temperature to adapt to the frigid waters found in Loch Ness."—Meredith, *Search at Loch Ness*, p. 121.

Sara's note card précis:

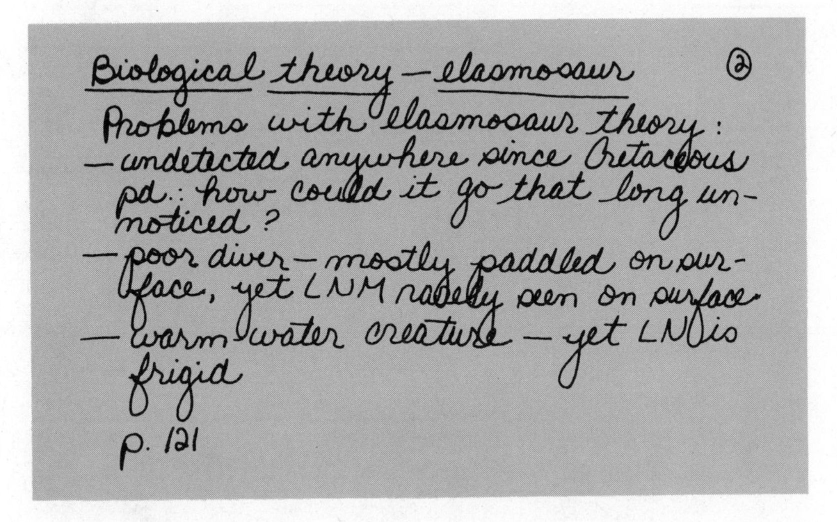
Biological theory—elasmosaur ②

Problems with elasmosaur theory:
—undetected anywhere since Cretaceous pd.: how could it go that long un-noticed?
—poor diver—mostly paddled on sur-face, yet LNM rarely seen on surface.
—warm water creature—yet LN is frigid

p. 121

As you take notes, be sure to distinguish between authors' facts and their opinions. Sara's material usually makes this distinction clear. She distinguishes between fact and opinion by underlining the author's opinions to separate them from the other information. Here is another note card Sara takes from *Search at Loch Ness*:

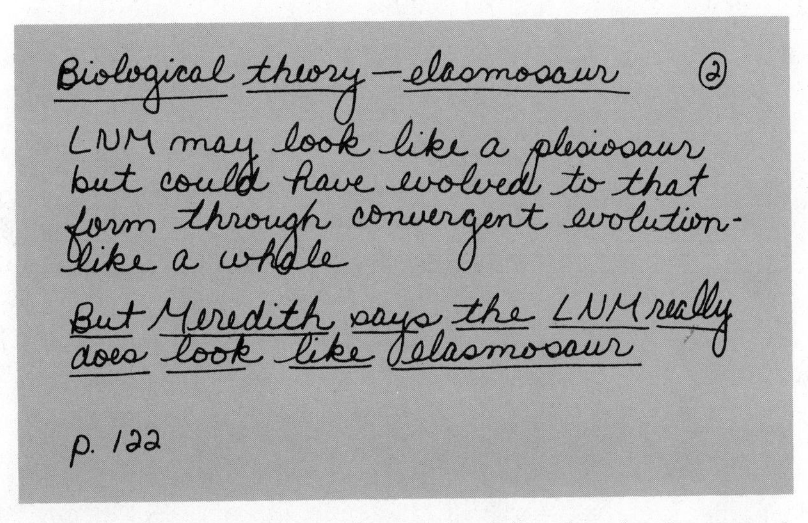
Biological theory—elasmosaur ②

LNM may look like a plesiosaur but could have evolved to that form through convergent evolution-like a whale

But Meredith says the LNM really does look like elasmosaur

p. 122

Margaret's sources express far more opinion than fact because of the nature of her topic, symbolism in Sherwood Anderson's *Winesburg, Ohio*. She deals directly with opinion on her note cards by citing by name the critic whose viewpoint she is summarizing. The following note card is drawn from a casebook article about the characters in *Winesburg, Ohio*.–[Irving Howe, "The Book of the Grotesque," *Winesburg, Ohio*: *Text and Criticism*, edited by John H. Ferres (New York: Viking, 1966), p. 413]:

Grotesques characterized (16)

Howe distinguishes between Anderson's grotesques and clods:

— grotesques: have sought the "truths" that disfigure them

— clods: unaware of such "truths"

— never tried; perhaps never realized

— those in charge are clods, as Will Henderson

p. 413

Phil's material deals mostly with fact but involves some hypothetical comment. He separates straight fact from opinion, judgment, or hypothesis by drawing a vertical line down the middle of a note card that includes both kinds of comment from a person he has interviewed:

Keith house—living room (3)

alternating brick—one row of dark red, one of light—used on fireplace, fpl. wall, and entire floor of lvrm.	C.K. got tired of that design after few years; clashed w/art collection

When you add a comment of your own to a note card, set it off with brackets (see Sara's note card, page 226) or perhaps a different color of ink. You may wish to add your own comment to a card for several reasons:

• You may not understand something that you are taking notes on; Sara made a note on her card that the author hadn't defined *echo-sounding*. She realizes that she will need to provide a definition, so she reminds herself via the comment in brackets.

• You may question or disagree with an opinion being expressed. Margaret finds herself doing this quite often because she is trying to match her own opinions on *Winesburg, Ohio* with those of critics.

• You may think of another subtopic that could be added to your paper as you read something that you haven't thought about before. Writing your idea down at once will preserve it for later consideration.

Accuracy and thoroughness in taking notes will save you the job of rechecking sources if doubts occur to you later. Accept the fact that you will not use all your notes in the paper when the time comes to write it. But do not overdo the note-taking process–quantity is not really the point here. The development of note cards offers you a means of thinking through your material and accumulating evidence for your research paper.

• **EXERCISE 4.**

A. Complete your bibliography cards from the list of working bibliography sources that you have developed. Compare with other members of your class the difference between the number of possible sources on your working bibliography list and the number of bibliography cards you actually have filled out. What are the reasons for this difference?

B. Verify correct form for bibliography cards by exchanging cards with two or three of your classmates and checking each others' accuracy in form.

C. Discuss any unusual form problems in class by illustrating on the chalkboard examples of each kind of bibliography source that class members have encountered in their research.

D. Take notes from any sources that appear to supply useful evidence for your research. Discuss note–taking problems of an unusual nature in class, using the chalkboard to illustrate approaches to note taking.

E. Submit bibliography cards and note cards once or twice to your teacher for verification of correct form and as evidence that you have completed your research.

PART 4

Step Four: Organizing the Paper

Before you begin to write your research paper, you must organize your notes into a logical framework. The guidelines on your note cards will facilitate the arrangement of your material into a coherent outline.

Sara begins the organizing process by sorting her note cards. She first lays the cards out in piles according to the guidelines she has used at the tops of the cards: Origins of the LNM, LNM Sightings, Photographing the LNM, LNM Biological Theories, and so forth. Margaret and Phil do the same.

The next step is to consider the organization of these divisions based on the controlling purpose of the paper. While you have taken notes with this controlling purpose in mind, you may have also changed your focus as you uncovered research material that suggested a shift in emphasis or subject matter. At this point you should review your notes to confirm your final controlling purpose. Although Sara's original controlling purpose was phrased as a question, she will now need to rephrase it as a statement.

When Sara began her research, she established this controlling purpose: How are modern methods of discovery helping to prove the existence of the Loch Ness monster? In reviewing her notes, she decides to make two changes. First, she inserts the word *scientific* in place of *modern*, for she has been impressed by the application of scientific methods to the search for the Loch Ness monster. Second, she realizes that the word *prove* is too strong, for absolute proof of the monster's existence remains unestablished at this point in Sara's research. So she rephrases her controlling purpose from a question to a statement as follows: *Controlling Purpose*: to suggest that scientific methods of detection are increasing the possibility of discovering and identifying the Loch Ness monster.

The crucial phrase here is *to suggest* because it controls precisely what Sara will need to do in her paper. Consider these other possible verbs for your controlling purpose: *analyze, compare and contrast, describe, discuss, examine, explain, explore, show.* Each of them has a precise meaning. Therefore you must select the verb carefully, because it commits you to doing just what it says. If you are going to *analyze*, for example, you will break your subject into parts and look at each part in relation to its contribution to the whole, since that is what *analysis* means.

Once you have established the controlling purpose, you are ready to set up the parts of the outline. Your teacher may require a *topic outline* or a *sentence outline*—or perhaps both. A topic outline divides your material in a manner somewhat as your guidelines have done; it uses single words and phrases as subheads. In a sentence outline, each point, major or minor, is a complete sentence. (See **Outline form** in the Language Handbook.)

Looking for a logical way to organize her material, Sara decides that because she will examine the search for the Loch Ness monster, she needs to organize her paper in a pattern that first describes the background of the phenomenon and then discusses the current theories about its existence. She establishes several basic points as she looks through her note cards. Then she determines just what can be developed under each point. Some of the material will not fit under any point, so she puts that material aside.

As Sara organizes her paper by putting her note cards into piles, she sees that her major divisions will not be of equal length. Nor do they need to be. She has more notes about sightings of the Loch Ness monster than about its supposed eating habits, for example. She tests the outline structure by rearranging points to see if they fit better. In listing the various theories about what kind of animal the monster might be, she considers a chronological order that would deal with the theories in the order in which they were reported. But rejecting that structure as artificial, Sara decides to list the theories in the order of the scientific evidence that supports them, from the least scientific to the most scientific. This order seems to Sara to fit the direction of her paper, which will emphasize the scientific developments in the search for the monster. Eventually she decides on these major outline divisions or heads:

I. Introduction
II. Historical Background and Sightings of the Loch Ness Monster
III. Concrete Evidence of the Monster's Existence
IV. Theories About the Nature and Behavior of the Monster
V. Conclusion

The three body divisions of Sara's outline (II, III, and IV) plus the introduction (I) and the conclusion (V) make up the five major sections in her outline. This organization should allow adequate subdivision of the paper without imposing a structure that treats every point as a major one. Seven or eight major sections would probably be too many for a paper of this length, for the material under each point would be brief and the treatment necessarily superficial. Two or three major sections might be too few because the direction in which the research moved would be minimal.

Now that she has determined the major sections, piling up her note cards accordingly, Sara subdivides each section of her outline. For example, she first divides section III, Concrete Evidence of the Monster's Existence, in this way:

A. Still photographs of the Loch Ness monster
B. Motion picture of the Loch Ness monster
C. Sonar tracings of the Loch Ness monster

But her research indicates to Sara that the sonar tracings are the most important evidence of the monster's existence, so she develops that section by further subdivision, deciding to omit references to the early still photographs altogether because such photographs could so easily be doctored or faked. Now her subdivision of section III looks like this:

A. Motion picture of the Loch Ness monster
B. Sonar tracings of the Loch Ness monster
    1. Early recordings by boats on the loch
    2. The 1972 Rines expedition
    3. The 1975 Rines expedition

Sara makes similar decisions about the rest of her paper, and her outline eventually reads as follows:

I. Introduction
    A. Background on Loch Ness
    B. Legendary reports of the Loch Ness monster
    C. Thesis
II. Modern Sightings of the Loch Ness Monster
    A. Single sightings
        1. 1934 Grant and Campbell reports
        2. 1938 MacLean report
        3. 1963 report
        4. Sightings on land
    B. Multiple sightings
    C. Loch Ness Investigation Bureau
III. Scientific Evidence About the Loch Ness Monster
    A. Evidence on film
    B. Sonar tracings
        1. Early recordings
        2. 1972 expedition
        3. 1975 expedition
IV. Biological Theories About the Monster
    A. Efforts to identify the monster
        1. Sea slug
        2. Marine bristle worm
        3. Eel
        4. Sirenian mammal
        5. Eogyrinus
        6. Elasmosaur
    B. Loch origin of monster
    C. Survival problems
V. Conclusion
    A. Composite portrait of the monster
    B. Evidence supporting its existence

Notice that in Sara's outline the number of subheads under each major section is not equal; rather, they vary with the amount of information she has to report. Notice how each section is divided; an A requires at least a B; a 1 requires at least a 2. In other words, there should always be two or more subtopics, or none at all. Since Sara will include evidence about only one motion picture, she cannot cite it as a 1 under section III–A, for she would have no 2 to follow it.

Phil's teacher requires a sentence outline, but his organizing process is similar to Sara's. He sorts his note cards into piles that enable him to develop a sequence that follows his controlling purpose of describing the Prairie style houses in his community and the reasons so few of them were built. Phil sets up a four-part outline. Besides an introduction and a conclusion, it includes two sections, one that describes six examples of Prairie style houses in Phil's community, and another that examines the reasons why more Prairie style houses were not built. Phil's sentence outline for this latter section reads as follows:

III. Prairie style houses were not built in the community after 1927, although a few modified versions were constructed after World War II.
   A. For many home builders and owners, Prairie style houses were regarded as too <u>avant garde.</u>
      1. Mediterranean, Greek Revival, and other styles were preferred as safer status symbols by most of the wealthy who built homes during the 1920s.
      2. Many people employed an architect on the basis of his prestige and followed his decision about the kind of home to be built.
         a. Most Prairie style architects did not have much prestige.
         b. Wright enjoyed great prestige, but he was also a highly controversial personality.
   B. Population and economic changes during the 1920s affected the construction of larger homes, including Prairie style houses.
      1. Improved public transportation and an increase in land costs combined to cause a sharp rise in the construction of apartment buildings instead of houses.
      2. Communities to the north began to increase their upper-middle class populations, and Prairie style houses began to be built there.
   C. The arrival of the Depression in 1929 stopped most home building for the next decade; World War II continued to prevent it until 1945.
   D. A few modified versions of Prairie style houses have been built since World War II.
      1. These houses are much smaller because

of construction costs and limits of lot sizes.
2. They do not use many of the same building materials as the true Prairie style houses.
3. Most new homes are mass-produced by contractors, who use simplified designs that will appeal to large numbers of people.

Although Phil's outline has four major sections, one fewer than Sara's, his outline looks longer than hers because each point is a complete sentence. He finds the outline harder to write than a topic outline would have been. But he sees that many of the sentences in his outline can now be transferred to his research paper as topic sentences for paragraphs. He also sees that he has developed many transitions in the outline that can be repeated in the paper itself. (See **Transitions** in the Language Handbook.)

• **EXERCISE 5.**

A. Determine if the original controlling purpose is still appropriate for the paper you will write. If necessary, adjust your controlling purpose to suit your change of emphasis.

B. Organize your note cards into a logical pattern from which you can develop an outline for your research paper. Consider two or three possible arrangements of your material.

C. Write an outline, either topic or sentence, depending upon which is most useful to you and which your instructor specifies.

D. In class, some students may write their outlines on the chalkboard and defend them as the most effective framework for their research. Compare the structure of your outline with those of your classmates. Look for weak spots in logic; check sequence and repetition; review the amount and variety of evidence and determine whether it supports the controlling purpose.

E. Before you submit your outline to your teacher for final approval, ask two or three classmates to read it for continuity and logic.

PART 5

Step Five: Writing the First Draft

As you sit down to write the first draft of your paper–often called the rough draft–develop an image of who your readers are so that you can use a writing style to suit them. Perhaps you feel your teacher is your only real reader, since the teacher will grade the paper. Your teacher will judge it, however, not simply by whether it appeals to him or her, but by whether it is clear and interesting to a general, uninformed reader. The style must be straightforward and not slangy or full of jargon. You will need a semiformal manner but not a stuffy or pedantic one.

Now may be the time to consider whether to bring yourself into the paper. Sara has strong opinions that the Loch Ness monster really does exist, but her research comes entirely from written sources. She may include an "in my opinion" phrase for emphasis and to separate her judgment from that of her sources, but that will be the limit of her direct appearance in the paper. Margaret believes some of Anderson's symbols in *Winesburg, Ohio* are weakly developed, but she feels that she can point this out while writing entirely in the third person. Phil, however, has done a great deal of personal research by visiting all six of the homes he will describe. Since much of what he will say comes from his eyewitness viewpoint, he may need to bring himself quite conspicuously into his paper. For example, he tries out these observations in his first draft:

> Like most Prairie style houses, the Keith house uses brick extensively on the interior as well as the exterior. The living room, for example, features a floor of alternating brick (a row of dark red brick, then a row of light red brick) that continues up the entire north wall dominated by the fireplace. The floor looked worn in spots to me, but the wall seemed untouched by fireplace smoke. Mrs. Keith told me she and her husband had liked the alternating brick pattern at first but eventually grew tired of it. "It clashed with our art collection," she added.(F3)

The "F3" footnote indication at the end of Phil's paragraph tells him he will need a footnote at that point and that the material comes from the source listed on bibliography card number 3.

Using the outline as a guide, write the first draft of your paper as quickly as possible. If the introduction puzzles you now, go on to the body sections and return to it later.

The first draft should be written in your own phrasing as much as possible. Much of this language will come from the note cards and from your outline, if it is a sentence outline. When you encounter material that will need to be footnoted, as Phil did in his paragraph, be sure to mark that spot in your paper with the source number. You will need to add the footnote information on the final draft even though you do not fill it out in detail now.

When you do use material from another source, you must be careful to give it credit in order to avoid plagiarism. In a shorter paper such as a book review, credit is usually given directly in the body of the text. In a longer paper such as this research paper, however, you need to footnote your sources in order to avoid the serious problem of using someone else's research without giving proper credit. Plagiarism problems may grow from the following circumstances:

1. directly copying a passage from a source without giving credit;

2. paraphrasing a source so closely that only a few words or phrases are changed;

3. partially using someone else's ideas and style without giving credit (although you may expand another's idea into one of your own, you still must give credit for the original idea).

Sometimes you will have trouble deciding whether to footnote information. When the material is so general that giving credit to a specific source seems impossible, a footnote may not be needed. Sara does not have to footnote the location of Loch Ness or her hypothesis that there is a lake monster, for example, because the knowledge is so common that to give specific credit would be impossible unless she used a direct quote or a close paraphrase. But she will footnote information about specific sightings of the monster, opinions of experts about the origins of the monster, and theories about its ability to live in the loch.

Margaret will need to cite *Winesburg, Ohio* when she refers to specific passages that she quotes or paraphrases, and she will credit critics whose analyses she employs as evidence. But she will not footnote her own judgments about the effectiveness of Anderson's symbols.

Phil will footnote his interviews with the residents of the houses he describes and the historical information that he obtains to explain how they came to be built and why their popularity was limited. But he will not need to footnote his own descriptions of the Prairie style houses that he visits because he is his own source.

While a missing footnote can constitute plagiarism, a research paper may also be over-footnoted. Generally, several sentences or even a whole paragraph from one source requires only one footnote at the end of the material. (But later on, the source may need to be footnoted again.) A direct quote must always be footnoted, however, even if it's just a few words. Refer to the sample research paper in the Appendix to see the way footnotes should appear in a paper.

• **EXERCISE 6.** Establish guidelines about the style of language in which you and your classmates will write your papers. To what extent will you use technical language and dialect? idiomatic language?

Write the first draft of your research paper.

Is your first draft written mainly in your own words? It should be. Have you included statements of your own opinion, where applicable? If so, is your opinion easily distinguished from that of your sources?

Have you clearly marked each sentence, phrase, or idea that will need to be footnoted in the final draft?

Share some samples of your first draft with classmates by writing excerpts on the chalkboard or discussing them in small groups. Do your classmates have a clear idea of what you are trying to say? If not, make necessary revisions.

Submit the first draft of your paper to your instructor, who will check it for style and structure before you write the final version.

PART 6

Step Six: Writing the Final Draft

With the aid of her teacher, Sara examined the rough draft of her research paper and located certain areas that needed improvement. Her major problem seemed to be wordiness and repetition. Occasionally her writing lacked precision. Her teacher suggested that Sara transpose her first two paragraphs, so that readers would be immediately introduced to the Loch Ness monster and learn the purpose of her paper. Following is the rough draft of the first two paragraphs with Sara's corrections. Notice how, in the edited version, the writing is tighter and more precise, with an opening paragraph that immediately draws the reader's attention.

First Draft

Loch Ness in northern Scotland is the largest freshwater lake in area in Great Britain. It is only about 24 miles long and up to one and a half miles wide and it more than compensates for this small surface area by having a remarkable depth, a maximum reported at 975 and 700 feet deep over much of its length. The sides go down precipitously away from the banks. The bottom has been proven to be mainly a flat, vegetation-free plain of silt. Salmon, sea trout, and elvers get into the loch and from there up several rivers running into it.

The Loch Ness monster has long been considered a myth. It has become more believable in the light of recent eyewitness accounts. Since the 1930s, many eyewitness accounts of this huge aquatic creature have used photographs,

Edited Revision:

The Loch Ness monster, long considered a myth, has become more believable in the light of recent eyewitness accounts. Since the 1930s, many sightings of this huge aquatic creature have been substantiated by photographs, motion pictures, and sonar tracings. Future explorations of the Loch Ness area, along with increasingly sophisticated detection equipment, should verify the existence of at least twenty such creatures.

This creature is named for Loch Ness in northern Scotland, one of the largest freshwater lakes in Great Britain. Although it is only about 24 miles long, and, in places, 1.5 miles wide, the loch is remarkably deep; its maximum depth is reported to be 975 feet, and it is 700 feet deep for much of its length. The sides of the loch slope

Your manuscript is both good and original; but the part that is good is not original, and the part that is original is not good.

Samuel Johnson

motion pictures, or sonar tracings. There will be future explorations of the Loch Ness area. There is also increasingly sophisticated detection equipment. Both of these should verify the existence of twenty creatures like the Loch Ness monster.

downward precipitously from the banks. The bottom is mainly flat, silty, and free of vegetation. Salmon, sea trout, and elvers (young eels) migrate from the sea into the loch and from there up several rivers running into it.

Besides transposing the paragraphs of her introduction, Sara has tightened her writing by using fewer sentences and relying on subordination to bring ideas more closely together. Her revised version of the thesis paragraph contains only three sentences, although the original had six. She retains five sentences in the paragraph about the loch itself but repunctuates, resulting in a more emphatic style that tells the reader what is most important. She also adds a parenthetical definition of "elvers" for readers who may not know that they are young eels. Finally, she changes her outline according to the revision.

• **EXERCISE 7.** Two or three days away from your first draft may help you to review it critically and to see places for improvement in style and content. As you work on the final version of your research paper, refer to the following checklist:

A. Check accuracy of facts.
B. Eliminate deadwood and unnecessary repetition.
C. Be sure your word choice is precise and that you say exactly what you mean to say.
D. Examine the topic sentence of each paragraph to make sure that it covers the entire paragraph. (See **Topic sentence** in the Language Handbook.)
E. Check transitions between paragraphs and between major and minor points. (See **Transitions** in the Language Handbook.)
F. Check for parallel structure within sentences and parts of sentences. (See **Parallel constructions** in the Language Handbook.)
G. Make sure the paper parallels the outline. If it does not, change either the paper or the outline so that they are parallel.
H. Read the paper aloud to yourself to make sure the sentences flow clearly and emphatically.
I. Ask someone else to read the paper as a representative of that general reader you are trying to reach.

Completing the Final Draft Pay particular attention to the final draft of the introduction and conclusion. Each of these sections will be a fairly long paragraph—or perhaps more than one (Sara has used three paragraphs in her introduction), for each must open or close a paper of considerable length. The introduction should develop any background or opening material that will be needed to begin the paper. It should define any terms that will be used throughout the paper. At some point, but not necessarily in the very beginning, the introduction will establish the thesis of the paper in a sentence or two that elaborates upon the controlling purpose of the outline. The introduction will also reveal the structure of the paper by referring to the major divisions of the outline. And it should immediately attract the reader's attention, as does the first paragraph of Sara's introduction. The introduction, then, should provide a reader with a solid understanding of just what your paper is going to do.

The conclusion of your paper needs to answer a basic question: "So what?" In other words, what is the significance of the information that you have just given to your reader? What is it that you wish to persuade the reader to think about your topic? In this final paragraph you may wish to summarize your research. But you also may want to synthesize it: to explain to your reader what your efforts add up to as a whole. Try to do that as clearly and emphatically as possible, since the last paragraph develops your reader's final impression about your research topic.

Once you are confident that the paper is as good as you can make it, you are ready to complete the final draft and assemble the other parts of the assignment. You will need to pay attention to rules of form, perhaps specified by your school and teacher, that follow the conventions of research paper presentation. These will concern each of the parts of the paper: the title page; a preface, which is optional; the outline/contents page; the body of the paper itself, including footnotes; the final bibliography; and, if needed, an appendix. Sara's complete research paper is in the Appendix of this book, along with forms for footnotes and bibliography. You will probably complete the text of the final draft before setting up the title page, contents outline, and bibliography, so let's examine that first.

If you can, type the final draft. If you cannot, be sure that your handwriting is legible. Use a good grade and weight of paper, leaving at least an inch of margin at the top, bottom, and both sides; and double space, indenting paragraphs five spaces. Number each page except the first at the upper right corner; there is no number on the first page of the text.

You will need to include footnotes in this final draft, so before you begin the paper, recheck to be sure that you know exactly where each footnote will go and that your numbering system is accurate. Type out the footnotes on scratch paper, using the correct form. (See **Footnote Forms** in the Appendix.) Although some teachers request that footnotes be listed together on a page at the end of the paper, many teachers require that they go at the bottom of each page on which the source is cited. This form is harder to do if you type, since you must gauge your space by counting typewritten lines as you go along to be sure that you leave enough room for the footnotes to fit on the page.

But it is also far more helpful to the reader of your paper, who won't have to thumb through the paper looking for the source. Footnotes are single-spaced and numbered consecutively throughout the paper. See the Appendix for examples of a paper with footnotes at the bottom of the text pages and of a footnote page that would appear at the back of a paper.

Once you have completed the final draft of the paper, only a few sections remain to be finished. The title page gives the title of the paper, your name, the name of the course for which you have written the paper, the date, plus anything else your teacher may specify. It serves as a cover sheet for the paper. A preface, if you wish to use one, follows the title page. It might include some kind of introductory comment that you feel is significant or interesting. The final outline, headed by a statement of your controlling purpose, serves as a contents page. It has no page numbers. The text itself follows the outline; begin numbering pages on the second page of the text, page 2. The final bibliography will appear after the last page of the body of your paper (unless all your footnotes are on one or more pages that follow the text; in that case, the bibliography follows the footnote page). Be sure each source that is footnoted is listed in the final bibliography. (See **Bibliography Forms** in the Appendix for a list of correct bibliographical forms.)

The bibliography identifies your sources more fully, credits them appropriately, and helps to establish the authenticity of your evidence. It also may lead an interested reader of your paper to additional material on the topic. If your teacher permits, your bibliography may include sources that you found helpful but did not actually cite in footnotes. Do not include in the bibliography those items from your working bibliography that were not useful. See the **Research Paper** in the Appendix for a sample bibliography page.

Occasionally a research paper may include an appendix. Phil has taken photographs of the six houses he has described, and he has drawn a map of his community to show their locations. His teacher permits him to include these items in an appendix at the back of the paper, following the final bibliography.

In evaluating your paper, your teacher will take a number of its elements into consideration: the quality of your research, the development of a logical thesis, the organizational structure, the use of evidence, the writing style, and the adherence to form requirements. If you meet these specifications successfully, the research-paper assignment should be a rewarding one for you.

• **EXERCISE 8.** Complete the final draft of your research paper, giving yourself time enough to have it proofread by one or two classmates before you submit it to your teacher. As you proofread your own paper or someone else's, determine if the introduction and the conclusion accomplish what they ought: introducing the topic and purpose of the research and summing it up. (See **Revision** in the Language Handbook.)

Chapters 23–28 Composition

Many of the sentences in the following paragraph contain errors. Match the number of the sentence with the letter of the error it contains. If a sentence has no error, write "Correct" after its number.

(1) My favorite way to spend a summer Sunday afternoon is at the Primate House at the zoo. **(2)** It's only a five-block walk, I compete for sidewalk space with joggers, bicyclers, and roller skaters. **(3)** First, I bid my respects to old Corby who bares his teeth, extends a half-eaten banana, and makes me feel that he's a visiter observing the antics at the Human Zoo. **(4)** He beckons me to join him in his cage. **(5)** With lettuce leaves, carrot spears, and a shredded box top strewn all over the floor. **(6)** Then I move on to Daisy, my favorite chimp, who holds a rubber toy and carries a baby chimp wrapped around her leg like a fat, brown bandage. **(7)** It seems to be part of her anatomy. **(8)** A freckled woman in a flowered bandanna informs anyone, who will listen, "that Daisy has adopted this baby since its real mother rejected it three weeks ago." **(9)** Acknowledging the fact that she is being the center of attention, Daisy scampers up to the top bars as is often the case during the next hour. **(10)** The freckled woman is one of those authorities who knows the names, ages, ailments, and escapades of each chimp. **(11)** "Freddy over there is nine years old and has never mated," she announces. **(12)** Meanwhile, Freddy sits on his haunches and proudly thumps his chest. **(13)** Lulu, the smallest of the adult chimps, swats her year-old child, who is simultaneously trying to grab a piece of rope, eat an apple, and pressing his nose against the window. **(14)** Finally grabbing the rope, the apple falls and the little chimp squeals. **(15)** Suddenly Freddy, who has been picking at the fur on his arm, ambers over to me in his funny chimp walk. **(16)** He points directly at my nose; I could swear he's laughing.

A. Wrong word
B. Spelling
C. Agreement
D. Comma splice
E. Fragment
F. Unnecessary punctuation
G. Reference of pronoun
H. Deadwood
I. Unparallel construction
J. Dangling modifier

Chapter 29 The Research Paper

The following true-false items are based on information from Chapter 29 and from the Appendix. Indicate a "T" or an "F" next to the number of each item.

1. In an outline, the number of subheads under each major section need not be equal.

2. It is not necessary to give credit for someone else's ideas, as long as you have expanded them into your own ideas.

3. Under certain circumstances, you may bring your personal opinions into a research paper.

4. It is not permissible to use direct quotes in your research paper.

5. The *New York Times Index* would be a good reference source for locating information on the Napoleonic Wars.

6. The first word that appears in a footnote is the author's last name.

7. A page citation for a book should be given in a footnote, but not in a bibliography.

8. A paraphrase is longer than a précis.

9. A working bibliography will contain more sources than a final bibliography.

10. If you have additional information such as photographs or maps, you could put them at the beginning of your research paper in the form of an appendix.

11. While a missing footnote can constitute plagiarism, a research paper may tend to be over-footnoted.

12. Both the controlling purpose and the outline may have to change as you develop your paper.

13. A critical edition contains the complete text of a work of literature, along with a collection of articles and essays about the work.

14. The major value in taking notes is to copy sources that cannot be taken out of the library.

15. The source number should be different for each bibliography card, although it may be the same for several note cards.

16. While a précis restates the author's ideas in your own words, a paraphrase summarizes those ideas in a briefer form.

17. In an outline, there must be more than one subhead under a larger heading.

18. When information is so general that giving credit to a specific source seems impossible, a footnote may not be needed.

19. Begin numbering again from *1* for each new page of footnotes.

20. The final outline, headed by a statement of your controlling purpose, serves as a contents page for your completed research paper.

Perfect Score: 36

Language Handbook

A

a, an

A and *an* are called "indefinite articles"; they function as noun determiners, signaling that a noun is to follow.

1. The choice between *a* and *an* depends on the beginning *sound*, not the beginning *letter*, of the following word. *A* is used before a consonant sound:

a heart	a C	a eulogy
a one-base hit	a unicorn	a hotel

An is used before a vowel sound:

an acorn	an M	an earphone
an orange	an understudy	an honor roll

2. The repetition of *a* or *an* before each item of a series helps make the items more distinct. "Each of the contestants was asked to bring a pen, a pencil, and a ruler" is more emphatic than "Each of the contestants was asked to bring a pen, pencil, and ruler."

(See also **Articles** and **Noun markers.**)

Abbreviations

Abbreviations are appropriately used in lists, footnotes, and technical writing. With certain exceptions, discussed below, they are not appropriate in ordinary writing.

1. *Mr., Mrs., Ms., Messrs., Mmes.,* and *Dr.* always appear as abbreviations when used as titles before names; *St.* (Saint) often is abbreviated. *Esq., Jr., Sr.* are usually abbreviated when they follow a name, as are *B.A., B.S., Ph.D.,* and other academic degrees:

Mr. James Summers, Sr.	Jennifer O'Reilly, B.A., Ph.D.
Mr. David S. Okada, Jr.	Messrs. Smith and Weiss
Loren D. Goodman, Esq.	Dr. Peterson
St. John	Robert Peterson, LL.D.

WRONG: The Dr. examined the Sr. partner.
RIGHT: The doctor examined the senior partner.
RIGHT: Dr. Wallace examined Mr. Clark, Sr.

2. In formal writing, titles such as *Reverend, Honorable, President, Profes-*

sor, and *Senator* are not abbreviated. In informal writing, they are abbreviated—but only when they come before initials or a given name:

FORMAL	INFORMAL
Reverend Clay R. Moore	Rev. Clay R. Moore
Honorable Charles Roth	Hon. Charles Roth
Professor Jean D. Sutter	Prof. J. D. Sutter

In newspapers and some magazines, however, where space is limited, the abbreviation is used alone with a surname: Rev. Moore, Prof. Sutter.

3. Certain indications of time—A.D., B.C., A.M., P.M.—are always abbreviated when used with figures:

A.D. 333 (*or* 333 A.D.)   57 B.C.   9:35 A.M.   11:20 P.M.

4. A few rather formal Latin expressions are almost always abbreviated. For example:

e.g.	*exempli gratia*	for example
et al.	*et alii*	and others
ca.	*circa*	about, approximately
i.e.	*id est*	that is
loc. cit.	*loco citato*	in the place cited
non seq.	*non sequitur*	it does not follow
pro tem.	*pro tempore*	for the time being
q.v.	*quod vide*	which see

In informal writing, the English equivalents of these Latin phrases are usually more appropriate.

5. Periods are used after abbreviations, except in these instances:

a. There is a growing tendency to omit periods with the abbreviations of names of government agencies and organizations commonly referred to by their initials: *FTC*, *AMA*, *USMC*, *ABA*, *UMT*. (See also **Acronym.**)

b. Periods are generally not used with scientific and technical abbreviations, which are regarded more as symbols than as abbreviations: *WTMJ*, *KFIZ* (in radio); $C_2H_2Cl_2$, N_2O, H_3PO_4 (in chemistry); *ctn*, *rad*, *cm* (in mathematics); *at wt*, *kwh*, *dc* (in physics).

c. When an abbreviation comes at the end of a sentence that is punctuated with a period, only one mark is used:

Sophocles died about the year 406 B.C.
But: Did you know that Sophocles' play *Antigone* won first place in a drama competition when it was first produced in 442 B.C.?

ability

After *ability*, use *to* and an infinitive:

Does Carl have the ability *to swim* across the English Channel?
[Not: the ability *of swimming*.]

Often the idea can be more simply expressed by using *can*:

Can Carl swim across the English Channel?

A noun following *ability* is preceded by *in*:

Sarah surprised us with her ability *in* mechanical drawing.
[Not: ability *for* mechanical drawing.]

above

The use of *above* as a noun, adjective, or adverb to refer to preceding material is appropriate in legal or business writing and in reference works:

The above is a brief delivered to Judge Parker.
The license numbers listed above are of cars abandoned in the city parking garage.

In other writing this use of *above* is avoided by many people, and the material is identified in some other way: "The quotations cited in the preceding paragraph . . . ," "The statistics shown in the chart . . . ," etc.

absolutely

In informal English, *absolutely* is used to mean "positively" or "unquestionably":

She is absolutely the happiest person in the world.

In conversation it is common as an overly emphatic, rather pompous "yes":

"Did you make a good impression at your first job interview?" "Absolutely."

In most writing (except for dialogue) *absolutely* should be used only in its original meaning, "completely; unconditionally":

The governor is absolutely committed to prison reform.
Is Ramon absolutely sure of the facts?

Absolute phrases

Absolute here means "independent"; the phrase, in other words, has no grammatical connection with the rest of the sentence. But it is related in meaning, since it adds descriptive details to the statement:

The lawn mowed, Cheryl came to the house for her pay.
Paul was lying on the porch, *his head covered with his shirt.*
Strawberries being so plentiful, we made up a large batch of jam.

Absolute phrases offer a writer an effective means of adding narrative and descriptive details in a minimum number of words. Such phrases, considered modifiers of the whole sentence, are always set off by commas. (See **Participial phrase.**)

Abstract and concrete words

Concrete words are words that name persons, places, and things that can be seen and touched: *tree, Rome, fingers, car, mother, kitten, dime.* The referents of these words actually exist in the real, physical world. Abstract words are words that name feelings, ideas, and actions—things that we cannot see or touch: *laughter, love, hate, avarice, pride, fear, jealousy.* The referents of these words do not actually exist—as specific physical objects—in the real world.

Accent

In words of more than a single syllable, one syllable is accented—or stressed—harder than the others. This increased emphasis is called the *primary*, or *main*, accent. Some dictionaries indicate this primary stress by a heavy slant mark placed after the accented syllable: /bär′bər/, /im′ə nənt/. Other dictionaries use a "high-set" straight mark placed before the accented syllable: /ˈbär-bər/, /ˈim-ə-nənt/.

Sometimes words of two or more syllables also have another syllable stressed, but with about half the force given to the primary accent. This lighter stress is called the *secondary* accent. It is indicated in some dictionaries by a light slant mark placed after the syllable: /ku̇k′bu̇k′/, /īs′brā′kər/. In other dictionaries this secondary accent is indicated by a "low-set" straight mark placed before the syllable: /ˈku̇k-ˌbu̇k/, /ˈīs-ˌbrā-kər/.

Accent marks

In formal writing, French words that have been added to English keep the accent marks used in their original French spelling:

ACUTE ACCENT:	attaché passé touché chargé d'affaires
CIRCUMFLEX ACCENT:	fête coup de grâce château rôle
GRAVE ACCENT:	suède à la mode

In writing that is not formal, the accent marks are usually dropped unless they are needed to indicate the pronunciation. In *fiancé* and *attaché*, for example, they are clearly useful in showing that these are words of three syllables, not two. But *fete* and *role* and *chateau* can be pronounced correctly without the aid of the marks.

accept, except

The similarity in sound causes these words to be confused. *Accept* means "take or receive; consent to receive; say *yes* to." It is always a verb:

I'm sure she will accept our invitation to dinner.

Except is most commonly used as a preposition meaning "but" or "other than":

Every car except ours was snow-laden.

In formal English *except* is also used as a verb meaning "take out; leave out; exclude; exempt; excuse":

I was excepted from jury duty because of my illness.

accompany

When *accompanied* means "escorted" or "attended," the preposition *by* is used:

The President was accompanied by his bodyguard and his press secretary.

When it means "supplemented," *with* is used:

The congregation accompanied the speaker's exhortations with loud "Amens."

Accusative case

See **Objective case.**

Acronym

A word formed from the initial letters or syllables of other words:

ACTION (from *A*merican *C*ouncil *T*o *I*mprove *O*ur *N*eighborhoods)
CARE (from *C*ooperative for *A*merican *R*emittances to *E*urope)
HURRAH (from *H*elp *U*s *R*each and *R*ehabilitate *A*merica's *H*andicapped)
NOW (from *N*ational *O*rganization for *W*omen)
radar (from *ra*dio *d*etecting *a*nd *r*anging)
SAC (from *S*trategic *A*ir *C*ommand)
OPEC (from *O*rganization of *P*etroleum *E*xporting *C*ountries)
UNESCO (from *U*nited *N*ations *E*ducational, *S*cientific, and *C*ultural *O*rganization)

Some acronyms, such as *radar*, provide a convenient name for a device or system. Others are mainly abbreviations of company or organization names, which may or may not suggest the purpose of the organization, as *CARE* does. But acronyms differ from abbreviations in that they are words rather than a series of letters which can be pronounced only as letters, like *N.A.A.C.P.* or *NBC*. (Compare **Blend.**)

Action verb

Words like *jump, think, hurl, worry,* and *rattle* are used mainly to "assert" or express physical or mental action:

Carlotta *jumped* over the flowerpot.
Jack *worried* about the history exam.

(See also **Linking verb.**)

Active and passive voice

A verb is said to be in the active voice when its subject is the doer of the action, and in the passive voice when its subject receives the action. A passive verb is a form of the verb *be* plus the past participle: *are made, were made, have been made, will be made,* etc. (Other forms are active.)

ACTIVE: My father made the delicious dessert for our party.
PASSIVE: The delicious dessert for our party was made by my father.

Although both active and passive verbs are useful, they are not equally effective in all situations. A sentence like "The earthquake destroyed every building on our street" would convey your meaning clearly and forcefully.

But suppose you want to emphasize the receiver of the action rather than the doer. You can get this emphasis by using a passive verb:

Every building on our street *was destroyed* by the earthquake.

Or suppose that the doer of the action is unknown or is too unimportant or too obvious to need mention in the context. The passive verb is preferable, for it permits you to express your meaning clearly and efficiently:

All stores and banks will be closed on Memorial Day. [It is obvious that the owners or the managers will close them.]
The flag should be at half-mast tomorrow. [The doer is unimportant.]

Except for situations like these, however, active verbs are preferable. They ordinarily make a sentence simpler, more direct, and more emphatic than passive verbs do:

AWKWARD PASSIVE VERBS	FORCEFUL ACTIVE VERBS
The Grand Canyon, Yellowstone Park, and the Painted Desert were visited by Jill and me last summer.	Last summer Jill and I visited the Grand Canyon, Yellowstone Park, and the Painted Desert.

Adage

See **Epigram.**

adapt, adopt

Adapt means "adjust" or "modify or alter for a different use." When *adapt* means "adjust," it is followed by *to:*

It was hard to adapt myself to daylight-saving time.

When *adapt* means "modify or alter for a different use," it is followed by *for* or *from:*

Can we adapt that long story for TV?
The ballet was adapted from a Russian folk tale.

Adopt means "take or use as one's own":

The town council adopted many energy-conserving plans.

Addresses

When an address appears in a list or in a sentence, commas are used to set off the various parts (the house number and street from the city, the city from the state and Zip code):

Ralph Nugent, 4006 Sherwood Drive, Kenosha, Wisconsin 53140
For copies of the talk, write to Ms. Lisa Novak, 1463 Elm Park Street, Whiting, Indiana 46394.

(For the forms of address in letters and on envelopes, see **Business letters.**)

Adjective

An adjective modifies a noun or pronoun; that is, it makes the meaning of the noun or pronoun more exact by describing or limiting it: an *arrogant* waiter, *orange* slacks, *most* newspapers, *Italian* opera, a *complaining* tenant, *that useless* vase, a *rigorous* exam, a *lively* dance.

1. Types. There are two general types of adjectives:

a. *Descriptive adjectives* modify nouns by telling a quality, a characteristic, or a condition of the persons or things named: a *stout* woman, *sweet* pickles, *black* and *white* flags, *mysterious* signals, a *golden* apple, a *soft-cooked* egg, the *brass* ring, a *dripping* faucet, the *forgotten* man. (Notice that *brass*, often used as a noun, is here used as an adjective; and that *dripping* and *forgotten*, parts of verbs, are here used as adjectives.)

b. *Limiting adjectives* point out persons or things in some way or indicate number or quantity: *these* bills, *this* pencil, *that* clerk, *my two* ties, *some* students, *thirteen* guests, a *double* dose.

(See also **Proper adjectives.**)

2. Position of adjectives. a. Adjectives ordinarily stand immediately before the word they modify:

a *gray* sky   the *overseasoned, undercooked* stew   *several* boys

b. In some instances, adjectives are placed after their nouns:

Ahead, we saw the woods, *dark* and *forbidding.* [For greater emphasis.]
His father, *purple* with rage, pointed to the crumpled fender. [Adjective is modified by other words.]
The court-*martial* is scheduled for the last week in May. [Adjective is part of a special compound word.]

c. When used as subject complements, adjectives follow the verb–either a form of the verb *be* or of some other linking verb (*feel, seem, become, sound, taste,* etc.):

I was *afraid.* The boys felt *silly.* His suspicions seem *ridiculous.*

(See **Linking verb.**)

3. Effective use of adjectives. "Think twice before you use an adjective," Carl Sandburg is said to have advised a writer. In following his advice, keep three points in mind. First, the adjectives you use should add to the meaning of your statements, making your word pictures more exact. Unless they do, they are excess baggage and are better omitted. For example, in the sentence "Before he was twenty, he was the author of a successful best seller," the adjective *successful* adds nothing to the meaning; all best sellers are by definition "successful."

Second, vague, general adjectives like *good, bad, awful, very,* and *nice* should be avoided, especially in writing; such adjectives seldom convey exact meanings.

Third, avoid overloading your writing with useless, repetitious modifiers, as in "He had great big enormous hands." Using three adjectives here merely clutters up the picture; *great* and *big* add nothing once you have said *enormous.*

4. Comparison. For a discussion of the use of adjectives in making comparisons, including adjectives like *unique*, *perfect*, *round*, *square*, *impossible*, see **Comparison of adjectives and adverbs,** section 3.

Adjective clause

A group of words containing a subject and verb that does the work of an adjective–that is, it modifies a noun or pronoun in the sentence. An adjective clause is usually introduced by a relative pronoun (*who*, *which*, *that*) or a relative adverb (*when*, *where*, *why*):

The classmate *who had planned the beach party* could not attend. [Modifies *classmate,* the antecedent of *who.*]
Blocking our way was a big truck *that had three flat tires.* [Modifies *truck,* the antecedent of *that.*]
Mr. Larson built his six-bedroom house at a time *when there were servants to help keep up a house.* [Modifies *time*, the antecedent of *when.*]

Often no introductory word is used: The statistics *he quoted* were impressive–and true. [Instead of: *that he quoted* or *which he quoted.*]

Adjective phrases

Prepositional, participial, and infinitive phrases are often used as adjectives, modifying a noun or pronoun in their sentences:

PREPOSITIONAL: Amy ordered a hamburger *with cheese.* [Modifies *hamburger;* tells what kind.]
PARTICIPIAL: Tina pretended not to see the dog *following her.* [Modifies *dog;* tells which one.]
PARTICIPIAL: The dresses *made of Dacron* were easier to iron. [Modifies *dresses;* tells which ones.]
INFINITIVE: Dan has no right *to open my mail.* [Modifies *right;* tells what kind.]

Adverb

1. Uses. a. Most adverbs are used to modify a verb, an adjective, an adverb, or a whole clause or sentence:

VERB MODIFIERS: Sis walked *gingerly.* [Tells how she walked.]
Sis walked *back.* [Tells where she walked.]
Sis looked *up*. [Tells where she looked.]
ADJECTIVE MODIFIERS: Sylvie is *almost* ready. [How ready?]
The bananas were *extremely* ripe. [How ripe?]
ADVERB MODIFIERS: She can pitch *rather* well. [How well?]
I can ski *pretty* proficiently now. [How proficiently?]
SENTENCE MODIFIERS: *Unfortunately,* she had moved.
Luckily, I have her address.

b. *Conjunctive adverbs* serve a double purpose—to join two clauses or sentences and also to indicate how the ideas in the two are related:

Huckleberry Finn has been widely read as an adventure story; *therefore* many people mistakenly think it is nothing more.

(See **Conjunctive adverbs.**)

c. *Interrogative adverbs* are used to introduce questions:

Why didn't you explain?
Where should we go to get good chili?

2. Types. Adverbs can be conveniently classified by meaning:

a. Adverbs of manner—tell how:

gracefully loudly carefully vigorously well abruptly

b. Adverbs of time—tell when:

later afterwards beforehand first last next

c. Adverbs of place and direction—tell where:

upstairs forward there north above up down

d. Adverbs of degree and measure—tell how much or to what extent:

nearly	very	entirely	surely	extremely
almost	less	much	quite	completely

(See **Intensifier.**)

3. Forms. Most adverbs are adjectives or participles plus the ending *-ly* (*swiftly, quietly, selfishly, resignedly, shyly).* But the *-ly* ending is not a sure sign that a word is an adverb; there are dozens of common adjectives that have an *-ly* ending: *friendly, homely, manly, cowardly, leisurely.* And a large number of adverbs have developed from Old English forms without a special ending to distinguish them: *now, quite, since, then, there, where,* etc.

A number of adverbs have two forms, one ending in *-ly* and one that is the same as the adjective form:

cheaply—cheap	highly—high	sharply—sharp
fairly—fair	loudly—loud	slowly—slow
hardly—hard	nearly—near	tightly—tight

Some of these pairs are used interchangeably: *Drive slowly* or *Drive slow, Don't talk so loudly* or *Don't talk so loud.* (Formal English is likely to use the *-ly* form of such words; informal English is likely to use the shorter form.) But others cannot be used interchangeably, since the two forms have quite different meanings:

He came *near.* But: It is *nearly* finished.
Kay tried *hard.* But: She *hardly* noticed us.
I aimed too *high.* But: Bill spoke *highly* of you.

4. Position. For the position of adverbs like *only, just, almost, even, hardly, nearly, scarcely* (in sentences like "He only ate one egg"), see **only.**

5. Effective use. Adverbs, like adjectives, should be used for a definite purpose–to make the meaning more exact, to give the reader a more vivid picture. Adverbs, like all words you use, should also be appropriate to the tone of your writing as a whole. For a specific suggestion concerning appropriateness, see **Conjunctive adverbs,** section 2.

6. Comparison. See **Comparison of adjectives and adverbs.**

Adverb clause

A group of words containing a subject and a verb that does the work of an adverb–that is, it serves as a modifier answering such questions as How? When? Why? Where? Under what condition? Adverb clauses are introduced by a subordinating conjunction: *when, so that, where, if, because, unless, after, wherever,* etc.

When he saw us the next day, he snubbed us. [Tells when he snubbed us.]
Mom left an extra key under the mat *so that Uncle Bill could get in.* [Tells why she left the key.]
Alberto makes trouble *wherever he goes.* [Tells where he makes trouble.]
If he doesn't stop loafing on the job, he'll be fired. [Tells under what condition he will be fired.]

An adverb clause at the beginning of a sentence is usually set off by a comma unless it is very short and there is no danger of misreading. Like single-word adverbs, these clauses modify verbs (He always does *as he pleases*), adjectives (It's later *than you think*), adverbs (She worked harder *than we did*), verbals (To eat *before the noon crowd arrives* would be good), or whole statements (*As he explained,* he was held up by traffic).

Adverbial nouns

Nouns often serve as adverbs, telling when, how much, how often, how far, and so on. But even though they do the work of adverbs, they are still considered nouns because they can be modified by adjectives and can have either a singular or plural form. (Some grammarians call these adverbial nouns simply "adverbials.")

Dad works *nights* now and every *Saturday.* [Tells when.]
The small ones cost only fifty *cents.* [Tells how much.]
We talked several *hours.* [Tells how long.]

Adverb phrases

Prepositional phrases and infinitive phrases are often used as adverb modifiers, answering such questions as How? When? Where? Why?

PREPOSITIONAL: Todd spoke *with a sneer.* [Tells how.]
We got there *before supper.* [Tells when.]
I ran *around the garage.* [Tells where.]
INFINITIVE: She had come up *to complain about the noise.* [Tells why.]

advice, advise

Advice is a noun that means "counsel" or "recommendation." Think of the word *ice* in *advice* to help you spell and pronounce this word:

Your advice will carry more weight if you practice what you preach.

Advise is a verb meaning "give advice" or "make a recommendation":

I'd advise you not to practice yoga on a full stomach.

-ae-, -oe-

The digraphs *-ae-* and *-oe-*, found in words that come from Greek and Latin, are both pronounced as if they were written *e* (a "long *e*" as in *equal* or a "short *e*" as in *echo*). Today the tendency is to simplify the spelling of such words to match their pronunciation:

ORIGINAL	SIMPLIFIED
aesthetic	esthetic
amoeba	ameba
anaemic	anemic
encyclopaedia	encyclopedia
mediaeval	medieval
subpoena	subpena

Very formal and technical writings generally keep the digraphs. And the digraph is always kept in Latin and Greek proper names (*Caesar*, *Oedipus*) and in Latin plurals (*antennae*, *larvae*).

Dictionaries frequently give both spellings. To find which is preferred for a particular word, consult a dictionary.

affect, effect

The similarity in sound causes these words to be confused. *Affect* is usually a verb; it is most frequently used to mean either "to influence" or "to pretend to have or feel":

After all, his selfish attitude does affect us all.
At the time, we affected a careless dress we were not comfortable with.

Effect is used chiefly as a noun meaning "result" or "consequence":

The threat of punishment had no effect on Scotty.

In formal English *effect* is also used as a verb meaning "to bring about or make happen":

The change to daylight-saving time was effected with little confusion.

afflicted

Followed by *with*, not *by*:

Job was certainly afflicted *with* many woes.

agree

The preposition to be used with *agree* depends on the meaning intended:

I agreed *with* Jo's review that the play was first-rate. [Had the same opinion as.]
We wanted Mother to agree *to* come home with us. [Consent to.]
The two doctors couldn't agree *on* the best surgical procedure. [Come to a common decision about.]
"You can have your rich food; it doesn't agree *with* me," he sighed. [Have a good effect on, suit.]
Larry's figures did not agree *with* Mr. Takeda's. [Correspond with.]

Agreement

In grammar, when we say that two words "agree," we mean that they are the same in person, number, case, or gender. In the sentence "Why was you boys late?" the subject and verb do not agree. The subject *you* is plural, and the verb *was* is singular. If the verb is changed to the plural form *were*, then the words agree: "Why were you boys late?"

1. A verb agrees with its subject in person and number:

I *am* always the last one to know. [First person singular verb *am* agrees with first person singular subject *I*.]

a. Phrases or clauses coming between the subject and the verb do not affect the subject-verb agreement. A singular subject requires a singular verb, and a plural subject a plural verb:

A long list of telephone numbers *was* the only clue they had. [Third person singular verb *was* agrees with third person singular subject *list*.]
All the words in the right-hand column *are* of Spanish origin. [Plural verb *are* agrees with plural subject *words*.]

(See **together with.**)

b. Compound subjects joined by *and* take a plural verb unless the parts of the subject mean only one person or are thought of as one thing:

The owner and the editor *determine* the paper's policy. [Two people.]
The owner and editor, Mr. Mochel, *writes* the editorials. [One person.]
Macaroni and cheese *tastes* best when it's hot.
The stress and strain *was beginning* to undermine his health.

c. When the parts of a compound subject are joined by *or*, *nor*, *either . . . or*, or *neither . . . nor*, the verb usually agrees with the nearer subject part:

Charles or Jorge *is* the man to see.
Neither criticism nor ridicule *disturbs* him.
Either the twins or Gary *is going* to take charge.
Either Gary or the twins *are going* to take charge.

But if the subject is plural in idea, a plural verb is often used in informal English, especially in questions and in negative sentences:

Have Karen or Ann arrived? [Formal: *Has* Karen or Ann arrived?]

Neither the president nor the vice-president *have signed* yet. [Formal: *has signed.*]

When the subjects are of different persons, in formal usage the verb agrees with the nearer part:

He or you *are* to drive. You or he *is* to drive.

People often avoid the necessity of such a choice of verb form by rewording the sentences:

You will drive, or he will. He will drive, or you will.

In sentences like the following, the verb agrees with the affirmative part, not the negative:

You, not I, *are invited.* I, not you, *am invited.*

People often avoid the problem by rewording the sentences:

You are invited, not I. I am invited, not you.

d. A collective noun (one that names a group of persons or things) may take either a singular or a plural verb. The verb is singular if the group is thought of as a unit, plural if the members of the group are acting as individuals:

The band *is going* to the Rose Bowl this year.
The band, as usual, *were straggling* into the auditorium in groups of two or three.

(See also **Collective nouns,** section 1.)

e. The meaning determines whether words like *half, all, one third, some, any, none, more, most, lot, part, rest,* and *number* take singular or plural verbs:

Half of the letters *have been mailed.* [Tells how many.]
Half of this letter *is* illegible. [Tells how much.]
One third of the students *live* on campus. [Tells how many.]
Two thirds of the stock *remains* unsold. [Tells how much.]

(See **number.**)

f. A subject plural in form but singular in meaning takes a singular verb:

Mumps *is* an infectious disease.
Three years *is* a long time to wait.
He said five dollars and thirty cents *was* the usual charge.
"Twelve Ways to Remember Everything" *sounds* like the best article.

g. Singular verbs are used with indefinite pronouns and adjectives–*each, every, either, neither, anyone, anybody, one, everyone, everybody, someone, somebody, nobody, no one.*

Each of the candidates *is introduced* in turn.
Everybody in the tents *was awakened* by the scream.
Someone *was whispering* my name.

Every one of the elms and oaks *has been sprayed.*
Neither of the clocks *keeps* accurate time.

h. The verb agrees with the subject regardless of the number of the subject complement:

His greatest delight *was* his children.
His children *were* his greatest delight.

i. Unusual word order does not affect agreement; the verb generally agrees with the subject, whether the subject follows or precedes it:

When *were* **you** in Mexico?
Last of all *comes* **Amahl** on his crutches.
Are there any **messages** for me?
Wasn't **anyone** willing to help?
The next day there *were* several **notices** and a new cafeteria **schedule** on the bulletin board. [A compound subject.]

In informal usage the expletive *there* is sometimes followed by a singular verb when the first part of the compound subject is singular:

The next day there was a new cafeteria schedule and several notices on the bulletin board.

j. The verb in a relative clause whose subject is *who, which,* or *that* agrees with the antecedent of the relative pronoun:

Tom is the only one of those debaters who *argues* logically. [Singular verb; the antecedent of *who* is *one.*]
Isn't Judy one of the three girls that *were told* to report? [Plural verb; the antecedent of *that* is *girls.*]

(See also **one of those who.**)

2. a. A pronoun generally agrees with its antecedent in person, number, and gender:

Emily checked every answer before *she* handed in *her* paper. [*She* and *her* agree with the antecedent *Emily*—third person singular, feminine.]
The boy looked back and waved *his* hand just before *he* turned the corner. [*His* and *he* agree with the antecedent *boy*—third person singular, masculine.]

b. Singular pronouns are generally used to refer to the indefinite pronouns *one, anybody, anyone, each, either, neither, everybody, everyone, somebody, someone, nobody,* and *no one,* as in the following examples:

Neither of the men felt that *he* was responsible.
Somebody had caught *her* heel on the rug.
Before anybody signs the contract, *he or she* should read the fine print. [Traditionally, *he* has been used with indefinite pronouns like *anybody,* but many writers prefer to use *he or she* and *his or her.*]

In informal conversation, plural pronouns are often used in such sentences, but the plurals are inappropriate in writing and in formal speech.

Sometimes the indefinite pronouns are so obviously plural in meaning that using singular pronouns to refer to them would sound ridiculous.

When *everybody* had arrived, Inga told **him** the good news.

In informal English a plural pronoun would be used in sentences like this. In formal English the sentence would be rephrased so as not to violate the grammatical agreement.

INFORMAL: When *everybody* had arrived, Inga told **them** the good news.
FORMAL: When *all the members* had arrived, Inga told **them** the good news.

(See also **he or she, his or her.**)

3. A demonstrative adjective agrees with its noun in number:

That kind of student spoils it for everyone else. [*That* is singular, to agree with the singular noun *kind.*]
His job is to analyze *these* various computer printouts for obvious programing errors. [*These* is plural, to agree with the plural noun *printouts.*]

(See **Demonstratives; kind, sort.**)

ain't

Used in nonstandard English as a contraction for *am not*, *is not*, *are not*, *has not*, *have not*.

Some authorities feel that *ain't* would be a useful addition to informal English, particularly as a contraction for *am I not*, a phrase that cannot be contracted easily (*amn't I* is hard to say). They defend *ain't I* as an appropriate colloquial expression in questions: "I'm going to ride with you, ain't I?" (For some reason *aren't I*, which is certainly no more "correct" grammatically than *ain't I*, is more readily accepted: "I'm going to ride with you, aren't I?") But because of the strong social and educational pressure against *ain't*, most users of standard English avoid it, even as a contraction for *am I not.*

The problem does not arise in formal English, which avoids contractions.

a la, à la

Originally French; now widely used as an English preposition meaning "in the manner of; in the style of":

The new star was wonderful–a comic à la Charlie Chaplin.

In formal writing and most fashion advertising the accent mark is kept: *à la.* Informal writing usually omits it.

alibi

In formal and legal usage *alibi* means "the plea or the fact that a person accused of a crime was in another place when it was committed":

Steve has an alibi; on the night in question, he was a hundred miles away.

In informal usage the meaning of *alibi* is much broader. It is used to refer to any excuse for any offense, important or unimportant, and also as a verb meaning "to make an excuse":

Jack had an alibi for not coming to football practice.
She alibied her way out of an unpleasant encounter.

all and its compounds

1. **All right** is used both as an adjective and as an adverb:

José will be all right after he rests awhile. [Modifies the noun *José.*]
Rose was there all right; I talked to her most of the night. [Adverb meaning "certainly."]
All right; you can have Grandmother's antiques. [Adverb meaning "very well; yes."]

The spelling *alright* is occasionally found in comic strips, advertisements, and familiar writing, but it is not yet generally accepted in either formal or informal writing. Always write the two words–*all right.*

2. **All ready.** When in doubt about writing *all ready* or *already* use this test: If you could use the word *ready* alone, without changing the meaning of the sentence, *all ready* is the one to use:

By midmorning we were all ready to start our trip.
Everyone was all ready to resign after that meeting.

Already is an adverb of time:

Mrs. Wong had already reported the test grades.

3. **All together.** The same test applies to choosing between *all together* and *altogether*. If the word *together* could be used alone, without changing the meaning, write *all together*:

The puppies were huddled all together in their basket.

Altogether is a rather formal adverb meaning "completely":

It is altogether fitting that the inventor should profit most.

4. **All-around** is a compound meaning "having many abilities, talents, or uses":

Jenny was truly an all-around athlete.

In informal English the form *all-round* is often used.

Alliteration

Literary device of repeating the same initial sound several times in rather close succession. Writers of poetry and literary prose often make use of alliteration to gain attention, to bind phrases together, or to create a musical effect:

Five ***m***iles ***m***eandering with a ***m***azy ***m***otion
–Samuel Taylor Coleridge, "Kubla Khan"

Alliteration gives many advertising and political slogans their catchy quality:

Protex Padlocks Protect Property. Good Government? Vote for Goode.

Inexperienced writers should be careful in their use of alliteration. Although it can be effective for special purposes, it is usually out of place in everyday factual writing. There it tends to attract attention to the words themselves and away from the ideas.

all of

The preposition *of* is usual with *all* before pronouns:

If all of you think that, all of you are wrong.
Fred drank all of it in one gulp.

All of is often used before nouns, also, though the *of* is not necessary and would probably be omitted in formal writing:

GENERAL USAGE: All of the children had to eat all of the food on their plates.
FORMAL WRITING: All the children had to eat all the food on their plates.

allow

In some local dialects *allow* is used to mean "declare; think; suppose":

DIALECT: I allow he means well.
STANDARD: I suppose he means well.

all right

See **all and its compounds,** section 1.

allude, refer

Both *allude* and *refer* mean "to speak of something in a way to turn attention to it." But *allude* means "to call attention *indirectly*," in contrast to *refer*, which implies a direct, open, specific mention:

Ann didn't dare say his name, but she was surely alluding to her boss when she said, "That old Scrooge always spoils our fun."

Allusion

A brief reference to a person, place, thing, or event that is familiar to most people. For example, suppose that in a magazine article a writer (who either had incontestable evidence or welcomed libel suits) alluded to a government employee, a Mr. Roe, as "a Benedict Arnold." Because almost everyone knows who Benedict Arnold was and why he is so well remembered, the writer's intended meaning would be immediately clear. They would know the writer was suggesting that, like Benedict Arnold, Mr. Roe was a traitor, a man willing to betray his country to its enemies, a man who deserved the contempt of his fellow citizens. Notice that this allusion suggests both what kind of man Mr. Roe is and how the writer feels about Mr. Roe.

History is not the only possible source of allusions; literature, art, religion, mythology, current events, and the entertainment world can also provide them. In the heat of an election campaign, for instance, you might hear one candidate accuse another of wanting to change society into a "brave new world" (an allusion to the novel of the same name by Aldous Huxley). Through allusion, the candidate suggests that if his or her opponent is elected, people's lives will become as mechanistic and controlled as those of Huxley's characters.

Allusions may appear in your everyday conversation. You might be told that someone has a Mona Lisa smile, an Achilles heel, the strength of Samson, or a sour grapes attitude–allusions to art, mythology, the Bible, and literature, respectively. The contexts in which these allusions are made will reveal whether they are meant to be humorous, derogatory, or simply informative. In any event, allusions provide a concise and vivid means of expression.

Keep in mind, however, that not all allusions are figurative. In the following sentence, for example, the reference to Watergate is a literal one, while the reference to Waterloo is figurative: "The events of Watergate led Nixon to his Waterloo."

As you listen to others or read what others have written, take special notice of how the allusions they use help make their meaning vivid and memorable. But don't stop there. Use allusions to give clarity and effectiveness to your own speech and writing.

allusion

See **illusion, allusion.**

almost

See **most, almost.**

Alphabetizing

Although business firms and publishers have their own rules to cover special situations, alphabetizing generally follows a few common conventions:

1. Names are listed with the surname first. When the surnames are the same, the order is decided by the first name or first initial. If necessary, the second name or initial is then considered:

Lewis, J. C.
Lewis, James L.
Lewis, James R.
Lewis, Jane A.
Lewiss, Cary

Surnames with prefixes are usually alphabetized under the prefix, not under the main part of the name:

De La Rosa, Ernesto
Delcore, James
De Marais, Felicia

In some systems, surnames with *Mac* and *Mc* are listed together under *Mac*; in other systems, they are grouped together in a separate section ahead of all other *M*'s. Currently the most common method is to list all such names in strict alphabetical order (Mabry, *MacCarthy*, Maritt, *McCrea*). Surnames with *St.* (St. Aubin, St. Pierre) are sometimes listed with the *Sa*'s (for *Saint*), sometimes with the *St*'s.

2. A title (whether the name of a book, magazine, short story, song, business firm, organization, and so on) is usually listed according to the first word that is not an article:

School for Scandal, The
Science Publications, Inc.
Senior Scholastic
Sentimental Journey, A
"Sir Patrick Spens"

3. An item in a book index is usually listed according to its important word–the one that users of the index would probably look for first:

Spelling, phonetics applied to, 132

The various phases of a topic are generally listed in alphabetical order after the entry item:

Theater, 293–299, 575–576; Drury Lane, 894, 1084; Elizabethan, 296; in London, 296, 364; in New York, 366–370

already

See **all and its compounds,** section 2.

also

Sometimes used as a connective in spots where *and* would be more appropriate and therefore more effective:

POOR: Aunt Em invested her money in Florida real estate, also in common stocks.

BETTER: Aunt Em invested her money in Florida real estate and in common stocks.

although, though

These two subordinating conjunctions have the same meaning and can be used interchangeably. In modern prose, *though* is much more common than *although*, whether the adverb clause comes at the beginning of a sentence or at the end:

Though (*or* Although) he gets nine hours of sleep every night, he needs several naps a day.
Mrs. Gordon worried about him, though (*or* although) their doctor advised her not to worry.

The spellings *tho* and *altho* are often used in familiar writing–letters, advertising, etc.—and are becoming increasingly common in informal writing. But the words should be spelled out in full in formal writing.

altogether

See **all and its compounds,** section 3.

alumnus

Alumnus means "a graduate or a former student of a school, college, or university." This borrowed word (meaning "foster son") keeps its original forms in English:

One male graduate:	alumnus	/ə lum′nəs/
Two or more:	alumni	/ə lum′nī/
One female graduate:	alumna	/ə lum′nə/
Two or more:	alumnae	/ə lum′nē/

Alumni is commonly used to refer to both men and women graduates (or former students) of a coeducational school.

To avoid the confusion that may arise in pronouncing the plural ending of these words, many people prefer to use the word *graduates.*

a.m., p.m.

Abbreviations for the Latin *ante meridiem* ("before noon") and *post meridiem* ("after noon"). These abbreviations are ordinarily used only when the time is given in figures:

The workshop lasted from 10:45 A.M. to 2:30 P.M. [Not: The workshop lasted from the A.M. to the P.M.]

Since A.M. means "before noon" and P.M. "after noon," it is redundant to say "The workshop lasted from 10:45 A.M. *in the morning* to 2:30 P.M. *in the afternoon.*" Drop one or the other.

(See **Hours.**)

M. is the abbreviation for *noon*: 12:00 M. There is no corresponding abbreviation for *midnight*; 12:00 P.M. is used.

In manuscript writing such as your handwritten papers, lower-case letters are generally used.

Ambiguity

An ambiguous construction is one that has two or more possible meanings. The most common causes of ambiguity are these:

1. Unclear reference of pronouns:

AMBIGUOUS: The jazz concert was held on the same night as the class play, so we had to miss it.

If this sentence appeared in context, the meaning would probably be clear. But to avoid any confusion, the writer should indicate more clearly the specific meaning intended:

CLEAR: We had to miss the jazz concert because it was held on the same night as the class play.
CLEAR: We had to miss the class play because it was held on the same night as the jazz concert.

2. Squinting and misplaced modifiers. A squinting modifier is ambiguous because it might refer to either the preceding or the following construction:

AMBIGUOUS: On the way home Tara told Uncle Lou several times she had borrowed his agate cuff links.
CLEAR: On the way home Tara told Uncle Lou several times that she had borrowed his agate cuff links.
CLEAR: On the way home Tara told Uncle Lou that several times she had borrowed his agate cuff links.

Misplaced modifiers, because of their position in the sentence, do not clearly modify the word they are intended to modify. They are also often a source of humor that the writer does not intend:

MISPLACED: I saw groups of magnificent cottonwood trees canoeing down the Mississippi River.
REVISED: Canoeing down the Mississippi River, I saw groups of magnificent cottonwood trees.

3. Incomplete expressions, especially in comparisons:

AMBIGUOUS: Dorothy liked Jon as much as Lorraine.
CLEAR: Dorothy liked both Jon and Lorraine.
CLEAR: Dorothy liked Jon as much as Lorraine did.
CLEAR: Dorothy liked Jon as much as she liked Lorraine.

American

Since no convenient adjective or noun can be formed from the name, the *United States*, citizens of the U.S. use *American*, from the name of the continent. This is an obviously inexact term, for citizens of other North American countries and of South America are "American" too. This use of the term for the people and the products of the U.S. only is often resented by other Americans. Despite inexactness and complaints, longstanding habit encourages the continued use of the term. But in situations where the usage might be considered offensive or misleading, it would be wise to substitute other words–for example, "a citizen of the United States" instead of "an American"; "a product of the United States" instead of "an American product."

American English

See **English, varieties of.**

among, between

See **between, among.**

amount, number

Amount is used in referring to "mass nouns"–nouns which name things that can be measured or weighed; *number* is used in referring to "count nouns"–nouns which name things that can be counted:

a small *amount* of cash
a large *amount* of dirt

a large *number* of soldiers
a small *number* of mud pies

(See also **number.**)

Ampersand (&)

The name for the sign which means "and." This sign is often used as a space saver in business writing and in charts and tables. The ampersand is not appropriate as a substitute for *and* in general writing.

In addressing or referring to a business firm, you should use the form the firm uses:

Hyde, Paine & Company

Greenberg, Hally and Co.

an

See **a, an.**

Analogy

A figure of speech in which a comparison is rather fully developed, suggesting several points of similarity:

Last summer, as I was driving from Tallahassee to Iowa, I missed my turn in downtown Dothan, Alabama, and drove several miles out of town headed west instead of north. When I finally realized that I was headed the wrong way, I turned around and went back to Dothan. I discovered the place where I had missed my turn. There was the turn-marker almost hidden by a branch of a tree. Cursing the Alabama Highway Department, I made the right turn and got on my way toward my destination.

I fancy that the same thing has happened to most people at one time or another when they were making a car trip. But I am sure that a similar kind of thing happens to every composition teacher every few minutes while he is reading student themes. He will be reading along the sentence . . . when all of a sudden he runs smack into a road block. He can't get through the rest of the sentence on the interpretation he is using. He has to turn around and go back to an earlier spot in the sentence. There he discovers the place where he missed his turn. This time, when he sees the sign, he reads it differently; he takes off in a different direction, and now proceeds successfully through the rest of the sentence. But he curses the Highway Department for not making its signs clearer. Next day in class he says, "Students, it is not enough that a sentence be capable of being understood. A good sentence must be incapable of being misunderstood even on a first reading." –Kellogg W. Kent. "Improving Sentence Structure." *English Journal* (April 1958) p. 206.

and

1. *And* is a coordinating conjunction that connects elements of equal grammatical value:

NOUNS:	Punch and Judy; an eagle, a birdie, and a hole in one
VERBS:	They huffed and puffed. She played and replayed the tape.
ADJECTIVES:	tall, thin, and graceful; a dark and stormy night
ADVERBS:	slowly and indignantly; He'll have to work faster and harder.
PHRASES:	around the corner and under a tree; arguing stupidly and getting nowhere
SUBORDINATE CLAUSES:	I wonder why he bought a motorcycle and where he got the money.
COORDINATE CLAUSES:	She heard one story and he heard another.

2. Inexperienced speakers and writers often use too many *and*'s, with resulting monotony. In some sentences a subordinating conjunction or a *but* or *yet* would express the idea more exactly than *and*:

INEXACT: The reporter from the *Natchez News* finally arrived with a photographer, and the excitement was just about over.

BETTER: When the reporter from the *Natchez News* finally arrived with a photographer, the excitement was just about over. [Or: The reporter from the *Natchez News* finally arrived with a photographer, but the excitement was just about over.]

In other sentences, *and* is used when no connective is needed:

Mother stared hard at Sam, and hoping he would turn around.

The participial phrase *hoping he would turn around* is a modifier of the subject *Mother.* Since it is not a second part of a compound verb, it should not be joined to the rest of the sentence by *and:*

Mother stared hard at Sam, hoping he would turn around.

A monotonous succession of *and*'s, as in the sentences below, can generally be avoided by "reducing" some of the details in such a way that all or most of the *and*'s can be dropped:

MONOTONOUS: After the game I was to meet Alyce, and we were going to her house and pick up her sister, and the three of us were going to the party together.

BETTER: After the game I was to meet Alyce and go with her to her house to pick up her sister because the three of us were going to the party together.

Though the expression *and so* is common (especially in speech), there is no need for using the *and* before the *so,* since it adds nothing to the meaning:

However, Ms. Storm had turned down her hearing aid, so she caught only my last two words. [Not: *and so* she caught only my last two words.]

3. *And* is sometimes effectively used at the beginning of a sentence, to place special emphasis on the idea that follows:

USUAL: This time Mr. Pérez threatened that some fine day he would get even with us, and he did.

MORE EMPHATIC: This time Mr. Pérez threatened that some fine day he would get even with us. And he did.

This device should not be overused, or it loses its effectiveness.

(For punctuation of compound sentences with *and* and of a series with *and*, see **Comma,** sections 1 and 3a.)

and etc.

See **etc.**

and/or

A business and legal expression that efficiently indicates three choices—both items mentioned *or* one of the items *or* the other item:

Please specify size and/or model number for each item on your order blank.

Because many people dislike its business connotation, *and/or* is seldom used in general writing.

and which, and who

And which and *and who* are appropriate only when joining a second relative clause to a first one:

We finally replaced our old TV set, which we had bought secondhand and which suffered from every known television ailment.

Using an *and which* or an *and who* (or *but which, but who*) when there is no preceding *which* or *who* clause is a mistake most writers make occasionally. Check your first drafts for sentences like these:

FIRST DRAFT: Dad spent time looking for a heat-efficient woodburning stove *and which* he could install in the bedroom.

REVISED: Dad spent time looking for a heat-efficient woodburning stove *which* he could install in the bedroom.

FIRST DRAFT: I myself liked Mrs. Vargas, the building manager, a crisp-mannered and crabby-voiced woman, *but who* was concerned about the tenants and did all she could to make life easier for them.

REVISED: I myself liked Mrs. Vargas, the building manager, *who* was crisp-mannered and crabby-voiced, *but who* was concerned about the tenants and did all she could to make life easier for them.

angle

A standard American English term for "point of view." Because *angle* has been so overused (especially as a slang term in sentences like "Jake knows all the angles" and "I wonder what his angle is"), it has acquired unfavorable connotations for many people that make it inappropriate for general writing. Use one of its synonyms–*point of view, aspect*, or *standpoint*:

OVERWORKED: This time let's consider the matter from the children's angle.

SAFER: This time let's consider the matter from the children's point of view.

Anglicizing

See **Borrowed words.**

angry

Angry at and *angry about* are used in referring to things:

Rita became angry at the cabdriver's arrogance.
The customers were angry about the false advertising.

In referring to persons, *angry with* is general:

I was angry with Joe; I wasn't angry with Jill.

But when the angry feeling is to be stressed, *at* is used:

At this final insult, I got so angry at her I hung up.

annoyed

We are annoyed *at* things and *with* people:

Joline Mae was annoyed at the frequent misspelling of her name.
Even Grandmother will be annoyed with her if she's late today.

By is used when the meaning is "pestered":

Every political speaker there was annoyed by hecklers.

Antecedent

The word, phrase, or clause to which a pronoun (or a relative adverb) refers. The pronoun agrees in person, number, and gender with its antecedent, which may precede or follow it:

Uncle Ben, who has wanted a dog, bought himself a schnauzer puppy. [*Uncle Ben* is the antecedent of the relative pronoun *who* and the reflexive pronoun *himself*.]
Even though she pretends to like them, Alice can't stand Mr. Alda and his son. [Here the antecedents follow the pronouns that refer to them: *she-Alice*; *them-Mr. Alda* and *son*.]
If someone calls, ask him or her to call later. [*Someone* is the antecedent of the pronouns *him* and *her*.]

anti-

See **Prefix.**

Anticipatory subjects

See **Expletives.**

Anticlimax

In writing, *climax* means the arrangement of two or more items in a rising order–from the least important to the most important, from the least forceful to the most forceful. *Anticlimax* means an abrupt departure from this order. In other words, the writer unexpectedly ends not with the most important item but with a trivial or commonplace one.

Anticlimax is sometimes used intentionally–and effectively–as a device for humor:

In spite of corpses, no one is really murdered [in Mrs. Rinehart's mystery stories], not because it isn't done, but because it hurts to get killed, and who wants to hurt anyone?–and besides, it makes a mess on the carpet. –Rex Stout. "These Grapes Need Sugar." *Vogue's First Reader.*

Used *unintentionally*, anticlimax can make a piece of writing seem ridiculous:

POOR: He was dismissed from the team, expelled from school, disowned by his father, and snubbed by a friend.

BETTER: He was snubbed by a friend, dismissed from the team, expelled from school, and disowned by his father.

(See **Climax.**)

Antonym

A word meaning the opposite of another word: *light* and *dark* are antonyms, as are *beautiful* and *ugly*, *pacify* and *enrage*, *under* and *over*, *thriftiness* and *wastefulness*, *sophisticated* and *naïve.*

anxious

When *anxious* means "eagerly desirous," it is followed by an infinitive or by *for*:

Lillian was anxious to perform well at her concert.
Aunt Georgia was anxious for their shop's success.

When *anxious* means "worried," it is followed by *about* or *at*:

Her mother was anxious about Caroline's melancholy moods.
The drama coach became anxious at Sue's bad laryngitis.

any and its compounds

1. *Any* is used as an adjective, as a pronoun, and as an adverb:

ADJECTIVE: No, I don't have any money.
PRONOUN: You won't need any; everything's free.
ADVERB: Are you feeling any better?

2. As a pronoun, *any* may be either singular or plural (and may take either a singular or a plural verb), depending on the meaning intended:

*Has*n't any of the galleys been checked yet? [Singular; speaker means "Isn't there even one that has been checked?"]
Go through the galleys and pull out any that *need* corrections. [Plural; speaker expects more than one to need corrections.]

3. *Anyone* and *anybody* always take singular verbs. They are referred to by singular pronouns in formal English and in most writing:

Anyone who *uses* that much sugar in *her* coffee *invites* tooth decay.
Anyone who *parks his* car in my space will wish *he* hadn't.
I think that anyone should feel free to say what *he* or *she thinks.*

In colloquial usage, however, plural pronouns are often used. (This is probably more true today since people have become aware of sexist language. The alternative is to use *he or she* and *his or her* to include both men and women; however, this use seems clumsy to some.)

Anybody that parks *their* car in my space will wish *they* hadn't.
I think that anyone should feel free to say what *they think.*

4. *Anybody, anyhow, anything,* and *anywhere* are always written as single words. *Anyone* and *anyway* usually are, but when each part has a separate meaning, they are written as two words. (*Any* is then an adjective.) The pronunciation gives a clue to the spelling. If *any* is stressed, the single-word form should probably be used:

STRESS ON *any*: He can outtalk anyone.
STRESS ON *one*: Any one of these ties would go with that suit.

STRESS ON *any*: Then Terry was late anyway.
STRESS ABOUT EQUAL: Any way you take it, it's a compliment.

5. Informal usage sometimes substitutes *anyplace* for *anywhere.* Nonstandard English uses *anywheres* and *anyways.*

Aphorism

See **Epigram.**

Apostrophe (')

1. The most common use of the apostrophe is in writing the possessive forms of nouns and of some of the indefinite pronouns:

his wife's fortune
anyone's guess
nobody's property
the ladies' coats
my sister-in-law's credit cards
the Ridges' house

The apostrophe is not used in the possessive form of the personal pronouns (*hers, its, ours, yours, theirs*) or of *who* (*whose*).

(See **Possessive case** for further examples.)

2. The apostrophe is used to show the omission of one or more letters in contractions:

can't she'd we'll it's (it is) you're he's

It also is used to indicate places in words in which the speaker does not pronounce certain sounds:

"Git movin', Rob, an' see if you can't finish more'n I did," said Jesse.

(See **Conversation.**)

3. An apostrophe is often used to form the plural of figures, symbols, letters of the alphabet, and words being discussed as words:

Europeans write their 7's with a small bar to distinguish them from *1*'s.
Edna and Mary each got B's on the final exam.
Miss Siegel had caught all five of my misspelled *occurred*'s.

(For further examples, see **Plurals of nouns,** section 9.)

Apostrophe

A figure of speech in which the absent are addressed as though present, the inanimate as though animate, or the dead as though living. The following is an apostrophe used for humorous effect:

> Beware, O asparagus, you've stalked my last meal.
> You look like a snake and slip down like an eel.
> I'd prefer drinking a bottle of turpentine,
> Rather than eating a tidbit so serpentine.
> —Wanda Fergus

Appendix

An addition at the end of a book. It may contain lists of definitions, biographical sketches, maps, charts, or other supplementary material like long tables and documents.

The English plural form *appendixes* is much more common now than the Latin plural *appendices* /ə pen′də sēz′/, used mainly in formal writing.

Appositives

1. *Apposition* means, literally, "a putting beside." An *appositive* is a second noun, or the equivalent of a noun, that is placed beside a first noun to explain it more fully. The appositive noun often has modifiers:

Carrie, *my cousin in Fresno,* runs a fruit stand.
His childhood hobby, *collecting coins,* has made him a rich man.
Her next bit of information, *that the cook had quit,* was incorrect.
Leo loved to use the expression *comme il faut.*

Introductory expressions—*such as, namely, or, like, that is, for example*—are sometimes used with appositives:

Certain euphemisms, such as *tonsorial artist* for *hairdresser*, are designed to boost the ego.

Some of the articles–for example, "Exciting and High-Paying Jobs"–didn't have to be assigned.

Occasionally an appositive is put before the noun it explains:

A dedicated soccer *enthusiast* all his life, Coach López was disappointed by the small turnout at the soccer movie.

Sometimes the appositive is separated from the noun it explains:

Carmen took her place on the mat across from the trapeze–a tiny but dynamic *figure*.

An appositive is sometimes used to sum up the idea expressed in a preceding group of words:

Cliff is always lending money to his friends–a *habit* that makes him vulnerable.

An appositive might sum up a preceding series of nouns:

Spaghetti, French fries, pecan pie, éclairs–high-calorie *foods* like these are what had made him gain twenty pounds.

Or a series of appositives may be used to explain a single noun:

Any reasonable excuse–a family *crisis, illness,* a *snowstorm*–will be accepted.

2. Appositives agree in case with the words they are in apposition with:

The lucky winners, Ted and *I*, got season passes for the baseball games. [The nominative-case pronoun *I* is used to agree with the subject noun *winners*.]
Unfortunately, Miss Hardy had appointed us–Ted and *me*–to be the clean-up crew. [The objective-case pronoun *me* is used to agree with the direct object *us*.]

3. For the punctuation of appositives, see **Comma,** section 6, and **Dash,** section 4.

Appropriateness

To be effective, English must be not only clear and lively, but also *appropriate.* Language is appropriate when it is suitable to the audience, to the subject, and to the situation. For example, a greeting like "Hiya, Stan my man" might be quite appropriate for a classmate. But it would be quite inappropriate for an elderly neighbor. "Hi, Mr. Levin" or "Good evening, Mr. Levin" would be far more suitable in addressing him. Similarly, the kind of language you would use in giving a report to the student council about a less-than-harmonious committee meeting would be very different from the kind of language you would use in a letter telling your best friend about the same meeting. Dignified, objective language would be appropriate for the first but out of place in the second.

As these examples suggest, there is not just one kind of English, appropriate for every speaking and writing situation; there are different kinds. In general, these different kinds of English can be sorted into three main types: formal, informal, and nonstandard. For a discussion of how these kinds of English differ and how they are used, see **Usage.**

Archaic

A term applied to words and expressions once common in the language but no longer in general use. Such expressions are now found only in books of an earlier period or in books that imitate the style of an earlier period: *eftsoons*, *gramercy*, *doeth*, *kerne*, *aroint*, *mage*. In general writing, they should be avoided.

Argumentum ad hominem

Here is an example of *argumentum ad hominem* ("an argument directed to the man"): In a TV news interview Mr. Zee, an automobile company executive, is asked to reply to a magazine article in which the author, a Dr. Redan, charges that automobiles are being made of shoddy materials. Mr. Zee makes a brief statement: "Redan's claims are ridiculous. What does a surgeon know about manufacturing cars? He should stay in his operating room."

Notice that instead of sticking to the point (the quality of materials used in making automobiles), Zee launches into an attack on Dr. Redan. Since it is likely that the average surgeon does not know much about car manufacturing (though this may not be true of Dr. Redan), an unwary listener might accept Zee's statement as a valid reply. But it is not. By shifting the attack to Dr. Redan, Zee is sidestepping the real question, the one he should be answering: Are cars being made of shoddy materials?

arise

Situations and difficulties and questions *arise*, but people *rise* (rather formal) or *get up*:

We doubt that such a problem will ever arise.
We were to rise (*or* get up) when the bride appeared.

In formal writing and in poetry, *arise* is sometimes used in referring to people.

around, round

In informal English *around* and *round* are used interchangeably. The tendency is to use *round* (or to clip the *a* of *around* so that it sounds like *round*):

My parents hope to fly round (*or* around) the world some day.
Anna tied a hemp cord round (*or* around) her waist.

Formal English generally uses *around* to mean "here and there" or "in every direction," and *round* to mean "in a circular or a reverse motion":

They walked around the shopping mall and then had dinner.
Whose spaceship was the first to fly round the earth?
Don't turn round now, but isn't that a movie star sitting behind us?

Articles

A, an, and *the,* sometimes called *noun markers,* are generally known as *articles. A* and *an* are *indefinite* articles; they point out any of a group (He grabbed *a* sandwich; I want *an* answer). *The* is the *definite* article; it points out a certain one of a group (*The* sandwich was stale; *The* answer was wrong).

Some grammarians regard articles as a class of adjectives. (See **a, an** and **the.**)

as

One of the most versatile words in our language, *as* has several uses:

1. The conjunction *as* introduces several kinds of adverbial clauses:

Just come dressed *as you are.* [Shows manner.]
I ran as fast *as I could.* [Shows degree.]
Sherry is as loud *as her sister (is).* [Shows comparison.]
As you enter, pick up one of the questionnaires by the door. [Means "when."]
The alarm went off *as he was preparing to go to bed.* [Means "while."]
Hungry *as she was,* she couldn't eat the squirrel stew. [Means "though."]

The conjunction *as* is a problem in writing. Because of the variety of its meanings, it is overused. Often a more exact conjunction would make the intended meaning immediately clear:

AMBIGUOUS: As Dad was in the living room watching TV, Ken and I rehearsed our skit in the kitchen.
BETTER: Since (*or* Because) Dad was in the living room. . . .
BETTER: While Dad was in the living room. . . .

2. As an adverb, *as* shows degree:

The watermelons are *as* cheap now as they will ever be.

3. Used as a relative pronoun, *as* usually follows *the same* or *such*:

Are your shoes *the same* size *as* mine [are]?
Scott had never seen *such* a sight *as* that back home.

In nonstandard English, the relative pronoun *as* is sometimes used for *who* or *that*:

NONSTANDARD: Anyone as has a ticket can attend.
STANDARD: Anyone who has a ticket can attend.

4. As a preposition, *as* means "in the role of" or "in the capacity of":

I wish I had seen Sir Laurence Olivier on the stage *as* Hamlet.
Last summer Bob worked *as* a waiter at the Corner Cupboard.

(See also **as . . . as; like, as.**)

as . . . as

1. When making a double comparison (like "as much as, if not more than") in speech, we often omit the second *as*:

He complained as much if not more than his wife.
Rudy's bite is as bad or worse than his bark.

In formal writing, this second *as* is generally included:

He complained as much as, if not more than, his wife.
Rudy's bite is as bad as or worse than his bark.

But many people consider these constructions rather clumsy and avoid them by stating the comparison thus:

He complained as much as his wife, if not more.
Rudy's bite is as bad as his bark or worse.

2. Guard against carelessly using *than* for the second *as* in a comparison like this:

We sold ten times *as* many banquet tickets *as* they did.
[Not: ten times *as* many banquet tickets *than* they did.]

3. In negative comparisons some formal writers use *not so . . . as*, but *not as . . . as* is the most common idiom in all styles:

FORMAL: Mr. Gorman is not *so* politically active *as* his family.
[Or: not *as* politically active.]
GENERAL: Mr. Gorman is not *as* politically active *as* his family.

as, like

For a discussion of the choice between *as* and *like* (Hold the guitar *as* he does; Hold the guitar *like* he does), see **like, as.**

as if, as though

In formal English, the subjunctive is generally used after *as if* or *as though*; in informal English, the indicative is often used:

FORMAL: She acted as if (as though) she *were* the supervisor.
INFORMAL: She acted as if (as though) she *was* the supervisor.

(For further discussion, see **Subjunctive.**)

as to

A commonly used, but clumsy, substitute for a single preposition—usually *on*, *about*, or *of*:

CLUMSY: The manager made one comment as to the charges of incompetence.
BETTER: The manager made one comment about the charges of incompetence.

Sometimes *as to* is simply deadwood and should be omitted in writing:

He was not certain [as to] how much the new fares would be.

at

Nonstandard English commonly adds an unnecessary *at* to questions beginning with *where*:

NONSTANDARD: Where are they at? Where is he working at?
STANDARD: Where are they? Where is he working?

athletics

Pronounced /ath let′iks/—three syllables, not four. When *athletics* refers to physical sports, games, and exercises, it generally takes a plural verb:

Athletics *are* popular at the state university—especially tennis and gymnastics.

When it refers to the principles of athletic training or a system of athletic training, it usually takes a singular verb:

In those days, athletics *was considered* unimportant.

Author card

See **Card catalog.**

Auxiliary verb

A verb used with another verb to help it express the exact meaning intended. An auxiliary verb helps show the tense, person, voice, and mood of the main verb. The most common auxiliaries are the forms of *be*, *have*, and *do* (*is* waiting, *has been* rewarded, *did* explain). Others frequently used are the "modals": *can*, *could*, *may*, *might*, *shall*, *should*, *will*, *would*, *must*. (See **Modals.**)

awful

See **Counter words.**

awhile, a while

One word when an adverb; two words when *while* is a noun in a prepositional phrase:

Stay *awhile* and watch me work. [Adverb modifying the verb *Stay*.]
Nham stayed for *a while* but then got bored and left. [*While* is object of the preposition *for*.]

Awkward writing

Awkwardness in writing may be the result of any one of a number of faults in sentence structure—vague pronoun reference, clumsy interruptions, shifted constructions, and so on. (See **Misplaced modifiers, Parallel constructions,** and **Reference of pronouns.**)

B B B B B B

Back-formations

Ordinarily a new form of a word is made by adding to an existing base form. For example, adding *-er* to the verb *talk* and *-y* to the noun *salt* resulted in two new forms–the noun *talker* and the adjective *salty.* But occasionally the opposite is true: A new form is made by dropping a part of an already existing form. For instance, the noun *peddler* was the original form. Dropping part of it resulted in the new verb form *peddle.* Similarly, dropping part of the already existing noun *donation* resulted in the new verb form *donate.* Forms made like this are called *back-formations.*

When a back-formation fills a need, as *peddle* and *donate* do, it usually is quickly accepted and used by all. But not every back-formation is welcomed with open arms. *Sculpt* from *sculpture*, for example, is considered correct only in informal usage; the verb *burgle* from *burglar* is considered slang. (See **enthuse.**)

back of, in back of

Both of these phrases are now established as standard usages in the United States, though many people consider the preposition *behind* more appropriate in writing, especially formal writing:

STANDARD: The child back of me cried during the entire movie.
[Or: in back of me, behind me.]

backward, backwards

Used interchangeably as adverbs:

Every other word in the message was spelled backward.
Every other word in the message was spelled backwards.

Only *backward* is used as an adjective:

With a backward glance at the audience, the tenor made his exit.

bad, badly

Bad is generally used as an adjective, *badly* as an adverb:

Kim had a bad scare.
Karl made a bad guess.

They were badly mistaken.
We played bridge badly.

In formal English and in informal writing, *bad*–not *badly*–is used as a predicate adjective following a linking verb:

He felt bad about breaking the vase.
The polluted lake smelled bad.

In informal speech, *badly* is often used as a complement, especially after the verb *feel*:

I felt badly about his being fired. [Written: felt bad.]

But this form is not appropriate in writing.

Informal English uses *badly* to mean "very much":

She needs some new clothes badly.

Bad and *badly* are both compared irregularly:

bad	worse	worst
badly	worse	worst

Bad grammar

A term of disapproval applied to all sorts of expressions ranging from "He ain't went yet" to "Who does he mean?" (instead of "Whom does he mean?") and "You can go now" (instead of "You may go now"). People who use this term to condemn *all* such expressions believe that there is just one kind of English that is "good," and that any departure from this one kind is "bad." They do not take into account that there are several kinds of English–each one good or appropriate for certain occasions, social groups, or geographical sections.

There is nothing wrong with these expressions in themselves. What makes them wrong is using them in situations where they are not appropriate. And then the objection to them is not that they are sins against grammar, but that they are sins against usage. For example, in informal speech "*Who* did she want?" and "The reason Sam was chosen was *because* he is tall" are appropriate. In formal English they are not. "*Whom* did she want?" and "The reason Sam was chosen was *that* he is tall" are the appropriate forms there.

Your goal should be to learn enough about the various kinds of English so that you can recognize and use the forms and the sentence structures that are appropriate at different times. (See **Usage.**)

Balanced sentences

Sentences in which two or more parts are noticeably similar in length and form. Using balanced sentences is an effective way to emphasize important ideas, especially ideas expressing comparisons and contrasts:

In science class, Ann's questions were welcomed as thought-provoking; in history class, they were dismissed as impertinent.

be

1. Forms. *Be* is a highly irregular verb with the following forms:

INFINITIVE:	(to) be
PRESENT PARTICIPLE:	being
PAST PARTICIPLE:	been
PRESENT:	I am, you are, he is; we, you, they are
PAST:	I was, you were, he was; we, you, they were
SUBJUNCTIVE:	be, were

2. As linking verb. *Be* is the most common linking verb, a verb that links a subject with a subject complement:

Roberta was a *sophomore* then. [Noun.]
The big piece is *mine.* [Pronoun.]
His face was *blank*. [Adjective.]

Pronoun complements after the verb *be* are in the nominative case in written English:

Yes, but it was *she* who paid for the window. [Not *her.*]
The first ones to volunteer were *he* and *I.* [Not *him* and *me.*]

In informal speech and writing "It's me" has practically replaced the formal "It is I." But other objective-case pronouns (*him*, *her*, *us*, *them*) are not as yet fully acceptable. (See **It's me.**)

3. As auxiliary verb. Forms of *be* are used with the present participles of other verbs to form the progressive-tense forms:

I am listening.
You have been hiding.
He has been lying.
We had been standing.
She will be smiling.
They were eating.

Forms of *be* are used with the past participles of other verbs to form the passive-verb forms:

I was delayed.
You have been paid.
It should have been cut.
She will be chosen.
They were mailed.
We had been saved.

In informal English one form of *be* is often used to serve both as a linking verb and as an auxiliary:

Dave *was* angry and beginning to show signs of his old temper.

In formal usage the form of *be* is repeated:

Dave *was* angry and *was* beginning to show signs of his old temper.

because

A subordinating conjunction used to introduce a clause that gives the reason for the statement in the main clause:

Because he was the oldest, he thought he could boss us around.

The conjunction *as* is often used instead of *because* in such clauses. But since *because* is more definite and emphatic than *as*, *because* is preferred in written English:

AMBIGUOUS: *As* Dad was busy working out his income tax, I decided it was better not to ask for money right then. [Seems at first to mean "while."]

DEFINITE: *Because* Dad was busy working out his income tax, I decided it was better not to ask for money right then.

In formal English the coordinating conjunction *for* is often used instead of *because*, especially when the clause is used to give evidence for or to explain the main statement:

INFORMAL: I knew we'd have a fire drill that period, because the fire chief had just pulled into the front parking area.

FORMAL: I knew we would have a fire drill that period, for the fire chief had just pulled into the front parking area.

(See **reason is because** and **as.**)

Begging the question

A speaker or writer who offers as evidence an assumption that needs to be proved is *begging the question.* Here is an argument that may remind you of your grade-school days: Rico says, "Why do I think Lisa cheats? Because she's a cheater; that's why."

To anyone but a child, this is a most unsatisfactory argument. Rico gives no real evidence to prove the truth of his conclusion about Lisa. Instead, he merely makes a statement that assumes *as already proved* the very point he is supposed to be proving. Rico, to use the logician's term, is *begging the question*–he is evading the issue by simply assuming as true a conclusion whose truth still needs to be proved. In begging the question, he is actually reasoning in a circle; his reasoning amounts to nothing more than "My conclusion is true because it is true."

Begging the question is usually done in a manner less blatant than Rico's. Often, only a careful listener can detect the faulty reasoning. Let us examine one high-school senior's attack on unannounced tests: "I think that pop quizzes are unfair because it is unreasonable to expect an unprepared student to perform well on a test." The argument restated is: Pop quizzes are unfair because an unprepared student cannot do well on them. The very words *unfair* and *unreasonable*, in this context, beg the question because they make assumptions that are yet to be proved. First of all, the senior is assuming that students will necessarily be caught unprepared by a pop quiz. Secondly, the senior has provided no valid argument against pop quizzes. Any of the following might provide a more legitimate argument against such quizzes:

1. While pop quizzes do test preparedness, they do not always measure actual knowledge and understanding of material.
2. Some students collapse under pressure; others require more time to organize their thoughts than a pop quiz allows.
3. Pop quizzes are usually geared to test superficial knowledge–not to evaluate a real grasp of the material.

being as, being that

Certain dialects use *being as* and *being that* in place of the conjunctions *since* and *because*, which are standard:

DIALECT: Being as Leo owned the ball and bat, we had to give in.
STANDARD: Since Leo owned the ball and bat, we had to give in.

DIALECT: Being that she seemed interested, we told her the story.
STANDARD: Because she seemed interested, we told her the story.

beside, besides

Beside is most commonly used as a preposition meaning "by the side of":

Finally, I turned to the man beside me and greeted him.

It is also used figuratively in certain rather formal idioms:

That is true, Harry, but quite beside the point.
He rushed at Tod, beside himself with rage.

Besides is used both as an adverb and as a preposition meaning "in addition (to)" or "except":

I typed her letter—and mailed it besides. [Adverb—"in addition."]
Besides being conceited, he is a bore. [Preposition—"in addition to."]
Nobody besides Emily had skis. [Preposition—"except."]

Besides is also used as a conjunctive adverb meaning "moreover":

Andy didn't feel like talking to Gloria; besides, he owed her a dollar and had only fifty cents.

between, among

Among implies more than two persons, places, or things:

She divided the money among the five of us.

Between is generally used to refer to only two:

The third-prize money was divided between Tomás and Gordon.

When used to refer to more than two, *between* suggests that the persons, places, or things are being considered two at a time:

A treaty between the four powers was drawn up.
She can't tell the difference between gingham, calico, and percale.

Between is followed either by a plural (between *halves*, between the *rows*) or by two expressions joined by *and*—not by *or* or *to*:

ILLOGICAL: I had to choose between asking her for the money *or* paying the bill myself.
LOGICAL: I had to choose between asking her for the money *and* paying the bill myself.

ILLOGICAL: Between Memorial Day *to* Labor Day, he earned two hundred dollars.
LOGICAL: Between Memorial Day *and* Labor Day, he earned two hundred dollars.

Although expressions like "between each cottage" and "between every quarter" are common in speech, it would be more logical to say:

There was an immense lawn between each cottage and the next.
The band performed between quarters. [Or: after every quarter.]

between you and me

In standard English the objective-case pronouns are used as objects of prepositions: *between you and me, between you and her, between you and him, between you and us, between you and them.*

Because so much emphasis is placed on the use of the nominative-case pronouns in sentences like "You and I should help," "Ann and he just left," "It was she," some people mistakenly think that "you and me" and "Ann and him" are always incorrect. So in an effort to be correct, they say "between you and I" and "between Ann and he," not realizing that in these phrases the objective forms, not the nominative, are called for: "between you and me," "between Ann and him."

Bible, bible

Bible is capitalized but not italicized or enclosed in quotation marks when it refers to the Holy Scriptures:

Whenever she was worried, Grandma turned to her Bible.

The word is neither capitalized nor italicized when it refers to a book that is regarded as an authority:

Roget's *Thesaurus* is the professional writer's bible.

These are the forms used in referring to parts of the Bible:

the Old Testament the New Testament
I Kings 10:6–12 [The 6th to the 12th verses in the 10th chapter of the First Book of Kings.]
The Last Supper is described in Matthew 26:20–29 and in John 13–17. [The 20th to the 29th verses in the 26th chapter of the Gospel of Matthew and the 13th to the 17th chapters of the Gospel of John.]

The adjective *Biblical* is often not capitalized: *biblical.*

Bibliography

See Appendix.

Big words

"Big words" are not necessarily long words. Instead they are uncommon, rather formal words that seem out of place in ordinary writing: *cogitate* (for *think*), *nefarious* (for *wicked*), *stentorian* (for *loud*), *inebriated* (for *drunk*). Big words tend to weaken the effectiveness of your writing by calling attention to themselves and away from what you are saying.
(See **Gobbledygook** and **Doublespeak.**)

blame

Both *blame . . . for* and *blame . . . on* are standard English. There is only a slight difference in meaning:

Everyone blamed Joel for the accident. [That is, everyone held him responsible, accused him of being at fault.]
Everyone blamed the accident on Joel. [That is, everyone claimed that he was responsible, ascribed the responsibility for the accident to him.]

Blend

A coined word made by telescoping two words into one:

glasphalt (*glass* and *asphalt*)
dumfound (from *dumb* and *confound*)
chortle (from *chuckle* and *snort*)
gasohol (from *gas* and *alcohol*)
blotch (from *blot* and *botch*)
medicare (from *medical* and *care*)

Until a blend has become accepted as part of the general vocabulary, as *motel* (from *motorist* and *hotel*) and *gerrymander* (from *Gerry* and *salamander*) have, it is more appropriate in informal writing than in formal. Blends are also called *portmanteau words* from the French *portmanteau*, meaning "a traveling bag with two compartments."

blond, blonde

As a noun, *blond* is a man; *blonde*, a woman:

The two youngest boys are blonds. My sister is a blonde.

Although the adjective is spelled with or without the final *e*, *blond* is the more common spelling:

She has blond hair and brown eyes.

born, borne

The past participle of *bear* in most of its meanings is *borne*:

The child had borne these hardships too long. ["Endured."]
Boy and balloon, borne aloft by the heavy gusts, quickly disappeared from view. ["Carried."]
She had borne five children. ["Given birth to."]

But *born* is the usual spelling in such sentences as:

My hamsters, Stop and Go, were born in September.
Lois is a born writer.
Born and raised in Illinois, Tasha loved the prairies.

borrow, lend

Borrow means "to get something from another person with the understanding that it is to be returned":

Rosalyn was reluctant to borrow my book over vacation.

Lend means "to let another have or use something temporarily":

If you lend me your coat I will have it cleaned before I return it.

In certain regional dialects *borrow* is used to mean "lend":

DIALECT: I'd have borrowed him the money, but I didn't have it.
STANDARD: I'd have lent him the money, but I didn't have it.

Borrow is usually followed by *from,* rarely by *of:*

We borrowed an extra chair from the neighbors upstairs.
Ken's mother had borrowed money of the credit union.

Borrow . . . off and *borrow . . . off of* are nonstandard.

NONSTANDARD: Jan's brother borrowed money off of the bank to buy a mobile home.

STANDARD: Jan's brother borrowed money from the bank to buy a mobile home.

Borrowed words

In the course of its history, English has borrowed words from many other languages. Some of these borrowings have been deliberate: scientists and scholars have often gone to foreign languages for names for new discoveries, ideas, or situations. Others have been brought in by groups of immigrants, introduced through commerce or trade, or picked up by large groups of citizens (soldiers, for example, or students) who have visited foreign lands. Some of these borrowed words retain their original forms and pronunciations (*soufflé, faux pas, mot juste, panettone*). But many of them—generally the most useful ones—are gradually Anglicized to bring their pronunciation (and sometimes their spelling) in line with English usage. (See section 3.)

1. Use. The reason for the common use of many borrowed words is that they supply a real need in our language. Many times they say in a word or two what it would take many English words to say—for example, *déjà vu,* "the illusion of having previously experienced something one is actually experiencing for the first time." Many times they are the only names we have for certain objects or ideas: *coup d'état, papier-mâché, kitsch, habeas corpus, kapok.* In other instances, they carry with them strong connotations that are extremely important in certain contexts: *macho, gemütlich, chutzpah, simpatico, terra incognita.* Borrowed words for which there are adequate English equivalents are not so likely to become common or *Anglicized,* retaining always a foreign flavor: *sans doute, Schrecklichkeit, vin rouge, coup d'oeil.* For these we can say *doubtless, horror, red wine, a quick glance.*

Borrowed words have greatly enriched English; in fact, it would be practically impossible to communicate without them. This sample list merely hints at the extent of these borrowings:

alligator (Spanish)
apropos (French)
arpeggio (Italian)
bamboo (Malay)
berserk (Old Norse)
blitz (German)
boomerang (Australian)
borsch (Russian)
boss (Dutch)
bungalow (Hindustani)
catastrophe (Greek)
dodo (Portuguese)
factory (Latin)
gape (Scandinavian)
typhoon (Chinese)
polka (Czech)
shawl (Persian)
slalom (Norwegian)
sputnik (Russian)
violin (Italian)

2. Italics. Borrowed words so commonly used that they have become part of the general vocabulary are written without italics. Those that have not been Anglicized and are still thought of as foreign words are usually italicized in print (underlined in writing):

en avant *fait accompli* *paparazzo* *sans pareil* *shalom*

When in doubt about whether to italicize a particular word or phrase, consult a dictionary. In recent dictionaries, borrowed words that are not part of the general English vocabulary are indicated by a double dagger (‡), by two parallel bars (||), by a label (*Italian*, *French*, *German*, etc.) preceding the definitions, or by being set in italics.

3. Pronunciation. The original pronunciation and form of some borrowed words has been retained: *garçon*, *auf Wiedersehen*, *coq au vin*, and *Gestalt*, for example. But many borrowed words—especially the ones that prove very useful but are hard to pronounce or spell—have been *Anglicized*, that is, given an English pronunciation or form. For instance, the French words *au gratin* /ō grȧ tᴀɴ′/ are generally given the pronunciation /ō grat′n/ or /ō grät′n/. The Italian *piazza* /pē ät′sə/ is usually pronounced /pē az′ə/. The Spanish *rebozo* /re bô′thô/ is usually pronounced /ri bō′zō/. And the word *employé*, borrowed from French, is commonly spelled without the accent mark: *employee* or *employe*.

both

Both is used to emphasize twoness:

His foster parents were both tennis instructors.
The Panthers and the Tigers both belong to the Valley League.

In speech *both* is sometimes used in sentences like these:

The novel and the movie were both alike.
Both Florence and Venice are equally fascinating.

But since *alike* in the first example and *equally* in the second express the intended meaning clearly, the word *both* is unnecessary. In writing, it should be omitted as a bit of deadwood.

In some regional dialects *both* is used in place of *two*:

DIALECT: The both girls went into engineering.
STANDARD: The two girls went into engineering.

both . . . and

Used as correlative conjunctions (conjunctions that work in pairs):

He was both ready and willing to help out.

(See **Correlative conjunctions.**)

boughten

Used in some regional dialects to distinguish articles bought at a store from those that are homemade:

DIALECT: This was Aunt Tilly's first boughten rug.
STANDARD: This was Aunt Tilly's first store-bought rug.

Brackets [ ]

Used mainly to enclose an explanation, comment, or correction that is inserted into quoted material:

"According to Alfred Korzybski [the author of *Science and Sanity*, an introduction to the subject of general semantics], a *static* culture, one in which generations pass without change, is a *doomed* culture."

bring, take

The choice between *bring* and *take* depends on the direction of the action. If the motion is toward the speaker, a form of *bring* is used:

If you're coming to the party, please bring me some ice.
He brought me a large bouquet of daisies.

If the motion is away from the speaker, *take* is used:

When you go home, be sure to take some cake.
If you cannot find your record, you can take mine to the party.

British usage

See **English, varieties of.**

Broad reference

A pronoun that refers to a preceding idea (expressed in a group of words) rather than to a specific, one-word antecedent is said to have "broad reference":

The next month the cost of living went up another 2 percent, *which* caused a serious problem for retired people with a small fixed income. [The *which* refers to the whole idea stated in the main clause.]

Bromide

A figurative term for a commonplace idea or a trite remark:

When it rains, it pours.
You can't teach an old dog new tricks.
Haste makes waste.

Since the literal meaning of *bromide* is "a medicine used to induce sleep," the term is an effective–though harsh–name for such expressions. (See **Cliché.**)

brunet, brunette

As a noun, *brunet* is a man; *brunette* is a woman:

The robber was a brunet. Was she always a brunette?

As an adjective, either *brunet* or *brunette* is used.

bunch

In formal English, *bunch* is used only to refer to things that grow together or can be fastened together:

a bunch of celery   a bunch of violets   a bunch of keys

In informal English, *bunch* is used to refer to a small group of anything–including people:

A bunch of boys went to the ice-cream shop together.

burned, burnt

The past tense and the past participle of *burn* are either *burned* or *burnt*:

She burned (*or* burnt) the last batch of cookies.
His cigarette had burned (*or* burnt) a hole in his jacket.

Burned is the more common form, except when the participle is used as an adjective before a noun:

I liked the lemon wafers with the burnt edges.

Business letters

1. The form of business letters. A business letter usually has six parts. Notice the placement and punctuation of the parts:

HEADING	10 Birch Lane Green Bay, Wisconsin 54303 July 12, 19__
INSIDE ADDRESS	Miss Marla Menoni Great Foods Publications 1320 Central Avenue St. Louis, Missouri 63144
SALUTATION	Dear Miss Menoni:
BODY	Please send me the "Fact Sheet on Home Canning," which was offered in your article, "Worldly Pickles," appearing in the June issue of *Great Foods Magazine*. I am enclosing 25¢ and a self-addressed envelope.
CLOSING	Yours truly,
SIGNATURE	Jill Shay

a. If the person to whom the letter is addressed has a title, it is included in the inside address, after the name. A rather long title may be put on a separate line below the name. (Most desk dictionaries have a special section telling the appropriate way to address mail to governors, senators, bishops, and so on.) If the letter is not directed to a particular person, the inside address consists of three lines.

Mr. Timothy Hardy
Director of Market Research
Banalco, Inc.
1000 Market Street
San Francisco, California 94109

The New Yorker Magazine, Inc.
25 West 43rd Street
New York, New York 10036

b. If the letter is not addressed to a particular person by name, until recently it had been the custom to use a masculine form of address—*Dear Sir* or *Gentlemen.* However, with the awareness today that the recipient may likely be a woman, alternative salutations are becoming accepted:

Dear Sir or Madam:
Ladies and Gentlemen:

Dear Bursar:
Dear Editor:
Dear Tri-State Company:

c. Since a typed business letter is single-spaced with double spaces between paragraphs, paragraph indentions are not needed and often are not used. However, some people prefer indenting the first word of typewritten paragraphs a half inch or an inch (five spaces or ten).

d. One of the conventional closings is generally used to end the letter:

Very truly yours, Sincerely, Cordially yours,

e. A man does not write the title *Mr.* before his signature, but a woman may write *Miss* or *Ms.* in parentheses before her name or add her married name below her signature to indicate how she would like to be addressed in the reply:

Very truly yours,

(Miss) May Luke

Cordially yours,

Ruth L. Pyrek

(Mrs. Henry A. Pyrek)

2. The envelope.

```
Carol Prattner
211 Taft Road, Apt. 211
Orem, Texas 84057

                    Mr. J. B. Otto, Manager
                    Sugargrove Farm
                    Rural Route 2, Box 27
                    Derby, Vermont 05829
```

3. Folding the letter. A business letter, usually written on paper 8½ × 11 inches, is generally folded in one of two ways, depending on the size of the envelope.

For a short envelope–

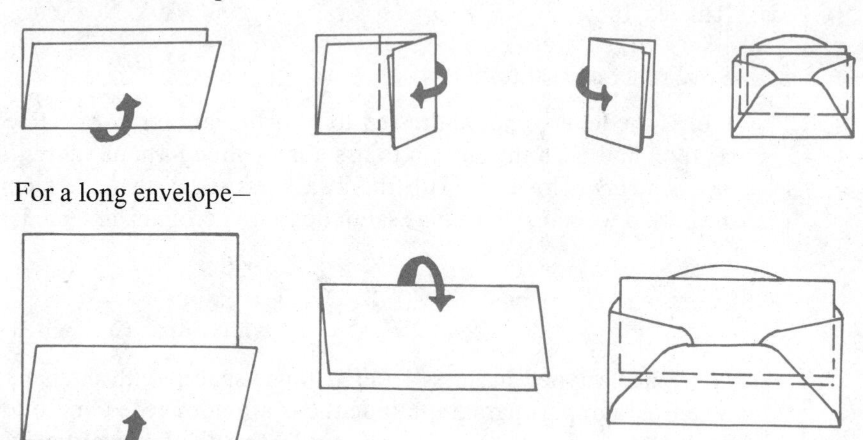

For a long envelope–

bust

Used in nonstandard English for *burst* or *break*:

NONSTANDARD: He dropped the teapot and busted the lid.
STANDARD: He dropped the teapot and broke the lid.

The expressions *bust a bronco*, *bust a trust*, *bust an officer* (reduce in rank) are labeled *Slang* in most dictionaries. But they are so generally used in informal English that they may be considered standard.

but

1. *But* is a coordinating conjunction used to connect two contrasting expressions. The words, phrases, or clauses joined by *but* should be of the same grammatical form:

ADJECTIVES: Neil was brash but likable.
ADVERBS: Mrs. Yaniz spoke briefly but convincingly.
PHRASES: Dr. Lee was in the building, but not in her office.
SUBORDINATE CLAUSES: I didn't choose the blue suit because I liked it better but because it cost less.
MAIN CLAUSES: We do all the work, but he takes all the credit.

The parts joined by *but* should actually be contrasting or opposite in thought. If they are not, *but* should not be used to join them:

CONTRASTING IDEAS: Joan's ankle was badly swollen, but she managed to come to work.

NOT CONTRASTING: The directions were printed in small type, *and* he couldn't read them without his glasses. [Not: *but* he couldn't read them.]

But should not be combined with a word like *however*, which adds nothing to its meaning:

Stan earned four hundred dollars last summer, but he didn't save a single penny. [Not: but *however* he didn't save.]

(For the punctuation of compound sentences with *but*, see **Comma,** section 1.)

2. *But* is sometimes used at the beginning of a sentence to emphasize the contrast between ideas:

Paul was one of the most ambitious students in the School of Design. He was enthusiastic, hard-working, and intelligent. But he had no talent.

Used too often, however, this introductory *But* gets tiresome and loses its effectiveness.

3. *But* is also used as a preposition meaning "except" and as a rather formal adverb meaning "only" or "no more than":

PREPOSITION: Everyone got the point but Elmer.
ADVERB: If I had but known, I would have warned her.
ADVERB: There were but five Democrats in the whole town.

Using *not* with *but* (in the sense of "no more than") makes a double negative:

There weren't but five Democrats in the whole town.

Though this double negative with *but* is found in informal speech, it is not appropriate in writing. There the *not* should be dropped. If the sentence then seems too formal in tone, the *but* can be changed to *only*:

There were only five Democrats in the whole town.

but that, but what

In informal written English *but that* is the usual conjunction in sentences like these:

There is no doubt but that Dale wrote the letter.
She has no doubt but that she will get the promotion.

In informal speech, *but what* (or *but* alone) is common:

There is no doubt but what Dale wrote the letter.
She has no doubt but she will get the promotion.

In formal English, *that* alone is preferred:

There is no doubt that Dale wrote the letter.
She has no doubt that she will get the promotion.

but which, but who

See **and which, and who.**

buy

Used with *from*, not with *off* or *off of*:

NONSTANDARD: Sid bought a ring and a tie off of the vendor.
STANDARD: Sid bought a ring and a tie from the vendor.

Buy off is an idiomatic phrase meaning "bribe":

The contractor tried to buy off the building inspector.

can, may

1. In informal English (both spoken and written) *can* is used to express permission as well as ability:

PERMISSION: Can I go with you?
You can't sleep in the park.
ABILITY: Sue can speak Chinese as well as she speaks English.
Their baby can't talk yet.

May is rarely used except to express possibility:

The wall may crack. He may be out of town.

2. In formal English *can* is generally used only to express ability:

Camels can go without water for a long time.
Can Mary drive a big truck?

To express permission, *may* is generally used:

May we have an early dinner?
You may report for duty tomorrow.

Canadian English

See **English, varieties of.**

cannot, can not

Both are used, but *cannot* is more common.

can't help but

A colloquial expression, common in everyday speech and in informal writing:

We can't help but enjoy the company.

In formal English, the expression *cannot help* followed by a gerund is more likely:

We cannot help enjoying the company.

capital, capitol

Capital always has the basic meaning of "chief; head; first in its class or in importance." As a noun, *capital* may refer to a city, to money or resources, or to property:

When I was in Richmond, the capital of Virginia, I visited several historic sites.
Her small company has a capital of $55,000.

As an adjective, *capital* may be used in ways such as the following:

Murder is a capital offense in many countries.
A moonlight swim? That's a capital idea!
Regina is a capital city.

When it is capitalized, *Capitol* refers to the building at Washington, D.C., in which Congress meets. When it begins with a lower-case letter, *capitol* refers to the building in which a state legislature meets. In either case, this word, as used in the United States, always applies only to a building in which the legislature meets. Many of these buildings have a dome; you might associate the *o* in *capitol* with the *o* in *dome* in order to help you spell this word:

The architectural students examined the domes on the capitols of several states.

Capital letters

1. Sentence capitals. a. The first word of a sentence is always capitalized.

b. In quotations, the first word of a quoted sentence is capitalized, but if the quoted sentence is interrupted by explanatory words (*he said, she answered,* etc.), the first word of its second part is not capitalized:

Uncle Bill said, "Eating out is too expensive."
"It wouldn't be," Aunt Hattie reminded him, "if you didn't always order prime rib. Why don't you stick to a hamburger?"
"I'd rather just stay home then," he replied. "Your hamburgers are better tasting than those in a restaurant."

c. A sentence enclosed in parentheses is capitalized when it stands *between* other sentences:

The Front Page presents newspaper people as a rough, tough, eccentric lot. (The main character is a reporter who can't be bothered to show up for his wedding trip because he is busy hiding an escaped criminal from the police.) Hecht and MacArthur, the authors, based the play on their own experiences as reporters in Chicago.

But when a sentence enclosed in parentheses comes *within* another sentence, it is not usually capitalized:

While Herzog was undergoing the worst tortures on the way back from the Himalayas (his hopelessly frozen fingers and toes were being amputated, and he was receiving painful injections that might or might not restore life to his arms and legs), he had only one fear—that he would never be able to go mountain climbing again.

2. Proper nouns and abbreviations of proper nouns are capitalized:

PEOPLE: Justice Louis D. Brandeis, Mary Cassatt, Eugene Debs

PLACES: Puerto Rico, Yellowstone National Park, Mount Holyoke

RACES, LANGUAGES, POLITICAL PARTIES: Mongoloid, Swahili, the Socialist Party, Republicans

CHURCHES, SYNAGOGUES, AND THEIR MEMBERS: St. Paul's Cathedral, Anshe Emet, Episcopalians, Baptists

BUSINESS FIRMS: Air Canada, General Foods Corporation, IBM Corporation

DAYS, MONTHS, HOLIDAYS, HOLY DAYS: Friday, May, Labor Day, Yom Kippur

ORGANIZATIONS: Girl Scouts of the U.S.A., Rotary International, Sigma Xi

INSTITUTIONS: Barat College, California Institute of Technology, Yale

SHIPS, SPACECRAFT, PLANES: H.M.S. *Victory*, *Nautilus*, *Sputnik II*, *Air Force One*

HISTORICAL EVENTS, PERIODS, DOCUMENTS: Revolutionary War, Dark Ages, Iron Age, Bill of Rights

BUILDINGS: Sun-Times Building, Washington Memorial, White House

TRADE NAMES: Clorox, Kodak, Chanel No. 5

SACRED FIGURES, BIBLE, PARTS OF THE BIBLE: God, our Father, Old Testament, Leviticus (See **Bible, bible.**)

3. Adjectives formed from proper nouns are generally capitalized, but the words they modify are not, unless they themselves are proper nouns:

Japanese customs   Shakespearean England   Danish furniture

4. The name of the planet earth is not capitalized when *the* precedes it; otherwise it is usually capitalized:

The *earth's* orbit is an ellipse and not a circle.
The third planet from the sun is *Earth.*

The names of all other planets (Jupiter, Venus, Saturn, etc.), which are derived from proper names, are always capitalized.

5. The names of the seasons are not capitalized:

In the *spring* we again postponed our trip to early *autumn.*

6. The points of the compass (south, north, southwest, etc.) are not capitalized when they indicate direction:

The library is *east* of the tracks; the high school is *west.*

They are generally capitalized, however, when used as the names of geographical regions:

She went to college in the *East*, but she hopes to live in the *West*.

7. School subjects are not capitalized unless they are names of languages or of specific numbered courses:

We signed up for *Italian* and *biology*.
I am also taking *Psychology 101*.

8. Words like *street, avenue, river, island, park, building, hospital, hotel, theater, bank, high school, junior*, and *senior* are not capitalized unless they are used as part of a proper noun:

His father owns the *bank* on that *street*; his uncle owns the *theater*.
You can get a good view of the *park* from the *hospital*.
The *juniors* and the *seniors* would like to run our *high school*.

But:			
	Century National Bank	Nile River	McCaskey High School
	Maple Street	Drake Hotel	Evanston Hospital
	Majestic Theater	Junior Prom	Luder's Island

Note: Many newspapers and magazines do not capitalize words like *street, avenue, park, island*, and *river* when they follow a proper noun: *Pine avenue, Laurel park, Passmore island, the Missouri river*. But in your school writing you will probably be expected to follow the more conservative practice of capitalizing the words.

9. Personal titles. Nouns showing office, rank, or profession (*senator, captain, archbishop, judge, coach*, etc.) are always capitalized when used with the name of a person and are usually capitalized when used alone in place of the person's name:

The contracts were approved by *Mayor Hodges*.
"Have you any statement for the press, *Mayor*?" she asked.
When did the *senator* sign the bill?
Art appreciation will be taught by *Professor Blake*. The *professor* I had last year retired.

The title of a country's highest executive is generally capitalized:

The *Prime Minister* called a cabinet meeting yesterday.
The *President* will speak to the nation on TV Tuesday evening.

10. Nouns showing family relationships. Capitalize words like *uncle, aunt, cousin, grandfather, mother, father*, etc., only when they are used with a person's name, or as a substitute for a person's name (unless it is preceded by a word such as *my, their, the, a, an*, etc.):

My *father* and *mother* disapprove of week-night visits–except to Uncle Dan's house.
"When you visit *Grandmother Sprague, Mother*, I'll be the cook."

11. Titles of articles, books, etc. The usual practice is to capitalize the first and last words of the title, all important words (nouns, pronouns, verbs, adverbs, adjectives), and all prepositions of more than four letters:

A Prison Without Walls	*A Tale of Two Cities*
"More Tomatoes with Cheese Recipes"	*The World We Live In*

12. Lines of poetry. In most poetry each line begins with a capital letter. But in much modern poetry this is not true. Remember that poetry must be copied exactly as it originally appeared—with or without capitals, however the poet wrote it.

13. See **O, oh.**

Card catalog

An alphabetical list of all the books in a particular library, arranged on cards in a series of drawers. In the catalog you can find (1) whether the library has a book of a certain title, (2) what books it has by a certain author, (3) what books it has on a given subject, and (4) where you will find a book on the library shelves.

The catalog usually contains at least three cards for every book: an *author* card, a *title* card, and a *subject* card. When you know the author of a book, you generally look for the author card. This is filed alphabetically by the author's last name, which appears at the top of the card. When you know the title of a book but not the author, you look for the title card. It is filed alphabetically according to the first important word of the title.

Sometimes you may want to find books on a certain subject, but you have no particular authors or titles in mind. Then you look in the catalog for subject cards, filed alphabetically according to the subject. Under every subject heading there are cards for the books in the library dealing with that subject. Moreover, a book may be listed under several different subject headings. (A study of American Indian crafts and dress, for example, might be listed under INDIANS OF NORTH AMERICA-COSTUME AND ADORNMENT and HANDICRAFT.) If you do not find the first subject heading you look for, try related subjects. (MORSE CODE may not be listed, but you may find books treating the subject under CIPHER AND TELEGRAPH CODES, COMMERCE, or TELEGRAPH.)

Look on the opposite page at the three catalog cards for Robert F. Marx's *Always Another Adventure.* The top lines differ, but otherwise the cards are exactly the same. The *call number* in the upper left corner of each tells where you will find the book in the library. The top line, **910.4,** is the Dewey classification number. (See **Dewey Decimal System.**) The second line, **M392,** is the author's initial and number. Since this call number is also printed on the spine of the book, it makes it very easy for you to find the book on the library shelves.

Catalog cards tell you other things that you may want to know about a book: the place and date it was published; the name of the publisher; the number of pages; whether it has illustrations, maps, appendixes; and all the subject headings it is listed under.

910.4 Marx, Robert F.
M392

Always another adventure [by] Robert
F. Marx. Cleveland, World [c1967]
332p. illus.

cuba
rers.

910.4 BURIED TREASURE.
M392

Marx, Robert F.
Always another adventure [by] Robert F.
Marx. Cleveland, World [c1967]
332p. illus.

1. Buried trea
diving. 3. Ad
I. Title.

910.4 Always another adventure.
M392

Marx, Robert F.
Always another adventure [by] Robert F.
Marx. Cleveland, World [c1967]
332p. illus.

1. Buried treasure. 2. Skin and scuba
diving. 3. Adventures and adventurers.
I. Title.

Caret (^)

A mark put in a line of manuscript to show that something should be inserted at that point:

had
Cliff ^ done a hard day's work and wanted to be paid.

You will rarely need to use carets in your papers if you take time to revise your first drafts carefully before making final copies. But in general (on exam papers, official forms, committee reports, etc.) there is no objection to your using carets to make corrections, if you do it neatly and not too often.

Case

1. Pronouns change in form depending on how they are used in a sentence. (When I saw *him, he* was wearing *his* badge on *his* arm. *She* was wearing *hers* on *her* coat when we saw *her*.) In grammar, this change of form to match a change in the function of a word is called a change in the "case" of the pronoun.

Personal pronouns (except *you* and *it*) and the pronoun *who* have three different case forms:

NOMINATIVE CASE: I, you, he, she, it, we, you, they; who
OBJECTIVE CASE: me, you, him, her, it, us, you, them; whom
POSSESSIVE CASE: mine, yours, his, hers, its, ours, yours, theirs; whose [The adjective forms are *my*, *your*, *his*, *her*, *its*, *our*, *your*, *their*; *whose*.]

a. The *nominative* forms are used as subjects and in appositives referring to subjects:

Ellen and *she* figured out the answer. [Not: Ellen and *her*.]
We boys won every game. [Not: *Us* boys.]
Who do you think ate the pie? [Not: *Whom. Who* is the subject of the verb *ate.*]
The two older girls–Judy and *she*–offered to baby-sit. [Not: *her.* The pronoun is in apposition with the subject *girls.*]
Is anyone else as bewildered as *I*? [*I* is the subject of the elliptical clause *as I am.*]
Aren't you shorter than *he*? [*He* is the subject of the elliptical clause *than he is.*]
"Who broke the typewriter?" "Not *I.*"

In casual conversation the objective form of the pronoun is commonly used in sentences like the last two–probably because the pronoun comes at the end of the sentence, where the objective-case form usually comes:

Aren't you shorter than him?
"Who broke the typewriter?" "Not me."

But in more careful speech, as well as in writing, the nominative-case forms are used.

Usage is divided when a pronoun is used as subject complement after the verb *be.* The nominative form is considered preferable in writing and careful speech:

Someone gave me those statistics–I am sure it was *he.*

But in casual conversation you will often hear the objective form:

Someone gave me those statistics–I'm sure it was *him.*

Some people feel that in many situations *he* (or *she*) is too formal to be appropriate and that *him* (or *her*) is too informal. Then they avoid the problem:

Someone gave me those statistics, and I'm sure he was the one.

(See also **It's me.**)

b. The *objective* forms are used as objects of verbs and prepositions and in appositives that refer to objects:

They wanted *him* and Nan to sit with them. [Not: *he.*]
She never pays any attention to *us* boys. [Not: *we* boys.]
"Did they call anyone?" "Yes, Ron and *me.*" [Not: *I.* The meaning is "They called Ron and me."]
You can come home with Kiku and *me.* [Not: *I.*]
I like both girls, Sue and *her*. [Not: *she.* The pronoun is in apposition with the object *girls*.]
I know Lisa better than *him.* [*Him* is the object of the elliptical clause *than I know him.*]

c. The *possessive* forms are used to show ownership:

Mine writes better than *yours.*
Whose won?

(See also **Gerund,** section 3.)

2. Nouns have only two case forms—a possessive and an ordinary form that is used for all other functions: *brother's*, *brother*; *Lynn's*, *Lynn*.

(See also **Nominative case; Objective case; Possessive case;** and **who, whom, whose.**)

case

Expressions with *case* are often merely deadwood that could easily be pruned away in revision:

[In] several [cases] freshmen were allowed to swim after school.
He has shown this same callousness before, in [the case of] his dealings with his clerks.
Although she has made several speeches, in not one [case] has Mayor Swift taken a stand on the tax question.

Cause and effect

See **Post hoc fallacy.**

center around (or about)

Center around and *center about* are informal idioms:

His life centers around his many school activities.

In formal English *center on* or *center in* is used:

The legends are centered on the supposedly haunted houses.
All power was centered in one person—the dictator.

center on, center in

See **center around (or about)**.

cf.

An abbreviation for the Latin *confer*. It is used in footnotes when the writer wants the reader to "compare" or "see" a given reference for further information.

Circumlocution

The use of a larger number of words than are necessary to express an idea clearly and effectively: "in a state of confusion" for "confused"; "filled with embarrassment" for "embarrassed"; "he was made the recipient of" for "he received."

Cities

In expository writing, the name of the country, state, or province need not be given when you are referring to well-known cities: *Athens, Florence,*

Montreal, London, Madrid, Paris, Versailles. But cities or towns that are not well known or have the same names as other cities should be fully identified if there is a possibility that readers may be puzzled or misled: *Athens, Tennessee*; *Florence, Colorado*; *London, Ohio*; *Versailles, Kentucky.*

Clause

A group of words that has a subject and a verb and is used as *part* of a sentence. (A simple sentence like "Sam found a twenty-dollar bill" has a subject and a verb, but we do not call it a clause, because it is a whole sentence, not part of a sentence.) There are two classes of clauses: *main* and *subordinate.*

1. Main clause (also called *independent* or *principal* clause). A main clause is one that, though part of a sentence, is grammatically independent; that is, it could stand alone as a sentence. The main clauses are italicized in these examples:

This term paper is Connie's, but *the other one is Hal's.*
The term paper that had the longest footnotes *was Connie's.*
When you call me at home, *be sure it's not after ten o'clock.*
Julia wondered what her mother might think.

2. Subordinate clause (also called *dependent* clause). A subordinate clause cannot stand alone as a sentence; it depends on the rest of the sentence to complete its meaning:

The term paper *that had the longest footnotes* was Connie's. [Adjective clause.]
When you call me at home, be sure it's not after ten o'clock. [Adverb clause.]
Julia wondered *what her mother might think.* [Noun clause used as object of the verb.]

Subordinate clauses, as the examples show, are always used in sentences as single words might be used–as adjectives, as adverbs, as nouns.

(For further examples and discussion, see **Adjective clause, Adverb clause, Noun clause, Compound sentence, Complex sentence.**)

Cliché

An expression that has been used so often that it has become commonplace and stale: *clean as a whistle, selling like hot cakes, knee-high to a grasshopper, gone but not forgotten, few and far between.* (See **Bromide.**)

Climax

Climax is the arrangement of a series of words, phrases, clauses, or sentences in an ascending order–that is, each item in the series is longer, more striking, more forceful, or more important in some way than the preceding item:

All that week at the lake it rained: Sometimes it was big, slow, single drops, making countless pockmarks on the surface of the water. Sometimes it was driving sheets of rain, raking across the beach in graceful waves. Sometimes it was a straight-down Niagara torrent so thick it blotted out everything but itself. [Order based on the amount and intensity of the rain.]

Climax is the natural order for arranging the items of a series unless there is some special reason for another order. Failure to use climactic order usually results in a weak passage or, if the last member of the series is conspicuously less important than the preceding ones, in anticlimax. (For a discussion of this point, see **Anticlimax.**)

Clipped words

Words made by dropping a syllable or more from another word are called *clipped words* or sometimes *clips.* They are used in informal speech and writing: *math, mums, flu, franks, photo, quad, rhino.* Some clips are shoptalk or slang: *electro, schizo, con, hood, rap.* Since clipped words are not abbreviations, they are not followed by periods.

Coherence

When a piece of writing has coherence (or is coherent), its ideas move in a smooth, straight, uninterrupted line from beginning to end. Sometimes, the word *continuity* is used instead of the word *coherence.*

Coining words

Making up a new word for a particular occasion (like *wear-you-outer, mini-spender, discomania*) or for general use (*me-tooism, gobbledygook, humongous*) is called *coining.* The made-up word is called a *coinage* or if it is never used again, a *nonce word.*

Collective nouns

A *collective noun* is one that though singular in form names a group of people or things:

band	committee	family	herd	squad
class	crowd	gang	mob	team

1. Agreement. When writers intend the collective noun to mean the group taken as a whole, they use a singular verb and pronoun:

The committee *is* ready to report *its* findings.

When writers intend the collective noun to mean the individual members of the group, they use a plural verb and pronoun:

The committee *were* still *arguing* about the merits of *their* various proposals.

2. Consistency. In speech we often use a collective noun with a singular verb and then inconsistently shift to a plural pronoun. But in writing, a collective noun should be treated consistently as either singular or plural:

The committee *has agreed* to alter *its* rules. [Not: *their* rules.]

Sometimes you will find that the meaning of a collective actually changes from singular to plural within a sentence. Then, rather than be inconsistent, substitute a regular plural noun for the collective:

INCONSISTENT: The band *has examined* the funds and *have* finally *agreed* to pay *their* own expenses.

CONSISTENT: The band members (*or* The members of the band) *have examined* the funds and *have* finally *agreed* to pay *their* own expenses.

Colloquial

Colloquial means "characteristic of conversation." When words and constructions are labeled *colloquial* in this book, it means that they are found chiefly in informal speech but are also generally considered appropriate in informal writing. (There are some colloquialisms that are not considered appropriate in writing; that point is made clear when such expressions are discussed in this book.)

The editors of some dictionaries of usage also use *Colloquial* to label words and phrases like *hot spot*, *kick him out*, *monkey around*, *old-timers*, *roughneck*, *skedaddle*, and *tag after*, which are used more often in speech than in writing. Remember when you see this label that, contrary to what many people think, the editors are not frowning on the use of the labeled word. They are simply indicating that the word is inappropriate in formal situations, though acceptable in most informal writing and completely appropriate in informal speech. (See also **Slang.**)

Colon (:)

The colon is a rather formal and emphatic mark that directs attention to what follows. As a "go ahead" sign it has three main uses:

1. A colon is used to introduce a list of appositives (at the end of a sentence) that the writer wants to emphasize:

Three Chaplin movies were shown at the festival: *City Lights, Modern Times,* and *The Gold Rush.* [The three names are in apposition with *movies*.]

At the end of the first week of the festival we had two worries: we were not making much money, and we had to look for another little theater. [The two clauses are in apposition with *worries.*]

Note: The colon is not used before a list unless the items are appositives. When they are simply subject complements or objects, no mark of punctuation should be used before them:

The three Chaplin movies shown at the festival were [ ] *City Lights, Modern Times,* and *The Gold Rush.* [The three names are subject complements.]

At the end of the first week of the festival we worried about [ ] not making much money and having to look for another small theater. [The two gerund phrases are objects of the preposition *about.*]

2. A colon is used to introduce a long or formal quotation in factual writing:

In his essay "Speaking of Translation," Maurice Valency says: "To translate word by word and phrase by phrase is virtually to court failure. The gifted translation depends more on magic than on labor."

3. A colon may be used between the clauses of a compound sentence when the second clause explains or illustrates the first:

Chris was lucky: she had the most lenient driving inspector and got her driver's license easily.
Not one of us in his class dared complain about the assignments: Mr. Novick would have withered us with his sarcasm.

4. The colon has several conventional uses:
a. After the salutation in a business letter:

Dear Mr. Hicks: Dear Miss Seiler: Dear Ms. Lum:

b. Between hours and minutes expressed in figures:

6:05 A.M. 7:45 P.M. at 8:30 this evening

c. Between volume and page numbers of a magazine:

Holiday, 47: 41–43

d. Between Biblical chapter and verse:

Luke 6:20 Ruth 1:1–14

Comma

The purpose of the comma is to help make what you write clear. You will find it useful to think of the comma as making a slight separation–just enough to keep words or phrases distinct. It represents the slight pause that we use automatically in speech to help get across our meaning.

Today the tendency in writing is to use as few commas as possible and still make the meaning clear. Narrative writing generally uses fewer commas than expository writing; formal writing generally uses more than informal.

The following sections point out places where commas are likely to be needed, to make reading easier or to prevent misreading.

1. In a compound sentence. A comma is generally used before the coordinating conjunction (*and*, *but*, *for*, *or*, *nor*, *yet*, *so*) that joins the two independent clauses of a compound sentence:

By eleven-thirty all the seats were filled, and people were standing in the side aisles and out on the sidewalk.

When the clauses are short and easily distinguishable, the comma is often omitted. This is especially true in informal narrative:

Jackie saw the wasp fly in and she ran for the door.
But: Jackie saw the wasp fly in, and out the back door she went. [Without the comma the clauses are not easily distinguishable. The sentence might first be read "Jackie saw the wasp fly in and out. . . ."]
He had to give up his painting or he would be unable to support his family.
But: He had to give up his painting, or his children would starve. [Without the comma the sentence might first be read "He had to give up his painting or his children. . . ."]

(For punctuating compound sentences when the clauses themselves contain commas, see **Semicolon,** section 2.)

2. To set off interrupting elements. Parenthetical expressions like *after all, it seems, of course, to be sure, as you know, I suppose*; nouns of address; words like *yes, no, oh, well*; and tags like *do you, don't they, can't he* added to statements to ask questions are all set off by commas:

Mr. Baxter, it seems, had threatened to call the superintendent.
Laura will be late, of course.
Sam tries to be fair, to be sure.
Get up, Sandy, and get ready. [Noun of address.]
You don't suppose humor would be inappropriate, do you?

Remember that expressions like *after all, it seems,* and *of course* are set off only when they are used parenthetically. When they are closely connected in meaning with other words in a sentence, they are not set off: "We arrived *after all* the excitement had calmed down." "Lately *it seems* that no one can please him."

Conjunctive adverbs (e.g., *however, moreover, nevertheless, consequently*) coming in the middle of a sentence or clause are considered parenthetical and are set off by commas:

The trip, however, was well worth the cost.

Many writers also set off conjunctive adverbs at the beginning of a sentence or clause, as parenthetical expressions or for emphasis:

He had absolutely no scruples in either his business or his social life; consequently, he had no friends and few admirers.

3. Between items in a series. a. Words, phrases, and clauses in a series are separated by commas:

My mother, aunt, and three cousins accompanied me to the hospital.
We found the illegible message scrawled on the garage door, beneath the mailbox, inside the desk drawer, and above the mantel.
He was a glutton for baked potatoes with sour cream, crackers with Roquefort cheese, and chocolate cheesecake.
Next figure out how much the trip would cost, how much time it would take, and how you could get the time and the money.

Commas are generally not used when all the items in the series are joined by conjunctions:

Then I had to buy a raincoat and a hat and an umbrella.

The comma before the last item of a series is often omitted, especially in newspaper and in business writing, which tend to use an "open" style of punctuation (in contrast to the "close" style of punctuation in most formal writing):

OPEN: Ed had a quarter, two dimes and four pennies.
CLOSE: Ed had a quarter, two dimes, and four pennies.

Choose whichever style you prefer. But remember always to use the comma before the last item if there is any possibility of confusion:

The proclamation was drafted by the two delegates from Taft High, Elizabeth Orso, and Jim Peterson.

Without the comma before *and*, it might seem that *Elizabeth Orso* and *Jim Peterson* were appositives identifying the two delegates. But the meaning intended in the sentence is that four people—not two—drafted the proclamation.

(For punctuating a series of items that contain commas themselves, see **Semicolon,** section 3.)

b. Commas are used between two or more adjectives in a series:

His talk was full of inaccurate, intolerant, inane remarks.

Since the three adjectives in this sentence are equal modifiers of *remarks*, each should have equal emphasis. Separating the three with commas shows that they are equal modifiers. At each comma the reader pauses and then gives the next adjective as much emphasis as the one before.

When the last adjective in a series is thought of as part of the noun, no comma is used before it:

His son-in-law was a fine young man.
Alan was a polite, generous, articulate young man.

In these sentences the adjective *young* is so closely connected in meaning with *man* that the writer considers the two words together as one noun (like *grand jury*, *small talk*, *hard coal*, *first aid*). The other adjectives in the sentences modify the word group *young man*—not *man* alone.

4. After introductory clauses and verbal phrases. a. An adverb clause that precedes the main clause is generally followed by a comma:

Whenever I questioned him, I got a lengthy answer.

When the adverb clause is short and closely related to the main clause, and the two clauses are easily distinguishable, the comma may be omitted:

If he enters he will win.
But: If he enters, the contest will attract an enormous crowd. [Without the comma the clauses are not easily distinguishable. The sentence might first be read "If he enters the contest...."]

Before the actor left he autographed my napkin.
But: Before the actor left, Mrs. Danvig asked him to autograph her napkin. [Without the comma the sentence might first be read "Before the actor left Mrs. Danvig...."]

b. A modifying verbal phrase at the beginning of a sentence is usually followed by a comma:

Inspired by her words, I vowed to become a doctor. [Participial phrase.]
To keep up with Julio, Pat had to study twice as hard as before. [Infinitive phrase.]

By lining up jobs early in spring, we had enough yard work to keep us busy all summer. [Gerund phrase.]

5. To set off nonrestrictive modifiers. *Restrictive modifiers*–those that are needed to identify which particular one or ones are meant–are not set off by commas:

The ushers refused to seat anyone who arrived late. [The adjective clause *who arrived late* is essential if the reader is to understand which particular people the ushers refused to seat.]

Nonrestrictive modifiers are not essential in getting across the basic meaning of the sentence. They add details, helping to explain or illustrate or describe, but the basic meaning would emerge without them. They are always set off:

My brother Jerry, who arrived late, had to wait in the lobby until the end of the first number. [Basic meaning: Jerry had to wait in the lobby. The adjective clause *who arrived late* adds an interesting and important bit of background information, but it is not essential in identifying who had to wait.]
She nodded her head in agreement, although she really didn't understand what the woman was saying. [Nonrestrictive adverb clause.]
Uncle Oscar, fatter than ever, met us at the bus station. [Nonrestrictive adjective phase.]
Finally Mrs. Pierson, swallowing her pride, apologized. [Nonrestrictive participial phrase.]
Maria was sitting in the back, her head bent over a puzzle with movable squares. [Absolute participial phrase; this construction is always nonrestrictive.]
Both our fathers were working the midnight shift, from midnight to eight. [Nonrestrictive prepositional phrase.]

Remember that a modifier may be either restrictive or nonrestrictive, depending on the meaning intended by the writer. In both of the following examples, the italicized modifiers are punctuated appropriately, each one for a different meaning:

A month later we checked the three boxes again. The cereal *packed in heavy foil* was still crisp; the others were quite limp. [The context makes it clear that there were several boxes of cereal; therefore the phrase *packed in heavy foil* is necessary to identify which particular cereal had stayed fresh.]
We searched the cupboards but found nothing except a box of cereal and a can of powdered milk. The cereal, *packed in heavy foil*, turned out to be quite fresh. [The context makes it clear that there was only one box; therefore *packed in heavy foil* is not being used to identify which particular cereal was meant. To show that the modifier is included simply as an explanatory detail, the writer sets it off.]

6. To set off appositives. Appositives are set off by commas when they are nonrestrictive–that is, when they are added to give additional information about the preceding noun:

The ambassador's favorite food was lox, a delicious smoked salmon.
Mr. Hale, the librarian at the college, was quite cooperative.

When the appositive is used to specify the particular person or thing, it is restrictive and is not set off:

his son Emil [He has more than one.]
the adjective *abominable*
Ethelred the Unready
his play *Private Lives*

7. For emphasis and contrast. a. Since a comma tends to make the reader pause, it is sometimes used before a construction that the writer wants to emphasize:

Maurie was immensely popular because of his lighthearted charm, and the late-model Corvette he drove. [Ordinarily a comma would not be put between the parts of a compound object of a preposition; here it is used to call attention to the second part.]

b. This use of the comma is especially common before contrasting expressions introduced by *not* or *but*:

He came upon a murky lagoon, not the sea he expected.
It was not tacos, but gyros, that was the most popular item on the menu.

c. With certain idioms like *the more . . . the greater*, *the fewer . . . the better* formal writing uses a comma for emphasis; informal writing does not:

FORMAL: The more the children begged, the less we listened.
INFORMAL: The bigger the plant the more likely it'll survive the winter.

8. For clearness. Often a comma is used to prevent reading together two parts of a sentence that do not belong together:

During recess, time whizzed by. [To prevent: During recess time. . . .]
The Inadas wanted her to eat, and drink some coffee before starting home. [To prevent: The Inadas wanted her to eat and drink some coffee. . . .]
All those who came, came with excellent credentials. [To prevent the reader from tripping over the repeated word.]

9. Routine uses of the comma. a. To set off the second and all following items in addresses and dates:

Honolulu, Hawaii
Miami Shores, Florida
Fort Wayne, Allen County, Indiana
Port-au-Prince, Haiti

Please send all manuscripts to Miss Sandra Kohl, 1921 Orrington Avenue, Evanston, Illinois 60201, before the May deadline.
January 14, 1976 [When the day of the month is not given, usage is divided—either January, 1976 or January 1976.]
On June 23, 1981, the watercolor classes will begin.

b. After the salutation in personal letters and the closing in all letters:

Dear Ozzie, Dear Miss Jens, Sincerely, Cordially yours,

c. In figures, to separate thousands, millions, etc.:

$6,170,166   32,000 students

d. To set off degrees and titles:

Elinor G. Flatley, D.D.S.   James MacNamara, Jr.
Leslie Bixby, Sr., will give the keynote speech.

e. To show omission of a word required to fill out a grammatical construction if confusion would result without the comma; if the meaning is clear, the comma may be omitted:

The Reynauds prefer hot chocolate for breakfast; the Engles, coffee. [Sentence would be hard to understand without the comma.]
Sally took the cake and he the last cookie. [Meaning is clear without the comma.]

10. Unnecessary commas. A comma should not be used:

a. Between the parts of a compound subject:

Out of the red sports car stepped a tall cowboy [ ] and a small child in a rabbit suit.

b. Between a subject and its verb:

Who will win the pennant this year [ ] is anybody's guess.

c. Between a verb and its object or complement:

In the evening we learned [ ] why he wasn't at the picnic.
The question in everyone's mind was [ ] where had he eaten?

d. Between the parts of a compound predicate—unless the comma is needed for clearness or is wanted for emphasis (as in section 7):

We struggled with the flat tire for an hour [ ] and then gave up.
Luis came along a little later [ ] and helped us.

e. At the end of a series of words, phrases, or clauses unless the series is part of a construction that requires a comma:

Selling her old guitar, stereo, and typewriter [ ] made moving easier.
But: Since she had saved for a new guitar, stereo, and typewriter, she was able to replace them. [The comma after *typewriter* is there to set off the introductory adverb clause.]

f. Between an adjective and the noun (or word group) it modifies:

I often have long, frightening [ ] nightmares.

g. Between a coordinating conjunction and the words that follow it—unless it is followed by an interrupting expression:

His wife is intuitive, creative, and [ ] intelligent.
Their son could drive, but [ ] he didn't have a driver's license.
But: Their son could have driven our car, but, it seems, he had had his license revoked.

h. Before an indirect question or an indirect quotation:

The baker asked [ ] who was next in line.
He told me [ ] that he never bakes pumpkin pies in July.

i. Before directly quoted words and phrases that are built right into the construction of a sentence:

Pete's response to the news was [ ] "Take five."
It took him a long time to get [ ] "sorta" out of his speech.

j. Before a title, unless it is used as a nonrestrictive appositive:

The author said [ ] "Glory Be" was her best short story.
At times like these she liked to quote the poem [ ] "Ozymandias."
But: The first story she wrote, "Instant Failure," was made into a movie.

k. Before *that* in a *so . . . that* construction:

Ms. Parks was so eager to get into the pool [ ] that she forgot to wear her bathing cap.

Comma splice

When you put two independent statements into one sentence, you ordinarily join them with a conjunction and a comma, or separate them with a semicolon. If you use a comma alone between the clauses, you have a comma splice. If you use no punctuation between the clauses, you have a run-on sentence. For a discussion of how to correct these writing faults, see **Run-on sentence.**

Commands and requests

1. Direct commands are expressed by the simple form of the verb (the infinitive form). The subject is not usually expressed unless special emphasis is wanted:

Jump!
Stand back.
Get me a towel, somebody.
Stacy, you ride with Sam and me.

The helping verb *do* is used in negative commands:

Don't just stand there.
Do not contradict him, Nancy.

Commands are usually punctuated with periods, unless the writer wants to suggest strong feeling by using an exclamation mark.

2. Softened commands or polite requests may be expressed in several different ways:

Do stop in on your way home.
Let's just ignore them.
You will make up the time before Friday, of course.

Often polite requests have the word order of questions—but these are generally punctuated with periods:

Will you please notify us today.
Would you please cancel our meeting.

common, mutual

See **mutual, common.**

Common noun

A noun used as the name of any one of a class or group of persons, places, or things: student, singer, puppy, city, river, hospital, desk, ink, star. (See **Proper noun.**)

compare

Differs from *contrast*, which always points out differences. *Compare* has two meanings: (1) Used with *to*, it means "point out similarities between," as in these examples:

He was at his most entertaining when he compared his classroom to a zoo. [He showed various ways in which the two were alike.]
Grandma, who has always been a movie fan, had fun comparing our camping experiences to *The Perils of Pauline.* [She described the ways in which our experiences resembled Pauline's.]

(2) Used with *with*, it means "point out similarities and differences between":

You will find it interesting to compare the novel with the movie.
Our assignment was to compare the *Tribune*'s account of the meeting with the write-up in the *Sun-Times.*

Comparison and contrast

One interesting and emphatic way of presenting material to a reader is to set two or more people, things, situations, or ideas side by side and point out their likenesses (comparison), their differences (contrast), or both.

Comparison of adjectives and adverbs

1. To show a greater degree of the quality or characteristic named by an adjective or adverb, *-er* or *-est* is added to the word or *more* or *most* is put before it:

ADJECTIVE:

POSITIVE:	Stan is quiet.
COMPARATIVE:	Stan is quieter than Dan.
SUPERLATIVE:	Stan is the quietest person in the class.
POSITIVE:	It was an exciting movie.
COMPARATIVE:	The second feature was more exciting than the first.
SUPERLATIVE:	These were the most exciting films I've ever seen.

ADVERB:

POSITIVE:	She always plays hard.
COMPARATIVE:	She always plays harder than you.
SUPERLATIVE:	She plays the hardest of all of us.
POSITIVE:	He speaks concisely.
COMPARATIVE:	He speaks more concisely than his teammate.
SUPERLATIVE:	Of all the debaters he speaks the most concisely.

The *-er* and *-est* endings are usual for words of one syllable and for many of two syllables. *More* and *most* are generally used with longer adjectives and adverbs, and with all adverbs ending in *-ly.* But for many words both forms are possible. Then the choice depends partly on the sound and partly on the emphasis wanted in a particular sentence:

Mother was *stricter* than Dad. [Emphasis is on the strictness.]
Dad was far *more strict* than Kathy's father. [Emphasis is on the degree of strictness.]

But both forms should not be used together, as in *more stricter* and *most strictest.* This "double comparison" was usual in Shakespeare's time but is nonstandard today.

Some adjectives and adverbs have irregular comparisons:

	POSITIVE	COMPARATIVE	SUPERLATIVE
ADJECTIVES:	bad	worse	worst
	far	farther, further	farthest, furthest
	good, well	better	best
	little	less, lesser	least
	much, many	more	most
ADVERBS:	well	better	best
	little	less	least
	much	more	most

The *comparative* forms are ordinarily used in comparing two things or people, and the *superlative* in comparing more than two:

Carol's idea was *better* than mine.
Is Bill really *more conservative* than his father?
Larry is the *weakest* swimmer on the team.
Of the three vases, Sue's was the *most graceful.*

But in informal speech, the superlative is often used for comparing two:

Both dresses are lovely, but I like the yellow one *best.*
Tell me which of the two meteorologists is *most likely* to be right.

2. A problem writers sometimes have in making comparisons (showing how or to what degree two or more things are alike or unlike) is phrasing them accurately enough for the reader to see immediately what things are being compared. When the phrasing is unclear or imprecise, a faulty comparison can result:

FAULTY: The marble in the vestibule is different from the rotunda. [Marble is being compared with a part of the building.]
CORRECTED: The marble in the vestibule is different from *that* in the rotunda.

FAULTY: His ability to produce new varieties of plants was almost as remarkable as Luther Burbank. [Ability is being compared with a man.]
CORRECTED: His ability to produce new varieties of plants was almost as remarkable as *Luther Burbank's.*

If comparisons are made between persons or things of the same class, be sure to use such phrases as "than any other," "than anyone else," or "than the other" with adjectives or adverbs in the comparative degree:

FAULTY: Probably O. Henry uses surprise endings in his stories more often *than any* fiction writer. ["Any fiction writer" includes O. Henry too.]

CORRECTED: Probably O. Henry uses surprise endings in his stories more often *than any other* fiction writer.

Phrases with "any" and "other" should *not* be used after adjectives and adverbs in the superlative degree:

FAULTY: Mr. Laskowski is the most learned *of any other judge* on the state Supreme Court. [Or: the most learned *of all the other judges.*]

CORRECTED: Mr. Laskowski is the *most learned judge* on the state Supreme Court. [Or: the most learned *of the judges*; the most learned *of all the judges.*]

3. In formal English, adjectives and adverbs like *perfect*, *perfectly*, *unique*, *fatal*, *round*, *dead*, *impossible* are generally used only in their exact, original meanings–that is, to name qualities that do not vary in degree. A thing is either perfect or not perfect, unique or not unique, dead or not dead. If it is perfect or unique or dead, something else cannot logically be *more* perfect, *more* unique, or *more* dead; it can only be *more nearly* perfect, *more nearly* unique, *more nearly* dead.

But in informal English these words are not always used in their exact, original sense. *Dead*, for instance, is used to mean not only "without life" but also "dull; quiet." *Unique* is used not only to mean "the only one of its kind" but also "rare; unusual; remarkable." *Impossible* is used not only to mean "not possible" but also "not easily possible." When the words are used in these broader meanings, they are often compared: It was the deadest spot on Rush Street. (See also **Tautology.**)

complement, compliment

Complement means "something that completes or makes whole":

Their personalities seem to complement one another; he's an extrovert, and she's an introvert.

Compliment has to do with courtesy and praise. It means "something good said about someone":

Mrs. Roth received numerous compliments on her speech.

Complement of a verb

See **Subject complement.**

Complex sentence

A sentence made up of one main clause and one or more subordinate clauses. The subordinate clauses are italicized in the following examples:

Stephen Baker was wearing an old army uniform *that was too small.*
When I saw Stephen Baker yesterday, he was wearing an old army uniform *that was too small.*

Compound-complex sentence

A sentence that contains two or more main clauses and one or more subordinate clauses:

When she arrived at the airport, her son met her, but he did not offer to carry her suitcase.
The two main clauses *her son met her* and *he did not offer to carry her suitcase* make the sentence compound. The subordinate clause *When she arrived at the airport* makes it compound-complex.

Compound predicate

A predicate consisting of two or more verbs (with or without complements and/or modifiers) that have the same subject:

In that year she *inherited* and *bequeathed* a million dollars.
Frank *looked* in, *caught* sight of Bennie, and *ducked* out the door.

Compound sentence

A sentence made up of two or more independent clauses (each could stand alone as a sentence). The clauses are joined either by a comma and a coordinating conjunction or by a semicolon:

The screws were very loose, and the chair fell apart.
There was great excitement in Pittsburgh; their team had won the World Series.

(See **Clause.**)

Compound subject

Two or more nouns (or noun equivalents) used as the subject of one verb:

Sarah and *Mike* studied math all afternoon.
Tulips, *daffodils*, and *lilacs* bloom about the same time each spring.

(For the agreement of verbs with compound subjects, see **Agreement,** sections 1b, 1c, and 1i.)

Compound words

Combinations of two or more words, some of which are written as one word (*blueprint*, *carefree*, *easygoing*, *heavyweight*, *killjoy*, *letterhead*, *roughneck*); some as hyphenated words (*blue-green*, *clean-shaven*, *flip-flop*, *ill-gotten*, *know-how*, *letter-perfect*, *wheeler-dealer*); and some as separate words (*blue law*, *cake flour*, *egg roll*, *grade school*, *jump shot*, *opera glasses*, *totem pole*). Regardless of how it is written, a compound word is thought of as a single word.

If you are not sure how to write a given compound, look it up in a recent dictionary. (See also **Hyphen** and **Plurals of nouns.**)

conclude

Used with *by* before a gerund:

Ms. Okuda concluded her lecture by assigning extra homework.

Used with *with* before a noun:

Aunt Rose always concludes her letters with "Peace, Rose."

Used with *from* when it means "infer":

We concluded from Dad's sad face that he had bad news.

Concrete and abstract words

Concrete words name persons, places, and things that can be seen and touched: *baby, beach, ice, desert, book, candy.* They contrast with abstract words, which name ideas, qualities, states: *happiness, greed, fear, pride, theocracy, failure.*

Conditions

In simple, straightforward conditions–those stating a condition that is likely or possible–indicative verb forms are used:

If Pham Thi *can play* with us, we'll have a strong team.
If you *will write* the article, we can beat the deadline.
If he *has* the money, he'll be glad to lend you a dollar or two.

When a condition is less likely or possible, the helping verb *should* or *would* or the past tense is used:

If we *should sell* all these plants, we would make a profit.
If we *sold* all these plants, we would make a profit.

In conditions that are contrary to fact–those that cannot be met–the subjunctive is often used in formal English, but rarely in informal:

If I *were* going, I would have told you. [Informal: If I *was* going.]
If Sam Kasias *were* here, things would change. [Informal: If Sam Kasias *was* here.]

(See also **Subjunctive.**)

Conjugation

A verb has various forms to show person, number, voice, mood, and tense. An orderly arrangement of these various forms of a particular verb is called a *conjugation.* For a typical conjugation, see **Tenses of verbs.**

Conjunctions

Connecting words used to join words, phrases, clauses, and sentences. For discussion of specific conjunctions, see the following items: **Coordinating conjunctions** (*and, but, for, yet, or, nor, so*); **Conjunctive adverbs** (*therefore, thus, moreover, consequently,* etc.); **Correlative conjunctions** (*both . . . and, either . . . or, neither . . . nor, not only . . . but also, whether . . . or*); **Subordinating conjunctions** (*after, because, so that, while,* etc.)

Conjunctive adverbs

1. Adverbs used as connectives to join two independent clauses (or sentences) by showing the relationship in meaning between them are called *conjunctive adverbs* (or *transitional adverbs* or *sentence connectors*):

It is well known that Mr. Tamez is a perfectionist whose standard is impossibly high; *however,* his students enjoy the challenge and work hard. [*However* points up the contrast between the clauses.]
Christina had worked diligently on her research paper; *therefore* she was confident she would get a good mark. [*Therefore* shows that the second clause is the result of the first.]

2. The most common conjunctive adverbs are:

accordingly	furthermore	later	now
besides	however	moreover	otherwise
consequently	indeed	nevertheless	still
finally	in fact	nonetheless	therefore

Some of these—*accordingly, consequently, furthermore, however, moreover, nevertheless, nonetheless, therefore*—are "heavy" connectives, rather stiff and formal. Simpler conjunctions are generally more appropriate in informal writing, especially narrative writing:

HEAVY: Everyone was envious of Meredith and me because we won two free dinners at the Country Jewel Diner. However, the dinners were limited to those costing three dollars or less. Consequently, we had to order hamburgers and, moreover, had to pay for our own beverages.

IMPROVED: Everyone was envious of Meredith and me because we won two free dinners at the Country Jewel Diner. But the dinners were limited to those costing three dollars or less, so we had to order hamburgers and pay for our own beverages.

3. When the clauses of a compound sentence are linked by a conjunctive adverb, a semicolon (not comma) is used between them—whether the adverb begins the second clause or comes within it:

I wrote to them about the vacancy, but they never responded; consequently, the apartment is now rented.
They waited for us through their free period; then they gave up.
Carlotta thought the hike was too long; she agreed, however, to meet us later.

When the adverb comes within the clause, as in the third example, it is generally set off by commas. When it comes first in the clause, as in the first two examples, it may or may not be followed by a comma. If the adverb is parenthetical, it is set off with a comma, otherwise not.

connected with, in connection with

Wordy phrases that often can be effectively replaced by a simple *in, for, with,* or *about*:

WORDY: Did the teacher say anything in connection with the poor grades on the quiz yesterday?
BETTER: Did the teacher say anything about the poor grades on the quiz yesterday?

WORDY: We were told the rules connected with using the swimming pool.
BETTER: We were told the rules for using the swimming pool.

Connotation

Besides its recognized dictionary meaning (its denotation), a word may have an additional shade of meaning (its connotation). *Statesman* and *politician*, for instance, both have the denotation "a person actively engaged in the business of government," but their connotations are different. *Statesman* suggests or connotes approval (a statesman is able, wise, high-principled); *politician* sometimes connotes disapproval (politicians may be scheming and opportunistic).

considerable

Although in speech a clear distinction is not always made between the adverb *considerably* and the adjective *considerable*, in both formal English and informal writing it is:

He influenced us considerably during that year. [Adverb modifying the verb *influenced.*]
She had considerable influence on the students. [Adjective modifying the noun *influence.*]

In nonstandard English *considerable* is used as an intensifier, but not in standard English:

NONSTANDARD: The whole play was considerable spooky.
STANDARD: The whole play was extremely spooky.

In informal speech *considerable* is sometimes used as a noun:

SPOKEN: The Loehmanns have done considerable for the community.
WRITTEN: The Loehmanns have done a great deal for the community.

Context

Used to mean (1) "the parts that come before or after a word or sentence," (2) "the whole passage, speech, or situation in which a word or sentence occurs." The context always determines the intended meaning of a particular word or sentence; therefore, to understand words and ideas exactly and completely, you must see them or hear them in context.

Contractions

Contractions are shortened forms of words, made by "telescoping" syllables when speaking the words; in writing, the letter or letters representing the omitted sounds are indicated by an apostrophe:

I have–I've	you are–you're	should have–should've
I am–I'm	he has–he's	they are–they're

do not–don't	we had–we'd	has not–hasn't
she will–she'll	it is–it's	could not–couldn't

Contractions are ordinarily out of place in formal writing. But because they are typical of conversational English, they often appear in informal writing–especially, of course, in the dialogue of stories and plays.

Conversation

A great deal of writing–exposition as well as narrative–can be made more interesting and vivid by the use of direct quotation and conversation. Notice how quotation enlivens this passage:

> Right then I remembered a few of the stories Pa had told me about his younger days. "Did you know about the time he won the gold spurs?" I asked.
>
> "Know about it?" Mr. Kingman laughed. "I was there, waiting for my turn to ride. Your dad drew a big, ornery buckskin horse and I told him he was crazier 'n a loco longhorn to get in the chute, let alone ride him. I never did see such a horse. Must have weighed thirteen hundred pounds."
>
> "That's what Pa says," I agreed. "Thirteen hundred!"
>
> "He darn near killed your dad," Mr. Kingman said softly.
>
> "But Pa stayed on for the full ten seconds, raked him and whipped him and gave him a whale of a ride!"
>
> "I'll say he did. And he wouldn't have been hurt, either, if that cinch hadn't let go. That horse just swelled up and snapped it."
>
> It had been a bad accident from what Ma told me. . . . –Bud Murphy. "Champion Stock." *Literary Cavalcade,* 1949.

Quoted speech is effective, of course, only if it sounds real. If you are interested in learning to write good conversation, start by observing carefully how you talk and how people around you talk. You will find that contractions, clipped expressions, and informal words and idioms are typical of everyday speech, and that the use of them will help make your written conversation sound natural. But don't overdo them. Though written conversation is based on real speech, it should not be a word-for-word reproduction. If you wrote down conversations as they were actually spoken, you would often end with a hodgepodge of apostrophes, distorted spellings (*cussin', champeen, gonna, jist, dese here, fergit, gimme, likker*), and coarse expressions. This would be confusing, distracting, and possibly offensive to your readers. In reproducing speech on paper, it is better to use just enough such spellings and expressions to *suggest* the way speech is supposed to sound. Take the following passage, for example:

> It was not until Babbitt was thick and disconsolate with mutton grease that he flung out:
>
> "I wound up a nice little deal with Conrad Lyte this morning that put five hundred good round plunks in my pocket. Pretty nice–pretty nice! And yet–I don't know what's the matter with me today. Maybe it's an attack of spring fever, or staying up too late at Verg Gunch's, or maybe it's just the winter's work piling up, but I've felt kind of down in the mouth all day

long. Course I wouldn't beef about it to the fellows at the Roughnecks' Table there, but you—Ever feel that way, Paul? Kind of comes over me; here I've pretty much done all the things I ought to: supported my family, and got a good house and a six-cylinder car, built up a nice little business, and I haven't any vices 'specially, except smoking–and I'm practically cutting that out, by the way. . . ." –Sinclair Lewis. *Babbitt.* New York: Harcourt Brace Jovanovich, 1950, pp. 60–61.

It is likely that a man like Babbitt would actually say *an'* for *and*, *whatsa matter* for *what's the matter*, *mebbe* for *maybe*, *cuttin'* for *cutting*, *kinda* for *kind of*, and so on. But these distorted spellings are not needed; for the use of such expressions as *good round plunks*, *beef about it*, *kind of down in the mouth* and the general rhythm and tone of the sentences strongly suggest the man's speech pattern, personality, and background.

A few words about the speaker, coming before or after his quoted words, sometimes help tell the story:

"All right, all right. I'm coming; I'm coming," he yelled, his irritation doubling with each step he took.

Jerome scooped up another handful of the slushy snow, packed it around the snowball Phil had handed him, and muttered maliciously, "When this hits old man Crawford, he'll know he's been hit."

But this kind of description or explanation should not be overdone. For instance, it isn't always necessary when labeling speeches to use a picturesque synonym for *said* (*grunted*, *murmured*, *squealed*, *thundered*, *stuttered*, *whimpered*). In fact, unless there is a good reason for using one of these more specific words, *said* is preferable because it is less conspicuous.

And you need not even indicate who is speaking if the conversation leaves no question in the reader's mind:

On the way back to the gym, Cory bumped into Dave. "Hi, Dave. Are the test grades posted yet?"

"Yup. They're on Mr. Russo's door."

"Did you see the list?"

"Yeah and I wish I hadn't."

"Why? Did you flunk?"

"No, I passed, but only just barely."

Some of the conventions of paragraphing and punctuating conversation are illustrated in the examples you have just read. More details can be found in **Quotation marks.**

Coordinating conjunctions

1. The coordinating conjunctions–*and*, *but*, *for*, *or*, *nor*, *yet*, *so*–are used to connect words, phrases, subordinate clauses, independent clauses, and sentences (parts of equal value):

WORDS: nuts and bolts; Tom, Dick, or Harry; small but strong; one or the other

PHRASES: by the people and for the people; watching the practice and finding fault with every play

SUBORDINATE CLAUSES:	They were looking for someone who had a sense of humor but who could be stern at times.
INDEPENDENT CLAUSES:	According to the polls Eaton didn't have a chance, yet he won by a landslide.
SENTENCES:	The young man promised Ms. Vaccaro he would be successful. And he was.

2. The conjunction *and* is badly overworked. Sometimes it is used when there is no need for it; sometimes it is used where another conjunction would express more exactly the relationship between two parts. For a discussion of this point, see **and.**

3. There is a special group of coordinating conjunctions that are used in pairs—*both . . . and, either . . . or, neither . . . nor, whether . . . or, not only . . . but also*. For a discussion of their use, see **Correlative conjunctions.**

Correction marks

In correcting your themes, your teacher may indicate some of the revisions that are needed by using certain abbreviations or symbols. The following list gives some of the most common correction marks. Each one is followed by a reference to an article in this book where you will find help in making the appropriate revisions.

Ab	**Abbreviations**	**Local**	**Localism**
Agr	**Agreement**	**Mis**	**Misplaced modifiers**
Amb	**Ambiguity**	**Par**	**Parallel constructions**
Apos	**Apostrophe**	**Pn**	Punctuation mark misused. See separate entries in this book.
Awk	**Awkward writing**		
Big W	**Big words**		
Cap	**Capital letters**	**Prep**	**Preposition**
CS	**Comma splice**	**Ref**	**Reference of pronouns**
Dang	**Dangling modifiers**	**RO**	**Run-on sentence**
Dead	**Deadwood**	**Sp**	**Spelling**
Div	**Division of words**	**Tense**	**Tenses of verbs**
Frag	**Sentence fragment**	**Wordy**	**Wordiness**

¶This symbol means a new paragraph is needed.

Correlative conjunctions

Coordinating conjunctions used in pairs:

not only . . . but also	whether . . . or	either . . . or
not only . . . but	both . . . and	neither . . . nor

The main purpose of these connecting words is to emphasize the fact that two items are involved. Therefore the two items that are connected should be "parallel"—or similar—in form. If the first conjunction is followed by a prepositional phrase, the second should be followed by a prepositional phrase; if the first is followed by a verb, the second should be followed by a verb, and so on.

NOT PARALLEL: Aunt Anna thought we should either *be loading* our car for the trip or *make* a lunch to eat on the way.
PARALLEL: Aunt Anna thought we should either *be loading* our car for the trip or (*be*) *making* a lunch to eat on the way.

NOT PARALLEL: My mother couldn't decide whether *to go* to work or *if she should go* to college full-time.
PARALLEL: My mother couldn't decide whether *to go* to work or *(to) go* to college full-time.
PARALLEL: My mother couldn't decide whether *she should go* to work or *(should) go* to college full-time.

NOT PARALLEL: Tak was either *going* with me or *with Amy.*
PARALLEL: Tak was going either *with me* or *with Amy.*
PARALLEL: Tak was either *going* with me or *staying* at home.

council, counsel

Council is "a group of people gathered together to accomplish a task." It is always a noun:

The city council met to discuss off-street parking during heavy snowfalls.

Counsel means "advice; the giving of advice." It may be a noun or a verb:

The banker's counsel about our home mortgage was valuable.
William G. Boyd counseled us about choosing the best textbooks available.

Counter words

Vague, general adjectives (like *nice*, *wonderful*, *cute*, *super*, *darling*, *awful*, *terrible*, *frightful*, *ghastly*) that are used not for their exact meanings but only for expressing approval or disapproval. Counter words are common—and useful—in conversation, but they are seldom appropriate in writing. There it is important to use words that express exact meaning, words that help to give the reader a specific picture.

Count nouns

See **amount, number.**

couple

Strictly, the noun *couple* means "two persons or things that are associated in some way":

Sally and Hal Cohen were the only couple who jogged with us.

Informally, *couple of* is used to mean "two or three; a few; several":

I think the recipe called for a couple of eggs.
She needed a couple of volunteers from our class.

In informal speech the *of* is often omitted:

Grandpa took a couple pills this morning.

But this usage is not considered appropriate in most writing.

criterion

A rule, standard, or test on which a decision or judgment is based. The plural is *criteria* or *criterions.*

Though *criteria* is sometimes used colloquially with a singular meaning, this use is avoided by careful writers and speakers:

Her main criterion for judging people is their political persuasion. [Not: Her main criteria for judging people. . . .]

Dangling modifiers

A modifier that has no word in the sentence which it can sensibly modify is said to be *dangling*:

DANGLING: *Having spent a summer in San Francisco,* the cable cars were quite familiar to me. [Who had spent a summer in San Francisco? The sentence seems to say that the cable cars had.]

REVISED: *Having spent a summer in San Francisco,* I was quite familiar with the cable cars. [Now there is a sensible word–*I*–for the modifier to relate to.]

Dash

Since dashes are conspicuous and emphatic marks of punctuation, they should be used sparingly–only when they serve a specific purpose, when no other marks will carry the intended meaning as well. They should not be used as substitutes for all other marks, as some writers use them.

1. A common use of the dash is to mark an abrupt change in the thought of a sentence:

"And if she thinks she can–oh, I'm sorry; I shouldn't gossip like this."
"Will you just–oh, never mind; I'll do it myself."

2. Dashes are used to set off parenthetical expressions–explanatory comments or side remarks–that make an abrupt interruption in the thought or structure of a sentence:

Our commencement speaker was Lillian Hellman–weren't we lucky?–and she gave a speech I'll always remember.
Citizen Kane was on–we watch Orson Welles every chance we can get–so we were glued to the TV.

Notice that the first word of the interrupting expression begins with a small letter, even though the interrupter is a complete sentence. A period is not used after an interrupter, but a question mark or an exclamation mark is–right before the second dash.

Parentheses, which are more formal than dashes, are sometimes used to set off interrupting expressions. Parentheses tend to lessen the emphasis, to make the interrupter seem less conspicuous. Dashes make the interrupters stand out more than parentheses would. In informal writing–unless it is serious expository writing–dashes are more common than parentheses, though both should be used sparingly.

3. Nonrestrictive modifiers are usually set off by commas. But when special emphasis is wanted, dashes are used. And dashes are usual if the modifiers themselves have commas:

He's the type who believes in telling the truth–when a lie won't help.
The big news–which angered the team, understandably–was that they would all be fined.

4. Nonrestrictive appositives are usually set off by commas; but when the writer wants to call special attention to an appositive or when the appositive phrase itself has commas, dashes are better:

Gita's entry–cauliflower, carrots, and pickled onions–won a special award.
The blood drive was headed by two research assistants–Faye Browning and Joe Burns.

If a comma were used instead of a dash in the second example sentence, a reader might think that the blood drive was headed by four persons. The dash shows clearly that the names are appositives identifying the two research assistants.

5. A dash is used before a word or phrase (like *these* or *all these*) that sums up a preceding list of items, to clearly mark the division between the list and the statement that follows:

The baby's sickness, the family's surliness, the baby-sitter's tardiness–all these explained, though they did not excuse, Mrs. Kay's impatience with her customers.

6. A double-length dash is used at the end of a sentence to show that it is left unfinished or that a speaker is interrupted. No period is used after the dash:

"But Mother," he began, "why can't we—"

7. In handwriting, distinguish between a dash and a hyphen by making the dash twice as long. On the typewriter, you will have to use two hyphens (with no space between the dash and the words flanking it), since the standard keyboard has no dash.

data

Pronounced /dā'tə/ or /dat'ə/. *Data* (from Latin) is the plural of the singular *datum*, which is rarely used. Since to most people its meaning is singular—"a group of facts" or "a mass of information"—*data* is generally used with a singular verb in informal English:

Without a broader sample the data *proves* nothing.

In formal English *data* is usually regarded as plural:

The data collected yesterday *confirm* our hypothesis.

However, in the United States the use of *data* as a singular has begun to gain acceptance.

Dates

The usual form for writing dates is:

August 13, 1945 September 10, 1980

The form *10 September 1980* (with no comma) is used by the armed services.

In personal letters and in business memos and forms, figures only are often used:

3/17/72 11/18/72

The month is put first, then the day of the month, then the year.

The *st*, *nd*, *rd*, *th* are now generally omitted from the day of the month when the day is given as a figure:

April 1 Not: April 1st
August 3 Not: August 3rd

In very formal style the day of the month is often written out in full when the year is not given:

October fifteenth July sixth

But the year is not written out in words except in formal social announcements or invitations, which are usually engraved or printed.

If it is necessary to save space (in business memos, for example), the names of months may be abbreviated. Here are some of the abbreviations in use:

Jan., Ja. Feb. Mar. Apr., Apl., Ap. Jun., Ju., Je.
Jul., Jl., Jy. Aug., Ag. Sept., Sep. Oct. Nov. Dec.

Dative case

Nouns or pronouns used as indirect objects of verbs are sometimes said to be in the *dative case*. Actually English (unlike Latin or German) has no distinctive form for the dative case. A noun used as an indirect object is in the ordinary case form and a pronoun is in the objective case form:

Father sold *Uncle Ed* the young gray mare.
Ly Nam gave *me* a beautifully crafted lacquered bowl.

Deadwood

A term used to describe words or phrases that add nothing to the meaning of a sentence:

At that [point in] time, my sister was [a very young child of] three years old and so small [in size], she was able to crawl out of the cave [on her hands and knees].

Declarative sentences

Sentences that make statements:

The fire started in the chemistry lab.
Mrs. Goldman asked us how the fire started.
She asked, "Why didn't someone sound the alarm?"
"We were scared stiff!" answered John.

Declension

The change in the form of nouns, pronouns, and adjectives to show *number* (dime–dimes, alumnus–alumni, mouse–mice); *case* (lady–lady's, she–her–hers); or *gender* (he–she–it, actor–actress). In a highly inflected language like Latin or German, declension plays an important part in grammar. But in English, where so few words change in form to show case or gender, declension plays a relatively small part.

Deductive reasoning

See **Inductive and deductive reasoning.**

Defining words

Many times in your writing you use words or phrases whose meaning your readers may not know. To make your meaning clear, you should find some way to explain what the words mean. If the word is abstract (like *equality*, *communism*, *selfishness*, *personality*), the best way to explain is to give concrete examples of what it means to you. If the word is concrete, you can often make its meaning clear by tucking in a synonym that your readers are likely to know. For example:

Even at these family get-togethers, we saw very little of Aunt Flora; right after dinner she would succumb to the vapors–an attack of nerves, we would say nowadays–and go off to her room.

By adding the synonym *an attack of nerves*, you make clear what Aunt Flora's indisposition was and still keep the expression *the vapors* with its Victorian flavor that helps readers get a vivid picture of the aunt.

There are two other common ways of clarifying the meaning of words–one direct and rather formal, the other indirect and informal:

The highlight of the second week, she wrote to Mrs. Urbanek, was a trip to Versailles in a char-à-banc. *Char-à-banc*, the French-derived word that she used just to impress Mrs. Urbanek, simply means a sightseeing bus.
The next morning we all piled into a large sightseeing bus–a *char-à-banc*, our British guide called it–for a memorable trip to the great palace at Versailles.

In the first example *char-à-banc* is defined directly; in the second, its meaning is made clear indirectly. This indirect method is preferable in narrative writing, since it does not interrupt the story with a formal definition.

In expository writing a formal definition is often best–especially to define a term for which there is no well-known synonym that will explain its meaning fully. In defining a word, give (1) its general class and (2) the characteristics that make it different from other things in that class:

Macramé [the word being defined] is a popular craft [the class it belongs to] in which knots are tied, usually in a geometric pattern [characteristics that distinguish macramé from other crafts].
A *lobby* is a group of persons who try to influence legislators to introduce or to vote for measures in behalf of a special interest.

The number of distinguishing details you should use depends on how much information you think your readers need to understand fully your intended meaning.

In your written work, avoid using *when* and *where* in defining words. Definitions like "Engraving is where you cut designs or letters in metal plates or blocks of wood and then print from them" and "A treaty is when two or more nations reach an agreement on terms concerning peace, trade, or alliance" make the meaning clear enough, but they sound amateurish. They are better stated in a more sophisticated way–by giving the general class first and then the distinguishing characteristics: "Engraving is the process of cutting. . . ." "A treaty is an agreement between two or more nations. . . ."

Definite article

The adjective *the* (called a *noun determiner* or *noun marker* by some grammarians). (See **the** and **a, an.**)

Degree (of adjectives and adverbs)

One of three stages in the comparison of adjectives and adverbs:

POSITIVE DEGREE:	cold	efficiently
COMPARATIVE DEGREE:	colder	more efficiently
SUPERLATIVE DEGREE:	coldest	most efficiently

(See also **Comparison of adjectives and adverbs.**)

Degrees

Academic degrees (titles granted by a college or university to show the completion of a required course of study or as an honor) are not ordinarily given with a person's name except in college publications or in reference works. (For punctuation of degrees see **Abbreviations,** section 1.)

Demonstrative adjectives and pronouns

This, that, these, those–used to specify or point out–are called demonstrative adjectives or demonstrative pronouns, depending on how they are used in a sentence:

ADJECTIVES: This pie has more calories than that cake.
These magazines belong on those shelves.

PRONOUNS: Why should that cost more than this?
Won't those last longer than these?

(See **kind, sort.**)

Denotation

The *denotation* of a word is its exact, literal meaning as contrasted with its *connotation*, the added meaning the word suggests or implies. The words *childish* and *childlike* have the same denotation ("characteristic of a child"), but their connotations differ. *Childish* suggests undesirable qualities such as immaturity and silliness; *childlike* suggests desirable qualities like trustfulness, simplicity, freshness, innocence.

Dependent clause

See **Clause,** section 2.

device, devise

Device is a noun referring to "something invented or designed for a particular purpose" or "a plan, scheme, or trick." Think of the word *ice* in *device* to help you spell and pronounce this word:

This clever little device will enable you to make flowers out of radishes.

Devise is a verb meaning "think out; plan; invent":

I would like to devise a robot who would do my homework, clean my room, and entertain my classmates with witty anecdotes.

Dewey Decimal System

To make it easy to find available material on a particular subject, most high-school libraries classify and arrange their books according to the Dewey Decimal System, devised by a New York librarian, Melvil Dewey, in 1876. In this system, all subject matter is divided into ten main classes and assigned certain numbers.

000-099 Generalities (encyclopedias, periodicals, etc.)
100-199 Philosophy & related disciplines (psychology, ethics, etc.)
200-299 Religion (Bible, churches, church history, etc.)
300-399 The social sciences (economics, law, education, etc.)
400-499 Language (grammar, derivations, etc., of various languages)
500-599 Pure sciences (mathematics, chemistry, astronomy, etc.)
600-699 Technology (applied sciences–agriculture, medicine, business, etc.)
700-799 The arts (sculpture, music, sports, theater, etc.)
800-899 Literature & rhetoric (novels, plays, essays, poetry, etc.)
900-999 General geography, history, collective biography, etc.

Each of these ten classes is subdivided into ten more specific groups:

700 The arts
710 Civic and landscape art
720 Architecture

730 Plastic arts; Sculpture
740 Drawing and decorative and minor arts
750 Painting and paintings
760 Graphic arts; Print making and prints
770 Photography and photographs
780 Music
790 Recreational and performing arts

Each of the ten groups is in turn divided into ten smaller fields:

790 Recreational and performing arts
791 Public performances
792 Theater (Stage presentations)
793 Indoor games and amusements
794 Indoor games of skill
795 Games of chance
796 Athletics and outdoor sports and games
797 Aquatic and air sports
798 Equestrian sports and animal racing
799 Fishing, hunting, shooting

Still smaller subdivisions are made by using decimals. For example, books dealing with the Olympic games are classified under the number 796.48; those dealing with mountain climbing, under 796.522.

In most small libraries, books of fiction are marked with an **F** and arranged on the shelves alphabetically by the last name of the author.

Individual biographies are marked **B** in some libraries; in others they are given number **92** or **920**. The biographies are arranged alphabetically by the last name of the person the book is about.

The Dewey classification number, which is part of the *call number*, is placed on the spine of the book. The call number is put in the upper left corner of the author, subject, and title cards in the card catalog. Once you know the call number of a certain book, you can easily find it on the shelves. (See also **Card catalog.**)

Dialect

Any identifiable varieties of speech that may differ from other speech patterns of the same language in pronunciation, grammar, or vocabulary. The United States, for example, has no one standard dialect that is preferred over all others. Each speech region–and there are many–has its own regional standard (the speech of the most respected).

From their studies of the various regions, dialectologists have determined that there are three general types of American speech. The three–Northern, Midland, and Southern–run across the country from east to west in more-or-less horizontal bands that tend to merge as they go farther toward the West Coast. Within these general areas are a number of distinctive subareas, such as New York City, Western Pennsylvania, Southern Mountain, and so on.

One of the first things you probably notice when you are introduced to people from another part of the country is that their speech sounds different from yours. You pronounce words differently. If you grew up in Atlanta, for example, and you encounter a native Detroit speaker for the first time, you may be struck by the hard *r*'s and, to you, unmusical intonation. On the other hand, the Detroiter will notice your "*r*-lessness" and "Southern drawl."

Some examples of regional vocabulary are:

string beans in the North; *green beans* and *string beans* in the Midland; *snap beans* and *snaps* in the South. Doughnuts are *fried cakes*, *nut cakes*, *rings*, and *olicooks* in the North; *crullers*, *fat cakes*, and *fossnocks* in the Midland; *cookies* in the South.

Not only do we find different words for the same object in the various speech regions, but people may state the same ideas in different ways, too: In the North, you *take* or *escort* someone someplace. In the Midlands you *take* or *see* someone someplace. In the South you *carry* someone someplace or *see them to* someplace.

Dialogue

For the use and punctuation of dialogue in writing, see **Conversation** and **Quotation marks.**

Diction

Manner of expressing one's ideas in words, including word choice and style of speaking.

die

Generally used with *of*–not *from* or *with*–before the name of an illness: He died *of* tuberculosis. But we say *died from a wound, died by violence, died through neglect, died from lack of care.*

different

In formal English and in informal writing, *different* is generally followed by *from*:

Kiyo's classes were different from her sister's.
The food was different from what they were used to on the farm.

Colloquial usage is divided; occasionally *from* is used, sometimes *to* (very common in England), and most often *than*:

His plans are different than anyone else's.

In both speech and writing, *different than* is becoming more common before a clause:

The food was different than they were used to on the farm.
The house was different than I had expected.

Direct address

The name or descriptive term by which persons (or animals) are addressed:

Ladies and gentlemen, let us reason together.

And where are you going, *young man*?
Stop dawdling, *Heidi*, and get dressed.

Words in direct address are set off by commas–one comma if they come at the beginning or the end of a sentence, and two commas if they come in the middle of a sentence.

Direct object

A noun or pronoun (or phrase or clause used as a noun) that tells who or what receives the action expressed by the verb is called a *direct object.* The direct object usually follows the verb, and it answers such questions as "What was it that Joan varnished?" or "Who was it that they disliked?"

Joan varnished the *table.*
They heartily disliked the *cashier.*
Ken enjoys *making a fool of himself.* [Gerund phrase.]
I can't remember *why he was fired.* [Noun clause.]

Occasionally, for emphasis, the object is put first in a sentence, before both the subject and the verb:

    O   S   V
The *buttons* she sewed on last.

Direct quotation

The actual words used by a speaker; in contrast with *indirect quotation,* in which the sense rather than the actual words is given:

DIRECT: "Why were you late for class, Lou?" asked Mr. Jones.
INDIRECT: Mr. Jones asked Lou why he was late for class.

(For punctuation, see **Quotation marks.**)

disinterested, uninterested

A distinction is generally made between these two words. *Disinterested* is used to mean "having no selfish interest or personal feelings in a matter and therefore no reason or desire to be anything but strictly impartial"; *uninterested* is used to mean "not interested":

She is disinterested in the matter and will give an unbiased report.
She is quite uninterested in hearing my side of the argument.

Ditto marks (″)

Ditto marks are used in accounts, lists, and tables to avoid repeating words that appear directly above:

derelict, derived from Latin
diplomat, ″ ″ French

Ditto marks are not appropriate in most of your written work (themes, tests, reports, letters) nor in footnotes or bibliographies.

dived, dove

Both forms are used as the past tense of *dive*; *dived* is more common, especially in writing.

Divided usage

The spellings, pronunciations, and constructions used by speakers and writers of the same education often differ. Whenever there are—in the same level of language—two or more forms that are equally acceptable, usage is said to be *divided.* There are many more of these divided usages than most people realize. Here are just a few:

IN SPELLING:	gaiety *or* gayety	monologue *or* monolog
	intern *or* interne	skillful *or* skilful

When a dictionary provides two spellings for a word, the first spelling is the more common.

IN PRONUNCIATION:	calm: /käm/ *or* /kälm/
	creek: /krēk/ *or* /krik/
	juvenile: /jü′və nəl/ *or* /jü′və nīl/
	status: /stā′təs/ *or* /stat′əs/
IN VERB FORMS:	Past tense: knelt *or* kneeled, pleaded *or* pled
	Past participle: shown *or* showed, beaten *or* beat

Remember that in all such instances of divided usage either of the forms is acceptable. Use whichever seems to you the most appropriate in a particular situation. You may choose the one that you think is preferred by your audience or, better still, the one that comes most naturally to you.

Division of words

You may occasionally have to divide words at the end of lines. Whenever it is necessary to divide a word, break it between syllables. The following rules will help you determine in general where the divisions should be made. If you are in doubt about a particular word, consult your dictionary.

1. Both parts of a divided word should be pronounceable; words of one syllable—*hemmed, strength, watched, through, twelve, you're, you'll*—should not be divided.

2. Words should not be divided so that a single letter stands by itself. For example, do not divide a word like *abash* (which would leave a lone *a* at the end of a line) or *slimy* (which would put a lone *y* at the beginning of a line).

3. As a rule, divide a word after a prefix or before a suffix:

bi-focal	in-justice	moral-ize
sub-contract	defeat-ist	intern-ment

4. As a rule, divide between double consonants:

crop-ping	jag-ged	fel-lows
neces-sity	cur-rent	guz-zling

But if the double consonants come at the end of the root word, they are not split; the division is made after the double consonants, before such endings as *-ing*, *-er*, and *-able*:

tell-ing   dress-er   surpass-able

5. Two consonants that come between two vowels may be divided if the consonants are pronounced separately:

tar-get   res-cued   gen-der   con-cert

6. Two vowels may be divided if they are pronounced separately:

vi-olence   cadmi-um   seri-ous   radi-ology

7. If two consonants or two vowels are pronounced as one sound, do not divide them:

hock-ey   mech-anism   fash-ion   ring-let

8. As a rule, divide between parts of a compound word:

motor-cycle   how-ever   table-cloth   law-breaker

If the compound word itself is actually spelled with a hyphen, divide at the hyphen to avoid the awkwardness of two hyphens in one word:

sober-minded   in-law   helter-skelter   safe-conduct

9. If a single consonant comes between two sounded vowels, the consonant generally is put at the beginning of a syllable with the second of the vowels:

se-dan   ma-ter-nal   To-le-do   de-fer

But if the preceding vowel is *short* and *accented*, the consonant is kept with that vowel:

sed′-entary   tep′-id   dec′-ade
mat′-ador   nov′-el   def′-erence

10. Try to avoid dividing words in a way that will at first glance cause readers to be confused about the meaning or pronunciation:

Not: rat-ional   But: ra-tional
miser-able   mis-erable

do

1. Besides its use as a predicate verb meaning "perform; make; accomplish; bring about; etc.," *do* has five uses (as a helping verb) where it has no definite meaning of its own:

a. For emphasis, especially in answer to a question or in a statement contradicting a preceding statement:

Yes, we *do* have to leave early.
But Richard Berry *did* leave early; David Miller left with him.

b. In asking questions:

Do you want to play tennis on Friday?
Did Bonnie say she could join us?

c. With negative verbs:

Don't wait for us longer than an hour.
He didn't say he could be here.

d. As a substitute for a verb that has just been used, to avoid repeating it:

His friends ski more often than he does.
Laura dared him to enter the slalom race; so he did.

e. In inverted sentences, after such adverbs as *rarely*, *little*, *hardly*:

Little did we know about the dangers of motorcycling.
Only rarely do we hear a bassoon concerto.

2. *Do* has many meanings and is part of many idiomatic phrases: you may *do* your hair or *do* the dishes; your sister may *do up* her week's wash or *do up* a package; you may have generous neighbors who *do well* by their relatives; after a man has *done time* for *doing a partner out of* large sums of money, he could *do without* the suspicious glances he gets and could *do with* a bit of kindness.

don't, doesn't

These contractions are universally used in informal writing, especially in sentences where *do not* or *does not* would seem too emphatic or where the rhythm seems smoother with the contraction.

In nonstandard English *don't* is used with a third-person singular subject (He don't count; It don't hold much). Educated speakers and writers avoid this usage, using *doesn't* with a third-person singular subject and *don't* only with a plural:

She doesn't believe it.	They don't believe it.
He doesn't count.	They don't count.
It doesn't hold much.	They don't own much.
Money doesn't grow on trees.	Dollars don't grow on trees.

Double comparison

See **Comparison of adjectives and adverbs,** section 1.

Double negative

In formal and in informal English two negative words are not used together to express one negative meaning. In nonstandard English this "double negative" construction is often used, especially when the negative meaning is to be emphasized:

NONSTANDARD: I didn't tell him nothing.
STANDARD: I didn't tell him anything.
STANDARD: I told him nothing.

NONSTANDARD: My parents won't never go out on New Year's Eve.
STANDARD: My parents won't ever go out on New Year's Eve.
STANDARD: My parents will never go out on New Year's Eve.

The objection to the double negative is not, as many people like to explain, that "two negatives make an affirmative." It is doubtful that anyone would ever mistake the intended meaning of "He won't never pay you back"—the double negative makes it only too clear. The real objection is that double negatives are just not used by educated people, except in a joking mood. Centuries ago double negatives were common in all levels of English; you have probably seen examples in Chaucer and in Shakespeare. But they are out of fashion now in the standard language.

Obvious double negatives like those in the examples above are easy to spot. Somewhat more tricky are those made with the adverbs *hardly*, *scarcely*, and *barely*, which have a negative meaning and should therefore not be combined with other negative words:

NONSTANDARD: The box was so heavy that Rolf couldn't hardly lift it.
STANDARD: The box was so heavy that Rolf could hardly lift it.

Double prepositions

In colloquial usage double prepositions like *off of* (for *off*), *inside of* (for *inside*), *outside of* (for *outside*) are common. In informal writing all of these but *off of* are acceptable, though the *of* is unnecessary and could neatly be dropped, since it adds nothing to the meaning. In formal English these double prepositions are avoided.

Doublespeak

The use of indirect or complex language, often to conceal an unpleasant truth or mislead others. Referring to a "fight" as "a conflict situation" is an example of doublespeak. Note the following examples of doublespeak:

Siblings are conflicted in their interpersonal relationships means that children of the same parent or parents don't like each other. Exogenous variables form the causal linkage that explains the poverty impact, the behavior modification, and the intergroup dissonance in the target area means that outside factors cause the poverty and the changes in people that lead to trouble in the neighborhood. A recommendation by a medical ethicist that a physician obtain an input from the patient's own value system means that the patient should be asked whether he wants the treatment. —Edwin Newman. *Strictly Speaking.* Indianapolis: The Bobbs-Merrill Co., Inc., 1974.

Doubling final consonants

See **Spelling,** section 1a.

doubt

In negative statements (where there is no real doubt) *doubt that* is used in formal English, *doubt but that* in informal writing, and *doubt but what* or *doubt but* in informal speech:

FORMAL: We do not doubt that Mayor Katz is able.

INFORMAL WRITING: We don't doubt but that Mayor Katz is able.
INFORMAL SPEECH: We don't doubt but what Mayor Katz is able.

In positive statements (where doubt really exists) *doubt whether* is used in formal English and *doubt if* in informal English:

FORMAL: I doubt whether it will snow tomorrow.
INFORMAL: I doubt if it will snow tomorrow.

When unbelief rather than doubt is intended, *doubt that* is used:

I doubt that it will snow tomorrow.

drought, drouth

Both forms are in good use; *drought* /drout/ is perhaps more common in formal English and *drouth* /drouth/ in informal.

drowned

In standard English, pronounced as one syllable /dround/—not two /droun'did/.

due to

Originally *due* was used only as an adjective, and in formal English it is still restricted to this use:

His late arrival was due to an earlier appointment across town.
[*Due* modifies *arrival; due to* means "caused by" or "attributable to."]

In informal English *due to* is commonly used as a preposition meaning "because of":

Due to their drills, the students knew what to do in case of fire.
Due to her age, Carla's parents wouldn't let her travel alone.

Since in spite of its commonness there is some prejudice against using *due to* as a preposition, it would be wise to avoid this use when writing for readers who you know are rather formal in language. You can easily substitute *because of* or *owing to*:

Because of her age, Carla's parents wouldn't let her travel alone.

each

1. *Each*, as an adjective or pronoun, is singular; it takes a singular verb and is referred to by singular pronouns:

Each mother *was given her* newborn baby's picture.
Each teacher *is assigned* a parking space of *his* or *her* own.
Each of the girls *wears her* hair in pigtails.

In colloquial usage, the pronoun *each* is sometimes regarded as a plural and is referred to by a plural pronoun:

After *each* of the contestants had had *their* say, a vote was taken.

But in formal writing, either singular or plural forms should be used together:

After *each* of the Mr. America contestants had had *his* say, a vote was taken.
After *all* of the contestants had had *their* say, a vote was taken.

2. *Each* is sometimes used as a pronoun in apposition with a plural subject:

Oak Hill and Bartville *each* have a new shopping center.
To finish in time, they *each* have to do their share of work.

Notice that in these sentences the pronoun *each* does not affect the number of the verb. Since the subjects are plural, the verbs (and the pronoun referring to the subject of the second sentence) are plural.

(See also **Agreement,** sections 1g and 2b.)

each other, one another

In formal English a distinction is sometimes made between these pronouns: *each other* is used in reference to two; *one another*, to more than two:

Our Siamese cat and their Pekinese eyed each other warily.
Incidentally, the three women on the staff trust and like one another.

Informal English does not make this distinction, using *each other* and *one another* interchangeably, to refer either to two or to more than two:

Our Siamese cat and their Pekinese eyed one another warily.
Incidentally, the three women on the staff trust and like each other.

Editorial

An article in a newspaper or magazine written or supervised by an editor, stating opinions and attitudes (of the editor, the publisher, or the owner) on a subject of current interest. Editorials are generally printed on a special page, called the "editorial page," to set them apart from other material. The problems or events discussed in newspaper editorials are usually covered in news stories in the same issue. The news stories are supposed to give just the facts, which the editorials interpret according to the political or social theories that the paper represents. Although most editorials are intended to influence opinion, they are sometimes written to inform or merely to entertain.

Editorial we

See **we,** section 2.

effect, affect

See **affect, effect.**

e.g.

See **for example.**

either, neither

1. The usual meaning of *either* is "one or the other of two":

ADJECTIVE: The debaters were good, but I didn't agree with *either* side.
PRONOUN: Bob and Mei were to meet us by noon, but I haven't seen *either* of them.

With reference to more than two, *any* or *any one* is generally preferable:

I want to study chemistry, biology, and physics in college. I could major in *any one* of these fields. [Not: *either* of these.]

The same distinction applies to the negative *neither. None* is used for more than two:

She checked both grocery stores, but *neither* had fresh coconuts.
I asked Hal and his sisters to go swimming with us, but *none* of them would. [Not: *neither* of them would.]

2. *Either* and *neither* are usually regarded as singular, although informal English sometimes uses plural verbs with them, especially in questions:

Is either of the twins home? [Informal: *Are* either of the twins home?]
Neither of us *has* a hall pass.

3. *Either* meaning "each" is formal English and is seldom used now:

RARE: There are flower beds on either side of the grand mall.
USUAL: There are flower beds on each side (*or* both sides) of the grand mall.

4. In all but a few sections of the United States, the pronunciations /ē'ŦHər/ and /nē'ŦHər/ are generally heard; /ī'ŦHər/ and /nī'ŦHər/ are regarded as affectations except in some New England communities or among families or groups in which they are naturally used.

either . . . or, neither . . . nor

Used as correlative conjunctions (linking words that work in pairs):

We must all either use less energy or suffer the consequences.
Neither corporations nor government agencies had quick solutions.

(See **Correlative conjunctions.**)

Either-or argument

Good or *bad, rich* or *poor, interesting* or *boring.* Thinking of persons or things in terms of opposites or extremes, in terms of *either-or* is fallacious reasoning. Rarely in real life do people and things fit neatly into one of two groups: the "bad guys" or the "good guys"; usually there is a middle ground that exists between the extremes. The writer or speaker who presents just two choices—"it has to be this or that," is quite likely oversimplifying the case. Sound solutions and answers can generally be found only by considering all the data, not just the extremes.

Ellipsis (. . .)

A punctuation mark of three spaced dots used to show an omission in writing or printing. (Plural: *ellipses.*)

1. An ellipsis is used chiefly to show where one or more words not essential to the meaning have been omitted from a quoted sentence:

The beginning writer must understand that slang . . . is effective only when used sparingly.

When an ellipsis comes at the end of a quoted sentence, a fourth mark is needed for the period:

A dictionary, then, is a record of existence. . . . Future historians will learn from dictionaries a great deal about twentieth-century life.

2. An ellipsis is sometimes used in narrative writing to show that a statement is left unfinished:

Because Emilia wanted to please both parents she had a dilemma. She knew that a stitch in time . . .

(See also **Dash.**)

Elliptical clauses

Clauses in which a word or words necessary for grammatical completeness but not for meaning are not used. The meaning of elliptical clauses is clear from other words in the sentence or from the context:

I worried about Carlos more than [I worried about] *them.*
I worried about Carlos more *than they* [worried about him].
When in Rome, do as the Romans do. [The meaning is obviously "When you are in Rome."]

(See **Dangling modifiers.**)

else

1. Since *else* follows the word it modifies, the sign of the possessive is added to *else* rather than to the modified word:

She always borrows someone else's textbook. [Not: someone's else.]
Everybody else's after-school activities seem more interesting to Josie.

2. In everyday speech, *else* is sometimes used for emphasis in sentences where it actually adds nothing to the meaning. This use is not appropriate in writing. You can check the use of *else* in this way: if it is followed by *but*, *except*, or *besides* and an object, *else* is deadwood and should be omitted:

There was nothing but potato chips in the pantry. [Not: nothing *else* but.]
I wish Carolyn would think of someone besides herself. [Not: someone *else* besides.]
But: I wish Carolyn would think of *someone else* for a change.

emigrate, immigrate

Emigrate means "to go from a country and settle in another." Associate the idea of going *out of* or *from* with *emigrate*:

I can trace my ancestors on my mother's side to an Abby Dean, who emigrated from Wessex in 1867.

Immigrate means "to come into a foreign country." Associate the beginning of this word, *im-*, with *in*:

Did you know that a number of those who immigrated to the United States in the eighteenth century were debtors or convicts?

Encyclopedias

Books or sets of books giving information, usually arranged alphabetically, on various branches of knowledge. Encyclopedias give authoritative general articles on persons, places, things, and events. The information is kept up to date by frequent (sometimes biannual) revisions of the articles or by annual supplements. Among the best known are these:

Collier's Encyclopedia (24 volumes, Volume 24 containing a Bibliography and Index; supplemented by *Collier's Encyclopedia Yearbook*)
The Columbia Encyclopedia (1 volume; a general encyclopedia with 75,000 entries in "compact" form, alphabetically arranged, with a cross-reference system to relate entries)
Compton's Encyclopedia and Fact-Index (26 volumes, with a portion of the Fact-Index included at the end of each volume. The Fact-Index contains some information on each subject and also serves as an index to longer articles.)
The Encyclopedia Americana (30 volumes, of which Volume 30 is the Index; supplemented by *The Americana Annual*)
The Encyclopaedia Britannica (30 volumes divided into the "Propaedia," a 1-volume outline of knowledge; the "Micropaedia," a 10-volume alphabetical listing of briefly defined facts which also serves as an index to longer articles; and the "Macropaedia," 19 volumes of lengthier articles for those looking for more detailed information on a subject. The Encyclopaedia is supplemented by *Britannica Book of the Year.* Many libraries may still have earlier editions of *The Encyclopaedia Britannica*, 24 volumes with the Atlas and Index in the last volume.)
Encyclopedia International (20 volumes, with Index included in the last volume)
The Lincoln Library of Essential Information (2 volumes, in which the material is organized in 12 "departments," each treating a major subject area, e.g., History, Economics and Useful Arts, Literature, Science, Biography)

Merit Students Encyclopedia (20 volumes, the Index in Volume 20 designed to help readers follow up any topic fully)
The World Book Encyclopedia (22 volumes, Volume 22 containing a Research Guide and Index; supplemented by *The World Book Year Book*)

In most of these encyclopedias a great majority of the articles are signed with the names (or the initials) of the subject-matter experts who worked on them–as authors, authenticators, reviewers, or consultants. The qualifications of each of these experts are listed in an index of contributors given at the beginning of each volume or in the first or last volume of the set.

End-stop

A mark of punctuation–usually a period, a question mark, or an exclamation mark–used at the end of a sentence. (See **Period, Question mark, Exclamation mark, Ellipsis,** and **Dash.**)

English, varieties of

American, Canadian, and English people speak English, but they do not speak exactly the same kind of English. The most extreme language differences are found, of course, in regional or provincial dialects. Someone from the United States might have a great deal of trouble understanding a person from Yorkshire, for instance, or a London cockney. The contrast between the standard language (the language of the majority of educated people) in English-speaking countries is less striking. But there still are differences to be noted.

In comparing American and British English, for example, one will notice a few variations in spelling. The English prefer the *-re* ending for words like *calibre, fibre, spectre.* They still keep the *-our* endings in words like *flavour* and *rumour.* They use *x* in words like *inflexion* and *connexion* (which are spelled *inflection* and *connection* in the United States). And they double more consonants (*medallist, focussing, libellous*).

There are a number of differences in vocabulary. For example:

AMERICAN	BRITISH
apartment	flat
checkers	draughts
closet	cupboard
corn	maize
dessert	sweet
detour	diversion
end of speed zone	end of prohibition
French fries	chips
garbage truck	dust cart
no passing	no overtaking
sedan	saloon car
sidewalk	pavement
subway	tube
tenderloin	undercut
thumbtack	drawing pin
truck	lorry

Words and phrases belonging peculiarly to the English are called *Briticisms*; those that belong peculiarly to U.S. speakers (*to monkey with, jaywalking, to debunk, had cold feet, to cough up, raise Cain, play possum, for keeps*) are called *Americanisms*. Such words and phrases are a frequent source of amusement in the two countries–and sometimes also a source of confusion. For instance, by taking words like *undercut* and *diversion* in their usual American sense, you might completely mistake the meaning intended by an English speaker.

You will notice only a few differences in grammar if you compare the standard spoken and written English of the two countries. Collective nouns, for example, are more likely to be plural in British usage: "The government *intend* to correct this"; "The cabinet *are* in accord." And where Americans would say "He felt like a fool," the English are likely to say "He felt a fool."

There are enough differences in pronunciation to make an "English accent" and an "American accent" clearly recognizable. The English have different values for the vowels, different stresses, and in general a more rapid speech and a tendency to slur syllables (like the *ar* in *dictionary* and *elementary*). American pronunciations are slower and fuller.

Just as British and American English differ in certain respects, Canadian English is distinct in many ways from English spoken in the United Kingdom and from English spoken in the United States. In Canada, for example, many people pronounce *vase* /vāz/, while the British say /väz/, and most people in the United States say /vās/. But although neither British nor American, Canadian speech patterns are, in some respects, a blend of both. Until recently, British spellings have predominated over American ones in Canada: *axe* for *ax*, *colour* for *color*, *cheque* for *check*. In recent years, however, American spellings are becoming more common.

There are hundreds of words native to Canada and other words with special meanings peculiar to the country. Some Canadianisms are used nationally, while others are largely regional. Certain terms are related to special fields of activity (from hockey and lacrosse come *blueline*, *rover*, *spearing*, *crosse*; from politics come *reeve*, *rural municipality*, *Grit*, *police village*). Other Canadianisms are names of regions (French Shore, Lakehead, Cariboo). Still others are borrowed words, with their forms changed slightly (from Canadian French come *chowder* [*chaudière*], *mush* [*marche*]).

As time goes by, the differences between these branches of the English language will probably tend to diminish. Modern developments in transportation and communication will bring speakers of English closer through a steady exchange of books, periodicals, movies, teachers, students, tourists, and entertainers. And each country will, in turn, make contributions that will enrich the English language.

ensure, insure

Ensure is preferred when the meaning is "make sure or certain":

Getting the support of the community *ensured* the success of the drive.

Insure is used to mean "arrange for money payment in case of loss, accident, or death." Remember *insure* in connection with *insurance*:

It cost us fifty dollars to *insure* our apartment.

enthuse

A verb formed from the noun *enthusiasm.* Although *enthuse* has gained wide acceptance as the colloquial expression for the more formal *be enthusiastic about* or *be enthusiastic over*, many people object to it and would avoid it in writing.

COLLOQUIAL: The manager enthused over the grand opening of the suburban office.

WRITTEN: The manager was enthusiastic about the grand opening of the suburban office.

Epigram

A short, pointed, often witty statement of a fact or opinion, either in verse or prose. Such statements are useful for focusing attention on a particular idea, making it easy to remember and to quote:

You should never wear your best trousers when you go out to fight for freedom and truth. –Henrik Ibsen. *An Enemy of the People*, act 4.
The cook was a good cook, as cooks go; and as cooks go she went. –H. H. Munro. *Reginald.* "Reginald on Besetting Sins."

Aphorisms are similar to epigrams, but are more likely to be abstract and not necessarily witty:

A good listener is not only popular everywhere, but after a while he gets to know something. –Wilson Mizner.

Proverbs are short, wise sayings, generally about character or conduct, that have been used for a long time by many people. Most proverbs have no known author. The terms *adage* and *maxim* are also used in reference to such sayings:

The cat in gloves catches no mice.
Keep your eyes wide open before marriage, half shut afterwards.
When the well's dry, we know the worth of water.

A special type of epigram is the *paradox*, which presents an idea in seemingly contradictory terms:

He who praises everybody, praises nobody. –James Boswell. *Life of Johnson.*

Esq. (Esquire)

A formal title of respect written after a man's name in the inside and outside addresses of a letter. *Esq.* is frequently used in England, where it signifies a definite social position. Its use in the United States and Canada–chiefly with names of professional men–has become rare, though it is still used occasionally, particularly with lawyers' names.

Preceding titles (Mr., Dr., Hon.) are not used when *Esq.* follows a name:

Clark McPherson, Esq.

et al.

An abbreviation of the Latin *et alii,* meaning "and others." It may be used in a footnote to indicate that a book has four or more authors, only the first of whom is named: Henrietta Smith et al. But the English *and others* is becoming more common: Henrietta Smith and others. (For punctuation, see the Appendix.)

etc.

1. *Etc.*, the abbreviation for the Latin *et cetera* (literally "and others"), is usually read *and so forth* or *et cetera* /et set′ər ə/. It is appropriate in reference and business usage:

Included in the woodwind group are the bassoons, clarinets, flutes, etc.
The *conifers*—pines, firs, spruces, larches, etc.—are cone-bearing trees.

As you can see from the examples given, only one period is necessary when *etc.* comes at the end of a sentence, but other punctuation marks are used after *etc.* according to the needs of the sentence. When *etc.* comes inside a sentence, it is set off by commas:

Pine, spruce, hemlock, etc., are softwoods.

2. *Etc.* is out of place in both formal and informal writing, which avoid abbreviations in general. If you want to write out the term, the English *and so forth* is less conspicuous—and better—than *et cetera.* But the best advice is to avoid all such terms. An *and so forth* weakens your writing by giving the impression that either you are too lazy to complete a list or you are bluffing—indicating that you know more than you actually do. One solution is to rephrase the sentence, using *such as* or some other expression to show that the list is not intended to be complete:

WEAK: To qualify as a detective-novel fan, you have to know the classic writers—Dorothy Sayers, Dashiell Hammett, etc.

BETTER: To qualify as a detective-novel fan, you have to know such classic writers as Dorothy Sayers, Ngaio Marsh, Dashiell Hammett, Raymond Chandler, and Rex Stout.

And etc. should never be used, since the *et* of *et cetera* means "and." Remember *et* also to fix the correct spelling of the abbreviation in your mind: *etc.*—not *ect.*

Euphemism

A mild, indirect word or phrase used instead of one that is more direct or harsh or that may have unpleasant connotations—*left us* for *died, those in the low-income bracket* for *the poor, guest house* for *boarding house, an equivocation* for *a lie.*

ever

In colloquial usage, *ever* is sometimes added after the interrogatives—*who, where, why, what, how, when*—for emphasis: "Who ever would have suspected him?" "Where ever did she park the car this time?" "What ever gave you that idea?" "How ever can they afford such a trip?"

In writing you will sometimes see the two words joined (*whoever, wherever, whatever . . .*).

every and its compounds

1. The adjective *every* and the pronouns *everybody* and *everyone* are grammatically singular; they take singular verbs and are usually referred to by singular pronouns:

Every member of our team *has his* or *her* own bowling ball.
Everybody who parks there *has* to leave *his* keys in *his* car.
All week everyone *is* on *her* best behavior.

In colloquial usage, plural pronouns are sometimes used to refer to *everybody* and *everyone*, especially when they are thought of as plural in meaning:

Everybody had figured out ahead of time what *they* would say.
Everybody on the committee had been uncooperative, though *they* hadn't realized it. [Not: *he* hadn't realized it. A plural meaning is clearly intended.]

In formal usage, singular pronouns would be used or–if the meaning is clearly plural–the sentence would be rephrased:

Every tenor knew ahead of time where *he* would stand on the platform.
All the members of the committee had been uncooperative, though *they* hadn't realized it.
Everyone on the committee had been uncooperative, though *none* of them had realized it.

(For further examples, see **Agreement,** sections 1g and 2b.)

2. *Everybody*, *everything*, and *everywhere* are written as one word. *Everyone* may be written as one word or two, depending on the meaning intended. The pronunciation can help you decide which form to use. If *every* is stressed, use the one-word form. If *one* receives an equal amount of emphasis or more, use two words:

Everyone commented on how successful the party was.
Every one of them was hoping to get the promotion.

When used as an adjective, *everyday* is one word; when *day* is a noun modified by *every*, two words are used:

Her bilious attacks were an everyday occurrence.
He raised and lowered the flag every day.

3. Informal usage sometimes substitutes *everyplace* for *everywhere*. There are several other useful informal idioms formed with *every* but, like *everyplace*, they should be avoided in formal speech and writing:

INFORMAL: There were cobwebs everyplace.
FORMAL: There were cobwebs everywhere.

INFORMAL: My hair was flying every which way.
FORMAL: My hair was flying in every direction.

INFORMAL: Every so often I have a taste for pomegranates.
FORMAL: Once in a while I have a taste for pomegranates.

ex-

See **Prefix.**

Exaggeration

See **Hyperbole.**

except

See **accept.**

Exclamation mark (!)

A mark used after a word, phrase, or sentence that the writer intends to be very emphatic. Such a word, phrase, or sentence is called an *exclamation*:

Help! Let me speak! She must hurry!
Not in there! Put it in the freezer!
That was a silly thing to say!

Exclamation marks are used more frequently in narrative writing than in other types. They should always be used thoughtfully and sparingly (and only one at a time!) because too many exclamation points weaken the emphasis they are intended to provide:

OVERDONE: The light finally changed! Buzz stepped on the gas, and the car shot forward! Just one more block!! Then at last they could relax!! Dr. Frank would take over!!

BETTER: The light finally changed. Buzz stepped on the gas, and the car shot forward. Just one more block! Then at last they could relax. Dr. Frank would take over.

Exclamatory sentences

Sentences used to express strong feeling:

What a coward he turned out to be!
This is a great party!

Expletives

It and *there* are called *expletives* when they begin sentences in which the real subject follows the verb:

It would be useful *to have all the reference books in one place.*
There should be one *dollar* in the sugar bowl.

Since the only function of *it* and *there* in sentences like these is to point ahead to (or "anticipate") the subjects, they are sometimes called "anticipatory subjects."

Expository writing

Writing intended primarily to inform others by explaining a process or idea, presenting and interpreting facts, and explaining reasons.

F F F F F F

Fact

See **Statement-of-fact.**

fact (the fact that)

Often used as a roundabout expression for *that*, which would express the same meaning more concisely:

Ms. Lafayette forgets [the fact] that French is not our native tongue. (See also **Deadwood.**)

Fallacies in reasoning

As a writer or speaker who wants others to accept your point of view on some matter, you have the obligation to provide well-reasoned, convincing evidence to support your conclusions. And as a reader or listener who is a straight thinker, you want to make very sure, before accepting any conclusion as valid, that it is based on sound evidence and reasoning. Some of the more common fallacies–errors in thinking–are treated under separate entries in this book. (See **Begging the question,** the **Post hoc fallacy, Ignoring the question, Argumentum ad hominem, Hasty generalization,** and **Either-or argument.**)

famous

Famous should not be used to label people who are obviously well known:

When he was young, my father lived next door to [the famous] Martin Luther King, Jr.

But if you were writing about someone whose fame was limited to a certain period of time or to a certain field that your readers might not be familiar with, *famous* would be appropriate:

The article is about Norma Shearer, a famous actress during the 1930s.
This is an original painting, done in New Mexico by the famous painter Georgia O'Keeffe.

(See also **notorious, famous.**)

farther, further

In formal English some people distinguish between these words, using *farther* to refer to physical distance and *further* to refer to abstract relationships of degree or quantity:

I won't walk farther until we discuss the purpose further.
He can't decide without further proof.

In informal English the distinction is not kept, and there seems to be a definite tendency for *further* to be used in all these senses.

Feature

A *feature* is a special story, article, column, comic strip, or cartoon in a newspaper or magazine. The feature, often prominently displayed, attracts attention because of its subject matter or because of the reputation of the writer.

A *feature story* is an unusual article or story whose appeal lies in some factor other than its news value. It holds attention by dramatizing the human-interest element contained in everyday incidents. Unimportant but interest-arousing incidents, such as the display of unusual bravery, courtesy, or discourtesy, are the kinds of subjects on which the feature writer of a newspaper thrives.

feel

For the use of *feel* as a linking verb, see **bad, badly.**

fewer, less

See **less, fewer.**

Fiction

Prose writings, particularly novels and short stories, that tell about imaginary people and events.

field (in the field of)

Often used unnecessarily in sentences like these:

They are looking for a teacher in [the field of] consumer education.
Last year Roger Kluz became interested in [the field of] chemistry.

Figurative and literal use of words

Words can be used in one of two ways, either literally or figuratively. In a literal sense we use them for their ordinary meanings:

As he was ducking under the barbed wire, several of the *barbs* tore into his thin shirt and scratched his back. [Metal barbs are projections that could cut through flesh.]

Words can also be used figuratively–that is, for meanings that are suggested by their literal meanings:

. . . Cowboy's jokes had *little tearing barbs that drew blood.* –Frank Bonham. *The Nitty Gritty.* [Cruelly sarcastic jokes hurt as badly as if they were actually accompanied by real barbs that could do physical harm.]

Figures (1, 61, 598 . . .)

See **Numbers** for the use of figures and the choice between figures and words in writing.

Figures of speech

Figures of speech are expressions in which words are used in an unusual sense, out of their literal meaning, or in an unordinary construction–to add beauty, force, or clarity. The most common figures are *simile* (He . . . buzzed about every hall and chamber, as idly restless and importunate as a blue-bottle fly on a warm summer's day. –Washington Irving, "The Specter Bridegroom"), *metaphor* (The average Ph.D. thesis is nothing but a transference of bones from one graveyard to another. –J. Frank Dobie. *A Texan in England*), and *personification* (I don't understand why . . . some days smile and others have thin slitted eyes and others still are days which worry. –John Steinbeck. *Journal of a Novel*).

fine

In "a fine woolen thread," "edged with fine lace," "a spool of fine wire," "earrings of fine gold," "a fine distinction," "ground into a fine powder," the adjective *fine* has a specific, exact meaning and is a useful and effective modifier. But *fine* (like *cute, wonderful, nice*) is often used as a counter word–a vague modifier that expresses only general approval. As a counter word, it has little value and is usually better omitted:

Steve Saftig proved to be a [fine,] devoted, understanding foster parent.

first

See **former, latter; first, last.**

First draft

The preliminary version of a paper in which the writer's ideas are generally presented in rough form. In subsequent drafts, the writer may add or omit material, correct mechanical errors, and improve the style and word choice.

fix

In general usage *fix* has several meanings: "fasten tightly" (fix the lamp on the wall), "set" (fixed the price at forty cents), "direct" (fixing his eyes on the top nail), "put definitely" (will fix the blame on us), "repair" (fixed the TV).

In informal English *fix* is used to mean "punish" or "get revenge on" (I'll fix him) and "an awkward situation" (helped him out of a fix). Both *fix* and *fix up* are used informally to mean "put in order" (fix your hair, fixed up the rec room). And although *fix* is in general usage to mean "repair," *fix up* used in the same sense is considered informal English.

Footnotes

See Appendix.

for

A comma is usually needed between two coordinate clauses joined by the conjunction *for*, to prevent misreading *for* as a preposition:

In the end I had to type both of the invoices, for Mrs. Reilly was called back to the hospital. [To prevent: In the end I had to type both of the invoices for Mrs. Reilly.]

(For the distinction between *for* and *because*, see **because.**)

Foreign words

See **Borrowed words.**

for example

The abbreviation used for *for example* is *e.g.* (from the Latin *exempli gratia*, meaning "for the sake of example"). *E.g.*, which rarely appears in informal writing, is particularly appropriate in scholarly papers, definitions, scientific writing, and legal documents. (For punctuation, see **namely and other introductory words.**)

Formal English

For a discussion of the characteristics and uses of this kind of English, see **Usage.**

Form classes

Through the years, various ways have been devised for classifying, or grouping, the words in the English language. One method, introduced by structural grammarians, is to divide the words in the language into two main groups: form-class words (words that primarily carry meaning) and function, or structure, words (words that primarily show relationships). (See **Function words.**)

The majority of English words fall into one of the four form classes, generally called nouns, verbs, adjectives, and adverbs. The classification is based on the forms of the words and their typical position in basic sentence patterns. For example, a word is classified as a noun if it meets one or more of these criteria: (1) if it has a typical noun ending like *-dom*, *-ism*, *-ment*, *-ness*; (2) if it has a singular, a plural, a singular possessive, and a plural possessive form (girl–girls–girl's–girls'); (3) if it is usually preceded by a noun marker like *a*, *an*, *the*, *some*, *her*; (4) if it will fit in one of the blanks in these sentence patterns: The _____ is good. He saw (the) _____.

Form classes are sometimes referred to as "open" classes, because new words are continually being added to them.

(See also **Words: classes of.**)

former, latter; first, last

Former and *latter* generally refer to two units only:

A newspaper reporter will interview Ms. Phyllis Smith and Mr. Richard Isenberger. The former is a spokeswoman for the union; the latter, the president of the school board.

First and *last* are used with three or more in a series:

Syndrome, *Destiny Waits*, and *The Wrong War* would all make interesting movies, though the first might seem too romantic to today's audiences and the last too starkly realistic. [Not: though the former . . . and the latter. . . .]

When used with a number, *first* precedes the number:

The first three in line each got an autographed record album.

Though *first* and *firstly* are both used as adverbs meaning "in the first place," *first* is generally preferred. When giving a list, say *first, second, third, last*:

First, the food at Waldo's, once of topnotch quality, is now just so-so. Second, the service is bad and is likely to get worse. Third, the prices. . . .

(See **last, latest.**)

Fractions

Fractions are written in figures when they are attached to other figures (13¼), when they are in a series that is being written in figures (8, 15, ¾, 910, 51, ½), and when they are in tables or reference material. Usually in ordinary writing they are written in words.

Fractions used as adjectives or adverbs are hyphenated:

A two-thirds majority is needed to pass a bill that has been vetoed by the governor.
The bushel was three-fourths full when he brought it home.

Usage is divided in writing fractions used as nouns:

Paul saves one half (*or* one-half) of what he earns.
Last semester two thirds (*or* two-thirds) of the class were girls.

But if the fraction contains a compound number from twenty-one to ninety-nine, the compound number is always hyphenated:

Tommy did not understand that twenty-one thirds is equal to seven.

Decimals are increasingly used in place of fractions in expository writing. They are always written in figures:

.897 .3 .50 3.14159

(See **Numbers.**)

Fragmentary sentences

For an explanation of fragmentary sentences, see **Sentence fragment.**

full, -ful

The adjective has two *l*'s: a *full* day, a *full* moon. The suffix has only one *l*: *helpful, tearful, wonderful.*

The standard plural of nouns ending in *-ful* is made by adding *-s*: *cupfuls, bucketfuls, handfuls, shovelfuls, teaspoonfuls.* Colloquially *cupsful, bucketsful*, etc., are sometimes heard.

Functional shift

In all languages, but more easily in English, the function of a word can be shifted—that is, a word can be used as more than one part of speech. For example, in the sentence "He grabbed the hammer" the word *hammer* functions as a noun (as direct object). In the sentence "He hammered the nail into the wood" the word *hammer*–with an *-ed* past ending added–functions as a verb (as predicate). And notice the various ways in which the word *short* functions in these four sentences:

AS ADJECTIVE: You have a short memory.
AS ADVERB: We ran short of milk.
AS NOUN: There was a short in the cable.
AS VERB: The cable shorted out.

Generally, as these examples indicate, no change is made in the word except the addition of inflectional endings (plural, possessive, past, etc.) where needed.

Function words

Some grammarians, especially structural grammarians, classify, or sort, the words of English into two main groups–form-class words and function words. (See **Form classes.**)

Among the various kinds of function words are prepositions (*under*, *with*, *at* ...), coordinating conjunctions (*and*, *but*, *or* ...), subordinating conjunctions (*that*, *because*, *while* ...), auxiliary verbs (*could*, *may*, *do* ...), and noun markers (*a*, *the*, *some* ...). Though function words carry some meaning, their primary job is to show relationships between words in sentences.

There are only about two hundred function words in English, grouped into fifteen or so categories. And since new words are rarely added to these groups, they are sometimes referred to as "closed" classes.

Future tense, future perfect tense

See **shall, will** and **Tenses of verbs.**

Gender

A classification of words to show whether they are masculine, feminine, or neuter.

1. In many languages nouns and the adjectives modifying them have special endings to show gender. However, in English there are relatively few nouns of this type: *brunet*, *brunette*; *host*, *hostess*; *widow*, *widower*.

2. Usually gender in English is indicated simply by the meaning of the word. Words referring to males are masculine (*he*, *son*, *nephew*, *godfather*, *stallion*); words referring to females are feminine (*she*, *daughter*, *niece*, *godmother*, *mare*); words referring to inanimate things are neuter (*it*, *book*, *telephone*, *honor*, *integrity*).

3. Many English nouns can be either masculine or feminine, depending on the person they refer to in a certain situation. Their gender is shown by the pronouns used with them:

We called our doctor and asked *her* if *she* had decided to operate. [The doctor here is feminine.]
The mayor tried to control *his* temper. [The mayor here is masculine.]

(See **he or she, his or her.**)

4. English often uses compounds to specify gender: *deliveryman*, *Girl Scout*, *Boy Scout*. Recently, however, many such gender specific compounds have been replaced (mailman⟶letter carrier; newsman⟶newscaster; salesman⟶salesperson).

5. Neuter nouns are sometimes given masculine or feminine gender through a type of personification:

Never again must war leave *his* scars on our land.

In informal usage particularly, intimacy or affection is frequently shown by making neuter objects feminine:

She may not be much to look at, but *she's* the best little car I've ever had.

Generalizations

General statements, principles, or rules inferred from particular facts or instances. When a generalization is based on enough facts or on enough particular instances, it is valid: "A balanced diet is an aid to good health." A generalization like this, which corresponds with facts, is sound and valuable.

A *hasty generalization* is a judgment made on the basis of too little evidence with only one or two facts or instances to support it. For example, at a party we meet an exchange student from England who reveals an amazing knowledge of literature, science, mathematics, history, and art. After an evening spent talking with her, we write a three-page composition whose controlling idea is "British students are better educated than American students." (And to "prove" it, we describe in detail the many accomplishments of the exchange student!)

In serious expository writing and speaking, every statement should be as valid as possible. This is particularly true when these statements are meant to influence others.

While you should guard against making inaccurate generalizations in your own speech and writing, you must be equally careful not to accept as true all of the generalizations that are hurled at you daily in books, in newspapers, over the radio, and on television. Challenge the generalizations you run across. Ask yourself such questions as: Is this statement always true?

What evidence is given to prove it is sound? Is it only partially true? Is it just one person's opinion? Why is the statement made? Is it intended to give me important information? Or is it used to persuade me to feel as the writer does so that I will think and do as he or she wants me to? (See **Inductive and deductive reasoning.**)

General usage

Words, forms, and constructions that are used in all kinds of English–formal, informal, and nonstandard. For a discussion, see **Usage.**

Genitive case

See **Possessive case.**

gentleman

See **man, woman.**

Gerund

A verb form ending in "ing" that is used as a noun.

1. A gerund can be used wherever a noun can be used:

SUBJECT:	*Jogging* is a popular form of exercise.
DIRECT OBJECT:	Gene Pinsky teaches *swimming* at the Y.
INDIRECT OBJECT:	He gives *gardening* all his free time.
SUBJECT COMPLEMENT:	My brother's favorite pastime is *sleeping.*
APPOSITIVE:	Phil's job, *umpiring*, isn't making him popular.
OBJECT OF PREPOSITION:	I have no great love for *ironing.*

Nouns are often used as modifiers: *reference* book–"a book for reference." Gerunds, too, may be used as modifiers: *bathing* suit–"a suit for bathing," *drinking* fountain–"a fountain for drinking."

2. Because a gerund is a verb form, it has some of the qualities of a verb. For example, a gerund may have a direct object:

We certainly enjoyed visiting *them.*
Angie plans on singing "This Land Is Your Land."

A gerund may be modified by an adverb:

Zito believes in living *frugally.* Plan on arriving *early.*

(See **Gerund phrase.**)

3. A pronoun form or a proper noun immediately preceding a gerund is usually in the possessive form:

Her wanting to be a veterinarian surprised her mother.
Lynn was surprised by *Elva's* nominating her for president.

Usage is divided when a common noun directly precedes a gerund. In formal English the possessive form is usual; in informal English, the ordinary form is often used:

FORMAL: My aunt was unhappy about my *cousin's* enlisting.
INFORMAL: My aunt was unhappy about my *cousin* enlisting.

The ordinary form is generally used for plural nouns:

He doesn't approve of employees working overtime.

When emphasis is wanted for the noun or pronoun rather than for the gerund that names the action, the ordinary form of the noun and the objective form of the pronoun are used:

Can you imagine *Arthur* enlisting? Can you imagine *him* enlisting?

4. A gerund used as the object of a preposition should be related to the subject. Otherwise, the phrase will dangle:

DANGLING: After locking the door, the phone began to ring.
CORRECTED: After locking the door, he heard the phone begin to ring.

(See **Dangling modifiers.**)

5. Do not confuse the gerund with the present participle. Both have the same form; but while the gerund is a verbal noun, the present participle is a verbal adjective:

GERUND: *Riding* the bus for two blocks seems pointless. [*Riding* names an action; it is the subject.]
PRESENT PARTICIPLE: *Riding* a cross-country bus, Bill set off on his vacation. [*Riding* modifies Bill.]

Gerund phrase

1. Gerunds, being verb forms, can have objects, complements, and adverb modifiers. These words, headed by a gerund, form a *gerund phrase.* The phrase–as a unit–functions as a noun in sentences:

Winning the contest made them instantly famous. [The gerund phrase is subject of the verb *made*; *contest* is the object of the gerund *Winning.*]
She was very tired of *having been manager for ten years.* [The gerund phrase is object of the preposition *of*; *manager* is the complement of the two-word gerund *having been*; and *for ten years* is an adverb phrase modifying the gerund.]
Louise Gersbacher's happiest moment was *climbing up to the summit.* [The gerund phrase is a subject complement after the linking verb *was*; *up* and *to the summit* are adverb modifiers of the gerund.]

2. A gerund phrase used as the object of a preposition should be related to the subject of the sentence. Otherwise, the phrase will dangle:

DANGLING: After waiting for two hours, my patience ran out.
REVISED: After waiting for two hours, I ran out of patience.

(See **Dangling modifiers.**)

get

1. The principal parts are *get, got, got* or *gotten*:

Theo can get the application forms at city hall.
Hermina and Mike got an A from Mrs. Polanski.
Call us as soon as you've got (*or* gotten) the good news from home.

In England the past participle *gotten*—once the usual form—has been replaced by *got*. But in America both forms are acceptable, although *gotten* is probably more commonly used. The choice between them depends on which form a person is in the habit of saying, on the rhythm of a sentence, or, in some cases, on the exact meaning of the sentence.

2. In informal usage *get* is often used as an emphatic helping verb in passive forms:

Laura Lempke is getting promoted to head cashier soon. [Less emphatic: Laura Lempke is being promoted.]
He got punished for talking back to Aunt Phyllis. [Less emphatic: He was punished.]

3. In colloquial usage *have got* (never *have gotten*) is sometimes used instead of *have* alone as an emphatic way of expressing obligation or possession:

I have got to go home early; you've got to find another helper.
Have you got an extra script? I haven't got one with me today.

In these sentences the *have* alone would carry the meaning, but many speakers feel it is not emphatic enough and so expand the verb to *have got*. This usage, though common in informal speech, is avoided in formal English.

Given names

See **Names.**

go

In colloquial usage *go and*—used when no actual movement is meant—is a common form of emphasis:

Knowing Annie, I bet she'll *go and* lie about it.
My dumb brother *went and* told Mom that Dad was giving her a very large box with something mink inside it.

This usage is appropriate in informal narrative writing, but not in most exposition or in formal writing. In these, the *go and* would be omitted:

"She'll lie about it," "My dumb brother told Mom."

Gobbledygook

A word (said to have been coined by the late Congressman Maury Maverick) for speech or writing that is hard to understand because technical terms, involved sentences, and "big words" have been used too much.

Gobbledygook, so called after the sound made by a turkey (a gobble followed by a gook), applies especially to government and business writing that sounds like this:

> The end result of the situation in question, which had been instituted by and later explicably denounced by the distinguished representatives of the committee, was of such moment that these selfsame individuals who were, in theory and in actuality, responsible for its genesis (and thus forced to bear the onus of the censure of the representatives of the fourth estate and thereafter, in natural consequence, that of the general populace) attempted to disavow their prior knowledge as individuals and as a group of the context in which, as historical precepts have instructed, subsequent events would, in all probability, develop.

(See **Big words.**)

Good English

Good English is language that most effectively serves the user's purpose. To be good, language must be clear, lively, and appropriate–to the subject and the situation, to the listener or the reader, to the speaker or the writer. For further discussion, see **Usage.**

good, well

Good is used as an adjective, *well* as either an adjective or an adverb:

ADJECTIVE: Mother's approval made us feel *good.* ["Pleasant."]
ADJECTIVE: How happy she was to feel *well* again! ["Not ill."]
ADVERB: We were surprised Dan presented his plan so *well.* ["In a satisfactory or favorable way."]

Nonstandard English almost always uses *good* in place of *well*:

NONSTANDARD: I don't sew *good* enough to make a jacket.
STANDARD: I don't sew *well* enough to make a jacket.

graduate from

Graduate from has generally replaced the formal and somewhat archaic idiom *to be graduated from*:

RARE: Tony was graduated from Banning High School in June, 1978.
USUAL: Tony graduated from Banning High School in June, 1978.

Nonstandard English sometimes uses the verb *graduate* alone (Tony graduated high school in June, 1978). This should be avoided.

H

Habitual action

Would is commonly used as a helping verb to express habitual action in the past:

On Saturday mornings we would go to the Laundromat.

Habitual action is also shown by *used to* or by the past tense and an adverb:

On Saturday mornings we used to go to the Laundromat.
On Saturday mornings we always went to the Laundromat.

had

Used (now rather rarely) in formal writing as the introductory word in a subordinate clause of condition:

RARE: Had the car been going faster, we would have gotten hurt.
USUAL: If the car had been going faster, we would have gotten hurt.

had better, had best

These are the usual idioms for making indirect commands and giving advice:

You had better talk to Steve Moline.
She'd better get home quickly with the ice cream.
He had best learn to control that hot temper.

In informal speech the *had* is sometimes dropped:

You better talk to Steve Moline.
She better get home quickly with the ice cream.
He best learn to control that hot temper.

In formal English and in most writing (unless you are reporting directly what a person said) the *had* should be used.

had ought

Had ought and *hadn't ought* are nonstandard forms of the standard *ought* and *ought not*:

NONSTANDARD: Irv had ought to try waiting on tables.
STANDARD: Irv ought to try waiting on tables.

NONSTANDARD: She hadn't ought to go to the football game with that cold.
STANDARD: She ought not to go to the football game with that cold.

had rather, would rather

Both expressions are used to show preference; the second is more emphatic and perhaps more common:

Erica had rather walk than wait for a ride.
I'm so tired today, I would rather sleep than eat.

In speech the *had* or *would* is often slurred or contracted (I'd rather sleep) so that it is impossible to tell which is being used.

half

The generally used idiom is *half a(n)*; the more formal is *a half*:

GENERAL: Even I can walk half a mile in half an hour.
FORMAL: Even I can walk a half mile in a half hour.

Expressions with the article *a* coming both before and after *half*, like *a half a piece* and *a half an ounce*, are common in speech. However, such repetition is unnecessary and not often used in writing.

hardly

See **Double negative.**

Hasty generalization

See **Generalizations.**

have

See **of,** section 3.

have got

See **get,** section 3.

he or she, his or her

The English language has traditionally used the masculine forms *he* and *his* to refer to antecedents that mean either or both men and women. There are, however, several ways to avoid using the masculine pronoun to refer to both men and women (see items 2, 3, and 4 following).

1. Traditionally, *he* has been used with indefinite pronouns like *anyone* and *everyone* and with antecedents that may refer to both men and women:

Everyone in Spanish class was told to practice rolling his *r*'s.
Each pianist brought his own music.

2. But many writers prefer to use *he or she* and *his or her*:

Everyone in class must have *his or her* adviser's permission.
Each singer brought *his or her* accompanist to the rehearsal.

3. People who regard *he or she* (and *his or her*) as cumbersome but dislike using *he* (and *his*) alone when women as well as men are meant, solve the problem by using a plural pronoun, a usage not totally accepted.

4. Possible ways of revising to avoid using the masculine pronoun with an indefinite referent are

ORIGINAL:	Each player performed his role competently.
RECAST INTO PLURAL:	The players performed their roles competently.
ORIGINAL:	Each shopper carefully selected his groceries.
ELIMINATE PRONOUN:	Each shopper carefully selected groceries.
ORIGINAL:	If one wants to lose weight, he should diet and exercise.
REPEAT PRONOUN:	If one wants to lose weight, one should diet and exercise.
USE SECOND PERSON PRONOUN:	If you want to lose weight, you should diet and exercise.

healthful, healthy

Formal English distinguishes between these words, using *healthful* to mean "giving health" or "good for the health," and *healthy* to mean "having or showing good health":

Val eats whole grains, honey, and other healthful foods.
He's not been healthy since his illness, and he needs a more healthful climate.

In informal English *healthy* is often used to mean "healthful":

We've learned that exercising is healthy.

here, there

Nonstandard English often adds an unnecessary *here* to *this* (and *there* to *that*):

NONSTANDARD: This here magazine is newer than that there one.
STANDARD: This magazine is newer than that one.

Often in conversation an expression such as *this umbrella here* or *that one there* is used to clarify or emphasize meaning:

"Which bus do you take?" "I ride this one here."
"Did your uncle bring anything?" "Yes, he baked that cake there."

These expressions, in which *here* and *there* function as adverbs rather than adjectives, are standard colloquial usage.

high school

Capitalized only when used as part of a proper name:

When we move, I'll have to transfer to Senn High School.

When used as an adjective, *high school* is often hyphenated:

The high-school cafeteria always serves nutritious foods.

himself, herself

See **Reflexive pronouns.**

Historical present

For the sake of vividness or liveliness the present tense is sometimes used in narratives about the past. This usage is called the "historical present":

Then Mother grabs the baby and I whistle for the dog and we race for the storm cellar. But just as we reach the house, I suddenly remember. . . .

Although it is quite common to use this method in telling stories aloud, as a rule you will find it easier and more effective to stick to the past tense in written narratives. Used throughout a story, the "historical present" can become quite monotonous. And unless you are careful, you may find yourself shifting without reason from present to past and then back–to the confusion of your reader.

home

Nonstandard English sometimes uses *to home* for the generally used *at home* or *home*:

NONSTANDARD: Dave telephoned Gail, but she wasn't to home.
STANDARD: Dave telephoned Gail, but she wasn't at home. [Or: wasn't home.]

Homographs

Words that have the same spelling but a different origin and definition: *sole* ("one and only"), *sole* ("the bottom or undersurface"), *sole* ("a kind of flatfish").

In most dictionaries homographs are entered separately, and a small superscript number is put after each (sole[1], sole[2], sole[3]) as a signal that there are other entries (or another entry) which may have the definition a person needs.

Homonyms

See **Homographs** and **Homophones.**

Homophones

Words that have the same pronunciation but different spellings and meanings: *ate–eight*; *know–no*; *rote–wrote.*

The meaning of such words is usually made clear by the context, but their spelling is likely to cause trouble. Keeping the words separated in your mind by visualizing them in phrases that give a clue to their meaning will help you spell them correctly:

they *ate* dinner	*eight* o'clock
be on time	a honey *bee*
beer and pretzels	a funeral *bier*
room and *board*	the audience was *bored*
buy savings bonds	a seat *by* the window
cite statistics	the *site* of the new library

an amazing *feat*
a *gilt* ornament
the *gnu* at the zoo
a *knight* in shining armor
know the answer
a sharp *pain*
pause before answering
spring *rains*
learn by *rote*
sew on a button
steal second base
to eat *too* much
write the *right* answer

wipe your *feet*
guilt or innocence
I *knew* it was *new*
late at *night*
yes and *no*
a *pane* of glass
the kitten's *paws*
a horse's *reins*
he *wrote* a note
sow seeds
nerves of *steel*
two tiny tots
a religious *rite*

Honorable

When used as a title of respect for persons in high political offices (members of Congress, judges, governors, mayors), *honorable* is capitalized, is usually preceded by *the*, and is followed by the first name or initials as well as the surname:

The report was submitted by the Honorable Leslie H. Seymour.

In addresses, when the first name or initials are used, *Honorable* may either be abbreviated or written out in full. Generally, the full spelling is preferable:

Hon. Leslie Seymour
Hon. L. H. Seymour

The Hon. Leslie Seymour
The Honorable Leslie Seymour

hopefully

Originally the adverb *hopefully* meant only "in a hopeful manner":

The dog waited hopefully for something to drop from the table.

But in recent years it has come to be used also in the sense of "it is hoped":

Hopefully, our team will make it to the basketball finals.
Our gym will be decorated, hopefully, by Thursday.

Although certain dictionaries now recognize this use of *hopefully* as standard, it would be wise to avoid it when you think it might annoy your audience and take their attention away from what you are saying.

Hours

Generally, hours are written in words:

Mrs. Tufo will come for us at half-past seven.
From eight-thirty until five o'clock, I picked apples.

When the time is to be particularly emphasized, figures are used:

Flight 247, scheduled to arrive at 8:15 this morning, was delayed.

With the abbreviations A.M. and P.M. (or a.m. and p.m.), figures are always used:

Your train will leave the station at 11:04 P.M. and arrive in New York City at 6:30 A.M.

Notice that a colon is used between hours and minutes written as figures, and that the phrase *o'clock* is not added after A.M. and P.M.

how come?

A colloquial shortening of "How does (did) it come that?": *How come* none of us were notified about the meeting?

however

See **Conjunctive adverbs.**

Hyperbole

/hī pėr'bə lē/ Exaggeration for the sake of effect and not meant to be taken literally:

I'm amazed. He ate at least a thousand hot dogs!
My nephew worked all night and prepared enough food for an army.

Hyphen (-)

A connecting mark used between words or parts of words.

1. With compound modifiers. A compound modifier (two or more words used as a single adjective) preceding a noun is generally hyphened:

grade-school memories — fresh-baked bread
lemon-yellow curtains — his good-for-nothing brother
her spare-the-rod-and-spoil-the-child attitude

If a compound modifier of this type comes after the noun or if its first part is an adverb ending in *-ly*, no hyphen is used:

My best memories are from *grade school.*
In the kitchen the curtains were a *lemon yellow.*
From that *slightly opened* window, we could smell *freshly baked* bread.

Compound proper adjectives or compound proper nouns used as adjectives are not hyphened:

Supreme Court decision — Memorial Day parade — Viet Nam War veteran

2. With numbers and fractions. Hyphens are used in compound numbers from twenty-one to ninety-nine:

thirty-seven — sixty-fourth attempt
There were twenty-five dollar bills in the wallet Larry found. [Compare with "twenty five-dollar bills ($100)"–in which the hyphen is used for a compound modifier.]

Fractions used as modifiers are always hyphened:

The gas tank was two-thirds full. [Adverb modifier.]
They'll need a three-fifths turnout to break even. [Adjective modifier.]

But usage is divided in writing fractions used as nouns:

We missed one half (*or* one-half) of the performance.
Three fourths (*or* three-fourths) of the members are seniors.

3. With prefixes. A hyphen is used:

a. Between a prefix and a proper noun or adjective:

pre-Victorian post-Reformation anti-Nazi un-American

b. Between a prefix ending in *i* and a root word beginning with *i*:

anti-imperialist semi-industrialized

c. After the prefixes *self-* and *ex-* (when *ex-* means "former" or "formerly"):

self-centered self-discipline ex-principal ex-commissioner

d. To avoid confusion with another word that has the same spelling but a different pronunciation and meaning:

We plan to *re-cover* that old sofa you hated. /rē kuv′ər/
She did not *recover* from that bout of flu quickly. /ri kuv′ər/
The William Crawfords want to *re-lease* their cabin next summer. /rē lēs′/
The police will *release* the men immediately. /ri lēs′/

4. With compound nouns. There is no simple rule for hyphenating ordinary compound nouns, since usage varies so widely. For example, although the compounds *show-off* and *dog-ear* are hyphened, *show window* and *dog tag* are written as two words. And related compounds–*showroom* and *doghouse*–are written as one word. Sometimes even the same word is spelled differently. In three different magazine articles you may find *race-track*, *racetrack*, and *race track*.

Many compound words go through three steps before they are written as one word. For example, in an article (published in 1891) in which James Naismith described a game he had invented, he wrote its name as two separate words–*basket ball.* Then for many years a hyphen was used–*basket-ball.* Finally the two words fused into one–*basketball.*

Since there is no simple rule to guide you in spelling compounds, the safest practice is to consult a recent dictionary for words you are in doubt about. If the dictionary does not list the compound you are looking for (either as one word or with a hyphen), write it as two words, without a hyphen.

5. For dividing words. A hyphen is used to mark the division of words at the end of a line of writing. The problem here is to divide the word between syllables. For a list of rules to guide you, see **Division of words.**

I i I i I i

I

I is written as a capital simply because in the old handwritten manuscripts a small *i* was likely to be lost or joined to a neighboring word. Contrary to a widespread belief, using *I* as the first word in a letter (or as the first word in a series of sentences in a paragraph) is not a sign of conceit. *I* can be used wherever it is needed to express ideas simply and clearly. People who use roundabout expressions to avoid using *I* usually turn out awkward, unnatural sentences that are far less effective than sentences with *I*:

AWKWARD: It is my belief that a good score will be given to me on the SAT.
BETTER: I believe I will score high on the SAT.

If every sentence in a paragraph you have written begins with *I*, you may feel that the pronoun is too conspicuous, that too many *I*'s will be annoying to your reader. By shifting a modifying phrase or clause to the beginning of two or three of the sentences, you can take the emphasis away from the *I*:

On my way to the library, I stopped at the gym to watch the wrestlers practice. [Rather than: I stopped at the gym on my way to the library to watch the wrestlers practice.]

Ibid.

An abbreviation of the Latin *ibidem*, meaning "in the same place." It is used in a footnote to refer to the work mentioned in the immediately preceding footnote. (See the Appendix.)

Idiom

An idiom is a combination of words that seems perfectly natural to the native speakers of a language but seems odd or peculiar to other people (usually because it has a meaning different from the literal meaning of the words):

break the ice
fall in love
fly off the handle
forget yourself
hit the spot
lose your mind
on the tip of my tongue
run out of ideas
catch a bus
crack a smile
look up a word
strike a bargain
walk on air
be on pins and needles
run across a friend
read between the lines

(For further discussion and examples, see **Preposition,** section 3.)

i.e.

An abbreviation of the Latin *id est*, meaning "that is." It is now seldom used except in reference works; *that is* is used instead. (For punctuation, see **namely and other introductory words.**)

if, whether

1. *If* is used to introduce a clause of condition; *whether* (with *or*) is used to introduce alternatives:

If we leave at noon, we'll be sure to get good seats.
If you see Wally, tell him to meet us at the pool.
Whether I pass or fail, I'll have to attend summer school.
Whether we want to or not, we should stay at Uncle Luke's farm.

2. In formal usage *whether* (usually with *or*) is used to introduce indirect questions and expressions of doubt:

INDIRECT QUESTION:	She asked whether Bill had been homesick.
INDIRECT QUESTION:	Al asked whether Lee could swim or not.
DOUBT:	I wonder whether Jim deserves to win the election.
DOUBT:	No one is sure whether Kay is snobbish or just shy.

In informal usage *if* rather than *whether* is generally used in such sentences:

She asked if Bill had been homesick.
Al asked if Lee can swim or not.
I wonder if Jim deserves to win the election.
No one is sure if Kay is snobbish or just shy.

Ignoring the question

A fallacy in argumentation in which the question at issue is disregarded, while extraneous statements are offered as "evidence." Such off-the-point arguments often gain acceptance because they appeal to the listeners' emotions, or because they come close enough to the real issues involved to pass as legitimate arguments. For example, "*Starborne* should have won the Academy Award. After all, it cost ten million dollars to make; the director is one of the world's best; the actors are the most popular; the story is based on a best-selling novel." The question actually at issue here is "Was *Starborne* the best picture of the year?" Yet not one of the statements the speaker makes (true as they may be) is relevant to the point at issue: the merits of the movie.

Notice how the following advertisement ignores the question by shifting from the real issue—whether or not Glitter is the most effective toothpaste—and addressing itself to off-the-point "proofs."

Glitter is the most effective toothpaste ever! Users agree it tastes better. Leading dentists approve Glitter. Glitter outsells other toothpastes.

Now analyze the preceding statements. Why is Glitter the most effective toothpaste? Because it tastes better. Now ask youself: "Tastes better than

what? Limburger cheese? three-day-old pizza? banana peels?" Next, we are told that leading dentists approve Glitter. How many dentists? Leading in what? Finally, we learn that Glitter outsells other toothpastes. Why? Is it cheaper? Which other toothpastes? An analysis of this advertisement reveals that all three "proofs" that Glitter is the most effective toothpaste ignore the question: the taste of a toothpaste, its approval by an indeterminate number of professionals, and its vague sales claims in no way prove it is the most effective toothpaste.
(See **Argumentum ad hominem,** the most common form of ignoring the question.)

illusion, allusion

An *illusion* is "a false impression" or "a deceptive appearance":

People traveling in the desert often have the illusion of seeing pools of water.
I wear vertical stripes to create an illusion of height.

An *allusion* is "an indirect reference to something or someone generally familiar":

Robert Graves's poetry is filled with classical allusions.
When Mr. Green said, "Down the rabbit hole," we didn't realize he had made an allusion to *Alice in Wonderland.*

Imagery

Imagery in writing is the use of words that appeal to the senses: sight, hearing, touch, smell, taste, and the sensation of movement from the muscles, joints, and tendons known as the kinesthetic sense. Although many words may appeal to more than one sense (*spiny cactus* to sight and touch; *toasted marshmallows* to sight, smell, and taste), usually one of the sense appeals is dominant, as in the following:

SIGHT:	snowcapped mountains, rainbow, blazing bonfire
HEARING:	whining puppy, ambulance siren, shrill whistle
TOUCH:	wet fur, crisp parchment, warm sand
SMELL:	fresh-cut lilacs, ammonia, pine needles
TASTE:	lemon-meringue pie, potato chips, barbecued chicken
KINESTHETIC:	pounding heart, parched throat, hiccoughs

Imagery is an important part of writing, and you will see it used in all but the most abstract discussions of ideas. Try to use images in your writing, but remember they are most likely to be effective when they come directly from your own experience. The things you are interested in–cars, travel, science, music, anything–should be the source of many images, images that you can use in writing about a variety of different topics.

Imitative words (Onomatopoeia)

A number of words imitate or suggest the sound associated with a certain thing or action: *beep, boom, crackle, crash, crunch, cuckoo, honk, pop, rasp, rattle, rustle, splash, tick-tock, whippoorwill.*

The use of imitative words to gain a special effect in writing is called *onomatopoeia* /on′ə mat′ə pē′ə/:

The clop-clop of the horse's hooves on the cobblestones provided the rhythm for the night sounds: ca-rick, splash, rustle.

immigrate

See **emigrate.**

Imperative mood

A verb in the imperative mood is used to give commands or to make requests:

Lock the garage door securely.

(See also **Commands and requests, Mood.**)

Imperative sentences

Sentences that give commands or make requests:

Don't stop to talk.
Please come home early.

(See also **Commands and requests.**)

Impersonal it

In talking about weather and time, we use *it* as an impersonal subject in sentences like these:

It started to snow just as school began.
It was four o'clock when Ms. Estrella dismissed us.

It is called impersonal because it does not refer to a definite person or thing.

imply, infer

Careful speakers and writers distinguish between these two words, using *imply* to mean "indicate without saying outright," and *infer* to mean "draw a conclusion by reasoning":

I was unhappy because Father implied that I was at fault.
I inferred from Father's letter that he felt this way.

However, *infer* has been used so often in the sense of "imply" that many dictionaries record "imply" as a secondary meaning of *infer*.

in, into, in to

In generally shows location (in a literal or a figurative sense); *into* generally shows direction:

The birds are in the nest.	The robins flew into their nest.
Al is in the Marine Corps.	Al went into the Marine Corps recently.

Colloquially *in* is often used for *into*:

Mosquitoes flew in the house.	The cat fell in the rain barrel.

Do not confuse the preposition *into* with the adverb *in* followed by the preposition *to*:

At noon we went into the cafeteria for lunch.
At noon we went in to lunch.

in back of

See **back of, in back of.**

Incomplete sentences

See **Sentence fragment; Sentences: major and minor types.**

Indefinite articles

The articles *a* and *an*, used to refer to any one of a group of persons, places, or things: *a* constable, *an* orchard, *a* typewriter, *an* encyclopedia. (See **a, an** and **the.**)

Indefinite it

Formal English and careful informal writing avoid the use of the indefinite *it*:

INDEFINITE: In this article it tells about the new plays on Broadway.
DEFINITE: This article is about the new plays on Broadway.

Indefinite pronouns

Pronouns used to refer to any one or more of a number of persons or things:

all	everybody	nothing
another	everyone	one, oneself
any	everything	other
anybody	few	several
anyone	many	some
anything	neither	somebody
both	nobody	someone
each	none	something
either	no one	such

(Some of the specific usage problems concerning these pronouns are discussed under separate listings of the words themselves. See also **Agreement,** sections 1g and 2b.)

Indention

Beginning a line in from the left-hand margin. Since an uneven margin makes a page look unsightly, the margin should be kept straight and the indentions consistent.

In longhand copy, paragraphs are indented about an inch; in typewritten copy, from five to ten spaces. These measurements may vary slightly according to the writer's taste or because of special need.

Hanging indention is the setting in of lines below the first line, as in outlines, newspaper headlines, and slant-style headings and addresses of letters. If a line of verse is too long for one line, indent the part brought over to the second line:

> True ease in writing comes from art, not
>   chance,
> As those move easiest who have learned to
>   dance.
>
> —Alexander Pope
> *Essay on Criticism*

Independent clause

(Also called *main* clause.) See **Clause,** section 1.

Indicative mood

The verb forms that are used in ordinary statements and questions about actual things and events are called verbs in the *indicative mood*:

Mr. Kowicki *has* a handlebar moustache.
Do I *bring* my own towel?
The school bus *does* not *take* that route.
I *can call* everyone after school.

(See **Mood.**)

Indirect object

A noun or a pronoun (or a phrase or clause used as a noun) that shows to whom or for whom an action is done:

The class will give the spelling *champion* a trophy.
Mart sent *him* a postcard from Holland.
The drama coach gave Esteban's *acting* high praise. [Gerund.]
Please give *whoever volunteers* a badge and petition forms. [Noun clause.]

Notice that the indirect object comes before the direct object and that it does not use the prepositions *to* or *for.*

Indirect question

A question that is put into the speaker's or writer's own words instead of being quoted as first heard or read. A period, not a question mark, is used after an indirect question, and there are no quotation marks:

INDIRECT: Ted asked us if we had ever visited the Grand Canyon.
DIRECT: Ted asked us, "Have you ever visited the Grand Canyon?"

Indirect quotation

A quotation that is reworded in the speaker's or writer's own words instead of being quoted as first heard or read. Quotation marks are not used to enclose an indirect quotation:

INDIRECT: Mrs. Kim said our club could meet in the back of her store.
DIRECT: Mrs. Kim said, "Your club can meet in the back of my store."

individual

See **person.**

Inductive and deductive reasoning

Inductive reasoning is the process of reasoning from particular instances or individual cases to a generalization. For example, suppose that over a period of time you have met a dozen or more people who were born and raised in the small town of Crestley or in the immediate area around it. In talking with these people, you were struck by their pronunciation of the name *Crestley.* They did not pronounce it /krest′lē/ as you did, but /krez′lē/—with a /z/ and without a /t/. From these dozen or more "sample" cases, you arrive at a generalization about all natives of Crestley: [If these dozen or more people pronounce *Crestley* the same way, with a /z/ and without a /t/, then it is quite likely that] "All natives of Crestley and the immediate area around it pronounce *Crestley* /krez′lē/—with a /z/ and without a /t/."

Such a generalization states a probability, of course, not a certainty. To make it a certainty, you would have to hear every Crestley-area native pronounce the name. However, the chances are that your generalization is valid. Even though you have not heard every Crestley native pronounce the town's name, every one you did hear used the same pronunciation, and a dozen or more would be a fairly representative number of natives of a small area.

(See **Generalizations.**)

Deductive reasoning is the process of applying a generalization to a particular instance or individual case. For example, suppose that you read in your newspaper that Dr. Paul Jonas, a native of Crestley, will appear on a television panel show that night. This reminds you of the generalization you had reached about Crestley natives, who pronounce *Crestley* with a /z/ and without a /t/. Applying this generalization to Dr. Jonas, you conclude (deduce) that, since he is a native of Crestley, he will also pronounce *Crestley* /krez′lē/—with a /z/, not a /t/.

This deductive thinking process can be stated in a three-part form, called a **syllogism.** It consists of a *major premise* (the generalization you begin with), a *minor premise* (the particular case), and a *conclusion* (the deductive inference that logically follows from the two premises). For example:

MAJOR PREMISE: [*If it is true that*] all natives of Crestley pronounce *Crestley* /krez′lē/—with a /z/ and without a /t/,

MINOR PREMISE: [*And if it is also true that*] Dr. Paul Jonas is a native of Crestley,

CONCLUSION: [*Then it must be true that*] Dr. Paul Jonas will pronounce *Crestley* /krez′lē/—with a /z/ and without a /t/.

Notice the bracketed *if*-clauses before the two premises. They are there to remind us that if either of the premises of a syllogism is not true, the conclusion cannot be true, of course. In any syllogism in which the premises are true and in which the reasoning is valid (as it is here), the conclusion will be valid.

(See **Fallacies in reasoning.**)

infer, imply

See **imply, infer.**

Infinitive

The simple form of the verb, usually preceded by *to*: *to laugh, to win, to argue*, help her (*to*) *pack.* Infinitives, alone or in phrases, are used as nouns (subjects, objects, complements), as adverbs, or as adjectives:

SUBJECT: *To err* is human.
OBJECT: The Joneses are planning *to move.*
COMPLEMENT: Our first impulse was *to quit.*
ADVERB: Is Ramon ready *to start?*
ADJECTIVE: Robert Nordhaus will want a garage *to rent.*

After certain verbs (*dare, help, need*) the *to* is sometimes not used:

Not one of my friends dared [*to*] *speak up.*
Why don't we help them [*to*] *decide*?

Infinitive phrase

Since infinitives are verb forms, they can have objects, complements, and adverb modifiers. Together with the infinitive, these words form an *infinitive phrase* which, like the infinitive alone, can be used as a noun, an adjective, or an adverb. For example:

To go ahead now would be unwise. [The infinitive is used as a noun, as subject of the verb *would be*; *ahead* and *now* are adverb modifiers of the infinitive *To go.*]
Harry had always planned *to be a doctor.* [The phrase is used as a noun, as object of the verb *had planned*; *doctor* is the complement of the infinitive *to be.*]
No one had any time *to help us.* [The phrase is used as an adjective modifying the noun *time*; *us* is the object of the infinitive *to help.*]
The coach dashed over to the referee *to complain about the call.* [The phrase is used as an adverb modifying the verb *dashed*; *about the call* is an adverb phrase modifying the infinitive *to complain.*]

An infinitive phrase used as a subject may follow the verb:

It would be unwise *to go ahead now.*
Wouldn't it be unwise *to go ahead now*?

It is not the subject in these sentences; the infinitive phrase is. (See **Expletives.**)

Objective-case pronouns are used for subject complements of infinitives that have subjects:

A number of people took Phyllis to be *me.* [*Phyllis* is the subject of the infinitive; *me* is the subject complement.]

The subject complement of an infinitive that has no expressed subject may have either the nominative or the objective form. The nominative is generally used in formal English; the objective in informal English:

FORMAL: I certainly would not want to be *he*.
INFORMAL: I certainly wouldn't want to be *him*.

(See also **Split infinitive** and **Tenses of verbs,** section 4.)

Inflection

In grammar, inflection means a change in the form of a word to show case (*he–him*), number (*desk–desks*), gender (*fiancé–fiancée*), person (*I leave–he leaves*), tense (*saw–seen*), or comparison (*newer–newest*).

Informal English

The language that educated people ordinarily use in speech and writing in all but formal situations. For discussion and examples, see **Usage,** section 2.

inside of

In informal English *inside of* is used in expressions of time:

INFORMAL: The reply came inside of a day. [Or: in a day.]
FORMAL: The reply came within a day.

The *of* is not necessary in such sentences as:

Have you ever been inside [of] the Statue of Liberty?

insure, ensure

See **ensure, insure.**

Intensifier

An adverb used to increase or lessen the force of an adjective or another adverb. An intensifier always comes immediately before the word it modifies:

scarcely hidden anger
terribly frigid night
rather quiet
knocked *very* slowly
talked *incredibly* fast
tried *quite* often

Intensive pronouns

Personal pronouns plus the suffix *-self* or *-selves*, used after a noun or pronoun to add emphasis:

Napoleon himself wouldn't have known how to fight that battle.
I don't understand her reasoning myself.

(See **myself.**)

Interjection

An exclamatory word or phrase: *oh, help, wow, good grief.* An emphatic interjection is followed by an exclamation mark; a mild interjection is followed by a comma:

Help! I'm going to fall.
Oh! Watch out below. [Or: Oh! watch out below.]
Good grief, it's not that important.

Interrogative adjectives

Adjectives used in asking questions: *which*, *what*, and *whose*.

Interrogative pronouns

Pronouns used in asking questions: *who*, *whose*, *whom*, *which*, *what*, and sometimes *whoever*, *whatever*.

Interrogative sentences

Sentences that ask for information:

Who is baby-sitting tonight? Can you come before it gets dark?

When a sentence is phrased as a statement but is meant as a question, it is followed by a question mark:

Your diet is a great success?

A polite request phrased as a question for the sake of courtesy is generally followed by a period rather than a question mark:

Will all the delegates please fill out these forms.

Intransitive verbs

Verbs whose meanings are complete without a direct object:

Dr. Phelps *operated* early in the morning.
Cheri *could* not *answer* for several minutes.

Linking verbs are always intransitive, merely connecting a noun, pronoun, or adjective with the subject:

My big sister *is* a friend.
The school bus *will be* his to drive next year.
We *were* late again this morning.

(See **Transitive and intransitive verbs.**)

Inverted sentences

The usual order in sentences is subject–verb, subject–verb–object, or subject–verb–complement. Sentences in which this order is changed are called *inverted sentences*:

Up the lazy river cruised the yacht. [Verb before subject.]
The gym shoes he dyed red. [Object first.]

Irony

A form of expression implying something different, even opposite, from what is actually said:

We had a marvelous time on our vacation: we had three flat tires going up; it rained every day; our tent leaked; some bears stole all our food; and we're still suffering from poison ivy.

irregardless

See **regardless.**

it

Informal English often uses *it* to refer to the idea of a preceding statement; formal English rarely does so:

INFORMAL: The whole team spent the afternoon helping Coach Braun paint his house and garage. It was worthwhile, we thought.

FORMAL: The whole team spent the afternoon helping Coach Braun paint his house and garage, a job we considered worthwhile.

(See **Indefinite it** and **Impersonal it.**)

Italics

In type, letters that slant to the right. (*This sentence is in italic type.*) In longhand and typewritten manuscript, italics are shown by underlining. (For specific uses of italics, see **Underlining.**)

its

The possessive form does not have an apostrophe:

The pennant was hung in its place. The dog whined for its food.

To avoid misspelling, associate *its* with *his* and *hers*, neither of which has an apostrophe.

it's

The contraction of *it is* or *it has. It's* is always spelled with an apostrophe:

It's your turn to speak. It's been lonely without you.

It's me

Formal grammarians explain that the verb *be* should always be followed by the nominative case: *It is I.* But in actual practice *It's me* is so generally used by educated people that it is now acceptable standard usage (even though some users of formal English still prefer *It is I*).

Though *It's me* is fully acceptable, *It's him*, *It's her*, *It's us*, and *It's them* are not.

J J J J

Jargon

Most commonly used in one of two senses. An early definition of jargon is "confused, meaningless talk or writing; unintelligible gibberish." A meaning that entered the language later is "the language of a special group, profession, or class." Professional or technical jargon is used by members of various vocations: theater, education, medicine, communications, trades, sports. The use of technical jargon among members of the group is expected, but overuse of jargon in general writing and speaking should be avoided.

She spoke such jargon–from TV, advertising, business, and elsewhere–I couldn't understand a word she said.
The car manufacturer spoke of "styling stability," jargon indicating that not much had changed in the car's outside looks.
My friend from Italy asked me what the football jargon "to clothesline" meant.

join together

The *together* is unnecessary, since *join* means "bring, come, or put together":

The little streams joined [together] to form the river.
The service clubs will join [together] to endorse the program.

Journalese

A style of writing found in some newspapers and magazines. Its chief characteristics (generally considered faults) are the overuse of "big words," roundabout expressions, and trite phrases.

judgment, judgement

Judgment is the more common spelling in the United States and Canada.

just

In informal English *just* is often used to mean "very; quite": Nancy's parents were just furious. Guard against overusing *just* in this sense in your written work. (For the position of *just*, see **only.**)

K

kid

Informal when used in either of these two senses: (1) as a noun meaning "child" or "young person"; (2) as a verb meaning "tease playfully" or "deceive; fool."

kind, sort

In formal English the singular adjectives *this* and *that* are used to modify the singular *kind* and *sort*:

This kind of novel appeals to seventh and eighth graders.
That sort of painting was developed during the Renaissance.

Similarly, formal usage requires that the plural adjectives *these* and *those* be used only when *kind* and *sort* are plural:

Eating these kinds of foods must be good for you.
Those sorts of foods only add to your weight.

Colloquially, the plural adjectives are often used with *kind* and *sort*:

Those kind of towels don't fluff-dry well.
A few more of these sort of dinner meetings would be welcome.

In spite of the fact that this usage is common in the speech of educated people, it still has only colloquial standing.

In both speech and writing, avoid the nonstandard *them kind*:

NONSTANDARD: You can cook them kind of apples.
STANDARD: You can cook that kind of apples.

kind of, sort of

In informal speech *kind of* and *sort of* are often used as adverbs meaning "rather; somewhat; almost; nearly":

It was so late at night, I was kind of reluctant to call her.
We were sort of anxious to get home quickly.

In written English the appropriate forms would be:

It was so late at night, I was rather reluctant to call her.
We were somewhat anxious to get home quickly.

kind of a, sort of a

Formal English omits the *a*:

Would this kind of course be popular with the students?
That sort of dance should appeal to all age groups.

But in informal English, especially in speech, *kind of a* and *sort of a* are common:

Would this kind of a course be popular with the students?
That sort of a dance should appeal to all age groups.

L L L L L L

lady

See **man, woman.**

last, latest

Formal English makes a distinction between these two words–using *last* to refer to the final item in a series, and *latest* to refer to the most recent item in a series that may or may not continue:

Did you read the last novel Hemingway wrote?
There is a questionnaire in the latest issue of the student paper.
Did you like Sondheim's latest song?

In informal English *last* is commonly used in place of *latest*:

There is a questionnaire in the last issue of the student paper.

But this usage should be avoided wherever it might be ambiguous:

AMBIGUOUS: Did you like Sondheim's last song? [This could mean Mr. Sondheim will not write another song.]

latter, last

See **former, latter; first, last.**

lay, lie

Notice the distinctions between these verbs:

lay, laid, laid–"to place," transitive (takes an object)
lie, lay, lain–"to recline," intransitive (no object)

You *lie* down on a sofa. Fluffy *is lying* on the radiator. Their farm *lies* just south of the railroad tracks. You *lay* carpet, *lay* your books on a table, *lay* your ideas before a committee. Yesterday you *lay* down for a nap, but you *laid* your watch on the dresser. Your brother *has lain* in the hammock all afternoon. Mr. Wolfe *has laid* a new, asphalt driveway.

Nonstandard English tends to use only the verb *lay* (*laid, laid*)—making it do the work of both these verbs. And sometimes in casual informal speech we use *lay* instead of *lie* in such an expression as "Lay down, Rover!" But this usage is inappropriate in careful speech and writing.

Lead

/lēd/ The introductory section of a news story, which tells the reader such important facts as *who* is concerned, *what* happened, *when*, *where*, and perhaps *how* or *why*. The lead may vary in length from one sentence to several paragraphs.

lead, led

The present tense of this verb is spelled *lead* and is pronounced to rhyme with *need.* The past tense (and past participle) is spelled *led* and rhymes with *red*:

All the roads lead to the main interstate highway.
Who did you say led the march to Washington?
She has led the party poorly for too many years.

Leading question

A question worded in such a way that it suggests the desired or expected answer:

You will help me with my homework, won't you?
You enjoyed Joanne's party, didn't you? [Compare: Did you enjoy Joanne's party?]

Leading questions are not permitted in a law court.

learn, teach

Nonstandard English often uses *learn* in the sense of *teach.* Standard English (formal and informal) does not:

NONSTANDARD: Will you learn me how to dance?
STANDARD: Will you teach me how to dance?
STANDARD: I'd like to learn how to dance from you.

leave, let

A common nonstandard idiom is the use of the verb *leave* (*left, left*) where formal and informal English would use the verb *let* (*let, let*). Remember that when you mean "permit" or "allow to pass, go, or come," *let* is the verb to use:

Let him learn from his own mistakes. [Not: *Leave* him learn.]
He *let* us off on the second floor. [Not: He *left* us off.]
Bruce *is letting* her use his stereo for the party. [Not: *is leaving* her use.]
Let me go, you big bully! [Not: *Leave* me go.]
Please *let* us pay for your ticket. [Not: *leave* us pay.]

With *alone*, however, either word is standard usage: "Leave the baby alone" or "Let the baby alone."

less, fewer

Formal English usually makes a distinction between these two words, using *fewer* to refer to number (to things that are counted), and *less* to refer to amount or quantity (to things that are measured):

Fewer than thirty people signed up for yoga exercises.
There were fewer cars in the lot today than yesterday.
Her mother needs less sleep than anyone I know.
We would use less gas if we all drove economy cars.

In informal English *less* is commonly used in place of *fewer*:

Less than thirty people signed up for yoga exercises.
There were less cars in the lot today than yesterday.

less, lesser

Both are comparatives of *little*, but they are not used interchangeably. *Less* refers to amount or quantity; *lesser*–a formal word–refers to value or importance:

No one is less willing to forgo immediate pleasures than he.
He was always asking us to choose the lesser evil.
Helen was a lesser official during the Harmony Party's administration.

let's us, let's don't

Since *let's* is a contraction of *let us*, another *us* should not be added to it. "Let's us eat" is repetitive–the same as saying "Let us us eat." Say "Let's eat," "Let's go home now."

In the negative, either *let's not* or *let's don't* is frequently used: "Let's not get upset." "Let's don't take the bus." Though *do* in the second example is not necessary to the meaning, the expression *let's don't* is a common and well-established idiom. (The expression *don't let's*–"Don't let's invite them"–is also occasionally used; here again, *do* is unnecessary for the meaning.)

Letters

For a discussion of the form of business letters, see **Business letters.**

Letters of the alphabet

The plurals of letters of the alphabet are formed by adding either *s* or *'s*, with *'s* being preferred after all small letters and those capital letters that would be confusing if *s* alone were added:

The baby knows her ABCs.
Do you spell that with one *r* or two *r*'s?
Trish has always gotten A's in math.

Notice that a letter used only as a letter (see the second sentence) is italicized–underlined in handwriting and typing.

Levels of usage

See **Usage.**

Library

See **Card catalog; Dewey Decimal System; Encyclopedias; Readers' Guide; Reference books.**

lie

See **lay, lie.**

lighted, lit

Both of these forms are used as the past tense and past participle of *light*:

Rex lit the candles.	The street lamps were lighted at dusk.
Ann had lit the bonfire.	Who has lighted the stage?

When the past participle is used as an adjective preceding a noun, *lighted* is more common: I expected lighted hallways.

like, as

1. In formal speech and writing *as*, *as if*, and *as though* are used as conjunctions—to introduce clauses:

His cousin was artistic and sensitive, just as he remembered.
Andrea ran as if her life were at stake.
It was as though no one had heard of human rights.

Informal English commonly uses *like* as a conjunction in such sentences:

His cousin was artistic and sensitive, just like he remembered.
Andrea ran like her life was at stake.
It was like no one had heard of human rights.

2. In both formal and informal English *like*—not *as*—is used as a preposition in phrases of comparison:

He walks like a penguin.	The dorm smells like a zoo.
The movie was not like the book.	Stu looks like his mother.

like for

In speech, especially in the southern United States, *like for* is common:

SPOKEN: I'd like for everyone to come to the party next Saturday.

In writing, the *for* is generally omitted:

WRITTEN: I would like everyone to come to the party next Saturday.

(See also **want.**)

line

Expressions with *line* are often clumsy and roundabout, and should be replaced by simpler, more direct wording:

ROUNDABOUT: On the matter of disciplining children, my parents' ideas seem to run along the same lines.

BETTER: On the matter of disciplining children, my parents' ideas seem similar.

Linguistics

The study of language, which includes such branches as phonology (dealing with sounds: phonetics and phonemics), morphology (the forms of words), syntax (the relationships of words and word groups in sentences), lexicography (the making of dictionaries), dialectology (regional and class dialects), semantics (the meaning of words and the relationship between language and thinking), usage (the use of variant word forms), rhetoric (the effective use of words), language history (the origins of words and relationships among languages).

Linking verb

A verb used chiefly to connect a subject with an adjective, pronoun, or noun that describes or means the same as the subject:

Congressman Sinclair's proposal *was* quite drastic. [Connects subject *proposal* with adjective *drastic.*]
The contact lens found on the gym floor *might have been* hers. [Connects subject *lens* with pronoun *hers.*]
Marisa *is* my best friend. [Connects subject *Marisa* with noun *friend.*]

Be is the most common linking verb. Other verbs frequently used as linking verbs are *act, appear, become, feel, go, grow, look, run, seem, smell, taste, turn.* Remember that when they are used as linking verbs (rather than as action verbs), they are followed by adjectives, not adverbs:

Willie felt *odd* about going to the quilting bee. [Not: *oddly*; it modifies *Willie*, not the verb *felt.*]
The leftover cheese dip looked *peculiar*. [Not: *peculiarly*; it modifies *dip*, not the verb *looked.*]

Litotes

/lī′tə tēz′/ or /lit′ə tēz′/ A type of understatement in which the writer or speaker says in negative form the opposite of what he or she really means:

A million dollars is no small piece of change. [Meaning: A million dollars is a lot of money.]
Lamar's pledge of support takes no little courage. [Meaning: Lamar's pledge of support takes great courage.]

loan

For many years considered to be only a noun (Becky applied for a government loan), *loan* is now generally used as a verb as well. In formal writing, however, many people still prefer the verb *lend*:

GENERAL: Anastasia's aunt loaned her money for college.
FORMAL: Anastasia's aunt lent her money for college.

Localism

A word or expression used in one section of a country, but not in others. Localisms are also called *provincialisms* or *dialectal expressions.*

(See **Dialect.**)

locate

Often used to mean "settle":

My brother and his wife want to locate in British Columbia.

However, this usage is generally avoided by careful writers.

Long variants

Needlessly long forms of words. Amateur writers sometimes add an extra prefix or suffix to a word that already carries the meaning they intend. They write *algebraic problems*, although *algebra problems* would be clear and acceptable. They write *adjudicate*, although *adjudge* expresses the meaning just as completely. Some other unnecessary long variants are:

beauteousness for *beauty*
potentiality for *potential*
paternalistic for *paternal*
blithesome for *blithe*
contemporaneous for *contemporary*
naturalistic when only *natural* is meant
habitude for *habit*
enkindle for *kindle*
intermingle when only *mingle* is meant
disputation when only *dispute* is meant
orientate for *orient*
hotness for *heat*

Loose sentence

A sentence in which the grammatical form and the essential meaning are complete before the end:

Phil left at eleven o'clock, muttering under his breath about long-winded speakers and vowing he'd never again attend a debate club meeting at night without his toothbrush and pillow.

This sentence could be stopped after "o'clock," "breath," "speakers," "meeting," "night," or "toothbrush" without destroying the sense of the main statement.

Loose sentences are typical of conversation. Used too consistently in writing, without an occasional *periodic sentence* for variety, they are likely to produce a roundabout and unemphatic style. (See **Periodic sentence.**)

lose, loose

These two words are frequently confused. Try to associate the spelling of each word with its pronunciation and meaning:

lose /lüz/—lose an umbrella, lose your place
loose /lüs/—a loose noose, loose clothing, pry loose

lot of, lots of

Informal expressions meaning "a great number or amount":

INFORMAL: A lot of people bought lots of those designer jeans.
FORMAL: Many people bought a great number of those designer jeans.

Main clause

See **Clause,** section 1.

Malapropism

A ridiculous misuse of words, caused by confusing two words that are similar in sound but different in meaning:

In a right triangle the side opposite the right angle is called the hippopotamus. [hypotenuse]
The cessation of the southern states was an immediate cause of the Civil War. [secession]
He died of a corollary thrombosis. [coronary]

Malapropisms are named after Mrs. Malaprop, a character in Sheridan's comedy *The Rivals* (1775), whose amusing misuse of words has made her one of the best-known comic characters in literature.

Malapropisms are sometimes used intentionally, particularly by certain TV personalities–for humorous effect. But they sound ridiculous when used unintentionally by someone who is ignorant or confused about word meanings. Guard against them in your speech and writing by checking unfamiliar words in a dictionary to make sure of their meanings. And listen carefully to expressions you pick up from others, to make sure of the words. *Eclectic* may sound like *epileptic*, but the expression is "an epileptic seizure"–not "an eclectic seizure."

man, woman

Now generally preferred to the more pretentious *gentleman* and *lady*, unless a note of special courtesy or respect is wanted. Originally, *gentleman* and *lady* were used in connection with the upper classes. But the original distinctions between *man* and *gentleman*, *woman* and *lady* seem to have practically disappeared in general U.S. usage. At times, in fact, it seems that the distinctions have been reversed; statements like "The women of the Opera Guild advertised for a lady to mend the costumes for *Rigoletto*" and "Are you the gentleman who delivers groceries to the man in the penthouse apartment?" are quite common.

Ladies and gentlemen is the customary formal expression in addressing an audience of both sexes.

Mass nouns

See **amount, number.**

may, can

See **can, may.**

may be, maybe

May be is a verb form; *maybe* (a shortening of *it may be*) is an adverb meaning "possibly; perhaps":

VERB: Fernonda's gown may be ready for the summer fete after all.
ADVERB: Maybe you should see a dentist about that sore tooth.

may of

In speech the words *may have* are often spoken so rapidly that they sound like *may of.* In writing, they should be spelled correctly: *may have* or *may've*—never *may of.*

The same is true of all other verb phrases with *have.* Write *should have* or *should've* (not *should of*), *would have* or *would've,* etc.

me

See **It's me** and **between you and me.**

Mechanics of writing

The technical part of writing, including such things as spelling, punctuation, forms of words, order of words, and sentence structure (as distinguished from the style, content, and organization).

medium

The singular is *medium*; the plural is *mediums* or *media.* The plural *media* is generally used in scientific writing and in referring to the *mass media* (the various forms of mass communication taken together).

You will occasionally see and hear the form *medias* used as the plural. But careful writers and speakers avoid this usage:

Film is one of the various *media* he wants to study. [Not: *medias.*]

They also avoid the use of *media* as a singular:

Are today's *media* responsive to public needs? [Not: *Is.*]
She got her start in the *medium* of radio journalism. [Not: *media.*]

Messrs.

The abbreviation of the French *messieurs* (meaning "gentlemen") is generally pronounced /mes'ərz/. In French it is /mā syœ'/. It is now chiefly used as the plural of Mr.:

Messrs. Chan and Willoughby are closing their Third Street office in March.

Metaphor

A figure of speech in which a comparison is implied rather than directly stated. In a metaphor the comparison is not introduced by *like* or *as*:

"Maybe life is a piece of cake," Earl said grudgingly, "but why did I have to get the crumbs." [There are two metaphors in this sentence: the first compares life in general to a piece of cake; the second compares Earl's own situation to cake crumbs or life's leftovers.]

Metonymy

/mə ton′ə mē/ A figure of speech in which the name of something closely associated with a thing is substituted for its name:

There has been no word from *10 Downing Street* about last night's explosion. [That is, the British Prime Minister has made no statement.]
At an early age, she felt drawn to the *stage.* [That is, to a career in the theater.]

(Compare **Synecdoche.**)

Misplaced modifiers

Sometimes a modifier is put in such a position in a sentence that the reader misunderstands what the writer is trying to say. For example, in "Jess decided to apologize for insulting Phil yesterday morning," *yesterday morning* seems to modify *insulting*—that is, that he had insulted Phil yesterday morning. But the meaning the writer intended was that Jess had decided to apologize yesterday morning, not that he had insulted Phil then. To make this meaning clear, the writer should move the modifying phrase away from the wrong word and closer to the word it does modify: "Yesterday morning, Jess decided to apologize for insulting Phil."

Sometimes a modifier seems to modify a word it could not sensibly modify:

Swimming round and round in the glass bowl, Roberto watched the goldfish.

To most readers this sentence would sound a bit ridiculous; they would be amused at the thought of Roberto swimming round and round in a glass bowl. Though the writer's intended meaning is obvious even with the misplaced modifier, the sentence could easily be improved by moving the phrase closer to the word that it is clearly intended to modify:

Roberto watched the goldfish swimming round and round in the glass bowl.

miss, misses

The title *Miss* (with a capital *M*) is always used with a name: *Miss Harrington, Miss Juanita Avila.* The noun *miss* (spelled with a small *m*) is used without a name as a term of address: "May I help you, miss?"

Misses is the plural title: *the Misses Lunt and Parker.* When the misses are from the same family, formal English refers to them as *the Misses Willis*; informal English often uses *the Miss Willises.* (See also **Ms.**)

Mixed figure of speech

Combining two figures of speech that are inconsistent or incongruous produces a "mixed figure." Such a figure ruins the effect of what otherwise might be an excellent bit of writing:

The flame that flickered in her eyes turned to stone as she listened to the news. [Fire does not turn to stone.]

Modals

The auxiliary verbs *can, could, may, might, shall, should, will, would, must* (used with a main verb to express certain shades of meaning) are sometimes called *modals.* (See **Auxiliary verb.**)

Modifiers

Words or groups of words that restrict, limit, or make more exact the meaning of other words. In the following examples the italicized words modify the words in small capitals:

a loud, raucous LAUGH — *a tomato* RED
the WOMAN *behind the counter* — *overly* SWEET
MONEY *to burn* — *freezing* COLD
Fiona *often* COMPETES *in Highland fling contests.*
Angered by Mr. Fane's bigoted comments, my dear FATHER yelled.
We welcome ANYONE *who can carry a tune and read music.*
THINK *twice before you sign that agreement in the small print.*

The modifiers of nouns and pronouns are usually adjectives, participles, adjective phrases, and adjective clauses. The modifiers of verbs, adjectives, and adverbs are adverbs, adverb phrases, and adverb clauses. (For discussions of the different modifiers, see the various items under their specific labels.)

Money

1. In ordinary writing (especially in a formal style), sums of money that can be expressed in two words are usually spelled out; others are put in figures:

Last month the price of bread rose eight cents a pound loaf.
The movie cost Billie four dollars, plus fifty cents for popcorn.
The gray suit in the window display was on sale for $99.99.
The Georges bought their house for $78,500.

If two or more sums are used in a sentence and only one can be expressed in two words, all are written in figures:

Celeste managed to save $53.65, but she still needed $100 to buy the turntable.

In technical, statistical, or business writing, exact sums are written in figures (even if they could be expressed in one or two words):

89 cents 89¢ $.89
Today only, all shoes are marked down to $15 a pair.
A haircut is $10.25; a wash and a set is $12.50; a permanent is $35.75.

Round sums (approximate sums in even units of hundreds or thousands) are usually spelled out:

At auction, this painting is expected to sell for around five hundred thousand dollars.
That hand-tooled saddle must have cost at least two thousand dollars.
Receipts from the church bazaar were over nine hundred dollars.

2. When the sum is used as an adjective modifier, it is generally spelled out (with a hyphen):

The *Daily Express* reported an eighty-thousand-dollar loss for April.
Voters are expected to reject the million-dollar school bond issue.
The ten-cent candy bar has gone the way of the dodo.

(See **Numbers.**)

Months

Except in reference books (where saving space is important) and in the headings of informal letters (where abbreviations may be used), the preferred usage is to write out in full the names of months:

Both Thomas Jefferson and John Adams died on July 4, 1826.
Between November 25 and January 18 you can reach me in care of the Ritz in Boston.
Her first book was published in June, 1978. [Or: in June 1978.]

(See **Dates.**)

Mood

The form of a verb that indicates the way in which the speaker or writer regards the sentence. A verb in the *indicative* mood shows that the sentence is regarded as a statement of fact: "Sonya *is planning* the surprise party for Marge." A verb in the *imperative* mood shows that the statement is regarded as a command: "*Close* that door." A verb in the *subjunctive* mood shows that the statement (or clause) is regarded as doubtful, improbable, or contrary to fact: "If I *were elected* President, I'd make you Secretary of State." (See also **Indicative mood, Imperative mood, Commands and requests, Subjunctive.**)

moral, morale

As an adjective *moral* means "good; virtuous; right." Used as a singular noun, *moral* means "a lesson of conduct." The plural noun *morals* refers to "principles in regard to conduct":

Your decision to return the money was a moral one.
I did not understand the moral of the story until you explained it.
His former employer recommended him as a person of high morals.

The noun *morale* refers to "a moral or mental condition or attitude":

The morale of the soldiers was high.

most, almost

In colloquial English *most* is commonly used as a clipped form of *almost*:

Most all of the seniors are attending the graduation exercises.
This year most every ornament on the Bocks' tree is handmade.
Our produce man most always has strawberries for his special customers.

Though common in speech, this usage is inappropriate in writing, except in reporting conversation. Otherwise, use *almost*: *almost all, almost every, almost always, almost anyone.*

mostly

An adverb meaning "for the most part; mainly; chiefly":

The cruise ship's passengers, mostly retired people, were delighted with the cuisine, the company, and the captain.

It is not appropriate as a substitute for *most* meaning "in or to the highest degree":

The people *most* upset about the airline's strike are those with plans to visit the islands during the holidays. [Not: The people *mostly* upset.]

Mr., mister

The title *Mr.* (generally abbreviated) is always used with a man's name or the name of his office: *Mr. Miller, Mr. Robert E. Evans, Mr. Secretary, Mr. Moderator.* The noun *mister*, meaning "sir," is a colloquial form of address. It is written out in full and not capitalized: "You left your headlights on, mister." In formal English *sir* would be used instead. (See **Messrs.**)

Mrs., missis

The title *Mrs.* is always used with a name: *Mrs. Milton, Mrs. Phillip Norton, Mrs. Angela Neuman.* The noun *missis* (or *missus*), meaning "wife" or "woman in charge of a household," is not appropriate in writing except to represent dialectal usage: "My missis sings in the church choir." "You'll have to ask the missis."

The title *Mrs.* should not be combined with another title. Good usage calls for *Mrs. Lynch, Dr. Lynch*, or *Professor and Mrs. Lynch.* Do not use *Mrs. Professor Lynch* or *Mrs. Dr. Lynch.*

MS.

MS. (also written *Ms.* and *ms.*) is the conventional abbreviation for manuscript–an author's copy of his or her work in handwriting or typewriting. (The plural forms are *MSS., Mss.*, and *mss.*)

Ms.

Ms. (generally pronounced /miz/) appears frequently before women's names in addresses. Like *Mr.*, which is used before the names of married and unmarried men, *Ms.* is used before the names of both married and unmarried women. Not surprisingly, the use of *Ms.* has been promoted by the movement for increased women's rights and adopted by business firms who find it useful when they do not know the marital status of a woman they are addressing.

must

Ordinarily used as an auxiliary verb (I must call Jane today), *must* is also used as a noun meaning "something necessary or vital" and as an adjective meaning "demanding attention or doing; necessary":

NOUN: The salesclerk persuaded Ron that the heavy-duty vacuum cleaner was a must for his workshop.
ADJECTIVE: For zookeepers, kindness and agility are almost must skills.

mutual, common

Many careful speakers and writers distinguish between these two words, using *mutual* to mean "each to the other; done, said, or felt by each toward the other" and *common* to mean "shared equally by each or all of a group":

Even before their famous duel, there was mutual antipathy between Alexander Hamilton and Aaron Burr. [Each disliked the other.]
The brothers have a common fondness for broccoli. [Each likes broccoli; it is a like they share in common.]

But in general usage *mutual* is used not only to mean "each to the other" but also "shared in common":

The brothers have a mutual fondness for broccoli.
My cousin and his fiancée were introduced by mutual friends.

myself

1. As a reflexive pronoun, *myself* is used as the object of the verb or of a preposition in a sentence whose subject is *I*:

I blamed myself. [Direct object.]
I made myself a mug of hot chocolate. [Indirect object.]
There I go again, talking to myself! [Object of preposition.]

2. As an intensive pronoun, *myself* is used for emphasis:

I myself would not stand for that kind of treatment.
I guess I'll have to do both the shopping and the cleaning myself.

Note: The preceding usage facts apply as well to other reflexive pronouns—*yourself*, *himself*, *herself*, etc.

3. In nonstandard and some colloquial English *myself* is used instead of *I* as the second part of a compound subject, but not in good written style:

NONSTANDARD AND COLLOQUIAL: Joanie and *myself* offered to take the hot meals to the shut-ins on Saturday.
WRITTEN: Joanie and *I* offered to take the hot meals to the shut-ins on Saturday.

In informal English *myself* is sometimes used instead of *me* as the second part of a compound object:

The director questioned Vladimir and *myself* about our acting experience.
Mrs. Wellingford told Gwennie and *myself* to begin arranging the flowers.
The movie theater was almost deserted except for Charlie and *myself*.

Though this usage is common in both speech and writing, many people avoid it and would use *me* instead:

The director questioned Vladimir and *me* about our acting experience.
Mrs. Wellingford told Gwennie and *me* to begin arranging the flowers.
The movie theater was almost deserted except for Charlie and *me*.

namely and other introductory words

1. Introductory expressions like *namely, viz., i.e., e.g.* are found chiefly in reference books and in rather formal expository writing. They are out of place in other kinds of writing, where less formal expressions–*for example, for instance, that is,* and *such as*–would be more appropriate. Often in informal writing it is most effective to omit a specific introductory word and simply give the examples, setting them off with a colon or a dash:

Nina raises many of the flowers she uses in making sachets: [such as] roses, lavender, babies' breath, and heather.
There is only one thing I really want for Christmas–[namely,] a black Scottish terrier puppy.

2. The punctuation used with these introductory words varies, depending on the kind of construction the words introduce. When the introductory word is followed by a clause, a semicolon or a colon is used:

Mr. Koberna said that we didn't have to write about the causes of the Revolutionary War; that is, we could fail history instead.
The farm club finally has reached a decision: namely, that the prize money from the fair will be used to buy and board a horse for members' use.

When the introductory word is not followed by a clause, either a dash or a comma is used:

Liz and I still have a great deal to do before we leave for music camp at Interlochen–for example, [to] buy trunks, [to] send address changes to our friends, and [to] pack clothes for three months in northern Michigan.
Uncle Tim recently purchased a herd of beefalo, that is, a herd bred from cattle and buffalo.

The introductory expression *such as* is not followed by a comma:

Many of the faculty members, such as [ ] Mr. Nassif, Mrs. Whalen, and Miss Scholl, have agreed to accept the seniors' challenge to a game of tag football.

Names

Given names are usually spelled out in full, although initials may be used. The second and other given names are not usually written out unless specifically needed (as in legal documents, wills, diplomas) to make identification more certain. Abbreviations such as *Geo.*, *Wm.*, and *Robt.* are no longer considered appropriate:

John D. Blair	J. D. Blair
William P. LaFrenz	W. P. LaFrenz
O. Robert Benjamin	O. R. Benjamin

Names of well-known people should generally be given in the form that is best known: Martin Luther King, Jr. (*not* M. L. King), J. William Fulbright (*not* James W. Fulbright), H. L. Mencken (*not* Henry Louis Mencken), Jimmy Carter (*not* James Carter).

(See also **Cities.**)

Narrative writing

A form of writing that relates an event or a story.

nature

Often deadwood that could be omitted with no loss in meaning:

As a young man Ebenezer Scrooge was not [of a] miserly [nature].
A big bully [by nature] as a child, Derek remained one as he grew up.

nauseated, nauseous

Nauseated is an adjective meaning "feeling sick":

Jerry felt nauseated at the sight of the carcasses hanging in the slaughterhouse.

Nauseous is an adjective meaning "causing to feel sick":

The nauseous odor emanating from the pipes forced the Elroys from their house.

necessary

Verbs like *must* and *have to* are often more direct and emphatic (though sometimes less courteous) than a construction with *necessary*:

INDIRECT: It is necessary for schoolchildren to be immunized against various diseases before enrolling.
DIRECT: Schoolchildren must be immunized against various diseases before enrolling.

necessity

The idiom is *necessity of doing* (or *for doing*) something—not *necessity to do* something:

Until heating costs rose, Mr. Simon couldn't see the necessity *of* (or *for*) insulating his house.

Need is more concise than *necessity*:

Until heating costs rose, Mr. Simon couldn't see the need of insulating his house.

need, needs

Although these are both third person singular forms of the verb *need*, they are used in different ways. *Needs* is the form in affirmative statements:

Rebecca needs to have her wisdom teeth extracted.

Need not and *does not need* are used in negative statements:

FORMAL: Rebecca need not have her wisdom teeth extracted.
INFORMAL: Rebecca does not need to have her wisdom teeth extracted.

In questions *need* or *does . . . need* is used:

FORMAL: Need he ridicule her learning to rebuild an engine?
INFORMAL: Does he need to ridicule her learning to rebuild an engine?

negotiate

Generally used to mean "arrange terms for":

Our diplomat has agreed to negotiate for the prisoners' release.

Negotiate is also used to mean "get past or over":

His arms full of groceries, Wilson couldn't negotiate the front door.

Although this usage is generally acceptable, many careful users of English would avoid it.

neither

See **either, neither** and **Correlative conjunctions.**

never

Never means "not ever; at no time." It should not be used when you simply mean *not*:

Poor Mother didn't even have time to read the financial page. [Not: Mother never even had time.]

(See also **Double negative.**)

Newspaper English

Good newspaper English is simply informal English applied to the recording and interpreting of events. It places a premium on accuracy and directness in telling a story and is written to be read easily and quickly. The essential information–who, what, when, where, why–is therefore usually given first, with details coming later. (See **Lead.**)

"Big words" and trite expressions are the two common faults of a careless style of newswriting called *journalese*:

A wave of excitement rippled through the crowd as the accused conflagrationist descended upon the courtroom.

A clearer way of putting it might be:

The spectators stirred as the accused arsonist entered the courtroom.

nice

In formal English *nice* means "exact; discriminating":

His nice sense of the language makes him a demanding editor.

Nice is also used as a counter word showing approval, with such a wide range of possible meanings that it is of little use in writing. In your written work substitute a more exact modifier wherever you can. (See **Adjective,** section 3.)

no-account

Colloquially used as a compound adjective: her *no-account* brother-in-law. In formal English, *worthless* or *shiftless* would be used: her *worthless* brother-in-law.

nohow

Used as an adverb in nonstandard English:

NONSTANDARD: With that bad cold, Joel can't sing nohow.
STANDARD: With that bad cold, Joel can't sing at all.

Nominative absolute

See **Absolute phrases.**

Nominative case

A noun or pronoun that is used as the subject or subject complement of a verb is said to be in the nominative case:

Leon and *I* said we'd help with the telephoning.
Mr. Randolph, who claims descent from a Virginia family, is *president* of the Sierra Historical Society.

I, you, he, she, it, we, you, they are the nominative forms of the personal pronouns; *who, which,* and *that,* of the relative pronouns. (See also **Case,** section 1.)

Nonce word

A word that is made up for a particular occasion and is not used again. If you called the problem affecting a clogged kitchen drain a *glurp, glurp* would be a nonce word.

none, no one

None may be either singular or plural, depending on the meaning intended:

None of this paper *is* acceptable. [No part of it is.]
We thought that none of the flower arrangements we saw *was* as original as Claire's. [Not a single one was.]
The professor complained that none of the freshmen *were* as proficient in English as they should be. [Not any of them were.]

When *none* tells how many (as in the third example), a plural verb is generally used, unless the idea of "not a single one" is to be emphasized (as in the second example).

No one is singular. It is sometimes used instead of *none*, for emphasis:

No one of the clerks deserves a promotion.

Nonrestrictive modifiers

Modifiers that are used not to identify the word they modify but merely to add a descriptive detail. Nonrestrictive modifiers are set off from the word they modify:

The brothers, *scolded into submission*, were sullenly silent.
Clarence, *who can't swim*, wants to be a physical education teacher.
Her arm, *which had been broken in three places*, mended slowly.

(For discussion, see **Restrictive and nonrestrictive.**)

Nonstandard English

The kind of English used by people who do not have much formal education or have not been much affected by the schooling they did have. For examples and an explanation of why this kind of English is not appropriate for general use, see **Usage,** section 3.

no place

Colloquially used for *nowhere*:

COLLOQUIAL: I got no place trying to explain my predicament in French to the *gendarme*.
WRITTEN: I got nowhere trying to explain my predicament in French to the *gendarme*.

not hardly, not scarcely

See **Double negative.**

not only . . . but also

See **Correlative conjunctions.**

Note taking

The most practical way to take notes for a research paper is on note cards, either 3″ x 5″ or 4″ x 6″. Take notes in ink, using one side of the card. Put on each card only one point—one fact or quotation or idea, or a few closely related facts that will probably be used in one part of the paper.

Fill out most note cards in your own words, taking advantage of the techniques of the *paraphrase* and the *précis* as forms of restating the material. A paraphrase is a restatement–in your own words–of an author's ideas. A précis summarizes the author's ideas and produces a condensed version of the original material that omits most examples and illustrations.

Quote directly only when the author's style seems as important as the meaning. When quoting, copy exactly each word and punctuation mark, enclosing the words in quotation marks.

At the top of each card use a *guideline* that indicates briefly what the note is about. At the end of your research, the guidelines will aid in the sorting of the notes and the outlining of the paper. (See **Paraphrase** and **Précis.**)

notorious, famous

Notorious means "widely known, but in an unfavorable way" (a notorious assassin); *famous* means "widely known for accomplishment or excellence" (a famous playwright).

Noun

A word used as the name of a person, place, thing, quality, action, or idea:

COMMON NOUNS: artist, hillside, rope, height, resignation, justice
PROPER NOUNS: Marie Curie, Gaspé Peninsula, Lake Chautauqua, Empire State Building

Noun clause

A group of words with a subject and verb used in a sentence in the same way a noun is used:

SUBJECT: *What I want and what I'll get* are two different things.
SUBJECT COMPLEMENT: The scene I like best is *when the old woman dies and her beautiful young spirit joins that of her lover in the blossoming apple orchard.*
DIRECT OBJECT: Caroline said *that she had lost fifteen pounds.*
INDIRECT OBJECT: Give *whoever opens the door* the prize.
OBJECT OF PREPOSITION: She will be delighted with *whatever you decide to give her.*
APPOSITIVE: Siggy's suggestion, *that we sponsor a Harvest Ball*, was voted down.

Noun markers

The words *a, an,* and *the* are sometimes called "noun markers" or "noun determiners" because they signal that a noun is coming:

A *group* of students followed **an** elderly *guide* through **the** lavishly decorated *rooms* of **the** *palace.*

Other words–for example, *my, your, his, her, our, their, this, that, some, few*–can also serve as noun markers: **her** *philodendron*, **that** ridiculous *article*, **few** completely correct *answers.*

no use

An informal idiom for *of no use*:

INFORMAL: Since I dislike travel, this map series is no use to me.
FORMAL: Since I dislike travel, this map series is of no use to me.

nowheres

A nonstandard form of *nowhere.*

Number

The form of a noun, pronoun, or verb that shows it to be singular or plural in meaning. (See **Plurals of nouns.**)

number

A number, meaning "several" or "many," takes a plural verb; *the number* takes a singular verb:

A number of precious gems *were missing* from the leather pouch.
The number of people moving to the country *is* increasing.

(See also **amount, number.**)

Numbers

1. In ordinary writing, numbers that can be expressed in one or two words are generally spelled out; other numbers are usually written in figures:

The mixed chorus has only eight boys and ten girls.
The ten miles home were longer than they had ever seemed before.
I'll expect you to read 175 pages a week.
We're about 325 miles west of Kansas City.

The form in which numbers are written should be consistent. If one of two or more numbers in a sentence cannot be expressed in two words or less, figures should be used for all:

The floats in this year's Rose Parade featured 134 types of roses, 58 varieties of green leaves, and 10 kinds of seeds and seed pods.

2. In statistical, technical, or business writing, figures are generally used, since expressing dimensions, weights, totals, distances, sums, and measures in figures makes it easier to work with the numbers:

8 ounces	5 teaspoons	98.6 degrees	18 acres	52 pecks
74 long tons	36 yards	2 by 4 feet	10 barrels	548 mph
18 carats	68 percent	125 meters	8 gallons	29 knots

3. A number at the beginning of a sentence should always be written out:

Ninety-four people waited in line to ride in the biplane.
Fifty percent of them were children.

If writing out the number is awkward, rephrase the sentence to change the position of the number:

AWKWARD: Eight hundred ninety-two thousand, five hundred and twenty people were questioned by the census takers.
IMPROVED: The census takers questioned 892,520 people.

4. The plural of figures is made by adding either an apostrophe and *s* or an *s* alone:

The dancers broke their line and formed squares of *8*'s. [But: of eights.]
Are these funny arrows really *7*s?

O, oh

O is ordinarily used with a noun in direct address. It is always capitalized; but since it is so closely related to the words used with it, it is not followed by a mark of punctuation:

What is your decision, O wise one?

Oh is an independent exclamation that may be followed by either a comma or an exclamation mark, depending on the stress wanted. It is capitalized at the beginning of a sentence, but not when used within the sentence:

Oh, by the way, Roland borrowed your sweater.
Oh! Hot fudge all over my white blouse!
We saw *The Music Man* last week, and, oh, how we enjoyed it.

Object

See **Direct object, Indirect object, Object of preposition.**

Object complement

The direct object of certain verbs–*consider*, *christen*, *elect*, *paint*, and *name*, for example–is often followed by an adjective or another noun. This word, the *object complement* of the sentence, explains or describes the direct object:

The duchess christened the ship *Gracious Reward.* [Tells what the duchess christened the ship.]
The critics didn't like it, but the audiences considered the show *fantastic.* [Tells what the audiences considered the show to be.]

Objective and subjective writing

A writer whose purpose is mainly to present facts about a topic and who does not let emotion or personal prejudice influence his or her statements is said to have an *objective* point of view and to be writing *objectively.* Good scientific and technical writing–most serious exposition, in fact–is objective.

A writer who wishes to present a topic from a personal point of view, emphasizing personal feelings and opinions along with plain facts, is said to have a *subjective* point of view and to be writing *subjectively*. Lyric poetry, informal essays, and autobiographies are almost always subjective.

Objective case

A noun (or its equivalent) that is used as the direct or indirect object of a verb, as the object of a preposition, or as an object complement is said to be in the objective case:

DIRECT OBJECT: She forgot my *birthday*.
INDIRECT OBJECT: Ms. Ferlinghetti gave *Dick Zerfas* a low grade.
OBJECT OF PREPOSITION: inside the *cave*
between *Boston* and *Washington, D.C.*
OBJECT COMPLEMENT: They called him a *traitor*.

Nouns do not have a special form for the objective case; the same form is used for both the nominative and the objective case. The personal pronouns (*I*, *he*, *she*, *we*, *they*) and the relative and interrogative pronoun *who* have separate forms for the objective case: *me*, *him*, *her*, *us*, *them*, and *whom*.

Object of preposition

A noun or pronoun (or a phrase or clause used as a noun) whose relationship to some other word in the sentence is shown by the preposition:

Sonja is in her *room*. [Noun–object of preposition.]
He became powerful by *directing events behind the scenes*. [Gerund phrase–object of *by*.]
Pay no attention to *what you hear*. [Noun clause–object of *to*.]

Obsolete

Dictionaries use the label *Obsolete* (often abbreviated *Obs.*) for a word or a particular meaning of a word that is no longer used in ordinary speech or writing, but exists in earlier writings: *wanhope* meaning "despair," *wlatsom* meaning "disgusting," *smoterlich* meaning "disreputable," *to transport* in the sense of "to kill."

o'clock

Usually added only to the actual hour: *nine o'clock*, but *ten to seven*, *two fifteen*, *a quarter to twelve*, *half-past one*. *O'clock* is generally not used with the abbreviations A.M. and P.M. or with figures.

of

1. *Of* is often used to show possession: the writings *of* Aristotle (*Aristotle's* writings). (See **Possessive case.**)

2. In colloquial English *of* is often used in the unnecessary doubling of prepositions: *inside of*, *outside of*, *off of*. *Inside of* and *outside of* are also used in informal writing, but not *off of*:

We got off [of] the bus at the wrong stop.

(See also **inside of,** for its use as applied to time.)

3. The contraction *'ve* (for *have*) is sometimes carelessly written *of*:

Greta and Ron *should've* called by now. [Not: *should of.*]
I *must've* left those records in the car. [Not: *must of.*]

off of

Nonstandard for *from* in a sentence like this:

NONSTANDARD: Shaun borrowed twenty dollars *off of* me this evening.
STANDARD: Shaun borrowed twenty dollars *from* me this evening.

oh

See **O, oh.**

OK, O.K.

Business and informal English for "correct; all right" and "approval":

The permissions department says it is OK to use these quotations.
Just give this your OK when you have a minute, please.

The verb forms are *OK*, *OK'd*, *OK'ing* (or *O.K.'d*, etc.):

Don't all personal checks have to be OK'd by the floor manager?

OK is sometimes spelled *okay. Oke* and *okeydoke* are slang.

Omission in a quotation

Indicated by the marks of ellipsis (. . .). (See **Ellipsis,** section 1.)

one

1. In formal speech and writing the pronoun *one* is used to mean people in general:

At times *one* should keep *one's* thoughts to *oneself.*

But to avoid the unpleasant repetition of *one* within a sentence, *he*, *his*, *him* (or *she*, *her*) are often used:

At times *one* should keep *his* thoughts to *himself.* [Or: *her* thoughts to *herself.*]

2. General usage prefers *we* or *you* to the impersonal and formal *one*:

At times *we* should keep *our* thoughts to *ourselves.*
You never know when *your* actions will return to help or hinder *you.*

(For further discussion, see **you.**)

3. *One* and *ones* are often used to avoid repeating a preceding noun:

Kitty can't decide whether to keep her old car or buy a new one.
These jars are nine dollars a dozen; the larger ones are twelve dollars a dozen.

4. In many sentences *one* is deadwood, taking attention away from the important word, and should be omitted in writing:

Phyllis's contribution was certainly [an] important [one].

(See also **every and its compounds,** section 2.)

one another

See **each other, one another.**

one of those who

The verb in the relative clause following *one of those who* (and similar expressions) agrees in number with the antecedent of the pronoun *who*:

Flora is the only one of those girls who *wants* to attend the cookout. [Singular verb; the antecedent of *who* is *one.*]
Candice is one of those hairdressers who *wash* their customers' hair as gently as their own. [Plural verb; the antecedent of *who* is *hairdressers.*]

In informal speech a singular verb is sometimes used in sentences like the second, since the idea uppermost in the speaker's mind is singular:

Candice is one of those hairdressers who washes her customers' hair as gently as her own.

only

Careful users of English put *only* (and adverbs like *almost, even, hardly, scarcely, just, nearly*) right before the word or words it modifies:

He had time to check only two pages of the standardized test.

In general usage, however, *only* is often placed before the verb:

He only had time to check two pages of the standardized test.

Whenever the intended meaning of a written sentence might not be clear because of the position of the adverb, be sure to put it before the word or words it modifies:

AMBIGUOUS: Mrs. Lee almost lost all her wheat in the warehouse fire.
CLEAR: Mrs. Lee lost almost all her wheat in the warehouse fire.

Onomatopoeia

See **Imitative words.**

onto, on to

Onto, written solid, is a preposition:

Karen stepped hesitatingly onto the high diving board.
Kip spent her summer vacation fastening nuts onto bolts at the car manufacturing plant.

When *on* is an adverb and *to* a preposition, they are two words:

Uncle Lloyd and Aunt Marguerite planned to drive on to Louisville in the morning.

Before moving on to his next point, the senator made sure the reporters noted what he had said.

Opinion

See **Statement of opinion.**

or

A coordinating conjunction that connects words, phrases, or clauses of equal grammatical value:

WORDS: I can't decide whether to play badminton or chess.
PHRASES: He's spending the holidays in Montana with relatives or in Iowa with his college roommate.
CLAUSES: He promised he would bring appetizers or help set the tables.

Two subjects joined by *or* take a singular verb when each is singular, a plural verb when both are plural:

A taco or a burrito *costs* less than an enchilada.
Tacos or burritos *cost* less than enchiladas.

When one subject is plural and the other singular, the verb agrees with the one standing nearer:

Perfume or colognes *are* her only extravagance.
Colognes or perfume *is* her only extravagance.

(For further examples, see **Agreement,** section 1c.)

oral, verbal

Strictly, *oral* means "spoken," and *verbal* means "in words, spoken or written." But *verbal* has been used so often in the limited sense of "spoken words" that dictionaries list "oral" as one meaning of *verbal*: *an oral agreement* and *a verbal agreement* mean the same.

The opposite of both *oral* and *verbal* is *written*:

I accept your verbal offer, but my office requires a written one.

other

Other is used in a comparison of things in the same class, but not in a comparison of things of different classes:

This Perry Mason mystery is better *than any other* Perry Mason I've ever read. [Same class.]
This new combine is more efficient *than* any ten field hands. [Different classes.]

If *other* were omitted from the first sentence, the statement would be illogical, since "any Perry Mason" would include the one under discussion.

Other is not used with a superlative:

Of all the foreign-language courses offered at Daleton High, Latin is the most popular. [Not: of *any other* foreign language course; of *all the other* foreign-language courses.]

ought

See **had ought.**

Outline form

An outline is a general plan of the material that has been or is to be presented in a speech or paper. The outline shows the order of the various topics, the relative importance of each, and the relationship between the various parts. Outlines are useful in studying material assigned for reading, since in an outline you can give in a clear concise form an overall view of the subject. But the chief value of outlines is to help you in planning talks or papers of your own.

There are three main types of outlines that you will find useful in preparing papers and talks of various kinds:

1. Work outline. For most of the papers you write or talks you give, an elaborate outline with parallel heads and subheads is not necessary. For a short paper, it is often sufficient merely to list the main topic to be discussed in each paragraph. This type of outline helps you to remember paragraph divisions as well as the main ideas you wish to cover; the details can be filled in as you write the paper itself. Or, if you are planning a longer paper or talk, you may wish to include both topics and subtopics in your outline. Since a work outline is not a showpiece, but merely a rough map to guide you in writing or speaking, the form in which it is written is not important. As long as the points are listed in an order that helps you present your ideas clearly, any outline form that you use is acceptable.

2. Topic outline. For some papers, you may have to submit a formal outline as part of your work. The most common type of formal outline required is the topic outline. The headings are given in brief phrases, clauses, or single words, and are numbered and lettered consistently, as in this example:

United States Citizenship and Naturalization (Title)

I. Citizens of the U.S. (Main head)
  A. Citizens of the U.S. only (Subhead)
    1. By birth (Sub-subhead)
      a. Through birthplace
      b. Through blood relationship
    2. By naturalization
    3. By act of Congress
      a. To waive naturalization requirements
      b. To grant honorary citizenship
    4. By treaty
  B. Citizens of both the U.S. and another country
II. Noncitizen residents of the U.S.
  A. Aliens
    1. Intending to become citizens
    2. Not intending to become citizens

B. Noncitizen nationals
C. Others
1. Stateless persons
2. Denaturalized or expatriated citizens

III. Naturalization of U.S. aliens
A. Declaration of intention
1. No longer required by law
2. Still required by professions in some states
B. Petition for naturalization
1. Required by Immigration and Naturalization Act of 1952
2. Required of petitioning alien
a. Age of eighteen years
b. U.S. residency of five years
c. State-of-naturalization residency of six months
d. Good moral character
e. Truthfulness of application
C. Investigation and interview
1. Immigration and Naturalization Service officers question
a. Alien
b. Two citizen witnesses
2. Officers test
a. Alien's simple literacy in English
b. Alien's knowledge of U.S. history
c. Alien's understanding of U.S. government
3. Officers recommend
a. Court approve alien's petition
b. Court deny alien's petition
D. Final hearings in court
1. If officers approved alien's petition, alien
a. Takes oath of allegiance
b. Receives certificate of naturalization
2. If officers denied alien's petition, alien
a. May first appeal to judge
b. May then appeal to next higher court
c. May finally appeal to Supreme Court

IV. Denaturalization and expatriation of naturalized U.S. citizens
A. Denaturalization for actions before naturalization, such as
1. Concealing facts on petition
2. Not intending permanent U.S. residency
3. Taking oath with mental reservations
4. Refusing to testify before a congressional committee
B. Expatriation for actions after naturalization, such as
1. Becoming a citizen of another country
2. Serving another country
a. In its armed forces
b. In its government
3. Voting in another country's elections
4. Formally renouncing U.S. citizenship
5. Deserting the U.S. armed forces during time of war

6. Avoiding U.S. military service
7. Committing treason

Notice the system used in a formal topic outline, the way numbers and letters are alternated—and indented—to show which items are of equal importance and how the various items are related. All items labeled with Roman numerals are main heads, giving the main divisions of the subject. All items marked by capital letters are equally important divisions of a main head, and so on, alternating between arabic numerals and small letters.

Notice, too, that items in the different groups are parallel in form. In the outline shown above, all the main heads are nouns modified by phrases. The A, B, and C subheads under I are also nouns modified by phrases. The four numbered items under A are prepositional phrases. The first item in any group determines the form; all following items in that group should be phrased the same way.

3. Sentence outline. A sentence outline is like a formal topic outline except that each head and subhead is expanded into a complete sentence. A sentence outline demands more thought than a topic outline because it requires you to put your ideas into specific, rather detailed statements. But for this very reason it will be more valuable to you than the sketchier topic outline.

out of date

Expressions like *out of date, out of doors, out of town* are hyphenated when they precede the noun they modify, but not when they follow:

Great-aunt Tess wore out-of-date clothes, but her ideas were *avant garde*.
By the time the consulting firm makes its recommendations, the information will be out of date.

over with

Used colloquially to mean "over" or "finished":

COLLOQUIAL: I can scarcely wait until this concert is over with.
WRITTEN: I can scarcely wait until this concert is over.

pair

The usual plural of *pair* is *pairs*:

My grandmother knitted two pairs of ski socks for me.

In business usage and in some informal speech the plural is often *pair* when it follows a number:

The Rock Island Library ordered ten pair of metal bookends.

Paradox

See **Epigram.**

Paragraphs

A paragraph–in expository writing–is a group of sentences developing one point, usually one phase of a larger topic. Since the number of sentences needed to make a particular phase clear will vary, paragraph length will vary, ranging from quite short to quite long. However, if a neatly developed paragraph turns out to be formidably long, modern writers are likely to split it into two (or more) parts, making the break between subpoints, where there is a natural break in the thought.

In narrative writing, details are not grouped around main points or phases but follow one another like links in a chain. Deciding where the paragraph breaks should come is largely a matter of judgment. Most writers begin a new paragraph to emphasize a particular action or scene or to show a change in time, in place, in mood. (It is also a general practice to start a new paragraph every time the speaker changes.) In most narratives the paragraphs are fairly short, since long paragraphs tend to slow the action down.

Parallel constructions

Ideas in a sentence that are of equal importance should be expressed in parallel (or grammatically similar) forms. Notice how, in each of the following sentence pairs, the original sentence has been revised so that the grammatical units are similar:

NOT PARALLEL: In the home repair course we learned *to rewire lamps*, *fixing leaky faucets*, and *how to caulk windows*.

PARALLEL: In the home repair course we learned how to *rewire lamps*, *fix leaky faucets*, and *caulk windows*.

NOT PARALLEL: I'd prefer *to fly* home to see my parents rather than *talking* to them on the telephone.

PARALLEL: I'd prefer *flying* home to see my parents rather than *talking* to them on the telephone.

NOT PARALLEL: Dr. Raube told me that I could cure my cold *by drinking* orange juice and *if I would get plenty of rest.*

PARALLEL: Dr. Raube told me that I could cure my cold *by drinking* orange juice and [*by*] *getting* plenty of rest.

Paraphrase

A restatement–in one's own words–of the ideas in a passage (written or spoken). When a writer uses rather involved or figurative or technical language or packs a great many ideas into a few concise sentences, even the best of readers need to weigh these words carefully to find all the meaning intended:

ORIGINAL	PARAPHRASE
Vanity is so frequently the apparent motive of advice that we, for the most part, summon our powers to oppose it without any very accurate inquiry whether it is right. It is sufficient that another is growing great in his own eyes at our expense and assumes authority over us without our permission; for many would contentedly suffer the consequences of their own mistakes rather than the insolence of him who triumphs as their deliverer.—Samuel Johnson. *The Rambler*, No. 87.	The desire to be admired so often seems to be the reason for someone's giving advice that we generally make up our minds to reject the advice without any very careful investigation to see whether it is good. It is enough that someone else is feeling self-important at our expense by assuming the right to tell us what to do without our consent; for many people would willingly put up with the results of their own mistakes rather than put up with the impertinence of a person who rejoices in being their rescuer.

Parentheses ( )

1. Parentheses are used to enclose added explanations or comments that the writer does not want to stand out conspicuously in a sentence. When the material in parentheses comes within a sentence, it is not begun with a capital letter or followed by a period, even if it is a sentence itself. But commas and semicolons are used, just as they would be in any sentence:

We saw Artie (my cousin, not my brother) at the auto show.
The two women have good working arrangements (Jan works mornings; Dana the afternoons) in their new jobs.

If the material enclosed in parentheses is a question or an exclamation, a question mark or an exclamation mark is used within the parentheses:

We should invite Laura (don't you agree?) to our party.
Jarmila (how tired she was!) fell asleep on the sofa.

Punctuation marks (commas, periods, semicolons, etc.) that belong to the sentence come after the parentheses, not before:

Grandma Moses (her full name was Anna Mary Robertson Moses), that fine primitive artist, is my favorite painter.
We will all miss our neighbors (they move to Florida in March).
Dan tutors Audrey in history (she's getting an A); she helps him with math.

2. Parenthetical material that is not in the body of a sentence begins with a capital letter and ends with a period (or question mark or exclamation mark):

Carla started her new job last week. (She's an editorial trainee at McNutt Publishing Company.) Her salary isn't high, but her chances for advancement are excellent.

3. Parentheses are often used to enclose letters or figures that mark items in a series:

The village council proposed three projects: (1) the refurbishing of monuments in Circle Park, (2) the landscaping of Village Square, and (3) the clearing of debris from Will's Dump.

4. Parentheses, dashes, and commas are all used to set off explanatory comments. In the sentence "Movie rights for Beau Casey's novel, *Whimpering Piccolo* (well received by the critics), have been purchased for fifty thousand dollars," the parentheses make the explanatory comment inconspicuous and show that it has only a slight bearing on the rest of the sentence. Dashes would emphasize an explanatory comment, while commas would show that the writer wanted it to be more closely related to other words in the sentence.

Parentheses are effective when they are used only occasionally. Used too often, they become tiresome and may distract the reader.

5. Parentheses should not be used to enclose words that you want omitted from a sentence. Draw a straight line through such words.

part

Used with *from* when it means "go away from; leave" and with *with* when it means "give up; let go":

It will be hard to part from friends when we graduate.
My parents refuse to part with their hoard of old magazines.

part (on the part of)

Often a clumsy substitute for *by*, *among*, *for*, and the like:

CLUMSY: The fear expressed *on the part of* the workers was that they would lose their jobs.
BETTER: The fear expressed *by* the workers was that they would lose their jobs.

Participial phrase

Like the participle itself, the participial phrase is a verb form used as an adjective, modifying nouns and pronouns:

Grabbing a sandwich from the tray, Tom made a dash to the pep rally. [The participial phrase modifies the noun *Tom*.]
Grapefruit *flown in from Florida* is the sweetest of all. [Modifies the noun *Grapefruit*.]

Sometimes the phrase also contains the word modified:

She accepted the news with nervousness, *her fingers twisting an errant wisp of hair.* [Participle *twisting* modifies noun *fingers*.]

Though generally used to modify a particular noun or pronoun, participles are sometimes used in phrases that relate to the whole sentence (to the situation) rather than to a particular word:

Speaking of the President, did you hear his speech last night?
Considering the importance of the research, more technicians will be hired.

Phrases like these are equivalent to subordinate clauses ("Since we are speaking of the President, did you hear his speech last night?"). Because they are not intended as modifiers of a particular word, they are not considered dangling modifiers.

(See **Dangling modifiers.**)

Participle

1. Forms. The present participle ends in *-ing*: *walking, dreaming, growing.* The past participle usually ends in *-ed, -t, -d, -en,* or *-n*: *sulked, kept, said, risen, thrown.*

2. Uses. a. Participles are used in forming various tenses of verbs:

Kay is dancing.
We have been shopping.
Father had been excited.
She should be tired.

b. When not part of a verb form, participles are used as verbal adjectives modifying nouns or pronouns:

a *swinging* sign
the *stolen* necklace
Waving, Arnetta stopped the *speeding* car. [*Waving* modifies *Arnetta, speeding* modifies *car.*]

party

See **person.**

passed

The past-tense form of the verb *pass* is *passed*:

Everyone in class *passed* that difficult quiz. [Not: Everyone in class *past.*]

Passive voice

See **Active and passive voice.**

Past tense, past perfect tense

See **Tenses of verbs.**

per

Per (Latin, "through; by") is used chiefly in business and technical English: *four times per diem, $65 per capita, 18 miles per gallon, 55 miles per hour, $9,200 per annum.*

In general usage an equivalent English expression is usually more appropriate: *four times a day, $65 for each person, 18 miles to a gallon, 55 miles an hour, $9,200 a year.*

percent, per cent

More commonly written as one word than as two, and not followed by a period: *a gain of 7 percent, a 12 percent interest rate.*

Colloquially *percent* is used in place of *percentage*:

COLLOQUIAL: A large percent of our graduates go to college.
WRITTEN: A large percentage of our graduates go to college.

Perfect tenses

The *present perfect tense* suggests an action begun at some point in the past and completed at the time of the statement: Max *has written* his English paper.

The *past perfect tense* shows that the action had been completed before a specific time or happening in the past: Max *had proofread* his paper before I even started writing mine.

The *future perfect tense* shows that the action will have been completed at some time in the future: With luck, I *will have finished* my English paper by next Thursday. (See **Tenses of verbs.**)

Period

1. The chief function of a period is to mark the end of a sentence that is not regarded as a question or an exclamation:

Mr. Baritz asked us where we were going.
Don't ask us; we don't know.
Will you please send us a copy of your transcript. [Intended as a polite request, not as a question.]

2. Periods have several conventional uses:

a. After abbreviations and initials:

Jan. N.J. Mr. Walter S. Redden, Jr.

b. Between dollars and cents when the dollar sign is used:

$1.50 $12,955.50 $.15 [But: 15 cents or 15¢]

c. Before decimals or between the whole number and the decimal:

.9 5.097 61.2%

3. Three spaced periods (. . .) are used to show the omission of words in a quotation. (See **Ellipsis.**)

4. A period coming at the end of a quotation is generally placed inside the quotation marks:

"The most amazing thing about it," Kiku said emphatically, "is its low cost."

(For periods with parentheses, see **Parentheses,** sections 1 and 2.)

Periodic sentence

A sentence in which the main thought is not complete until the end:

We all found it hard to believe that Gerri Hilt–the same Gerri who had flunked general mathematics and skipped most of her classes in business at

Hatcher High—had become an accountant with a prominent San Francisco firm.

Because the reader has to wait for the main idea until after reading all the minor details upon which the idea is based, the effect of a periodic sentence is one of suspense.

Used occasionally, periodic sentences add a pleasant variety and emphasis to writing. Used too often, though, they give an unnatural, stilted tone. (See also **Loose sentence.**)

Person

Personal pronouns change form to indicate person:

FIRST PERSON, THE ONE SPEAKING:	I, me, mine; we, us, ours
SECOND PERSON, THE ONE SPOKEN TO:	you, yours
THIRD PERSON, THE ONE SPOKEN OF:	he, him, his; she, her, hers; it, its; they, them, theirs

In English the only change in the form of verbs to indicate person occurs in the third person singular: I speak, you speak, he *speaks*; we, you, they speak.

The verb *be* is exceptional: I *am*, you *are*, he *is*; we, you, they *are.*

person

Person is the word generally used to refer to a human being. Many people use *individual* interchangeably with *person*; but *individual* is a rather heavy and pretentious word to use unless the person referred to is being contrasted with others, or his or her distinctiveness is being emphasized:

PRETENTIOUS: She was an extremely fastidious individual.
BETTER: She was an extremely fastidious person.

Though *party* is used colloquially to mean "person" (The *party* who called wouldn't leave his name), this use is not generally considered acceptable. *Party*, used in legal English, means "each of the persons or sides in a contract or lawsuit."

Personal pronouns

Pronouns whose forms show person; that is, the forms show whether the speaker (first person), the one spoken to (second person), or the one spoken of (third person) is meant: *I*; *you*; *he*, *she*, *it*; *we*; *they*. (See also **Case,** section 1, and **Gerund,** section 3.)

Personification

A figure of speech in which a lifeless thing or quality is spoken of as if alive:

My cruel little car has never treated me fairly; I do everything to keep it happy and well, but the moody little machine lets me down frequently.

phenomenon

The usual meaning is "an observable fact, event, or circumstance": The return of the swallows to Capistrano is an annual phenomenon. The plural is *phenomena*: Cyclones, hurricanes, and tornadoes are three of the most devastating of nature's phenomena.

Phenomenon is also used to mean "something or someone extraordinary." Used in this sense, the plural is generally *phenomenons*: The haunting of the house on the hill is one of the neighborhood phenomenons.

Phrases

A phrase is a group of words without a subject and verb, used as a single word in a sentence:

PREPOSITIONAL PHRASE: Arrange your flowers *on the kitchen counter.* [Used as an adverb modifying *Arrange.*]

PARTICIPIAL PHRASE: *Speaking politely*, the motorist tried to contradict the police officer. [Used as an adjective modifying *motorist.*]

GERUND PHRASE: *Fishing without a license* is prohibited. [Used as the subject of *is prohibited.*]

INFINITIVE PHRASE: Dale wants *to read that book.* [Used as the direct object of *wants.*]

Plagiarism

Using the words, ideas, or expressions of others as if they were your own. Plagiarism problems may grow from the following circumstances:

1. Directly copying a passage from a source without giving credit.
2. Paraphrasing a source so closely that only a few words or phrases are changed.
3. Partially using someone else's ideas and style without giving credit (you may expand another's idea into one of your own, but you must give credit for any idea you use that is not your own).

When you use material from another source, you must give it credit. In a shorter paper such as a book review, this credit is usually given directly in the text. In a longer piece of writing such as a research paper, however, you will need to footnote your sources. (See **Footnotes** in the Appendix.)

plenty

Plenty is colloquial when used as an adverb or as an adjective modifier preceding a noun:

ADVERB: We were plenty worried.
Our house is plenty big enough for extra guests.

ADJECTIVE: She always had plenty money for trips.
We'll need plenty volunteers to paint the hall.

These modifier uses are avoided in formal English.

Plurals of nouns

1. Most nouns are regular, forming their plurals with *s*:

dancer–dancers	tea–teas	judge–judges
Dr. Crane–the Cranes	tray–trays	monkey–monkeys

2. Nouns ending in *sh*, *s*, *x*, *z*, or *ch* (when pronounced as /ch/ and not as /k/) add *es*:

bush–bushes	moss–mosses	wrench–wrenches
dish–dishes	tax–taxes	couch–couches
census–censuses	waltz–waltzes	Meyers–Meyerses

3. Nouns ending in *y* preceded by a consonant change the *y* to *i* and add *es*:

ferry–ferries	jury–juries	army–armies
enemy–enemies	buddy–buddies	canary–canaries

Names of people are exceptions to this rule:

I must know at least four *Jerrys*. [Not: *Jerries*.]
The *Anthonys* weren't home last night. [Not: *Anthonies*.]

4. Nouns ending in *o* preceded by a vowel add *s*:

folio–folios	curio–curios	zoo–zoos
radio–radios	stereo–stereos	tattoo–tattoos

But nouns ending in *o* preceded by a consonant vary. Some add *s*, others *es*, and still others either *s* or *es*:

WITH *s*:	piano–pianos	hypo–hypos	auto–autos
WITH *es*:	tomato–tomatoes	hero–heroes	veto–vetoes
WITH *s* OR *es*:	hobo–hobos or hoboes	motto–mottoes or mottos	
	zero–zeros or zeroes		

5. Nouns ending in *f* and *fe* also vary:

WITH *s*:	serf–serfs	roof–roofs	waif–waifs
	safe–safes	sheriff–sheriffs	
WITH *ves*:	sheaf–sheaves	shelf–shelves	life–lives
WITH *s* OR *ves*:	scarf–scarfs or scarves	hoof–hoofs or hooves	

6. A few nouns form their plural by a change in spelling:

die–dice	child–children	mouse–mice
goose–geese	woman–women	tooth–teeth

7. Some nouns borrowed from foreign languages have English endings, others foreign endings, and still others have both:

ENGLISH PLURALS:	kimono–kimonos	boomerang–boomerangs
	luau–luaus	troika–troikas
FOREIGN PLURALS:	genesis–geneses	bronchus–bronchi
	phylum–phyla	monsieur–messieurs
	kibbutz–kibbutzim	alumna–alumnae
	crisis–crises	alumnus–alumni
	diagnosis–diagnoses	bonus–bonuses

BOTH: abacus–abacuses or abaci
genus–genera or genuses
larynx–larynges or larynxes
appendix–appendixes or appendices
bolshevik–bolsheviks or bolsheviki

In scientific and formal writing, the foreign plurals of words that have both forms are more likely to be used. But in other situations the English plurals are more common and are the appropriate forms to use.

8. Compound words vary. When they are written as one word, the plural is usually formed by adding *s* or *es* to the end:

onlooker–onlookers
toothbrush–toothbrushes

When the parts are separate or hyphenated, the principal part is usually made plural:

board of health–boards of health
knight-errant–knights-errant
square dance–square dances
son-in-law–sons-in-law
man-of-war–men-of-war
ice cream–ice creams

But in these compound words the principal parts are not made plural:

sit-in–sit-ins
shake-up–shake-ups
lean-to–lean-tos
six-year-old–six-year-olds

9. Either *s* or *'s* is added to numbers, signs, letters, and words discussed as words. The *'s* is preferred after all lower-case letters and those capital letters that would be confusing if *s* alone were added:

two *9*s *or* two *9*'s
five *s *or* five *'s
the 1800s *or* the 1800's
your ABCs *or* your ABC's
There are three consecutive double letters in *bookkeeper*: two *o*'s, two *k*'s and two *e*'s.
Jim's *5*'s look like *s*'s.
Her *and*'s and *uh*'s were very annoying.

10. A few nouns have the same form for both singular and plural:

one Sioux and one Vietnamese–two Sioux and six Vietnamese
one deer–several deer
Last month Russia launched four spacecraft; one spacecraft was manned.

p.m.

Abbreviation for the Latin *post meridiem*, "after noon." (See **a.m., p.m.**)

Poetry (quoted)

When quoting poetry in your writing, copy it exactly as it was originally written, keeping each line, capital letter, and punctuation mark. If the quotation consists of only one line or part of a line, it is put in quotation marks and written into the text. If two lines or more are quoted, they are usually set below the text and indented from each margin. When they are set off in this way, no quotation marks are needed. (If, because of lack of space, more than one line is incorporated in the text, the end of each line is usually indicated by a short diagonal mark [/] separating it from the following line.)

When possible, a line of poetry should be written complete on one line of your paper. If it is necessary to carry a long line over, it should be indented deeper than the other lines. (See also **Indention.**)

Portmanteau words

See **Blend.**

Possessive adjectives

When *my*, *your*, *his*, *her*, *its*, *our*, *your*, and *their*, possessive forms of the personal pronouns, modify a noun, some grammarians classify them as possessive adjectives:

my error	his courage	our graduation	their Siamese cat

Other terms used in classifying these words are pronominal adjectives or noun markers.

Possessive case

1. Forms. The possessive case (sometimes called the genitive case) is formed in various ways:

a. Singular nouns and indefinite pronouns add an apostrophe and *s*:

girl's coat
Dana's help
sister-in-law's hobby

Postmaster General's duties
someone's good name
anybody's guess

With singular proper names ending in *s*, usage is divided. Sometimes only an apostrophe is added: Dickens' characters. But most often both an apostrophe and *s* are used except with the names *Jesus* and *Moses* and Greek names of more than one syllable ending in *es*:

Dickens's characters
Peter Sellers's autograph

Dickens' characters
Peter Sellers' autograph

But: Jesus' disciples and Diogenes' lantern

b. Plural nouns ending in *s* add only the apostrophe:

boxes' labels	Davises' farm	witches' potions
spiders' webs	Millers' geese	teachers' salaries

But plural nouns not ending in *s* add both the apostrophe and *s*:

children's nursery	henchmen's loyalty	alumni's votes

c. To show joint ownership, the last noun is made possessive:

Terry and Jerry's room [They share it.]
Mr. Lee and Mr. Wild's drugstore [They own it together.]
her mother and father's vacation [They went together.]

But to show separate ownership, each noun is made possessive:

Sarah's and Jenny's bicycles
Mr. Roth's and Mr. Wild's cars
her sister's and brother's suitcases

d. The personal pronouns and the relative and interrogative *who* have special possessive forms, spelled without the apostrophe:

USED BEFORE NOUNS: my, your, his, her, its, our, their; whose
USED ALONE: mine, yours, his, hers, its, ours, theirs; whose

e. The possessive may also be formed by using a phrase with *of*:

the dedication of Dr. Obata [Dr. Obata's dedication]
the innocence of a child [a child's innocence]

The *of*-possessive is more common with names of inanimate objects than the *'s*-form, but both are used. The *'s*-form is more common with names of people, although both are used:

the handle of the umbrella — the umbrella's handle
Amelia Earhart's spirit — the spirit of Amelia Earhart

In general, choose the form that sounds best in the sentence.

f. The *'s*-form and the *of*-form are often combined, especially with *this* or *that*:

that habit of Andy's — those pals of my brother's
this book of Jackie's — these plans of Mother's

2. Uses. Although the principal use of the possessive case is to show ownership (*Laura's headache, her drawings, Henry Gordon's freckles*), it is also used to show a number of other relationships:

DESCRIPTION: a foreigner's viewpoint, the taste of nutmeg
DOER OF AN ACT: Walter's teasing, the judge's instructions, the instructions of the judge
RECIPIENT OF AN ACT: Miss Hanson's promotion, Lincoln's assassination
AUTHORSHIP: Anne Bradstreet's poetry, the poetry of Anne Bradstreet
MEASURE: a week's work, a quarter's worth, a baker's dozen

Possessive pronouns

The possessive forms of the personal pronouns and of *who* are *mine, yours, his, hers, its, ours, theirs*; *whose*. (Compare **Possessive adjectives** and **Pronominal adjectives.**)

Post hoc fallacy

The error of thinking that Happening A must be the cause of Happening B merely because Happening A came first is called the *post hoc* fallacy. (The name comes from the Latin phrase *post hoc, ergo propter hoc,* which means "after this, therefore because of it.") Notice the *post hoc* thinking in this argument, given by George's father:

"Well, I should have known better last month than to let George buy that motorcycle. The very day he got it his chemistry grade plummeted. We'll just have to lock the cycle in the garage, since it's obvious that getting that thing cost him his place on the honor roll. I really should have known. . . ."

You are George's lab partner and know that several other factors—not the cycle—contributed to his low chemistry grade: he had missed three days of class discussion because of illness; he had botched an important experiment and was therefore late in handing in a report; having crammed all of the night before, he had done less well than usual on the six weeks' test; and so on. His father had mistakenly assumed that, since George's poor grade *followed* his acquiring the motorcycle, the poor grade was *caused* by his getting the motorcycle.

The *post hoc* fallacy is easy to fall into. Before we can figure out a solution to many of the problems that concern us, we must know what caused the problems. But in our hurry to reach a solution, we often tend to oversimplify matters, to act as if a given event has just a single cause—a preceding event. The truth is that there are generally many causes, many preceding events, which contribute to any given result. Moreover, the mere fact that event A precedes event B in time does not mean that there is necessarily a causal connection between the two.

Unless we keep these points in mind, we will (like the imaginary father above) present arguments that are fallacious.

pre-

Prefix meaning "before in place, time, or rank." Generally words with *pre-* are written without a hyphen: *prejudge, precondition, predestine, preschool, preset.* But a hyphen is usually used when the part following *pre-* is a proper name: *pre-Revolutionary War, pre-Reformation.*

Usage varies when the part of the word following *pre-* begins with an *e.* Such words are sometimes hyphened or written with a dieresis (*pre-election, preëlection*; *pre-establish, preëstablish*), but it is becoming more common to write them as solid words (*preelection, preestablish*).

precede, proceed

Precede, meaning "to go or come before," is often confused in spelling with *proceed*, meaning "to go on after having stopped" or "to move forward":

The flower girl will precede the bride down the aisle.
The President's motorcade proceeded to the convention site.

Précis

You may often want to give the gist of something you have read or heard: a book, a magazine article, a speech, a movie, a discussion, or a conversation. If you write an accurate and brief summary of such material in your own words, keeping the author's or speaker's original point of view, you are writing a précis. (*Précis*, pronounced /prā′sē/ or /prā sē′/, is spelled the same in the singular and plural, but the plural is pronounced with a final /z/ sound—/prā′sēz/.)

For an average paragraph the précis might be only a sentence, or it may

run to half the length of the passage summarized. The important thing is to include in a clear, brief statement all the major ideas expressed by the author or speaker without distorting his or her point of view. For an example, compare the following paragraph–taken from Robert Louis Stevenson's "An Apology for Idlers"–with the précis given after it:

It is surely beyond a doubt that people should be a good deal idle in youth. For though here and there a Lord Macaulay may escape from school honors with all his wits about him, most boys pay so dear for their medals that they never afterward have a shot in their locker, and begin the world bankrupt. And the same holds true during all the time a lad is educating himself, or suffering others to educate him. It must have been a very foolish old gentleman who addressed Johnson at Oxford in these words: "Young man, ply your book diligently now, and acquire a stock of knowledge; for when years come upon you, you will find that poring upon books will be but an irksome task." The old gentleman seems to have been unaware that many other things besides reading grow irksome, and not a few become impossible by the time a man has to use spectacles and cannot walk without a stick. Books are good enough in their own way, but they are a mighty bloodless substitute for life. It seems a pity to sit, like the Lady of Shalott, peering into a mirror, with your back turned on all the bustle and glamour of reality. And if a man reads very hard, as the old anecdote reminds us, he will have little time for thoughts.

It is not wise to force young people to spend all their time on their studies. There should be a time for idleness as well, for free time gives a young person a chance to experience life at firsthand before growing too old.

Some passages are more difficult to summarize than others, depending on the material and the author's style. Until you master the technique, it may be best to follow these steps:

a. Read the passage carefully, but as quickly as possible, for the overall meaning. If necessary, reread the difficult parts.

b. Reread the passage, focusing your attention on key words and connectives, and checking the meaning of those you do not know.

c. List mentally or on paper the major ideas of the passage.

d. In your own words, write a summary of these ideas. As far as possible, avoid the words and phrasing used by the author or speaker, though you will have to use certain key words because they are essential to the meaning. Usually all details, figures of speech, and examples are omitted.

e. Reread the passage and your précis to see where you can further compress the meaning or economize on words. Check carefully to see that you have not changed the point of view of the passage or otherwise changed the author's intended meaning.

Once you have become skilled in writing précis, you can combine or even omit some of these steps, especially in summarizing simple material. In dealing with more complex material, though, you will find that following these steps will bring the best results. The time you spend practicing précis-writing will be repaid in increased ability to understand what you read and to express clearly and compactly what you learn.

Predicate

The verb and the words used with it to make a statement about the subject of a sentence or clause:

Cat *purred.*
Eduardo's family *is very close and loving.*
The boys *played football all day.*
You *should learn to drive defensively.*
A year later Kurt *felt bad effects from his leg injury.*

Two or more verbs used with one subject are known as a *compound predicate*:

Rachel *walked* her dog, *fed* her cat, and *jogged* a mile before coming to work.

prefer

The better idiom is *prefer . . . to*:

Ann prefers swimming *to* jogging. [Not: Ann prefers swimming *more than* jogging.]
Don prefers Beethoven's symphonies *to* Tchaikovsky's.

With infinitives, in order to avoid a repetition of *to*, *rather than* is used:

I would prefer to stay at home tonight *rather than* [to] go out in that below-zero weather.

Prefix

A word, syllable, or syllables put at the beginning of a word to change its meaning or to form a new word. For example, adding *dis-* (meaning "not") to *honest* makes *dishonest*, meaning "not honest."

Knowing the meaning of the common prefixes is often a help in figuring out the meaning of new words you run across. The following list gives a few of the more common prefixes and illustrates one meaning of each:

a- (not): atonal, atypical, asocial
ante- (before): anteroom, antebellum, antedate
anti- (against): antiseptic, anti-Populist, antigravity
bi- (two): bivalve, bicentennial, bifocal
circum- (around): circumscribe, circumnavigate, circumlocution
co- (together): coeducational, copartnership, co-worker
dis- (not): disenchanted, dislocate, discredit
ex- (former): ex-judge, ex-member, ex-president
fore- (before): foredoom, forecast, foreknowledge
hyper- (excessively): hypertension, hyperthyroid, hypercritical
in- (not): insensitive, inflexible, inexpert
inter- (between; among): interracial, interstate, interchange
mal- (bad): malcontent, maladjusted, malodor
mis- (wrong): misbehave, misunderstand, mistrust
non- (not): nonstandard, nonsmoker, non-English
pre- (before): prepackage, premedical, pre-Columbian
re- (again): reheat, reenter, rename

semi- (half): semitropical, semiprecious, semiyearly
super- (over; above): supernova, supersaturate, supersensitive
trans- (across): transplant, transcontinental, transoceanic
tri- (three): triangle, tricolor, triennial

(See also **pre-, re-,** and **semi-.**)

Preposition

1. A preposition is a word used to show the relation between a noun or its equivalent (called the *object of the preposition*) and some other word in the sentence, as in the following examples:

The tall man *beside* me blocked my view. [Shows the relationship between *me* and the noun *man.*]
Jaime walked *around* the block while we stopped to shop. [Shows the relationship between *block* and the verb *walked.*]

2. Among the most common prepositions are:

above	because of	down	in front of	through
after	behind	for	of	till
around	between	from	on	to
at	by	in	over	with

But remember that it is the use of a word, not its form, that determines what part of speech it is. *After*, for example, is often a preposition (Ollie will speak *after* the intermission); but it may also be a subordinating conjunction (We planned to go swimming *after* we mowed the lawn) or an adverb (They lived happily ever *after*).

3. The right preposition to use after certain words depends sometimes on the meaning intended. We say, for example, "call *at* his office," "call *down* an employee for an error," "call *for* a package," "call *from* a public phone," "call *in* a consultant," "call *on* us for help." At other times, the right preposition is a matter of idiom. We say "detrimental *to* our cause," not "detrimental *for*"; "mourn *over* a loss," not "mourn *of*"; "model *in* clay," not "model *from.*"

Ordinarily you learn the idiomatic prepositions to use with common words by hearing or seeing them in phrases. Words not in your everyday vocabulary may raise questions. Here is a list of such words and the idiomatic prepositions to use with them. (For words not in this list or not entered as separate items, you should consult a dictionary.)

apathy *toward* studies
caution *against* danger
complied *with* the rules
atmosphere conducive *to* work
emigrate *from* Poland
eligible *for* parole
engrossed *in* her research
familiarity *with* Romance languages
fond *of* his cousins
fondness *for* opera
forgetful *of* his friends
immigrate *to* Australia
intolerant *of* his relatives
motive *for* the crime
neglectful *of* his duty
observant *of* the customs
conduct offensive *to* us
peculiar *to* this county

perceptive *in* domestic matters
possibility *of* snow
take responsibility *for* her deeds
sparing *of* advice
sue *for* divorce
translate *from* the Spanish
translate *into* Swahili
vulnerable *to* criticism
wallow *in* the mud
wary *of* his motives

Keep in mind that when two words requiring different prepositions are used with a single object, both prepositions should be given:

May was conscious *of* but unmoved *by* their problems. [Not: May was conscious but unmoved by their problems.]

But when the two words require the same preposition, it need not be repeated:

Terry acknowledged, with thanks, their *kindness* and *help* to her.

4. It was once a general practice for textbooks to warn against ending a sentence with a preposition–and many writers, as a result, wrote quite awkward and unnatural sentences in an effort to avoid doing so. The taboo against the final preposition holds only in certain cases: (1) in sentences like "Where were your car keys at?" and "Where did Pete go to?"–in which the prepositions are not needed; (2) in sentences like "We finally met the girl about whom Kathy had been talking about"–in which either the second *about* or the first should be dropped; (3) in sentences like "What letter of the alphabet do I look prose fiction up under?"–in which the two prepositions at the end sound awkward.

Except for cases like these three, there is no reason for hesitating to end sentences with prepositions. "Where does Sasha come from?" is far more natural and less awkward than "From where does Sasha come?" Except in very formal writing, a sentence like "Mr. Henry has a great deal to worry about" is preferable to "Mr. Henry has a great deal about which to worry." And in a sentence like "The motion has not yet been voted on" the preposition not only fits smoothly and naturally at the end, but would be impossible to shift from that position without rewording the sentence.

Prepositional phrase

A preposition and its object, which together serve as a modifier–either adjective or adverb:

The little girl *with braided hair* is my sister. [Used as an adjective modifying *girl.*]
Pearl's new bike was locked *in the toolshed.* [Used as an adverb modifying *was locked.*]

Present tense

See **Tenses of verbs.**

Principal parts of verbs

The various tenses of a verb are formed from its principal parts: the infinitive (*jump*), the past tense (*jumped*), and the past participle (*jumped*).

Most verbs are "regular"–that is, both the past tense and past participle are formed by adding *-ed* to the infinitive (*call*, *called*, *called*). But there are some verbs–"irregular verbs"–whose principal parts are formed in other ways. Because of their irregularity, the forms of these verbs sometimes cause trouble for speakers and writers.

Here is a list of the more common troublesome verbs:

INFINITIVE	PAST TENSE	PAST PARTICIPLE
arise	arose	arisen
awake	awoke, awaked	awoke, awaked
be	was	been
bear	bore	borne (born: "given birth to")
beat	beat	beaten, beat
become	became	become
begin	began	begun
bend	bent	bent
bid ("offer")	bid	bid
bid ("order")	bade, bid	bidden, bid
bind	bound	bound
bite	bit	bitten, bit
bleed	bled	bled
blow	blew	blown
break	broke	broken
bring	brought	brought
broadcast	broadcast, broadcasted	broadcast, broadcasted
build	built	built
burn	burned, burnt	burned, burnt
burst	burst	burst
buy	bought	bought
catch	caught	caught
choose	chose	chosen
cling	clung	clung
come	came	come
cost	cost	cost
creep	crept	crept
deal	dealt	dealt
dig	dug	dug
dive	dived, dove	dived
do	did	done
draw	drew	drawn
dream	dreamed, dreamt	dreamed, dreamt
drink	drank	drunk
drive	drove	driven
eat	ate	eaten
fall	fell	fallen
feed	fed	fed
fight	fought	fought

find	found	found
flee	fled	fled
fling	flung	flung
fly	flew	flown
forbid	forbade, forbad	forbidden, forbid
forget	forgot	forgotten, forgot
freeze	froze	frozen
get	got	got, gotten
give	gave	given
go	went	gone
grind	ground	ground
grow	grew	grown
hang ("put to death")	hanged	hanged
hang ("suspend")	hung	hung
hear	heard	heard
hide	hid	hidden, hid
hold	held	held
hurt	hurt	hurt
kneel	knelt, kneeled	knelt, kneeled
knit	knitted, knit	knitted, knit
know	knew	known
lead	led	led
lean	leaned	leaned
leap	leaped, leapt	leaped, leapt
leave	left	left
lend	lent	lent
let	let	let
light	lighted, lit	lighted, lit
lose	lost	lost
mean	meant	meant
mistake	mistook	mistaken
pay	paid (of ropes: payed)	paid (payed)
plead	pleaded, pled	pleaded, pled
prove	proved	proved, proven
put	put	put
read	read	read
ride	rode	ridden
ring	rang	rung
rise	rose	risen
run	ran	run
say	said	said
see	saw	seen
seek	sought	sought
sew	sewed	sewed, sewn
shake	shook	shaken
shine ("glow; gleam")	shone, shined	shone, shined
shine ("polish")	shined	shined

show	showed	shown, showed
shrink	shrank, shrunk	shrunk, shrunken
sing	sang, sung	sung
sink	sank, sunk	sunk
slay	slew	slain
sleep	slept	slept
slide	slid	slid, slidden
sling	slung	slung
slink	slunk	slunk
sow	sowed	sown, sowed
speak	spoke	spoken
speed	sped, speeded	sped, speeded
spell	spelled, spelt	spelled, spelt
spit	spat, spit	spat, spit
spring	sprang, sprung	sprung
stand	stood	stood
steal	stole	stolen
stick	stuck	stuck
sting	stung	stung
stink	stank, stunk	stunk
stride	strode	stridden
strike	struck	struck, stricken
string	strung	strung
strive	strove, strived	striven
swear	swore	sworn
sweat	sweat, sweated	sweat, sweated
swell	swelled	swelled, swollen
swim	swam	swum
swing	swung	swung
take	took	taken
teach	taught	taught
tear	tore	torn
tell	told	told
throw	threw	thrown
tread	trod	trodden, trod
understand	understood	understood
wake	waked, woke	waked
wear	wore	worn
weave	weaved	weaved
weave (of cloth)	wove	weaved, woven
weep	wept	wept
win	won	won
wind	wound	wound
wring	wrung	wrung
write	wrote	written

In standard English, the forms in the second column (not the third) are used alone, as the simple past tense:

Wendy *did* her chores early. [Not: Wendy *done.*]
Sam *saw* the shirt he wants. [Not: Sam *seen.*]
Then we *began* to harmonize. [Not: we *begun.*]

The forms in the third column (not in the second) are used with auxiliary, or helping, verbs:

We *have sung* the wrong response. [Not: we *have sang.*]
Pete *had drunk* the quart of milk. [Not: Pete *had drank.*]
Mother *was worn* out from nursing Grandmother. [Not: Mother *was wore* out.]

principal, principle

Let the *a* in *principal* remind you that the adjective *principal* (meaning "chief") ends in *al*: *his principal objection, our principal economic problem.* Then if you remember that the *principal* of a school is the "principal person," that the *principal* in your bank is the "principal sum," and that the *principals* in a play or movie are the "principal actors," you will spell all these nouns correctly with an *a.*

To spell the noun *principle* right, remember that it means "a rule of conduct" and, like *rule*, ends in *le.*

prior to

Sometimes used when the simpler word *before* would be better:

HEAVY: Prior to buying our car, we looked at all the new models.
BETTER: Before buying our car, we looked at all the new models.

Progressive verb forms

See **Tenses of verbs,** section 2g.

Pronominal adjectives

In the sentence "When the volunteers arrived, Mr. Murdoch gave them the instruction sheets," *them* is a pronoun used as the indirect object of the verb *gave.* In the sentence "The volunteers took their responsibilities seriously," *their* has two uses–as a pronoun referring to the volunteers and as an adjective modifier of *responsibilities.* Pronouns that are also used as adjectives are sometimes called *pronominal adjectives.* (See also **Possessive pronouns.**)

Pronouns

Words that represent persons, places, or things without naming them. There are several kinds of pronouns: demonstrative, indefinite, intensive, interrogative, personal, possessive, reflexive, relative.

For more detailed information on the various kinds and uses of pronouns, see **Agreement,** section 2; **Case,** section 1; entries on particular pronouns (for example, **every and its compounds; who, whom, whose**); and entries on types of pronouns (**Relative pronouns, Reflexive pronouns, Indefinite pronouns,** etc.).

Pronunciation

Wherever pronunciations have been given throughout this book, the following symbols have been used. The key to these symbols is given below:

a	hat, cap	o	hot, rock
ā	age, face	ō	open, go
ä	father, far	ô	order, all
		oi	oil, voice
b	bad, rob	ou	house, out
ch	child, much		
d	did, red		
		p	paper, cup
		r	run, try
e	let, best	s	say, yes
ē	equal, be	sh	she, rush
ėr	term, learn	t	tell, it
		th	thin, both
f	fat, if	TH	then, smooth
g	go, bag		
h	he, how		
		u	cup, butter
i	it, pin	u̇	full, put
ī	ice, five	ü	rule, move
j	jam, enjoy		
k	kind, seek	v	very, save
l	land, coal	w	will, woman
m	me, am	y	young, yet
n	no, in	z	zero, breeze
ng	long, bring	zh	measure, seizure

ə represents:
a in about
e in taken
i in pencil
o in lemon
u in circus

FOREIGN SOUNDS

Y as in French *du.* Pronounce (ē) with the lips rounded as for (ü).

à as in French *ami.* Pronounce (ä) with the lips spread and held tense.

œ as in French *peu.* Pronounce (ā) with the lips rounded as for (ō).

N as in French *bon.* The N is not pronounced, but shows that the vowel before it is nasal.

H as in German *ach.* Pronounce (k) without closing the breath passage.

Proofreaders' marks

See inside back cover.

Propaganda

Propaganda is the systematic attempt by a person or group to persuade others to accept certain opinions, principles, or beliefs. Since words are the chief medium of propaganda, readers (and listeners) must be constantly alert. Facts and even statistics can be presented in such ways that they lose their true significance and seem to prove what the propagandist wants them to prove–unless readers can see through any attempts to mislead and can think clearly for themselves.

Propaganda may be presented in any form of writing–in novels, advertising, and poetry–and in various kinds of oral expression–radio and TV addresses, political speeches, drama, motion pictures. It may be used to advance a good cause by truthful and legitimate means, but in general the term is applied to writing or speaking that resorts to deceit and distorting facts to achieve its purpose.

Some of the more common methods used by propagandists that you should learn to detect are the following:

a. *Emotionalizing*, appealing to such emotions in the reader or hearer as hate, fear, greed, patriotism, or love of family.

b. *Generalizing*, making broad statements that permit a variety of interpretations or that are true only in a few exceptional instances: "Americans are rich," "Big business exploits the working people," "Large unions hurt the country," "Good mothers serve Whyte's White Bread," and so on. (See also **Generalizations.**)

c. *Name calling*, labeling a person or idea with a term of unfair or unpleasant connotations: "sexist," "radical," "egghead," "strikebreaker," "clotheshorse."

d. *Distorting facts*, giving only one side of a picture or confusing the issue so much that the average person will get only the meaning the propagandist wants.

As a good reader or listener you must try to separate facts and honest opinion from propaganda and to arrive at your own opinions uninfluenced by the deceptions that are hidden in many of the words that you read and hear. As an intelligent person you will want to arrive at convictions through your own reasoning power.

Proper adjectives

Adjectives that are formed from proper nouns and proper nouns that are used as adjectives are capitalized:

Elizabethan costume
South American songs
Chinese elm
Boston bull terrier
Spenserian sonnet
Shantung silk
Bunsen burner
Roquefort cheese

When a proper adjective no longer suggests its origin, it is treated as a simple adjective and is not capitalized:

bowie knife
casaba melon
graham crackers
damask rose
quixotic idea
worsted suit

Proper noun

The name of a particular person, place, or thing. Proper nouns are always capitalized: *Caroline, Carl Sandburg, Spain, the Dead Sea, the Lincoln Memorial.* (See **Common noun.**)

prophecy, prophesy

Prophecy /prof′ə sē/ is the noun; *prophesy* /prof′ə sī/ is the verb:

NOUN: The astrologer's prophecy frightened Marion.
VERB: Many people have prophesied the end of the world.

proved, proven

Proved is the usual past participle of *prove*, but *proven* is also used, especially as an adjective:

Jack Dunn has proved to be an invaluable mechanic.
Father wanted to know the proven method for maintaining the lawn.

Proverb

See **Epigram.**

provided, providing

Both are used (often with *that*) as conjunctions meaning "on the condition that":

Mrs. Apelian will drive us to the beach provided we get an early start. [Or: provided that, providing (that).]

Provincialism

See **Localism.**

Pun

A figure of speech in which a word is used humorously in two senses at the same time:

In *Romeo and Juliet*, the witty Mercutio, stabbed and dying, puns with his last breath: "Ask for me tomorrow, and you shall find me a grave man."
A celebrity, upon having a drink spilled on her designer dress, admonished the offender never to darken her Dior again.

The best puns play on both sound and meaning. A reasonable amount of punning adds variety to writing. Overdone, puns lose their effectiveness.

Punctuation

See the articles on the various marks of punctuation: **Colon, Comma, Dash, Ellipsis, Exclamation mark, Parentheses, Period, Question mark, Quotation marks, Semicolon.**

quay

Place where ships load and unload. The standard pronunciation is /kē/, although some people, misled by the spelling, pronounce the word /kwā/ or /kā/.

Question

See **Interrogative sentences, Question mark.**

Question mark (?)

1. Uses. a. A question mark is used at the end of a sentence that the writer intends as a question:

Don't you want breakfast?
That course has been canceled?
Why are you in Seattle?
She's not a member, is she?

b. A question mark may be used after each item in a series of interrogative expressions, for emphasis:

Who will hire the band? the caterers? the florist? the pavilion?

c. A question mark, generally in parentheses, may be used as an editorial mark to show that a statement of fact is questionable or a date is only approximate:

The first English printer, William Caxton, was born in 1422 (?).
The forces of King Harold II of England (1022?–1066) were defeated by William the Conqueror's at the Battle of Hastings.

2. With other punctuation. a. When a question mark and quotation marks fall together, the question mark is placed inside the closing quotation mark if it applies to the quoted sentence, and outside if it applies to the complete sentence:

Suddenly Henry shouted, "All right, where is the key?"
Who was with you when you said, "I'm going to be a star"?

When both the complete sentence and the quoted sentence are questions, only one question mark is used–inside the closing quotation mark:

How did Joyce find the nerve to ask Jeff, "Will you be my steady?"
Can you guess who shouted, "Who's for a game of touch football?"

b. When a parenthetical question within a question is set off by dashes or enclosed in parentheses, the question mark is put before the second dash or inside the parentheses:

We're reading Coleridge's *The Rime of the Ancient Mariner*–does anyone else, these days?–before going on to Dickens's *Bleak House.*
Ralph W. Hilton (isn't he handsome?) and Leila Andropoulos have the leads in the spring play.

c. When a question mark and parentheses fall together at the end of a sentence, the question mark goes inside the parentheses if it applies only to the parenthetical material, outside if it applies only to the rest of the sentence:

Calliope has been offered a hundred-thousand dollar contract by Beauty Products, Inc. (can you believe it?). [Notice that another punctuation mark must be used to end the complete sentence.]
Have you ever been a patient in the hospital (I hope not)?

When both the complete sentence and the parenthetical material are questions, only one mark is used–outside the parentheses:

Will you tell the lieutenant the truth now (or will you lie)?

3. Unnecessary question marks. a. A question mark is not used after indirect questions or polite requests that are phrased as questions:

Clarice asked Giuseppe if he would be able to attend the fair.
Will you please call the plumber while I'm out.

b. A question mark in parentheses used to indicate sarcasm or irony is a weak, amateurish device and is better omitted:

My brave little cousin had to be brought home early from the Cub Scout campout; he was afraid of the dark. [Not: My brave (?) little cousin.]

Quotation marks (" ")

1. Quotation marks are used to enclose the exact words of a speaker:

"Why aren't you wearing your new western boots?" I asked Alex.

"Well," he replied, "because I returned them."

I was amazed. "But we all agreed they were the best-looking, best-made boots we'd ever seen," I said.

"True," he remarked as he opened the box he was carrying. "In fact, they were so good-looking that you and Manny and Rick and Marv whizzed down and bought boots just like them. So I returned them and got these for hiking instead."

"Alex," I mused, having a brainstorm, "I think these new boots of yours are even better looking than the western ones!"

a. Notice that introductory and explanatory expressions (*he replied, I said*) are set off by a comma, or, if they interrupt the quoted sentence, by two commas. If a quoted sentence ends with a question mark or an exclamation point, though, that mark alone serves; no comma is added.

b. All sentences belonging to one uninterrupted quotation are put in one set of quotation marks. (See paragraph four of the preceding example.)

c. Periods and commas are always put inside the closing quotation marks:

As we entered, Lorna beamed, "I appreciate your arriving early."
Leon offered, "I'll fix the handle of your racquet," as he reached for the tape.

d. Semicolons are always put just outside the closing quotation marks:

When asked, Cleo said, "No"; consequently, she wasn't on the committee.

e. A question mark or an exclamation point is put inside the quotation marks if it applies only to the quoted matter, outside if it applies to the complete sentence that contains the quotation:

Clutching his quarter, the little boy asked, "How much is a hot dog?"
Beating the door, the woman howled, "I've been robbed!"
Hasn't Mr. Greeves said, "Let sleeping dogs lie"?
Watch out if Andy whispers, "Fire drill"!

When both the sentence and the quotation ending the sentence are questions or exclamations, only one mark is used–inside the closing quotation marks:

Weren't you there when Phil asked, "What's up?"
Let's all jump when Chris shouts, "Now!"

f. A new paragraph is generally used for each change of speaker, as in the example conversation at the beginning of this article. But when short bits of conversation are given to illustrate a point, rather than for their own sake, they may be put together in one paragraph:

Robert Benchley, the American humorist, is famous for being as funny in everyday life as he was in print. For example, though he had a reputation as a big tipper, he once received less than adequate service at a Paris hotel. As Benchley was leaving, the hotel doorman for the first time opened a taxi door for him and, with hand extended expectantly, smiled, "You're not going to forget me, sir?" "No," said Benchley soberly, clasping his hand and shaking it heartily. "I'll write you every day."

When a quoted passage is made up of more than one paragraph, opening quotation marks are put at the beginning of each paragraph, but closing marks are put only at the end of the last paragraph.

2. Quotation marks are used to enclose any direct quotation from another writer. Before such quotations, which are not part of a conversation, a colon rather than a comma is generally used, especially if the quotation is more than one sentence:

Mark Twain and his boyhood friends were envious when one of their number ran away from home to become an apprentice on a steamboat: "If ever a youth was cordially admired and hated by his comrades, this one was. No girl could withstand his charms. He 'cut out' every boy in the village. When his boat blew up at last, it diffused a tranquil contentment among us such as we had not known for months. But when he came home the next week, alive, renowned, and appeared in church all battered up and bandaged, a shining hero, stared at and wondered over by everybody, it seemed to us that the partiality of Providence for an undeserving reptile had reached a point where it was open to criticism." —Mark Twain. *Life on the Mississippi.*

A very long quoted passage is often presented without quotation marks, especially in typed and printed material. Then the whole passage is indented; in typed matter it is single-spaced, and in printed matter it is often set in smaller type than the rest of the text.

3. Quotation marks are generally used to enclose titles of chapters of books, magazine articles, essays, short stories, short poems, and songs:

Hardy's short story "The Grave by the Handpost" is from a book entitled *The Waiting Supper and Other Tales.*
Can you whistle a few bars of "Greensleeves"?

(See **Titles of books, articles, etc.**)

4. Quotation marks may be used to call the reader's attention to words that the writer is defining or explaining, and to special or technical terms that may be new to the reader:

"Quicksilver" is another term for the metal mercury.

In geology, a "hogback" is a low, sharp ridge with steep sides.
In this report, the word "ton" will refer to the 2,240-pound long ton.

(Many writers prefer to italicize such words. See **Underlining.**)

5. Use single quotation marks for a quotation within a quotation:

"But someone yelled 'Fire!' " Maureen protested.
"I love it when Sidney Carton says 'It is a far, far better thing I do,' " said Nanette.
"Oh, Leroy said 'I will volunteer' all right," said Felicia, "but no one heard him."

6. Unnecessary quotation marks. a. Quotation marks are not used to enclose *indirect* quotations:

Ms. Klein announced that the report group had come to an impasse. [Not: Ms. Klein announced that "The report group had come to an impasse."]

However, even when you are reporting someone's speech indirectly, you may want to emphasize the fact that certain of the words you use are the exact words spoken; then you may put those words in quotation marks. If you have no particular reason for emphasizing that they are the exact words, there is no need to use quotation marks.

Like Thoreau, he never discovered "the companion that was so companionable as solitude."
Most of his conversation consisted of two words–either "yep" or "nope." [If the quotation marks were omitted here, these words would be italicized. See **Underlining,** section 2.]

b. It is rarely a good idea to enclose in quotation marks words or phrases that seem a little informal or slangy for the context. If a word is appropriate, using it requires no apology; if it isn't appropriate, it should not be used at all:

The new popcorn machine is a real "rip-off." [Omit the quotation marks; the phrase is perfectly appropriate in this informal context.]
Altogether it behooves our government leaders to "take the bull by the horns" and pass effective legislation. ["Take the bull by the horns" is inappropriate in this formal context. Either substitute a phrase such as *take command*, or rewrite the sentence.]

c. The use of quotation marks to indicate sarcasm or irony is a weak and amateurish device and should be avoided:

Mabelle's poor old aunt has a villa in Cannes and a chauffeur for her Rolls Royce. [Not: Mabelle's "poor" old aunt.]

R

radio

The verb and noun forms are regular: *radioed, radioing, radios, radio's.*

raise

See **rise, raise.**

re-

Words made with the prefix *re-*, meaning "again," are usually written as solid—or single—words: *refreeze, rehabilitate, reorganize.* But the prefix is hyphened: (1) When the form without the hyphen has a different meaning:

react too quickly	re-act the part of Hamlet
reform a criminal	re-form your opinions
restore stolen property	re-store the supplies
resolve to do better	re-solve the problem

(2) When the prefix is to be especially emphasized:

I've re-written this paragraph five times, but it still isn't right.

Usage varies when the part following *re-* begins with an *e*. Such words are sometimes hyphened or written with a dieresis (*re-employ, reëmploy; re-explain, reëxplain*), but it is becoming more common to write them as solid words (*reemploy, reexplain*).

Readers' Guide

One of the best sources of information on subjects of current interest is magazine articles. A valuable help in finding the articles quickly and easily is the *Readers' Guide to Periodical Literature.* The *Guide* is an index of all articles, stories, and poems that have appeared in over a hundred magazines. The articles are listed alphabetically, both by subject and by author. Here is a typical subject entry:

DEER
Big ones are back! B. Vogt. il map Nat Wild-life 16:4-13 O '78
Deer: farmers' friend or foe? D. J. Decker and T. L. Brown. il Conservationist 33:27-9 Ja '79
Saga of the toy deer; National Key Deer Refuge. H. Ryden. il Audubon 80:92-103 N '78
Short ungulates. G. C. Whittow. il Natur Hist 87:44-9 bibl(p 111) My '78
View from the castle; Père David's deer. S. D. Ripley. Smithsonian 9:6 Ag '78
Whitetail truths. J. Weiss. il Outdoor Life 162: 68-75+ S '78
See also
Caribou
Elk

A key at the front of the *Guide* explains the abbreviations and symbols that are used. The first item under the subject "Deer," for example, means that the article "Big Ones Are Back!" by B. Vogt, appears in Volume 16 of *National Wildlife.* The article appears on pages 4 through 13 of the October 1978 issue and contains both illustrations and a map. The last article listed, by J. Weiss, is illustrated and appears in Volume 162 of *Outdoor Life*, on pages 68 through 75 of the September 1978 issue. The + sign after the page numbers means that the article is continued on later pages of the same issue. After *See also* is a list of subjects under which additional articles related to the subject "Deer" can be found.

The author entry for Hope Ryden, who wrote the third article listed, looks like this:

RYDEN, Hope
Saga of the toy deer. il Audubon 80:92-103 N '78

Readers' Guide is always up to date, since it is issued not only in hardbound volumes covering a one-year period, but also in paper-bound supplements indexing articles in the latest magazines. If the article you want or need is a recent one, look in the latest supplement. If you need other material, look in the hardbound cumulative volume.

real, really

In formal English and informal writing *real* is used only as an adjective, and *really* as an adverb:

Can you determine which is the real Lautrec painting?
Kim's acting is really professional.

In colloquial usage *real* is often used as an adverb meaning "very," but this use is not appropriate in writing:

COLLOQUIAL: Everyone was real happy when the winner was announced.
WRITTEN: Everyone was very happy when the winner was announced. [Or: Everyone really was happy when the winner was announced.]

reason is because

In formal English the expression "the reason is" is followed by a noun or a noun clause beginning with *that*:

The reason Mimi is no longer a dancer is her ill *health.* [Noun.]
The reason Mimi is no longer a dancer is *that she has ill health.* [Noun clause.]

Note that a smoother sentence results when the phrase "the reason" is omitted entirely:

Mimi is no longer a dancer because of her ill health.
Mimi is no longer a dancer because she has ill health.

In informal speech and frequently in informal writing many people use the more natural connective *because* with "the reason is" because this connective more obviously stresses the idea of reason:

The reason Mimi is no longer a dancer is *because of her ill health.*
The reason Mimi is no longer a dancer is *because she has ill health.*

Reasoning

See **Fallacies in reasoning.**

reckon

A localism for *think* or *suppose*:

LOCALISM: I reckon I should have read the assignment.
GENERAL: I suppose I should have read the assignment.

Redundancy

The use of unnecessary words, especially of words that repeat an idea expressed elsewhere in the sentence:

Then the conductor [he] took our tickets.
We were to arrive at 9:30 A.M. Saturday [morning].
The telescope will track the comet as it ascends [upwards] until it is no longer visible [to the eye].

refer back

Though *refer back* is commonly used, the *back* is unnecessary in most sentences:

To support his point, Monroe referred [back] to act 3, scene 3.

Reference books

Besides the encyclopedias, which supply background information on almost every subject, libraries have a number of other reference books that are useful for different purposes.

To find facts about important people, consult the following:

Who's Who (mainly contemporary British biographies)
Who's Who in America
Current Biography (annual volumes and monthly supplements)
Webster's Biographical Dictionary (people of all countries and times)
American Authors: 1600–1900 (by Kunitz and Haycraft)
Twentieth Century Authors (by Kunitz and Haycraft)
Contemporary Authors (a bio-bibliographical guide to current writers)

To find miscellaneous information, statistics, records, etc., look through one of these:

The World Almanac and Book of Facts
Information Please Almanac
Reader's Digest Almanac and Yearbook

To find maps, statistics, and other geographical information, see:

Goode's World Atlas
Rand McNally-Cosmopolitan World Atlas
Hammond's Ambassador World Atlas

Reference of pronouns

A pronoun has little specific meaning of its own; it gets its exact meaning from the word or words to which it refers (its antecedent). Therefore, if you are to make your intended meaning clear, the reference of the pronouns you use must be clear.

1. When the antecedent of a pronoun is not definitely stated, the reference is said to be *vague.* Correct a vague pronoun reference by replacing the pronoun with a noun:

NO ANTECEDENT: Nick liked to read about horseback riding, although he had never been on *one.*

CLEAR: Nick liked to read about riding, although he had never been on a *horse.*

If the antecedent is "hidden"—that is, if it is a noun used as a modifier or as a possessive—the reference will also be vague and perhaps confusing:

CONFUSING: As a tailor, Freida specialized in suit construction, but she seldom made *them* for herself.

CLEAR: As a tailor, Freida specialized in suit construction, but she seldom made *suits* for herself.

CONFUSING: The rejections were a blow to the young writer's ego, who had thought he'd written a best seller.

CLEAR: The rejections were a blow to the ego of the young writer, who had thought he'd written a best seller.

Pronouns such as *which*, *this*, and *that* are sometimes used to refer to a group of words or a whole idea rather than to a single noun antecedent:

Mr. Nevins sang well, *which* made him popular with the senior choir.

But if there is in the sentence any single noun to which the pronoun might seem to refer, the sentence should be revised to make the intended meaning clear:

CONFUSING: Dora Feldman consulted a palm reader about her will, *which* her relatives disapproved of.

CLEAR: Dora Feldman's relatives disapproved of her consulting a palm reader about her will.

2. The use of *it* and *they* without a definite antecedent is common in everyday speech. But in writing, the *indefinite* use of these pronouns should be avoided:

FAULTY: In *Huckleberry Finn it* tells about a boy and a runaway slave on a raft drifting down the Mississippi River.

BETTER: *Huckleberry Finn* tells about a boy and a runaway slave on a raft drifting down the Mississippi River.

FAULTY: Since school enrollment has been decreasing, *they* need fewer teachers now than ten years ago.

BETTER: Since school enrollment has been decreasing, fewer teachers are needed now than ten years ago.

3. Sometimes a pronoun is placed so that it might refer to either of two antecedents. You can correct *ambiguous* pronoun references (a) by replacing the pronoun with a noun; (b) by moving the pronoun closer to the intended antecedent; or (c) by rephrasing the sentence:

CONFUSING: The partnership of Chef Maurier and Monsieur Timbale ended in July, when *he* left to open his own restaurant.

CLEAR: The partnership of Chef Maurier and Monsieur Timbale ended in July, when *Timbale* left to open his own restaurant.

CONFUSING: Mrs. Miranda forgot to call Ms. Shell when *she* was in Seattle.

CLEAR: When *she* was in Seattle, Mrs. Miranda forgot to call Ms. Shell. [Or: When Ms. Shell was in Seattle, Mrs. Miranda forgot to call *her*.]

CONFUSING: Craig decided not to go to the party with Angelo, because *he* had a bad cold.

CLEAR: Craig, *who* had a bad cold, decided not to go to the party with Angelo.

A sentence that contains two or more pronouns referring to different antecedents may also be ambiguous. Often the only way the ambiguity can be removed is by rewriting the sentence:

CONFUSING: Moira Finnigan heartily disliked Rita O'Laughlin even though *she* always treated *her* fairly.

CLEAR: Although Rita O'Laughlin always treated her fairly, Moira Finnigan heartily disliked her. [Or, if the other meaning is intended: Moira Finnigan heartily disliked Rita O'Laughlin but always treated her fairly.]

Referent

The meaning of any word lies in what the word stands for—or "refers" to. Whatever person or thing the word refers to is called its *referent* /ref′ər ənt/ or /ri fėr′ənt/.

Reflexive pronouns

Pronouns with the ending *self* or *selves*: *myself, yourself, himself, herself, itself, oneself, ourselves, yourselves, themselves*. They are called *reflexive pronouns* because the action of the verb is turned back on the subject:

They weighed *themselves.* [Direct object.]
Gary scrambled *himself* some eggs. [Indirect object.]
I was furious with *myself.* [Object of preposition.]

The forms *hisself, ourself, theirself,* and *theirselves* are nonstandard. (For a discussion of usage, see **myself.**)

regard, regards

The standard idioms are *in regard to* and *with regard to* ("In regard to your request, we are sending you our new catalog and our revised price list"). In nonstandard English *in regards to* and *with regards to* are often used ("In regards to your question").

regardless

The ending *-less* gives *regardless* a negative meaning: "without regard to." Adding the prefix *ir-* —*irregardless*—makes a double negative. Though *irregardless* is often heard, it is not considered good usage and should be avoided in writing:

STANDARD: Senator Wilson will abstain regardless of her party's wishes.

In colloquial usage *regardless* is used as an adverb meaning "anyway" or "no matter what": You be at the family gathering tomorrow, *regardless.*

Relative adverb

When an adverb like *where, when, why, since,* or *after* is used to introduce an adjective clause, it is called a *relative adverb*:

The inn *where* we recuperated is high in the Swiss Alps.
He arrived at the airport five minutes *after* her plane had left.

Relative clause

Since adjective clauses are usually introduced by a relative pronoun (*who, which, that*) or a relative adverb (*where, when, why, after*) that refers, or "relates," to an antecedent, they are often called *relative clauses.* For example:

I can even remember the coat *that you tried on at Harrod's.* [Modifies the antecedent *coat.*]
Do you remember the morning *when we first saw the Cathedral of Notre Dame*? [Modifies the antecedent *morning.*]

A succession of relative clauses in one sentence is likely to be awkward. In revising first drafts, watch out for sentences that follow a "house that Jack built" pattern:

AWKWARD: The money bags that were discovered in a well that is on a farm that is near the old house that is supposed to be haunted were part of a shipment that was stolen last month from an armored truck.

BETTER: The money bags discovered in a well on a farm near the old house that is supposed to be haunted were part of a shipment stolen last month from an armored truck.

(For punctuation of relative clauses, see **Comma,** section 5.)

Relative pronouns

The pronouns *who, whose, whom, which,* and *that*—used in introducing adjective clauses. Ordinarily *who* is used to refer to persons, *which* to refer to things, and *that* to refer to persons or things:

Anyone *who* (or *that*) wants to be a good French horn player must practice regularly.
The pages *that* (or *which*) the scholar pored over were mottled and crumbling.

remember

Standard English does not use *of* after the verb *remember*:

NONSTANDARD: I don't remember of reading that.
STANDARD: I don't remember reading that.

Repetition

Intentionally repeating a word, a thought, or a sound is often an effective way to gain emphasis in speech or writing. For example, repeating prepositions, possessive adjectives, or articles before the various nouns in a series can help to emphasize each noun's distinctiveness:

WITHOUT REPETITION	EFFECTIVE REPETITION
As a result of the hurricane, the families lost their cars, furniture, houses, and hope.	As a result of the hurricane, the families lost their cars, their furniture, their houses, and their hope.

Similarly, the intentional repetition of key words can help to suggest emotion or strong feeling:

We shall fight on the beaches, landing grounds, fields, streets, and hills, and never surrender.	We shall fight on the beaches, we shall fight on the landing grounds, we shall fight in the fields and in the streets, we shall fight in the hills; we shall never surrender. –Sir Winston Churchill, Speech on Dunkirk, House of Commons, June 4, 1940.

But repetition that serves no purpose, that occurs mainly because of carelessness or haste, is likely to be distracting and annoying to readers. Make it a point to remove distracting repetitions when revising your papers.

Reports

Business, technical, and official reports should be impersonal and businesslike in tone. They should be complete, of course, but also as concise as possible. When you are writing such reports, go straight to the point. Set down all facts, opinions, and recommendations briefly and clearly. Be sure also to distinguish between facts and opinions. Wherever you express a personal opinion, make clear that it is one, and back up your judgment with sound reasons.

Mechanical devices–like putting information into the form of tables, diagrams, graphs; and listing, labeling, or numbering ideas or steps–are often useful. This is especially true in committee reports, where the ideas of several people have to be combined into a clear, concise piece of writing. Look at the following example:

REPORT OF THE COMMITTEE
ON IMPROVING
SCHOOL-BUS SERVICE

Date: October 15, 19--

To: Dunbar High School Student Council

Subject: Ways to provide adequate and prompt school-bus service.

This report was requested by the Student Council following complaints from students and parents about the overcrowding on some of the buses and the frequent lateness of most of the buses.

Our committee was appointed by the Council president on September 15, 19--.

Procedure: The committee investigated the situation and conferred with Mr. Felix Kerl, assistant superintendent and director of school services; Mrs. Loretta Matz, principal of Dunbar High School; Mr. Harvey Zeller, assistant principal of Burnside Junior High School; and Mrs. Marvin Grorby, PTA representative.

Recommendations: The recommendations of the committee are as follows:

1. New bus routes should be worked out so that no bus will carry more students than it can seat. Mr. Kerl agrees, and his staff is already working on new routes and schedules.

2. Dunbar and Burnside students should insofar as possible be assigned to separate buses so that a bus will not need to make two school stops, which lengthens each run by at least fifteen minutes, and so that the bus schedules can conform better to the different opening and closing times of the two schools. Mr. Kerl, Mrs. Matz, and Mr. Zeller will support this request.

3. Classes going on field trips should not use school buses if they will not return to school by 2:45 p.m., in time for the buses to begin their regular afternoon runs. Classes going on field trips that extend beyond school hours should apply to the PTA Enrichment Program for funds to charter a bus. Mrs. Matz and Mrs. Grorby concur and will help work out the necessary procedures.

4. The Student Council should help relieve congestion at the afternoon departure time by working out an assigned place for each bus to load and by providing signs identifying the buses.

The committee urges the Council to accept these recommendations and take action at once.

Respectfully submitted,

Eloise Johnson, Chairwoman
Raymond Neidlinger
Richard E. Moose
Carolyne Robinson

Research paper

A report that incorporates the writer's findings and thoughts about a subject. The writer narrows the subject to a manageable size for a 1,500 to 3,000 word paper. He or she then makes a systematic investigation of the subject, relying primarily on books and magazine articles, but occasionally using personal interviews or television programs as sources of information. Refer to the Appendix for more information.

resign

Usually followed by *from*, though sometimes immediately by the object:

A strong clash of personalities caused Ruth Stephens to resign from the design committee. [Or: to resign the design committee.]

Resolution

A formal statement of opinion adopted by a committee, club, or other organization. It is used typically for group expressions of sympathy, thanks, and so on, and for recommendations of action. The style is formal and impersonal, and the wording is standardized:

WHEREAS, The Student Council of George Washington High School has been sponsored for the past nine years by Miss Sophie Wetzel; and

WHEREAS, The Council is aware of and grateful for her devotion and for her efforts on its behalf; and

WHEREAS, The Council has been informed of her plans to retire at the end of the current semester, therefore be it

Resolved, That a special committee be formed to draw up plans for a suitable farewell party and an appropriate gift for Miss Wetzel; and be it further

Resolved, That the committee be instructed to report its recommendations at the next scheduled meeting of this Council.

James M. Martin, Secretary

Restrictive and nonrestrictive

A *restrictive* modifier–one that is used to tell which particular person or thing is meant–is not set off by commas from the word it modifies:

Someone *in the jewelry department* was singing.
The man *wearing the toupee* is a television star.
The paintings *stolen from the museum* were returned.
The one food *that I can't eat* is strawberries.
Fritz is the only tour guide *who speaks both German and English.*
Was that the night *when the mirror cracked?*

But a *nonrestrictive* modifier–which is used merely to add a descriptive or explanatory detail–is set off from the word it modifies:

We found Gus at his favorite haunt, *in the jewelry department.*
Ricardo, *wearing the toupee,* was a real scene-stealer.
Dairy products, *which I can't eat,* are used in many recipes.
Marilyn, *who speaks both German and English,* was a popular guide with tourists in the Black Forest.
Was that the only time you were frozen with fear, *when the mirror cracked?*

Adverb clauses that tell the particular time, place, reason, purpose, manner, condition, etc., are *restrictive* and are not set off:

We had to leave the reception *before the band arrived.*
Hilary parked the car *where she thought we'd be sure to find it.*
I'm having my hair cut *because I can't do a thing with it.*
They ran through the routine once again *so that the new model could learn it.*
Sally acts *as if she understands contemporary art.*
Charles said to call *if we needed help with the antenna.*
Findlay was so well bandaged *that he looked like an Egyptian mummy.*

Adverb clauses that merely add explanatory details or comments (which could be omitted without changing the basic meaning of the sentence) are *nonrestrictive* and should be set off from the rest of the sentence:

They left right after the dinner, *before the band arrived.*
Hilary had parked the car next to the exit, *where we couldn't miss seeing it.*
I'm having Mr. Jay cut my hair, *because he's faster than Anita.*
Nell seemed preoccupied, *as if she hadn't expected us.*
Counselor Harmon is pleading the case, *though she usually prefers to do the briefs.*
I intend to get a dog, *whether you like it or not.*

(For further discussion and examples, see **Comma,** section 5; **Dash,** section 3; and **Parentheses,** sections 1 and 4.)

Reverend

A term of respect for members of the clergy. In formal English it is preceded by *the*, and must be followed by the first name, initials, or title of the person as well as his last name:

the Reverend John Norris	the Rev. John Norris
the Reverend J. C. Norris	the Rev. John C. Norris
the Reverend Mr. Norris	the Rev. Dr. Norris

In informal English *Reverend* is sometimes used with only the last name:

Reverend Norris	the Reverend Norris

The use of *reverend* as a noun meaning "a member of the clergy" (The reverend will sit to the left of the bride's mother) is increasingly found in informal English.

Revision

It is a good idea to allow a little time to elapse before going over the first draft of any work; you can generally be much more objective about your writing if you take a short rest from it. Then, when you do come back to the paper, start by reading it straight through without stopping.

It is at this point you might decide that, except for correcting a few misspellings and deleting one or two commas, the writing requires no further work. It is finished. If there are any doubts about this decision, you might get a second opinion by reading your work to someone whose judgment you trust. If that person approves your writing, your job is over.

More often, however, as you read your writing through, your eye will fall on spots that you decide could be improved with minor revision. Once in a great while you may decide that a fairly major change is in order–switching two sections, for example, or dropping a section, or shifting emphasis.

Asking questions like the following ones can help you evaluate your work:

Questions about writing:
Is the opening paragraph likely to catch the readers' interest?
Are the sentences smoothly linked so that the reader can move effortlessly from beginning to end without a break?
Are there any awkward sentences?
Is any of the writing wordy? Are there words and phrases that can be deleted? Are there places where one word could be substituted for two or more?
Have specific, picture-making words been used wherever possible and appropriate?
Does the closing paragraph give a note of finality without seeming tacked on?

Questions about mechanics:
Are there any mistakes in grammar, sentence structure, usage?
Are there any errors in spelling, punctuation, capitalization?

After completing a research paper or other longer composition, you may wish to consider the following questions:

Questions about structure:
Do the ideas presented follow one another logically in view of the controlling purpose?

Have readers been told first the things they should know first?
Has appropriate emphasis been given to various topics, making clear by their position and by the amount of space allotted to them which are more and which less important?

Questions about content:
Is the controlling purpose clear?
Have I included enough material to make my controlling purpose clear and the body of my paper interesting, clear, and convincing, or are there some thin spots?
Is all the material relevant; that is, does every paragraph in the paper help explain or illustrate or develop the controlling purpose?
Is any of the material irrelevant?
Are all special and technical terms explained?
Does the paper ever seem to assume knowledge on the part of readers that they might not actually have?
Has the factual information all been checked for accuracy?

(See also individual entries such as **Agreement, Balanced sentences, Parallel constructions,** and **Run-on sentence.**)

Rhetoric

Rhetoric is sometimes used as a disparaging term for inflated, wordy, insincere speech or writing. But used by linguists, the term refers to the study and practice of the effective use of language. It deals with the selection of those words and constructions that will most clearly and effectively convey a writer's or speaker's meaning on a particular subject, to a particular audience, for a particular purpose.

Rhetorical question

A question asked only for effect–usually to emphasize a point, to suggest an opinion, or to introduce a topic. No direct answer is expected (since it is, of course, obvious):

Everyone agrees that the inflationary trend of our economy must be halted. And almost everyone seems to have a theory about how to do it. Economists make frequent, and often conflicting, suggestions. Members of Congress make speeches, urging each other to endorse numerous, and often conflicting, measures. Editorial writers use tons of print offering their solutions. But how much has actually been done to turn the economy around?

rise, raise

Rise (*rose, risen*) is intransitive and does not take an object; *raise* (*raised, raised*) is transitive and takes an object:

The rate of inflation *is rising* rapidly.
Donna, did you *raise* your hand?
The sun *rises* in the east.
The question you *have raised* is an interesting one, Jim.

Root

A word or part of a word that is used as a base for forming other words, as *new* is the root of *renew, newly*; *ject* is the root of *reject, object, projectile, injection.*

round

See **around, round.**

route

Generally pronounced /rüt/ (rhymes with *suit*), but /rout/ (rhymes with *trout*) is used in the army and for newspaper and delivery routes.

Run-on sentence

When you put two independent statements into one sentence, you ordinarily join them with a conjunction and a comma or separate them with a semicolon. If you use a comma alone between the clauses, you have a comma splice; if you use no punctuation, you have a run-on sentence. There are four ways in which a run-on sentence can be corrected:

1. Repunctuate with a period:

RUN-ON: John and Linda are buying furniture now they're getting married in March.

REVISED: John and Linda are buying furniture now. They're getting married in March.

2. Repunctuate with a semicolon:

RUN-ON: It's funny that Manuel can't carry a tune his father was once in the Metropolitan Opera chorus.

REVISED: It's funny that Manuel can't carry a tune; his father was once in the Metropolitan Opera chorus.

3. Insert a coordinating conjunction (*and, but, for, or, nor, yet*) to make a compound sentence:

RUN-ON: John D. Blair used to enjoy taking long trips he doesn't anymore.

REVISED: John D. Blair used to enjoy taking long trips, but he doesn't anymore.

4. Rephrase the run-on, using a subordinate conjunction or a verbal phrase to show the exact relationship between the ideas:

RUN-ON: The throng crowded around the rider and horse they had just won the Kentucky Derby.

REVISED: The throng crowded around the rider and horse, who had just won the Kentucky Derby.

REVISED: The throng crowded around the rider and horse because they had just won the Kentucky Derby.

RUN-ON: Professional dancing demands much of aspiring dancers this includes talent, hard work, and determination.

REVISED: Professional dancing demands much of aspiring dancers, including talent, hard work, and determination.

saint

Saint is abbreviated with proper names (*St. Anthony, St. Jude*). The plural *saints* is abbreviated *SS.* or *Sts.* (*SS. Stephen and James, Sts. Gregory and Basil*). Sometimes the French feminine form *sainte* is used (*Sainte Jeanne d'Arc*) with the abbreviation *Ste.*

same

Same as a pronoun is no longer used in such business expressions as "Please send us your check for same." Current usage prefers *it* or *them*:

Please complete the enclosed application, and return *it* by Thursday. [Not: return *same.*]

Sarcasm

A remark made with the intention of hurting someone's feelings by taunting, ridiculing, mocking, or sneering at them. Sarcastic remarks are often ironical (saying one thing but meaning another):

"Well," said the master chef after the nervous young student had finally produced a tray of rolls that were not burned, "you're quite a Julia Child, aren't you?"

But sarcasm may also be direct:

"Why certainly, Mr. Peabody," the barber snapped sarcastically at his crotchety customer. "I'll be happy to cut your hair. Which one?"

Since sarcasm is often indicated by the tone of the voice, it sometimes passes unnoticed in writing. In dialogue, if it is not unmistakably indicated by the context, writers often label it, as in the second example. But usually the sarcasm is obvious. (See also **Irony.**)

Satire

The use of ridicule, irony, or sarcasm to make fun of a person, a custom, an idea, or an institution. This "fun-making" may be harmless, intended only to amuse the reader or listener, or it may be a bitter attack intended to discredit by ridicule the person or thing at which it is aimed. It may be concerned with a trivial and laughter-provoking subject, such as the latest in wearing apparel for dogs; or it may expose the weaknesses of the social and political customs and policies of a nation.

say, state, talk

Say is a general word for speaking: The guide *said* that the volcano is dormant. *State* implies a more formal, orderly communication: Dr. Gilbert *stated* her reasons for declining the nomination. *Talk* implies conversation, especially of an informal kind: Everyone at the snack shop *was talking* about Bob's getting a tryout with the Bruins. (For the use of *say* in reporting conversation, see **Conversation.**)

scarcely

See **Double negative.**

scarcely . . . when

The idiom is *scarcely . . . when*, not *scarcely . . . than*:

The movie audience had *scarcely* recovered from the monster's first appearance *when* he leaped out at the hero again.

School subjects

The name of a school or college course is not capitalized unless it is the name of a language or of a specifically numbered course:

You should have taken Latin instead of botany.
Only ten students are enrolled in Physics 3.

Schwa (ə)

The *schwa* /shwä/ is the symbol used in this book and in many recent dictionaries to simplify the system of showing pronunciation: *aroma*—/ə rō′mə/, *seller*—/sel′ər/. The schwa represents the neutral vowel sound of many unstressed syllables:

a as in *about* *i* as in *pencil* *u* as in *circus*
e as in *taken* *o* as in *lemon*

Seasons

The names of the seasons—*spring*, *summer*, *fall*, *winter*, *midsummer*, and so on—are not capitalized except for emphasis in some poetry or nature essays.

secretive

There are two different words with this spelling: one derived from the word *SEcret* and generally pronounced /sē′krə tiv/; another derived from the word *seCRETE* and always pronounced /si krē′tiv/.

seem

Can't seem is a useful informal idiom for the more formal and logical *seem unable*:

INFORMAL: Gloria can't seem to remember her lines.
FORMAL: Gloria seems unable to remember her lines.

self

As a prefix *self-* is usually hyphenated to the root word:

self-control   self-preservation
self-evident   self-pity

But there is no hyphen in words like *selfish* and *selfless*, in which *self* is the root to which the endings *-ish* and *-less* have been added.

For the use of pronouns ending in *self* (*myself, yourself, himself,* etc.), see **Intensive pronouns** and **Reflexive pronouns.**

Semantics

The scientific study of the meanings of words and the relationship between language and thinking.

semi-

Prefix meaning "half" (*semitone*), "occurring twice within a certain period" (*semiyearly*), or "partially" (*semiconscious*). Before proper nouns or words that begin with an *i*, a hyphen is used: *semi-Romanized, semi-industrial.*

Semicolon

1. A semicolon is used to separate the clauses of a compound sentence when they are not joined by a coordinating conjunction (*and, but, for, or, nor, yet*):

I can't get this stain out; you will have to buy another shirt.
That card is too sentimental; take a look at this one.

Remember that connectives like *then, still, however, moreover, nevertheless, consequently* are not coordinating conjunctions but conjunctive adverbs. Main clauses joined by these adverbs are separated by a semicolon:

First write the outline; then you should have no trouble with the paper.
The restaurant owner hated to drop clams from his menu; however, the red tide made it imperative.

2. A semicolon is often used (instead of a comma) between main clauses joined by *and, but,* etc., if either clause contains a comma:

Barrant H. Sweet, chairman of the fund-raising drive, has announced this year's financial goals; Dale Heid, last year's chairman, has agreed to serve as business advisor.
Ms. Danielson, the firm's oldest lawyer, can be difficult to please; but Bob Watkins, her paralegal assistant, insists that she is a wonderful boss.

3. A semicolon is used (instead of a comma) between items of a series if the items contain commas:

In five days, the fast-traveling tourists saw London, England; Edinburgh, Scotland; and Copenhagen, Denmark.
The panel of judges included: Ms. Sandra Ferguson, president of Pivots Unlimited Model Agency; Mr. John E. Pichel, merchandising head of Wil-

son, Fleary and Cott department stores; and Dr. Edith M. Toohey, curator of costumes and textiles at the Institute of Applied Arts.

Sentence fragment

A piece of a sentence that has been detached from the sentence to which it belongs and punctuated as a separate sentence:

FRAGMENT: I spent ten minutes looking for my glasses. *Forgetting that they were perched on top of my head.* [Participial phrase.]

A sentence fragment can easily be corrected by joining it to the sentence it was cut off from:

CORRECTED: I spent ten minutes looking for my glasses, forgetting that they were perched on top of my head.

Here are some other common fragments:

FRAGMENT: The store refused to take back the skirt. *Because the zipper was now broken.* [Adverb clause.]
CORRECTED: The store refused to take back the skirt, because the zipper was now broken.

FRAGMENT: This pair of boots is just the thing for my sister. *Who loves handsome footwear.* [Adjective clause.]
CORRECTED: This pair of boots is just the thing for my sister, who loves handsome footwear.

FRAGMENT: Tomorrow I'm going to the movies with Anne-Marie. *Our exchange student from Belgium.* [Appositive.]
CORRECTED: Tomorrow I'm going to the movies with Anne-Marie, our exchange student from Belgium.

FRAGMENT: Paul and his family spent the summer in Maine. *And never tried eating lobster or steamed clams.* [Part of a compound verb.]
CORRECTED: Paul and his family spent the summer in Maine and never tried eating lobster or steamed clams.

(Compare **Sentences: major and minor types,** section 2.)

Sentences: classifications

English sentences can be sorted, or "classified," in several different ways. Here we will review three common ones:

1. By pattern. Sentences can be classified by their basic patterns. Most English sentences are built on just a few basic patterns:

a. SUBJECT—VERB [S—V]:

The leaves fell. It will probably storm.
Claudia skipped quickly up the steps.

b. SUBJECT—VERB—OBJECT [S—V—O]:

She taught physics. He had lost his shoe.

c. SUBJECT—VERB—INDIRECT OBJECT—OBJECT [S—V—IO—O]:

Beth told me a secret.
The pianist flashed the audience a pleased smile.

d. SUBJECT—LINKING VERB—COMPLEMENT [S—LV—C]:

Chiyoko seems tired.
Shōgun is a book about medieval Japan.

e. SUBJECT—VERB—OBJECT—OBJECT COMPLEMENT [S—V—O—OC]:

I painted the background dark green.
The supervisor, Mrs. Spencer, called him a dolt.

2. By number and kind of subject-verb units. Classified by this method, sentences fall into four groups:

a. *Simple sentences*—sentences containing only one subject and one verb—either or both of which may be compound:

The *horn* **sounded.**
The white *cat* and the gray *squirrel* **eyed** each other warily.
Dolores **knocked** on the door and **entered.**
Christine and *I* **baked** cookies, **steamed** a pudding, and **frosted** the cake.

b. *Compound sentences*—sentences made up of two or more main clauses (each could stand alone as a sentence). The clauses are joined either by a comma and a coordinating conjunction or by a semicolon:

Adam **nominated** Theresa Sabatini, and *I* **nominated** William P. Campbell.
The *stable* **advertised** riding lessons for beginners; otherwise, *I* **would** never **have ventured** out on horseback.

c. *Complex sentences*—sentences containing one main clause and one or more subordinate clauses:

Nadine took us to the antique shop *that she had discovered.*
We wondered too late *why the prices were so low.*
When the settee arrives, shall we show you the cracked rung *we found*?

d. *Compound-complex sentences*—sentences containing two or more main clauses and one or more subordinate clauses:

Ralph might have understood what you were getting at, but I didn't. [Two main clauses joined by *but* and one subordinate clause—*what you were getting at.*]

(See also **Clause** and the individual entries for the sentences in this classification.)

3. By purpose.

a. *Declarative sentences* are used to make statements:

Many jockeys weigh less than a hundred pounds.
On Tuesday the telephone seemed never to stop ringing.

b. *Imperative sentences* are used to express commands or requests:

Beware of the dog.
Pick me up at eight o'clock, please.

c. *Interrogative sentences* are used to ask questions:

What's playing at the Cinema tonight?
How long will this assignment take?

d. *Exclamatory sentences* are used to express strong feeling:

We won!
What a wonderful time we had at the party!
That boulder is rolling our way!

(For further examples, see the individual entries for the sentences in this classification.)

Sentences: major and minor types

Over the centuries that English has been a language it has developed a wide range of sentence patterns for communicating meaning. We express our thoughts, feelings, and ideas by putting words together in groups arranged according to these patterns. We do this without conscious effort, of course, since we learned the sentence patterns by imitation as we were growing up, and they are as much a part of us as our vocabulary.

Grammarians classify the sentence patterns in a number of different ways. One way is into *major* and *minor* types.

1. Major-type sentences. The sentence patterns most commonly used belong to the major type. They are sentences like these:

Cybil laughed.
Until last fall we went apple picking there every year.
Maestro Van Ghent is considered a leading interpreter of Mahler's symphonies.
Did Peter ever show her a piece of rock the astronauts brought from the moon?
Out slithered the snake, coiling and rattling its tail.
The Browns painted their cottage gray.
You finish your spinach, dear, or Popeye will be upset.[1]
How tall Malcolm has grown!
It isn't easy to work with some people, especially those as particular as Millicent Simpson.
If she can't find a dress for the dance, she will probably make or borrow one.
After sorting the china, Pablo folded linens and emptied the trash so that there would be little to do when the movers arrived.

These are representative samples of major-type sentences. As you can

---

[1] Usually the subject in a command or request is not expressed: "Finish your spinach, dear. . . ."

see, they differ from one another in several respects: The first, for example, has no modifiers; the last (a complex sentence) has many, including two adverb clauses. Some have a direct object. In addition, one has an indirect object and one an object complement. Others have a subject complement. One is a compound sentence with two coordinate clauses. One has a long appositive at the end, another a participial-phrase modifier. But all of them–long or short–are alike in one respect: All have a *subject* and a *verb.* These are the basic elements, the parts that serve as a framework to which all other parts are related.

2. Minor-type sentences. A common definition of a sentence is "a group of words that contains a subject and a verb and that is grammatically complete." Because the great majority of our sentences are of the major type, centered on a subject and a verb, this definition is a practical and useful guide–nine tenths of the time. But like many definitions that have been simplified for general use, it is not quite accurate, since it does not take into account many sentences that lack a subject or a verb or both, yet are perfectly good sentences. For example:

Easy come, easy go.
Cash or charge?
What an inexcusable way for him to behave!
Good luck!

There are two ways of explaining sentences that do not fit the usual definition. A common practice is to explain that the sentences are "elliptical"–that is, words necessary for grammatical completeness but not for meaning have been omitted. For instance, the answer to the question "Where is Mrs. Hanson?" might be "She is in the library." It is more likely to be simply "In the library"–since the subject *She* and the verb *is* are clearly understood. By supplying the understood words, you can make the elliptical sentence fit the usual definition.

Many modern grammarians prefer another explanation. They point out that though the typical English sentence has a subject and a verb, there are many sentences of a "minor" type, without these elements. Nothing, they explain, is left out of these sentences; and no words need be "understood" in analyzing them. They are natural forms of expression and just as "correct" as the major sentences, though of more limited use. Here are some of the common kinds of minor-type sentences. Notice that the first four groups are forms used primarily in speech and would usually appear in writing only to record conversation.

a. Exclamations and interjections:

Good night. Help! Ouch! Ah!
Happy New Year. Oh, no! What a beautiful dog!

b. Requests and commands:

More juice, please.
Ham with mustard on rye to go.
Quickly!
Your attention, please.

c. Specific answers to questions:

["When is curtain time?"] "At eight o'clock."
["What color is their springer spaniel?"] "Liver and white."
["How many head of cattle does he run?"] "About three hundred."
["Where is Mother?"] "In the den doing the income tax."

d. Questions:

["John wants to meet you."] "When?"
["We're having macaroni and cheese instead of spaghetti."] "Why?"

e. "Equational" sentences:

Win a few, lose a few.
Lucky at cards, unlucky at love.
Cold hands, warm heart.
Out of the frying pan, into the fire.

f. "Appositional" sentences (in which a subject complement is set beside the subject without a linking verb):

Beatrice a movie star? An amusing idea, that.

g. Transitional sentences (to bridge the gap between one part of a speech or composition and another):

So much for the plot. Now for the acting in the new play, *Run In Slowly.*

Notice that though the sentences differ greatly in form, they all have one thing in common–all are, in their contexts, independent units that stand alone to express the intended meaning.

Sequence of tenses

See **Tenses of verbs,** section 3.

Series

For the punctuation of items in a series, see **Comma,** section 3, and **Semicolon,** section 3.

set, sit

See **sit, set.**

shall, will

For many years the following two-part rule has been taught: To show simple future, use the auxiliary *shall* in the first person and *will* in the second and third (I shall apply for the job, You will swim in the first race, He will probably be the new editor). To show determination, reverse the pattern, using *will* in the first person and *shall* in the second and third (I will pass physics this time, You shall regret cheating me, He shall apologize for insulting my brother). But the rule, even though memorized by many, is rarely followed. Speakers of standard English generally use *will* in all persons to show both simple future and determination. *Shall* is seldom used except for special emphasis.

Shifted constructions

For examples of shifted (or nonparallel) constructions, see **Parallel constructions** and **Correlative conjunctions.**

Ships' names

In most books and generally in formal writing, the names of ships (aircraft, submarines) are capitalized and italicized (underlined in handwriting): the *Titanic* (ship), *Air Force One* (airplane), the *Triton* (submarine), the *Tinkerbelle* (sailboat). Use this style in your written work. The names of trains, however, are generally no longer italicized.

In some informal writing, especially in newspapers, such names are treated simply as proper names, capitalized but not italicized (or underlined): the Lusitania (ship), the Valkyrie (airplane), Apollo 10 (spaceship).

In all writing, names indicating the make and class of cars, planes, missiles, helicopters, and so on, are generally capitalized but not italicized: Pontiac Catalina (car), CF-104 Starfighter (plane), Minuteman (missile), Westland Scout (helicopter).

Shoptalk

Shoptalk is the special vocabulary used by people in a certain occupation. Stagehands, for example, use terms like *keystone*, *proscenium*, *dutchman*, *ratchet*, and *to size.* Electricians deal with *cathodes*, *resistance*, *circuits*, and *amps.* Hockey players talk about *icing the puck*, *stick handling*, *face-offs*, and *hat tricks.* Stockbrokers are concerned with *blue chips*, *quotations*, *payout ratios*, and *bull* and *bear markets.*

Shoptalk, then, consists of names for materials, processes, people, and tools in a special job. The names may be technical, like *trephine* in medicine or *parallax* in photography. More often they are clipped or made-up words, like *lip sync* in television, *blurb* in advertising, and *typo* and *cut* in printing.

Hobbies and other special interests of any kind involve shoptalk too. Ham radio operators use terms like *rig*, *transceiver*, and *patch*, and such expressions as *73* (meaning "regards"), *QSG* ("Have you a doctor nearby?"), and *Calling CQ* ("Does anybody anywhere feel like talking–about anything?"). Coin collectors discuss *galvanos*, *double-struck coins*, *cabinet pieces*, and *clad coinage.*

Sometimes shoptalk words move into the general vocabulary. In recent years, for instance, space flights and lunar landings have introduced many terms from the field of space exploration. People have been quick to take over such space shoptalk as *A-OK*, *go* ("All systems are go"), *to splash down*, and *to scrub*. And they are quite familiar with terms like *blastoff*, *countdown*, *launching pad*, *lunar module*, *docking*, and *EVA*.

But as a rule, shoptalk is not appropriate in speaking or writing that is intended for a general audience. To such a group it would be meaningless. Unless shoptalk is clearly defined, it is appropriate only for an audience familiar with the field in which it is used.

(See also **Jargon.**)

sic

Sic /sik, sēk/ (Latin for *thus*, *so*; underlined in handwriting) is used to show that a mistake has been copied exactly as it appeared in the original:

The topic for the education seminar was "Why Johnny Can't Speel [*sic*]."

similar to

A wordy way of saying *like*:

WORDY: Fashion-watchers say the new designer's style is similar to the great Balenciaga's.

BETTER: Fashion-watchers say the new designer's style is like the great Balenciaga's.

Simile

A figure of speech in which a comparison between two unlike things is introduced by *like* or *as*:

Those mussels taste like foam rubber.
I feel as low as a snake with fallen arches.

Simple sentence

A sentence that has only one subject and one verb, either or both of which may be compound, is called a *simple sentence*:

The duke bowed.
A year ago at this time, Jill Clark and I bicycled to the lake and picnicked on the shore at least twice a week.

(See also **Sentences: classifications,** section 2.)

sit, set

Sit (*sat*, *sat*, *sitting*) is generally intransitive and does not take an object; *set* (*set*, *set*, *setting*) is generally transitive and takes an object:

Was it you who *sat* in the meringue pie?
Why had Clara *set* it on the stoop?

But in certain constructions, *sit* takes an object and *set* does not:

Sit the baby in her carriage.
The sun *sets* before six o'clock now.
The red hens *are setting*, but the white ones refuse to.

situated

Often deadwood that should be pruned away in writing:

The municipal swimming pool is [situated] three blocks east of Harrison High.

(See **Deadwood.**)

size, sized

In advertising, the form *size* is commonly used: large-*size* beach blankets, a quart-*size* bottle, an economy-*size* tin. In general writing the more formal *sized* is usual: a medium-*sized* pullover, three small-*sized* root beers. Often the word is better omitted altogether: large beach blankets, three small root beers.

Slang

The breezy, colorful, timely language we call *slang* can be found in both the standard and nonstandard levels of English. Everyone, young or old, who likes humor and novelty and color also likes slang–especially good slang. Used skillfully, it adds liveliness and sparkle to anyone's speech. Part of its attraction, of course, is that slang gives the people who use it a feeling of being "with it," of being up on the very latest thing.

The chief attraction slang has for people is novelty. It is fun to hear an idea phrased in a new, unusual, streamlined way. But after hundreds of repetitions, the novelty wears off; the slang loses its freshness and sparkle. The history of most slang expressions is that they are born–they are overused–they become stale–and they die an early death.

That is one reason why slang is often ineffective in speech and usually inappropriate in writing–especially in writing that is meant to last for some time. Today a novel filled with the slang of the Twenties not only sounds dated but is in part meaningless. (Do *sockdolager*, *lounge lizard*, or *cake-eater* mean anything to you? And if you read that "Lydia thought Craig was the cat's pajamas," would you know whether Craig was being complimented or insulted?)

Then too a great many slang expressions are so general that they hardly have any meaning at all beyond a vague indication of approval or disapproval. Using such words adds no more to your speech or writing than does calling everything you like "wonderful" and everything you dislike "awful." Words like *neat*, *dreamy*, *groovy*, and *punk*, *lousy*, *crummy* are slang of this kind and add little to style or meaning.

Occasionally a slang term becomes an accepted part of the language, instead of fading into meaninglessness or oblivion. *Bonus*, for instance, was once stockbrokers' slang. *Carpetbagger* originally was a slang term of disapproval, but today anyone referring to the days in American history when carpetbaggers were active would use that name, even in a formal context. *Hobo*, *highbrow*, and *killjoy* are some other examples of slang that have become acceptable.

Slang is usually more appropriate in speech than in writing. But if not overused, it can be appropriate in informal writing meant for current reading–in a sports column, for example, or a feature article. Slang may also be needed in writing fiction, to make the speech of certain characters in a story seem real and believable.

But slang should always be used with caution. A safe prescription is this: In conversation with friends, use it, but in small doses. Use it even more sparingly in informal writing, making sure that what you use is appropriate to the subject and will not annoy or bore readers. Do not use it at all in formal speech or writing.

If you read a great deal and listen with interest to the speech of people who use language well, you will gradually develop a reliable judgment about the appropriateness of slang. Then, when you feel sure a slang expression is effective, you will probably be right.

slow, slowly

Both *slow* and *slowly* are used as adverbs. Use whichever sounds better:

Please drive slow so that I can read the street signs.
The aged mule ambled slowly toward the gate.

so

1. In speech *so* is often used to introduce clauses of purpose:

COLLOQUIAL: They moved to a new neighborhood so the children could walk to school.
WRITTEN: They moved to a new neighborhood so that the children could walk to school.

So is common in clauses of result, which written English would usually introduce by *so that* or change to a *since* (or *because*) construction:

COLLOQUIAL: None of the supply shops carried the exact spangles we wanted, so we had to order them from a store in New York.
WRITTEN: None of the supply shops carried the exact spangles we wanted, so that we had to order them from a store in New York.
WRITTEN: Since none of the supply shops carried the exact spangles we wanted, we had to order them from a store in New York.

2. The overuse of *so* to connect sentences is sometimes referred to as the "so-habit." It is especially common in speech, particularly in narrative accounts:

Loren and I wanted to see a movie, so we drove to the Palace so we could see what was showing there. We had seen the movie at the Palace, so we drove to the Cinema, but we'd seen the one there too. So then we decided to buy a newspaper so we could see what was showing at the other theaters. So we drove to a newsstand. But by that time it was nine o'clock, so we couldn't have seen a complete movie anywhere. So we went bowling instead.

Sentences like these should be rewritten to avoid the overuse of *so*.

3. The use of *so* as an intensive is mainly colloquial; in written English it is usually avoided or the comparison completed:

COLLOQUIAL: It is raining so hard!
WRITTEN: It is raining so hard that we'll have to cancel the outing.

so-called

When *so-called* is used, quotation marks are not needed, because they would duplicate the idea: *a so-called intellectual*, not *a so-called "intellectual."*

So-called is usually hyphened when it comes before the word it modifies, but not when it follows: His sophistication, *so called*, impresses no one over six years old.

some and its compounds

1. *Some* is most often used as an adjective or a pronoun:

ADJECTIVE: I see there are some changes in the batting order.
PRONOUN: Some are all right, but some are disappointing.

Some is also used colloquially as an adverb meaning "somewhat; little":

COLLOQUIAL: Now and then his old war wound bothers him some.
WRITTEN: Now and then his old war wound bothers him a little.

2. *Someone* and *somebody* are grammatically singular; they take singular verbs and are usually referred to by singular pronouns:

If someone in the audience *is* a doctor, will *he* or *she* please come to the stage door?
Surely somebody *is* willing to give you *his* version of the accident.

(For further discussion, see **Agreement,** sections 1g and 2b.)

3. *Somebody*, *somehow*, *something*, *somewhat*, and *somewhere* are always written as single words. *Someone*, *sometime*, and *someday* may be written as one word or two, depending on the meaning intended. Pronunciation will give a clue to the right spelling. If the stress is on *some*, the one-word form is used. For example:

STRESS ON *some*: You should read Saki's short stories someday.
STRESS ON *day*: Let's meet for lunch some day next week.

4. In informal English *someplace* is often used instead of *somewhere. Somewheres* is nonstandard.

sooner . . . than

Than, not *when*, is used as a connective after *no sooner*:

No sooner had the Fitzgeralds' guest begun to sing *than* their Irish wolfhound began to howl. [Not: *No sooner* had the Fitzgeralds' guest begun to sing *when.*]

sort

See **kind, sort; kind of, sort of; kind of a, sort of a.**

so . . . that

Even though several words come between *so* and *that*, no comma should precede *that*:

Pam Motto was so excited when she realized her team had scored the winning goal [ ] that she fell on the ice.

species

Has the same form in both singular and plural: a *species*, many *species*. Pronounced /spē'shēz/ or sometimes /spē'sēz/.

Specie /spē'shē/ or /spē'sē/, meaning "money in the form of coins," is a different word, a collective noun without a plural form.

Spelling

The argument that many of our celebrated writers and great men and women have been notably poor spellers does not alter the fact that accurate spelling has become a generally applied test of literacy–one of the minimum requirements of an educated person. Not only your future employers, but anyone who reads your writing, will expect you to be able to spell.

To be a good speller does not mean you have to be a perfect speller, one who without help can spell correctly every word he or she uses. It does mean that you should master the spelling of simple, everyday words (*all right*, *February*, *government*, *height*, *hundred*, *nickel*, *toward*) and that you should form the habit of referring to a good dictionary for less common words whose spelling you may be unsure of (*amethyst*, *boutonniere*, *paraphernalia*).

1. One of the best ways to improve your spelling is to master a few general rules that apply to large groups of common words:

a. Doubling final consonants. When a suffix beginning with a vowel is added to a one-syllable word that ends in a single consonant preceded by a single vowel, the final consonant is doubled:

drum + er = drummer
ram + ed = rammed
mar + ing = marring
big + est = biggest
clan + ish = clannish
can + ery = cannery

If the word has more than one syllable, the final consonant is doubled only if the accent is on the last syllable:

in fer' + ed = inferred
pro pel' + er = propeller
re gret' + ing = regretting
con cur' + ent = concurrent
re but' + al = rebuttal
re mit' + able = remittable

(But: ac cred'it + ed = accredited; cor'ner + ing = cornering.)

b. Final silent e. A final silent *e* is generally dropped before a suffix that begins with a vowel:

fine + ed = fined
blue + er = bluer
profane + ing = profaning
dictate + or = dictator
excite + able = excitable
desire + ous = desirous
palate + able = palatable
issue + ance = issuance

There are a few exceptions: the *e* is kept in words like *dyeing* and *singeing* (to keep them distinct from *dying* and *singing*) and in words like *noticeable* and *courageous* (to keep the /s/ sound of the *c* and the /j/ sound of the *g*).

Before a suffix beginning with a consonant, the final *e* is usually kept:

rue + ful = rueful
pleasure + less = pleasureless
wholesome + ness = wholesomeness
sincere + ly = sincerely
move + ment = movement
safe + ty = safety

A number of common words are exceptions: *ninth*, *truly*, *duly*, *argument*, *wholly*.

c. Words with y. A final *y* preceded by a consonant is changed to *i* before a suffix that begins with a consonant:

queasy + ly = queasily
lusty + ness = lustiness
duty + ful = dutiful
worry + ment = worriment
remedy + less = remediless
dandy + fy = dandify

The same change is made before the suffixes *-ed*, *-er*, *-es*, *-est*:

spy + ed = spied
ugly + er = uglier
terrify + es = terrifies
showy + est = showiest

But before the suffix *-ing*, the *y* is kept:

spying frying liquefying justifying

d. Adding prefixes. The prefixes *dis-*, *mis-*, and *un-* end with a single consonant. When they are attached to a base word beginning with the same letter, there will be two *s*'s or two *n*'s. Otherwise there will be only one:

dis + service = disservice
mis + spent = misspent
mis + spell = misspell
un + needed = unneeded
un + neighborly = unneighborly
dis + inherit = disinherit
mis + apply = misapply
mis + calculate = miscalculate
un + salted = unsalted
un + kind = unkind

e. Adding suffixes. No letter is dropped from the base word when the suffix *-ness* or *-ly* is added:

mean + ness = meanness
craven + ness = cravenness
national + ly = nationally
eternal + ly = eternally

But remember that if the base word ends in *y* preceded by a consonant, the *y* is changed to *i*: *huskiness*, *warily*.

f. Ei and ie. Use *ie* when the sound is long *e* (as in *me*):

piece believer grief yield
shriek relieves achieved niece

A few common words are exceptions: *leisure*, *seize*, *weird*.

Use *ei* after *c*, or when the sound is not long *e*:

deceiver height heir foreigner
conceived forfeit weight eighty
receiving neighbor heinous reindeer

The most common exceptions are *friend*, *mischief*, *handkerchief*, *sieve*, *view*, *fiery*, *financier*.

2. Often pronouncing words correctly will help you with the spelling. For example, if you pronounce *athletic* and *remembrance* correctly as three syllables, you will not put an extra vowel in the words ("athaletic" and "rememberance"). If you look at *perspire* and *children* carefully and pronounce them correctly, you will not be tempted to transpose the letters in them ("prespire" and "childern").

If you remember that *tian* (as in *Christian*) spells a /chən/ sound, you will not use *tian* in spelling words like *curtain*, *mountain*, *certain*, and *captain*–which end with a /tən/ sound (not /chən/). If you remember that the /shən/ sound in words like *expression* and *session* and *admission* is spelled with *ssion*, you will use two *s*'s in these words. But you will use only one *s* in words like *conclusion*, *confusion*, and *illusion*–since they end with the sound /zhən/. Make it a practice to compare the way words sound with the way they are spelled. The pronunciations are not always foolproof clues, but they help with many groups of words of similar sound.

3. For single words whose spelling is hard or seems unreasonable or illogical, try to figure out some formula to fix the spelling in your mind. Notice, for example, the "cola" in *chocolate* and the "bullet" in *bulletin.* Don't forget the "ear" in *hear*. Remember that you should "gain" from a *bargain.* Any device, no matter how nonsensical it may seem, that helps you with the spelling of a difficult word is valuable.

4. Finally, since many misspellings are due to carelessness or haste rather than ignorance, make it a point to proofread all your written work carefully before handing it in. Keep a list of all words that you habitually misspell and check your papers especially for those. Wanting to be a good speller is half the battle.

Split infinitive

Putting an adverb modifier between *to* and the infinitive form of the verb results in what is called a "split infinitive":

Mr. Aga told us to quickly read our notes before the quiz.
Dorothy was too stunned to fully understand what had happened.

Split infinitives that sound awkward are to be avoided in writing:

AWKWARD: It is difficult to heartily laugh at a joke one does not find amusing.
BETTER: It is difficult to laugh heartily at a joke one does not find amusing.

But otherwise there is no point in revising a sentence just to avoid splitting an infinitive. Good writers, in fact, prefer using split infinitives in sentences where not doing so would result in ambiguity or awkwardness:

CLEAR: I was too tired to really care how the late movie ended.
UNCLEAR: I was too tired really to care how the late movie ended.
AWKWARD: I was too tired to care really how the late movie ended.

Squinting modifier

A modifier that is ambiguous because it could refer to a preceding or to a following construction:

SQUINTING: The cafeteria is handing out chocolate bars to graduating seniors only today.

CLEAR: The cafeteria is handing out chocolate bars to graduating seniors today only.

CLEAR: The cafeteria is handing out chocolate bars to only graduating seniors today.

Standard English

The language used by educated people. For a discussion, see **Usage.**

state

See **say, state, talk.**

Statement-of-fact

Each of the following is a statement-of-fact:

The chalkboard in our math class is green.
The chalkboard in our math class is black.

Carbon tetrachloride removes paint stains.
Carbon tetrachloride does not remove paint stains.

The telegraph was invented by an American, Samuel Morse.
An Italian, Guglielmo Marconi, invented the telegraph.

As you can see by comparing the examples in each pair, a statement-of-fact is not necessarily a true statement. It is, however, a statement whose truth or falsity can be proved. Because such statements deal only with "fact"—that is, with persons, places, objects, occurrences, or processes that actually exist or did exist—their truth or falsity can be established by objective means. Many statements-of-fact can be proved true or false by personal observation or by experimentation. However, we seldom do the experimenting ourselves because reliable reports by experts in their field are available to us in reference books.

Statement of opinion

Suppose that in gathering material for a paper on your local schools, you hear or read the following statements:

Lemont High School, designed for 700 students, now has an enrollment of 1,000.
Lemont students are getting an inferior education.

Though both of these statements provide "information," they are of quite different types. The first is a statement-of-fact whose truth or falsity can be proved. The second is a statement of opinion that cannot be proved true or false. It is an expression of personal opinion, a personal view. While opinions can be vigorously defended (or attacked), they cannot be proved (or disproved), as factual statements can generally be.

This is not to say that all opinions are worthless. Some are worthless, of course, but opinions that are sound are valuable to us, especially when we are discussing matters for which we do not have all the facts. In determining the soundness of a particular opinion, we should consider: first, how authoritative the source is; second, whether the opinion is supported by facts; third, what motivated the opinion.

stationary, stationery

Stationary means "standing still" or "not movable":

The light fixture was stationary.

Stationery is writing materials such as paper and envelopes. (It may help you to remember that this stationery has an *er* just like pap*er*.)

I don't like this lavender stationery, but it's all I have on hand.

Story

The word *story* is most commonly applied to a narrative of imaginary happenings—to a short story or a novel. It is also used to refer to a narrative of actual events—to a newspaper story, for example.

Editorials, reviews, essays, treatises, and so on, are not narratives, but pieces of expository writing—writing that discusses ideas or explains processes. The word *story* should not be applied to them.

street

In many newspapers *street* is not capitalized as part of an address: *221B Baker street.* In other forms of writing it is: *221B Baker Street.* But in your school writing you will probably be expected to follow the more conservative practice of capitalizing the word.

The abbreviation *St.* or *st.* is not used except to save space in texts or reference works and occasionally in letter headings.

Structural grammar

A grammatical study that is concerned primarily with describing the system of structural signals that help communicate meaning in language. In English these signals are word order, derivational endings, inflectional endings, function words, and intonation. The complete meaning of a communication is conveyed by the meaning of the words used (lexical meaning) and the structure signals used (structural meaning).

Subject

The subject names the person or thing about which the verb makes a statement or asks a question. The subject may be simple, a single word, or compound, two or more words, joined by a conjunction:

SIMPLE: The *dog* ran alongside its jogging master.
COMPOUND: The *dog*, *rabbits*, and *rooster* lived in comparative harmony.

(See also **Agreement,** section 1.)

Subject complement

A word that completes the meaning of a linking verb or of a transitive verb in the passive voice. The subject complement is usually a noun or a pronoun that refers to the same person or thing as the subject, or an adjective that modifies the subject:

NOUN: The boy who went ballooning is *Ralph.*
NOUN: Shirley was named head *cheerleader.*
PRONOUN: Was it *you* who inquired about her father?
ADJECTIVE: His new car is stoplight *red.*

Subjunctive

The subjunctive form of the verb is used in certain set phrases and in parliamentary motions:

Heaven *forbid*! If I *were* you . . . Far *be* it from me . . .
I move that the minutes *be accepted* as read.

In addition, the subjunctive is used in formal English:
(1) In wishes:

Tyrrell often wishes he *were* more athletic.
I wish he *were* less shy.

(2) In *if*-clauses that are highly doubtful or contrary to fact:

If Lester *were* program chairman, the meetings would be jammed.
She acts as if she *were* uninterested, but I know she is curious.
If Don *were* one year younger, he could fly half fare. [But: If Don *was* at the drugstore, he must have made the phone call. (Here the subjunctive is not used, since the writer feels it is probable Don was at the drugstore.)]

(3) In *that*-clauses after verbs of *insisting*, *asking*, *ordering*, *requesting*, and such expressions as *it is necessary* and *it was urged*:

Mother insisted that Marsha *go* to the style show.
It is not necessary that Luellen *write* the letter.

But the subjunctive is far less common than it once was. In informal English the indicative is often used in wishes and in statements contrary to fact:

Tyrrell often wishes he *was* more athletic.
I wish he *was* less shy.
If Lester *was* program chairman, the meetings would be jammed.
She acts as if she *was* uninterested, but I know she is curious.
If Don *was* one year younger, he could fly half fare.

And in both formal and informal English, people frequently avoid the subjunctive in *that*-clauses, by expressing the idea in another way:

Mother insisted that Marsha *should go* to the style show.
It is not necessary for Luellen *to write* the letter.

To show that a wish or condition refers to a past time, the helping word *had*, not *would have*, is used:

I wish he had won. [Not: *would have won.*]
If she had been appointed manager, I would have resigned. [Not: *would have been appointed.*]

(See **Mood.**)

Subordinate clause

See **Clause,** section 2.

Subordinating conjunctions

Subordinating conjunctions connect dependent, or subordinate, clauses with main clauses:

He doesn't understand *why* he can't go.
Gina left *because* we did.

Among the most common subordinating conjunctions are:

after	because	since	unless
although	before	so that	when
as	how	that	where
as if	if	though	while
as long as	in order that	till	why

The relative pronouns (*who*, *which*, *that*) and the interrogative pronouns (*who*, *which*, *what*) serve as subordinating conjunctions:

RELATIVE: The calligraphy *that* Charlie does is elegant.
INTERROGATIVE: I asked the cameraman *what* the commotion was about.

such

Colloquially, *such* is used as an intensive:

It was such an obvious falsehood.

In writing that is at all formal this use is avoided or the comparison is completed:

It was an extremely obvious falsehood.
It was *such* an obvious falsehood *that* everyone laughed.

such as

When used to introduce examples, *such as* is not followed by a comma:

Books such as [ ] *Bleak House* and *War and Peace* take awhile to read.
Any time spent learning basic household skills, such as [ ] cooking and sewing, can prove a wise investment for boys and girls.

Suffix

An addition made at the end of a word to form another word of different meaning or function:

-able:	laughable, readable	*-ize*:	categorize, humanize
-en:	shorten, whiten	*-less*:	painless, useless

-er:	cleaner, farmer	*-ly*:	suddenly, usually
-ful:	beautiful, wonderful	*-ment*:	punishment, treatment
-fy:	classify, purify	*-ness*:	awareness, softness
-ish:	boyish, foolish	*-ship*:	membership, ownership

Superlative degree

See **Comparison of adjectives and adverbs.**

sure

Sure is used primarily as an adjective:

Homemade pasta is a sure sign of good cooking.
Are you sure of your data?

Sure used as an adverb meaning "yes" or "certainly" is a colloquialism. It is frequently heard in conversation, but is inappropriate in writing (except in dialogue):

"Want to go for a pizza?" "Sure."
"I sure miss Howard's wry sense of humor."

suspicion

Used as a verb, *suspicion* is nonstandard:

NONSTANDARD: Captain Fergus suspicions a conspiracy.
STANDARD: Captain Fergus suspects a conspiracy.

swell

See **Counter words.**

Syllogism

A syllogism /sil′ə jiz′əm/ is a form of deductive reasoning. A categorical syllogism (there are other kinds not covered here) consists of three parts: a *major premise* (the general statement), a *minor premise* (the particular case), and a *conclusion* (the deductive inference that logically follows from the two premises). For example:

MAJOR PREMISE: All graduates of Fuller Technical School are experts in auto mechanics.
MINOR PREMISE: Luther Ellis is a graduate of Fuller.
CONCLUSION: Therefore Luther Ellis is an expert in auto mechanics.

[Notice that each statement in the syllogism contains a "subject term" and a "predicate term" connected by a linking verb:

IN THE MAJOR PREMISE: *graduates of Fuller* are *experts in auto mechanics*
IN THE MINOR PREMISE: *Luther Ellis* is *graduate of Fuller*
IN THE CONCLUSION: *Luther Ellis* is *expert in auto mechanics*

Notice also that the entire syllogism contains only three different terms, each used twice: *graduate(s)* and *expert(s)* and *Luther Ellis.* Each of the three terms names a different class of things. All categorical syllogisms are based on this pattern of three terms, each used twice.]

In determining whether or not a syllogism is valid, examine the premises and the conclusion. If either of the premises is not true, the conclusion cannot be true, of course. But in any syllogism in which the premises are true and in which the reasoning is valid, the conclusion will be valid. In the previous syllogism, for example, if all Fuller graduates are indeed experts in auto mechanics, and if Luther Ellis is actually a Fuller graduate, then the conclusion—that Luther Ellis is an expert in auto mechanics—is inevitable and valid.
(See also **Inductive and deductive reasoning.**)

Synecdoche

/si nek′də kē/ A figure of speech in which the writer names (1) a part when the whole is intended, or (2) the whole when only a part is intended:

Mrs. Stearns hired four extra *hands* for her spring plowing. [That is, she hired four extra workers.]
Is Chicago in the World Series? [That is, is a Chicago baseball team in the World Series.]

(Compare **Metonymy.**)

Synonym

Synonyms are words that have the same basic meaning, but suggest slightly different things. That is, they have much the same denotation but different connotations:

famous—renowned—celebrated—illustrious—eminent
praise—extol—eulogize—commend—applaud
prudent—circumspect—discreet—cautious—politic
scent—aroma—fragrance—odor—bouquet

The best way to build up your fund of synonyms is to observe and use the new words that you come across in reading and conversation. But when in your writing you need a synonym for a specific word, it may be necessary to use a special reference book. Some good ones are:

Webster's New Dictionary of Synonyms (Springfield, Mass., 1968)
Funk & Wagnalls Standard Handbook of Synonyms, Antonyms, and Prepositions (New York, 1947)
The Synonym Finder (Emmaus, Pa., 1978)
Roget's International Thesaurus (New York, 1977)
Roget's Thesaurus of English Words and Phrases (New York, 1965)

The first two not only list synonyms but make clear what their different connotations are. The last three simply list the words without making any real distinctions between them.

Most standard dictionaries also give help with synonyms.

Syntax

Syntax refers to the relationship of words and word groups in sentences. Some entries in this book that deal with matters of syntax are **Noun clause, Indirect object, Object of preposition, Linking verb, Tenses of verbs.**

TTTTTT

talk

See **say, state, talk.**

Tautology

The needless repetition of an idea:

The tweed jacket was too large [in size] for me.
The T'ang jar was perfect [and flawless].
Wild geese swam [in the water] in Small Pond.

(See also **Deadwood.**)

teach

See **learn, teach.**

Tenses of verbs

1. Forms. The form of a verb helps to show the time of the action. Though there are only three divisions of time–present, past, and future–English has six "tenses" to show various distinctions within these divisions. The simple present tense and past tense forms are single words: he *gives*, he *gave*. All other tense forms are phrases in which helping verbs are combined with a part of the main verb. The following table shows the forms most commonly used to show time distinctions:

		Active	*Passive*
PRESENT TENSE		he gives	he is given
		he is giving	he is being given
		he does give	
PAST TENSES	Past	he gave	he was given
		he was giving	he was being given
		he did give	
	Present perfect	he has given	he has been given
		he has been giving	
	Past perfect	he had given	he had been given
		he had been giving	

FUTURE TENSES	Future	he will give he will be giving	he will be given
	Future perfect	he will have given he will have been giving	he will have been given

2. Uses. a. The *present* tense is used not only to show that the action takes place at the present time, but also to make a statement that is generally true, regardless of time:

Five times nine *equals* forty-five.
The sun *is* ninety-three million miles from earth.
Trees *lose* their leaves in autumn.

Occasionally the present tense is used to tell of things that happened in the past, especially when the speaker or writer wants to make the past events seem more vivid. This use of the present tense is called the *historical present*. You may wish to use the historical present tense in writing papers, reports, and reviews:

The witches in *Macbeth serve* as omens.
Ed *is* on first, Al on second, and Casey *hits* into a double play!

b. The simple *past* tense form is used for action completed in the past:

Larry *talked* about his garden yesterday.
Josie *scored* well on the Law Boards.

To show customary or repeated action in the past, a form with *used to* or *would* is used:

The Zilliacs *used to take* the train to Mexico City each spring.
Mrs. McHenry *would walk* old Gypsy every afternoon.

c. The *future* tense, which shows that the action will occur in the future, is usually formed with the helping verb *shall* or *will.* But it can be formed in other ways. The present tense form, used in combination with an adverb of time, is common:

Next week we *begin* painting the boat.
Bill Cosby *is opening* at the Blackthorne *Saturday.*

A form of *go* or *be* plus an infinitive are also used to refer to future time:

Carla *is to play* the part of Titania.
The recital *is about to begin.* The seniors *are going* to raise funds.

d. The *present perfect* tense indicates an action begun in the past and extending to the time the statement is made:

You *have heard* the chorus sing "June Is Bustin' Out All Over."
Abe Mosher *has been* class representative three semesters.

e. The *past perfect* tense indicates an action completed earlier than some other past action:

We *had fished* that stream before the sun rose.
The cabinetmaker *had mended* the antique cradle that we bought.

f. The *future perfect* tense indicates an action to be completed at some definite time in the future:

The parade *will have begun* by the time we get to town.
Will you *have finished* the sculpture in time for the art show?

g. The *progressive* tense forms (made with the helping verb *be* and the present participle) are used to show continuing action:

I *was watching* television last night when you called.
Douglas Smith *is hiking* along the Appalachian Trail this summer.
They *have* both *been looking* at calculators.
Kirby *will be playing* first chair violin in the concert tonight.

h. The *emphatic* tense forms (made with the helping verb *do* and the infinitive) are used for emphasis and in negative statements and questions:

I *do think* we should have chosen navy blue instead of turquoise.
Annie Jacobs *does* not *study* four hours each evening.
Does Gillian *expect* to study in Florence next year?

3. Sequence of tenses. When the verb in the main clause is in the present tense, the verb in the subordinate clause is in whatever tense expresses the meaning intended:

Rosa *concedes* that these tortillas *are* floury.
We *doubt* that they *plan* to buy a baby alligator.
Drew *claims* that Amy *will lose* her new watch within a week.
The student council *is hinting* that it *may propose* a dress code.

When the verb in the main clause is in a past tense, the verb in the subordinate clause is also in a past tense form, except in a sentence like the last in the following group:

Rosa *conceded* that the tortillas *were* floury.
We *doubted* that they *planned* to buy a baby alligator.
Then we *remembered* that the sun *rises* in the east and *sets* in the west. [The fact stated in the subordinate clause is true regardless of time.]

In telling about two past actions, one of which was completed some time before the other, use the past perfect tense, not the simple past, for the earlier of the two actions:

They *thought* that we *had taken* the negatives to be developed. [Not: *took* the negatives. . . .]

4. Tenses of verbals. Participles and infinitives have two tenses, the present (*giving, being given*; *to give, to be given*) and the perfect (*having given, having been given*; *to have given, to have been given*).

The perfect tense is used to show action that took place before the action of the main verb:

Having promised to attend, Sue felt she must.
I am disappointed *to have missed* the meeting.

Otherwise the present tense is used:

Wondering why she'd been invited, Marguerite stepped from the carriage.
We had wanted *to swim*, but the water was too cold. [Not: *to have swum*. The intention—which we had in the past—was *to swim*, not *to have swum*.]

terrible

Colloquial in the sense of "bad; unpleasant; annoying": a *terrible* gossip, a *terrible* headache. Avoid this use in writing. (See also **Counter words.**)

than

1. In formal English the case of the pronoun after *than* in elliptical clauses of comparison depends on the use of the pronoun in the clause. The nominative form is used if the pronoun is the subject; the objective form is used if the pronoun is the object:

Nanette is a more aggressive salesperson than *he* [is].
Jerry likes my cousin more than [he likes] *me*.

In colloquial usage the objective form of the pronoun is often used in sentences like the first one (Nanette is a more aggressive salesperson than *him*). However this usage is not considered appropriate in writing or in formal speech.

Using the right form of the pronoun is often important in avoiding ambiguity. A sentence like "He trusts Floyd more than me," for example, might mean "He trusts Floyd more than I do" or "He trusts Floyd more than he trusts me." If in your writing you consistently use *I* when you mean the first, and *me* when you mean the second, you will make your intended meaning clear.

2. *Than* is the idiomatic conjunction after *no sooner*:

I had *no sooner* answered the phone *than* the doorbell rang. [Not: *when* the doorbell rang.]

But *when*—not *than*—is used after *barely*, *hardly*, or *scarcely*:

I had *scarcely* answered the phone *when* the doorbell rang.

than, then

Since *than*, when spoken rapidly and without stress, is pronounced /ᴛʜən/, careless writers tend to spell it *then.* Remember that *then* is an adverb of time (*Then* Casey stole third), and *than* a conjunction (Millie weighs more *than* her sister Peggy).

than whom

In the phrase *than whom* (meaning "compared to whom"), *than* is a preposition and *whom* the object of the preposition. The phrase is formal and old-fashioned, and many people avoid it as rather awkward:

AWKWARD: Professor Quirk, than whom there are few astronomers more knowledgeable on the subject of black holes, will head a symposium in November.

BETTER: Professor Quirk, one of the most knowledgeable astronomers on the subject of black holes, will head a symposium in November.

that

1. Conjunction. *That* should usually be repeated with each of a series of parallel subordinate clauses:

After his first week at Hunter, Guy called home to say *that* college was great, *that* his roommates were friendly, and *that* he needed more money.

But *that* should not be repeated within a single clause:

Courtney remarked *that* if Terry wanted to go [that] he could drive.

2. Adverb. In general usage *that* (or *this*) is commonly used as an adverb modifying adjectives and adverbs of quantity and extent:

Never before had I eaten *that* many fried shrimp.
How could anyone run *that* fast in hiking boots?

In colloquial usage *that* is also used to modify other adjectives and adverbs:

I didn't realize I was *that* hungry. [Formal: *as hungry as that.*]

In the speech of some localities *that* is used instead of *so . . . that*:

LOCAL: I was that exasperated with her I snubbed her in the hall.
GENERAL: I was so exasperated with her [that] I snubbed her in the hall.

(For pronoun use, see **this, that,** section 1.)

that, which

That is usually preferred as a relative pronoun in restrictive clauses, and *which* in nonrestrictive:

Ogunquit is the town in Maine that we like the best.
Ogunquit, which is in Maine, is our favorite seaside resort.

that is

A connective used to introduce examples or explanations. When it introduces a clause, it is usually preceded by a semicolon (sometimes a dash) and followed by a comma:

This diploma ought to have my parents' names on it too; that is, without their help I wouldn't have it.

When it introduces words or phrases, commas are used:

The choir will sing the last two selections *a cappella*, that is, without instrumental accompaniment.

In informal writing the *that is* would often be omitted before a short construction:

Only one thing kept Louise from going on the ski trip to Vail, [that is,] not knowing how to ski.

the

1. When spoken without stress, *the* is pronounced /ᴛʜə/ before consonants, and /ᴛʜi/ before vowels. When stressed, as in "Bilbo's Basement is *the* campus hangout," it is pronounced /ᴛʜē/.

2. Repeating *the* before the various nouns in a series emphasizes their distinctness:

The time, the money, and the inconvenience were offered as excuses. [Compare: The time, money, and inconvenience were. . . .]

3. *United States* is preceded by *the*: *the* United States.

4. *The* is used as an adverb in expressions like "the bigger the better." In formal writing, a comma is used in such expressions: "The more enthusiastic the audience, the more inspired the performance." In informal writing, the comma is generally omitted. (See also **Articles.**)

theater, theatre

In Canada, the British Isles, and most other English-speaking countries, *theatre* is the common spelling. In the United States, *theater* is more common except in proper names of long standing: the Abbey Theatre, the Hampstead Theatre Club. The standard pronunciation is /thē′ə tər/; the nonstandard, /thē ā′tər/.

their, theirs

Both are possessive forms of *they. Their* is used before nouns; *theirs* (no apostrophe) is used alone:

Her sister borrowed *their* car to attend the reunion.
Theirs is the small white house on the right.

their, there, they're

Their is a possessive form of *they.* (See **they.**) *There* is an introductory word, singular or plural depending upon the number of the subject it introduces. It is also an adverb indicating *where.* (See **there is, there are.**) *They're* is the contracted form of *they are.* (See **they.**)

Their telephone number is 345-6789.
There is a mouse in their basement.
There are many reasons for the strike.
The car is there in the ditch.
They're planning a visit to Charleston in April.

theirself, theirselves

Nonstandard for *themselves.*

them

Used only in nonstandard English as a demonstrative adjective and pronoun:

NONSTANDARD: *Them* sandals are pretty.
STANDARD: *Those* sandals are pretty.

NONSTANDARD: *Them* are the scallop shells.
STANDARD: *Those* are the scallop shells.

themselves

See **Reflexive pronouns** and **Intensive pronouns.**

then

When used as a conjunctive adverb, joining the two clauses of a compound sentence, *then* should be preceded by a semicolon:

After the explosion, there was a moment of silence; then there was frantic activity.

If *and then* is used to make a closer connection, a comma separates the clauses:

Sid filled the jars with chili sauce, and then he sealed them tightly.

(See also **than, then.**)

therefore

See **Conjunctive adverbs.**

there is, there are

1. When the subject following the introductory word *there* is singular, a singular verb is used; when the subject is plural, a plural verb is generally used:

There *is* a set of old cookie cutters in this drawer.
There *were* only two racks of coats on sale.
There *were* four zebras and a giraffe in the enclosure. [Compound subject.]

When the first part of a compound subject following *there* is singular, a singular verb is sometimes used:

There *was* a giraffe and four zebras in the enclosure.

2. Though the occasional use of sentences beginning with *there is* adds variety, an overuse tends to make writing unemphatic:

UNEMPHATIC: There was an owl perched on the lamppost.
EMPHATIC: An owl was perched on the lamppost.

UNEMPHATIC: There were flames and smoke billowing out of the burning garage.
EMPHATIC: Flames and smoke were billowing out of the burning garage.

they

In speech, often used as an indefinite pronoun (one without a specific antecedent), but this use is not considered appropriate in writing:

COLLOQUIAL: They make and sell delicious mints at this department store.
WRITTEN: This department store makes and sells delicious mints.

COLLOQUIAL: They have raised the price of gasoline again.
WRITTEN: The price of gasoline has been raised again.
WRITTEN: The dealers have raised the price of gasoline again.

thing

Often deadwood that should be omitted:

WORDY: Fortunately, his joblessness wasn't a usual thing.
IMPROVED: Fortunately, his joblessness wasn't usual.

WORDY: The first thing you do is gather dried leaves and berries.
IMPROVED: First you gather dried leaves and berries.

this, that

1. The pronouns *this* and *that* are often used to refer to the whole idea of a preceding group of words:

Mrs. Antonio was working intently on her opening statement, and *that* was why she didn't hear the sirens.

But this use should be avoided if there is any danger that the reader may think the pronoun refers to a particular noun in the group:

AMBIGUOUS: Marietta embroidered her jeans with her own initials. *This* was her mother's idea. [That she embroider her jeans? Or that she use her initials?]
CLEAR: Marietta embroidered her jeans with her own initials–a design her mother suggested.

2. In everyday speech *this* is sometimes used as an emphatic definite article (instead of the usual *the*):

Then *this* big oaf almost pushes me down *this* flight of stairs!

This use is out of place in writing except in quoting conversation.

this here, that there

Used only in nonstandard English for *this* and *that*:

NONSTANDARD: This here tree is a hawthorn. That there one is a maple.
STANDARD: This tree is a hawthorn. That one [there] is a maple.

till, until

Both have the same meaning; choose whichever best fits the rhythm of the sentence. *Until* is more usual at the beginning of sentences:

Until I saw the Parthenon, I never appreciated architecture.
I never appreciated architecture *till* (or *until*) I saw the Parthenon.

Titles of books, articles, etc.

1. Formal usage. a. In most books, in some magazines, and in most school writing, the titles of books, pamphlets, movies, radio and television programs, plays and poems published as separate volumes, and the names of newspapers and magazines are put in italics—underlined in writing:

Book: *Far from the Madding Crowd*
Pamphlet: *Turkey: How to Prepare It*
Movie: *Shane*
TV program: *The Muppet Show*
Newspaper: The *Christian Science Monitor*
Magazine: *Time*
Long Play: *The Importance of Being Earnest*
Long Poem: *The Faerie Queene*

b. The titles of artistic works (paintings, statues, concertos, operas, ballets, musical comedies) are also put in italics:

Painting: Vallotton's *Street Scene in Paris*
Statue: Moore's *King and Queen*
Opera: *Faust*
Ballet: *Rodeo*

c. Titles of short stories, articles, essays, short poems, and songs are enclosed in quotation marks:

Story: Saki's "Tobermory"
Article: "Ethics in the Classroom"
Poem: Donne's "Song"
Song: "I've Grown Accustomed to Her Face"

2. Informal usage. In some magazines and newspapers the titles of books, movies, magazines, etc., are treated as proper names—capitalized but not italicized or enclosed in quotation marks. In other periodicals the titles are capitalized and put in quotation marks. For your school writing, follow the formal style of italicizing such titles.

to, too, two

Do not confuse the spellings of *to*, the preposition; *too*, the adverb; and *two*, the number:

Rosie and Dan are going to the circus.
Can we come too?
The sleeves are too short.
Lamb chops and ham are my two favorite meats.

together with

A phrase beginning with *together with* (or *along with, as well as, with*) is sometimes added to a singular subject. When the phrase is used in a clearly parenthetical way, it does not affect the number of the verb:

Dr. Lobl, together with four trustees, *opposes* the selection of the new university president. [Not: *oppose.*]

When the phrase is not intended as a parenthetical addition, usage varies. In informal English, a plural verb is often used, since the singular subject and the phrase are felt to be the same as a compound subject:

In some versions of the story, a glass slipper together with a rose *lead* the prince to his true love.

Formal English sticks to the singular verb or changes the *together with* to *and* and then uses a plural verb:

In some versions of the story, a glass slipper and a rose *lead* the prince to his true love.

too

See **very, too.**

Topic outline

See **Outline form,** section 2.

Topic sentence

A statement, in general terms, of the central idea of a paragraph or group of paragraphs. It serves the writer as a guide in determining what details are needed to make the central idea clear to readers, as well as what details are irrelevant.

Though the usual place for a topic sentence is at the beginning of a paragraph, it may also come at the end. Occasionally if the writer feels that the central idea will be clear to readers without being explicitly stated, he or she does not include a topic sentence. In narrative writing topic sentences are rare.

toward, towards

Both forms are standard.

Transformational-generative grammar

A grammar system intended to account for the production (the "generating") of every possible sentence in a language. According to this system there are in English two kinds of sentences–kernel sentences and transformations, or derived sentences. Kernel sentences are short, report-type statements that fall into a few basic patterns. Transformations–all other sentences–are built, or "derived," from kernel sentences according to a limited set of rules (shifting, deleting, or inserting words and phrases, for example, or combining two or more kernels).

Transitions

Devices that enable the reader to understand the writer's intended relationship of one sentence to the next in a paragraph or of one paragraph to the next in a longer composition.

One goal of writers is a coherent text that proceeds logically and smoothly. The first transitional aid is, then, a sensible ordering of the items or ideas in the paragraph. That is, point A comes before point B because A occurred before B, or because A led to or caused B, or because B illustrates and expands A.

A logical pattern alone, however, is not enough. Writers cannot expect readers to bridge the gaps among a succession of isolated sentences. The writer must link the sentences with transitional devices so that they flow smoothly from one idea to the next, uniting the paragraph into one coherent work. Some of the most commonly used transitional devices are the following:

Direct links. Direct links are connecting words or phrases that show precisely how one sentence ties in with another. In a narrative paragraph, for example, expressions such as these might prove useful: *first*, *in a few minutes*, *soon*, *afterward*, *meanwhile*, *next*, and *then*.

For a descriptive paragraph, a writer might use such transitional terms as these: *to the left*, *at the top of the hill*, *inside*, *below*, *directly to the east*, *straight ahead*, *in the foreground*, *just behind*, and *beside*.

As Jacob's eyes became accustomed to the dark, he began to distinguish objects in the room. *Straight ahead* loomed a huge wardrobe. Immediately *to the left* of it stood a large, ornately carved chair, upholstered in crimson. An enormous carpet of oriental design lay *beside* his bed on the stone floor.

If the paragraph is about a contrast between two things, words like the following can help the reader see what the writer intends: *yet*, *however*, *in spite of*, *then . . . now*, *at first . . . later*, *nevertheless*, *on the contrary*, *notwithstanding*, and *on the other hand*.

The price of gold, gems, and silver continued to soar. *On the other hand*, the value of the dollar and of many stocks dropped regularly.

In a paragraph listing reasons or examples, transitions can be made from one point to the next with expressions such as these: *for instance, in the first place, in addition, for example, furthermore,* and *similarly.*

Interest in the existence of legendary monsters seems never to entirely disappear. *For instance,* just last summer an expedition trained in fresh-water photography set out for Scotland with special underwater cameras and highly technical equipment in a quest for the Loch Ness monster. *Similarly,* photographs and plaster casts of large footprints discovered in a Louisiana bayou caused a stir this past autumn.

Including too many direct links may lead to an overly stiff or formal composition. But used carefully and appropriately, transitional terms provide one good means of filling the gaps between ideas, thereby ensuring that the reader associates them in the way the writer intended.

Indirect links. A good way to avoid overuse of direct links is through less noticeable transitions: using pronouns to substitute for words in preceding sentences, repeating key words and phrases, or occasionally using synonyms to echo terms used earlier.

1. In the spring, *hedgerows* become living green walls on either side of the road. In some instances, *they* are so high that *their* longer shoots begin to arch over the narrow country roads forming lacy canopies.
2. Perhaps one solution for the future can be found in the development of *model towns.* Each *model town* will be designed to enhance its natural site, as well as to accommodate the needs of the people who will live in it.
3. *Gloria Darling* has come out of retirement to appear in a new film version of *Great Expectations.* When asked why, the *former stage and screen star* replied that she was now "long enough in the tooth" to play the part of Miss Havisham realistically.

At times, transitional devices that are stronger than those already mentioned may be needed. When consecutive paragraphs do not appear to be closely related, for example, a transitional sentence or even a short transitional paragraph may be necessary to show the relationship.

Transitive and intransitive verbs

A verb is called *transitive* when it is used with an object to complete its meaning:

Kevin *held* the vase.
Mack *dribbled* the ball.
I *was calling* my friend.

A verb is called *intransitive* when it does not need an object to complete its meaning or when the receiver of the action is not named:

The rooster *crowed.*
Martina *will arrive* late.
The buzzer *sounded* fifteen minutes early.

Linking verbs (those that merely link an adjective or noun to the subject) are regarded as intransitive:

Their date *was* a disaster.
The judges *seemed* sleepy.

Many verbs are used either transitively or intransitively, usually with different meanings:

TRANSITIVE: Herbert *sings* sea chanteys while working on his boat.
INTRANSITIVE: Luciano *sings* professionally.

Trite expressions

Usually figures of speech that through constant overuse have lost their original effectiveness. They may be expressions that have been around for many years, such as *in the nick of time* or *last but not least*; or they may be more current expressions that have caught on too quickly and too well, such as *that's not my bag* or *he's a together dude.* The overuse of such expressions marks writing as amateurish.

try and, try to

Although the formal idiom is *try to*, informal English has long used *try and*:

FORMAL: Try to remember to bring a pencil next time.
INFORMAL: Try and remember to bring a pencil next time.

type, type of

In speech, especially in business, *type* is often used as an adjective: a certain *type* computer, a different *type* job, this *type* form. But in formal English and in nonbusiness writing, *type of* is preferred: a certain *type of* computer, a different *type of* job, this *type of* form.

Underlining

Underlining in longhand and typewritten copy corresponds to the use of italic type in printed matter.

1. Titles of books and magazines are underlined:

Have you read Middlemarch?
She ought to dress well; the only magazines she reads are Vogue and Harper's Bazaar.

(For more details about this use, see **Titles of books, articles, etc.**)

2. Any word that a writer wishes to emphasize may be underlined (italicized in print), but this kind of emphasis loses its force if used too frequently:

It's one of those towns where the *only* place to go is the post office.
Do you mean you *walked* the distance between Morris and Rayburn?

3. Letters, figures, and words used not for their meaning but as words are generally underlined, especially in books and articles on language:

There is a *u* in *fourth* but not in *forty*.
The *29* should have been in the first paragraph and the *30* in the second.

4. Foreign words and phrases are often underlined to distinguish them from ordinary English:

Lucy hasn't drunk black coffee since she was introduced to *café au lait* in France.

Understatement

A figure of speech in which words less strong than expected are used. Understatement generally lends emphasis to an idea:

A Lamborghini and the trip to Italy to pick it up might be a nice graduation present.

(See also **Litotes.**)

uninterested

See **disinterested, uninterested.**

unique

In strict formal usage *unique* means "the only one of its kind" and therefore cannot be compared. In informal usage it has become generalized to mean "rare or unusual," and is compared with *more* or *most* or modified by *very* or *rather*:

This embroidered fabric is more unique than that striped.
Nicky found a rather unique fur coat at the rummage sale.

(See also **Comparison of adjectives and adverbs,** section 3.)

United States

As the name of a country *United States* is singular and is preceded by the article *the*:

In the past the favorable rate of exchange has encouraged tourists from many countries to visit the United States.

For lack of a better word, *United States* is also used as an adjective, as in *the United States Postmaster General*, although *the Postmaster General of the United States* is less awkward. (See also **American.**)

Unity

Writing is said to have unity when it gives a oneness of effect. Unity results from (1) selecting material that is pertinent to the subject and (2) presenting it so that it produces a single effect or impression.

until

See **till, until.**

up

Informal English often uses *up* after certain verbs though it adds no new element to the meaning:

We tied [up] the horses to a bush on the river bank.
Let's join [up] now, before the rush.

In formal writing this use of *up* would be avoided.

Usage

Usage–the ways in which words are actually used–determines whether the words are appropriate or inappropriate English. The different kinds of English that people use can be sorted out into three major categories: *formal English*, *informal English*, and *nonstandard English.* Two of these kinds–formal and informal–belong to what is called the **standard level** of English. The third kind–nonstandard–does not.

1. Formal English. Formal English is the kind of English that educated people use on formal occasions. You will occasionally hear it–in sermons, graduation speeches, scholarly addresses, public speeches by government officials, and so on. But it is used more often in writing than in speaking, especially in writing meant for the clergy, doctors, lawyers, scientists, educators, and others whose interests are intellectual. You will find it in academic and technical writing (scholarly magazines, reports of experiments, certain textbooks, theses, legal papers, business reports) and also in certain literature (essays, some fiction and biography, and some poetry).

It is a common mistake to think that formal writing is necessarily stiff and artificial. Good formal writing is not. It may be more dignified and more bookish than ordinary writing. And it must be read more carefully than ordinary writing. But it is not stilted or pompous. Rather, the careful word choice and sentence construction add to the richness and precision of the writer's expression.

Of course, if you use formal English inappropriately–say in a thank-you note for a birthday gift or in a conversation with friends–it will sound unnatural and ridiculously stiff. But it is highly effective where it is appropriate: (1) in discussing difficult, abstract ideas for restricted audiences, as in a literary criticism; (2) in dealing with complex technical and scientific matters, as in a medical report; (3) in speaking or writing on any occasion that calls for a dignified tone, as in a dedication speech.

2. Informal English. Informal English lies between the two extremes of formal and nonstandard English. In speaking, it is the comfortable kind of

English that educated people ordinarily use. In writing, it is the speech of educated people tidied up–with an eye to pleasing the reader.

Informal English is the kind of English you will find most useful. It is the normal language of the classroom. It is appropriate for almost all personal and business letters, and for most social affairs. In fact, you will probably never find that informal English is really inappropriate for you (although there may be occasions in your life when formal English would be more effective). Informal English is the most important kind for you to know and to use.

3. Nonstandard English. Nonstandard English is the English used by people who have not had much formal education–or whose education has had little effect on their speech and writing. It is mainly spoken English, because the millions of people who use it do not often find it necessary to write except in personal matters. (When it does appear in print it is usually in the dialogue of stories and plays or in comic strips.)

Despite what you may have learned, nonstandard English is not necessarily "bad" English. It is simply one kind of English–and it serves a great many people perfectly well. But for most educated people it is both inadequate and inappropriate. Their work and their personal interests usually involve constant use of language. They have to read and write and talk about complex matters. They have to express things exactly, and in a way that meets the approval of other educated people. For them, nonstandard English just would not do the job.

4. General usage. In the preceding discussions of the three main kinds of English, the chief emphasis is on the differences between them–yet there are actually more similarities than differences. There are only a few words and constructions that mark the differences between nonstandard or informal or formal. The rest of the words and constructions are in **general usage.** Everyone uses such words and constructions, no matter what kind of English he or she is speaking or writing.

All writers and speakers, for instance, use the ordinary names of things–like *street*, *chair*, *house*, *running*, *jumping*. Everyone forms the plural of *friend*, *boy*, *chair*, *pencil*, and other regular nouns by adding *s*. All of our sentences fall into a few basic patterns: subject–verb–object, for example. The greater part of our language, then, raises no questions; it can cause you no trouble since it is always appropriate–in any situation.

used to

Though the *d* is not pronounced, it should not be omitted in writing:

Sergei *used to* play in the percussion section of the Cleveland Symphony. [Not: Sergei *use to*.]

But the negative and interrogative forms are usually made with *did* and *use* (without the *d*):

I *did* not *use* (or *didn't use*) to like cabbage or liver. [More formal: I *used not* to like.]
Did he *use* to appear in television commercials?

Used to could is a nonstandard idiom:

NONSTANDARD: Darlene can't dance all night like she used to could.
STANDARD: Darlene can't dance all night as she once could. [Or: as she used to be able to.]

V

Variant

A different form or spelling of a word. Spellings such as *buses—busses, catalogue—catalog*; pronunciations such as /rüt/—/rout/, /tə mā′tō/—/tə mä′tō/; and constructions such as *the student's—of the student, sillier—more silly, had knelt—had kneeled* are variants.

Though most variant forms are equally good, there may be slight differences in the shade of meaning expressed or in the degree of formality that makes one or another more appropriate. The form *amoebae*, for example, is preferred in formal English, *amoebas* in informal.

Variety

Variety, which is necessary for interesting writing, can be gained by varying sentence length, sentence order, and sentence types. (See **Parallel constructions, Periodic sentence, Balanced sentences, Repetition, Climax.**)

Verb

A word or group of words used to "assert" or express action or being:

ACTION: Hugh *was climbing* the ladder when one of the rungs *cracked.*
BEING: Stacy *is* a fine sports reporter.

For discussion and examples see **Agreement,** section 1; **Auxiliary verb; Principal parts of verbs;** and **Tenses of verbs.**

Verb-adverb combinations

In the sentence "The car rolled back into the garage," *back* is an adverb. It has the usual adverb use: it modifies the verb *rolled*, telling *where.* But in "The steel companies rolled back prices," *back* (although technically an adverb) is semantically part of the verb. *Rolled* means "moved on wheels," but the combination *rolled back* means "reduced to a previous level"; it has nothing to do with moving on wheels.

English has many such verb-adverb combinations, two-part verbs that have a meaning different from the literal meaning of their parts:

VERB AND MODIFIER	TWO-PART VERB
I ran up to the attic.	They *ran up* a big bill.
Mom put the cat out.	Please *put out* your campfire.
We live down in Bay City.	He'll *live down* this disgrace.

Sometimes the two-part verb is separated, as in "He'll *live* this disgrace *down.*" But the verb in this example is still *live down* rather than *live* (modified by *down*), as in "We live down in Bay City."

The examples cited and hundreds of other verb-adverb combinations are in common use, especially in informal and colloquial English. In formal English single words are likely to be preferred: *investigate* for *look into*, *persuade* for *win over*, *conclude* for *wrap up*. In informal English, however, the emphatic rhythm of the verb-adverb combinations are often preferred.

verbal

See **oral, verbal.**

Verbals

Verb forms that are used as nouns (*Wanting* isn't *getting*), adjectives (a *frightening* experience), or adverbs (Joe came *to hear* the recital). For further information, see **Gerund, Gerund phrase; Participle, Participial phrase; Infinitive, Infinitive phrase.**

Verb phrases

Verbs that consist of more than one word (also called *phrasal verbs*):

are learning	will have moved	is being taught
could sing	might have chosen	will have been gone

Some grammarians use the term *verb phrase* to stand for a main verb and any complements and modifiers it may have.

very, too

1. In formal English *very* and *too* are not used in sentences like "They were very disturbed by our refusal" and "She was too involved in the matter to be objective," in which *very* and *too* modify a past participle directly. In such sentences formal English uses intensifiers like *very much*, *too much*, *greatly*, *highly*, etc.: "They were *very much* disturbed by our refusal." "She was *too closely* involved in the matter to be objective." Informal English makes no such distinctions.

2. *Very* has been so commonly overused that it has little value as an intensive. Avoid using it unless you are sure that it really adds meaning to your statement:

WEAK: Even the sailboat seemed very happy, skimming along very quickly over the very blue water.

IMPROVED: Even the sailboat seemed happy, skimming along quickly over the blue water.

viewpoint

Viewpoint is an economical substitute for *point of view* (though some purists object to its use as unidiomatic). In sentences in which *point of view* would be followed by another *of* (from the point of view of the surgeon), *viewpoint* would perhaps be less clumsy (from the surgeon's viewpoint, from the viewpoint of the surgeon).

viz.

Abbreviation of the Latin *videlicet* /və del′ə set/, meaning "that is to say" or "namely." *Viz.* is used only in rather formal documents or reference works. It is usually read "namely."

Voice

A form of the verb that shows whether the subject is the doer of the action named by the verb (active voice: Henry Higgins *taught* Eliza) or is the receiver of the action (passive voice: Eliza *was taught* by Professor Higgins).

vs.

An abbreviation for the Latin *versus*, meaning "against." *Vs.* (sometimes *vs* without the period) is most often used in headlines and writing about sports events (Chicago Bears vs. Green Bay Packers). In other writing, the full form–*versus*–is more common.

In law the abbreviation *v.* is used (The State of Ohio v. Richard Roe).

wait on, wait for

Wait on used in the sense of "wait for" is dialectal:

DIALECT: Polly mentioned to Carlos that we'd wait on him in the tearoom.

STANDARD: Polly mentioned to Carlos that we'd wait for him in the tearoom.

STANDARD: Since it was their last night at the mountain lodge, the Baileys gave the girl who had waited on them a large tip. [Meaning "served."]

want

The use of *want for* (He wants for me to drive) is common among speakers in the southern United States and is occasionally heard in other regions. But the *for* is generally omitted in writing:

WRITTEN: We want you to enjoy yourselves.
SPOKEN: We want for you to enjoy yourselves.
NONSTANDARD: We want you should enjoy yourselves.

(See also **like for.**)

Want is colloquial for *should*, *ought*, or *had better*:

You want to remember to send a thank-you letter.
You want to be careful there, balancing on the railing.

Want meaning "lack" or "need" is formal, and is chiefly a British usage:

Those roses want more sunlight than they are getting.

want in, off, out, up, etc.

These are localisms for *want to come in*, *want to get off*, *want to go out*, and so on:

LOCAL: I think La Rue wants in.
GENERAL: I think La Rue wants to come in.

LOCAL: He wanted off at Fort Street, but the bus didn't stop.
GENERAL: He wanted to get off at Fort Street, but the bus didn't stop.

way, ways

In everyday speech, *ways* is often used instead of *way* in a sense of "distance":

COLLOQUIAL: George left the car a little ways down the road.
WRITTEN: George left the car a little way down the road. [More formal: a short distance.]

Way is informal in the sense of "condition" or "state":

Beau was in a bad way after the racing accident.

we

1. *We* is sometimes used as an indefinite pronoun referring to people in general:

We live in a complex society, and we often long for simpler times.
We tend to dislike foods we have not tasted.

2. In editorials and other featured columns of newspapers and magazines, *we* is often used by a writer to suggest that his or her ideas and opinions represent those of the entire editorial staff (even though the writer may be expressing personal views).

This editorial *we* is sometimes used in familiar and informal writing, especially of a light tone. But used only to avoid using *I*, *we* is conspicuous and is better avoided.

we boys, us girls, etc.

Whether to use the nominative form *we* or the objective form *us* in such expressions depends on the function of the pronoun in the sentence:

Only *we* girls were in the house at the time. [Subject of the verb.]
It was *we* boys who were eating those apples. [Subject complement.]
The coach cautioned *us* players about the wet court. [Direct object.]
Mindy gave *us* bridesmaids pearl bracelets. [Indirect object.]
The ball sailed right into the midst of *us* bleacher bums. [Object of preposition.]

well

See **good, well.**

whatever, wherever, whyever

See **ever.**

when, where, in definitions

See **Defining words,** last paragraph.

where

Although in informal speech *where* is sometimes used in place of *that,* it is not appropriate in writing:

I read in the paper this morning *that* the old Thoren house is coming down.
[Not: I read . . . *where* the old Thoren house. . . .]

where . . . at, where . . . to

Though used in certain dialects, the *at* and *to* are generally omitted in standard English:

Where is my hat? [Not: Where is my hat *at*?]
Where can those seed packets have gone? [Not: have gone *to*.]

whether

See **if, whether.**

which

1. As a relative pronoun, *which* is used for things and for collective nouns referring to people (*team, delegation, family, audience, class*) when the group, not the individuals, is meant:

The back storm door, which we never lock, flew open in the wind last night and crashed against the house.
The audience, which had seemed lethargic throughout the first act, became alive and appreciative during the second.

When individual members of the group are meant, *who* is used:

The jury, who were as varied a group of people as the defense attorney had ever seen, were variously attentive, indifferent, and asleep.

(See also **that, which.**)

Which is used to refer to the whole idea expressed in a preceding group of words:

The Turners always arrive early, which flusters their hostesses.
This sleepy-looking mare is a real firecracker, which surprises most riders.

But this use should be avoided if there is any danger that the reference of *which* will not be clear; that is, if *which* may seem to refer to a particular noun in the group instead of to the group as a whole:

NOT CLEAR: Leila Martin was practicing a march on her new piano, which was to be a surprise for her father.
CLEAR: The march Leila Martin was practicing on her new piano was to be a surprise for her father.

Whose is often used as the possessive of *which*, instead of the more awkward *of which*:

This Victorian house, *whose* interior has been completely redecorated, was built in 1876 by the town's first postmaster. [Or: the interior *of which.*]

2. *Which*-clauses are subordinate clauses and should not be carelessly joined to a main statement by *and* or *but*:

CARELESS: His was an easygoing, agreeable disposition, and which made him many friends.
BETTER: His was an easygoing, agreeable disposition, which made him many friends.

CARELESS: For Noel, they bought a 1977 car, but which had only 22,500 miles on it.
BETTER: For Noel, they bought a 1977 car, which had only 22,500 miles on it.

(See also **and which, and who.**)

while

1. *While* is used mainly as a subordinating conjunction introducing adverbial clauses of time:

While I was on the phone, the cake in the oven burned.

2. *While* is also used, although rather weakly, in the sense of "though" or "but":

While I don't like the allergy shots, they seem to be helping me.
This office is more spacious, while that one has a window.

3. *While* is used colloquially and in journalese for *and*, a construction avoided in careful writing:

According to the consumer reporter, ground beef at Fred's Meat Market averages $2.25 a pound, while at other neighborhood grocery chains its cost is even higher. [Better: *and* at other neighborhood. . . .]

(See also **awhile, a while.**)

who, whom, whose

1. The pronoun *who*–used both as a relative and as an interrogative–refers to people and sometimes to animals:

The stylist who cut my hair has opened his own salon.
Calico Cass, who spends most of her days in the bay window, complained loudly when the sill was painted.

2. When the relative or interrogative pronoun is the subject or the subject complement of the verb, the nominative form *who* (or its compound *who-ever*) is used:

The couple who ran the inn turned out to be cousins of our cousins. [Subject of *ran* in the adjective clause *who ran the inn.*]
Who was given the combination to the safe? [Subject of *was given.*]
Give whoever comes to the door a popcorn ball. [Subject of *comes* in the noun clause *whoever comes to the door.*]
We didn't know who he was. [Subject complement in the noun clause *who he was.*]

The objective form *whom* (or its compound *whomever*) is used as direct object and as object of a preposition:

Bertie couldn't decide whom he would take to the football game. [Object of *would take* in the noun clause *whom he would take. . . .*]
Give the extra floral arrangements to whomever you wish. [Object of *wish* in the noun clause *whomever you wish.*]
The people whom they turned to for help responded generously. [Object of *to* in the adjective clause *whom they turned to for help.*]

When the interrogative pronoun used as the object of a verb or preposition comes at the beginning of a sentence or clause, informal English generally uses *who*, while formal English uses the objective form *whom*:

FORMAL: Whom did the newspaper send to the peace conference?
INFORMAL: Who did the newspaper send to the peace conference?

FORMAL: For whom did you arrange the limousine?
INFORMAL: Who did you arrange the limousine for?

FORMAL: We tried to remember whom Maurice had selected.
INFORMAL: We tried to remember who Maurice had selected.

When the relative pronoun is the object of a verb or preposition, formal English uses the objective form *whom*. In informal English the *whom* is often omitted or *that* is used:

FORMAL: He listed the famous ballerinas whom he had trained.
INFORMAL: He listed the famous ballerinas [that] he had trained.

FORMAL: Isn't Jane Regal the congresswoman to whom Barry Bower introduced us?
INFORMAL: Isn't Jane Regal the congresswoman [that] Barry Bower introduced us to?

Interrupting expressions like *I thought*, *you remember*, and *did you say* do not affect the use of *who* in its own clause:

Do you know who I thought would be nominated? [Not *whom*; *who* is the subject of *would be nominated.*]
Harry Jackson, whom you remember nobody liked at first, is now quite popular. [Not *who*; *whom* is the object of *liked.*]
There was no doubt about who Dad thought would win. [Not *whom*; *who* is the subject of *would win.*]

The form you should use in a particular context depends, of course, on the situation. On formal occasions–during an interview, in giving an address or report before a group, in a research paper or other serious expository writing–use the forms preferred in formal English. In informal situations–in conversations with friends, in personal letters, in informal narratives–the forms used in informal English are appropriate.

The possessive form *whose* shows ownership:

Whose is the house with the overgrown yard?
Will the couple whose little girl is waiting for them in Lost and Found please pick her up?

(For *whose* as the possessive of *which*, see **which,** section 1.)

3. When *who* is the subject of a relative clause, its verb agrees in number with its antecedent:

Nell is the only one of the scholarship semifinalists who *is* enrolled in a cooking class. [Antecedent is *one.*]
Mr. Hall is one of those people who always *manage* to say the wrong thing. [Antecedent is *people.*]

(For further examples and discussion, see **one of those who.**)

will

See **shall, will.**

woman, lady

See **man, woman.**

wonderful

Used exactly, *wonderful* means "causing wonder; marvelous; remarkable": the *wonderful* majesty of the Taj Mahal. *Wonderful* is also used informally as a counter word of approval: *wonderful* vacation. (See **Counter words.**)

Word division

See **Division of words.**

Wordiness

The use of more words than are needed to express ideas clearly and accurately results in weak, often vague, writing. The commonest types of wordiness are:

1. Circumlocution—using several words or roundabout phrasing to say what might be said more directly, in fewer words:

WORDY: With respect to its historical accuracy, the film is sound.
BETTER: The film is historically accurate.

WORDY: Their new living room has a floor that is made of woods of different shades arranged in a geometric pattern.
BETTER: Their new living room has a parquet floor.

WORDY: Owing to the fact that I had not yet completed the assignment for my class in algebra, I found myself unable to attend the pep rally held on that evening.
BETTER: Because I hadn't finished my algebra assignment, I couldn't go to the pep rally that evening.

2. Deadwood—words that add nothing to the meaning:

The sweatshirt was too large [in size] for Milly.
Did the police ever discover the [true] facts about the robbery?

Words: classes of

A common way to classify, or sort out, the words in the English language is into eight classes, or parts of speech: nouns, verbs, adjectives, adverbs, pronouns, prepositions, conjunctions, and interjections. This classification is based on the meaning and use of a word in a sentence, as well as its form.

world

Deadwood in such expressions as "in the social world," "in the world of finance." "In society" or "in finance" is enough.

would of

A misspelling of *would've* (*would have*).

would rather

See **had rather, would rather.**

ye, the

The *ye* in such names as *Ye Olde Wayside Inn* is simply the archaic form of *the.* It is correctly pronounced /ᴛʜē/, not /yē/. (In Old English writing, the sound /ᴛʜ/ was represented by a single symbol, the letter thorn: þ. Early printers who did not have this symbol substituted the letter *y*, which somewhat resembled the letter thorn.)

yes, no

These adverbs may modify sentences (*Yes*, Hank has a scholarship) or may stand by themselves as complete sentences. ("Have you seen my sweater?" "*No.*") Remember that when *yes* or *no* modifies a sentence it is always set off by a comma.

yet

Yet is used chiefly as an adverb:

He has not yet been thanked. Has the mail arrived yet?

It is also used as a coordinating conjunction, equivalent to *but*. Then it is preceded by a comma:

Thelma wanted to sing in the trio, yet she hated to audition.

you

In informal speech and writing *you* is commonly used as an indefinite pronoun, referring to people in general:

You cannot enter Russia without a visa.
Finally you top each parfait with whipped cream.

In formal English *one* is preferred, or else a different construction:

One cannot enter Russia without a visa.
Finally each parfait is topped with whipped cream.

The indefinite *you* should be avoided whenever it might be misunderstood as personal rather than impersonal—especially if the misunderstanding would turn a generalization into an insult, as in the sentence "You should bathe frequently."

you-all

You-all (often contracted *y'all*) is widely used by speakers in the southern United States as the plural of *you.*

your, you're

Do not confuse the possessive form *your* (your parents) with the contraction *you're* (you are). Remember that an apostrophe is never used in forming the possessives of the personal pronouns.

yourself, yourselves

The reflexive forms of *you.* (See **Reflexive pronouns** and **myself.**)

FOOTNOTES

Writers use footnotes to give credit for material they have taken from other sources. In informal writing, credit is often given directly in the text. But in more formal papers, such as research papers, a writer does not want to slow the reader by stopping to cite sources in the text itself. Footnotes supply these citations, but in an inconspicuous place such as the bottom of the page or at the end of the paper.

Footnotes are necessary for reporting the source of material that a writer quotes directly or indirectly. Occasionally they are also used to elaborate upon a detail that is mentioned in the text, especially when that elaboration would require the writer to go off on a tangent in the text itself. Sometimes a footnote will be used to express an opinion different from the one that is quoted in the text. When statistics or figures or other highly specific information is taken from another source, the footnote is used to give that source credit.

Consecutive Arabic numerals (1, 2, 3, 4) are used to mark footnotes in a paper; the numbering system runs throughout the paper and does not begin again at each new page. When typing footnotes, place the number slightly above the item to be footnoted by turning the carriage very slightly toward you. A footnote number in the body of the paper is added at the end of the material and goes outside most punctuation marks, including quotation marks; but it may be placed inside a dash. For example:

> In the beginning of "Sophistication," George Willard "wants to come close to some other human, to touch someone with his hands, be touched by the hands of another"[1]—but who. . . . [from Sherwood Anderson's "Sophistication" in Winesburg, Ohio: Text and Criticism, edited by John H. Ferres (New York: Viking, 1966), p. 235.]

There are two places for the footnotes. Some teachers prefer them at the bottom of each page of text on which they appear; others prefer them all together on a separate page or pages at the end of the paper. See the sample research paper on pages 507–523 for footnotes at the bottom of the page and pages 501–502 for an example of footnotes listed together at the end of the paper.

When footnotes appear at the bottom of the page, separate them from the text by a line extending across the page from the left margin to the right margin. For example:

> The nineteenth-century biographer of Charlotte Brontë, Mrs. Gaskell, wrote in a letter that at Haworth Parsonage, where the Brontës lived, "The wind goes piping and wailing and sobbing round the square, unsheltered house in a very strange unearthly way."[10]
>
> ---
>
> [10] Roger Lancelyn Green, Authors & Places: A Literary Pilgrimage (New York: Putnam, 1963), p. 80.

Some teachers allow a dividing line shorter than the one illustrated.

If you are footnoting at the bottom of each page, be careful that only those references actually cited on a specific page are footnoted at the bottom of that page. Because the footnote numbers should align with the indention of each paragraph, indent each footnote five spaces (or the number specified by your teacher); observe the text margin at the right. If a footnote runs on to a second or third line, bring those lines back to the left margin and single-space them. Double-space between footnotes, however.

When you cite a source for the first time in your paper, the basic footnote will contain the author's (or authors') full name, the title underlined or enclosed in quotation marks and volume or edition number (if applicable), publication data (place of publication, publishing company, and date), and the page or pages where the material was found. That will sometimes result in a rather complicated footnote. But when citing the same source thereafter in your paper, you may use a much simpler form: just the author's last name and the page number. If you are using more than one work by that author, add the specific title each time to avoid confusion. Use a shortened form of a long title if you wish, but be consistent in using that form.

Sometimes a footnote will simply repeat the immediately preceding citation, although perhaps from a different page. When that happens, the use of *Ibid.*, the Latin abbreviation for *ibidem*, meaning "in the same place," is customary. Because *Ibid.* is an abbreviation, follow it with a period; because it is a foreign word, underline it. If the page number differs from the previous citation, use a comma after *Ibid.* and write the page number:

> [4]Sherwood Anderson, Winesburg, Ohio (New York: Viking, 1960), p. 47.
>
> [5]Ibid.
>
> [6]Ibid., p. 22.
>
> [7]Edgar Lee Masters, New Spoon River Anthology (Riverside, New Jersey: Macmillan, 1968), p. 56.
>
> [8]Anderson, p. 40.

Note that publication information may be shortened for the footnote so long as it remains clear. The name of a well-known city, for example, need not be followed by the state or country in which it is located, but a less well-known town should be further identified. You need not use the full name of the publishing company, but be sure to use enough so that the firm is easily identifiable. You may also use abbreviations such as *Univ.* for *University.*

If there are footnotes on the final page of your paper, they should still go at the bottom of the page even though the text may end long before that point. Position the last footnote so that its final line is one inch above the bottom of the page.

Footnote Forms

BOOKS

(The footnotes occasionally contain abbreviations defined in the section titled Reference Terms.)

A. One author:

[1]Phillip Knightley, The First Casualty: The War Correspondent As Hero, Propagandist, and Myth Maker (New York: Harcourt Brace, 1975), p. 171.

B. Two authors:

[2]Earl English and Clarence Hach, Scholastic Journalism, 6th ed. (Ames, Iowa: Iowa State Univ. Press, 1978), p. 27.

C. Three authors:

[3]Floyd C. Watkins, William B. Dillingham, and Edward T. Martin, Practical English Handbook, 4th ed. (Boston: Houghton Mifflin, 1973), p. 105.

D. Four or more authors: if the book has more than three authors, you need list the name of the first only, followed by the abbreviation *et al.* (*et alii*), Latin for "and others":

[4]Wilfrid L. Guerin et al., A Handbook of Critical Approaches to Literature, 2nd ed. (New York: Harper Row, 1979), p. 87.

E. No author: if the book lists no author, begin with the title:

[5]The Song of Roland, trans. Frederick Bliss Luquines (Riverside, New Jersey: Macmillan, 1960), p. 10.

F. An author using a pseudonym: you may supply the author's real name in parentheses if you wish:

[6]George Orwell (Eric Blair), Animal Farm (New York: Harcourt Brace, 1954), p. 52.

G. One editor: if the book lists an editor but no author, write the editor's name followed by (ed.):

[7]Earl Rovit (ed.), Saul Bellow: A Collection of Critical Essays (Englewood Cliffs, New Jersey: Prentice-Hall, 1975), p. 83.

H. Two editors:

[8]Charles Feidelson, Jr., and Paul Brodtkorb, Jr. (eds.), Interpretations of American Literature (New York: Oxford Univ. Press, 1959), p. 211.

See footnotes C and D, page 496 for the form to use when you have a book with three or more editors. Be sure to include (eds.) after the names.

I. When you have the names of both the author and an editor or translator, the name of the editor or translator, preceded by ed. or trans. (for "edited by" or "translated by"), follows the title of the work:

[9]Sophocles, Three Theban Plays, trans. Theodore H. Banks (New York: Oxford Univ. Press, 1956), p. 68.

J. The name of a special edition of a work follows the title:

[10]William Shakespeare, Romeo and Juliet, A New Variorum Edition, ed. Horace Howard Furness (1871: rpt. New York: Dover, 1963), pp. 5–6 (I.i. 1–26).

(Note that a reprint [rpt.] of an old edition requires notation of the original date as well as publication facts of the reprint. As a courtesy to your reader, who may not have the same edition of Shakespeare's plays, include act, scene, and line numbers.)

K. A series name follows the title of the source:

[11]John Donne, John Donne's Poetry, An Annotated Text with Critical Essays, Critical Editions Series, ed. Arthur L. Clements (New York: Norton, 1966), p. 113.

L. To refer to only one book with a specific title that is part of a work of several volumes under a general title, list the author, specific title, and volume number, followed by the general title:

[12]George Orwell, An Age Like This, Vol. 1: The Collected Essays, Journalism, and Letters of George Orwell (New York: Harcourt Brace, 1971), p. 309.

M. To cite one chapter or section of a complete work by an author:

[13]Lewis Thomas, "Notes on Punctuation," The Medusa and the Snail (New York: Viking, 1979), pp. 125–129.

N. To cite one piece in a collection of different pieces all by the same author:

[14]E. B. White, "The Years of Wonder," The Points of My Compass: Letters from the East, the West, the North, the South (New York: Harper Row, 1962), p. 206.

O. To cite an article by one author in a larger work, such as a casebook or critical edition, that has been edited by someone else, list the author of the article; the title of the article in quotation marks; title of the larger work underlined; followed by the name of the editor (preceded by ed.); the publication information; and the page number:

[15] George Plimpton, "The Story Behind a Nonfiction Novel," Truman Capote's In Cold Blood: A Critical Handbook, ed. Irving Malin (Belmont, California: Wadsworth, 1968), p. 35.

P. To cite a specific poem in a volume of poetry, write the name of the poet, the title of the poem in quotation marks, the title of the book underlined, the editor if there is one, and the publication information, followed by the page number:

[16] Theodore Roethke, "The Waking," The Collected Poems of Theodore Roethke (Garden City, New York: Doubleday, 1975), p. 104.

Q. When citing classical references, it is customary to indicate books within a longer work with small Roman numerals. If the work is not divided into books, any divisions are indicated with Arabic numerals. Page numbers are not cited, but line numbers are:

[17] Homer, The Iliad, trans. Richmond Lattimore (Chicago: Univ. of Chicago Press, 1961), xii., ll. 10–15.

R. Citations of religious scripture, including the Bible and other works, should list the name of the book within the larger work, the chapter, and the verses. Editions of the Bible other than the King James version should be noted in parentheses:

[18]Leviticus 2:2-7.

[19]Corinthians 5:1–5 (Revised Standard Version).

Some teachers prefer a shorter form of footnoting that excludes the publication information. Footnote A (page 496) in the shorter form would read as follows:

[1]Phillip Knightley, The First Casualty: The War Correspondent As Hero, Propagandist, and Myth Maker, p. 171.

The reasoning behind this style preference is that the full information about the source appears in the bibliography and thus need not be included in the footnotes too. The longer form is more generally accepted, however, so be sure to find out which your instructor prefers.

ARTICLES: Magazines, Encyclopedias, Pamphlets, Newspapers

A. To cite an article from a magazine, journal, newspaper, or other periodical, list the author's name; the title of the article in quotation marks; the name of the periodical underlined; the date of issue and the page or pages:

[1]Thomas Y. Canby, "The Search for the First Americans," National Geographic, September 1979, p. 330.

B. If the author's name is not given, begin the footnote with the title of the article:

[2]"Defender of the Dollar," Time, October 22, 1979, p. 23.

C. An entry in an encyclopedia should be cited with the author's name, the title of the article, the encyclopedia, and year of publication. A page citation is not necessary:

[3]Elias Bredsdorff, "Hans Christian Andersen," Encyclopedia Americana, 1978.

D. If an encylopedia entry lists no author, begin the footnote with the name of the article:

[4]"Sherwood Anderson," Grolier Universal Encyclopedia, 1965.

E. Large encyclopedias usually have many editors, who need not be listed in footnotes. But when a specialized encyclopedia has one editor, his or her name should be included:

[5]Richard Harrier, "Imagery," The Reader's Encyclopedia of Shakespeare, ed. Oscar J. Campbell, 1966.

F. The citation of a pamphlet or report should begin with the author's name and then include the title underlined, the place and date of publication, and the page(s):

[6]Robert H. Fossum, William Styron: A Critical Essay (Grand Rapids, Michigan: 1968), p. 35.

G. A bylined article in a newspaper should begin with the writer's name, followed by the headline in quotation marks; the name of the newspaper underlined; the date, and the page. Whenever possible the section and column numbers should be given too:

[7]William Safire, "The Road to Morocco," New York Times, October 25, 1979, p. A19, col. 1.

H. A newspaper article with no author listed should begin with the headline of the article:

[8]"Agency Transfers Linked to Politics," New York Times, October 25, 1979, p. A20, col. 3.

OTHER FORMS

A. When you interview someone, list the name of the person interviewed, his or her identification if applicable, the place, and the date:

[1]Interview with Lawrence B. Perkins, former president, Perkins & Will Architects, Chicago, Illinois, January 9, 1980.

B. If the interview was conducted by telephone, specify that:

[2]Telephone interview with Prof. Kenneth Kaye, Department of Education, University of Chicago, March 11, 1980.

C. When you footnote an unpublished letter that you have received from a source, list the name of the writer, his or her profession or position, and the date:

[3]Letter from John Hersey, author, April 4, 1977.

D. If the letter has been written to someone other than yourself, indicate that in the footnote:

[4]Letter from Frank Lloyd Wright, architect, to Catherine V. Keith, a client, September 12, 1924.

E. To refer to information in a personal or private file, include a description of the material and its location as specifically as possible:

[5]Original sketches for the house at 2227 Simpson Street, Evanston, Illinois, 1923–24, now in the possession of Catherine V. Keith.

F. To cite a thesis or dissertation, list the author, the title (in quotation marks), the university where the work was completed, the date, and the page:

[6]Barbara R. Radner, "The Guided Tour As Mediation Between Museums and Schools: Current Practices and a Proposed Alternative," (unpublished Ph.D. dissertation, Department of Education, University of Chicago), June 1978, p. 121.

G. To refer to the notes on a record album, list the author's name, the title of the notes, the name of the album, the recording company, and the date:

[7]William Flanagan, "Notes," _Twelve Poems of Emily Dickinson_ by Aaron Copland, Columbia Records, 1966.

H. To credit an original source when you have taken the material from a secondary source that has quoted it, list first the name of the author and the title of the original source and page, and next the place from which you quoted it:

[8]Edmund Wilson, "The Ambiguity of Henry James," Hound and Horn, April–June 1934, p. 385, quoted in Gerald Willen (ed.), A Casebook on Henry James's The Turn of the Screw (New York: Crowell, 1969), p. 115.

Footnotes Listed on a Page at the End of a Research Paper

[1]Sherwood Anderson, Winesburg, Ohio, 2nd ed. (New York: Viking, 1960), p. 28.

[2]Walter B. Rideout, "The Simplicity of Winesburg, Ohio," Winesburg, Ohio: Text and Criticism, ed. John H. Ferres (New York: Viking, 1966), p. 293.

[3]Anderson, p. 46.

[4]Ibid., p. 47.

[5]Ibid., p. 163.

[6]William A. Sutton, The Road to Winesburg: A Mosaic of the Imaginative Life of Sherwood Anderson (Metuchen, New Jersey: Scarecrow, 1972), p. 156.

[7]Anderson, p. 235.

[8]Ibid., p. 205.

[9]Ibid., p. 243.

[10]Sutton, p. 204.

[11]Ibid., p. 219.

[12]Anderson, p. 119.

[13]Ibid., p. 77.

[14]Sutton, p. 223.

[15]Anderson, pp. 242–243.

[16]Sutton, p. 208.

[17]Anderson, p. 236.

[18]Ray Lewis White, The Achievement of Sherwood Anderson (Chapel Hill: Univ. of North Carolina, 1966), p. 101.

[19]Anderson, p. 41.

[20]Rex Burbank, Sherwood Anderson (Boston: Twayne, 1964), pp. 73–74.

[21]Anderson, p. 223.

[22]Burbank, pp. 73–74.

BIBLIOGRAPHY

The bibliography at the end of a research paper, an article, or book gives proper credit to the sources from which the material has been taken and provides the reader with an alphabetized list of further reading on the topic if he or she is interested. See the bibliography at the end of the sample research paper, page 523.

The bibliography at the end of your research paper will probably be shorter than the working bibliography used during the research process. Some sources on the working bibliography were probably of no use once you began to write the paper; others could not be located. Most teachers will require that the final bibliography list only the sources that are actually footnoted in the paper. Some teachers, however, will permit you to list sources that are not footnoted but which you feel were of general help in writing the paper. If you include these sources in your final bibliography, do so sparingly; otherwise it will appear as though you are trying to pad your bibliography in order to make it seem more impressive.

Study the examples below and note the differences in form between a basic footnote and a basic bibliography entry.

Footnote

[1]William Justema, The Pleasures of Pattern (New York: Reinhold, 1968), p. 98.

Bibliography entry

Justema, William. The Pleasures of Pattern. New York: Reinhold Book Corporation, 1968.

In the bibliography entry, the author's last name comes before the first and a period instead of a comma follows the name. A period also follows the title of the source in a bibliography entry. The publication data are not enclosed by parentheses as they are in a footnote, and the full name of the publishing firm is included. A period, rather than a comma, follows the publication data. There is no page reference in a bibliography entry for a book. Note too the arrangement of the bibliography entry. The first line is flush with the left margin, but the second and subsequent lines are indented five spaces. A bibliography entry is single-spaced with double-spacing between entries.

You have two choices when organizing a list of bibliography entries. You may divide the material into different categories: books, periodicals, encyclopedias, pamphlets, and a miscellaneous category for such items as speeches, films, and interviews. Each of these subheadings should be centered and the sources arranged alphabetically by author within each group. If your bibliography is fairly long and divides easily into different categories, this arrangement is effective. But a short bibliography or one that draws most of its material from one kind of source might look better as a single list with entries alphabetically listed by author. When an entry has no author, it is listed alphabetically by title. Consult your teacher for the most effective way of organizing your bibliography.

Bibliography Forms

1. A book by one author:

Atlas, James. Delmore Schwartz: the Life of an American Poet. New York: Farrar, Straus & Giroux, 1977.

2. A book by more than one author:

Cockelreas, Joanne, and Dorothy Logan. Writing Essays About Literature. New York: Holt, Rinehart and Winston, 1971.

3. A book that lists no author but one or more editors:

Ellmann, Richard, and Charles Feidelson, Jr. (eds.). The Modern Tradition: Backgrounds of Modern Literature. New York: Oxford University Press, 1965.

4. A book in which you have used only one chapter:

Kazin, Alfred. "The Earthly City of the Jews." Bright Book of Life: Novelists and American Storytellers from Hemingway to Mailer. Boston: Little, Brown and Co., 1977.

(Because the chapter is cited in a footnote, it is often not cited in the bibliography entry.)

5. An article from a critical edition or casebook:

Clark, Eleanor. "Old Glamour, New Gloom." Arthur Miller: Death of a Salesman: Text and Criticism. Ed. Gerald Weales. New York: The Viking Press, 1967.

(Note that Ed. is capitalized because it follows a period.)

6. A second or subsequent edition of a book:

Lester, James D. Writing Research Papers. 2nd ed. Glenview, Illinois: Scott, Foresman and Company, 1976.

7. An article from a magazine by one author:

Lewis, Donald M. "Testing and Its Legal Limits—the Florida Decision." Today's Education, November/December 1979, pp. 25–28.

(Be sure to include all the pages on which the article appears.)

8. An article from a magazine by two or more authors:

Lasson, Robert, and David Eynon. "Spinning Off the Bard." Esquire, November 1979, pp. 54–55.

9. An article from a magazine that lists no author is alphabetized by title:

"Notes and Comment." The New Yorker, October 29, 1979, p. 29.

10. A pamphlet or report when the author is listed:

Bosley, Harold A. Job and J.B. Evanston, Illinois: The First Methodist Church, n.d.

(The n.d. stands for "no date." See the reference terms following this section.)

11. A pamphlet or report when the author is not listed:

Annual Report, The Newspaper Fund. Princeton, New Jersey: Dow Jones and Co., 1979.

12. An encyclopedia article when the author is listed:

Quinn, Edward. "Macbeth." The Reader's Encyclopedia of Shakespeare. Ed. Oscar J. Campbell. New York: Thomas Y. Crowell, Co., 1966.

13. An encyclopedia article that does not list the author:

"The Question of Israel." The Random House Encyclopedia, 1977.

14. A newspaper article when the author is listed:

Chambers, Marcia. "Choosing Schools Is a Dilemma for Middle-Class New Yorkers." New York Times, October 28, 1979, pp. 1, 60.

15. A newspaper article that lists no author is alphabetized by title:

"One Week's Toll." Chicago Tribune, October 28, 1979, section 2, p. 1.

16. A source that is not in print form:

Keith, Catherine V. Interview. February 4, 1980, Chicago, Illinois.

Lousma, Jack. Speech, "Space and Beyond." October 19, 1979, New Trier Township High School East, Winnetka, Illinois.

When you list more than one entry by an author in a bibliography, the second and subsequent entries need not repeat the author's name. Instead a line at the beginning of the entry is used to indicate that the author's name is being repeated. For example:

Tuchman, Barbara. A Distant Mirror. New York: Alfred A. Knopf, 1978.

____________. The Guns of August. New York: Dell Publishing Co., 1963.

REFERENCE TERMS

Research papers frequently use abbreviations and foreign terms–usually Latin–to condense information. While you may not use most of these terms in your own research paper, you may need to know what they mean when you come across them in the works of others.

bk., bks.	book or books
c., ca.	*circa*, meaning "about" or "approximately"; generally appears with dates: c. 1315.
c. or ©	copyright
cf.	*confer*, meaning "compare with"; used to refer the reader to something else in the text or in another source.
c., ch., chs.	chapter or chapters
col., cols.	column or columns
comp.	compiled or compiler
ed., eds.	editor or editors; edition or editions; edited by
e.g.	*exempli gratia*, Latin for "for example"
enl.	enlarged
esp.	especially
et al.	*et alii*, Latin for "and others"
et seq.	*et sequens* and *et sequentes*, Latin for "and the one following" and "and those that follow"

ex., exs.	example, examples
f., ff.	and the following (lines or pages); usually replaces *et seq.*
fn.	footnote
ibid.	*ibidem*, Latin for "in the same place"; refers to the immediately preceding footnote.
idem	Latin for "the same"; may be used in place of *ibid.* if the footnote is on the same page.
i.e.	*id est*, Latin for "that is"
illus.	illustrated, illustrator, illustration(s)
l., ll.	line, lines
ms., mss.	manuscript, manuscripts
n., nn.	note, notes
n.b., N.B.	*nota bene*, Latin for "note well"
n.d.	no date
no., nos.	number, numbers
n.p.	no place of publication
op. cit.	*opere citato*, Latin for "in the work cited"; used in footnotes when several entries are listed between the first mention of a source and a subsequent reference to it.
p., pp.	page, pages
par., pars.	paragraph, paragraphs
passim	Latin for "here and there throughout the work"
pref.	preface
pseud.	pseudonym, a pen name
rev.	review, reviewed by; revised by, revision
sec., sect., secs.	section, sections
ser.	series
sic	Latin for "as it is"; in brackets, *sic* means that the writer is interrupting the quotation to point out that it is being copied exactly as it appeared, even though it contains an error or questionable fact.
st.	stanza
tr., trans.	translator, translation, translated by
viz.	*videlicet*, Latin for "namely"
vol., vols.	volume, volumes
vs.	*versus*, Latin for "against"
vs.	verse

SAMPLE RESEARCH PAPER: TITLE PAGE

THE LOCH NESS MONSTER

Myth or Reality?

by Sara Nevarez

Submitted in partial fulfillment of the requirements

of Senior English

Centerville High School

March 17, 1980

OUTLINE

Controlling Purpose: to suggest that improved methods of scientific detection are increasing the possibility of discovering the Loch Ness monster.

I. Introduction
   A. Thesis
   B. Background on Loch Ness
   C. Legendary reports of the monster
II. Modern Sightings of the Loch Ness Monster
   A. Single sightings
      1. 1934 Grant and Campbell reports
      2. 1938 MacLean report
      3. 1963 report
      4. Sightings on land
   B. Multiple sightings
   C. Loch Ness Investigation Bureau
III. Scientific Evidence About the Loch Ness Monster
   A. Evidence on film
   B. Sonar tracings
      1. Early recordings
      2. 1972 expedition
      3. 1975 expedition

IV. Biological Theories About the Monster

    A. Efforts to identify the monster

        1. Sea slug

        2. Marine bristle worm

        3. Eel

        4. Sirenian mammal

        5. Eogyrinus

        6. Elasmosaur

    B. Loch origin of monster

    C. Survival problems

V. Conclusion

    A. Composite portrait of the monster

    B. Evidence supporting its existence

The Loch Ness Monster: Myth or Reality?

The Loch Ness monster, long considered a myth, has become more believable in the light of recent eyewitness accounts. Since the 1930s, many sightings of this huge aquatic creature have been substantiated by photographs, motion pictures, and sonar tracings. Future explorations of the Loch Ness area, along with increasingly sophisticated detection equipment, should verify the existence of at least twenty such creatures.

This creature is named for Loch Ness in northern Scotland, one of the largest freshwater lakes in Great Britain. Although it is only about 24 miles long, and, in places, 1.5 miles wide, the loch is remarkably deep; its maximum depth is reported to be 975 feet, and it is 700 feet deep for much of its length. The sides of the loch slope downward precipitously from the banks. The bottom is mainly flat, silty, and free of vegetation. Salmon, sea trout, and elvers (young eels) migrate from the sea into the loch and from there up several rivers running into it.[1]

Even before the Highlands of Scotland became known to the outside world at the beginning of the Middle Ages, there were legends of large aquatic creatures in the Scottish lochs. The legend of the kelpie or water horse was widely believed and still persists today. This creature was said to

---

[1]Nicholas Witchell, The Loch Ness Story (London: Penguin, 1975), pp. 9–11.

occupy lonely lochs and to lure weary travelers to their death.[2] The first record of a large animal in Loch Ness was in A.D. 565 when St. Columba, the Irish missionary who brought the Christian religion to Scotland, was said to have encountered a fierce monster in the loch and frightened it off.[3] Similar sketchy accounts of monsters, "floating islands," and "leviathan creatures" appeared occasionally in journals and other records.[4] The people living near the loch have always suspected that there were large living creatures in the loch, and mothers used to warn their children not to take a ride on any horselike animal that approached the shore.[5]

Not until 1933, following the completion of a roadway along the northern shore, did the world hear about the Loch Ness monster. Since then there have been reports of sightings every year by scientists and laity alike. Over the last fifty or so years, descriptions of the monster have remained relatively consistent. On August 12, 1934, Mr. P. Grant had a sighting at 10:45 A.M. from Abriachan Pier. He wrote:

---

[2] Ibid., pp. 12–13.

[3] Peter Costello, In Search of Lake Monsters (New York: Coward, McCann & Geoghegan, 1974), pp. 25–26.

[4] John Wiley, Jr., "Cameras, sonar close in on denizen of Loch Ness," Smithsonian, June 1976, p. 97.

[5] Ibid., p. 101.

> I saw the object appear in the water about 120 yards from the shore. I had no glasses or camera but was able to make out clearly the monster's head which appeared to be like that of a goat. On top of the head were two stumps resembling a sheep's horns broken off. The neck was about forty inches long, and where neck and body met appeared considerable swelling which resembled a fowl with a full crop. The color of the body was . . . dark brown and appeared to be light underneath. The skin appeared to be smooth, the markings were like that of a lizard. The animal appeared to have flippers on the fore part of the body, and these were extended straight forward and were not being used. The eyes appeared to be mere slits like the eye of a darning needle. I watched the creature for almost five minutes; then it submerged. It was moving at a speed of about 8 m.p.h., and there was no wash or commotion in the water, but after it had disappeared, air bubbles appeared at the front and the rear. Length of the body was 20 feet.[6]

In another sighting about that time, Alex Campbell, now a retired game warden, who reports seeing the monster on seventeen different occasions, testified:

> It was mid-May 1934. I was looking across the water, and, heavens, there was this terrific upsurge about 200 to 250 yards distant. And then this huge neck appeared, six feet at least above the water, with a small head that kept turning nervously. Oh, the head was just going. I said, "This is fantastic." . . . As soon as the bow of a trawler appeared, the creature saw it, and swoosh, for heaven's sake, what a dive![7]

---

[6]Witchell, pp. 47–48.

[7]William S. Ellis, "Loch Ness: the Lake and the Legend," National Geographic, June 1977, pp. 759 and 763.

The following report is most unusual, since apart from enjoying a very clear view of one of the animals, the witness also observed the creature apparently feeding. The report is from the July 1, 1938 issue of the Inverness Courier:

> . . . Mr. MacLean, who was standing at the shore near the mouth of the Altsigh Burn, watching to see whether any trout were rising as he was contemplating fishing, said in an interview: "In a moment I saw an extraordinary sight. It was the monster's head and neck less than twenty yards from me, and it was without a doubt in the act of swallowing food. . . ."[8]

One of the most exciting sightings occurred in 1963 when the witnesses went after the monster in a small boat:

> . . . We decided that the best thing would be to get the boat out and try to intercept it (the monster). . . . The thing was still coming down the loch, and as we got closer we could see more details of it. There was a long neck coming about six feet out of the water and a head which reminded me rather of a horse, though bigger and flatter. The body was made up of three low humps—about thirty to forty feet in all, and about four feet high. The color was dark, and the skin looked rough. . . .[9]

Most often seen in the water, these creatures have also repeatedly been sighted on land. On January 5, 1934, Mr.

---

[8] Witchell, p. 59.

[9] Ibid., p. 68.

W. Arthur Grant, a 21-year-old veterinary student, was returning home on his motorcycle when he almost ran into a creature he described in these words:

> I was almost on it when it turned what I thought was a small head on a long neck in my direction. The creature apparently took fright and made two great bounds across the road and then went faster down to the loch, which it entered with a huge splash. . . . The body was very hefty, and I distinctly saw two front flippers, and there seemed to be two other flippers which were behind and which it used to spring from. The tail would be from five to six feet long and very powerful; the curious thing about it was that the end was rounded off. The total length of the animal would be fifteen to twenty feet. . . . It looked like a hybrid. . . . It had a head rather like a snake or an eel, flat at the top, with a large oval eye, longish neck and somewhat longer tail. . . . In color it was black or dark brown and had a skin rather like that of a whale. . . .[10]

Many people believe that there is only one monster that is unique to Loch Ness. Actually, scientists theorize that there must be at least twenty to maintain the species.[11] And the instances of multiple sightings, as well as varying accounts of size and color, suggest that there is certainly more than one. A sighting of more than one monster was made by another Mr. Campbell on July 19, 1958, when he saw one large black hump heading diagonally toward the far side of the loch, churning the surface around it, while a

---

[10]Ibid., pp. 96–97.

[11]Wiley, p. 104.

second black hump was lying comparatively quietly near St. Benedict's Abbey.[12]

The Loch Ness Investigation Bureau, founded in 1962 and disbanded ten years later, was a team of volunteers who surveyed the loch and collected and analyzed eyewitness sightings. After a witness had completed a forty-five-point sighting form, a member of the Bureau conducted an interview. Those unwilling to supply their name or address were rejected immediately. Over three thousand reports were gathered.[13] Yet there may be many valuable sightings that, because of scepticism about the existence of a Loch Ness monster, have not been reported: those claiming to have seen the monster have often been considered crazy, drunk, or stupid.

Better than an undocumented report, of course, is concrete evidence. Through the fifty or so years of modern sightings, there have been many good still photographs, motion pictures, and sonar tracings of large living animals in Loch Ness. Lately, there has been some success with underwater photography.

The first good motion picture was taken in 1960 by an aeronautics engineer, Tim Dinsdale. The film shows one of

---

[12] Witchell, p. 56.

[13] Meredith Wheeler, "The Lure of Loch Ness," Chicago Daily News, June 15, 1972.

the creatures swimming across the loch parallel to the shore. In 1966, the film was submitted to the Royal Air Force's Joint Air Reconnaissance Center for evaluation. The Reconnaissance Center experts stated in a report that the object filmed was not a boat or submarine, which suggests that it probably was an "animate object." The report also says that the object was standing about three feet above the water when first sighted and that a cross section through the object would not be less than six feet wide and five feet high. It also states that the original hump was between twelve and sixteen feet in length and was traveling at between seven and ten miles per hour.[14] In 1972, the same film was submitted to the American computer enhancement experts who found that two other parts of the body broke the surface in addition to the main hump.[15]

Many times these creatures have been traced with radar or sonar by boats on the loch. In March 1964, a fishing boat, Girl Norma, recorded a 30-foot-long object at a depth of about 250 feet. In August 1966, the yacht Pharma tracked on its radar a moving object estimated at about 30

---

[14] Wiley, pp. 99–100.

[15] Witchell, pp. 113–114.

feet long. In April 1969, the echo sounder of the trawler Ha-Gurn detected a very large object over 700 feet down.[16]

In 1972, an expedition, led by Dr. Robert H. Rines and consisting of a team from his Academy of Applied Science, used an underwater stroboscopic camera and Raytheon sonar equipment to get sonar tracings and a picture of the monster. Here is the account of Peter Davies, skipper of the boat:

> . . . There were a lot of fish in the bay which were appearing on the chart as tiny little dots about the size of a pinhead. . . . It was about 1:45 A.M. . . . [Suddenly we] noticed that the fish dots were becoming streaks, as if the fish were all moving rapidly away from the area. Then it started—a big black trace started to appear. To begin with, we thought it must be two or three fish close together. But then it got bigger and blacker and thicker. . . . something huge was moving down there. . . .[17]

Another expedition made in 1975 by the Rines team shows conclusive evidence that a large creature lives in Loch Ness. An underwater strobe camera was suspended on a rope line to a depth of forty-five feet below the boat. At 4:32 A.M. on June 20, a torso shot was taken showing a long, curving neck and the front part of a large body with two flippers. At 11:45 A.M. a picture was taken of the head from a distance of only four feet.[18] Occupying the left-hand

---

[16] Ibid., p. 122.

[17] Ibid., p. 130.

[18] Wiley, pp. 101–102.

section of the frame, the head was more or less in profile: the open mouth of the animal showed what appeared to be teeth inside; a prominent, long ridge ran down the center of the face into a thick-looking upper lip; two nostril-shaped marks were above the upper lip, one on either side of the central ridge. Most remarkable of all, there were two clearly defined stalks or tubes protruding from the top of the head.[19]

From the photographic evidence and eyewitness sightings, various theories emerge about what the monster may be. Some think it is an enormous and unknown variety of sea slug—a type of mollusk. Such a creature could shape its bulk into the one, two, three, or more humps seen by different witnesses. In addition, a sea slug could easily appear to have a head and neck, and the sea slug's method of jet propulsion could account for the high speeds the monster seems to be able to attain, as well as the tremendous amount of water turbulence it causes.[20] Other authorities think it is a marine bristle worm. Among the highest forms of worm life, it has appendages called <u>false feet</u> and a well-developed head with jaws. Moreover, the worm's body can convolute to form humps, such as those seen on the surface of the loch. Some believe "Nessie" is a

---

[19] Witchell, p. 149.

[20] Doug Walsh, "Loch Ness Monster: Fact or Fiction?" <u>Senior Scholastic</u>, May 18, 1976, pp. 28–29.

very large eel. Eels can "fold up like accordions," which could account for the sightings of many humps. Eels breed by laying eggs, which hatch out into three-inch larvae. Yet a six-foot-long larva has been found and is on display in Copenhagen, Denmark. An eel growing from such a larva would be ninety feet long.[21] However, all these invertebrate theories seem to collapse when one considers the land sightings. Creatures of the monster's size would appear to need a backbone and skeleton to support their bodies on land.[22] Another theory is that "Nessie" is a "carnivorous, sea-going mammal of the Sirenian order."[23] Yet another theory is that "Nessie" belongs to a family of amphibians called Eogyrinus and believed to have been extinct for 250,000,000 years.[24]

Some scientists believe the monster resembles a plesiosaur, a flippered reptile with a long neck. The elasmosaur, a type of plesiosaur, which lived during the Cretaceous period, 135 to 65 million years ago, seems especially similar to the monster. Its long neck had seventy-six vertebrae, and its body was broad and flat. It

---

[21] Mary Fiore, "Searching for the Loch Ness Monster," Boys' Life, July 1972, p. 50.

[22] Witchell, p. 143.

[23] Fiore, p. 50.

[24] Ronald Kotulak, "Loch Ness Monster Gains Respectability," Chicago Tribune, January 5, 1976, p. 16.

was about forty feet long, the same size as the monster seems to be, and it moved with flippers, as the monster is said to do. The elasmosaur had a small, round head, as the monster appears to have, and fed on fish, using its neck to reach for them, as the monster is described as doing. That action may explain the sudden movement of the monster's humps reported by so many witnesses: it could be lunging to snare fish.[25]

But there are problems with the elasmosaur theory. There is no proof that elasmosaurs have existed since the Cretaceous period. Could such animals go that long unnoticed? Elasmosaurs were poor divers, paddling mostly on the surface, yet the lake monsters are rarely seen on the surface. And elasmosaurs were warm-water creatures, but Loch Ness is a cold body of water.[26] It might be possible, however, that the monster looks like an elasmosaur only because it evolved into a similar form through what scientists call convergent evolution.[27] (Whales are an example of convergent evolution. They are mammals, yet have the shape of a fish.)

How did the creatures get into the loch? One possibility is that as the ice melted at the end of the last ice age (about 10,000 years ago), the level of the sea was raised, flooding

---

[25] Dennis L. Meredith, Search at Loch Ness (New York: Quadrangle, 1977), pp. 120–121.

[26] Ibid., p. 121.

[27] Ibid., p. 122.

many coastal valleys. The land, when freed of the weight of ice, slowly rose, separating the sea from the inland water. It is possible that when Loch Ness was linked to the sea, a group of these animals swam into its sheltered waters and remained there. Eventually the land rose, and Loch Ness became an enclosed lake; consequently, the return route to the sea was blocked. As the water slowly lost its saline content, the creatures adapted to their new freshwater existence. The only other possibility is that the creatures entered Loch Ness after it was cut off from the sea.[28]

Obviously, no single animal could survive over the hundreds of years of reported sightings, so the animals must be present in sufficient numbers to assure reproduction and to withstand attrition from disease and other natural causes. However, could a group of these animals survive in Loch Ness? The theory that Loch Ness monsters are predators stems from the low levels of plant life in the loch. Although vegetation is lacking, fish could provide an adequate food supply for the Loch Ness monsters. The loch, as noted before, contains an abundance of sea trout, eels, and salmon (along with stickleback and char), and among these, salmon could be a key source of food for a colony of predators. Scientists calculate that prior to spawning, Loch Ness could contain up to 13 million adult salmon. The periodic nature of this food supply would

---

[28] Witchell, pp. 139–140.

present no problem because many aquatic carnivorous animals feed heartily during annual cycles when food is plentiful; such animals fast during lean times.[29]

From the hundreds of eyewitness accounts and from the many authenticated photographs, a composite emerges of a creature with a long, slender neck, a small, "snakelike" head, a reasonably heavy body, a long, powerful tail, and four diamond-shaped flippers or paddles. Different witnesses have reported a varying number of humps, from a one-humped "upturned boat" appearance to a two- or three-humped back. The size of the animals seems to range from about fifteen or twenty feet to a maximum of perhaps fifty feet.[30]

In 1976, "Nessie" was given a scientific name to protect her/him/them from poachers. The name is Nessiteras Rhombopteryx, which means "new marvel with a diamond-shaped fin."[31] If the evidence presented has not convinced you of the existence of the Loch Ness monster, I think you will be convinced within the next five years. Scientific interest is increasing, and each year the tactics of the hunt and the new equipment grow more ingenious and sophisticated. Someday someone will be in the right place at the right time with the right equipment. Wouldn't you love to be there when it finally happens?

---

[29] Robert H. Rines, "Search for the Loch Ness Monster," Technology Review, March/April 1976, pp. 32–33.

[30] Witchell, p. 138.

[31] Wiley, p. 97.

BIBLIOGRAPHY

Books

Costello, Peter. In Search of Lake Monsters. New York: Coward, McCann & Geoghegan, Inc., 1974.

Meredith, Dennis L. Search at Loch Ness. New York: Quadrangle/The New York Times Book Co., 1977.

Witchell, Nicholas. The Loch Ness Story. London: Penguin Books, 1975.

Periodicals

Doherty, J. "Real Nessie?" Wildlife, March 1976, pp. 38–39.

Ellis, William S. "Loch Ness: The Lake and the Legend." National Geographic, June 1977, pp. 759–779.

Fiore, Mary. "Searching for the Loch Ness Monster." Boys' Life, July 1972, pp. 24–25, 50.

"Loch Ness Monster." Science Digest, March 1976, pp. 8–9.

Rines, Robert H. "Search for the Loch Ness Monster." Technology Review, March/April 1976, pp. 25–40.

Walsh, Doug. "Loch Ness Monster: Fact or Fiction?" Senior Scholastic, May 18, 1976, pp. 28–29.

Wiley, J. "Cameras, sonar close in on denizen of Loch Ness." Smithsonian, June 1976, pp. 96–105.

Newspaper Articles

Kotulak, Ronald. "Loch Ness Monster Gains Respectability." Chicago Tribune, January 5, 1976, p. 16.

Wheeler, Meredith. "The Lure of Loch Ness." Chicago Daily News, June 15, 1972.

INDEX

Items included in the *Language Handbook* are not listed in this index unless they appear in exercises in the chapters. Items not listed in this index can be readily found in the *Language Handbook,* which is arranged alphabetically.

A

B

C

D

E

F

G

H

I

K

L

M

N

O

P

Q

R

S

T

U

V

W

Y

Proofreaders' Marks

Example	Mark	Meaning
the Senator	lc	Lower-case the capital letter
senator Watkins	cap	Capitalize the lower-case letter
ATLANTIC	c/lc	Initial capital with lower-case letters
Time	ital	Indicate italics by underlining
motor cycle	⁀	Close up
She jumped off of the wall.		Delete
Paul called me Big Brover.	stet	Let it stand
in 25 years	sp	Spell out
I want talk with you.	^	Something left out
Mrs Maddox	⊙	Insert period
my teacher Mr. Steiner	^,	Insert comma
groceries milk, butter, and jam	(:)	Insert colon
We seldom see each other however, we are still friends.	;/	Insert semicolon
Why did you say that	?/	Insert question mark
Mr. Lupas smile	’	Insert apostrophe
Kevin said, If you go. . . .	“	Insert open quotation marks
“We should begin, she said.	”	Insert closed quotation marks
high school classes	|=|	Insert hyphen
the following chart see page 1	(/)	Insert parentheses
freind	∾	Transpose
	¶	New paragraph
	No ¶	No new paragraph
Allright	#	Insert space